CONTENTS

■ **PART 3**
CONSUMERS IN THEIR SOCIAL
AND CULTURAL SETTINGS/261

We are proud to herald in the twenty-first century with our seventh edition, which examines the full range of consumer behavior in the context of the incredibly dynamic, high-tech global environment in which we live. Instantaneous satellite transmissions spread the word on new products and fashions simultaneously across the globe to an increasingly wired global population. The volume and diversity of Internet marketing seems to explode daily, while regional and global marketing expands rapidly and geometrically. The variety of service and product offerings seems boundless.

The population of students and professors has never before been so diverse, so savvy, so experienced, so technologically literate. Never before have research sources—journals, articles, archives, and esoteric compilations—been so available, on stream, on-line, in hand.

And therein lay our challenge. For this streamlined age, we had to produce a streamlined book. We did a wide-ranging, encyclopedic search of the literature, selected the latest and most relevant articles for our new citations, pared back on old citations, and managed to reduce the book from 21 chapters to 16 chapters, with little sacrifice in coverage.

In this new edition we have intensified our emphasis on marketing strategy, using both a theoretical and an applications-oriented approach. Always true believers in the marketing concept, we have tried our best to meet the needs of our consumers—students, marketing practitioners, and professors of consumer behavior—by providing a text that is highly readable and that clearly explains the relevant concepts on which the discipline of consumer behavior is based. We have supplemented this material with a great many "real-world" examples in order to demonstrate how consumer concepts are used by marketing practitioners to develop and implement effective marketing strategies. The book is amply illustrated with timely, effective marketplace examples.

To make the seventh edition as useful as possible to both graduate and undergraduate students, we have sought to maintain an even balance of basic behavioral concepts, research findings, and applied marketing examples. We are convinced that providing structure and direction for effective market segmentation is a major contribution of consumer behavior studies to the practice of marketing. To this end, we have paid particular attention to revising and refining the discussion on market segmentation.

This seventh edition of *Consumer Behavior* is divided into four parts, consisting of 16 chapters. Part 1 provides the background and tools for a strong and comprehensive understanding of the consumer behavior principles that follow. Chapter 1 introduces the reader to the study of consumer behavior, its diversity, its development, and the role of consumer research. It contains a detailed discussion of ethical considerations in marketing and consumer practices. The first chapter also introduces a simple model of consumer behavior decision making which provides the framework for understanding and relating the consumer behavior principles studied throughout the book. Chapter 2 provides readers with a detailed overview of the critical consumer research process and the techniques associated with consumer behavior research, including a discussion of positivist and interpretivist research methods. Chapter 3 presents a comprehensive examination of market segmentation.

Part 2 discusses the consumer as an individual. It begins with an exploration of consumer needs and motivations, recognizing both the rational and emotional bases of many consumer actions. Chapter 5 discusses the impact of a full range of personality theories on consumer behavior and explores consumer materialism, fixated consumption, and compulsive consumption behavior. The chapter considers the related concepts of "self" and "self-image" and includes a new discussion of "virtual personality" and self. Chapter 6 provides a comprehensive examination of the impact of consumer perception on marketing strategy and the importance of production positioning and repositioning. The chapter is followed by a discussion of consumer learning, limited and extensive information processing, and the applications of involvement theory to marketing practice. This chapter includes a new section on measures of consumer learning. After an in-depth examination of consumer attitudes (now one comprehensive chapter), part 2 concludes with a discussion of communication and persuasion, and links consumers as individuals to the world and people around them.

Part 3 is concerned with the social and cultural dimensions of consumer behavior. It begins with a newly combined discussion of consumer reference groups (including virtual groups and communities), family role orientations, and changing family lifestyles. Chapter 11 presents consumers in their social and cultural milieus (including the emergence of the new "techno class"), and investigates the impact of societal and subcultural values, beliefs, and customs on consumer behavior. Part 3 concludes with an extensive discussion of cross-cultural marketing within an increasingly global marketplace.

Part 4 explores various aspects of consumer decision making. It begins with a comprehensive discussion of personal influence, opinion leadership, and the diffusion of innovations. Next, it describes how consumers make product decisions and explores the newly important practice of relationship marketing. This section examines in detail the simple model of consumer decision making that was briefly introduced in chapter 1, and ties together the psychological, social, and cultural concepts discussed throughout the book. It includes a greatly expanded exploration of consumer gifting behavior, and concludes with an examination of the expanding research focus on individual consumption behavior and the symbolic meanings of consumer possessions.

OVERVIEW OF MAJOR CHANGES

The text has been thoroughly updated and revised, yet substantially shortened to focus attention on critical consumer behavior concepts and to highlight the linkages between interrelated principles and processes. Some of the major changes are as follows.

- Chapters 8 and 9 have been combined into chapter 8, "Consumer Attitude Formation and Change." The new chapter 8 streamlines the flow of the text and strengthens the link between closely related material. Key principles from the previous edition have been retained and updated and enhanced by new tables, illustrations, and numerous examples that show marketing strategy in action.
- Chapters 11 and 12 have been combined to form chapter 10, "Reference Groups and Family Influences." This chapter carefully traces the influence of both nonfamily and family groups on consumer behavior. All the critical concepts pertaining to reference group membership and the influence of reference groups and the family remain, presented with complete definitions

and explanations along with specific marketing examples. New and revised tables and illustrations highlight principles and issues of particular importance.

- Chapters 17 and 18 have been combined to form chapter 15, "Consumer Influence and the Diffusion of Innovations." As a result of this change, students can more clearly see the linkage between two interrelated issues—the influence that others have on a consumer's behavior and the dynamic processes that shape the consumer's acceptance of new products and services. Definitions and examples of key concepts have been retained and enhanced with many new tables and figures; selected sections have been streamlined and updated in recognition of emerging ideas and practices.
- To streamline the text and focus students' attention on consumer behavior issues directly related to marketing strategy, chapters 20 and 21 have been eliminated and examples of the application of consumer behavior principles to not-for-profit marketing and public policy issues have been integrated throughout the new edition.
- Every chapter features numerous new examples, advertisements, figures, tables, and diagrams. These have been carefully designed to bring consumer behavior principles to life and to show how marketers actually apply consumer theories and research in the development and implementation of effective marketing strategies.

SUPPLEMENTS

The following state-of-the-art supplements package has been created to support the seventh edition of *Consumer Behavior*.

Instructor's Manual

This helpful teaching resource, prepared by James V. Dupree of Grove City College, contains chapter objectives, lecture outlines, chapter summaries, and answers to end-of-chapter questions and exercises.

Test Item File

Extensively revised for the seventh edition, the Test Item File, also prepared by James V. Dupree, contains more than 1500 items, including multiple-choice, true-false, and essay questions that are graded for difficulty and page-referenced to the text. The test items are also available through the Prentice Hall Test Manager program (Windows version).

PowerPoint Slides and Acetate Color Transparencies

A PowerPoint 4.0 set containing more than 200 electronic slides covers key concepts and includes complete lecture notes and illustrative tables and figures from the text.

This material is also available in a full set of acetate color transparencies for those professors who prefer to use an overhead projector in class.

Advertisement Transparencies

New to this edition, a set of over 75 acetate color transparencies of recent ads, both domestic and international, is provided together with teaching notes for each ad.

On-Line Cases

Four part-ending video cases, and four chapter-end cases, together with supporting questions and teaching notes, are located on-line at **www.prenhall.com/schiffman**.

Each video case explores consumer behavior issues as they are managed by Sputnik, Nascar, Yahoo!, and Kodak. A 10-minute, company-based video segment supports each part-ending case.

In addition to these exciting video cases, we offer four chapter-end cases. Each two-pages, in length explore the concepts presented in various chapters throughout the text.

Web Exercises

The seventh edition also offers Web-based exercises for each chapter in the text. Located on-line at **www.prenhall.com/schiffman**, each Web question challenges students to use the Internet to resolve consumer behavior issues.

Consumer Behavior Video Library

Prentice Hall has produced four company-based video segments to accompany this edition. Each video is approximately 10 minutes in length and profiles consumer behavior concepts as they are managed by companies such as Sputnik, Nascar, Yahoo!, and Kodak. Each video supports a comprehensive part-ending case.

Instructor's CD-ROM

A great lecture presentation tool, this easy–to–use software works with PowerPoint 7.0 and includes, for each chapter, PowerPoints, videoclips, and ads together with complete lecture notes, preview questions, and discussion questions.

Comprehensive Web Site: www.prenhall.com/phbusiness/phlip

Prentice Hall is proud to offer the best Web resource in the industry for both professors and students. "PHLIP" is a comprehensive Web site that supports Prentice Hall Business Publishing. As one of the featured titles on PHLIP, *Consumer Behavior*, Seventh Edition offers bimonthly updates by chapter, including timely readings and Internet links. A password-protected professor resource section allows adopters to download the *Instructor's Manual* and PowerPoint files, along with a set of four video cases, four chapter-end questions, and Internet exercises. PHLIP, developed by Dan Cooper of Marist College, also includes a feedback feature and bulletin board for professors teaching the consumer behavior course. Additional teaching resources are available in the "faculty lounge" feature.

Student resources include updates, access to study tips, software help, and related Web site links. PHLIP can also be used to organize homework and out-of-class exercises and projects for students.

ACKNOWLEDGEMENTS

Of the many people who have been enormously helpful in the preparation of this seventh edition of *Consumer Behavior*, we are especially grateful to our own consumers— the graduate and undergraduate students of consumer behavior and their professors, who have provided us with invaluable experiential feedback to our earlier editions.

We would like to thank our close friends and colleagues in the Department of Marketing at Baruch College for their continued support, encouragement, and friendship. We are grateful to the following professors for their continuous suggestions and highly constructive comments: Steve Gould of Baruch College; Benny Barak and Elaine Sherman, Hofstra University; Martin Topol, Pace University; Harold Kassarjian, UCLA; David Brinberg, Virginia Polytechnic Institute; John Holmes, Simmons College; Joel Saegert, The University of Texas at San Antonio; Lewis Hershey, Eastern Missouri State College; William R. Dillon, Southern Methodist

CHAPTER 1

Introduction: Diversity in the Marketplace

■■■■■■■■■■■■■■■■■■■■■■■■■■■■■■■■■■■

At the dawn of the twenty-first century, the global marketplace is a celebration in diversity. People differ not only among cultures, but within cultures. Where newcomers to the United States once sought *assimilation* in the American society by adopting American customs and language, they now value *transnationalism*, and shuttle back and forth between the homes and the lives they left and the new lives they found. Second- and third-generation Americans continue to observe their own ethnic customs, rituals, and language within the context of the larger American society. Multiculturalism has become the cornerstone of American society and a major contributing factor to the diversity of consumer behavior. Consumers differ not only in the usual ways—by age and gender, by education and occupation, by marital status and living arrangements—but also in their activities and interests, their preferences and opinions, the foods they eat and the products they buy. And marketers make it their all-consuming business to understand, to predict, and to satisfy the needs and wants of consumers—whatever they're like, whatever they want, wherever they live.[1]

There is diversity not only among consumers, but among marketers; not only among producers, but among sellers. Traditional retailers, from department stores to mom-and-pop stores, are still around. So are the mass merchandisers, the discount stores, and the off-price stores. But there has been a shift from mass marketing to niche marketing to direct marketing, from custom catalogs to television shopping to cyber shopping. Where U.S. producers once focused almost exclusively on the domestic market, the larger global market now beckons, and marketers employ marketing strategies designed to be as effective in Bombay as they are in Boston.

There is great diversity in advertising media. In addition to the traditional broadcast and print media, we have ethnic media within a great variety of alternative media. Marketers of every size and every product have established Web sites on the Internet, and more and more consumers turn to the World Wide Web for product information and advice. For alternative media, the future clearly is *now*.

With all of the diversity that surrounds us, the profusion of goods and services offered to us, and the freedom of choice available to us, one may wonder how individual marketers actually reach us with their highly specific marketing messages. How do they know which people to target, where and how to locate them, and what message would be most effective?

The answer, of course, is **consumer research.** Recognizing the high degree of diversity among us, consumer researchers seek to identify the many similarities—or *constants*—that exist among the peoples of the world. For example, we all have the same kinds of biological needs, no matter where we are born—the needs for food, for nourishment, for water, for air, and for shelter from the elements. We also acquire needs after we are born. These needs are shaped by the environment and the culture in which we live, by our education, and by our experiences. The interesting thing about acquired needs is that there are usually many people who experience the same needs. This commonality of need or interest constitutes a *market segment*, enabling the marketer to design specific products and/or promotional appeals to satisfy the needs of that segment. **Market segmentation** also enables the marketer to vary the image of its product, so that each market segment perceives the product as better fulfilling its specific needs than competitive products.

One of the most important constants among all of us, despite our differences, is that above all we are consumers. We use or consume on a regular basis food, clothing, shelter, transportation, education, equipment, vacations, necessities, luxuries, services, even ideas. As consumers, we play a vital role in the health of the economy—local, national, and international. The purchase decisions we make affect the demand for basic raw materials, for transportation, for production, for banking; they affect the employment of workers and the deployment of resources, the success of some industries and the failure of others. There is no question that consumer behavior has become an integral factor in the ebb and flow of all business in a bustling world economy.

The term *consumer* often is used to describe two different kinds of consuming entities: the **personal consumer** and the **organizational consumer**. The *personal consumer* buys goods and services for his or her own use (e.g., an electronic notebook), for the use of the household (a VCR), or as a gift for a friend (a videogame). In each of these contexts, the products are bought for final use by individuals, who are referred to as *end users* or *ultimate consumers*. The second category of consumer—the *organizational consumer*—includes profit and not-for-profit businesses, government agencies (local, state, and national), and institutions (e.g., schools, hospitals, and prisons), all of which must buy products, equipment, and services in order to run their organizations.

Despite the importance of both categories of consumers—individuals and organizations—this book will focus on the individual consumer, who purchases for his or her own personal use or for household use. End-use consumption is perhaps the most pervasive of all types of consumer behavior, for it involves every individual, of every age and background, in the role of either buyer or user, or both.

▪▪▪▪▪ CONSUMER BEHAVIOR AS AN ACADEMIC DISCIPLINE AND AN APPLIED SCIENCE

The study of **consumer behavior** as a separate marketing discipline began when marketers realized that consumers did not always act or react as marketing theory suggested they would. Despite a sometimes "me too" approach to fads and fashions, many consumers rebelled at using the identical products that everyone else used. Instead, they preferred differentiated products that they felt reflected their own special needs, personalities, and lifestyles. Even in industrial markets, where needs for goods and services were always more homogeneous than in consumer markets, buyers were exhibiting diversified preferences and less predictable purchase behavior.

Other factors that contributed to the growing interest in consumer behavior were the accelerated rate of new product development, the consumer movement, public policy concerns, environmental concerns, and the opening of national markets throughout the world.

THE MARKETING CONCEPT

The field of consumer behavior is rooted in a marketing strategy that evolved in the late 1950s, when some marketers began to realize that they could sell more goods, more easily, if they produced only those goods they had already determined that consumers would buy. Instead of trying to persuade customers to buy what the firm had already produced, marketing-oriented firms found that it was a lot easier to produce only products they had first confirmed, through research, that consumers wanted. Consumer needs and wants became the firm's primary focus. This consumer-oriented marketing philosophy came to be known as the **marketing concept**.

The key assumption underlying the marketing concept is that, to be successful, a company must determine the needs and wants of specific target markets and deliver the desired satisfactions better than the competition. The marketing concept is based on the premise that a marketer should make what it can sell, instead of trying to sell what it has made. The *selling concept* focuses on the needs of the seller; the *marketing concept* focuses on the needs of the buyer.

The widespread adoption of the marketing concept by American business provided the impetus for the study of consumer behavior. To identify unsatisfied consumer needs, companies had to engage in extensive marketing research. In so doing, they discovered that consumers were highly complex individuals, subject to a variety of psychological and social needs quite apart from their survival needs. They discovered that the needs and priorities of different consumer segments differed dramatically, and in order to design new products and marketing strategies that would fulfill consumer needs, they had to study consumers and their consumption behavior in depth. Thus, the marketing concept underscored the importance of consumer research and laid the groundwork for the application of consumer behavior principles to marketing strategy.

THE SCOPE OF CONSUMER BEHAVIOR

The study of consumer behavior focuses on how individuals make decisions to spend their available resources (time, money, effort) on consumption-related items. That includes *what* they buy, *why* they buy it, *when* they buy it, *where* they buy it, *how often* they buy it, and how often they *use* it. Consider a simple product such as a personal fax machine. Consumer researchers want to know what kinds of consumers buy fax machines for home use. What features do they look for? What benefits do they seek? What types of documents do they fax and for what reasons? How likely are they to replace their old models when new models with added features become available? The answers to these questions can provide fax manufacturers with important input for product scheduling, design modification, and promotional strategy.

In addition to studying consumer uses and postpurchase evaluations of the products they buy, consumer researchers also are interested in how individuals dispose of their once-new purchases. For example, after consumers have used a product, do they store it, throw it or give it away, sell it, rent it, or lend it out? (Think: What do consumers really do with their obsolete cell phones and laptops?) The answers to these questions are important to marketers, because they must match their production to the frequency with which consumers buy replacements. The answers are also important to society as a whole, because solid waste disposal has become a major environmental problem that marketers must address in their development of new products and packaging. Recycling is no longer a sufficient response to the problem. Many manufacturers have begun to remanufacture old components to install in new products, because remanufacturing is often cheaper, easier, and more efficient than recycling.[2]

CONSUMER BEHAVIOR HAS INTERDISCIPLINARY ROOTS

Consumer behavior was a relatively new field of study in the mid- to late 1960s. Because it had no history or body of research of its own, marketing theorists borrowed heavily from concepts developed in other scientific disciplines, such as psychology (the study of the individual), sociology (the study of groups), social psychology (the study of how an individual operates in groups), anthropology (the influence of society on the individual), and economics to form the basis of this new marketing discipline. Many early theories concerning consumer behavior were based on economic theory, on the notion that individuals act rationally to maximize their benefits (satisfactions) in the purchase of goods and services. Later research discovered that consumers are just as likely to purchase impulsively, and to be influenced not only by family and friends, by advertisers and role models, but also by mood, situation, and emotion. All of these factors combine to form a comprehensive model of consumer behavior that reflects both the cognitive and emotional aspects of consumer decision making.

▪▪▪▪ A SIMPLIFIED MODEL OF CONSUMER DECISION MAKING

The decision-making process can be viewed as three distinct but interlocking stages: the input stage, the process stage, and the output stage. These stages are depicted in the simplified model of consumer decision making in Figure 1-1.

The *input* stage influences the consumer's recognition of a product need and consists of two major sources of information: the firm's *marketing efforts* (the product itself, its price, its promotion, and where it is sold) and the external *sociological influences* on the consumer (family, friends, neighbors, other informal and noncommercial sources, social class, and cultural and subcultural memberships). The cumulative impact of each firm's marketing efforts, the influence of family, friends, and neighbors, and society's existing code of behavior, are all inputs that are likely to affect what consumers purchase and how they use what they buy.

> *For example, if a college student (let's call him Mark) knows that a professor he admires uses an IBM Thinkpad laptop, knows that his parents want to buy him a special gift for his upcoming birthday, and then sees a CompUSA advertisement announcing a laptop sale, he may decide that a new Thinkpad is exactly what he needs and wants.*

The *process* stage of the model focuses on how consumers make decisions. The *psychological factors* inherent in each individual (motivation, perception, learning, personality, and attitudes) affect how the external inputs from the input stage influence the consumer's recognition of a need, prepurchase search for information, and evaluation of alternatives. The experience gained through evaluation of alternatives, in turn, affects the consumer's existing psychological attributes.

> *Consider our friend Mark, the college student. Recognizing his "need" for a new IBM laptop, he immediately visits three large computer stores in his area, looks at the various Thinkpad models, and compares their prices. Concerned that a newer model may be introduced shortly, Mark decides to buy from a traditional retailer rather than a deep discounter because it offers a 30-day money-back guarantee, giving him the opportunity to upgrade if a more suitable model becomes available. His evaluation of the terms of sale may affect his earlier belief that the lowest-priced retailer is always the best.*

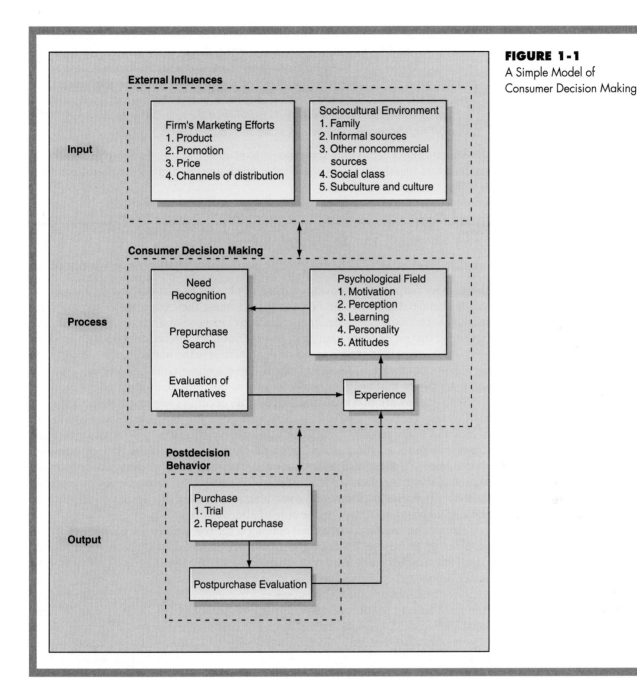

FIGURE 1-1

A Simple Model of
Consumer Decision Making

The *output* stage of the consumer decision-making model consists of two closely related postdecision activities: *purchase behavior* and *postpurchase evaluation*. Purchase behavior for a low-cost, nondurable product (for example, a new shampoo) may be influenced by a manufacturer's coupon and may actually be a trial purchase; if the consumer is satisfied, he may repeat the purchase. The trial is the exploratory phase of purchase behavior in which the consumer evaluates the product through direct use. A repeat purchase usually signifies product adoption. For a relatively durable product such as a laptop ("relatively" durable because of the rapid rate of obsolescence), the purchase is more likely to signify adoption.

However, in our friend Mark's case, the ability to return his IBM Thinkpad selection within 30 days for a full refund suggests that he does have a trial period during which to make the final product decision. The postpurchase evaluation of the product feeds directly into the consumer's experience in the *process* stage of the model. *In Mark's case, it may mean that he becomes a loyal IBM customer, or that he becomes a loyal customer of the retailer, or he may decide that his next computer will be a desktop model.*

The consumer decision-making model is examined in greater depth in chapter 16, where it ties together in great detail the psychological and sociocultural concepts explored throughout the book.

ETHICS IN MARKETING

The primary purpose for studying consumer behavior as part of a marketing curriculum is to understand why and how consumers make their purchase decisions. These insights enable marketers to design more effective marketing strategies. Some critics are concerned that an in-depth understanding of consumer behavior makes it possible for unethical marketers to exploit human vulnerabilities in the marketplace. In short, they are concerned that knowledgeable insights into consumer behavior give marketers an unfair advantage that enables them to engage in unethical marketing practices.

We are all aware that unethical practices do occur in every marketplace, at every level of the marketing mix: in the design of products, in packaging, in pricing, in advertising, and in distribution. They also occur at the other side of the marketing equation, when consumers act unethically in their dealings with marketers. Although most studies of **marketing ethics** focus on marketers' practices, some researchers are beginning to study consumer ethics. Tables 1-1 and 1-2 list various types of unethical marketing behavior, together with some blatant examples. Occurrences such as these make it important to reflect on the role of ethics in marketing.

There is no universally accepted definition for the term *ethics*. A study of ethical philosophies reveals two different groups of theories: teleological theories and deontological theories. **Teleology** deals with the moral worth of a behavior as determined by its consequences. According to teleology, to be ethical, a decision should be based on what is best for everyone involved. **Utilitarianism**, a teleological theory, can be summarized as "the greatest good for the greatest number." According to this theory, it would be perfectly ethical for a pharmaceutical company to conceal potentially harmful side effects of a new diet drug that may affect just a few people, so long as a large number of people are likely to benefit. To utilitarians, ethics are evaluated on the basis of a cost–benefit analysis: if the benefits to society (or to a specific segment of society) exceed the costs—that is, if more people would benefit than would be harmed—a behavior is considered ethical. However, a cost–benefit analysis should explore not only the financial but also the human consequences of a business decision, in both the short term and the long term. It is especially important that responsible decision makers anticipate all negative consequences that may occur and take action to avert such outcomes.

Deontology deals with the methods and intentions involved in a particular behavior. Deontological theories focus on the results of a particular action, and they tend to place greater weight on personal and social values than on economic values. Kant's *categorical imperative* is a deontological theory that suggests that individuals should be willing to have their actions become universal laws that would apply equally to themselves as to all others.[3] The reverse of the "golden rule," which most of us learned in grammar school, aptly

---

TABLE 1-1 Unethical Marketing Behavior

TYPES OF UNETHICAL MARKETING BEHAVIOR

PRODUCT	EXAMPLES
• Safety	Manufacture of flammable stuffed animals
• Shoddy goods	Products that cannot withstand ordinary wear and tear
• Inadequate warranties	Warranties with insufficient time or parts coverage
• Environmental pollution	Dumping hazardous wastes
• Mislabeled products	Flavored sugar water sold as apple juice for babies
• Development	Bribery of FDA officials to secure agency approval of generic pharmaceuticals
• Manufacturing	Unauthorized substitutions in generic drugs after FDA approval
• Brand "knock-offs"	Counterfeit branded goods sold as genuine brands

PRICE	
• Excessive markups	High prices used by retailers to connote quality
• Price differentiation	Yield-management pricing of airline tickets, resulting in day-to-day differential pricing of adjacent seats
• Price discrimination	Favored pricing to preferred racial or ethnic groups

PROMOTION	
• Exaggerated claims	Razor blade manufacturer advertises that its razors offer "the closest shave known to man"
• Tasteless advertising	Sexual innuendos and gender disparagement (e.g., a beer company targeted college males with ads on "how to scam babes")
• Inappropriate targeting	Inner-city billboards for luxury products (e.g., $125 sneakers)
• Deceptive advertising	Ads for cereal claiming it prevents heart disease
• Persuasive role models for inappropriate products	Celebrity spokespersons in beer, liquor, and cigarette ads targeted to youths
• Naive audiences	Billboards for cigarettes and alcohol in poor urban neighborhoods, where many people are dying from related causes
	Ads on children's TV for nutritionally unsound products (sugary cereals, candy, etc.)
• Captive audiences	Mandatory viewing of TV commercials by students in schools subscribing to closed channel newscasts
• Telemarketing	Offers of fabulous prizes in return for credit-card purchases of touted goods

DISTRIBUTION	
• Fraudulent sales	Phony markdowns based on "kited" retail list prices
• Bait-and-switch tactics	Luring consumers with ads for low-priced merchandise and switching them to higher-priced models
• Direct marketing	Deceptive, misleading product size and performance claims

PACKAGING	
• Deceptive quantities	Some marketers use "packaging-to-price" tactics that mask a decrease in product quantity while maintaining the same price and traditional product size

---

expresses the notion of ethical behavior in marketing: *Do not do unto others what you would not have others do unto you (or your loved ones).* Of the two dominant traditions, deontology is favored by most moral philosophers today.

Ethics clearly is a two-way street. For the marketing process to work beneficially for all of society, marketers and consumers alike must understand and practice ethical behavior.

ETHICS AND SOCIAL RESPONSIBILITY

The corporate environment and corporate philosophy are crucial determinants of ethical behavior among an organization's employees. Many companies have developed explicit codes of ethics that set the tone for decision making throughout the organization.

TABLE 1-2 Unethical Consumer Practices

- Shoplifting
- Switching price tags
- Returning clothing that has been worn
- Abusing products and returning them as damaged goods
- Redeeming coupons without the requisite purchase
- Redeeming coupons that have expired
- Returning products bought at sale and demanding the full-price refund
- Stealing belts from store clothing
- Cutting buttons off store merchandise
- Returning partially used products for full store credit
- Abusing warranty or unconditional guarantee privileges
- Damaging merchandise in a store and then demanding a sales discount
- Duplicating copyrighted materials (e.g., books, videotapes, or computer software) without permission

The New York Life Insurance Company, for example, distributes to its employees a Statement of Purpose, which includes the following: "We adhere to the highest ethical standards in all of our business dealings." Research shows that ethical practices by employees are very much a product of the corporate environment.

Many trade associations have developed industrywide codes of ethics because they recognize that industrywide self-regulation is in every member's best interests, in that it deters government from imposing its own regulations on the industry.

A number of companies have incorporated specific social goals into their mission statements and include programs in support of these goals as integral components of their strategic planning. They believe that ethics and social responsibility are important components of organizational effectiveness. Most companies recognize that socially responsible activities improve their image among consumers, stockholders, the financial community, and other relevant publics. They have found that ethical and socially responsible practices are simply good business, resulting in a favorable image and, ultimately, in increased sales. The converse is also true: Perceptions of a company's lack of social responsibility negatively affect consumer purchase decisions. Examples of company policies that influence consumer patronage include corporate environmental concerns, political activities, and the company's reputation for fairness, sexism, or equality. Figure 1-2 includes excerpts from a brochure issued by Ben & Jerry's.

FIGURE 1-2
Example of a Company Policy Statement Stressing Social Responsibility.

Ben & Jerry's is dedicated to the creation and demonstration of a new corporate concept of linked prosperity. Our mission consists of 3 interrelated parts:

PRODUCT MISSION

To make, distribute and sell the finest quality all natural ice cream and related products in a wide variety of innovative flavors made from Vermont dairy products.

ECONOMIC MISSION

To operate the company on a sound financial basis of profitable growth, increasing value for our shareholders and creating career opportunities and financial rewards for our employees.

SOCIAL MISSION

To operate the company in a way that actively recognizes the central role that business plays in the structure of society by initiating innovative ways to improve the quality of life of a broad community: local, national and international.

UNDERLYING THE MISSION

Is the determination to seek new and creative ways of addressing all three parts, while holding a deep respect for individuals inside and outside the company, and for the communities of which they are a part.

© Ben & Jerry's Homemade Holdings, Inc. 1999. Ben & Jerry's is a trademark of Ben & Jerry's Homemade Holdings, Inc.

THE SOCIETAL MARKETING CONCEPT

Given the fact that all companies prosper when society prospers, many people believe that all of us, companies as well as individuals, would be better off if social responsibility was an integral component of every marketing decision. Indeed, in an era of environmental deterioration, homelessness, drug addiction, AIDS, casual gun use, and countless other societal ills, the marketing concept as we know it—fulfilling the needs of target audiences—is sometimes inappropriate. This is particularly true in situations in which the means for need satisfaction, the product or service provided (e.g., drugs, tobacco, or prostitution), can be harmful to the individual or to society. A reassessment of the traditional marketing concept suggests that a more appropriate conceptualization for the times in which we live would balance the needs of society with the needs of the individual and the organization. The **societal marketing concept** requires that all marketers adhere to principles of social responsibility in the marketing of their goods and services; that is, they must endeavor to satisfy the needs and wants of their target markets in ways that preserve and enhance the well-being of consumers and society as a whole. Thus, a restructured definition of the marketing concept calls on marketers to *fulfill the needs of the target audience in ways that improve society as a whole, while fulfilling the objectives of the organization.*[4] According to the societal marketing concept, fast-food restaurants would not sell food that is high in fat and starch and low in nutrients (e.g., hamburgers or fries), despite strong consumer acceptance of these products. Nor would marketers advertise alcoholic beverages or cigarettes to young people, or use young models or professional athletes in liquor or tobacco advertisements, because celebrities so often serve as role models for the young.

A serious deterrent to widespread implementation of the societal marketing concept is the short-term orientation embraced by most business managers in their drive for increased market share and quick profits. This short-term orientation derives from the fact that managerial performance usually is evaluated on the basis of short-term results. The societal marketing concept of necessity requires a long-term perspective. It recognizes that all companies would be better off in a stronger, healthier society, and that companies that incorporate ethical behavior and social responsibility in all of their business dealings attract and maintain loyal consumer support over the long term.

THE PLAN OF THIS BOOK

In an effort to build a useful conceptual framework that both enhances understanding and permits practical application of consumer behavior principles to marketing strategy, this book is divided into four parts: part I gives an Introduction to the Study of Consumer Behavior, part II discusses the Consumer as an Individual, part III examines Consumers in Their Social and Cultural Settings, and part IV synthesizes all of the variables discussed earlier into the Consumer Decision-Making Process.

Chapter 1 introduced the reader to the study of consumer behavior as an interdisciplinary science that investigates the consumption-related activities of individuals. It described the reasons for the development of consumer behavior as an academic discipline and as an applied science. And it introduced a simplified model of consumer decision-making that links together all of the personal and group influences that affect consumption decisions. Chapter 2 examines the methodology of consumer research, including the assumptions underlying qualitative and quantitative research approaches. Chapter 3 discusses the process of market segmentation, including the demographic, sociocultural, and psychographic bases for segmenting markets.

Part II focuses on the psychological characteristics of the consumer. Chapter 4 discusses how individuals are motivated, chapter 5 examines the impact of individual personality characteristics on consumer behavior, chapter 6 explores consumer perception, chapter 7 examines how consumers learn, chapter 8 discusses consumer attitudes, and chapter 9 concludes part II with an examination of the communications process and consumer persuasion.

Part III focuses on consumers as members of society, subject to varying external influences on their buying behavior, such as their group and family memberships (chapter 10), social class (chapter 11), and the broad cultural and specific subcultural groups to which they belong (chapters 12 and 13). The importance of cross-cultural consumer research to international marketing is explored in chapter 14.

Part IV examines the consumer decision-making process. Chapter 15 discusses the consumer's reactions to innovation and change, and describes the process by which new products are adopted and become diffused throughout society. The book concludes with chapter 16, an in-depth discussion of consumer decision making that shows how all the psychological and sociocultural variables discussed in parts II and III influence the consumer's decision-making process.

SUMMARY

The global marketplace is a study in diversity—diversity among consumers, producers, marketers, retailers, advertising media, cultures, and customs. However, despite prevailing diversity, there also are many similarities. Segmenting target audiences on the basis of such similarities makes it possible for marketers to design marketing strategies with which their target consumers identify.

The study of consumer behavior enables marketers to understand and predict consumer behavior in the marketplace; it is concerned not only with what consumers buy, but also with why, when, where, how, and how often they buy it. Consumer research is the methodology used to study consumer behavior; it takes place at every phase of the consumption process: before, during, and after the purchase.

Consumer behavior is interdisciplinary; that is, it is based on concepts and theories about people that have been developed by scientists in such diverse disciplines as psychology, sociology, social psychology, cultural anthropology, and economics.

Consumer behavior has become an integral part of strategic market planning. The belief that ethics and social responsibility should also be integral components of every marketing decision is embodied in a revised marketing concept—the societal marketing concept—that calls on marketers to fulfill the needs of their target markets in ways that improve society as a whole.

DISCUSSION QUESTIONS

1. Describe the interrelationship between the consumer behavior discipline and the marketing concept.
2. Discuss the differences involved in marketing fax machines to personal consumers and to organizational consumers.
3. You are the brand manager of a new line of lightweight digital cameras. Describe how an understanding of consumer behavior is useful to you in terms of market segmentation strategy.

4. Is it ethical for marketers to promote expensive sneakers to inner-city youth? Explain your answer.
5. Compare the marketing concept with the societal marketing concept. Do you think marketers should adopt the societal marketing concept? In which industries does the immediate adoption of the societal marketing concept appear to be necessary?

KEY TERMS

- **Consumer behavior**
- **Consumer research**
- **Deontology**
- **Market segmentation**

- **Marketing concept**
- **Marketing ethics**
- **Organizational consumer**
- **Personal consumer**

- **Societal marketing concept**
- **Teleology**
- **Utilitarianism**

NOTES

1. Deborah Sontag and Celia W. Dugger, "The New Immigrant Tide: A Shuttle Between Worlds," *New York Times*, 19 July 1998, A1, 29–31.
2. See, for example, Claudia H. Deutsch, "Second Time Around and Around: Remanufacturing Is Gaining Ground in Corporate America," *New York Times*, 14 July 1998, C1.
3. Immanuel Kant, *Groundwork of the Metaphysics of Morals*, trans. H. J. Paton (New York: Harper & Row, 1964).
4. Philip Kotler, *Marketing Management Analysis: Planning and Control*, 9th ed. (Upper Saddle River, NJ: Prentice Hall, 1997).

CHAPTER 2
Consumer Research

■ ■

The field of consumer research developed as an extension of the field of marketing research, focusing almost exclusively on consumer behavior rather than on other aspects of the marketing process. Just as the findings of marketing research were used to improve managerial decision making, so too were the findings of consumer research. The initial reason for studying consumer behavior was to enable marketers to predict how consumers would react to promotional messages and to understand why they made the purchase decisions they did. Marketers assumed that if they knew everything there was to know about the consumer decision-making process, they could design marketing strategies and promotional messages that would influence the consumer in the desired way (that is, to purchase the marketer's product or service).

CONSUMER RESEARCH PARADIGMS

The early consumer researchers gave little thought to the impact of mood, emotion, or situation on consumer decisions. They believed that marketing was simply applied economics, and that consumers were rational decision makers who objectively evaluated the goods and services available to them and selected only those that gave them the highest utility (satisfaction) at the lowest cost.

Despite their assumptions that consumers were logical problem solvers who engaged in careful thought processes (i.e., information processing) to arrive at their consumption decisions, researchers soon realized that consumers were not always consciously aware of why they made the decisions they did. Even when they were aware of their basic motivations, consumers were not always willing to reveal those reasons. Then, in 1939, a Viennese psychoanalyst named Ernest Dichter began to use Freudian psychoanalytic techniques to uncover the hidden motivations of consumers. By the late 1950s, his research methodology (called *motivational research*), which was essentially qualitative in approach, was widely adopted by consumer researchers. As a result of Dichter's work and subsequent research designed to search deep within the consumer's psyche, consumer researchers today use two different types of research methodology to study consumer behavior—**quantitative research** and **qualitative research**.

QUANTITATIVE RESEARCH

Quantitative research is descriptive in nature and is used by researchers to understand the effects of various promotional inputs on the consumer, thus enabling marketers to "predict" consumer behavior. This research approach is known as **positivism**, and consumer researchers primarily concerned with predicting consumer behavior are known as *positivists*. (Other terms used to describe the positivist research paradigm include *modernism, logical empiricism, operationalism*, and *objectivism*.[1] The research methods used in positivist research are borrowed primarily from the natural sciences and consist of experiments, survey techniques, and observation. The findings are descriptive, empirical, and, if collected randomly (that is, using a probability sample), can be generalized to larger populations. Because the data collected are quantitative, they lend themselves to sophisticated statistical analysis.

QUALITATIVE RESEARCH

Qualitative research methods consist of depth interviews, focus groups, metaphor analysis, collage research, and projective techniques (discussed later in the chapter). These techniques are administered by a highly trained interviewer-analyst who also analyzes the findings—thus, they tend to be somewhat subjective. Because sample sizes are necessarily small, findings cannot be generalized to larger populations. They are primarily used to obtain new ideas for promotional campaigns.

Interpretivism

A number of academicians from the field of consumer behavior, as well as from other social science disciplines from which the consumer behavior field developed, have become more interested in the act of consumption rather than in the act of buying (that is, decision making). They view consumer behavior as a subset of human behavior, and increased understanding as a key to reducing some of the ills associated with consumer behavior (the so-called "dark side" of consumer behavior), such as drug addiction, shoplifting, alcoholism, and compulsive buying behavior. Interest in understanding consumer experiences has led to the term **interpretivism**, and the researchers who adopt this paradigm are known as *interpretivists, experientialists*, or *postmodernists*.[2] (Other terms used to describe this approach to consumer behavior include *naturalism, humanism*, and *postpositivism*.)[3]

Interpretivists engage in qualitative research. Among the research methodologies they use are ethnography, semiotics, and depth interviews. *Ethnography* is a technique borrowed from cultural anthropology in which the researchers place themselves— participate—in the society under study in an effort to absorb the meaning of various cultural practices. Ethnography lends itself easily to the study of all kinds of consumer behavior, including how individuals buy products and services.[4] (For example, in shopping for a cell phone, do consumers show more interest in clarity of sound or in phone size and weight?) Interpretivists are also very interested in *semiotics*—the study of symbols and the meanings they convey.[5] It is important for marketers to understand the meanings that nonverbal symbols convey to the target audience to be certain that their promotional symbols and logos enhance, rather than detract from, the persuasiveness of the message. The illustration in Figure 2-1 symbolizes and thus underscores the gracefulness of the advertised product.

Depth interviews are an important part of the interpretivist research process. The findings of an interpretive depth interview are likely to be unique to the specific researcher–consumer interaction, because interpretivist researchers sometimes play

FIGURE 2-1
Nonverbal Symbolism
Enhances the Message

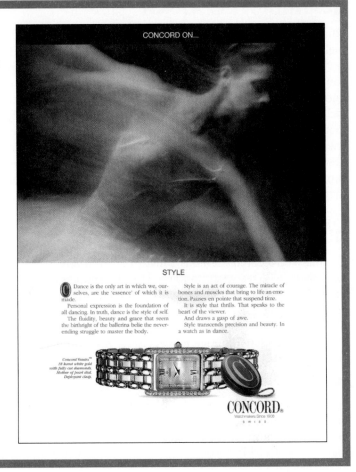

an active role in the interview process. Both interpretivist research and positivist research are often used to help make business decisions. Table 2-1 compares the purposes and assumptions of positivist research and interpretivist research

COMBINING QUALITATIVE AND QUANTITATIVE RESEARCH FINDINGS

Because of the limitations of qualitative research findings, some marketers use a combination of quantitative and qualitative research to help make strategic marketing decisions. They use qualitative research findings to discover new ideas and to develop promotional strategy, and quantitative research findings to predict consumer reactions to various promotional inputs. Sometimes ideas stemming from qualitative research are tested empirically and become the basis for the design of quantitative studies.

Marketers have discovered that, rather than conflicting, these two research paradigms are really complementary in nature. The prediction made possible by positivist research and the understanding provided by qualitative research together produce a richer and more robust profile of consumer behavior than either research approach used alone.[6] The combined findings enable both for-profit and not-for-profit marketers to design more meaningful and effective marketing strategies. Together they also provide a firmer basis for public policy decisions.

TABLE 2-1 Comparisons between Positivism and Interpretivism

PURPOSE

| Positivism | Prediction of consumer actions |
| Interpretivism | Understanding consumption practices |

METHODOLOGY

| Positivism | Quantitative |
| Interpretivism | Qualitative |

ASSUMPTIONS

Positivism

- Rationality: consumers make decisions after weighing alternatives
- The causes and effects of behavior can be identified and isolated
- Individuals are problem solvers who engage in information processing
- A single reality exists
- Events can be objectively measured
- Causes of behavior can be identified; by manipulating causes (i.e, inputs), the marketer can influence behavior (i.e., outcomes)
- Findings can be generalized to larger populations

Interpretivism

- There is no single, objective, truth
- Reality is subjective
- Cause and effect cannot be isolated
- Each consumption experience is unique
- Researcher/respondent interactions affect research findings
- Findings are often not generalized to larger populations

THE CONSUMER RESEARCH PROCESS

The major steps in the consumer research process include (1) defining the objectives of the research, (2) collecting and evaluating secondary data, (3) designing a primary research study, (4) collecting primary data, (5) analyzing the data, and (6) preparing a report on the findings. Figure 2-2 depicts a model of the consumer research process.

DEVELOPING RESEARCH OBJECTIVES

The first step in the consumer research process is to carefully define the objectives of the study. Is it to segment the market for wide-screen television? To find out consumer attitudes about on-line shopping? To determine what percentage of households use e-mail? It is important for the marketing manager and the researcher to agree at the outset on the purposes and objectives of the study to ensure that the research design is appropriate. A carefully thought-out statement of objectives helps to define the type and level of information needed.

For example, if the purpose of the study is to come up with new ideas for products or promotional campaigns, then a qualitative study is usually undertaken, in which respondents spend a significant amount of time face-to-face with a highly trained professional interviewer-analyst who also does the analysis. Because of the high costs

FIGURE 2-2

The Consumer Research
Process

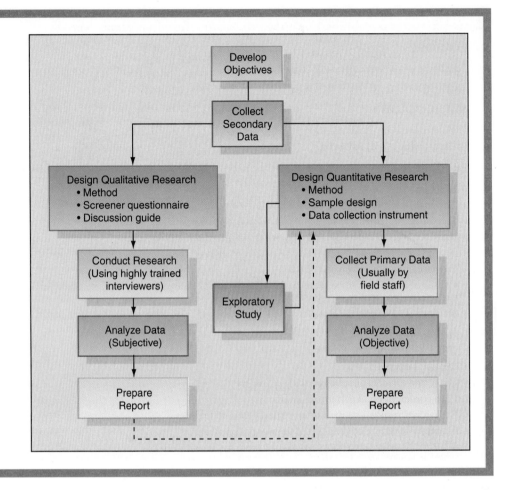

of each interview, a fairly small sample of respondents is studied; thus, the findings are not projectable to the marketplace. If the purpose of the study is to find out how many people in the population (that is, what percentage) use certain products and how frequently they use them, then a quantitative study that can be computer-analyzed is undertaken. Sometimes, in designing a quantitative study, the researcher may not know what questions to ask. In such cases, before undertaking a full-scale study, the researcher is likely to conduct a small-scale exploratory study to identify the critical issues to include in the data collection instrument (e.g., questionnaire).

COLLECTING SECONDARY DATA

A search for **secondary data** generally follows the statement of objectives. Secondary information is any data originally generated for some purpose other than the present research objectives. It includes findings based on research done by outside organizations, data generated in-house for earlier studies, and even customer information collected by the firm's sales or credit departments. Locating secondary data is called secondary research. (Original research performed by individual researchers or organizations to meet specific objectives is called **primary research**.) Secondary research findings sometimes provide sufficient insight into the problem at hand to eliminate the need for primary research. Most often, it provides clues and direction for the design of primary research. Government agencies, private population data firms, marketing research companies, and advertising agencies are all important sources of secondary market data. For example, the U.S. Census of Housing and Population collects data on the age, education, occupation, and income of residents of areas as small as a city block. Additional information on rents, places of work, automobile ownership, and patterns of migration is provided by the government in studies of census tracts within major metropolitan areas. Behaviorscan and the A. C. Nielsen Company regularly supply subscribers such as General Foods, Nabisco, and Procter & Gamble with brand-by-brand sales data for products sold in food and drug stores. Other marketing information routinely published by syndicated market research firms shows key demographic changes by census tracts (e.g., Census Update) or breaks down such data by postal zip codes (ZIProfile).

Retailers and not-for-profit organizations often have directly relevant demographic and usage information available in their own records. They can use credit and charge account data or mail-order records to identify just who their customers are, what products and brands they purchase, and how frequently they buy. Subscription and donor lists serve the same purpose for not-for-profit organizations and charities. Table 2-2 lists some major sources of secondary data.

If more detailed information on purchasing patterns or product usage is needed or if psychological or sociocultural consumer information is sought, then primary data must be collected. Research to secure such information is more costly and more time consuming than secondary research but is likely to yield a more accurate picture than studies based on secondary data alone.

DESIGNING PRIMARY RESEARCH

The design of a research study is based on the purposes of the study. If descriptive information is needed, then a quantitative study is likely to be undertaken; if the purpose is to get new ideas (for instance, for repositioning a product), then a qualitative study may be in order. Because the approach for each type of research differs in terms of method of data collection, sample design, and type of data collection instrument used, each research approach is discussed separately below.

Quantitative Research Designs

The design of a quantitative research study includes the method for collecting the data, the sample design, and construction of the data collection instrument (a questionnaire, for example).

Data Collection Methods   There are three basic ways to collect primary data in quantitative research: by observing behavior, by experimentation (in a laboratory or in the field, such as in a retail store), or by survey (that is, by questioning people).

Observational Research.   Observational research is an important method of consumer research, because marketers recognize that the best way to gain an in-depth understanding of the relationship between people and products is by watching them in the process of buying and using products. Many large corporations and advertising agencies use cultural anthropologists to observe and often videotape consumers in stores, malls, and their own homes (that is, to engage in *ethnographic research*). By watching people interact with products, observational researchers gain a better understanding of what the product symbolizes to a consumer and greater insight into the bond between people and products that is the essence of brand loyalty. Observational research is also widely used by interpretivist researchers to understand the buying and consumption process.

TABLE 2-2 Major Sources of Secondary Data

INTERNAL SOURCES

Internal sources include company profit-loss statements, balance sheets, sales figures, sales-call reports, invoices, inventory records, and prior research reports.

GOVERNMENT PUBLICATIONS

Statistical Abstract of the U.S., updated annually, provides summary data on demographic, economic, social, and other aspects of the American economy and society.

County and City Data Book, updated every three years, presents statistical information for counties, cities, and other geographical units on population, education, employment, aggregate and median income, housing, bank deposits, retail sales, etc.

U.S. Industrial Outlook provides projections of industrial activity by industry and includes data on production, sales, shipments, employment, etc.

Marketing Information Guide provides a monthly annotated bibliography of marketing information.

Other government publications include the *Annual Survey of Manufacturers; Business Statistics; Census of Manufacturers; Census of Population; Census of Retail Trade, Wholesale Trade, and Selected Service Industries; Census of Transportation; Federal Reserve Bulletin; Monthly Labor Review; Survey of Current Business;* and *Vital Statistics Report.*

PERIODICALS AND BOOKS

Business Periodicals Index, a monthly, lists business articles appearing in a wide variety of business publications.

Standard and Poor's Industry Surveys provides updated statistics and analyses of industries.

Moody's Manuals provide financial data and names of executives in major companies.

Encyclopedia of Associations provides information on every major trade and professional association in the United States.

Marketing journals include the *Journal of Marketing, Journal of Marketing Research*, and *Journal of Consumer Research.*

Useful trade magazines include *Advertising Age, Chain Store Age, Progressive Grocer, Sales and Marketing Management*, and *Stores.*

Useful general business magazines include *Business Week, Fortune, Forbes*, and *Harvard Business Review.*

COMMERCIAL DATA

A. C. Nielsen Company provides data on products and brands sold through retail outlets (Retail Index Services), data on television audiences (Media Research Services), magazine circulation data (Neodata Services, Inc.), etc.

Market Research Corporation of America provides data on weekly family purchases of consumer products (National Consumer Panel); data on home food consumption (National Menu Census); and data on 6,000 retail, drug, and discount retailers in various geographical areas (Metro Trade Audits).

Selling Areas-Marketing, Inc., provides reports on warehouse withdrawals to food stores in selected market areas (SAMI reports).

Simmons Market Research Bureau provides annual reports covering television markets, sporting goods, proprietary drugs, etc., giving demographic data by sex, income, age, and brand preferences (selective markets and media reaching them).

Burke Marketing Services, Inc., provides TV campaign testing in controlled marketing labs, marketing modeling, retail store audits, physiological measures of advertising stimuli, pre- and post-TV copy testing, and custom survey research.

Markets Facts, Inc., provides consumer mail panel, market test-store audit services, shopping mall facilities, WATS telephone interviewing, and ad hoc survey research.

Other commercial research houses selling data to subscribers include the Audit Bureau of Circulation, Audits and Surveys, Dun &Bradstreet, Opinion Research, Roper-Starch, and Arbitron.

Source: Adapted from Philip Kotler, *Marketing Management: Analysis, Planning, Implementation, and Control*, 9th ed. (Upper Saddle River, NJ: Prentice Hall, 1997).

Experimentation. It is possible to test the relative sales appeal of many types of variables such as package designs, prices, promotional offers, or copy themes through experiments designed to identify cause and effect. In such experiments (called *causal research*), only one variable is manipulated at a time (the *independent variable*), while all other elements are kept constant. A controlled experiment of this type ensures that any difference in outcome (the *dependent variable*) is due to different treatments of the variable under study and not to extraneous factors. For example, if IBM wanted to test the sales appeal of black laptops versus ivory-colored laptops, it could select two computer stores (or groups of stores) matched in terms of size, appearance, and type of neighborhood, and place a display of black laptops in one and the same model in ivory in the other. (Note that in each instance, the model of the computer displayed is held constant.) If one store sells significantly more units than the other during a specific time frame, the researcher could conclude that the difference in sales was due solely to the specific color of the computer, because all other factors (such as model, price, type of customer, and type of promotional appeal) were kept constant. —*or in the field*

Experiments are also conducted in laboratories with the use of special instrumentation, such as eye cameras that study the eye movement of subjects as they view competitive advertisements.[7]

Surveys. If researchers wish to ask consumers about their purchase preferences, they can do so in person, by mail, by telephone, or on-line. Each of these survey methods has certain advantages and certain disadvantages that the researcher must weigh when selecting the method of contact (see Table 2-3). *— Sample survey to check accuracy of reference info.*

Personal interview surveys most often take place in the home or in retail shopping areas. The latter, referred to as *mall intercepts*, are used more frequently than home interviews because of the high incidence of not-at-home working women and the reluctance of many people today to allow a stranger into their home.

Telephone surveys are also used to collect consumer data; however, evenings and weekends are often the only times to reach the working homemaker, who tends to be less responsive to calls that interrupt dinner, television viewing, or general relaxation. The difficulties of reaching people who have unlisted telephone numbers have been solved through random-digit dialing, and the costs of a widespread telephone survey are often minimized by using toll-free telephone lines. Other problems arise, however, from the increased use of answering machines and caller ID to screen calls, especially among the young affluent market segment. Some market research companies have tried to automate telephone surveys, but many respondents are even less willing to interact with an electronic voice than with a live interviewer.

Mail surveys are conducted by sending questionnaires directly to individuals at their home. One of the major problems of mail questionnaires is a low response rate, but researchers have developed a number of techniques to increase returns, such as

TABLE 2-3 Comparative Advantages of Mail, Telephone, and Personal Interview Surveys

	MAIL	TELEPHONE	PERSONAL INTERVIEW	ON-LINE
Cost	Low	Moderate	High	Low
Speed	Slow	Immediate	Slow	Fast
Response rate	Low	Moderate	High	Self-selection
Geographic flexibility	Excellent	Good	Difficult	Excellent
Interviewer bias	N/A	Moderate	Problematic	N/A
Interviewer supervision	N/A	Easy	Difficult	N/A
Quality of response	Limited	Limited	Excellent	Excellent

enclosing a stamped, self-addressed envelope, using a provocative questionnaire, sending prenotification letters and follow-up letters. A number of commercial research firms that specialize in consumer surveys have set up "panels" of consumers who, for a token fee, agree to complete the research company's mail questionnaires on a regular basis. Sometimes panel members are also asked to keep diaries of their purchases.

On-line surveys are sometimes conducted on the Internet. Respondents are directed to the marketer's (or the researcher's) Web sites by computer ads or home pages; thus, the samples tend to be self-selected and the results therefore cannot be projected to the larger population. (The CNN site plainly states that its "poll is not scientific and reflects the opinion of those Internet visitors who have chosen to participate.")[8] Most computer polls ask respondents to complete a profile consisting of demographic questions that enable the researchers to classify the responses to the substantive product or service questions.

Researchers who conduct computer polling believe that the anonymity of the Internet encourages respondents to be more forthright and honest than they would be if asked the same questions in person or by mail. Some survey organizations cite the inherent advantages of wide reach and affordability in on-line polling.

Data Collection Instruments   Data collection instruments are developed as part of a study's total research design to systematize the collection of data and to ensure that all respondents are asked the same questions in the same order. Data collection instruments include questionnaires, personal inventories, attitude scales, and, for qualitative data, discussion guides. Data collection instruments are usually pretested and "debugged" to assure the validity and reliability of the research study. A study is said to have **validity** if it does, in fact, collect the appropriate data needed to answer the questions or objectives stated in the first (Objectives) stage of the research process. A study is said to have **reliability** if the same questions, asked of a similar sample, produce the same findings. Often a sample is systematically divided in two, and each half is given the same questionnaire to complete. If the results from each half are similar, the questionnaire is said to have *split-half reliability*.

Questionnaires.   For quantitative research, the primary data collection instrument is the questionnaire, which can be sent through the mail to selected respondents for self-administration or can be administered by field interviewers in person or by telephone. In order to motivate respondents to take the time to respond to surveys, researchers have found that questionnaires must be interesting, objective, unambiguous, easy to complete, and generally not burdensome. To enhance the analysis and facilitate the classification of responses into meaningful categories, questionnaires include both substantive questions that are relevant to the purposes of the study, and pertinent demographic questions.

The questionnaire itself can be *disguised* or *undisguised* as to its true purpose; a disguised questionnaire sometimes yields more truthful answers and avoids responses that respondents may think are expected or sought. Questions can be open-ended (requiring answers in the respondent's own words) or closed-ended (the respondent merely checks the appropriate answer from a list of options). Open-ended questions yield more insightful information, but are more difficult to code and to analyze; closed-ended questions are relatively simple to tabulate and analyze, but the answers are limited to the alternative responses provided (that is, to the existing insights of the questionnaire designer). Great care must be taken in wording each question to avoid biasing the responses. The sequence of questions is also important: The opening questions must be interesting enough to "draw" the respondent into participating, they must proceed in a logical order, and demographic (classification) questions should be placed at the end, where they are more likely to be answered. The format of the questionnaire and the wording and sequence of the questions affect the validity of the responses and, in the case of mail questionnaires, the number (rate) of responses received. Questionnaires usually offer respondents confidentiality or anonymity to dispel any reluctance about self-disclosure.

Personal Inventories. Sometimes, instead of a list of questions, the data collection instrument presents a series of statements—a *personal inventory*—to which respondents are asked to indicate their degree of agreement or disagreement. The basic difference between an inventory and a questionnaire is that the inventory presents a list of statements, while the questionnaire asks a series of questions.

Attitude Scales. Researchers sometimes present respondents with a list of products or product attributes for which they are asked to indicate their relative feelings or evaluations. The instruments most frequently used to capture this evaluative data are called *attitude scales*. The most frequently used attitude scales are *Likert scales*, *semantic differential scales*, and *rank-order scales*.

The *Likert scale* is by far the most popular form of attitude scale because it is easy for researchers to prepare and to interpret, and simple for consumers to answer. They check or write the number corresponding to their level of "agreement" or "disagreement" with each of a series of statements that describe the attitude-object under investigation. Figure 2-3 presents an example of a five-point Likert scale. Note that the scale consists of an equal number of agreement–disagreement choices on either side of a neutral choice. A principal benefit of the Likert scale is that it gives the researcher the option of considering the responses to each statement separately, or of combining the responses to produce an overall, summated score. Because of this property, the Likert scale is often called a *summated scale*.

The *semantic differential scale*, like the Likert scale, is relatively easy to construct and administer. The scale typically consists of a series of bipolar adjectives (such as good/bad, hot/cold, like/dislike, or expensive/inexpensive) that are anchored at the

FIGURE 2-3
Example of a Likert Scale

Please place the number that best indicates how strongly you agree or disagree with each of the following statements about shopping on-line in the space to the left of the statement.

1 = Agree Strongly
2 = Agree
3 = Neither Agree nor Disagree
4 = Disagree
5 = Disagree Strongly

_____ a. It is fun to shop on-line.
_____ b. Products often cost more on-line than they are worth.
_____ c. It is a good way to find out about new products.
_____ d. I'm afraid to give out my credit card number on-line.
_____ e. I can shop whenever I want—even at 2 o'clock in the morning.
_____ f. Some Web sites really encourage you to browse.
_____ g. It's easy to compare different makes and models on-line.

ends of an odd-numbered (e.g., five- or seven-point) continuum. Respondents are asked to evaluate a concept (or a product or company) on the basis of each attribute by checking the point on the continuum that best reflects their feelings or beliefs. Sometimes an even-numbered scale is used to eliminate the option of a neutral answer. An important feature of the semantic differential is that it can be used to develop graphic consumer profiles of the concept under study. Figure 2-4 depicts semantic differential profiles of three on-line service providers. Semantic differential profiles are also used to compare consumer perceptions of competitive products, and to indicate areas for product improvement when perceptions of the existing product are measured against perceptions of the "ideal" product.

With *rank-order scales*, subjects are asked to rank items such as products (or retail stores or Web sites) in order of preference in terms of some criterion, such as overall quality or value for the money. Rank-order scaling procedures provide important competitive information and enable marketers to identify needed areas of improvement in product design and product positioning. Figure 2-5 illustrates how rank-order scales can be utilized in consumer research.

FIGURE 2-4

Semantic Differential Profiles of Three Pay-Per-Movie Services

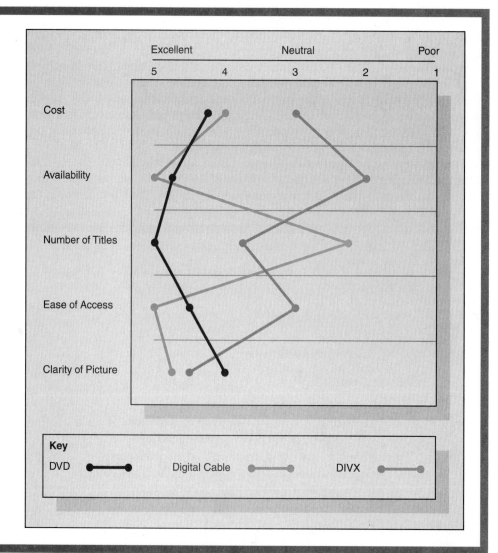

A. Please rank the following e-mail providers in terms of ease of access by placing a 1 in front of the service you think is best, a 2 alongside the second best, and continuing until you have ranked all six service providers.

_____ America Online
_____ Netscape
_____ Microsoft Explorer
_____ AT&T Worldnet
_____ Juno
_____ Erols

B. Rank the following computer manufacturers in terms of hotline help by placing a 1 next to the one who provides the best telephone help, a 2 next to the second best, until you have ranked all six.

_____ IBM
_____ Dell
_____ Compaq
_____ Hewlett Packard
_____ Gateway
_____ NEC

Qualitative Research Designs

In selecting the appropriate research format for a *qualitative* study, the researcher takes into consideration the purpose of the study and the types of data needed. Although the research methods used may differ in composition, they all have roots in psychoanalytic and clinical aspects of psychology, and they stress open-ended and free-response types of questions to stimulate respondents to reveal their innermost thoughts and beliefs.

Data Collection Methods The choice of data collection techniques for qualitative studies includes depth interviews, focus groups, projective techniques, and metaphor analysis. These techniques are regularly used in the early stages of attitude research to pinpoint relevant product-related beliefs or attributes and to develop an initial picture of consumer attitudes (especially the beliefs and attributes they associate with particular products and services).

Depth Interviews. A depth interview is a lengthy (generally 30 minutes to an hour), nonstructured interview between a respondent and a highly trained interviewer, who minimizes his or her own participation in the discussion after establishing the general subject to be discussed. (However, as noted earlier, interpretative researchers often take a more active role in the discussion.) Respondents are encouraged to talk freely about their activities, attitudes, and interests in addition to the product category or brand under study. Transcripts, videotapes, or audiotape recordings of interviews are then carefully studied, together with reports of respondents' moods and any gestures or "body language" that they might have used to convey attitudes or motives. Such studies provide marketers with valuable ideas about product design or redesign and provide insights for positioning or repositioning the product. For purposes of *copytesting*, respondents might be asked to describe in depth various ads they are shown. Other techniques include *autodriving* in which researchers show respondents photos, videos, and audiotapes of their own shopping behavior and ask them to explicitly comment on their consumption actions.[9]

Focus Groups. A focus group consists of 8 to 10 respondents who meet with a moderator-analyst for a group discussion "focused" on a particular product or product category (or any other subject of research interest). Respondents are encouraged to discuss their interests, attitudes, reactions, motives, lifestyles, feelings about the product or product category, usage experience, and so forth.

Because a focus group takes about 2 hours to complete, a researcher can easily conduct two or three focus groups (with a total of 30 respondents) in 1 day, while it might take that same researcher 5 or 6 days to conduct 30 individual depth interviews. Analysis of responses in both depth interviews and focus groups requires a great deal of skill on the part of the researcher. Focus-group sessions are invariably taped, and sometimes videotaped, to assist in the analysis. Interviews are usually held in specially designed conference rooms with one-way mirrors that enable marketers and advertising agency staff to observe the sessions without disrupting or inhibiting the responses.

Respondents are recruited on the basis of a carefully drawn consumer profile (called a *screener questionnaire*) based on specifications defined by marketing management, and usually are paid a fee for their participation. Sometimes users of the company's brands are clustered in one or more groups, and their responses are compared to those of nonusers interviewed in other groups.

Some focus groups take the form of *collage research*, in which the participants are given scissors, paste, paper, and magazines, and asked to make a collage representing themselves, as well as their relationship with the product category under study.

Some marketers prefer focus groups to individual depth interviews because it takes less time overall to complete the study, and they feel that the freewheeling group discussions and group dynamics tend to yield a greater number of new ideas and insights than depth interviews. Other marketers prefer individual depth interviews because they feel that respondents are free of group pressure and thus are less likely to give socially acceptable (and not necessarily truthful) responses, are more likely to remain attentive during the entire interview, and—because of the greater personal attention received—are more likely to reveal private thoughts. Figure 2-6 presents a

FIGURE 2-6
Selected Portions
of a Discussion Guide

1. Why did you decide to use your current cellular company? (Probe)
2. How long have you used your current cellular company? (Probe)
3. Have you ever switched services? When? What caused the change? (Probe)
4. What do you think of the overall quality of your current service? (Probe)
5. What are the important criteria in selecting a cellular service? (Probe)

Examples of Probe questions:
   a. Tell me more about that . . .
   b. Share your thinking on this . . .
   c. Does anyone see it differently . . .

portion of a discussion guide that might be used in a focus-group session to gain insights into the attitudes of consumers toward various cellular service providers. The findings would be equally relevant to the positioning of a new cellular service provider or the repositioning of an existing provider.

Projective Techniques. Projective techniques are designed to tap the underlying motives of individuals despite their unconscious rationalizations or efforts at conscious concealment. They consist of a variety of disguised "tests" that contain ambiguous stimuli, such as incomplete sentences, untitled pictures or cartoons, ink blots, word-association tests, and other-person characterizations. Projective techniques are sometimes administered as part of a focus group, but more often are used during depth interviews. A projective test can take the form of a word-association test ("What is the first word you think of when I say 'beer'?"), or a sentence completion test ("When I go to a ball game, I . . ."). Or, the respondent may be asked to complete, describe, or explain the meaning of various ambiguous stimuli. The theory behind projective tests is that respondents' inner feelings influence how they perceive such stimuli. The stories they tell or the sentences they complete are actually projections of their inner thoughts, even though subjects may attribute their responses to something or someone else. Thus, their responses are likely to reveal their underlying needs, wants, fears, and motives, whether or not the respondents are fully aware of them.

Metaphor Analysis. A new stream of consumer research suggests that most communication is nonverbal, and that people do not think in words, but in images.[10] If consumers' thought processes consist of a series of images, or pictures in their mind, then it is likely that many respondents cannot adequately convey their feelings and attitudes about the research subject (such as a product or brand) through the use of words alone. Therefore, it is important to enable consumers to represent their images in an alternate, nonverbal form—through the use, say, of sounds, music, drawings, or pictures. The use of one form of expression to describe or represent feelings about another is called a *metaphor*. A number of consumer theorists have come to believe that people use metaphors as the most basic method of thought and communication. In **metaphor analysis**, respondents are given magazines, scissors, paste, and paper and asked to cut out pictures from magazines that represent their "feelings" about the product category under study. They then organize these clippings into a "meaningful" collage, which is then explicated with the help of the researcher. The *collage research* method described earlier is a form of metaphor analysis. For example, a recent study explored the nature and study of nostalgia through the use of consumer collages.[11] The collages were created by small groups consisting of graduate students and included images based on both their personal and their cultural memories. The findings from this study are useful in the merchandising of nostalgia products (such as the hula hoop) or in the reissue of items of cultural nostalgia like the movie *Gone With the Wind*.

The *Zaltman Metaphor Elicitation Technique (ZMET)* combines collage research and metaphor analysis to bring to the surface the mental models and the major themes or constructs that drive consumer thinking and behavior.[12] Part of the construct elicitation process calls for the respondent to identify how any two of three stimuli presented are similar to each other but different from the third stimulus. This technique, called the *Kelly Repertory Grid*, brings to the surface the variables that the respondent uses to make sense of the meaning of a product category, a specific brand, or other consumption-related situation.[13]

Consumer values also play an important role in understanding consumer behavior in the marketplace. Several research techniques are used to study personal values. For example, a *means-end chain* can be used to identify the linkages that exist between the attributes of a product (the "means"), the consequences for the consumer provided by the attributes, and the consumer's personal values (the "ends" or goals) sought through use of the product category. This technique offers advertisers a way to position products by associating the *means* (the product's physical characteristics) with the consumer's desired *ends* (valued states).[14]

The research technique known as *laddering* provides researchers with insights into how consumers translate the attributes of products into meaningful associations tied to personal values.[15] Laddering involves a tailored interviewing format using a series of directed probes, with the express goal of determining sets of linkages that exist across the range of product attributes, anticipated consequences, and personal values. These association networks, or "ladders," represent combinations of perceived elements that enable consumers to distinguish between and among products in a given product category.

Sampling An integral component of a research design is the sampling plan. Specifically, the sampling plan addresses three questions: whom to survey (the sampling *unit*), how many to survey (the sample *size*), and how to select them (the sampling *procedure*). Deciding whom to survey requires explicit definition of the universe or boundaries of the market from which data is sought so that an appropriate sample can be selected (such as working mothers). Interviewing the correct target market or potential target market is basic to the validity of the study.

The size of the sample is dependent both on the size of the budget and on the degree of confidence that the marketer wants to place in the findings. The larger the sample, the more likely the responses will reflect the total universe under study. It is interesting to note, however, that a small sample can often provide highly reliable findings, depending on the sampling procedure adopted. (The exact number needed to achieve a specific level of confidence in the accuracy of the findings can be computed with a mathematical formula that is beyond the scope of this discussion.)

If the researcher wants the findings to be projectable to the total population, then a **probability sample** should be chosen; if it is sufficient to have the findings "representative" of the population, then a **nonprobability sample** can be selected. Table 2-4 summarizes the features of various types of probability and nonprobability designs.

TABLE 2-4 Probability and Nonprobability Sampling Designs

PROBABILITY SAMPLE

Simple random sample	Every member of the population has a known and equal chance of being selected.
Systematic random sample	A member of the population is selected at random and then every "nth" person is selected.
Stratified random sample	The population is divided into mutually exclusive groups (such as age groups), and random samples are drawn from each group.
Cluster (area) sample	The population is divided into mutually exclusive groups (such as blocks), and the researcher draws a sample of the groups to interview.

NONPROBABILITY SAMPLE

Convenience sample	The researcher selects the most accessible population members from whom to obtain information (e.g., students in a classroom).
Judgment sample	The researcher uses his or her judgment to select population members who are good sources for accurate information (e.g., experts in the relevant field of study).
Quota sample	The researcher interviews a prescribed number of people in each of several categories (e.g., 50 men and 50 women).

DATA COLLECTION

As indicated earlier, qualitative studies usually require highly trained social scientists to collect data. A quantitative study generally uses a field staff that is either recruited and trained directly by the researcher or contracted from a company that specializes in conducting field interviews. In either case, it is often necessary to verify whether the interviews have, in fact, taken place. This is sometimes done by a postcard mailing to respondents asking them to verify that they participated in an interview on the date recorded on the questionnaire form. Completed questionnaires are reviewed on a regular basis as the research study progresses to ensure that the recorded responses are clear, complete, and legible.

ANALYSIS

In qualitative research, the moderator or test administrator usually analyzes the responses received. In quantitative research, the researcher supervises the analysis. Open-ended responses are first coded and quantified (that is, converted into numerical scores); then all of the responses are tabulated and analyzed using sophisticated analytical programs that correlate the data by selected variables and cluster the data by selected demographic characteristics.

REPORT PREPARATION

In both qualitative and quantitative research, the research report includes a brief executive summary of the findings. Depending on the assignment from marketing management, the research report may or may not include recommendations for marketing action. The body of the report includes a full description of the methodology used and, for quantitative research, also includes tables and graphics to support the findings. A sample of the questionnaire is usually included in the appendix to enable management to evaluate the objectivity of the findings.

CONDUCTING A RESEARCH STUDY

In designing a research study, researchers adapt the research process described in the previous sections to the special needs of the study. For example, if a researcher is told that the purpose of the study is to develop a segmentation strategy for a new on-line dating service, he or she would first collect secondary data, such as population statistics (e.g., the number of men and women on-line in selected metropolitan areas within a certain age range, their marital status and occupations). Then, together with the marketing manager, the researcher would specify the parameters (that is, define the sampling unit) of the population to be studied (for instance, single, college-educated men and women between the ages of 18 and 45 who live or work within the Boston metropolitan area). A qualitative study (e.g., focus groups) might be undertaken first to gather information about the target population's attitudes and concerns about meeting people on-line, their special interests, and the specific services and precautions they would like an on-line dating service to provide. This phase of the research should result in tentative generalizations about the specific age group(s) to target and the services to offer.

The marketing manager then might instruct the researcher to conduct a quantitative study to confirm and attach "hard" numbers (percentages) to the findings that emerged from the focus groups. The first-phase study should have provided sufficient insights to develop a research design and to launch directly into a large-scale survey. If, however, there is still doubt about any element of the research design, such as question wording or format, they might decide first to do a small-scale exploratory study. After refining the questionnaire and any other needed elements of the research design, they would launch a full-scale quantitative survey, using a probability sample that would allow them to project the findings to the total population of singles (as originally defined). The analysis should cluster prospective consumers of the on-line dating service into segments based on relevant sociocultural or lifestyle characteristics and on media habits, attitudes, perceptions, and geodemographic characteristics.

SUMMARY

The field of consumer research developed as an extension of the field of marketing research to enable marketers to predict how consumers would react in the marketplace and to understand the reasons they made the purchase decisions they did. Consumer research undertaken from a managerial perspective to improve strategic marketing decisions is known as positivism. Positivist research is quantitative and empirical and tries to identify cause-and-effect relationships in buying situations. It is often supplemented with qualitative research.

Qualitative research is more concerned with probing deep within the consumer's psyche to understand the motivations, feelings, and emotions that drive consumer behavior. Qualitative research findings cannot be projected to larger populations, but are used primarily to provide new ideas and insights for the development of positioning strategies. Interpretivism, a qualitative research perspective, is generally more concerned with understanding the act of consuming itself rather than the act of buying (consumer decision making). Interpretivists view consumer behavior as a subset of human behavior, and increased understanding as

a key to eliminating some of the ills associated with destructive consumer behavior.

Each theoretical research perspective is based on its own specific assumptions and uses its own research technologies. Positivists generally use probability studies that can be generalized to larger populations. Interpretivists tend to view consumption experiences as unique situations that occur at specific moments in time; therefore they cannot be generalized to larger populations. The two theoretical research orientations are highly complementary and, when used together, provide a deeper and more insightful understanding of consumer behavior than either approach used alone.

The consumer research process—whether quantitative or qualitative in approach—generally consists of six steps: defining objectives, collecting secondary data, developing a research design, collecting primary data, analyzing the data, and preparing a report of the findings. The researcher must make every effort to ensure that the research findings are reliable—that a replication of the study would provide the same results—and valid (that they answer the specific questions for which the study was originally undertaken).

DISCUSSION QUESTIONS

1. Why might a researcher prefer to use focus groups rather than depth interviews? When might depth interviews be preferable?

2. Under what circumstances might the availability of secondary data make primary research unnecessary? What are some common sources of secondary data?

3. Which research paradigm (positivist or interpretivist) is more focused on discovering "objective" facts? Do both paradigms produce facts?

4. How would the interpretation of survey results change if the researcher used a probability sample rather than a nonprobability sample?

5. Secondary data in the form of information about consumers' buying habits is collected by many research firms and sold to marketers. Some people believe that collecting and selling such data is unethical and constitutes invasion of privacy. Do you agree or disagree? Why?

6. Probability sampling is not an issue in qualitative research. Why?

EXERCISES

1. Have you ever been selected as a respondent in a marketing research survey? If yes, how were you contacted? Why do you think you, in particular, were selected? Did you know or could you guess the purpose of the survey? Do you know the name of the company or brand involved in the survey?

2. Identify a purchase you have made that was motivated primarily by your desire to obtain a special "feeling" or an "experience." Would the positivist or interpretivist research paradigm be a more appropriate way to study your consumption behavior? Explain your answer.

3. A. Develop a questionnaire to measure students' attitudes toward the instructor in this course.

    (1) Prepare five statements to be evaluated on a Likert scale.

    (2) Prepare five semantic differential scales to measure student attitudes. Can the same dimensions be measured by using either scaling technique? Explain your answer.

  B. Administer the questionnaire you developed to several students in your class. Discuss any response-related problems you encountered.

KEY TERMS

- **Depth interview**
- **Focus group**
- **Interpretivism**
- **Metaphor analysis**
- **Nonprobability sample**

- **Positivism**
- **Primary research**
- **Probability sample**
- **Projective techniques**
- **Qualitative research**

- **Quantitative research**
- **Reliability**
- **Secondary data**
- **Validity**

NOTES

1. Richard Lutz, "Positivism, Naturalism, and Pluralism in Consumer Research: Paradigms in Paradise," *Advances in Consumer Research* 16 (Provo, UT: Association for Consumer Research, 1989), 17; Bobby J. Calder and Alice M. Tybout, "Interpretive, Qualitative, and Traditional Scientific Empirical Consumer Behavior Research," in *Interpretive Consumer Research*, ed. Elizabeth C. Hirschman (Provo, UT: Association for Consumer Research, 1989), 199–208.

2. John Sherry, "Postmodern Alternatives: The Interpretive Turn in Consumer Research," in *Handbook of Consumer Behavior*, ed. H. Kassarjian and T. Robertson (Upper Saddle River, NJ: Prentice Hall, 1991); Morris B. Holbrook and John O'Shaughnessy, "On the Scientific Status of Consumer Research and the Need for an Interpretive Approach to Studying Consumption Behavior," *Journal of Consumer Research* 15 (December 1988): 398–402; Morris Holbrook and Elizabeth C. Hirschman, "The Experiential Aspects of Consumption: Consumer Fantasies, Feelings, and Fun," *Journal of*

Consumer Research, 9, 2 (1982): 132–40; Julie L. Ozanne and Laurel Anderson Hudson, "Exploring Diversity in Consumer Research," in *Interpretive Consumer Research*, ed. Elizabeth C. Hirschman (Provo, UT: Association for Consumer Research, 1989), 1–9; and Laurel Anderson Hudson and Julie L. Ozanne, "Alternative Ways of Seeking Knowledge in Consumer Research," *Journal of Consumer Research* 14 (March 1988): 508–21.

3. See, for example, Shelby D. Hunt, "Naturalistic, Humanistic, and Interpretive Inquiry: Challenges and Ultimate Potential," in *Interpretive Consumer Research*, ed. Elizabeth C. Hirschman (Provo, UT: Association for Consumer Research, 1989), 185–98; Melanie Wallendorf and Russell Belk, "Assessing Trustworthiness in Naturalistic Consumer Research," in *Interpretive Consumer Research*, ed. Elizabeth C. Hirschman (Provo, UT: Association for Consumer Research, 1989), 69–84; Elizabeth C. Hirschman, "Humanistic Inquiry in Marketing Research, Philosophy, Method, and Criteria," *Journal of Marketing Research* 23 (August 1986): 237–49; Paul F.

Anderson, "On Method in Consumer Research: A Critical Relativistic Perspective," *Journal of Consumer Research* 13 (September 1986): 155–73; and Timothy B. Heath, "The Reconciliation of Humanism and Positivism in the Practice of Consumer Research: A View from the Trenches," *Journal of the Academy of Marketing Science* 20, 2 (1992): 107–18.

4. See Ronald Paul Hill, "Ethnology and Marketing Research: A Postmodern Perspective," Proceedings, AMA Educators' Conference, vol. 4 (1993): 257–61; also Eric J. Arnould and Melanie Wallendorf, "Market-Oriented Ethnography: Interpretation Building and Marketing Strategy Formulation," *Journal of Marketing Research* 31 (November 1994): 484–504.

5. Anil Pandya and A. Venkatesh, "Symbolic Communication among Consumers in Self-Consumption and Gift Giving: A Semiotic Approach," in *Advances in Consumer Research*, vol. 19, ed. John F. Sherry and Brian Sternthal (Provo, UT: Association for Consumer Research, 1992), 147–54; David Mick, "Consumer Research and Semiotics: Exploring the Morphology of Signs, Symbols, and Significance," *Journal of Consumer Research* 13, 2 (1986): 196–213; and Winfred Noth, "The Language of Commodities: Groundwork for a Semiotics of Consumer Goods," *International Journal of Research in Marketing* 4, 3 (1988): 173–86.

6. Not all researchers agree that interpretive research enhances traditional quantitative and qualitative market research. See, for example, Stephen Brown, "No Representation without Taxation: Postmodern Marketing Research," Proceedings, American Marketing Association Educators' Conference (Summer 1995): 256–62.

7. Warren F. Kuhfeld, Randall D. Tobias, and Mark Garratt, "Efficient Experimental Design with Marketing Research Applications," *Journal of Marketing Research* 31 (November 1994): 545–57.

8. Matt Richtel, "On-Line Polling Is More Business Than Science," *The New York Times*, 9 July 1998, E3.

9. Deborah D. Heisley and Sidney J. Levy, "Autodriving: A Photoelicitation Technique," *Journal of Consumer Research* 18 (December 1991): 257–72.

10. William J. Havlena and Susan L. Holak, "Exploring Nostalgia Imagery Through the Use of Consumer Collages," *Advances in Consumer Research*, 23 (1996): 35–42.

11. The following discussion is drawn from Gerald Zaltman, "Rethinking Market Research: Putting People Back In," *Journal of Marketing Research*, 34 (November 1997): 424–37 and from Gerald Zaltman and Robin Higie Coulter, "Seeing the Voice of the Customer: Metaphor-Based Advertising Research," *Journal of Advertising Research* (July–August 1995): 35–51.

12. Zaltman and Coulter, "Seeing the Voice."

13. George A. Kelly, *A Theory of Personality* (New York: W. W. Norton, 1963).

14. Jonathan Gutman, "A Means-End Chain Model Based on Consumer Categorization Processes," *Journal of Marketing* 46 (Spring 1982): 60–72.

15. Thomas J. Reynolds and Jonathan Gutman, "Laddering Theory, Method, Analysis, and Interpretation," *Journal of Advertising Research* (February–March 1988): 11–31.

CHAPTER 3
Market Segmentation

■ ■

Market segmentation and diversity are complementary concepts. Without a diverse marketplace composed of many different peoples with different backgrounds, countries of origin, interests, and needs and wants, there would be little reason to segment markets. Diversity in the global marketplace makes market segmentation an attractive, viable, and potentially highly profitable strategy. The necessary conditions for successful segmentation are a large enough population with sufficient money to spend (general affluence) and sufficient diversity to lend itself to partitioning into sizable segments on the basis of demographic, psychological, or other strategic variables. The presence of these conditions in the United States, Canada, Western Europe, Japan, Australia, and other industrialized nations makes these marketplaces extremely attractive to global marketers.

When marketers provide a range of product or service choices to meet diverse consumer interests, consumers are better satisfied, and their overall happiness, satisfaction, and quality of life are ultimately enhanced. Thus, market segmentation is a positive force for both consumers and marketers alike.

WHAT IS MARKET SEGMENTATION?

Market segmentation can be defined as the process of dividing a market into distinct subsets of consumers with common needs or characteristics and selecting one or more segments to target with a distinct marketing mix. Before the widespread acceptance of market segmentation, the prevailing way of doing business with consumers was through **mass marketing**—that is, offering the same product and marketing mix to all consumers. The essence of this strategy was summed up by the entrepreneur Henry Ford, who offered the Model T automobile to the public "in any color they wanted, as long as it was black."

If all consumers were alike—if they all had the same needs, wants, and desires, and the same background, education, and experience—mass (undifferentiated) marketing would be a logical strategy. Its primary advantage is that it costs less: Only one advertising campaign is needed, only one marketing strategy is developed, and usually only one standardized product is offered. Some companies, primarily those that deal in agricultural products or very basic manufactured goods, successfully follow a mass-marketing strategy. Other marketers, however, see major drawbacks in an undifferentiated marketing approach. When trying to sell the same product to every prospective customer with a single advertising campaign, the marketer must portray its product as a means for satisfying a common or generic need, and often ends up appealing to no one. A washing machine may fulfill a widespread need to clean dirty laundry, but a standard-size washing machine may be too big for a grandmother who lives alone and too small for a family of six. Without market differentiation, both the grandmother and the family of six would have to make do with the very same model, and, as we all know, "making do" is a far cry from being satisfied.

The strategy of segmentation allows producers to avoid head-on competition in the marketplace by differentiating their offerings, not only on the basis of price, but also through styling, packaging, promotional appeal, method of distribution, and superior service. Marketers have found that the costs of consumer segmentation research, shorter production runs, and differentiated promotional campaigns are usually more than offset by increased sales. In most cases, consumers readily accept the passed-through cost increases for products that more closely satisfy their specific needs.

Market segmentation is just the first step in a three-phase marketing strategy. After *segmenting* the market into homogeneous clusters, the marketer then must select one or more segments to *target*. To accomplish this, the marketer must decide on a specific *marketing mix*—that is, a specific product, price, channel, and/or promotional appeal for each distinct segment. The third step is **positioning** the product so that it is perceived by the consumers in each target segment as satisfying his or her needs better than other competitive offerings.

WHO USES MARKET SEGMENTATION?

Because the strategy of market segmentation benefits both sides of the marketplace, marketers of consumer goods are eager practitioners. For example, consider two very diverse product categories—automobiles and shampoos. Toyota targets its Celica automobile, with its sporty styling, minimal rear seat, and small trunk, to young singles; and targets its Avalon, a much larger vehicle, at the family car buyer needing a roomier vehicle. Procter & Gamble targets its shampoos to different segments of the hair care market. For example, Procter & Gamble's Pert is targeted to the person who wants a single product that will both clean and condition hair; and Head & Shoulders is targeted to individuals who are concerned about dandruff.

Market segmentation also has been adopted by retailers. A great example is The Gap, Inc. The Gap targets different age, income, and lifestyle segments in a diversity of retail outlets. The Gap and Super Gap stores are designed to attract a wide age range of consumers who seek a casual and relaxed style of dress. Gap targets upscale consumers through its Banana Republic stores and somewhat downscale customers with its Old Navy Clothing Company stores. It targets young parents (who are also likely to be Gap or Banana Republic shoppers) with its Baby Gap and Gap Kids stores.[1] The Gap is mindful of catering to the needs of specific market components and acknowledging their unique or particular buying patterns. In this spirit, it is securing additional sales from time-harried New Yorkers by offering a Gap-to-Go menu targeting customers residing in Manhattan or the Hamptons on Long Island, who can either call or fax in their orders for a limited variety of basic or staple products. If ordered early enough in the day, Gap-to-Go delivers the products that same day to the customer's home or office.

Hotels also segment their markets and target different chains to different market segments. For example, Marriott operates the *Fairfield Inns* (for short stays) and *Residence Inns* (apartment-like accommodations for extended stays) for the value- or budget-oriented traveler, *Courtyard* for the price-conscious businessperson, *Marriott Hotels* for full-service business travelers, *Marriott Resorts* for leisure and vacation guests, *Marriott Time Sharing* for those seeking affordable resort ownership, and *Marriott Senior Living* environments for elderly people. Marriott also owns the company that operates the luxury *Ritz-Carlton* hotel chain. Similarly, the Holiday Inn hotel chain operates units under the names *Holiday Inn* and *Holiday Inn Hotels and Suites*, as well as *Holiday Inn Express* (budget hotels), *Holiday Inn Select* (business-oriented hotels), *Holiday Inn SunSpree Resort* (full-activity hotels in vacation areas), and *Holiday Inn Garden Court*.[2]

Industrial manufacturers also segment their markets, as do not-for-profit organizations and the media. For example, Boeing produces different models of aircraft to meet the needs of the airlines, air charter services, the military, and airfreight companies. Charities such as the Heart Fund or the Red Cross frequently focus their fund-raising efforts on "heavy givers." Some Performing Arts Centers segment their subscribers on the basis of *benefits sought* and have succeeded in increasing attendance through specialized promotional appeals.

HOW MARKET SEGMENTATION OPERATES

Segmentation studies are designed to discover the needs and wants of specific groups of consumers, so that specialized goods and services can be developed and promoted to satisfy each group's needs. Many new products have been developed to fill gaps in the marketplace revealed by segmentation research. For instance, Bayer, makers of the One-A-Day vitamins, has developed a variety of products that are designed to appeal directly to different age and gender market segments in terms of their specific vitamin requirements.

Segmentation studies also are used to guide the redesign or **repositioning** of a product or the addition of a new market segment. For example, Nintendo, very successful in capturing a large share of the children's market for its electronic games, now seeks to attract adult users. The ongoing ad campaign appeals to potential adult game players by promising them "kid-like" fun, a notion that many adults find appealing. Similarly, Wolverine, perhaps best known as a manufacturer of men's work boots, now markets a work boot especially designed for women's feet (see Figure 3-1).

In addition to filling product gaps, segmentation research is used by marketers to identify the most appropriate media in which to place advertisements. Almost all media vehicles—from TV and radio stations to newspapers and magazines—use segmentation research to determine the characteristics of their audience and to publicize their findings in order to attract advertisers seeking a similar audience. For example, Time Warner has created a separate division to market magazines to baby boomers (for example, *In Health*, *Parenting*, *Cooking Light*, and *Martha Stewart Living*). The titles reveal why these magazines would be of interest to "aging" baby boomers. In a somewhat similar fashion, *Business Week* targets different segments with special editions of its magazine. Not only does an advertiser have the choice of placing an ad in geographically-based editions (for example, worldwide, continental, regional, state, and city versions of each issue), but the magazine also offers an Industrial/Technology edition (for individuals working in industries such as manufacturing and mining), an Elite edition (targeted to subscribers living in high-income zip codes and to senior management titles receiving the magazine at their offices), and a Small Business Enterprise edition. New magazines are constantly being created to meet the unfulfilled needs of specific market segments. For example, *Mode* (a fashion magazine for the full-figured woman) has created clothing and advertising messages that stress the fashionability of its products, which are targeted to a market segment consisting of full-figured women.[3]

FIGURE 3-1

Wolverine Branches Out from Its Traditional Male Market Segment

BASES FOR SEGMENTATION

The first step in developing a segmentation strategy is to select the most appropriate base(s) on which to segment the market. Nine major categories of consumer characteristics provide the most popular bases for market segmentation. They include geographic factors, demographic factors, psychological factors, psychographic (lifestyle) characteristics, sociocultural variables, use-related characteristics, use-situation factors, benefits sought, and hybrid segmentation forms, such as demographic-psychographic profiles, geodemographic factors, and values and lifestyles. Hybrid segmentation formats each use of a combination of several segmentation bases to create rich and comprehensive profiles of particular consumer segments (e.g., a specific age range, income range, lifestyle, and profession). For example, *The Bump Fighter Shaving System*, manufactured by the American Safety Razor Company, is a razor designed specifically for "African American Males," while the Honda Prelude is targeted to young, moderate to higher income singles and young marrieds. Table 3-1 lists the nine segmentation bases, divided into specific variables with examples of each. The following section discusses each of the nine segmentation bases. (Various psychological and sociocultural segmentation variables are examined in greater depth in later chapters.)

TABLE 3-1 Market Segmentation Categories and Selected Variables

SEGMENTATION BASE	SELECTED SEGMENTATION VARIABLES
GEOGRAPHIC SEGMENTATION	
Region	Southwest, Mountain states, Alaska, Hawaii
City size	Major metropolitan areas, small cities, towns
Density of area	Urban, suburban, exurban, rural
Climate	Temperate, hot, humid, rainy
DEMOGRAPHIC SEGMENTATION	
Age	Under 12, 12–17, 18–34, 35–49, 50–64, 65–74, 75–99, 100+
Sex	Male, female
Marital status	Single, married, divorced, living together, widowed
Income	Under $25,000, $25,000–$34,999, $35,000–$49,999, $50,000–$74,999, $75,000–$99,000, $100,000 and over
Education	Some high school, high school graduate, some college, college graduate, postgraduate
Occupation	Professional, blue-collar, white-collar, agricultural, military
PSYCHOLOGICAL SEGMENTATION	
Needs-motivation	Shelter, safety, security, affection, sense of self-worth
Personality	Extroverts, novelty seekers, aggressives, low dogmatics
Perception	Low-risk, moderate-risk, high-risk
Learning-involvement	Low-involvement, high-involvement
Attitudes	Positive attitude, negative attitude
PSYCHOGRAPHIC	
(Lifestyle) Segmentation	Economy-minded, couch potatoes, outdoors enthusiasts, status seekers
SOCIOCULTURAL SEGMENTATION	
Cultures	American, Italian, Chinese, Mexican, French, Pakistani
Religion	Catholic, Protestant, Jewish, Moslem, other
Subcultures (Race/ethnic)	African American, Caucasian, Asian, Hispanic
Social class	Lower, middle, upper
Family life cycle	Bachelors, young marrieds, full nesters, empty nesters
USE-RELATED SEGMENTATION	
Usage rate	Heavy users, medium users, light users, nonusers
Awareness status	Unaware, aware, interested, enthusiastic
Brand loyalty	None, some, strong
USE-SITUATION SEGMENTATION	
Time	Leisure, work, rush, morning, night
Objective	Personal, gift, snack, fun, achievement
Location	Home, work, friend's home, in-store
Person	Self, family members, friends, boss, peer
BENEFIT SEGMENTATION	Convenience, social acceptance, long lasting, economy, value-for-the-money
HYBRID SEGMENTATION	
Demographic/psychographic	Combination of demographic and psychographic profiles of consumer segments profiles
Geodemographics	"Money and Brains," "Black Enterprise," "Old Yankee Rows," "Downtown Dixie-Style"
SRI VALS™	Actualizer, fulfilled, believer, achiever, striver, experiencer, maker, struggler

VALS™ is an example of a demographic/psychographic profile. PRIZM is an example of a geodemographic profile.

GEOGRAPHIC SEGMENTATION

In **geographic segmentation**, the market is divided by location. The theory behind this strategy is that people who live in the same area share some similar needs and wants, and that these needs and wants differ from those of people living in other areas. For example, certain food products and/or varieties sell better in one region than in others (for example, canned tuna sells best in the Northeast; mild salsa sells best in the East, while hot salsa sells best in the West; Cincinnati residents prefer chicken noodle soup, while El Paso residents prefer chicken with rice). Geographic preferences may also extend to brands, with the East and West Coasts preferring Skippy peanut butter, the Midwest preferring Jif, and the South buying more Peter Pan.[4]

Some regional consumption differences can be accounted for by climate. The Sunbelt regions of the South and West represent better opportunities for selling bathing suits and in-ground pools than the Snowbelt regions of the North and East, where snowblowers and children's sleds are likely to be better sellers.

Some marketing scholars have argued that direct mail merchandise catalogs, national toll-free telephone numbers, satellite television transmission, global communication networks, and the Internet have erased all regional boundaries, and that geographic segmentation should be replaced by a single global marketing strategy. Clearly, any company that decides to put its catalog on the Internet makes it easy for individuals all over the world to browse and become customers. For example, scuba diving equipment retailers in New York and Chicago have posted their catalogs on the Web, advertise their Web addresses in scuba diving magazines, and gladly accept orders from both U.S. and overseas customers. For the consumers who shop on the Internet, it makes little difference if on-line retailers are around the corner or halfway around the world—the only factor that differs is the shipping charge.

Other marketers have, for a number of years, been moving in the opposite direction and developing highly regionalized marketing strategies. For example, Campbell's Soup segments its domestic market into more than 20 regions, each with its own advertising and promotion budget. Within each region, Campbell's sales managers have the authority to develop specific advertising and promotional campaigns geared to local market needs and conditions, using local media ranging from newspapers to church bulletins. They work closely with local retailers on displays and promotions and report that their **micromarketing** strategies have won strong consumer support.

Marketers have observed divergent consumer purchasing patterns among urban, suburban, and rural areas. Throughout the United States, more furs and expensive jewelry are sold in cities than in small towns. Even within a large metropolitan area, different types of household furnishings and leisure products are sold in the central city and in the suburbs. Convertible sofas and small appliances are more likely to be bought by city apartment dwellers; suburban homeowners are better prospects for lawn mowers and barbecue grills. Probably the best example of successful segmentation based on geographic density is the giant Wal-Mart operation. Wal-Mart's basic marketing strategy was to locate discount stores in small towns (often in rural areas) that other major retail chain operations were ignoring at the time.

In summary, geographic segmentation is a useful strategy for many marketers. It is relatively easy to find geographically-based differences for many products. In addition, geographic segments can be easily reached through the local media, including newspapers, TV and radio, and regional editions of magazines.

DEMOGRAPHIC SEGMENTATION

Demographic characteristics, such as age, sex, marital status, income, occupation, and education, are most often used as the basis for market segmentation. *Demography* refers to the vital and measurable statistics of a population. Demographics help to *locate* a target market, whereas psychological and sociocultural characteristics help to *describe* how its members *think* and how they *feel*. Demographic information is often the most accessible and cost-effective way to identify a target market. Indeed, most secondary data, including census data, are expressed in demographic terms. Demographics are easier to measure than other segmentation variables; they are invariably included in psychographic and sociocultural studies because they add meaning to the findings. *American Demographics Magazine* publishes each month research dealing with demographic issues, and a number of its articles relate demographic variables to other segmentation bases.

Demographic variables reveal ongoing trends that signal business opportunities, such as shifts in age, gender, and income distribution. For example, demographic studies consistently show that the "mature-adult market" (the 50-plus market) has a much greater proportion of disposable income than its younger counterparts. This factor alone makes consumers over age 50 a critical market segment for products and services that they buy for themselves, for their adult children, and for their grandchildren.

Age

Product needs and interests often vary with consumers' age. For instance, while adults of all ages join health clubs primarily to "improve or maintain their health," there are some other interesting motivations that set adult age segments apart with regard to joining a health club. Specifically, it appears that younger adults (those 18–34 years of age) join health clubs in part because they desire to "look good," those who are between 35 and 54 years of age join to "deal with stress," and those who are 55 and older join for "medical-physical therapy."[5] Because of such age-motivational differences, marketers have found age to be a particularly useful demographic variable for market segmentation. Many marketers have carved themselves a niche in the marketplace by concentrating on a specific age segment. For example, Oscar Mayer Foods has been very successful with its *Lunchables* brand of prepackaged meals targeted to 4-to-9 year olds, that it is now extending the concept to adult meals with the introduction of six varieties of *Lunchables Deli-Carryouts*. Each of the six varieties will include bread, meat, cheese, condiments, side dish, and dessert, and will also be available in low-fat versions.[6]

Age, especially chronological age, implies a number of underlying forces. In particular, demographers have drawn an important distinction between *age effects* (occurrences due to chronological age) and *cohort effects* (occurrences due to growing up during a specific time period). Examples of the *age effect* are the heightened interest in leisure travel that often occurs when people (single and married) reach middle age (their late fifties or early sixties) and in the interest in learning to play golf. While people of all ages learn and play golf, it is particularly prevalent among people in their fifties. These two trends are examples of age effects because they especially seem to happen as people reach a particular age category.

In contrast, the nature of *cohort effects* is captured by the idea that people hold onto the interests they grew up to appreciate. If 10 years from today it is determined that many rock-and-roll fans are over 50, it would not be because older people have suddenly altered their musical tastes, but that the baby boomers who grew up with rock and roll have become older.[7] As Bill Whitehead, CEO of the advertising agency Bates North America, noted: "When baby boomers are 70, they'll still eat pizza and still listen to the [Rolling] Stones."[8] It is important for marketers to be aware of the distinction between age effects and cohort effects: One stresses the impact of aging, while the second stresses the influence of the period when one is born and shared related experiences with others of the same age (i.e., experienced the same general history—music, TV shows, and emerging technology).

The notion of segmenting a market based upon cohort effects has been bolstered by a categorization system called *Cohorts II*, which first classifies consumer households into one of 27 types configured on the basis of gender and marital status. In addition, Cohorts II considers age, family income, occupation, home ownership, and the presence of children in the home. The Bombay Company, a national retailer of furniture and home accessories, has used the Cohorts II scheme. The company found that almost half of all Bombay's customers came from only five of the 27 Cohorts II groups; an analysis of this information was used to determine who should receive future direct-mail pieces.[9]

Sex

Gender is quite frequently a distinguishing segmentation variable. Women have traditionally been the main users of such products as hair coloring and cosmetics, and men have been the main users of tools and shaving preparations. However, sex roles have blurred, and gender is no longer an accurate way to distinguish consumers in some product categories. For example, women are buying household repair tools, and men have become significant users of skin care and hair products. It is becoming increasingly common to see magazine ads and TV commercials that depict men and women in roles traditionally occupied by the opposite sex. For example, many ads reflect the expanded child-nurturing roles of young fathers in today's society.

Much of the change in sex roles has occurred because of the continued impact of dual-income households. One consequence for marketers is that women are not so readily accessible through traditional media as they once were. Because working women do not have much time to watch TV or listen to the radio, many advertisers now emphasize magazines in their media schedules, especially those specifically aimed at working women (e.g., *Working Woman* and *Working Mother*). Direct marketers also have been targeting time-pressured working women who use merchandise catalogs, convenient 800 numbers, and Internet sites as ways of shopping for personal clothing and accessories, as well as many household and family needs.

Marital Status

Traditionally, the family has been the focus of most marketing efforts, and for many products and services, the household continues to be the relevant consuming unit. Marketers are interested in the number and kinds of households that buy and/or own certain products. They also are interested in determining the demographic and media profiles of household decision makers (the persons involved in the actual selection of the product) to develop appropriate marketing strategies.

Marketers have discovered the benefits of targeting specific marital status groupings, such as singles, divorced individuals, single parents, and dual-income married couples. For instance, singles, especially one-person households with incomes greater than $35,000, comprise a market segment that tends to be above average in the usage of products not traditionally associated with supermarkets (e.g., cognac, books, loose tea) and below average in their consumption of traditional supermarket products (for example, catsup, peanut butter, mayonnaise). Such insights can be particularly useful to a supermarket manager operating in a neighborhood of one-person households, when deciding on the merchandise mix for the store. Some marketers target one-person households with single-serving prepared foods (e.g., Lipton Cup-a-Soup) and others with miniappliances such as small microwave ovens and two-cup coffee makers. (The family as a consuming unit is discussed in greater detail in chapter 10.)

Income, Education, and Occupation

Income has long been an important variable for distinguishing between market segments. Marketers commonly segment markets on the basis of income because they feel that it is a strong indicator of the ability (or inability) to pay for a product or a specific

model of the product. For instance, initially marketers of under-$1,000 home comput-
ers felt that such products would be particularly attractive to homes with modest
family incomes. However, these low-priced PCs also proved to be quite popular with
higher income families who wanted additional computers for younger family members.

Income is often combined with other demographic variables to more accurately
define target markets. To illustrate, high income has been combined with age to identify the important *affluent elderly* segment. It also has been combined with both age
and occupational status to produce the so-called *yuppie* segment, a sought-after subgroup of the baby boomer market. College students (who represent age and educa-
tional-occupational variables) are also a highly sought after segment. Figure 3-2

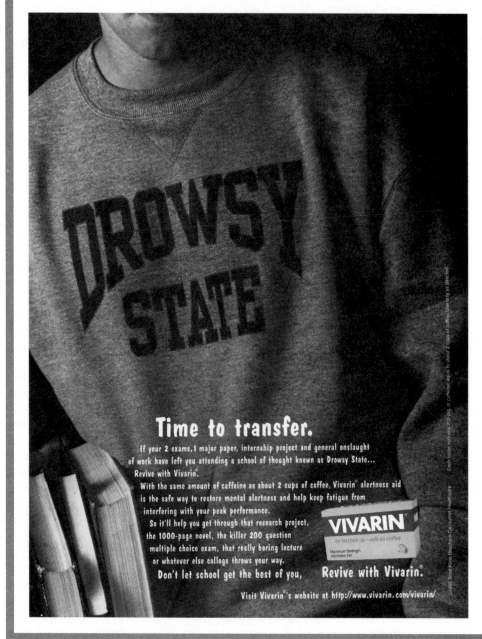

FIGURE 3-2
Appeal to College Stu-
dents—An "Educational-
Occupational" Segment

shows an ad targeted to college students, who are known to "pull an all-nighter" when a term paper is due the next morning.

Education, occupation, and income tend to be closely correlated in almost a cause-and-effect relationship. High-level occupations that produce high incomes usually require advanced educational training. Individuals with little education rarely qualify for high-level jobs. Insights on media preferences tend to support the close relationship among income, occupation, and education. Specifically, prime-time TV watching appears to be strongest in households whose members have incomes of less than $20,000, no high school diploma, and are unemployed, whereas newspaper readership is strongest among those with household incomes of $75,000 or more, among college graduates, and among those in executive-managerial professions.[10]

PSYCHOLOGICAL SEGMENTATION

Psychological characteristics refer to the inner or intrinsic qualities of the individual consumer. Consumer segmentation strategies are often based on specific psychological variables. For instance, consumers may be segmented in terms of their *motivations, personality, perceptions, learning,* and *attitudes.* (Part 2 examines in detail the wide range of psychological variables that influence consumer decision making and consumption behavior.)

PSYCHOGRAPHIC SEGMENTATION

Marketing practitioners have heartily embraced *psychographic research*, which is closely aligned with psychological research, especially personality and attitude measurement. This form of applied consumer research (commonly referred to as *lifestyle analysis*) has proven to be a valuable marketing tool that helps identify promising consumer segments that are likely to be responsive to specific marketing messages.

The psychographic profile of a consumer segment can be thought of as a composite of consumers' measured activities, interests and opinions (**AIOs**). As an approach to constructing consumer psychographic profiles, AIOs research seeks consumers' responses to a large number of statements that measure *activities* (how the consumer or family spends time, e.g., working, vacationing, hiking), *interests* (the consumer's or family's preferences and priorities, e.g., home, fashion, food), and *opinions* (how the consumer feels about a wide variety of events and political issues, social issues, the state of education, the future). In their most common form, AIO-psychographic studies use a battery of statements (a **psychographic inventory**) designed to identify relevant aspects of a consumer's personality, buying motives, interests, attitudes, beliefs, and values. Table 3-2 presents a portion of a psychographic inventory from a recently designed study of "techno-road-warriors," businesspeople who spend a high percentage of their workweek on the road, equipped with laptop computers, pagers, cellular telephones, and electronic organizers. Table 3-3 presents a hypothetical psychographic profile of a techno-road-warrior. The appeal of psychographic research lies in the frequently vivid and practical profiles of consumer segments that it can produce (which will be illustrated later in this chapter).

The results of psychographic segmentation efforts are frequently reflected in firms' marketing messages. For instance, Apple Computer has employed a largely visual advertising campaign that uses photographs of highly recognizable "world-class personalities"—all known for their creative and individualistic thinking and contributions. An aim of the campaign is to communicate the notion that these historically important individuals have dared to "think different," and that in the same spirit the consumer segment that uses Apple computers is also willing to "think different" (see

TABLE 3-2 A Portion of an AIO Inventory Used to Identify Techno-Road-Warriors

Instructions: *Please read each statement and place an "x" in the box that **best** indicates how strongly you "**agree**" or "**disagree**" with the statement.*

	AGREE COMPLETELY						DISAGREE COMPLETELY
I feel that my life is moving faster and faster, sometimes just too fast.	[1]	[2]	[3]	[4]	[5]	[6]	[7]
If I could consider the "pluses" and "minuses," technology has been good for me.	[1]	[2]	[3]	[4]	[5]	[6]	[7]
I find that I have to pull myself away from e-mail.	[1]	[2]	[3]	[4]	[5]	[6]	[7]
Given my lifestyle, I have more of a shortage of time than money.	[1]	[2]	[3]	[4]	[5]	[6]	[7]
I like the benefits of the Internet, but I often don't have the time to take advantage of them.	[1]	[2]	[3]	[4]	[5]	[6]	[7]
I am generally open to considering new practices and new technology.	[1]	[2]	[3]	[4]	[5]	[6]	[7]

Figure 3-3). Following a different approach to psychographic segmentation, Old Spice is targeting the active sports lifestyle with its High Endurance deodorant product (see Figure 3-4). Psychographic segmentation is discussed later in the chapter, where we consider hybrid segmentation strategies that combine psychographic and demographic variables to create rich descriptive profiles of consumer segments.

SOCIOCULTURAL SEGMENTATION

Sociological (group) and *anthropological* (cultural) variables—that is, **sociocultural variables**—provide further bases for market segmentation. For example, consumer markets have been successfully subdivided into segments on the basis of stage in the family life cycle, social class, core cultural values, subcultural memberships, and cross-cultural affiliation.

Family Life Cycle

Family life cycle segmentation is based on the premise that many families pass through similar phases in their formation, growth, and final dissolution. At each phase, the family unit needs different products and services. Young single people,

TABLE 3-3 A Hypothetical Psychographic Profile of the Techno-Road-Warrior

- Goes on the Internet 6-plus times a week
- Sends and/or receives 15 or more e-mail messages a week
- Regularly visits Web sites to gather information and/or to comparison shop
- Often buys personal items via 800 numbers and/or over the Internet
- May trade stocks and/or make travel reservations over the Internet
- Earns $100,000 or more a year
- Belongs to several rewards programs (for example, frequent flyer programs, hotel programs, rent-a-car programs)

FIGURE 3-3
A Psychographic-Lifestyle
Appeal from Apple

for example, need basic furniture for their first apartment, while their parents, finally free of child rearing, often refurnish their homes with more elaborate pieces. Family life cycle is a composite variable based explicitly on *marital* and *family status*, but implicitly reflects *relative age, income,* and *employment status.* Each of the stages in the traditional family life cycle (*bachelorhood, honeymooners, parenthood, postparenthood,* and *dissolution*) represents an important target segment to a variety of marketers. (Chapter 10 discusses the family life cycle in greater depth and shows how marketers cater to the needs and wishes of consumers in each stage of the life cycle.)

FIGURE 3-4
Old Spice Targets Aggressive
Sports Enthusiasts

Social Class

Social class (or relative status in the community) can be used as a base for market segmentation, and is usually "measured" by a weighted index of several demographic variables, such as education, occupation, and income. The concept of *social class* implies a hierarchy in which individuals in the same class generally have the same degree of status, while members of other classes have either higher or lower status. Studies have shown that consumers in different social classes vary in terms of values, product preferences, and buying habits. Many major banks and investment companies, for example, offer a variety of different levels of service to people of different social classes (e.g., private banking services to the upper classes). Figure 3-5 illustrates how one investment company appeals to upper-class customers with the suggestion that investment portfolios should be diversified "across a broad range of asset classes, including domestic equities, bonds, . . . and international equities." In contrast, a financial program targeted to a lower social class might talk instead about savings accounts or certificates of deposit. Chapter 11 discusses in depth the use of social class as a segmentation variable.

FIGURE 3-5
Appealing to an Affluent
Social Class Segment

Exceptional Service.
What all banks promise.
What few actually deliver.

At The Huntington, a promise made is a promise kept. Please call for an appointment.

Huntington Private Banking

Huntington Trust

Curt Wells 263-4447   Gail S.T. Webster 263-3393

Culture, Subculture, and Cross-Culture

Some marketers have found it useful to segment their domestic and international markets on the basis of cultural heritage, because members of the same culture tend to share the same values, beliefs, and customs. Marketers who use cultural segmentation stress specific, widely held cultural values with which they hope consumers will identify (e.g., for American consumers, *youthfulness*, and *fitness and health*). Cultural segmentation is particularly successful in international marketing, but it is important for the marketer to understand fully the target country's beliefs, values, and customs (the cross-cultural context).

Within the larger culture, distinct subgroups (subcultures) often are united by certain experiences, values, or beliefs that make effective market segments. These groupings could be based on a specific demographic characteristic (such as race, religion, ethnicity, or age) or lifestyle characteristic (working women, golfers). In the United States, African Americans, Hispanic Americans, Asian Americans, and the elderly are important subcultural market segments.

Culturally distinct segments can be prospects for the same product, but often are targeted more efficiently with different promotional appeals. For example, a bicycle might be promoted as an efficient means of transportation in Asia and as a health-and-fitness product in the United States. Refrigerators are sold in Arctic regions as a way of keeping food from freezing and in temperate and tropical climates as a way of keeping food cold. A recent cross-cultural study of 25,000 adolescents in 41 countries found that teens average about 6 hours a day watching TV, most use computers, and both boys and girls consider basketball to be their favorite sport.[11] (Chapters 12, 13, and 14 examine cultural, subcultural, and cross-cultural bases of market segmentation in greater detail.)

USE-RELATED SEGMENTATION

An extremely popular and effective form of segmentation categorizes consumers in terms of product, service, or brand *usage* characteristics, such as level of usage, level of awareness, and degree of brand loyalty.

Rate of usage segmentation differentiates among heavy users, medium users, light users, and nonusers of a specific product, service, or brand. For example, research has consistently indicated that between 25 and 35 percent of beer drinkers account for more than 70 percent of all beer consumed. For this reason, most marketers prefer to target their advertising campaigns to *heavy users*, rather than spend considerably more money trying to attract *light users*. This also explains the successful targeting of light beer to heavy drinkers on the basis that it is less filling (and thus can be consumed in greater quantities) than regular beer.

Marketers of a host of other products have also found that a relatively small group of heavy users accounts for a disproportionately large percentage of product usage; targeting these heavy users has become the basis of their marketing strategies. Other marketers take note of the gaps in market coverage for light and medium users and profitably target those segments.

Awareness status encompasses the notion of consumer awareness of the product, interest level in the product, readiness to buy the product, or whether consumers need to be informed about the product. Figure 3-6 presents an ad for Gillette's Sensor Excel shaving system that is designed to create both awareness and interest among a segment of consumers who normally use disposable razors.

Sometimes, *brand loyalty* is used as the basis for segmentation. Marketers often try to identify the characteristics of their brand-loyal consumers so that they can direct their promotional efforts to people with similar characteristics in the larger population. Other marketers target consumers who show no brand loyalty ("brand switchers"), in the belief that such people represent greater market potential than consumers who are loyal to competing brands. Also, almost by definition, consumer innovators—often a prime target for new products—tend *not* to be brand loyal. (Chapter 15 discusses the characteristics of consumer innovators.)

Increasingly, marketers stimulate and reward brand loyalty by offering special benefits to consistent or frequent customers. Such frequent usage or relationship programs often take the form of a membership "club" (e.g., Hertz Number 1 Club Gold, American Airlines Platinum Level, or Marriott's Rewards). Relationship programs tend to provide special accommodations and services, as well as free extras, to keep these frequent customers loyal and happy.

FIGURE 3-6
Creating Awareness and
Interest Among Consumers
in Another Market Segment

USAGE-SITUATION SEGMENTATION

Marketers recognize that the occasion or situation often determines what consumers will purchase or consume. For this reason, they sometimes focus on the **usage situation** as a segmentation variable.

The following three statements reveal the potential of situation segmentation: "When Eric gets a good report card, I always buy him a special present"; "When I'm away on business for a week or more, I try to stay at an Embassy Suites hotel"; "I always buy my wife a big box of candy on Valentine's Day." Under other circumstances, in other situations, and on other occasions, the same consumer might make other choices. Some situational factors that might influence a purchase or consumption choice include whether it is a weekday or weekend (e.g., going to a movie); whether there is sufficient time (e.g., use of regular mail or express mail); whether it is a gift for a girlfriend, a parent, or a self-gift (a reward to one's self).

Some marketers try to instill the notion of the suitability of certain products for certain situations; others try to break consumer habits. In an effort to increase Coke consumption, the Coca-Cola Company challenged the customer usage of coffee as a breakfast and midmorning adult drink, and promoted the idea of using its popular caffeinated

FIGURE 3-7
Ad Asking Consumers to Celebrate the Occasion by Buying a Diamond Necklace

Coke Classic as a morning drink. And with today's emphasis on drinking bottled water, one company added caffeine to its bottled water, promoting its Water Concepts' Water Joe, a line of caffeinated bottled water, as a breakfast drink available nationwide.[12] The Diamond ad in Figure 3-7 is also an example of situational segmentation. The ad asks consumers to celebrate the occasion by buying a diamond necklace.

Many products are promoted for special usage occasions. The greeting card industry, for example, stresses special cards for a variety of occasions that seem to be increasing almost daily (Grandparents' Day, Secretaries' Day, etc.). The florist and candy industries promote their products for Valentine's Day and Mother's Day, the diamond industry promotes diamond rings as an engagement symbol, and the wristwatch industry promotes its products as graduation gifts.

BENEFIT SEGMENTATION

Marketing and advertising executives constantly attempt to identify the one most important benefit of their product or service that will be most meaningful to consumers. Examples of benefits that are commonly used include: *financial security* (Met Life), *comfort* (Bausch & Lomb disposable contact lenses), *good health* (Egg Beaters egg substitute), *proper fit* (Wrangler women's jeans), and *backache relief* (Advil).

Changing lifestyles play a major role in determining the product benefits that are important to consumers, and provide marketers with opportunities for new products and services. For example, the microwave oven was the perfect solution to the needs of dual-income households, where neither the husband nor the wife has the time for lengthy meal preparation. Food marketers offer busy families the *benefit* of breakfast products that require only seconds to prepare.

Benefit segmentation can be used to position various brands within the same product category.[13] The classic case of successful benefit segmentation is the market for toothpaste: Aim is targeted to parents as a good-tasting toothpaste that will encourage children to brush longer; Viadent is targeted to adults as a means of removing tartar (a cosmetic benefit) and plaque (a health benefit). Figure 3-8 suggests that the primary benefit derived from using Rembrandt toothpaste is whiter teeth.

FIGURE 3-8
Ad Offering Consumers the Primary Benefits of Whiter Teeth

A DRAMATICALLY
WHITER SMILE IN 30 DAYS.

GUARANTEED.

Dazzling White is the first toothpaste and bleaching gel in one that dramatically bleaches teeth whiter (proven in clinical test after clinical test). 94% of dentists say they would recommend it.* Simply brush your teeth and quickly see dramatic results. Safe. Easy. Clinically proven.

Call us at 1-800-548-3663 for more information and visit us at www.rembrandt.com
*94% of those dentists responding to a dental survey intend to recommend Dazzling White to their patients. ©1998 Den-Mat Corp.

REMBRANDT
DAZZLING WHITE™
TOOTHPASTE AND BLEACHING GEL IN ONE

HYBRID SEGMENTATION APPROACHES

Marketers commonly segment markets by combining several segmentation variables, rather than relying on a single segmentation base. This section examines three hybrid segmentation approaches that provide marketers with richer and more accurately defined consumer segments that can be derived from using a single segmentation variable. These include psychographic-demographic profiles, geodemographics, and VALS 2.

Psychographic-Demographic Profiles

Psychographic and demographic profiles are highly complementary approaches that work best when used together. By combining the knowledge gained from both demographic and psychographic studies, marketers are provided with powerful information about their target markets.

Demographic-psychographic profiling has been widely used in the development of advertising campaigns to answer three questions: "Whom should we target?" "What should we say?" "Where should we say it?" To help advertisers answer the third question, many advertising media vehicles sponsor demographic-psychographic research on which they base very detailed *audience profiles*. Table 3-4 presents a selected demographic and psychographic profile of the *PC Magazine* subscriber. By offering media buyers such carefully defined dual profiles of their audiences, mass media publishers and broadcasters make it possible for advertisers to select media whose audiences most closely resemble their target markets. Advertisers are increasingly designing ads that depict in words and/or pictures the essence of a particular target-market lifestyle or segment that they want to reach. In this spirit, Timex appeals to specific active and outdoor lifestyles (see Figure 3-9).

Geodemographic Segmentation

This type of hybrid segmentation scheme is based on the notion that people who live close to one another are likely to have similar financial means, tastes, preferences, lifestyles, and consumption habits (similar to the old adage, "Birds of a feather flock together"). Some syndicated market research firms specialize in producing computer-generated geodemographic market "clusters" of like consumers. Specifically, these firms have clustered the nation's 250,000-plus neighborhoods into lifestyle groupings based on postal zip codes. Clusters are created based on consumer lifestyles, and a specific cluster includes zip codes that are composed of people with similar lifestyles widely scattered throughout the country. Marketers use the cluster data for direct-mail campaigns, to select retail sites and appropriate merchandise mixes, to locate banks and restaurants, and to design marketing strategies for specific market segments. Table 3-5 presents five examples of geodemographic clusters.

Geodemographic segmentation is most useful when an advertiser's best prospects (in terms of consumer personalities, goals, and interests) can be isolated in terms of where they live. However, for products and services used by a broad cross-section of the American public, other segmentation schemes may be more productive.

SRI Consulting's Values and Lifestyle System (VALS™)

Drawing on Maslow's need hierarchy (see chapter 4) and the concept of social character, in the late 1970s researchers at SRI Consulting developed a generalized segmentation scheme of the American population known as the values and lifestyle (**VALS**) system. This original system was designed to explain the dynamics of societal change, but was quickly adapted as a marketing tool.

TABLE 3-4 Selected Psychographic/Demographic Characteristics of the *PC Magazine* Subscriber

DEMOGRAPHICS	PERCENT
SEX (BASE 990)	
Men	86
Women	13
AGE	
Under 25	5
25–34	18
35–44	29
45–54	31
55–64	12
65 or older	5
Mean age	44.1
EDUCATION	
Some college or less	27
Graduate college	27
Education beyond college graduate	46
EMPLOYMENT STATUS	
Employed by someone else	68
Self-employed	21
Other	11
OCCUPATION/BUSINESS DEPARTMENTS	
Computer related-professional	22
Senior or corporate management	16
Engineering-related professional	13
Administrative/manufacturing, accounting, finance, purchasing, advertising, marketing, sales	26
Others	23
INCOME	
Under $30,000	7
$30,000–$49,999	15
$50,000–$74,999	24
$75,000–$99,000	19
$100,000 or more	24
Mean income	$87,700
PRIMARY RESIDENCE	
Own	74
Rent	18
Other	3
No answer	5

PSYCHOGRAPHICS	PERCENT
USE A COMPUTER	**100**
At home	96
At work	89
On vacation/traveling	46
SELECTED USE OF COMPUTER	
Word processing	96
Connect to Internet	86
E-mail	84
For work	80
Accounting/record keeping	75
Reference	68
Recreation/games	66
PORTABLE DEVICES USES WHEN TRAVELING ON BUSINESS	
Laptop/notebook computer	57
Cellular phone	47
Beeper or pager	30
Personal Digital Assistant/electronic organizer	14
TRAVEL FOR BUSINESS/PLEASURE	
Business Travel	
5 or more days per month	31
5 or more nights away from home per month	17
Pleasure/Vacation Travel	
15 or more days per year	37
Mean number of days per year	15.5
MEMBER OF FREQUENT FLYER PROGRAMS	**90**
FINANCIAL SERVICES	
Currently own	
Mutual funds	48
Stocks	44
Bonds	24
Life insurance/annuities	44
Currently use	
Brokerage services	36
On-line investment services	16
Retirement/financial planning	41

RESPONSE OF SELECTED CONSUMER PSYCHOGRAPHIC STATEMENTS	PERCENT Describe Completely
Research before choose brand of new product to buy	41
Other people ask my opinion about which computer products to buy	41
Usually buy products based on quality, not price	26
Prefer products that are latest in new technology	26
Among group I am one of first to try new product	19

SELECTED SPORTS/ACTIVITIES PLAYED/PARTICIPATED IN PAST YEAR	
Walking/running/jogging	63
Exercise/fitness/weight training	44
Bicycling	37
Swimming	37
Golf	27
Fishing	23
Boating/sailing	19
Skiing	19
Tennis	14

HOBBIES/OTHER ACTIVITIES PARTICIPATED IN	
Listen to music	77
Reading	61
Going to movies	60
Surfing the Internet	50
Games-videos on computer	48
Gardening	32
Going to the theater	32
Cooking	30
Photography	30
Collecting stamps/coins	11
Sewing needlecraft	6

Source: *1997 Lifestyles Study*, PC Magazine Subscriber Study, Ziff-Davis, Inc., June 1997.

In 1989 SRIC revised the VALS system to focus more explicitly on explaining consumer purchase behavior. The current VALS typology classifies the American population into eight distinctive subgroups (segments) based on consumer responses to 35 attitudinal and 4 demographic questions. Figure 3-10 depicts the VALS classification scheme and offers a brief profile of the consumer traits of each of the VALS segments. The major groupings (from left to right in Figure 3-10) are defined in terms of three major *self-orientations* and (from top to bottom) a new definition of resources: the *principle-oriented* (consumers whose choices are motivated by their beliefs, rather than by desires for approval), the *status-oriented* (consumers whose choices are guided by the actions, approval, and opinions of others), and the *action-oriented* (consumers who are motivated by a desire for social or physical activity, variety, and risk taking). Each

TABLE 3-5 Sample Geodemographic Clusters

BLUE BLOOD ESTATES
- 0.8% of United States households
- Predominant employment: Professional
- Elite super-rich families
- Key education level: College grads
- Adult age range: 35–44, 45–54, 55–64

CHARACTERISTICS: America's wealthiest suburbs are populated by established executives, professionals, and heirs to "old money." These people are accustomed to privilege and live in luxury, often surrounded by servants. A tenth of this group are multimillionaires. The next level of affluence is a sharp drop from this pinnacle. Blue blood estate people belong to a country club, own mutual funds ($10,000+), purchase a car phone, watch TV golf, and read business magazines.

MID-CITY MIX
- 1.3% of United States households
- Predominant employment: Service, white-collar
- African American singles and families
- Key educational level: High school, some college
- Adult age range: 35–54

CHARACTERISTICS: These individuals and families are geographically centered in the Northeast and Great Lakes regions. They are ethnically diverse and a mix of white- and blue-collar employment. These rowhouse neighborhoods on the urban fringe are two-thirds black and have a high incidence of college enrollment. They go to pro basketball games, have veterans life insurance, eat canned hashes, listen to religious/gospel music, and read fashion/sports magazines.

GRAY COLLARS
- 2.1% of United States households
- Adult age range: 55–64, 65+
- Median household income: $31,400
- Aging couples in inner suburbs

CHARACTERISTICS: For nearly two decades, we read about the decline of the Great Lakes industrial "Rust Belt." Decimated by foreign takeovers in the steel and automobile industries, the area lost a million jobs. Although most of the kids left, their highly skilled parents stayed and are now benefitting from a major U.S. industrial resurgence. They buy 1950's nostalgia, own CDs, eat canned cooked hams, listen to radio football, and read health/fitness magazines.

YOUNG INFLUENTIALS
- 1.1% of United States households
- Predominant employment: Professional, white-collar
- Upwardly mobile singles and couples
- Key education level: College grads
- Adult age range: Under 24, 25–34

CHARACTERISTICS: This cluster is dubbed the "Young Urban Professional." Before getting married they were the educated, high-tech, metropolitan sophisticates, the "swingers" and childless live-in couples, whose double incomes bought the good life in Boomtown U.S.A. They are the last of the Yuppies. They go to college basketball games, have an American Express card, often drink imported beer, listen to progressive rock radio, and read style/fashion magazines.

SHOTGUNS AND PICKUPS
- 1.6% of United States households
- Predominant employment: Blue-collar, farm
- Rural blue-collar workers and families
- Key education level: High school, grade school
- Adult age range: 35–44, 45–54

CHARACTERISTICS: The least affluent of the "Country Families" clusters, members of this group are found in the Northeast, the Southeast, in the Great Lakes and Piedmont industrial regions. They lead the "Country Families" group in blue-collar jobs; the majority are married with school-age children. They are church-goers who also enjoy bowling, hunting, sewing, and attending auto races, smoke pipe tobacco, have medical loss of income insurance, drink Canadian whisky, listen to country radio, and read hunting/car and truck magazines.

Source: Courtesy of Claritas Inc. (PRIZM and 62 Cluster nicknames are registered trademarks of Claritas Inc.). Reprinted by permission.

of these three major self-orientations represent distinct attitudes, lifestyles, and decision-making styles. Resources (most to least) refers to the range of psychological, physical, demographic, and material means and capacities consumers have to draw upon, including education, income, self-confidence, health, eagerness to buy, and energy level. Figure 3-11 presents information on the percentage of individuals in each of the eight VALS segments who participated in selected sports in a recent year. For instance, the findings reveal than *Actualizers, Experiencers*, and *Achievers* are more likely to participate in thrill-oriented sports than other segments. Table 3-6 shows the size of each of the eight VALS segments as a percent of the population (also see www.future.sri.com).

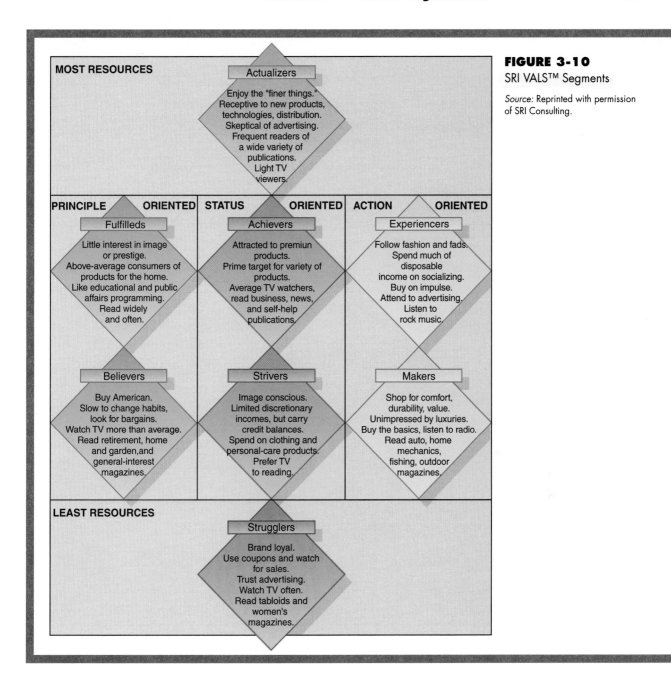

FIGURE 3-10
SRI VALS™ Segments

Source: Reprinted with permission
of SRI Consulting.

In terms of consumer characteristics, the eight VALS segments differ in some important ways. For instance, *Believers* tend to buy American-made products and are slow to alter their consumption-related habits, while *Actualizers* are drawn to top-of-the-line products and to new products, especially innovative technologies (for example, they might be early buyers of such products as tiny palm-held computers). VALS linkages with the Simmons annual survey of the American Household and other databases provides national product, service, and media data for each VALS consumer segment. GeoVALS™, a site location program, provides the American household and other data-bases, while a sister program provides the percent of each VALS consumer type in each residential zip code to help marketers identify where concentrations of their customers live. SRIC also offers Japan-VALS, specific to the Japanese consuming market.

FIGURE 3-11

VALS™ 2 Segments and
Participation in Selected
Sports

Source: Rebecca Piirto Heath,
"You Can Buy A Thrill: Chasing
the Ultimate Rush," *American
Demographics*, June 1997, p. 48.
www.demographics.com. © 1997
PRIMEDIA-Interec, Stamford, CT.
Reprinted with permission.

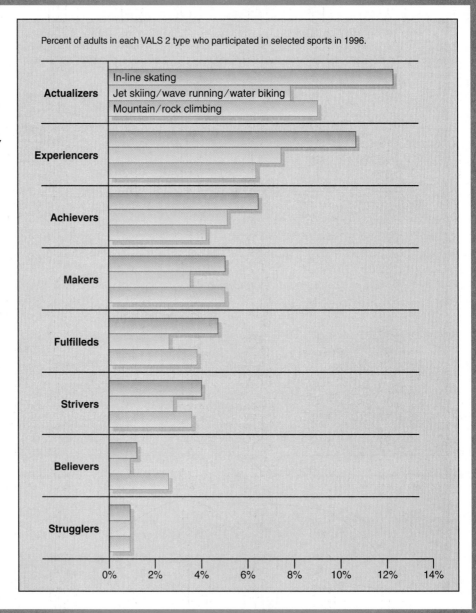

Percent of adults in each VALS 2 type who participated in selected sports in 1996.

VALS™ SEGMENT	PERCENT OF POPULATION
Actualizer	11.7%
Fulfilled	10.5
Believer	17.0
Achiever	14.7
Striver	11.8
Experiencer	12.9
Maker	12.0
Struggler	9.5

TABLE 3-6 The Size of Each VALS™ Segment as Percent of the United States Population

Source: VALS™/Simmons.

CRITERIA FOR EFFECTIVE TARGETING OF MARKET SEGMENTS

The previous sections have described various bases on which consumers can be clustered into homogeneous market segments. The next challenge for the marketer is to select one or more segments to target with an appropriate marketing mix. To be an effective target, a market segment should be (1) identifiable, (2) sufficient (in terms of size), (3) stable or growing, and (4) accessible (reachable) in terms of both media and cost.

IDENTIFICATION

To divide the market into separate segments on the basis of a series of *common* or *shared* needs or characteristics that are relevant to the product or service, a marketer must be able to identify these relevant characteristics. Some segmentation variables, such as *geography* (location) or *demographics* (age, gender, occupation, race), are relatively easy to identify or are even observable. Others, such as *education, income,* or *marital status*, can be determined through questionnaires. However, other characteristics, such as *benefits sought* or *lifestyle*, are more difficult to identify. A knowledge of consumer behavior is especially useful to marketers who use such intangible consumer characteristics as the basis for market segmentation.

SUFFICIENCY

For a market segment to be a worthwhile target, it must consist of a sufficient number of people to warrant tailoring a product or promotional campaign to its specific needs or interests. To estimate the size of each segment under consideration, marketers often use secondary demographic data, such as that provided by the United States Census Bureau (available at many libraries and on-line via the Internet), or they undertake a probability survey whose findings can be projected to the total market. (Consumer research methodology was described in chapter 2.)

STABILITY

Most marketers prefer to target consumer segments that are relatively stable in terms of demographic and psychological factors and needs and that are likely to grow larger over time. They prefer to avoid "fickle" segments that are unpredictable in embracing fads. For example, teens are a sizable and easily identifiable market segment, eager to buy, able to spend, and easily reached. Yet, by the time a marketer produces merchandise for a popular teenage fad, interest in it may have waned.

ACCESSIBILITY

A fourth requirement for effective targeting is accessibility, which means that marketers must be able to reach the market segments they want to target in an economical way. Despite the wide availability of special-interest magazines and cable TV programs, marketers are constantly looking for new media that will enable them to reach their target markets with minimum waste of circulation and competition. One way this can be accomplished is via the Internet. Upon the request of the consumer, a growing number of Web sites periodically send e-mail messages concerning a subject of special interest to the computer user. For example, a Houston, Texas, resident who likes to take short vacation trips, might have Continental Airlines e-mail her the coming weekend's special airfare, hotel, and rent-a-car deals.

IMPLEMENTING SEGMENTATION STRATEGIES

Firms that use market segmentation can pursue a *concentrated* marketing strategy or a *differentiated* marketing strategy. In certain instances, they might use a **counterseg-mentation** strategy.

CONCENTRATED VERSUS DIFFERENTIATED MARKETING

Once an organization has identified its most promising market segments, it must decide whether to target one segment or several segments. The premise behind market segmentation is that each targeted segment receives a specially designed marketing mix; that is, a specially tailored product, price, distribution network, and/or promotional campaign. Targeting several segments using individual marketing mixes is called *differential marketing*; targeting just one segment with a unique marketing mix is called *concentrated marketing*.

Differentiated marketing is a highly appropriate segmentation strategy for financially strong companies that are well established in a product category and competitive with other firms that also are strong in the category (e.g., soft drinks, automobiles, or detergents). However, if a company is small or new to the field, concentrated marketing is probably a better bet. A company can survive and prosper by filling a niche not occupied by stronger companies. For example, Viadent toothpaste has become a leader in the small but increasingly important submarket of the overall tooth care market that focuses on products that fight gingivitis and other gum diseases.

COUNTERSEGMENTATION

Sometimes, companies find that they must reconsider the extent to which they are segmenting their markets. They might find that some segments have contracted over time to the point that they do not warrant an individually designed marketing program. In such cases, the company seeks to discover a more generic need or consumer characteristic that would apply to the members of two or more segments, and recombine those segments into a larger single segment that could be targeted with an individually tailored product or promotional campaign. This is called a *countersegmentation* strategy. Some business schools with wide course offerings in each department were forced to adopt a countersegmentation strategy when they discovered that students simply did not have enough available credits to take a full spectrum of in-depth courses in their major area of study. As a result, some courses had to be canceled each semester because of inadequate registration. For some schools, a countersegmentation strategy effectively solved the problem (e.g., by combining *advertising*, *publicity*, *sales promotion*, and *personal selling* courses into a single course called *Promotion*).

SUMMARY

Market segmentation and diversity are complementary concepts. Without a diverse marketplace, composed of many different peoples with different backgrounds, countries of origin, interests, needs, and wants, there really would be little reason to segment markets.

Before the widespread adoption of the marketing concept, mass marketing (offering the same product or marketing mix to everyone) was the marketing strategy most widely used. Market segmentation followed as a more logical way to meet consumer needs. Segmentation is defined as the process of dividing a potential market into distinct subsets of consumers with a common need or characteristic and selecting one or more segments to target with a specially designed marketing mix. Besides aiding in the development of new products, segmentation studies assist in the redesign and repositioning of existing products, in the creation of promotional appeals, and the selection of advertising media.

Because segmentation strategies benefit both marketers and consumers, they have received wide support from both sides of the marketplace. Market segmentation is now widely used by manufacturers, by retailers, and by the nonprofit sector.

Nine major classes of consumer characteristics serve as the most common bases for market segmentation. These include geographic factors, demographic factors, psychological factors, psychographic characteristics, sociocultural variables, use-related characteristics, use-situation factors, benefits sought, and hybrid forms of segmentation (for example, psychographic-demographic profiles, such as VALS™, and geodemographic factors, such as PRIZM™). Important criteria for segmenting markets include identification, sufficiency, stability, and accessibility. Once an organization has identified promising target markets, it must decide whether to target several segments (differentiated marketing) or just one segment (concentrated marketing). It then develops a positioning strategy for each targeted segment. In certain instances, a company might decide to follow a countersegmentation strategy and recombine two or more segments into one larger segment.

DISCUSSION QUESTIONS

1. What is market segmentation? How is the practice of market segmentation related to the marketing concept?

2. How are market segmentation, targeting, and positioning interrelated? Illustrate how these three concepts can be used to develop a marketing strategy for a product of your choice.

3. Discuss the advantages and disadvantages of using demographics as a basis for segmentation. Can demographics and psychographics be used together to segment markets? Illustrate your answer with a specific example.

4. Many marketers have found that a relatively small group of heavy users accounts for a disproportionately large amount of the total product consumed. What are the advantages and disadvantages of targeting these heavy users?

5. Under which circumstances and for what types of products should a marketer segment the market on the basis of: (a) awareness status, (b) brand loyalty, and (c) use-situation?

6. Some marketers consider benefit segmentation as the segmentation approach most consistent with the marketing concept. Do you agree or disagree with this view? Why?

7. Club Med is a prominent company in the vacation and travel industry. Describe how the company can use demographics and psychographics to identify TV shows and magazines in which to place its advertisements.

8. How can a marketer for a chain of health clubs use the VALS™ segmentation profiles to develop an advertising campaign? Which segments should be targeted? How should the health club be positioned to each of these segments?

9. For each of the following products, identify the segmentation base that you consider best for targeting consumers: (a) coffee, (b) soups, (c) home exercise equipment, (d) portable telephones, and (e) nonfat frozen yogurt. Explain your choices.

10. Apply the criteria for effective segmentation to marketing a product of your choice to college students.

EXERCISES

1. Select a product and brand that you use frequently and list the benefits you receive from using it. Without disclosing your list, ask a fellow student who uses a different brand in this product category (preferably, a friend of the opposite sex) to make a similar list for his or her brand. Compare the two lists and identify the implications for using benefit segmentation to market the two brands.

2. Does your lifestyle differ significantly from your parents' lifestyle? If so, how are the two lifestyles different? What factors cause these differences?

3. Do you anticipate any major changes in your lifestyle in the next 5 years? If so, into which VALS segment are you likely to belong 5 years from now? Explain.

4. The owners of a local health-food restaurant have asked you to prepare a psychographic profile of families living in the community surrounding the restaurant's location. Construct a 10-question psychographic inventory appropriate for segmenting families on the basis of their dining-out preferences.

5. Find three print advertisements that you believe are targeted at a particular psychographic segment. How effective do you think each ad is in terms of achieving its objective? Why?

KEY TERMS

- **AIOs (Activities, Interests, Opinions)**
- **Benefit segmentation**
- **Countersegmentation**
- **Demographic characteristics**
- **Demographic segmentation**
- **Differentiated marketing**

- **Geographic segmentation**
- **Hybrid Segmentation**
- **Mass marketing**
- **Market segmentation**
- **Micromarketing**
- **Positioning**
- **Psychographic inventory**

- **Psychographic segmentation**
- **Psychological segmentation**
- **Repositioning**
- **Sociocultural segmentation**
- **Use-related segmentation**
- **Usage-situation segmentation**
- **VALS**

NOTES

1. Nina Munk, "Gap Gets It," *Fortune*, August 3, 1998, 68–82.
2. Bruce Orwall, "Multiplying Hotel Brands Puzzle Travelers," *Wall Street Journal*, April 17, 1996, B1, B2.
3. Carol Krol, "Full-Figured Women a Great Fit for 'Mode,'" *Advertising Age*, February 23, 1998, S16.
4. Florence Fabricant, "The Geography of Taste," *New York Times Magazine*, March 10, 1996, 40–41.
5. Martin G. Letscher, "Sports Fads and Trends," *American Demographics*, June 1997, 54.
6. Judann Pollack, "Oscar Mayer Lunchables Creates Adult Versions," *Advertising Age*, November 11, 1996, 8.
7. Geoffrey Meredith and Charles Schewe, "The Power of Cohorts," *American Demographics*, December 1994, 22–31.
8. Michael M. Phillips, "Selling by Evoking What Defines a Generation," *Wall Street Journal*, August 13, 1996, B1.
9. Jock Bickert, "Cohorts II: A New Approach to Market Segmentation," *Journal of Consumer Marketing*, 14, 1997, 362–363.
10. Rebecca Piirto, "Cable TV," *American Demographics*, June 1995, 42.
11. Jane L. Levere, "The Media Business—Advertising," *New York Times*, June 11, 1996, D8.
12. Gerry Khermouch, "New Age Bevs Get Caffeine Injection," *Brandweek*, October 14, 1996, 16.
13. Russell Haley, "Benefit Segmentation: A Decision-Oriented Research Tool," *Marketing Management* 4, Summer 1995, 59–62; Dianne Cermak, Karen Maru File, and Russ Alan Prince, "A Benefit Segmentation of the Major Donor Market," *Journal of Business Research*, February 1994, 121–30; Gordon McDougall and Terrence Levesque, "Benefit Segmentation Using Service Quality Dimensions: An Investigation in Retail Banking," *International Journal of Bank Marketing*, 1994, 15–23; and Joel S. Dubow, "Occasion-Based Versus User-Based Benefit Segmentation: A Case Study," *Journal of Advertising Research*, March–April 1992, 11–18.

PART 2

THE CONSUMER AS AN INDIVIDUAL

Chapters 4 through 8 provide the reader with a comprehensive picture of consumer psychology. These chapters explain the basic psychological concepts that account for individual behavior and demonstrate how these concepts influence the individual's consumption-related behavior. Chapter 9 shows how communication links consumers as individuals to the world and people around them.

PART 2 DISCUSSES THE CONSUMER AS AN INDIVIDUAL.

CHAPTER 4
Consumer Motivation

■ ■

Human needs—consumer needs—are the basis of all modern marketing. Needs are the essence of the marketing concept. The key to a company's survival, profitability, and growth in a highly competitive marketing environment is its ability to identify and satisfy unfulfilled consumer needs better and sooner than the competition.

Marketers do not create needs, though in some instances they may make consumers more keenly aware of unfelt needs. Successful marketers define their markets in terms of the needs they presume to satisfy, not in terms of the products they sell. This is a market-oriented, rather than a production-oriented, approach to marketing. A marketing orientation focuses on the needs of the buyer; a production orientation focuses on the needs of the seller. The marketing concept implies that the manufacturer will make only what it knows people will buy; a production orientation implies that the manufacturer will try to sell what it decides to make.

Marketers who base their offerings on a recognition of consumer needs find a ready market for their products. The popularity of farmers' markets in the United States is grounded in their appeal to consumers' needs for freshness, quality, and flavor—needs that too often are not met by large food marketers, who focus on centralized purchasing, warehousing, and convenience. There are countless examples of products that have succeeded in the marketplace because they fulfilled consumer needs; there are even more examples of products and companies that have failed because they did not recognize or understand consumer needs.

This chapter discusses basic needs that operate in most people to motivate behavior. It explores the influence such needs have on consumption behavior. Later chapters in Part 2 explain why and how these basic human motives are expressed in so many diverse ways.

MOTIVATION

Motivation can be described as the driving force within individuals that impels them to action. This driving force is produced by a state of tension, which exists as the result of an unfulfilled need. Individuals strive both consciously and subconsciously to reduce this tension through behavior that they anticipate will fulfill their needs and thus relieve them of the stress they feel. The specific goals they select and the patterns

FIGURE 4-1

Model of the Motivation Process

Source: From Jeffrey F. Dugree et al., "Observations: Translating Values into Product Wants," *Journal of Advertising Research* 36, 6 (November 1996): p. 93. Reprinted by permission of the American Marketing Association.

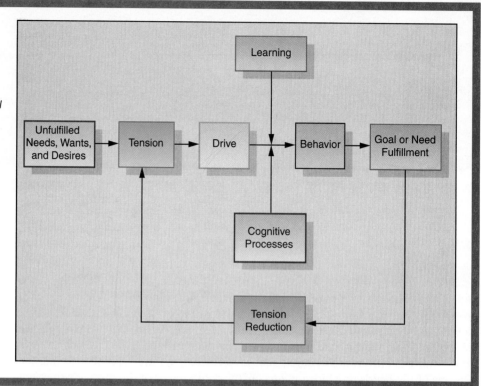

of action they undertake to achieve their goals are the results of individual thinking and learning. Figure 4-1 presents a model of the motivational process. It portrays motivation as a state of need-induced tension that "drives" the individual to engage in behavior that he or she believes will satisfy the need and thus reduce the tension. Whether gratification is actually achieved depends on the course of action being pursued. For instance, if a high school girl expects to become a great tennis player by wearing the same brand of sneakers that Jennifer Capriati wears, she is likely to be disappointed; if she takes tennis lessons and practices diligently, she may succeed.

The specific goals that consumers wish to achieve, and the courses of action they take in order to attain these goals, are selected on the basis of their thinking processes (cognition) and previous learning.

NEEDS

Every individual has needs: some are innate, others are acquired. **Innate needs** are physiological (that is, *biogenic*); they include the needs for food, water, air, clothing, shelter, and sex. Because they are needed to sustain biological life, the biogenic needs are considered **primary needs** or motives.

Acquired needs are needs that we learn in response to our culture or environment. These may include needs for self-esteem, prestige, affection, power, and learning. Because acquired needs are generally psychological (i.e., *psychogenic*), they are considered **secondary needs** or motives. They result from the individual's subjective psychological state and from relationships with others. For example, all individuals need shelter from the elements; thus, finding a place to live fulfills an important primary need for a newly transferred executive. However, the kind of home she rents or buys may be the result of secondary needs. She may seek a place in which she and her husband can entertain large groups of people (and fulfill social needs); she may want to live in an exclusive community to impress her friends and family (and fulfill ego needs). The place where an individual ultimately chooses to live thus may serve to fulfill both primary and secondary needs.

GOALS

Goals are the sought-after results of motivated behavior. As Figure 4-1 indicated, all behavior is goal-oriented. Our discussion of motivation in this chapter is in part concerned with **generic goals**—that is, the general classes or categories of goals that consumers see as a way to fulfill their needs. If a person tells his parents that he wants to get a graduate degree, he has stated a generic goal. If he says he wants to get a graduate degree in engineering from MIT, his goal has become product-specific. Marketers are particularly concerned with **product-specific goals**—the specifically branded products and services that consumers select as their goals. An executive may want to buy a luxury car to signify to his friends that he is a success. The Chrysler Company wants to make his generic goal product specific; they want him to choose the Chrysler LHS luxury car.

Most trade association advertising promotes generic goals—i.e., the use of the product category. Individual members of a trade association promote their own specific labeled products (i.e., product-specific goals). For example, members of the National Fluid Milk Processor Promotion Board are delighted that the "milk mustache" campaign has been so effective in encouraging consumers to drink milk (see Figure 4-2). An individual member of the trade association would want to persuade consumers to drink its own brand of bottled milk. Marketers who support their industry trade associations recognize the importance of promoting both generic and product-specific goals.

Means-end analysis is another way to view the needs-goals paradigm.[1] Individuals set desired *ends* (goals) on the basis of their personal values, and they select *means* (or behaviors) that they believe will help them achieve their desired ends. Take the personal value *good health*. An individual may see certain behaviors (e.g., exercise, proper nutrition, cleanliness) as the means to achieving good health (the goal or desired end). A marketer of specific products within the "means" product category (e.g., home exercise equipment, low-fat foods, or antibacterial soaps) would want to persuade people who are concerned with the goal of good health to use its specific product to achieve that goal.[2] A Kellogg's ad proclaims, "A bowl of cereal can grow strong bones and teeth." In other words, the marketer tries to convert the consumer's generic goal into a product-specific goal. Table 4-1 illustrates how a means-end analysis would permit a marketer to promote its specific product by associating it with a generic goal.[3]

The Selection of Goals   For any given need, there are many different and appropriate goals. The goals selected by individuals depend on their *personal experiences, physical capacity, prevailing cultural norms* and *values*, and the goal's *accessibility* in the physical and social environment. For example, an individual may have a strong hunger need. If he is a young college athlete, he may envision a thick sirloin steak as his goal object; if his doctor has advised him to avoid red meat, he may settle for a thick tuna steak instead. If he has a toothache, he may not be able to chew a steak; he may have to select hamburger. If he has never tasted steak—if it is outside his realm of personal experience—he probably would not even think of steak, but instead would select a food that has previously satisfied his hunger.

Finally, the goal object has to be both socially acceptable and physically accessible. If our college athlete was having dinner with his mother, she might disapprove of his eating red meat and insist he eat fish or chicken instead. If he were shipwrecked on an island with

FIGURE 4-2
Generic Appeal

This may be
the land of plenty, but
there's something
Americans, especially
teenagers, aren't getting
enough of – calcium.
This could lead to
osteoporosis. So what's
the best way to
load up on calcium?
Drink lowfat or
fat free milk. We always
keep a full thermos
in the cabinet.

MILK
Where's your mustache?

no food provisions or living animals, he could not realistically select steak as his goal object, although he might fantasize about it. If he were in India, where cows are considered sacred, he would not be able to eat steak, because to do so would be considered sacrilege. He would have to select a **substitute goal** more appropriate to the social environment.

An individual's own perception of himself or herself also serves to influence the specific goals selected. The products a person owns, would like to own, or would not like to own are often perceived in terms of how closely they reflect (are congruent with) that person's *self-image*. A product that is perceived as matching a consumer's self-image has a greater probability of being selected than one that is not. Thus, a man who perceives himself as young and "cool" may drive a Porsche; a woman who perceives herself as rich and conservative may drive a Mercedes. The types of houses people live in, the cars they

TABLE 4-1 Means-End Analysis

PRODUCTS AND MEANS EXPRESSING GOOD HEALTH VALUE

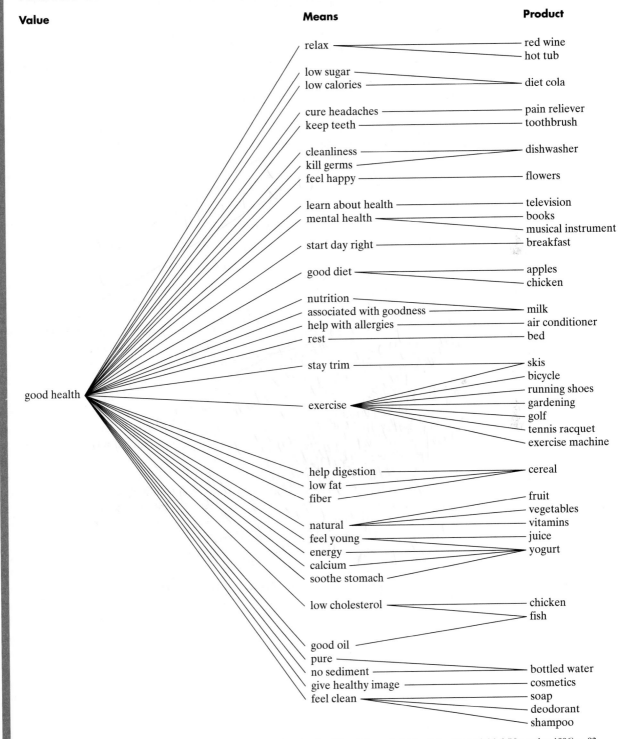

Source: Jeffrey F. Durgee et al., "Observations: Translating Values into Product Wants" *Journal of Advertising Research* 36, 6 (November 1996): p. 93.

drive, the clothes they wear, the very foods they eat—these specific goal objects are often chosen because they symbolically reflect the individual's self-image while they satisfy specific needs. (The relationship of self-concept to product choice is discussed more fully in chapters 5 and 6.)

INTERDEPENDENCE OF NEEDS AND GOALS

Needs and goals are interdependent; neither exists without the other. However, people are often not as aware of their needs as they are of their goals. For example, a teenager may not consciously be aware of his social needs but may join a photography club to meet new friends. A local politician may not consciously be aware of a power need but may regularly run for public office. A college student may not consciously recognize her need for achievement but may strive to attain a straight A grade point average.

Individuals are usually somewhat more aware of their physiological needs than they are of their psychological needs. Most people know when they are hungry, thirsty, or cold, and they take appropriate steps to satisfy these needs. The same people may not consciously be aware of their needs for acceptance, for self-esteem, for status. They may, however, subconsciously engage in behavior that satisfies their psychological (acquired) needs.

POSITIVE AND NEGATIVE MOTIVATION

Motivation can be **positive** or **negative** in direction. We may feel a driving force *toward* some object or condition, or a driving force *away* from some object or condition. For example, a person may be impelled toward a restaurant to fulfill a hunger need, and away from motorcycle transportation to fulfill a safety need.

Some psychologists refer to positive drives as needs, wants, or desires, and to negative drives as fears or aversions. However, although positive and negative motivational forces seem to differ dramatically in terms of physical (and sometimes emotional) activity, they are basically similar, in that both serve to initiate and sustain human behavior. For this reason, researchers often refer to both kinds of drives or motives as needs, wants, and desires. Some theorists distinguish *wants* from *needs* by defining wants as product-specific needs. Others differentiate between desires, on the one hand, and needs and wants on the other. They believe that consumer desires involve "powerful emotions and fervent passion," which are expressed through the use of positive and negative metaphors.[4] One study pointed out that consumers frequently use food metaphors to express both positive and negative consumption desires (e.g., a "delicious" movie, or "not my cup of tea").[5]

Goals, too, can be positive or negative. A positive goal is one toward which behavior is directed; thus it is often referred to as an approach object. A negative goal is one from which behavior is directed away, and is referred to as an avoidance object. Since both **approach** and **avoidance goals** can be considered objects of motivated behavior, most researchers refer to both simply as goals. Consider this example: A middle-aged woman may have a positive goal of fitness and joins a health club to work out regularly. Her husband may view getting fat as a negative goal, and so he joins a jogging club. In the former case, the wife's actions are designed to achieve the positive goal of health and fitness; in the latter case, her husband's actions are designed to avoid a negative goal—a flabby physique. The ad depicted in Figure 4-3A offers readers a positive goal; the ad in Figure 4-3B depicts a negative goal.

Sometimes people become motivationally aroused by a threat to or elimination of a behavioral freedom (for example, the freedom to make a product choice without undue influence from the seller). This motivational state is called *psychological reactance*

and is usually manifested by a negative consumer response.[6] A classic example occurred in 1985 when the Coca-Cola Company changed its traditional formula and introduced "New Coke." Many people reacted negatively to the notion that their "freedom to choose" had been taken away, and they refused to buy the New Coke. Company management responded to this unexpected psychological reaction by reintroducing the original formula as "Classic Coke," and gradually phased out the New Coke.

FIGURE 4-3A
Positive Motivation

FIGURE 4-3B
Negative Motivation

RATIONAL VERSUS EMOTIONAL MOTIVES

Some consumer behaviorists distinguish between so-called **rational motives** and **emotional motives**. They use the term *rationality* in the traditional economic sense, which assumes that consumers behave rationally when they carefully consider all alternatives and choose those that give them the greatest utility. In a marketing context, the term *rationality* implies that consumers select goals based on totally objective criteria, such as size, weight, price, or miles per gallon. Emotional motives imply the selection of goals according to personal or subjective criteria (for example, pride, fear, affection, or status).

The assumption underlying this distinction is that subjective or emotional criteria do not maximize utility or satisfaction. However, it is reasonable to assume that consumers always attempt to select alternatives that, *in their view*, serve to maximize satisfaction. Obviously, the assessment of satisfaction is a very personal process, based on the individual's own need structure, as well as on past behavioral and social (or learned) experiences. What may appear irrational to an outside observer may be perfectly rational in the context of the consumer's own psychological field. For example, a product purchased to enhance self-image (such as a fragrance) is a perfectly rational form of consumer behavior if the consumer will feel better about herself for wearing it. If the behavior does not seem rational to the person at the time it is undertaken, obviously he or she would not do it.

Consumer researchers who subscribe to the *positivist* research perspective tend to view all consumer behavior as rationally motivated, and they try to isolate the causes of such behavior so that they can predict, and thus influence, future behavior. *Experientialists* are often interested in studying the hedonistic pleasures that certain consumption behaviors provide, such as fun, or fantasy, or sensuality. They study consumers in order to gain insights and understanding of the behaviors consumers take in various unique circumstances.

■■■■ THE DYNAMIC NATURE OF MOTIVATION

Motivation is a highly dynamic construct that is constantly changing in reaction to life experiences. Needs and goals are constantly growing and changing in response to an individual's physical condition, environment, interactions with others, and experiences. As individuals attain their goals, they develop new ones. If they do not attain their goals, they continue to strive for old goals, or they develop substitute goals. Some of the reasons why need-driven human activity never ceases include the following: (1) Many needs are never fully satisfied; they continually impel actions designed to attain or maintain satisfaction. (2) As needs become satisfied, new and higher-order needs emerge that cause tension and induce activity. (3) People who achieve their goals set new and higher goals for themselves. Figure 4-4 bases its appeal on the achievement of new and higher goals.

NEEDS ARE NEVER FULLY SATISFIED

Most human needs are never fully or permanently satisfied. For example, at fairly regular intervals people experience hunger needs that must be satisfied. Most people regularly seek companionship and approval from others to satisfy their social needs. Even more complex psychological needs are rarely satisfied. For example, a person may partially or temporarily satisfy a power need by working as assistant to the CEO of a *Fortune* 500 company, but this small taste of power may not sufficiently satisfy her need; thus she may strive for her own decision-making position in the company. In this instance, temporary goal achievement does not adequately satisfy the need for power, and the individual strives harder in an effort to satisfy the need more fully.

NEW NEEDS EMERGE AS OLD NEEDS ARE SATISFIED

Some motivational theorists believe that a hierarchy of needs exists and that new, higher-order needs emerge as lower-order needs are fulfilled.[7] For example, a man who has largely satisfied his basic physiological needs may turn his efforts to achieving acceptance among his new neighbors by joining their political clubs and supporting their candidates. Once he is confident that he has achieved acceptance, he then may seek recognition by giving lavish parties or building a larger house.

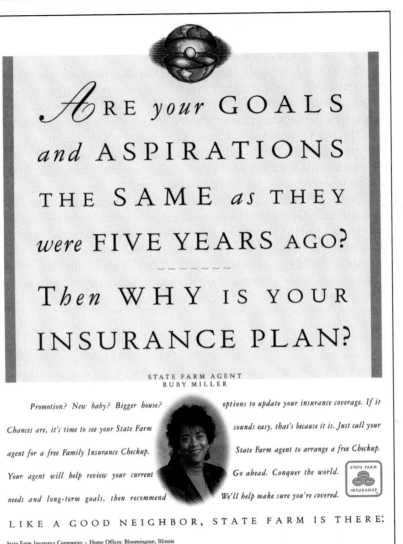

FIGURE 4-4
New and Higher Goals
Motivate Behavior

Marketers must be attuned to changing needs. Car manufacturers who continually promote the prestige value of their automobiles may fail to recognize that consumers often look beyond material possessions to satisfy their needs for prestige—for example, to charitable gift giving or to public service. For this reason, some manufacturers of luxury cars stress different need satisfactions (such as family enjoyment or safety) as reasons for buying a new model.

SUCCESS AND FAILURE INFLUENCE GOALS

A number of researchers have explored the nature of the goals that individuals set for themselves.[8] In general, they have concluded that individuals who successfully achieve their goals usually set new and higher goals; that is, they raise their **levels of aspiration**. This may be due to the fact that their success in reaching lower goals makes them more confident of their ability to reach higher goals. Conversely, those who do not reach their goals sometimes lower their levels of aspiration. Thus, goal selection is often a function of success and failure. For example, a college senior who is not accepted into medical school may try instead to enter dental school; failing that, he may study to be a pharmacist.

The nature and persistence of an individual's behavior are often influenced by expectations of success or failure in reaching certain goals. Those expectations, in turn, are often based on past experience. A person who takes good snapshots with an inexpensive camera may be motivated to buy a more sophisticated camera in the belief that it will enable her to take even better photographs. In this way, she eventually may upgrade her camera by several hundred dollars. On the other hand, a person who has not been able to take good photographs is just as likely to keep the same camera or even to lose all interest in photography.

These effects of success and failure on goal selection have strategy implications for marketers. Goals should be reasonably attainable. Advertisements should not promise more than the product will deliver. Products and services are often evaluated by the size and direction of the gap between consumer expectations and objective performance. Thus, even a good product will not be repurchased if it fails to live up to expectations, however unrealistic they may be. Similarly, a consumer is likely to regard a mediocre product with greater satisfaction than it warrants if its performance exceeds her expectations.

SUBSTITUTE GOALS

When an individual cannot attain a specific goal or type of goal that he or she anticipates will satisfy certain needs, behavior may be directed to a *substitute goal*. Although the substitute goal may not be as satisfactory as the primary goal, it may be sufficient to dispel uncomfortable tension. Continued deprivation of a primary goal may result in the substitute goal assuming primary-goal status. For example, a man who has stopped drinking whole milk because he is dieting may actually begin to prefer skim milk. A woman who cannot afford a BMW may convince herself that a Mazda Miata has an image she clearly prefers. Of course, in this instance, the substitute goal may be a defensive reaction to frustration.

FRUSTRATION

Failure to achieve a goal often results in feelings of frustration. At one time or another, everyone has experienced the frustration that comes from the inability to attain a goal. The barrier that prevents attainment of a goal may be personal to the individual (e.g., limited physical or financial resources), or it can be an obstacle in the physical or social environment (e.g., a rock slide). Regardless of the cause, individuals react differently to frustrating situations. Some people manage to cope by finding their way around the obstacle or, if that fails, by selecting a substitute goal. Others are less adaptive, and may regard their inability to achieve a goal as a personal failure. Such people are likely to adopt a **defense mechanism** to protect their egos from feelings of inadequacy.

Defense Mechanisms

People who cannot cope with frustration often mentally redefine their frustrating situations in order to protect their self-images and defend their self-esteem. For example, a young woman may yearn for a European vacation she cannot afford. The coping individual may select a less expensive vacation trip to Disneyland or to a national park. The person who cannot cope may react with anger toward her boss for not paying her enough money to afford the vacation she prefers, or she may persuade herself that Europe is unreasonably expensive for Americans this year. These last two possibilities are examples, respectively, of *aggression* and *rationalization*, **defense mechanisms** that people sometimes adopt to protect their egos from feelings of failure when they do not attain their goals. Other defense mechanisms include *regression, withdrawal, projection, autism, identification*, and *repression*.

Aggression Individuals who experience frustration may resort to aggressive behavior in attempting to protect their self-esteem. This was aptly illustrated by two British yachtsmen who, disappointed at their poor showing in a sailing competition, burned their boat and swam ashore. Frustrated consumers have boycotted manufacturers in an effort to improve product quality, and have boycotted retailers in an effort to have prices lowered.

Rationalization Sometimes, individuals redefine a frustrating situation by inventing plausible reasons for being unable to attain their goals. Or, they may decide that the goal is not really worth pursuing. Rationalizations are not deliberate lies, since the individual is not fully aware of the cognitive distortion that occurs as a result of the frustrating situation.

Regression Sometimes people react to frustrating situations with childish or immature behavior. A shopper attending a bargain sale, for example, may fight over merchandise and even rip a garment that another shopper will not relinquish, rather than allow the other person to have it.

Withdrawal Frustration is often resolved by simply withdrawing from the situation. For instance, a person who has difficulty achieving officer status in an organization may simply quit that organization. Furthermore, he may rationalize his resignation by deciding the organization is not true to its stated ideals and that its other members are somewhat shallow. In addition, he may decide he can use his time more constructively in other activities.

Projection An individual may redefine a frustrating situation by projecting blame for his or her own failures and inabilities on other objects or persons. Thus, the golfer who misses a stroke may blame the caddy or the golf clubs; the driver who has an automobile accident may blame the other driver or the condition of the road.

Autism Autism, or autistic thinking, refers to thinking that is almost completely dominated by needs and emotions, with little effort made to relate to reality. Such daydreaming, or fantasizing, enables the individual to attain imaginary gratification of unfulfilled needs. A person who is shy and lonely, for example, may daydream about a romantic love affair.

Identification Sometimes people resolve their feelings of frustration by subconsciously identifying with other persons or situations that they consider relevant. Marketers have long recognized the importance of this defense mechanism and frequently use it as the basis for advertising appeals. That is why *slice-of-life* commercials and advertisements are so popular. Such advertisements often portray a stereotypical situation in which an individual experiences a frustration and then overcomes the problem by using the advertised product. If the viewer can identify with the frustrating situation, he or she may very likely adopt the proposed solution and buy the product advertised. Figure 4-5 invites readers frustrated with their aging appearance to identify with people who have had cosmetic surgery.

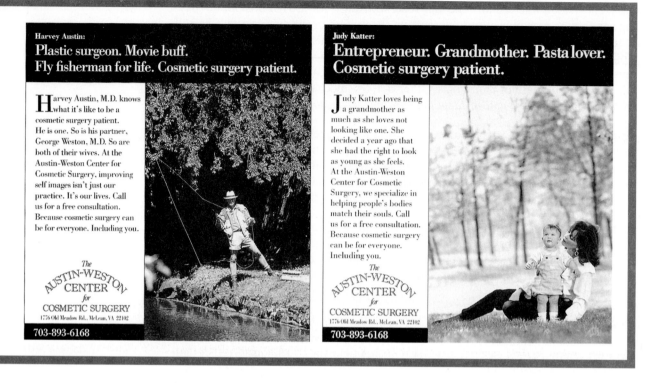

Harvey Austin:
Plastic surgeon. Movie buff.
Fly fisherman for life. Cosmetic surgery patient.

Harvey Austin, M.D. knows what it's like to be a cosmetic surgery patient. He is one. So is his partner, George Weston, M.D. So are both of their wives. At the Austin-Weston Center for Cosmetic Surgery, improving self images isn't just our practice. It's our lives. Call us for a free consultation. Because cosmetic surgery can be for everyone. Including you.

The
AUSTIN-WESTON
CENTER
for
COSMETIC SURGERY
1776 Old Meadow Rd., McLean, VA 22102

703-893-6168

Judy Katter:
Entrepreneur. Grandmother. Pasta lover.
Cosmetic surgery patient.

Judy Katter loves being a grandmother as much as she loves not looking like one. She decided a year ago that she had the right to look as young as she feels. At the Austin-Weston Center for Cosmetic Surgery, we specialize in helping people's bodies match their souls. Call us for a free consultation. Because cosmetic surgery can be for everyone. Including you.

The
AUSTIN-WESTON
CENTER
for
COSMETIC SURGERY
1776 Old Meadow Rd., McLean, VA 22102

703-893-6168

FIGURE 4-5
Identification with Cosmetic
Surgery Patients

Repression Another way that individuals avoid the tension arising from frustration is by repressing the unsatisfied need. Thus, individuals may "forget" a need; that is, they force the need out of their conscious awareness. Sometimes repressed needs manifest themselves indirectly. A couple who cannot have children may surround themselves with plants or pets. The wife may teach school or work in a library; the husband may do volunteer work in a boys' club. The manifestation of repressed needs in a socially acceptable form is called *sublimation*, another type of defense mechanism.

This listing of defense mechanisms is far from exhaustive. People have virtually limitless ways of redefining frustrating situations to protect their self-esteem from the anxieties that result from experiencing failure. Based on their early experiences, individuals tend to develop their own characteristic ways of handling frustration. Marketers often consider this fact in their selection of advertising appeals. Figure 4-6 shows how Lotus products can ease the many frustrations of a sales rep's day.

Multiplicity of Needs

A consumer's behavior often fulfills more than one need. In fact, it is more likely that specific goals are selected because they fulfill several needs. We buy clothing for protection and for modesty; in addition, our clothing fulfills an enormous range of personal and social needs. Usually, however, there is one overriding (prepotent) need that initiates behavior. For example, a woman may want to lose weight because she wants to wear more stylish clothing; she also may be concerned about high blood pressure. In addition, she has noticed her husband admiring shapely girls on the beach. If the cumulative amount of tension produced by each of these three reasons is sufficiently strong, she will truly diet. However, just one of the reasons (for instance, her husband's straying eye) may serve as the triggering mechanism; that would be the prepotent need.

FIGURE 4-6
Identification

Needs and Goals Vary among Individuals

One cannot accurately infer motives from behavior. People with different needs may seek fulfillment through selection of the same goal; people with the same needs may seek fulfillment through different goals. Consider the following examples. Five people who are active in a consumer advocacy organization may each belong for a different reason. The first may be genuinely concerned with protecting consumer interests; the second may be concerned about an increase in counterfeit merchandise; the third may seek social contacts from organizational meetings; the fourth may enjoy the power of directing a large group; and the fifth may enjoy the status provided by membership in an attention-getting organization.

Similarly, five people may be driven by the same need (e.g., an ego need) to seek fulfillment in different ways. The first may seek advancement and recognition through a professional career; the second may become active in a political organization; the third may run in the Boston marathon; the fourth may take professional dance lessons; and the fifth may seek attention by monopolizing classroom discussions.

AROUSAL OF MOTIVES

Most of an individual's specific needs are dormant much of the time. The arousal of any particular set of needs at a specific moment in time may be caused by internal stimuli found in the individual's physiological condition, by emotional or cognitive processes, or by stimuli in the outside environment.

Physiological Arousal

Bodily needs at any one specific moment in time are based on the individual's physiological condition at that moment. A drop in blood sugar level or stomach contractions will trigger awareness of a hunger need. Secretion of sex hormones will awaken the sex need. A decrease in body temperature will induce shivering, which makes the individual aware of the need for warmth. Most of these physiological cues are involuntary; however, they arouse related needs that cause uncomfortable tensions until they are satisfied. For example, a shivering man may turn up the heat in his home to relieve his discomfort; he also may make a mental note to buy flannel pajamas. Research suggests that television programs often generate physiological arousal in viewers (e.g., hunger) that affects the impact of ensuing commercials.[9]

Emotional Arousal

Sometimes daydreaming results in the arousal or stimulation of latent needs. People who are bored or frustrated in trying to achieve their goals often engage in daydreaming (autistic thinking), in which they imagine themselves in all sorts of desirable situations. These thoughts tend to arouse dormant needs, which may produce uncomfortable tensions that drive them into goal-oriented behavior. A young woman who daydreams of being a captain of industry may enroll in graduate business school. A young man who dreams of becoming a novelist may sign up for a writing workshop.

A memorable advertising campaign for Calvin Klein's perfume, *Obsession*, relied on the emotional arousal of needs. A series of 30-second TV commercials portrayed men and women in situations of feverish, all-consuming intensity. Although most perfume advertising talks about the fragrance or scent of the product, these commercials were capped with the phrase, "Ahhh . . . the smell of it," further stressing the all-consuming lust portrayed.[10]

Cognitive Arousal

Sometimes, random thoughts can lead to a cognitive awareness of needs. An advertisement that provides reminders of home might trigger instant yearning to speak with one's parents. This is the basis for many long-distance telephone company campaigns that stress the low cost of international long-distance rates. Figure 4-7 depicts an ad directed at cognitive arousal.

Environmental Arousal

The set of needs an individual experiences at a particular time are often activated by specific cues in the environment. Without these cues, the needs might remain dormant. For example, the 6 o'clock news, the sight or smell of bakery goods, fast-food commercials on television, the end of the school day—all of these may arouse the "need" for food. In such cases, modification of the environment may be necessary to reduce the arousal of hunger.

A most potent form of situational cue is the goal object itself. A woman may experience an overwhelming need for a new television set when she sees her neighbor's new wide-screen home theater; a man may suddenly experience a "need" for a new car when passing a dealer's display window. Sometimes, an advertisement or other environmental cue produces a psychological imbalance in the viewer's mind. For example, a man who prides himself on his gardening may see an advertisement for a tractor mower that apparently works more efficiently than his own rotary mower. The ad may make him so unhappy with his old mower that he experiences severe tension until he buys himself a new tractor model.

When people live in a complex and highly varied environment, they experience many opportunities for need arousal. Conversely, when their environment is poor or deprived, fewer needs are activated. This explains why television has had such a mixed effect on the lives of people in underdeveloped countries. It exposes them to various lifestyles and expensive products that they would not otherwise see, and it

FIGURE 4-7
Cognitive Arousal of Needs

awakens wants and desires that they have little opportunity or even hope of satisfying. Thus, while television enriches many lives, it also serves to frustrate people with little money or education or hope, and may result in the adoption of such aggressive defense mechanisms as robbery, boycotts, or even revolts.

There are two opposing philosophies concerned with the arousal of human motives. The *behaviorist* school considers motivation to be a mechanical process; behavior is seen as the response to a stimulus, and elements of conscious thought are ignored. An extreme example of the stimulus-response theory of motivation is the impulse buyer who reacts largely to external stimuli in the buying situation. According to this theory, the consumer's cognitive control is limited; he or she does not act, but *reacts* to stimuli in the marketplace.[11] The *cognitive* school believes that all behavior is directed at goal achievement. Needs and past experiences are reasoned, cate-gorized, and transformed into attitudes and beliefs that act as predispositions to behavior. These predispositions are focused on helping the individual satisfy needs, and they determine the actions that he or she takes to achieve this satisfaction.

▪▪▪▪ TYPES AND SYSTEMS OF NEEDS

For many years, psychologists and others interested in human behavior have attempted to develop exhaustive lists of human needs. Most lists of human needs tend to be diverse in content as well as in length. Although there is little disagreement about specific physiological needs, there is considerable disagreement about spe-cific psychological (that is, psychogenic) needs.

In 1938, the psychologist Henry Murray prepared a detailed list of 28 psychogenic needs that have served as the basic constructs for a number of widely used personality tests (for instance, the Edwards Personal Preference Schedule). Murray believed that everyone has the same basic set of needs, but that individuals differ in their pri-ority ranking of these needs. Murray's basic needs include many motives that are assumed to play an important role in consumer behavior, such as acquisition, achieve-ment, recognition, and exhibition (see Table 4-2).

Lists of human motives often are too long to be of practical use to marketers. The most useful kind of list is a limited one, in which needs are sufficiently generic in title to subsume more detailed human needs. Although some psychologists have sug-gested that people have different need priorities based on their personalities, their experiences, their environments, and so forth, others believe that most human beings experience the same basic needs, to which they assign a similar priority ranking.

HIERARCHY OF NEEDS

Dr. Abraham Maslow, a clinical psychologist, formulated a widely accepted theory of human motivation based on the notion of a universal **hierarchy of human needs**.[12] Maslow's theory identifies five basic levels of human needs, which rank in order of importance from lower-level (**biogenic**) needs to higher-level (**psychogenic**) needs. The theory postulates that individuals seek to satisfy lower-level needs before higher-level needs emerge. The lowest level of chronically unsatisfied need that an individual experi-ences serves to motivate his or her behavior. When that need is "fairly well" satisfied, a new (and higher) need emerges that the individual is motivated to fulfill. When this need is sat-isfied, a new (and still higher) need emerges, and so on. Of course, if a lower-level need experiences some renewed deprivation, it may temporarily become dominant again.

Figure 4-8 presents Maslow's hierarchy of needs in diagrammatic form. For clar-ity, each level is depicted as mutually exclusive. According to the theory, however, there is some overlap between each level, as no need is ever completely satisfied. For this rea-son, although all levels of need below the level that is currently dominant continue to motivate behavior to some extent, the prime motivator—the major driving force within the individual—is the lowest level of need that remains largely unsatisfied.

Physiological Needs

In the hierarchy-of-needs theory, physiological needs are the first and most basic level of human needs. These needs, which are required to sustain biological life, include food, water, air, shelter, clothing, sex—all the biogenic needs, in fact, that were listed as primary needs earlier.

TABLE 4-2 Murray's List of Psychogenic Needs

NEEDS ASSOCIATED WITH INANIMATE OBJECTS

Acquisition
Conservancy
Order
Retention
Construction

NEEDS THAT REFLECT AMBITION, POWER, ACCOMPLISHMENT, AND PRESTIGE

Superiority
Achievement
Recognition
Exhibition
Inviolacy (inviolate attitude)
Infavoidance (to avoid shame, failure, humiliation, ridicule)
Defendance (defensive attitude)
Counteraction (counteractive attitude)

NEEDS CONCERNED WITH HUMAN POWER

Dominance
Deferrence
Similance (suggestible attitude)
Autonomy
Contrariance (to act differently from others)

SADO-MASOCHISTIC NEEDS

Agression
Abasement

NEEDS CONCERNED WITH AFFECTION BETWEEN PEOPLE

Affiliation
Rejection
Nurturance (to nourish, aid, or protect the helpless)
Succorance (to seek aid, protection, or sympathy)
Play

NEEDS CONCERNED WITH SOCIAL INTERCOURSE (THE NEEDS TO ASK AND TELL)

Cognizance (inquiring attitude)
Exposition (expositive attitude)

Source: Adapted from Henry A. Murray, "Types of Human Needs," in David C. McClelland, *Studies in Motivation* (New York: Appleton-Century-Crofts, 1955), 63–66. Reprinted by permission of Irvington Publishers, Inc.

According to Maslow, physiological needs are dominant when they are chronically unsatisfied: "For the man who is extremely and dangerously hungry, no other interest exists but food. He dreams food, he remembers food, he thinks about food, he emotes only about food, he perceives only food, and he wants only food."[13] For many people in this country, the biogenic needs are generally satisfied, and higher-level needs are dominant. Unfortunately, however, the lives of the many homeless people in major cities and in physically devastated areas are focused almost entirely on satisfying their biogenic needs: the need for food, clothing, and shelter from the elements.

FIGURE 4-8

Maslow's Hierarchy of
Needs

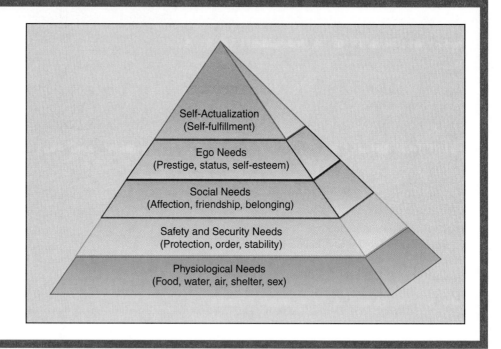

Safety Needs

After the first level of need is satisfied, safety and security needs become the driving force behind an individual's behavior. These needs are concerned with much more than physical safety. They include order, stability, routine, familiarity, and control over one's life and environment. Health and the availability of health care are important safety concerns. Savings accounts, insurance policies, education, and vocational training are all means by which individuals satisfy the need for security (see Figure 4-9). Ironically, in response to the physical safety need aroused by a growing crime rate in the 1990s, personal protection companies have promoted a variety of self-defense products (e.g., pepper sprays, handguns, mace, personal bodyguards) as ways of expressing love and holiday cheer.[14]

Social Needs

The third level of Maslow's hierarchy includes such needs as love, affection, belonging, and acceptance. People seek warm and satisfying human relationships with other people and are motivated by love for their families (see Figure 4-10). Because of the importance of social motives in our society, advertisers of personal care products often emphasize this appeal in their advertisements.

Egoistic Needs

When social needs are more or less satisfied, the fourth level of Maslow's hierarchy becomes operative. This level is concerned with egoistic needs. These needs can take either an inward or an outward orientation, or both. *Inwardly-directed ego needs* reflect an individual's need for self-acceptance, self-esteem, success, independence, personal satisfaction with a job well done. *Outwardly-directed ego needs* include the needs for prestige, reputation, status, and recognition from others. The presumed desire to "keep up with the Joneses" is a reflection of an outwardly-oriented ego need.

FIGURE 4-9
Appeal to the Safety Need

Need for Self-Actualization

According to Maslow, most people do not satisfy their ego needs sufficiently to ever
move to the fifth level—the need for self-actualization (self-fulfillment). This need
refers to an individual's desire to fulfill his or her potential—to become everything he
or she is capable of becoming. In Maslow's words, "What a man can be, he must be."[15]
This need is expressed in different ways by different people. A young man may
desire to be an Olympic star and work single-mindedly for years to become the best
in his sport. An artist may need to express herself on canvas; a research scientist may
strive to find a new drug that eradicates cancer (see Figure 4-11). Maslow noted that
the self-actualization need is not necessarily a creative urge, but that it is likely to take
that form in people with some capacity for creativity. Advertisements for art lessons,
banking services, and even for military recruitment often try to appeal to the self-actu-

Perfect holiday setting.

Bordeaux, always à propos.

▶◀

A propos. Is there any better reason to raise a glass of Bordeaux than to celebrate the holiday season? Perfect at parties with family and friends. And as you welcome in the New Year whether at home on the couch or out on the town, why not raise a glass or two. Because the wine you pour says so much more, when it comes from the region simply known as Bordeaux. When you toast to the old and welcome the new, remember to enjoy yourself sensibly this holiday season. Satisfy your thirst for more information on Bordeaux wines. Visit our web site at **www.bordeaux.com**

FIGURE 4-10
Appeal to the Social Need

alization need. Some of our largest companies hire motivation experts to encourage their highly paid employees to look beyond their paychecks to find gratification and self-fulfillment in the workplace—to view their jobs as the way to become "all they can be."[16] Figure 4-12 shows an ad for shoes based on a self-actualization appeal.

FIGURE 4-11
Appeal to Self-Actualization

An Evaluation of the Need Hierarchy

Maslow's hierarchy-of-needs theory postulates a five-level hierarchy of prepotent human needs. Higher-order needs become the driving force behind human behavior as lower-level needs are satisfied. The theory says, in effect, that dissatisfaction, not satisfaction, motivates behavior.

The need hierarchy has received wide acceptance in many social disciplines because it appears to reflect the assumed or inferred motivations of many people in our society. The five levels of need postulated by the hierarchy are sufficiently generic

FIGURE 4-12
A Self-Actualization
Appeal

C A B L E & C o .

The Art of Movement Defined.

Destination is not a finite place.
Rather, it's a compass by which you judge
how far you've come.
Motion does not scare you.
Indeed, it's where you draw the energy to strive,
to achieve, to explore.
No distance is too great. No territory too vast.

No discovery too new.
Space is something you've mastered.
In style.
Because that's the only way you move. Always.
And that's a powerful state.
For if not for men like you, the horizon would
indeed be a place somewhere near.

CABLE & Co.
The Art of Movement

The Cable & Co. "Drives" are designed, constructed and hand finished by the world's finest craftsmen and are available at
SAKS FIFTH AVENUE • BLOOMINGDALES • MACY'S • BULLOCKS • PARISIAN • NEIMAN MARCUS
and other fine specialty and department stores
For the store nearest you please call 1-800-624-2020
©1995 Cable & Co., 39 West 56th St, New York, NY 10019

to encompass most lists of individual needs. The major problem with the theory is that it cannot be tested empirically; there is no way to measure precisely how satisfied one need must be before the next higher need becomes operative. The need hierarchy also appears to be very closely bound to our contemporary American culture (that is, it appears to be both culture- and time-bound).

Despite these criticisms, Maslow's hierarchy is a useful tool for understanding consumer motivations and is readily adaptable to marketing strategy, primarily because consumer goods often serve to satisfy each of the need levels. For example, individuals buy houses, food, and clothing to satisfy physiological needs; they buy

In summary, individuals with specific psychological needs tend to be receptive to advertising appeals directed at those needs. They also tend to be receptive to certain kinds of products. Thus, a knowledge of motivational theory provides marketers with additional bases on which to segment their markets.

▪▪▪▪ THE MEASUREMENT OF MOTIVES

How are motives identified? How are they measured? How do researchers know which motives are responsible for certain kinds of behavior? These are difficult questions to answer because motives are hypothetical constructs—that is, they cannot be seen or touched, handled, smelled, or otherwise tangibly observed. For this reason, no single measurement method can be considered a reliable index. Instead, researchers usually rely on a combination of various qualitative research techniques to try to establish the presence and/or the strength of various motives.

Some psychologists are concerned that many measurement techniques do not meet the crucial test criteria of *validity* and *reliability*. (Remember, validity ensures that the test measures what it purports to measure; reliability refers to the consistency with which the test measures what it does measure.)

As discussed in chapter 2, the findings of qualitative research methods are highly dependent on the analyst; they focus not only on the data themselves but also on what the analyst thinks they imply. By using a combination of assessments (called *triangulation*) based on behavioral data (observation), subjective data (self-reports), and qualitative data (projective tests, collage research, etc.), many consumer researchers feel more confident that they are achieving more valid insights into consumer motivations than they would by using any one technique alone. Though some marketers are concerned that qualitative research does not produce hard numbers that objectively "prove" the point under investigation, others are convinced that qualitative studies are more revealing than quantitative studies. However, there is a clear need for improved methodological procedures for measuring human motives.

MOTIVATIONAL RESEARCH

The term **motivational research**, which should logically include all types of research into human motives, has become a "term of art" used to refer to qualitative research designed to uncover the consumer's subconscious or hidden motivations.[22] Based on the premise that consumers are not always aware of the reasons for their actions, motivational research attempts to discover underlying feelings, attitudes, and emotions concerning product, service, or brand use. Table 4-3 describes the "personalities" consumers have attributed to selected products; these findings were uncovered through motivational research studies.

Sigmund Freud's psychoanalytic theory of personality (discussed in chapter 5) provided the foundation for the development of motivational research. This theory was built on the premise that unconscious needs or drives—especially biological and sexual drives—are at the heart of human motivation and personality. Freud constructed his theory from patients' recollections of early childhood experiences, analysis of their dreams, and the specific nature of their mental and physical adjustment problems.

Dr. Ernest Dichter, formerly a psychoanalyst in Vienna, adapted Freud's psychoanalytical techniques to the study of consumer buying habits. Up to this time, marketing research had focused on *what* consumers did (i.e., quantitative, descriptive studies). Dichter used qualitative research methods to find out *why* they did it. Marketers were quickly fascinated by the glib, entertaining, and usually surprising explanations offered for consumer behavior, especially since many of these explanations

TABLE 4-3 Selected Product Personality Profiles Uncovered by Motivational Research

BAKING
An expression of femininity and motherhood, baking evokes pleasant, nostalgic memories of the odors pervading the house when one's mother was baking. To many, a woman is subconsciously and symbolically going through the act of giving birth when baking a cake, and the most fertile moment occurs when the baked product is pulled out of the oven.

ICE CREAM
Ice cream is associated with love and affection. It derives particular potency from childhood memories, when it was given to a child for being "good" and withheld as an instrument of punishment. People refer to ice cream as something they "love" to eat. Ice cream is a symbol of abundance; people prefer round packaging with an illustration that runs around the box panel because it suggests unlimited quantity.

POWER TOOLS
Power tools are a symbol of manliness. They represent masculine skill and competence and are often bought more for their symbolic value than for active do-it-yourself applications. Ownership of a good power tool or circular saw provides a man with feelings of omnipotence.

BEER
For most people, beer is an active, alive, sensuous beverage that provides the drinker with a feeling of security. People generally describe the beer they like as "alive," "foamy," and "sparkling," and disliked brands as "flat," "dead," or "stale."

Source: Adapted from *Handbook of Consumer Motivations*, by Ernest Dichter. Copyright 1964, McGraw-Hill Book Company. Used with permission of McGraw-Hill Book Company.

were grounded in sex. For example, marketers were told that cigarettes and Lifesaver candies were bought because of their sexual symbolism, that men regarded convertible cars as surrogate mistresses, and that women baked cakes to fulfill their reproductive yearnings.[23] Before long, almost every major advertising agency in the country had a psychologist on staff to conduct motivational research studies.

By the early 1960s, however, marketers realized that motivational research had some drawbacks. Because of the intensive nature of qualitative research, samples necessarily were small; thus, there was concern about generalizing findings to the total market. Also, marketers soon realized that the analysis of projective tests and depth interviews was highly subjective. The same data given to three different analysts could produce three different reports, each offering its own explanation of the consumer behavior examined. Critics noted that many of the projective tests that were used had originally been developed for clinical purposes, rather than for studies of marketing or consumer behavior. (One of the basic criteria for test development is that the test be developed and validated for the specific purpose and on the specific audience profile from which information is desired.)

Other consumer theorists noted additional inconsistencies in applying Freudian theory to the study of consumer behavior. First, psychoanalytic theory was structured specifically for use with disturbed people, whereas consumer behaviorists were interested in explaining the behavior of "typical" consumers. Second, Freudian theory was developed in an entirely different social context (nineteenthth-century Vienna), while motivational research was introduced in 1950s postwar America.[24] Finally, too many motivational researchers imputed highly exotic (usually sexual) reasons to rather prosaic consumer purchases. Marketers began to question their recommendations (e.g., Is it better to sell a man a pair of suspenders as a means of holding up his pants or as a "reaction to castration anxiety"? Is it easier to persuade a woman to buy a garden hose to water her lawn or as a symbol of "genital competition with males"?).

Evaluation of Motivational Research

Despite these criticisms, motivational research is still regarded as an important tool by marketers who want to gain deeper insights into the *whys* of consumer behavior than conventional marketing research techniques can yield. Since motivational research often reveals unsuspected consumer motivations concerning product or brand usage, its principal use today is in the development of new ideas for promotional campaigns, ideas that can penetrate the consumer's conscious awareness by appealing to unrecognized needs. For example, in trying to discover why women bought traditional roach sprays rather than a brand packaged in little plastic trays, researchers asked women to draw pictures of roaches and write stories about their sketches. They found that, for many of their respondents, roaches symbolized men who had left them feeling poor and powerless. The women reported that spraying the roaches and "watching them squirm and die" allowed them to express their hostility toward men and gave them feelings of greater control.[25]

Motivational research also provides marketers with a basic orientation for new product categories, and enables them to explore consumer reactions to ideas and advertising copy at an early stage to avoid costly errors. Furthermore, as with all qualitative research techniques, motivational research findings provide consumer researchers with basic insights that enable them to design structured, quantitative marketing research studies to be conducted on larger, more representative samples of consumers.

Despite the drawbacks of motivational research, there is new and compelling evidence that the unconscious is the site of a far larger portion of mental life than even Freud envisioned. Research studies show that the unconscious mind may understand and respond to nonverbal symbols, form emotional responses, and guide actions largely independent of conscious awareness.[26]

Though they are not usually identified as motivational research techniques, there are a number of associated qualitative research techniques that are used to delve into the consumer's unconscious or hidden motivations. These include collage research, metaphor analysis, means-end analysis, and laddering. (These techniques were discussed in chapter 2.) All of these qualitative research techniques provide invaluable insights to marketers who want to know the hidden motives underlying consumer behavior.

SUMMARY

Motivation is the driving force within individuals that impels them to action. This driving force is produced by a state of uncomfortable tension, which exists as the result of an unsatisfied need. All individuals have needs, wants, and desires. The individual's subconscious drive to reduce need-induced tension results in behavior that he or she anticipates will satisfy needs and thus bring about a more comfortable internal state.

All behavior is goal oriented. Goals are the sought-after results of motivated behavior. The form or direction that behavior takes—the goal that is selected—is a result of thinking processes (cognition) and previous learning. There are two types of goals: generic goals and product-specific goals. A generic goal is a general category of goal that may fulfill a certain need; a product-specific goal is a specifically branded or labeled product that the individual sees as a way to fulfill a need. Product-specific needs are sometimes referred to as wants.

Innate needs—those an individual is born with—are physiological (biogenic) in nature; they include all the factors required to sustain physical life (e.g., food, water, clothing, shelter, sex). Acquired needs—those an individual develops after birth—are primarily psychological (psychogenic); they include love, acceptance, esteem, and self-fulfillment. For any given need, there are many different and appropriate goals. The specific goal selected depends on the individual's experiences, physical capacity, prevailing cultural norms and values, and the goal's accessibility in the physical and social environment.

Needs and goals are interdependent and change in response to the individual's physical condition, environment, interaction with other people, and experiences. As needs become satisfied, new, higher-order needs emerge that must be fulfilled.

Failure to achieve a goal often results in feelings of frustration. Individuals react to frustration in two ways: "fight" or "flight." They may cope by finding a way around the obstacle that prohibits goal attainment or by adopting a substitute goal (fight); or they may adopt a defense mechanism that enables them to protect their self-esteem (flight). Defense mechanisms include aggression, regression, rationalization, withdrawal, projection, autism, identification, and repression.

Motives cannot easily be inferred from consumer behavior. People with different needs may seek fulfillment through selection of the same goals; people with the same needs may seek fulfillment through different goals. Although some psychologists have suggested that individuals have different need priorities, others believe that most human beings experience the same basic needs, to which they assign a similar priority ranking. Maslow's hierarchy-of-needs theory proposes five levels of prepotent human needs: physiological needs, safety needs, social needs, egois-

tic needs, and self-actualization needs. Other needs widely integrated into consumer advertising include the needs for power, affiliation, and achievement.

There are three commonly used methods for identifying and "measuring" human motives: observation and inference, subjective reports, and qualitative research (including projective techniques). None of these methods is completely reliable by itself. Therefore, researchers often use a combination of two or three techniques in tandem to assess the presence or strength of consumer motives. Motivational research is qualitative research designed to delve below the consumer's level of conscious awareness. Despite some shortcomings, motivational research has proved to be of great value to marketers concerned with developing new ideas and new copy appeals.

DISCUSSION QUESTIONS

1. a. "Marketers don't create needs; needs preexist marketers." Discuss this statement.
    b. Can marketing efforts change consumers' needs? Why or why not?

2. Consumers have both innate and acquired needs. Give examples of each kind of need and show how the same purchase can serve to fulfill either or both kinds of needs.

3. Specify both innate and acquired needs that would be useful bases for developing promotional strategies for: (a) global positioning systems, (b) Harley Davidson motorcycles, and (c) recruiting college seniors to work for a high-technology company.

4. Why are consumers' needs and goals constantly changing? What factors influence the formation of new goals?

5. How can marketers use consumers' failures at achieving goals in developing promotional appeals for specific products and services? Give examples.

6. Most human needs are dormant much of the time. What factors cause their arousal? Give examples of ads for audio/video equipment that are designed to arouse latent consumer needs.

7. For each of the situations listed in Question 3, select one level from Maslow's hierarchy of human needs that can be used to segment the market and position the product (or the company). Explain your choices. What are the advantages and disadvantages of using Maslow's hierarchy for segmentation and positioning applications?

8. a. How do researchers identify and "measure" human motives? Give examples.
    b. Does motivational research differ from qualitative research? Discuss.
    c. What are the strengths and weaknesses of motivational research?

EXERCISES

1. You are a member of an advertising team assembled to develop a promotional campaign for a new digital camera. Develop three headlines for this campaign, each based on one of the levels in Maslow's need hierarchy.

2. Find an advertisement that depicts a defense mechanism. Present it in class and discuss its effectiveness.

3. Explain briefly the needs for power, affiliation, and achievement. Find three advertisements for different products that are designed to appeal to these needs.

KEY TERMS

- **Approach versus avoidance goals**
- **Biogenic versus psychogenic needs**
- **Defense mechanisms**
- **Generic versus product-specific goals**
- **Innate versus acquired needs**
- **Levels of aspiration**
- **Maslow's hierarchy of human needs**
- **Motivational research**
- **Positive versus negative motivation**
- **Prepotent need**
- **Primary versus secondary needs**
- **Rational versus emotional motives**
- **Substitute goals**

NOTES

1. Jonathon Gutman, "A Means-End Chain Model Based on Consumer Categorization Processes," *Journal of Marketing* 46 (Spring 1982): 60–72.

2. Jeffrey F. Durgee et al., "Observations: Translating Values into Product Wants," *Journal of Advertising Research* 36, 6 (November 1996): 90–99.

3. Ibid.

4. Russell W. Belk et al., "Metaphors of Consumer Desire," *Advances in Consumer Research* 23 (1996): 368–73.

5. Ibid.

6. Jack W. Brehm, "Psychological Reactance: Theory and Applications," *Advances in Consumer Research* 16 (1989 Association for Consumer Research): 72–75.

7. See Abraham H. Maslow, "A Theory of Human Motivation," *Psychological Review* 50 (1943): 370–96; Abraham H. Maslow, *Motivation and Personality* (New York: Harper & Row, 1954); and Abraham H. Maslow, *Toward a Psychology of Being* (New York: Van Nostrand Reinhold, 1968), 189–215.

8. A number of studies have focused on human levels of aspiration. See, for example, Kurt Lewin et al., "Level of Aspiration," in *Personality and Behavior Disorders*, ed. J. McV. Hunt (New York: Ronald Press, 1944); Howard Garland, "Goal Levels and Task Performance, a Compelling Replication of Some Compelling Results," *Journal of Applied Psychology* 67 (1982): 245–48; Edwin A. Locke, Elizabeth Frederick, Cynthia Lee, and Philip Bobko, "Effect of Self-Efficacy, Goals and Task Strategies on Task Performance," *Journal of Applied Psychology* 69, 2 (1984): 241–51; Edwin A. Locke, Elizabeth Frederick, Elizabeth Buckner, and Philip Bobko, "Effect of Previously Assigned Goals on Self-Set Goals and Performance," *Journal of Applied Psychology* 72, 2 (1987): 204–11; and John R. Hollenbeck and Howard J. Klein, "Goal Commitment and the Goal-Setting Process: Problems, Prospects and Proposals for Future Research," *Journal of Applied Psychology* 2 (1987): 212–20.

9. Surendra N. Singh and Gilbert A. Churchill Jr., "Arousal and Advertising Effectiveness," *Journal of Advertising* 16, 1 (1987): 4–10.

10. Pat Sloan, "Klein's Sultry Avedon Ads for Obsession Hit TV," *Advertising Age*, March 25, 1985, 104; and Michael McWilliams, "Calvin Bests Fellini with Obsession Spots," *Advertising Age*, April 8, 1985, 81.

11. Peter Weinberg and Wolfgang Gottwald, "Impulsive Consumer Buying as a Result of Emotions," *Journal of Business Research* 10 (1982): 43.

12. Maslow, "A Theory of Human Motivation," 380.

13. Ibid., 380.

14. J. Pederzane, "Visions of Perpetrators Dancing in Their Heads," *New York Times*, 18 December, 1994, 2E.

15. Maslow, "A Theory of Human Motivation," 380.

16. Adam Bryant, Looking for Purpose in a Paycheck" *New York Times*, 21 June 1998, Sec. 4, p. 1.

17. Rudy Schrocer, "Maslow's Hierarchy of Needs as a Framework for Identifying Emotional Triggers," *Marketing Review* 46, 5 (February 1991): 26, 28.

18. See, for example, David C. McClelland, *Studies in Motivation* (New York: Appleton-Century-Crofts, 1955).

19. David C. McClelland, "Business Drive and National Achievement," *Harvard Business Review* (July–August 1962): 99; "Achievement Motivation Can Be Developed," *Harvard Business Review* 5, 24 (November–December 1965): 18; and Abraham K. Korman, *The Psychology of Motivation* (Upper Saddle River, NJ: Prentice Hall, 1974), 190.

20. A. G. Greenwald, "Ego Task Analysis: An Integration of Research on Ego-Involvement and Self-Awareness," in *Cognitive Social Psychology*, A. H. Hastorf and A. M. Isen, ed. (New York: Elsevier-North Holland, 1982), 109–47.

21. Judith M. Harackiewicz, Carol Sansone, and George Manderlink, "Competence, Achievement Orientation, and Intrinsic Motivation: A Process Analysis," *Journal of Personality and Social Psychology* 48 (1985): 493–508.

22. Ernest Dichter, *A Strategy of Desire* (Garden City, NY: Doubleday, 1960).

23. For additional reports of motivational research findings, see Dichter, *A Strategy of Desire*; Vance Packard, *The Hidden Persuaders* (New York: Pocket Books, 1957); and Pierre Martineau, *Motivation in Advertising* (New York: McGraw-Hill, 1957).

24. Jeff B. Murray and Deborah J. Evers, "Theory Borrowing and Reflectivity in Interdisciplinary Fields," *Advances in Consumer Research* 16 (1988): 652–57.

25. Daniel Goleman, "New View of Mind Gives Unconscious an Expanded Role," *New York Times*, 7 February 1984, C1–2.

26. Ronald Alsop, "Agencies Scrutinize Their Ads for Psychological Symbolism," *The Wall Street Journal*, 11 June, 1987, 27. See also David Mick, "Consumer Research and Semiotics: Exploring the Morphology of Signs, Symbols and Significance," *Journal of Consumer Research* 13 (September 1986): 196–213.

CHAPTER 5
Personality and Consumer Behavior

■ ■

Marketers have long tried to appeal to consumers in terms of their personality characteristics. They have intuitively felt that what consumers purchase, and when and how they consume, are likely to be influenced by personality factors. For this reason, advertising and marketing people have frequently depicted (or incorporated) specific personality traits or characteristics in their advertising messages. Some recent examples are an appeal to personal creativity for the Philips CD recorder (headline: "I've made a CD as unique as I am."), an appeal to the inner self for Senscience hair care products (headline: "Inner strength means outer beauty."), an appeal to spontaneity for the Ford Escort ZX2 (headline: "Excuse yourself from the predictable."), an appeal to demanding people for Evian natural spring water ("This is no place for compromise."), an appeal to complexity of personality for Calvin Klein's Contradiction line of body products (headline: "She is always and never the same."), and an appeal to positive personality traits for Montecristo cigars (headline: "Consistent. Worldly. Knows no equal. And that's just the Cigar.").

This chapter is designed to provide the reader with an understanding of how *personality* and self concept are related to various aspects of consumer behavior. It examines what personality is, reviews several major personality theories, and describes how these theories have stimulated marketing interest in the study of consumer personality. The chapter considers the important topic of *brand personality*, and concludes with an exploration of how the related concepts of *self* and *self-image* influence consumer attitudes and behavior.

■ ■ ■ ■ WHAT IS PERSONALITY?

The study of **personality** has been approached by theorists in a variety of ways. Some have emphasized the dual influence of heredity and early childhood experiences on personality development; others have stressed broader social and environmental influences and the fact that personalities develop continuously over time. Some theorists prefer to view personality as a unified whole; others focus on specific traits. The wide variation in viewpoints makes it difficult to arrive at a single definition. However, we propose that personality be defined as those inner psychological characteristics that both determine and reflect how a person responds to his or her environment.

The emphasis in this definition is on *inner characteristics*—those specific qualities, attributes, traits, factors, and mannerisms that distinguish one individual from other individuals. As discussed later in the chapter, the deeply ingrained characteristics that we call personality are likely to influence the individual's product choices: They affect the way consumers respond to marketers' promotional efforts, and when, where, and how they consume particular products or services. Therefore, the identification of specific personality characteristics associated with consumer behavior has proven to be highly useful in the development of a firm's market segmentation strategies.

THE NATURE OF PERSONALITY

In the study of personality, three distinct properties are of central importance: (1) personality reflects *individual differences*; (2) personality is *consistent and enduring*; and (3) personality can *change*.

Personality Reflects Individual Differences

Because the inner characteristics that constitute an individual's personality are a unique combination of factors, no two individuals are exactly alike. Nevertheless, many individuals may be similar in terms of a single personality characteristic, but not in terms of others. For instance, some people can be described as "high" in *venturesomeness* (willing to accept the risk of doing something new or different), while others can be described as "low" in *venturesomeness* (for example, afraid to buy a really new product). Personality is a useful concept because it enables us to categorize consumers into different groups on the basis of one or even several traits. If each person were different in terms of all personality traits, it would be impossible to group consumers into segments, and there would be little reason for marketers to develop products and promotional campaigns targeted to particular segments.

Personality Is Consistent and Enduring

An individual's personality tends to be both consistent and enduring. Indeed, the mother who comments that her child "has been stubborn from the day he was born" is supporting the contention that personality has both consistency and endurance. Both qualities are essential if marketers are to explain or predict consumer behavior in terms of personality.

While marketers cannot change consumers' personalities to conform to their products, if they know which personality characteristics influence specific consumer responses, they can attempt to appeal to the relevant traits inherent in their target group of consumers.

Even though consumers' personalities may be consistent, their consumption behavior often varies considerably because of the various psychological, sociocultural, environmental, and situational factors that affect behavior. For instance, while an individual's personality may be relatively stable, specific needs or motives, attitudes, reactions to group pressures, and even responses to newly available brands may cause a change in the person's behavior. Personality is only one of a combination of factors that influence how a consumer behaves.

Personality Can Change

Under certain circumstances personalities change. For instance, an individual's personality may be altered by major life events, such as the birth of a child, the death of a loved one, a divorce, or a significant career promotion. An individual's personality changes not only in response to abrupt events, but also as part of a gradual maturing process— "He's growing up, he is less wild," says an aunt after not seeing her nephew for 5 years.

THEORIES OF PERSONALITY

This section briefly reviews three major theories of personality: (1) **Freudian theory**, (2) **neo-Freudian theory**, and (3) **trait theory**. These theories have been chosen for discussion from among many theories of personality because each has played a prominent role in the study of the relationship between consumer behavior and personality.

FREUDIAN THEORY

Sigmund Freud's **psychoanalytic theory of personality** is the cornerstone of modern psychology. This theory was built on the premise that *unconscious needs or drives*, especially sexual and other biological drives, are at the heart of human motivation and personality. Freud constructed his theory on the basis of patients' recollections of early childhood experiences, analysis of their dreams, and the specific nature of their mental and physical adjustment problems.

Id, Superego, and Ego

Based on his analyses, Freud proposed that the human personality consists of three interacting systems: the **id**, the **superego**, and the **ego**. The *id* was conceptualized as a "warehouse" of primitive and impulsive drives—basic physiological needs such as thirst, hunger, and sex—for which the individual seeks immediate satisfaction without concern for the specific means of satisfaction. The ad for Ray-Ban™ scratch-resistant glass lenses (see Figure 5-1) captures the exciting "forces" associated with the primitive drives of the *id*. The positioning and appearance of the models (including the long nails) add to this sense of excitement.

In contrast to the id, the *superego* is conceptualized as the individual's internal expression of society's moral and ethical codes of conduct. The superego's role is to see that the individual satisfies needs in a socially acceptable fashion. Thus, the superego is a kind of "brake" that restrains or inhibits the impulsive forces of the id.

Finally, the *ego* is the individual's conscious control. It functions as an internal monitor that attempts to balance the impulsive demands of the id and the sociocultural constraints of the superego. Figure 5-2 represents the interrelationships among the three interacting systems. In addition to specifying a structure for personality, Freud emphasized that an individual's personality is formed as he or she passes through a number of distinct stages of infant and childhood development. These are the *oral, anal, phallic, latent,* and *genital* stages. Freud labeled four of these stages of development to conform to the area of the body on which he believed the child's sexual instincts are focused at the time.

According to Freudian theory, an adult's personality is determined by how well he or she deals with the crises that are experienced while passing through each of these stages (particularly the first three). For instance, if a child's oral needs are not adequately satisfied at the first stage of development, the person may become fixated at this stage, and as an adult display a personality that includes such traits as dependence and excessive oral activity (e.g., gum chewing and smoking). When an individual is fixated at the anal stage, the adult personality may display other traits, such as an excessive need for neatness.

Freudian Theory and "Product Personality"

Researchers who apply Freud's psychoanalytic theory to the study of consumer personality believe that human drives are largely *unconscious* and that consumers are primarily *unaware* of their true reasons for buying what they buy. These researchers tend to see consumer purchases and/or consumption situations as a reflection and an

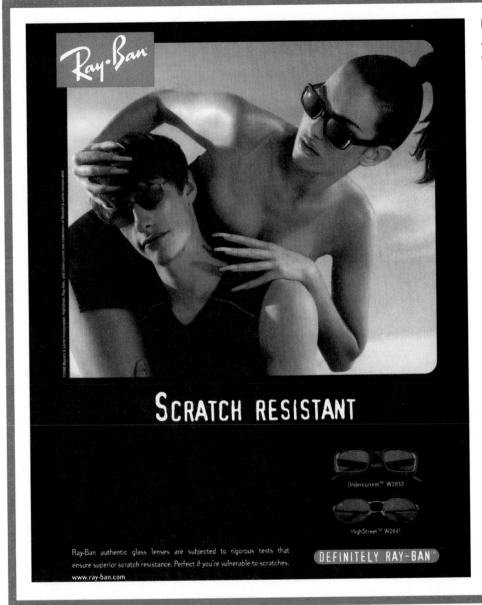

FIGURE 5-1
Ad Portraying the "Forces"
of the Id

extension of the consumer's own personality. In other words, they consider the consumer's appearance and possessions—grooming, clothing, jewelry, and so forth—as reflections of the individual's personality. (The related topics of *brand personality*, and the *self* and *self-images* are considered later in the chapter.)

NEO-FREUDIAN PERSONALITY THEORY

Several of Freud's colleagues disagreed with his contention that personality is primarily instinctual and sexual in nature. Instead, these neo-Freudians believed that *social relationships* are fundamental to the formation and development of personality. For instance, Alfred Adler viewed human beings as seeking to attain various rational goals, which he called *style of life*. He also placed much emphasis on the individual's efforts to overcome feelings of *inferiority* (i.e., by striving for superiority).

FIGURE 5-2

A Representation of the Interrelationships among the Id, Ego, and Superego

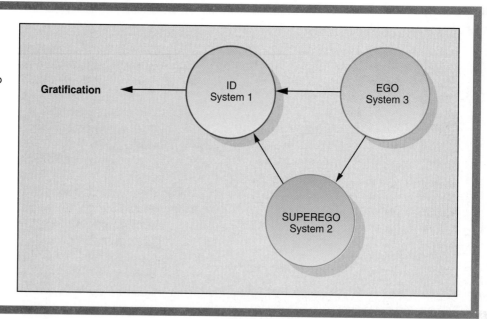

Harry Stack Sullivan, another neo-Freudian, stressed that people continuously attempt to establish significant and rewarding relationships with others. He was particularly concerned with the individual's efforts to reduce tensions, such as *anxiety*.

Like Sullivan, Karen Horney was also interested in anxiety. She focused on the impact of *child-parent* relationships, and the individual's desire to conquer feelings of anxiety. Horney proposed that individuals be classified into three personality groups: **compliant**, **aggressive**, and **detached**.[1]

1. *Compliant individuals* are those who move *toward* others (they desire to be loved, wanted, and appreciated).
2. *Aggressive individuals* are those who move *against* others (they desire to excel and win admiration).
3. *Detached individuals* are those who move *away* from others (they desire independence, self-reliance, self-sufficiency, and freedom from obligations).

A personality test based on Horney's theory (the CAD) has been developed and tested within the context of consumer behavior.[2] The initial CAD research uncovered a number of tentative relationships between college students' scores and their product and brand usage patterns. For example, highly *compliant* students were found to prefer name brand products such as Bayer aspirin; students classified as *aggressive* showed a preference for Old Spice deodorant over other brands (seemingly because of its masculine appeal); and highly *detached* students proved to be heavy tea drinkers (possibly reflecting their desire not to conform). Recent research found that children who scored high in self-reliance—who preferred to do things independently of others (i.e., *detached* personalities)—were *less* likely to be brand loyal and were more likely to try different brands.[3]

Many marketers use some of these neo-Freudian theories intuitively. For example, marketers who position their products or services as providing an opportunity to belong or to be appreciated by others in a group or social setting would seem to be guided by Horney's characterization of the *compliant* individual. Figure 5-3 shows an ad for Yahoo; its headline, "Doesn't the thought of 20 new friends sound terrific?" targets it directly to compliant individuals—those who are attracted to the idea of meeting new people.

Doesn't the thought of 20 new friends sound terrific?

Yahoo! Chat

At any given moment, 24 hours a day, there are literally thousands of people waiting to talk to you. Maybe some will stick. Free at www.yahoo.com

Do You Yahoo!?

FIGURE 5-3
Ad Applying Horney's
Compliant Personality

TRAIT THEORY

Trait theory constitutes a major departure from the *qualitative* measures that typify the Freudian and neo-Freudian movements (e.g., personal observation, self-reported experiences, dream analysis, projective techniques).

The orientation of trait theory is primarily *quantitative* or *empirical*; it focuses on the measurement of personality in terms of specific psychological characteristics, called traits. A *trait* is defined as "any distinguishing, relatively enduring way in which one individual differs from another."[4] Trait theorists are concerned with the construction of personality tests (or inventories) that enable them to pinpoint individual differences in terms of specific traits.

Selected *single-trait personality* tests (which measure just one trait, such as self-confidence) are often developed specifically for use in consumer behavior studies. These tailor-made personality tests measure such traits as **consumer innovativeness** (how receptive a person is to new experiences), **consumer materialism** (the degree of the consumer's attachment to "worldly possessions"), and **consumer ethnocentrism** (the consumer's likelihood to accept or reject foreign-made products).

Trait researchers have found that it is generally more realistic to expect personality to be linked to how consumers *make their choices* and to the purchase or consumption of a *broad product category*, rather than a specific brand. For example, there is more likely to be a relationship between a personality trait and whether or not an individual *owns* a convertible sports car, than between a personality trait and the *brand* of convertible sports car purchased.

The next section shows how trait measures of personality are used to expand our understanding of consumer behavior.

PERSONALITY AND UNDERSTANDING CONSUMER DIVERSITY

Marketers are interested in understanding how personality influences consumption behavior, because such knowledge enables them to better understand consumers and to segment and target those consumers who are likely to respond positively to their product or service communications. Several specific personality traits that provide insights about consumer behavior are examined next.

CONSUMER INNOVATIVENESS AND RELATED PERSONALITY TRAITS

Marketing practitioners try to learn all they can about **consumer innovators**—those who are likely to be first to try new products, services, or practices—for the market response of such innovators is often a critical indication of the eventual success or failure of a new product or service.

Personality traits that have been useful in differentiating between consumer innovators and noninnovators include *consumer innovativeness*, *dogmatism*, *social character*, *optimum stimulation level*, and *variety-novelty seeking*. (Chapter 15 examines nonpersonality characteristics that distinguish between consumer innovators and noninnovators.)

Consumer Innovativeness

Consumer researchers have endeavored to develop measurement instruments to gauge the level of consumer innovativeness, because such personality trait measures provide important insights into the nature and boundaries of a consumer's willingness to innovate.[5] Table 5-1 presents a six-item measure of consumer innovativeness that has been designed to have flexible boundaries in terms of the domain being studied; that is, the scale can be used to study a broad product category (like personal computers); a subproduct category (like notebook computers); or a product type (three-pound mini-notebook computers).

Dogmatism

Consumer responses to distinctively unfamiliar products or product features (i.e., level of dogmatism—a personality-linked behavior) is of keen interest to many marketers,

TABLE 5-1 A Consumer Innovativeness Scale

In general, I am among the last in my circle of friends to buy a new (rock album[a]) when it appears.[b]

If I heard that a (new rock album) was available in the store, I would be interested enough to buy it.

Compared to my friends, I own few (rock albums).[b]

In general, I am the last in my circle of friends to know the (titles of the latest rock albums).[b]

I will buy a new (rock album), even if I haven't heard it yet.

I know the names of (new rock acts) before other people do.

Note: Measured on a 5-point "agreement" scale.

[a]The product category and related wording is altered to fit the purpose of the researcher.

[b]Items with a ([b]) are negatively worded and are scored inversely.

Source: Ronald E. Goldsmith and Charles F. Hofacker, "Measuring Consumer Innovativeness," *Journal of the Academy of Marketing Science* 19 (1991), 212. Copyright © 1991 Academy of Marketing Science. Reprinted by permission.

especially marketers of technologically "rich" products. **Dogmatism** is a personality trait that measures the degree of rigidity (versus openness) that individuals display toward the unfamiliar and toward information that is contrary to their own established beliefs.[6] A person who is *highly dogmatic* approaches the unfamiliar defensively and with considerable discomfort and uncertainty. At the other end of the spectrum, a person who is *low in dogmatism* will readily consider unfamiliar or opposing beliefs.

Consumers who are low in dogmatism (*open-minded*) are more likely to prefer innovative products to established or traditional alternatives. In contrast, highly dogmatic (*closed-minded*) consumers are more likely to choose established, rather than innovative, product alternatives.

Highly dogmatic consumers tend to be more receptive to ads for new products or services that contain an appeal from an authoritative figure. To this end, marketers have used celebrities and experts in their new-product advertising to make it easier for potentially reluctant consumers (noninnovators) to accept the innovation. In contrast, low-dogmatic consumers (who are frequently high in innovativeness) seem to be more receptive to messages that stress factual differences, product benefits, and other forms of product-usage information.

Social Character

The personality trait known as *social character* has its origins in sociological research, which focuses on the identification and classification of individuals into distinct sociocultural "types." As used in consumer psychology, social character is a personality trait that ranges on a continuum from **inner-directedness** to **other-directedness**. Inner-directed consumers tend to rely on their own "inner" values or standards in evaluating new products and are likely to be consumer innovators. Conversely, other-directed consumers tend to look to others for direction on what is "right" or "wrong"; thus, they are *less* likely to be consumer innovators.

Inner- and other-directed consumers are attracted to different types of promotional messages. Inner-directed people seem to prefer ads that stress product features and personal benefits (enabling them to use their own values and standards in evaluating products), while other-directed people prefer ads that feature an approving social environment or social acceptance (in keeping with their tendency to look to others for direction). Thus, other-directed individuals may be more easily influenced because of their natural inclination to go beyond the content of an ad and think in terms of likely social approval of a potential purchase.

Optimum Stimulation Level

Some people seem to prefer a simple, uncluttered, and calm existence, while others prefer an environment crammed with novel, complex, and unusual experiences. Consumer research has examined how such variations in individual needs for stimulation may be related to consumer behavior. Research has found that high **optimum stimulation levels** (OSLs) are linked with greater willingness to take risks, to try new products, to be innovative, to seek purchase-related information, and to accept new retail facilities than low OSLs.

OSL scores also seem to reflect a person's desired level of lifestyle stimulation.[7] For instance, consumers whose actual lifestyles are equivalent to their OSL scores appear to be *quite satisfied*, while those whose lifestyles are understimulated (that is, their OSL scores are greater than the lifestyle they are currently living) are likely to be *bored*. Those whose lifestyles are overstimulated (their OSLs are lower than current reality) are likely to seek *rest* or *relief*. This suggests that the relationship between consumers' lifestyles and their OSLs is likely to influence their choices of products or services and how they manage and spend their time. For instance, a person who feels bored (an understimulated consumer) is likely to be attracted to a vacation that offers a great deal of activity and excitement. In contrast, a person who feels overwhelmed (an overstimulated consumer) is likely to seek a quiet, isolated, relaxing, and rejuvenating vacation.

Variety-Novelty Seeking

A personality-driven trait quite similar to and related to OSL is **variety** or **novelty seeking**.[8] There appear to be many different types of consumer variety seeking: *exploratory purchase behavior* (e.g., switching brands to experience new and possibly better alternatives), *vicarious exploration* (e.g., securing information about a new or different alternative and then contemplating or even daydreaming about the option), and *use innovativeness* (using an already adopted product in a new or novel way).[9]

The use innovativeness trait is particularly relevant to technological products (such as home electronics products), where some models offer an abundance of features and functions, while others contain just a few essential features or functions. For example, a consumer with a high variety-seeking score might purchase a stereo system with more features than a consumer with a lower variety-seeking score. Consumers with high variety-seeking scores are also more likely to be attracted to brands that claim to have novel or multiple uses or applications (Figure 5-4).

Marketers, up-to-a-point, benefit by offering additional options to consumers seeking more product variety, because consumers with a high need for variety tend to search for marketers that provide a diverse product line (offering much choice).[10] However, a point may be reached where a marketer might offer too many products, with too many features. In such a case, the consumer may be turned off and avoid a product line with too much variety. Ultimately, marketers must walk the fine line between offering consumers too little and too much choice.

The stream of research examined here indicates that the consumer innovator differs from the noninnovator in terms of personality orientation. A knowledge of such personality differences should help marketers select target segments for new products and then to design distinctive promotional strategies for specific segments.

COGNITIVE PERSONALITY FACTORS

Consumer researchers have been increasingly interested in how **cognitive personality** factors influence various aspects of consumer behavior. In particular, two cognitive personality traits—**need for cognition** and **visualizers versus verbalizers**—have been useful in understanding selected aspects of consumer behavior.

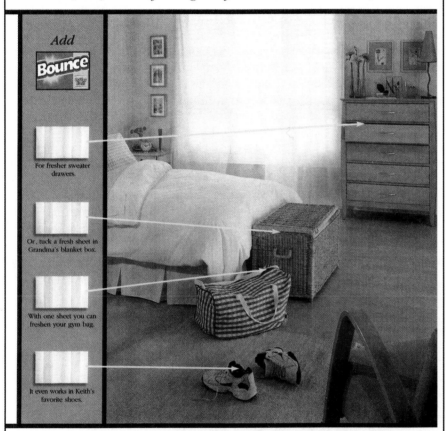

FIGURE 5-4
Ad Appealing to Novelty-
and Variety-Seeking
Personalities

Need for Cognition

A promising cognitive personality characteristic is **need for cognition** (NC). It measures a person's craving for or enjoyment of *thinking*. Available research indicates that consumers who are *high* in NC are more likely to be responsive to the part of an ad that is rich in product-related information or description; consumers who are relatively *low* in NC are more likely to be attracted to the background or peripheral aspects of an ad, such as an attractive model or well-known celebrity.[11] Related research suggests that consumers who are high in NC are likely to spend more time *processing* print advertisements, which results in superior brand and ad claim recall.[12] These research insights provide advertisers with valuable guidelines for creating advertising messages (including supporting art) that appeal to a particular target group's *need for cognition.*

Visualizers versus Verbalizers

Cognitive personality research classifies consumers into two groups: *visualizers* (consumers who prefer visual information and products that stress the visual, such as membership in a videotape club) or *verbalizers* (consumers who prefer written or verbal information and products, such as membership in book clubs or audiotape clubs). Some marketers stress strong visual dimensions in order to attract visualizers (see Figure 5-5); others raise a question and provide the answer, or feature a detailed description or point-by-point explanation to attract verbalizers (see Figure 5-6).

FROM CONSUMER MATERIALISM TO COMPULSIVE CONSUMPTION

Consumer researchers have become increasingly interested in exploring various interrelated consumption and possession traits. These traits range from *consumer materialism* to *fixated consumption behavior* to *consumer compulsive behavior.*

FIGURE 5-5
Schick Ad Targets Visualizers

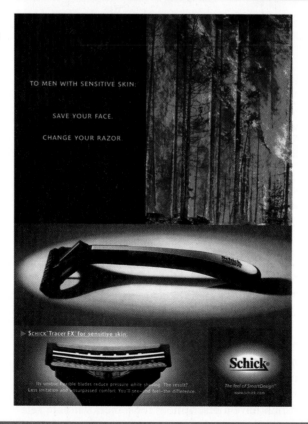

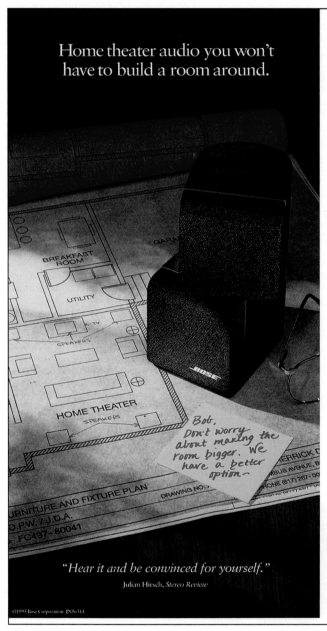

Home theater audio you won't have to build a room around.

"Hear it and be convinced for yourself."
Julian Hirsch, *Stereo Review*

Bob,
Don't worry about making the room bigger. We have a better option—

Bose® Acoustimass® Home Theater Speakers. If you're trying to build a home theater system, there are more reasons than ever to consider Acoustimass speakers.

These little 6" speakers have already made a big impact on the way people think about sound. And now that you need up to five speakers to enjoy home theater, using these Virtually Invisible® speakers makes even more sense.

Instead of being overwhelmed by a room full of big, bulky speakers, you'll be overwhelmed by sound. Not only by its sheer power, but because it's so true-to-life. From explosive sound effects to the most intimate sigh, Acoustimass speakers reproduce surround sound with lifelike realism.

You get powerful home theater without having to rearrange your room to accommodate big speakers. And that leaves more space for all the people who'll want to join you after they hear a movie or big game on Acoustimass speakers.

To learn more about Acoustimass home theater speakers, call for Bose dealers near you. That is, if there's room for more exciting audio in your life.

1-800-444-BOSE Ext. xxx

BOSE®
Better sound through research®

FIGURE 5-6
BOSE Targets Verbalizers

Consumer Materialism

Materialism (the extent to which a person is considered "materialistic") is a topic frequently discussed in newspapers, in magazines, and on TV (e.g., "Americans are very materialistic") and in everyday conversations between friends ("He's so materialistic!"). Materialism, as a personalitylike trait, distinguishes between individuals who regard possessions as essential to their identities and their lives, and those for whom possessions are secondary.[13] Researchers have found some general support for the following characteristics of materialistic people: (1) they especially value acquiring and showing-off possessions; (2) they are particularly self-centered and selfish; (3) they seek lifestyles full of possessions (e.g., they desire to have lots of "things," rather than a simple uncluttered lifestyle); and (4) their many possessions do not give them greater personal satisfaction (that is, their possessions do not lead to greater happiness).[14] Table 5-2 presents sample items from a materialism scale.

Fixated Consumption Behavior

Somewhere between materialism and compulsion with respect to buying or possessing objects is the notion of *being fixated* with regard to consuming or possessing. Like materialism, *fixated consumption behavior* is in the realm of normal and socially acceptable behavior. Fixated consumers do not keep their objects or purchases of interest a secret; rather, they frequently display them, and their involvement is openly shared with others who have a similar interest. In the world of serious collectors (Barbie dolls, Beanie Babies, rare antique quilts, or almost anything else that has drawn collectors), there are countless millions of *fixated consumers* pursuing their interests and trying to add to their collections. Take the case of Zippo lighters. There are tens of thousands of collectors of Zippo lighters. These dedicated collectors belong to Zippo clubs, chat on the Internet, and attend swap meets to exchange stories about Zippo lighters (e.g., how it saved soldiers' lives in a war); and to trade Zippo lighters to enhance their collections. Figure 5-7 presents an ad for a limited edition, collectable Zippo lighter.

Fixated consumers typically possess the following characteristics: (1) a deep (possibly "passionate") interest in a particular object or product category; (2) a willingness to go to considerable lengths to secure additional examples of the object or product category of interest; and (3) the dedication of a considerable amount of discretionary time and money to searching out the object or product.[15] This profile of the fixated consumer describes many collectors or hobbyists (for instance, coins, stamps, antiques, vintage wristwatches, or fountain pens). Research exploring the dynamics of

TABLE 5-2 Sample Items from a Materialism Scale

SUCCESS

The things I own say a lot about how well I'm doing in life.
I don't place much emphasis on the amount of material objects people own as a sign of success.[a]
I like to own things that impress people.

CENTRALITY

I enjoy spending money on things that aren't practical.
I try to keep my life simple, as far as possessions are concerned.[a]
Buying things gives me a lot of pleasure.

HAPPINESS

I'd be happier if I could afford to buy more things.
I have all the things I really need to enjoy life.[a]
It sometimes bothers me quite a bit that I can't afford to buy all the things I'd like.

Note: Measured on a 5-point "agreement" scale.

[a]Items with an ([a]) are negatively worded and are scored inversely.

Source: From Marsha L. Richins and Scott Dawson, "A Consumer Values Orientation for Materialism and Its Measurement: Scale Development and Validation." *Journal of Consumer Research* 19 (December 1992), 310. Reprinted by permission of The University of Chicago Press as publisher.

FIGURE 5-7
Zippo Target Collectors
Edition Lighter

the fixated consumer (in this case, coin collectors) revealed that, for fixated consumers, there is not only an enduring involvement in the object category itself but also a considerable amount of involvement in the *process of acquiring* the object (sometimes referred to as the "hunt").[16]

Compulsive Consumption Behavior

Unlike materialism and fixated consumption, **compulsive consumption** is in the realm of abnormal behavior—an example of "the dark side of consumption." Consumers who are compulsive have an addiction; in some respects they are out of control, and their actions may have damaging consequences to them and to those around them. Examples of compulsive consumption problems are uncontrollable gambling, drug addiction, alcoholism, and various food and eating disorders.[17] From a marketing and consumer behavior perspective, *compulsive buying* can also be included in any list of compulsive activities. To control or possibly eliminate such compulsive problems generally requires some type of therapy or clinical treatment.

There have been some research efforts to develop a screener-inventory to pinpoint compulsive buying behavior. Table 5-3 presents sample questions from several of these scales.[18] Evidence suggests that some consumers use self-gifting, impulse buying, and compulsive buying as a way to influence or manage their moods, i.e., the act of purchasing may alter a negative mood to a more positive one ("I'm depressed, I'll go out shopping and I'll feel better").[19]

CONSUMER ETHNOCENTRISM: RESPONSES TO FOREIGN-MADE PRODUCTS

In an effort to distinguish between consumer segments that are likely to be receptive to foreign-made products and those that are not, researchers have developed and tested the *consumer ethnocentrism* scale, called CETSCALE (see Table 5-4).[20] The CETSCALE has been successful in identifying consumers with a predisposition to accept (or reject) foreign-made products. Consumers who are highly *ethnocentric* are likely to feel that it is inappropriate or wrong to purchase foreign-made products because of the resulting economic impact on the domestic economy, whereas nonethnocentric consumers tend to evaluate foreign-made products—ostensibly more objectively—for their extrinsic characteristics. For example, a recent article suggests that some older American consumers, in remembrance of World War II, still refuse to purchase German- and/or Japanese-made products, while some German and Japanese consumers may feel similarly about American-made products.[21]

Marketers successfully target ethnocentric consumers in any national market by stressing a nationalistic theme in their promotional appeals (e.g., "Made in America" or "Made in France"), because this segment is predisposed to buy products made in their native land. Honda, the Japanese automaker, in an indirect appeal to ethnocentric Americans, has advertised that its Accord wagon is "Exported from America" to other markets.

TABLE 5-3 Sample Items from Scales to Measure Compulsive Buying

VALENCE, D'ASTOUS, AND FORTIER COMPULSIVE BUYING SCALE
1. When I have money, I cannot help but spend part or the whole of it.
2. I am often impulsive in my buying behavior.
3. As soon as I enter a shopping center, I have an irresistible urge to go into a shop to buy something.
4. I am one of those people who often responds to direct mail offers (e.g., books or compact discs).
5. I have often bought a product that I did not need, while knowing I had very little money left.

FABER AND O'GUINN COMPULSIVE BUYING SCALE
1. If I have any money left at the end of the pay period, I just have to spend it.
2. I felt others would be horrified if they knew my spending habits.
3. I have bought things though I couldn't afford them.
4. I wrote a check when I knew I didn't have enough money in the bank to cover it.
5. I bought something in order to make myself feel better.

Source: Gilles Valence, Alain d'Astous, and Louis Fortier, "Compulsive Buying: Concept and Measurement," *Journal of Consumer Policy* 11 (1988), 419–33; Ronald J. Faber and Thomas C. O'Guinn, "A Clinical Screener for Compulsive Buying," *Journal of Consumer Research* 19, December 1992, 459–69; and Leslie Cole and Dan Sherrell, "Comparing Scales to Measure Compulsive Buying: An Exploration of Their Dimensionality," in *Advances in Consumer Research* 22, ed. Frank R. Kardes and Mita Sujan, (Provo, UT: Association for Consumer Research, 1995): 419–27.

TABLE 5-4 The Consumer Ethnocentrism Scale—CETSCALE

1. American people should always buy American-made products instead of imports.
2. Only those products that are unavailable in the U.S. should be imported.
3. Buy American-made products. Keep America working.
4. American products, first, last, and foremost.
5. Purchasing foreign-made products is un-American.
6. It is not right to purchase foreign products, because it puts Americans out of jobs.
7. A real American should always buy American-made products.
8. We should purchase products manufactured in America instead of letting other countries get rich off us.
9. It is always best to purchase American products.
10. There should be very little trading or purchasing of goods from other countries unless out of necessity.
11. Americans should not buy foreign products, because this hurts American business and causes unemployment.
12. Curbs should be put on all imports.
13. It may cost me in the long run but I prefer to support American products.
14. Foreigners should not be allowed to put their products on our markets.
15. Foreign products should be taxed heavily to reduce their entry into the United States.
16. We should buy from foreign countries only those products that we cannot obtain within our own country.
17. American consumers who purchase products made in other countries are responsible for putting their fellow Americans out of work.

Notes: Response format is a 7-point Likert-type scale (strongly agree = 7, strongly disagree = 1). Range of scores is from 17 to 119. Calculated from confirmatory factor analysis of data from 4-area study.

Source: Terence A. Shimp and Subhash Sharma, "Consumer Ethnocentrism: Construction and Validation of the CETSCALE," *Journal of Marketing Research* 24 (August 1987): 282. Reprinted by permission.

BRAND PERSONALITY

Early in this chapter, as part of our discussion of Freudian theory, we introduced the notion of *product personality*. Consumers also subscribe to the notion of *brand personality*, that is, they attribute various descriptive "personality-like" traits or characteristics to different brands in a wide variety of product categories. For instance, with some help from frequent advertising, consumers tend to see Volvo as representing *safety*, Perdue (chickens) as representing *freshness*, Nike as *the athlete in all of us*, and BMW as *performance driven*.[22] In a similar fashion, the brand personality for Levi's 501 jeans is "dependable and rugged," "real and authentic," and "American and Western." Such personalitylike images of brands reflect consumers' visions of the "inner-core" of many strong brands of consumer products. As these examples reveal, a brand's personality can either be functional ("provides safety") or symbolic ("the athlete in all of us").[23]

BRAND PERSONIFICATION

Some marketers find it useful to create a **brand personification**, which tries to recast consumers' perception of the attributes of a product or service into a "human-like character." For instance, in focus group research, well-known brands of dishwashing liquid have been likened to "demanding task masters" or "high-energy people." Many consumers express their inner feelings about products or brands in terms of their association with known personalities. Identifying consumers' current brand-personality links or creating personality links for new products are important marketing tasks.[24]

To "personify and humanize its model consumer," Celestial Seasonings Inc., the leading specialty tea maker in the United States, refers in its advertising to "Tracy Jones." And just who is Tracy Jones? According to Celestial Seasonings, she is "female, upscale, well-educated, and highly involved in life in every way."[25]

Mr. Coffee, a popular brand of automatic-drip coffeemakers, also illustrates a consumer-brand link. In this case, an unexpected finding from focus group research was the observation that consumers were referring to Mr. Coffee as if the product were a *person* (e.g., "He makes good coffee." "He's got a lot of different models and prices.").[26] After careful consideration, the marketers decided to explore the possibility of creating a *brand personification*. Initial consumer research indicated that "Mr. Coffee" was seen as being: "dependable," "friendly," "efficient," "intelligent," and "smart."

Figure 5-8 presents a *brand personality framework* that reflects extensive consumer research designed to pinpoint the structure and nature of a brand's personality. The framework suggests that there are five defining *dimensions* of a brand's personality ("sincerity," "excitement," "competence," "sophistication," and "ruggedness"), and 15 *facets* of personality that flow from the five dimensions (for instance, "down-to-earth," "daring," "reliable," "upper class," and "outdoors").[27] If we carefully review these brand personality dimensions and facets, it appears that this framework tends to accommodate the brand personalities pursued by many consumer products.

PRODUCT PERSONALITY AND GENDER

A product personality, or persona, frequently endows the product or brand with a gender. For instance, Celestial Seasonings' Tracy Jones was given a feminine persona; whereas Mr. Coffee was given a masculine personality. The assigning of a gender as part of a product's personality description is fully consistent with the marketplace reality that products and services, in general, are viewed by consumers as having genders. A study that asked Chinese consumers to categorize various products in terms of gender, found that Chinese consumers perceived coffee and toothpaste to be masculine products; whereas bath soap and shampoo were seen as feminine products.[28]

Armed with knowledge of the perceived gender of a product or a specific brand, marketers are in a better position to select visuals and text copy for various marketing messages.

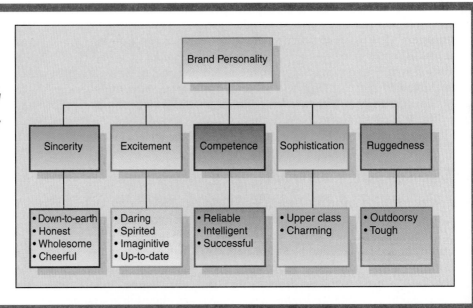

FIGURE 5-8

A Brand Personality Framework

Source: Jennifer L. Aaker, "Dimension of Brand Personality," *Journal of Marketing Research,* 35 (August 1997): 352. Reprinted by permission of the American Marketing Association.

PERSONALITY AND COLOR

Consumers not only ascribe personality traits to products and services, but they also tend to associate personality factors with specific colors. For instance, Coca-Cola is associated with red, which connotes excitement. Blue bottles are often used to sell wine because the color blue appeals particularly to female consumers, and they buy the majority of wine.[29] Yellow is associated with "novelty," and black frequently connotes "sophistication."[30] For this reason, brands wishing to create a sophisticated persona (such as Minute Maid juices or Pasta LaBella) or an upscale or premium image (e.g., Miller Beers' Miller Reserve) use labeling or packaging that is primarily black. A combination of black and white communicates that a product is carefully engineered, high tech, and sophisticated in design. IBM has consistently used an all-black case with a few selected red buttons and bars to house its very successful Thinkpad laptops. Nike has used black, white, and a touch of red for selected models of its sport shoes. This color combination seems to imply "advanced-performance sports shoes." Recently, M&M/Mars has exploited the folklore that its green M&Ms are aphrodisiacs by creating a green female M&M character that it has featured in some of its ads.[31]

Many fast-food restaurants use combinations of bright colors, like red, yellow, and blue, for their roadside signs and interior designs. These colors have come to be associated with fast service and inexpensive food. In contrast, fine dining restaurants tend to use sophisticated colors like gray, white, shades of tan, or other soft, pale, or muted colors to reflect the feeling of fine, leisurely service. Consumer research sponsored by a marketer of popular-priced casual wear found that dark colors like gray, dark blue, and black, were preferred to pastel colors in wintry northeastern and midwestern markets. However, when the multimarket study reached sunny Phoenix, Arizona, a reversal occurred—the darker colors fell into disfavor, and rose, pinks, yellows, and turquoise became the preferred colors. Further research revealed that many people seek to contrast the somber backdrop of the desert with multicolor pastel clothing and home furnishings. Table 5-5 presents a list of various colors, their personality-like meanings, and associated marketing insights. To discover such insights, researchers use a variety of qualitative measurement techniques, such as *observation*, *focus groups*, *depth interviews*, and *projective techniques* (discussed in chapter 2).

SELF AND SELF-IMAGE

Consumers have a variety of enduring images of themselves. These self-images, or "perceptions of self," are very closely associated with personality in that individuals tend to buy products and services and patronize retailers whose images or "personalities" closely correspond to their own self-images. In essence, consumers seek to depict themselves in their brand choices.[32] In this final section, we examine the issue of *one* or *multiple* selves, explore the *makeup* of the self-image, the notion of **extended self**, and the possibilities or options of *altering the self-image*.

ONE OR MULTIPLE SELVES

Historically, individuals have been thought to have a single self-image and to be interested, as consumers, in products and services that satisfy that single self. However, it is more accurate to think of consumers as having **multiple selves**.[33] This change in thinking reflects the understanding that a single consumer is likely to act quite differently with different people and in different situations. For instance, a person is likely to behave in different ways with parents, at school, at work, at a museum opening, or

TABLE 5-5 The Personalitylike Associations of Selected Colors

COLOR	PERSONALITY LINK	MARKETING INSIGHTS
BLUE	Commands respect, authority	• America's favored color • IBM holds the title to blue • Associated with club soda • Men seek products packaged in blue • Houses painted blue are avoided • Low-calorie, skim milk • Coffee in a blue can perceived as "mild"
YELLOW	Caution, novelty, temporary, warmth	• Eyes register it fastest • Coffee in yellow can tasted "weak" • Stops traffic • Sells a house
GREEN	Secure, natural, relaxed or easygoing, living things	• Good work environment • Associated with vegetables and chewing gum • Canada Dry ginger ale sales increased when it changed sugar-free package from red to green and white
RED	Human, exciting, hot, passionate, strong	• Makes food "smell" better • Coffee in a red can perceived as "rich" • Women have a preference for bluish red • Men have a preference for yellowish red • Coca-Cola "owns" red
ORANGE	Powerful, affordable, informal	• Draws attention quickly
BROWN	Informal and relaxed, masculine, nature	• Coffee in a dark-brown can was "too strong" • Men seek products packaged in brown
WHITE	Goodness, purity, chastity, cleanliness, delicacy, refinement, formality	• Suggests reduced calories • Pure and wholesome food • Clean, bath products, feminine
BLACK	Sophistication, power, authority, mystery	• Powerful clothing • High-tech electronics
SILVER, GOLD, PLATINUM	Regal, wealthy, stately	• Suggests premium price

Source: From Bernice Kanner, "Color Schemes." *New York* magazine, 3 April 1989, 22–23. Copyright 1996, New York Magazine. Distributed by Los Angeles Times. Reprinted by permission.

with friends at a nightclub. The healthy or normal person is likely to display a somewhat different personality in each of these different situations or social **roles**. In fact, acting exactly the same in all situations or roles—not adapting to the situation at hand—may be considered a sign of an abnormal or unhealthy person.

In terms of consumer behavior, the idea that an individual embodies a number of different "selves" (that is, has multiple self-images) suggests that marketers should target their products and services to consumers *within the context of a particular "self,"* and in certain cases, a choice of different products for different *selves*. (The notion of a consumer having multiple selves or playing multiple roles supports the application of use-situation as a segmentation base discussed in chapter 3.)

THE MAKEUP OF THE SELF-IMAGE

Consistent with the idea of multiple self-images, each individual has an image of himself or herself as a certain kind of person, with certain traits, skills, habits, possessions, relationships, and ways of behaving. As with other types of images and personality, the individual's self-image is unique, the outgrowth of that person's background and experience. Individuals develop their self-images through interactions with other people—initially their parents, and then other individuals or groups with whom they relate over the years.

Products and brands have symbolic value for individuals, who evaluate them on the basis of their consistency (congruence) with their personal pictures or images of themselves. Some products seem to match one or more of an individual's self-images; others seem totally alien. It is generally believed that consumers attempt to preserve or enhance their self-images by selecting products and brands with "images" or "personalities" that they believe are congruent with their own self-images and avoiding products that are not.[34] This seems to be especially true for women; research reveals that more women than men (77 percent versus 64 percent) feel that the brands that they select reflect their personalities.[35]

Given this relationship between brand preference and consumers' self-images, it is natural that consumers use brands to help them in their task of defining themselves. Research indicates that consumers who have strong links to particular brands—a positive self-brand connection—see such brands as *representing an aspect of themselves*. For marketers, such *connections* are certainly an important step in the formation of consumer loyalty and a positive relationship with consumers.[36]

A variety of different self-images have been recognized in the consumer behavior literature. In particular, many researchers have depicted some or all of the following kinds of self-image: (1) **actual self-image** (how consumers in fact see themselves), (2) **ideal self-image** (how consumers would like to see themselves), (3) **social self-image** (how consumers feel others see them), and (4) **ideal social self-image** (how consumers would like others to see them).

It also seems useful to think in terms of a fifth type of self-image, **expected self-image** (how consumers expect to see themselves at some specified future time). The *expected self-image* is somewhere between the *actual* and *ideal* self-images, a future-oriented combination of "what is" (the actual self-image) and what consumers would like "to be" (the ideal self-image). Moreover, because the expected self-image provides consumers with a realistic "opportunity" to change the *self*, it is likely to be more valuable to marketers than the actual or ideal self-image as a guide for designing and promoting products.

In different contexts (that is, in different situations and/or with respect to different products), consumers might select a different self-image to guide their attitudes or behavior. For instance, with some everyday household products, consumers might be guided by their actual self-image; whereas, for some socially enhancing or socially conspicuous products, they might be guided by their social self-image. When it comes to a so-called fantasy product, they might be guided by either their ideal self-images or ideal social self-images.

The concept of self-image has strategic implications for marketers. For example, marketers can segment their markets on the basis of relevant consumer self-images and then position their products or services as symbols of such self-images. Such a strategy is fully consistent with the marketing concept in that the marketer first assesses the needs of a consumer segment (with respect to both the product category and to an appropriate symbol of self-image) and then proceeds to develop and market a product or service that meets both criteria.

THE EXTENDED SELF

The interrelationship between consumers' self-images and their possessions (that is, objects they call their "own") is an exciting topic. Specifically, consumers' possessions can be seen to "confirm" or "extend" their self-images. For instance, acquiring a desired or sought-after pair of "vintage" Nike sneakers might serve to expand or enrich a Japanese teenager's image of "self." The teenager might now see herself as "being more desirable, more fashionable, and more successful," because she has a pair of the sought after "vintage sneakers" (often one of the previous year's hard-to-get styles). In a similar manner, if the wristwatch that a teenager (let's call him Stuart) received as a gift from his grandfather was stolen, Stuart is likely to feel diminished in some way. Indeed, the loss of a prized possession may lead Stuart to "grieve" and to experience a variety of emotions, such as frustration, loss of control, the feeling of being "violated," even the loss of magical protection. Table 5-6 presents sample items from a measurement instrument designed to reflect how particular possessions (e.g., a mountain bike) might become part of one's extended self.

The previous examples suggest that much human emotion can be connected to valued possessions. In such cases, possessions are considered extensions of the self. It has been proposed that possessions can extend the self in a number of ways: (1) *actually*, by allowing the person to do things that otherwise would be very difficult or impossible to accomplish (e.g., problem solving by using a computer); (2) *symbolically*, by making the person feel better or "bigger" (receiving an employee award for excellence); (3) by *conferring status* or *rank* (e.g., among collectors of rare works of art because of the ownership of a particular masterpiece); (4) by *bestowing feelings of immortality* by leaving valued possessions to young family members (this also has the potential of extending the recipients' "selves"); and (5) by *endowing with magical powers* (e.g., a cameo pin inherited from one's aunt might be perceived as a magic amulet bestowing good luck when it is worn).[37] Figure 5-9 illustrates a number of these concepts. It presents examples from an ongoing series of print advertisements that stress how a Patek Philippe wristwatch

---

TABLE 5-6 Sample Items from an Extended Self-Survey*

My _____ holds a special place in my life.

My _____ is central to my identity.

I feel emotinally attached to my _____.

My _____ helps me narrow the gap between what I am and try to be.

If my _____ was stolen from me I will feel as if part of me is missing.

I would be a different person without my _____.

I take good care of my _____.

I trust my _____.

*A six-point agree-disagree scale was used.

Source: Kimberly J. Dodson, "Peak Experiences and Mountain Biking: Incorporating the Bike in the Extended Self," *Advances in Consumer Research*, 1996. Reprinted by permission.

(considered by many to be the world's finest wristwatch) might be seen as something that you never really "own," but that you possess for a while and then pass along to the next generation.

ALTERING THE SELF

Sometimes consumers wish to change themselves to become a different or "improved" self. Clothing, grooming aids or cosmetics, and all kinds of accessories (such as sunglasses, jewelry, or even tattoos) offer consumers the opportunity to modify their appearances (to create a "makeover") and thereby to alter their "selves." In using *self-altering products*, consumers are frequently attempting to express their individualism or uniqueness by creating a new self, maintaining the existing self (or preventing the loss of self), and extending the self (modifying or changing the self). Sometimes, consumers use self-altering products or services to conform to or take on the appearance of a particular type of person (such as a military person, a physician, a business executive, or a college professor).

Altering one's self, particularly one's appearance or body parts, can be accomplished by cosmetics, hair restyling or coloring, getting a tattoo, switching from eyeglasses to contact lenses (or the reverse), or undergoing cosmetic surgery. Figure 5-10 presents an ad for Jane Cosmetics. The headline reinforces the importance of taking charge of one's appearance, when it declares that "sure, real beauty comes from within . . . now, whatcha gonna do about the outside?"

FIGURE 5-9

Patek Philippe Appeals to Target Consumers' Sense of "Extended Self"

FIGURE 5-10
Ad Suggesting That the
Consumer Alter Herself

VANITY AND CONSUMER BEHAVIOR

Closely related to self-image is the idea of personal vanity. Using a "vanity scale" (Table 5-7), researchers have investigated both *physical vanity* (an excessive concern for and/or a positive—or inflated—view of one's physical appearance) and *achievement vanity* (an excessive concern for and/or a positive or inflated view of one's personal achievements). They have found both these ideas related to materialism, use of cosmetics, concern with clothing, and country club membership.[38]

TABLE 5-7 Sample Items from a Vanity Scale

PHYSICAL-CONCERN ITEMS
1. The way I look is extremely important to me.
2. I am very concerned with my appearance.
3. It is important that I always look good.

PHYSICAL-VIEW ITEMS
1. People notice how attractive I am.
2. People are envious of my good looks.
3. My body is sexually appealing.

ACHIEVEMENT-CONCERN ITEMS
1. Professional achievements are an obsession with me.
2. Achieving greater success than my peers is important to me.
3. I want my achievements to be recognized by others.

ACHIEVEMENT-VIEW ITEMS
1. My achievements are highly regarded by others.
2. I am a good example of professional success.
3. Others wish they were as successful as me.

Source: Richard G. Netemeyer, Scot Burton, and Donald R. Lichtenstein, "Trait Aspects of Vanity: Measurement and Relevance to Consumer Behavior." *Journal of Consumer Research* 21, March 1995, 624. Reprinted by permission of The University of Chicago Press as publisher.

VIRTUAL PERSONALITY OR SELF

With the widespread interest in using the Internet as a form of entertainment and as a social vehicle to meet new people with similar interests, there has been a tremendous growth in the use of on-line chat rooms. People who visit chat rooms are able to carry on real-time conversations about themselves and topics of mutual interest with people from all over the globe. Since at the present time most "chats" are actually "text conversations," rather than live video broadcasts, the participants commonly never get to see each other. This creates an opportunity for chat room participants to try out new identities or to change their identities while on-line. For instance, one can change from male to female (known as "gender swapping"), from old to young, or from married to single; from white-collar professional to blue-collar worker, or from grossly overweight to svelte. In terms of personality, one can change from mild-mannered to aggressive, or from introvert to extrovert. The possibilities are almost endless.

The notion of a **virtual personality** or **virtual self** provides an individual with the opportunity to try on different personalities or different identities, much like going to the mall and trying on different outfits in a department or specialty store. If the identity fits, or the personality can be enhanced, the individual may decide to keep the new personality in favor of his or her old personality. According to one expert, the Internet is redefining human identity, creating an "on-line self."[39] From a consumer behavior point of view, it is likely that such opportunities to try out a new personality, or alter the "self" may result in changes in selected forms of purchase behavior; which may in turn offer marketers new opportunities to target various "on-line selves."

SUMMARY

Personality can be described as the psychological characteristics that both determine and reflect how a person responds to his or her environment. Although personality tends to be consistent and enduring, it may change abruptly in response to major life events, as well as gradually over time.

Three theories of personality are prominent in the study of consumer behavior: psychoanalytic theory, neo-Freudian theory, and trait theory. Freud's psychoanalytic theory provides the foundation for the study of motivational research, which operates on the premise that human drives are largely unconscious in nature and serve to motivate many consumer actions. Neo-Freudian theory tends to emphasize the fundamental role of social relationships in the formation and development of personality. Alfred Adler viewed human beings as seeking to overcome feelings of inferiority. Harry Stack Sullivan believed that people attempt to establish significant and rewarding relationships with others. Karen Horney saw individuals as trying to overcome feelings of anxiety and categorized them as compliant, aggressive, or detached.

Trait theory is a major departure from the qualitative (or subjective) approach to personality measurement. It postulates that individuals possess innate psychological traits (for instance, innovativeness, nov-

elty seeking, need for cognition, materialism) to a greater or lesser degree, and that these traits can be measured by specially designed scales or inventories. Because they are simple to use and to score and can be self-administered, personality inventories are the preferred method for many researchers in the assessment of consumer personality. Product and brand personalities represent real opportunities for marketers to take advantage of consumers' connections to various brands they offer. Brands often have personalities—some even include "humanlike" traits and even gender. These brand personalities help shape consumer responses, preferences, and loyalties.

Each individual has a perceived self-image (or multiple self-images) as a certain kind of person with certain traits, habits, possessions, relationships, and ways of behaving. Consumers frequently attempt to preserve, enhance, alter, or extend their self-images by purchasing products or services and shopping at stores they perceive as consistent with their relevant self-image(s) and by avoiding products and stores they perceive are not. With the growth of the Internet, there appear to be emerging "virtual selves" or "virtual personalities." Consumer experiences with chat rooms sometimes provides an opportunity to explore new or alternative identities.

DISCUSSION QUESTIONS

1. How would you explain the fact that, although no two individuals have identical personalities, personality is sometimes used in consumer research to identify distinct and sizable market segments?

2. Contrast the major characteristics of the following personality theories: (a) Freudian theory, (b) Neo-Freudian theory, and (c) trait theory. In your answer, illustrate how each theory is applied to the understanding of consumer behavior.

3. Describe personality trait theory. Give five examples of how personality traits can be used in consumer research.

4. How can a marketer of cameras use the research findings that the target market consists primarily of inner-directed or other-directed consumers? Of consumers who are high (or low) on innovativeness?

5. Describe the type of promotional message that would be most suitable for each of the following personality market segments and give an example of each: (a) highly dogmatic consumers, (b) inner-directed consumers, (c) consumers with high optimum stimulation levels, (d) consumers with a high need for recognition, and (e) consumers who are visualizers versus consumers who are verbalizers.

6. Is there likely to be a difference in personality traits between individuals who readily purchase foreign-made products and those who prefer American-made products? How can marketers use the consumer ethnocentrism scale to segment consumers?

7. A marketer of health foods is attempting to segment his or her market on the basis of consumer self-image. Describe the four types of consumer self-image and discuss which one(s) would be most effective for the stated purpose.

EXERCISES

1. How do your clothing preferences differ from those of your friends? What personality differences might explain why your preferences are different from those of other people?

2. Find three print advertisements based on Freudian personality theory. Discuss how Freudian concepts are used in these ads. Do any of the ads personify a brand? If so, how?

3. Administer the nine items from the materialism scale (listed in Table 5-2) to two of your friends. In your view, are their consumption behaviors consistent with their scores on the scale? Why or why not?

KEY TERMS

- **Actual self-image**
- **Brand personification**
- **Cognitive personality**
- **Compliant, aggressive, and detached personality groups**
- **Compulsive consumption**
- **Consumer ethnocentrism**
- **Consumer innovativeness**
- **Consumer innovators**
- **Consumer materialism**
- **Dogmatism**

- **Expected self-image**
- **Extended self**
- **Freudian theory**
- **Id, superego, and ego**
- **Ideal self-image**
- **Ideal social self-image**
- **Inner-directedness**
- **Multiple self or multiple selves**
- **Need for cognition**
- **Neo-Freudian personality theory**
- **Optimum stimulation levels**

- **Other-directed consumers**
- **Other-directedness**
- **Personality**
- **Psychoanalytic theory of personality**
- **Roles**
- **Social self-image**
- **Trait theory**
- **Variety- or novelty-seeking trait**
- **Virtual personality or self**
- **Visualizers versus verbalizers**

NOTES

1. For example, see Karen Horney, *The Neurotic Personality of Our Time* (New York: Norton, 1937).

2. Joel B. Cohen, "An Interpersonal Orientation to the Study of Consumer Behavior," *Journal of Marketing Research* 6 (August 1967): 270–78; Arch G. Woodside and Ruth Andress, "CAD Eight Years Later," *Journal of the Academy of Marketing Science* 3 (Summer–Fall 1975): 309–13; see also Jon P. Noerager, "An Assessment of CAD: A Personality Instrument Developed Specifically for Marketing Research," *Journal of Marketing Research* 16 (February 1979): 53–59; and Pradeep K. Tyagi, "Validation of the CAD Instrument: A Replication," in *Advances in Consumer Research* vol. 10, ed. Richard P. Bogazzio and Alice M. Tybout (Ann Arbor, MI: Association for Consumer Research, 1983), 112–14.

3. Morton I. Jaffe, "Brand-Loyalty/Variety-Seeking and the Consumer's Personality: Comparing Children and Young Adults," in *Proceedings of the Society for Consumer Psychology*, ed. Scott B. MacKenzie and Douglas

M. Stayman (La Jolla, CA: American Psychological Association, 1995), 144–51.

4. J. P. Guilford, *Personality* (New York: McGraw-Hill, 1959), 6.

5. Ronald E. Goldsmith and Charles F. Hofacker, "Measuring Consumer Innovativeness," *Journal of the Academy of Marketing Science* 19 (1991): 209–21; Suresh Subramanian and Robert A. Mittelstaedt, "Conceptualizing Innovativeness as a Consumer Trait: Consequences and Alternatives," in *1991 AMA Educators' Proceedings*, ed. Mary C. Gilly and F. Robert Dwyer et al., (Chicago: American Marketing Association, 1991), 352–60; and "Reconceptualizing and Measuring Consumer Innovativeness," in *1992 AMA Educators' Proceedings*, ed. Robert P. Leone and V. Kumor, et al. (Chicago: American Marketing Association, 1992), 300–307.

6. Milton Rokeach, *The Open and Closed Mind* (New York: Basic Books, 1960).

7. P. S. Raju, "Optimum Stimulation Level: Its Relationship to Personality, Demographics, and Exploratory Behavior," *Journal of Consumer Research* 7 (December 1980): 272–82; Leigh McAlister and Edgar Pessemier, "Variety Seeking Behavior: An Interdisciplinary Review," *Journal of Consumer Research* 9 (December 1982): 311–22; Edgar Pessemier and Moshe Handelsman, "Temporal Variety in Consumer Behavior," *Journal of Marketing Research* 21 (November 1984): 435–44; Erich A. Joachimsthaler and John L. Lastovicka, "Optimal Stimulation Level-Exploratory Behavior Models," *Journal of Consumer Research* 11 (December 1984): 830–35; Elizabeth C. Hirschman, "Experience Seeking: A Subjectivist Perspective of Consumption," *Journal of Business Research* 12 (1984): 115–36; Jan-Benedict E. M. Steenkamp and Hans Baumgartner, "The Role of Optimum Stimulation Level in Exploratory Consumer Behavior," *Journal of Consumer Research* 19 (December 1992): 434; and Russell G. Wahlers and Michael J. Etzel, "A Consumer Response to Incongruity between Optimal Stimulation and Life Style Satisfaction," in *Advances in Consumer Research* vol. 12, ed. Elizabeth C. Hirschman and Morris B. Holbrook (Provo, UT: Association for Consumer Research, 1985), 97–101.

8. Satya Menon and Barbara E. Kahn, "The Impact of Context on Variety Seeking in Product Choices," *Journal of Consumer Research* 22 (December 1995): 285–95.

9. Elizabeth C. Hirschman, "Innovativeness, Novelty Seeking and Consumer Creativity," *Journal of Consumer Research* 7 (1980): 283–95; and Wayne Hoyer and Nancy M. Ridgway, "Variety Seeking as an Explanation for Exploratory Purchase Behavior: A Theoretical Model," in *Advances in Consumer Research*, vol. 17, ed. Thomas C. Kinnear, (Provo, UT: Association for Consumer Research, 1984), 114–19.

10. Barbara E. Kahn, "Dyanamic Relationships with Customers: High-Variety Strategies," *Journal of the Academy of Marketing Science* 26 (Winter 1998): 47–53.

11. Richard Petty et al., "Personality and Ad Effectiveness: Exploring the Utility of Need for Cognition," in *Advances in Consumer Research*, vol. 15, ed. Michael Houston (Ann Arbor, MI: Association for Consumer Research, 1988), 209–12.

12. Ayn E. Crowley and Wayne D. Hoyer, "The Relationship Between Need for Cognition and Other Individual Difference Variables: A Two-Dimensional Framework," in *Advances in Consumer Research*, vol. 16, ed. Thomas K. Srull (Provo, UT: Association for Consumer Research, 1989), 37–43; and James W. Peltier and John A. Schibrowsky, "Need for Cognition, Advertisement Viewing Time and Memory for Advertising Stimuli," *Advances in Consumer Research* 21 (1994): 244–50.

13. Russell W. Belk, "Three Scales to Measure Constructs Related to Materialism," and Russell W. Belk, "Materialism: Trait Aspects of Living in the Material World," *Journal of Consumer Research* 12 (December 1985): 265–80.

14. Marsha L. Richins and Scott Dawson, "A Consumer Values Orientation for Materialism and Its Measurement: Scale Development and Validation," *Journal of Consumer Research* 19 (December 1992): 303–16.

15. Ronald J. Faber and Thomas C. O'Guinn, "A Clinical Screener for Compulsive Buying," *Journal of Consumer Research* 19 (December 1992): 459–69.

16. Ibid. Also, see Stacey Menzel Baker and Robert A. Mittelstaedt, "The Meaning of the Search, Evaluation, and Selection of 'Yesterday's Cast-Offs': A Phenomenological Study into the Acquisition of the Collection," in *1995 AMA Educators' Proceedings*, ed. Barbara B. Stern and George M. Zinkan (Chicago: American Marketing Association, 1995), 152.

17. Elizabeth C. Hirschman, "The Consciousness of Addiction: Toward a General Theory of Compulsive Consumption," *Journal of Consumer Research* 19 (September 1992): 155–79.

18. Leslie Cole and Dan Sherrell, "Comparing Scales to Measure Compulsive Buying: An Exploration of Their Dimensionality," in *Advances in Consumer Research* vol. 22, ed. Frank R. Kardes and Mita Sujan (Provo, UT: Association for Consumer Research 1995), 419–27.

19. Ronald J. Faber and Gary A. Christenson, "Can You Buy Happiness?: A Comparison of the Antecedent and Concurrent Moods Associated with the Shopping of Compulsive and Non-Compulsive Buyers," in *1995 Winter Educator's Conference* vol. 6, ed. David W. Stewart and Naufel J. Vilcassin (Chicago: American Marketing Association, 1995), 378–79.

20. Terence A. Shimp and Subhash Sharma, "Consumer Ethnocentrism: Construction and Validation of the CETSCALE," Journal of Marketing Research, 24 (August 1987), 280–89; Richard G. Netemeyer, Srinivas Durvaula, and Donald R. Lichtenstein, "A Cross-National Assessment of the Reliability and Validity of the CETSCALE," *Journal of Marketing Research* 28 (August 1991): 320–27.

21. Subhash Sharma, Terence A. Shimp, and Jeongshin Shin, "Consumer Ethnocentrism: A Test of Antecedents and Moderators," *Journal of the Academy of Marketing Science* 23 (1995): 27.

22. David Martin, "Branding: Finding That 'One Thing," *Brandweek*, 16 February 1998, 18.

23. Subodh Bhat and Srinivas K. Reddy, "Symbolic and Functional Positioning of Brands," *Journal of Consumer Marketing* 15 (1998): 32–43.

24. Jennifer L. Aaker, "Dimension of Brand Personality," *Journal of Marketing Research* 35 (August 1997): 347–56.

25. Tim Triplett, "When Tracy Speaks, Celestial Listens," *Marketing News*, 24 October 1994, 14.

26. David M. Morawski and Lacey J. Zachary, "Making Mr. Coffee," *Quirk's Marketing Research Review* 6 (March 1992): 6–7, 29–33.

27. Jennifer L. Aaker, "Dimension of Brand Personality," 351–52.

If the company had decided to make the silver polish effective for 40 days, it would have sacrificed a good deal of repeat purchase frequency. If it had decided to make the polish effective for 23 days (just 3 extra days of product life), its claim of "lasts longer" would not be perceived as true by most consumers. Making the product improvement just equal to the j.n.d. thus becomes the most efficient decision that management can make.

Marketing Applications of the j.n.d.

Weber's law has important applications in marketing. Manufacturers and marketers endeavor to determine the relevant j.n.d. for their products for two very different reasons: (1) so that negative changes (e.g., reductions in product size or quality, or increases in product price) are not readily discernible to the public (they remain below the j.n.d.) and (2) so that product improvements (such as improved or updated packaging, larger size, or lower price) are very apparent to consumers without being wastefully extravagant (i.e., they are at or just above the j.n.d.).

Marketers often want to update their existing package designs without losing the ready recognition of consumers who have been exposed to years of cumulative advertising impact. In such cases, they usually make a number of small changes, each carefully designed to fall below the j.n.d., so that consumers will perceive minimal difference. For example, Betty Crocker, the General Mills symbol, has been updated seven times since it first appeared in 1936 (see Figure 6-1.).

Pepsi redesigned its packaging in 1997 to update its look. Its new cola cans are bright royal blue, with the word Pepsi in white lettering rising vertically up the side of the can. In order to provide continuity in perceived appearance, the company initially introduced the new packaging (and ads) in a lighter blue, which it gradually intensified, making its globe logo more prominent.

FIGURE 6-1
Sequential Changes in the Betty Crocker Symbol Fall Below the j.n.d.

Coca-Cola also redesigned its signature red cans and labels in order to keep the brand looking fresh and new. At the same time, it was concerned that customer loyalists—who had rebelled at the introduction of the "New Coke" in 1985—not erroneously perceive the newly designed can as a new taste formulation.

To better compete in a global marketplace that has been radically altered by computer technology, many companies are updating their corporate logos to convey the notion that they are timely, fast-paced, and at the top of their respective product class. Many of the new corporate icons feature some element that conveys motion—streaking, slashing, orbiting. Microsoft's windows, for example, appear to float through space and to break into pieces. While some companies make minor changes (below the j.n.d.) to promote continuity, others have deliberately changed their traditional block lettering and dark colors in favor of script typefaces, bright colors, and hints of animation—taking their cues from pop icons like MTV. Mobil gasoline, for example, is animating its 77-year-old icon, Pegasus the flying horse, as part of a comprehensive image campaign that is simultaneously trying to target younger consumers while it evokes fond memories of an idealized past among older consumers.

Lexmark International Inc., which bought the office supplies and equipment line from the International Business Machine Corporation in March 1991, agreed to relinquish the IBM name by 1996. Recognizing the need to build a brand image for Lexmark while they moved away from the well-known IBM name, Lexmark officials conducted a four-stage campaign for phasing in the Lexmark name on products. As Figure 6-2 indicates, Stage 1 carried only the IBM name, Stage 2 featured the IBM name and downplayed Lexmark, Stage 3 featured the Lexmark name and downplayed IBM, and Stage 4 features only the Lexmark name. Figure 6-3 shows a Lexmark ad with the transition complete.

FIGURE 6-2
Gradual Changes in
Brand Name Below the
j.n.d.

Another interesting example is Ivory soap, which was introduced in 1879. The subtle packaging changes Ivory introduced over the years were each small enough to avoid notice, but the package managed to retain a contemporary look. The latest Ivory package is considerably different from the original, but the changes made at each step of the way were designed so skillfully that the transition has been hardly noticeable to consumers.

When it comes to product improvements, marketers very much want to meet or exceed the consumer's differential threshold; that is, they want consumers to readily perceive any improvements made in the original product. Marketers use the j.n.d. to determine the amount of improvement they should make in their products. Less than the j.n.d. is wasted effort because the improvement will not be perceived; more than the j.n.d. may be wasteful because it reduces the level of repeat sales.

SUBLIMINAL PERCEPTION

In chapter 4, we spoke of people being motivated below their level of conscious awareness. People are also *stimulated* below their level of conscious awareness; that is, they can perceive stimuli without being consciously aware that they are doing so. Stimuli that are too weak or too brief to be consciously seen or heard may nevertheless be strong enough to be perceived by one or more receptor cells. This process is called **subliminal perception** because the stimulus is beneath the threshold, or "limen," of conscious awareness, though obviously not beneath the absolute threshold of the receptors involved. (Perception of stimuli that are above the level of conscious awareness technically is called supraliminal perception, though it is usually referred to simply as perception.)

Subliminal perception created a great furor in the late 1950s, when it was reported that consumers were being exposed to subliminal advertising messages they were not aware of receiving. These messages purportedly were persuading people to buy goods and services without being aware of why they were motivated to do so. The effectiveness of so-called subliminal advertising was reportedly tested at a drive-in movie in New Jersey in 1957, where the words "Eat popcorn" and "Drink Coca-Cola" were flashed on the screen during the movie.[4] Exposure times were so short that viewers were unaware of seeing a message. It was reported that during the 6-week test period, popcorn sales increased 58 percent and Coca-Cola sales increased 18 percent. However, no scientific controls were used, and researchers were never able to replicate the results. Nevertheless, public indignation at the possibility of such manipulation was so widespread that both the Federal Communications Commission and the United States Congress conducted hearings to determine whether subliminal advertising should be outlawed. The resultant publicity reawakened academic interest in the subject of subliminal perception.

Research Findings Concerning Subliminal Perception

A series of highly imaginative laboratory experiments that followed the public hearings gave some support to the notion that individuals could perceive below the level of their conscious awareness, but found no evidence that they could be persuaded to act in response to such subliminal stimulation. For example, one researcher found that while the simple subliminal stimulus COKE served to arouse thirst in subjects, the subliminal command, DRINK COKE, did not have a greater effect, nor did it have any behavioral consequences.[5] Other experiments had similar results; they supported the finding that individuals could perceive below their level of conscious awareness, but that subliminal stimuli did not affect their purchase intentions.

Interest in the field of subliminal perception was renewed in the mid-1970s with the charge that advertisers were using subliminal embeds in their print ads to persuade consumers to buy their advertised brands. It was alleged, for example, that liquor advertisers were trying to increase the subconscious appeal of their products by embedding sexually suggestive symbols in ice cubes floating in a pictured drink.[6] However, research findings indicate that sexually oriented embeds do not influence consumer preferences.[7] Several experiments into the effectiveness of subliminal messages in television commercials concluded that it would be very difficult to use the technique on television, but that even if subliminal messages were to have "some influence," it would be much less effective than overt advertising messages, and would likely interfere with consumers' memory for a brand name.[8]

The self-help audiocassette industry is based on the premise of subliminal persuasion. Consumers are spending millions of dollars annually on self-help tapes in the belief that they can learn a foreign language, break a bad habit, improve their willpower or their memory, or take off weight. The tapes play relaxing music (or the sound of ocean waves) and contain subliminal messages not perceptible to the ear but supposedly recognizable to the subconscious mind. Most of the tapes come with a written script of the subliminal messages (for example, "I chew slowly," "I eat less," "I am capable," "I act decisively").

Evaluating the Effectiveness of Subliminal Persuasion

Despite the many studies undertaken by academicians and researchers since the 1950s, there is no evidence that subliminal advertising persuades people to buy goods or services. A review of the literature indicates that subliminal perception research is based on two theoretical approaches. According to the first theory, constant repetition of very weak (i.e., subthreshold) stimuli has an incremental effect that enables such stimuli to build response strength over many presentations. This would be the operative theory when weak stimuli are flashed repeatedly on a movie screen or played on a soundtrack or audiocassette. The second approach is based on the theory that subliminal sexual stimuli arouse unconscious sexual motivations. This is the theory behind the use of *sexual embeds* in print advertising. But no studies have yet indicated that either of these theoretical approaches have been effectively used by advertisers to increase sales. However, there is some indication that subliminal advertising may provide new opportunities for modifying antisocial behavior through public awareness campaigns that call for individuals to make generalized responses to suggestions that enhance their personal performance or improve their attitudes.[9]

In summary, although there is some evidence that subliminal stimuli may influence affective reactions, there is no evidence that subliminal stimulation can influence consumption motives or actions. There continues to be a big gap between perception and persuasion. A recent review of the evidence on subliminal persuasion indicates that the only way for subliminal techniques to have a significant persuasive effect would be through long-term repeated exposure under a limited set of circumstances, which would not be economically feasible or practical within an advertising context.[10]

As to sexual embeds, most researchers are of the opinion that "What you see is what you get"; that is, a vivid imagination can see whatever it wants to see in just about any situation. And that pretty much sums up the whole notion of perception: Individuals see what they want to see (e.g., what they are motivated to see) and what they expect to see. To correct any misperceptions among the public that subliminal advertising does, in fact, exist, the advertising community occasionally sponsors ads like the one depicted in Figure 6-4, which ridicule the notion that subliminal techniques are effective or that they are used in advertising applications.

Several studies concerned with public beliefs about subliminal advertising found that a large percentage of Americans know what subliminal advertising is, they believe it is used by advertisers, and that it is effective in persuading consumers to buy.[11] This misperception should be of concern to marketers because, true or not, these beliefs influence consumer attitudes toward advertising.

Because of the absence of any evidence that subliminal persuasion really works, no state or federal laws have been enacted to restrict the use of subliminal advertising. The Federal Communications Commission has adopted the position that "covert messages by their very nature are against the public interest." Clearly, that position covers both paid (commercial) subliminal advertisements and unpaid (public service) subliminal messages.

▪▪▪▪ DYNAMICS OF PERCEPTION

The preceding section explained how the individual receives sensations from stimuli in the outside environment and how the human organism adapts to the level and intensity of sensory input. We now come to one of the major principles of perception:

FIGURE 6-4

Subliminal Embeds Are in the Eye of the Beholder

Raw sensory input by itself does not produce or explain the coherent picture of the world that most adults possess. Indeed, the study of perception is largely the study of what we subconsciously add to or subtract from raw sensory inputs to produce our own private picture of the world.

Human beings are constantly bombarded with stimuli during every minute and every hour of every day. The sensory world is made up of an almost infinite number of discrete sensations that are constantly and subtly changing. According to the principles of sensation, intensive stimulation "bounces" off most individuals, who subconsciously block (i.e., adapt to) the receipt of a heavy bombardment of stimuli. Otherwise, the billions of different stimuli to which we are constantly exposed might serve to confuse us totally and keep us perpetually disoriented in a constantly changing environment. However, neither of these consequences tends to occur, because perception is not a function of sensory input alone. Rather, perception is the result of two different kinds of inputs that interact to form the personal pictures—the perceptions—that each individual experiences.

One type of input is physical stimuli from the outside environment; the other type of input is provided by individuals themselves in the form of certain predispositions (expectations, motives, and learning) based on previous experience. The combination of these two very different kinds of inputs produces for each of us a very private, very personal picture of the world. Because each person is a unique individual, with unique experiences, needs, wants, desires, and expectations, it follows that each individual's perceptions are also unique. This explains why no two people see the world in precisely the same way.

Individuals are very *selective* as to which stimuli they "recognize"; they subconsciously *organize* the stimuli they do recognize according to widely held psychological principles, and they *interpret* such stimuli (they give meaning to them) subjectively in accordance with their needs, expectations, and experiences. Let us examine in some detail each of these three aspects of perception: the **selection**, **organization**, and **interpretation** of stimuli.

PERCEPTUAL SELECTION

Consumers subconsciously exercise a great deal of selectivity as to which aspects of the environment (which stimuli) they perceive. An individual may look at some things, ignore others, and turn away from still others. In actuality, people receive or perceive only a small fraction of the stimuli to which they are exposed. Consider, for example, a woman in a supermarket. She may be exposed to over 20,000 products of different colors, sizes, and shapes; to perhaps 100 people (looking, walking, searching, talking); to smells (from fruit, meat, disinfectant, or people); to sounds within the store (cash registers ringing, shopping carts rolling, air conditioners humming, and clerks sweeping, mopping aisles, stocking shelves); and to sounds from outside the store (planes passing, cars honking, tires screeching, children shouting, car doors slamming). Yet she manages on a regular basis to visit her local supermarket, select the items she needs, pay for them, and leave, all within a relatively brief period of time, without losing her sanity or her personal orientation to the world around her. This is because she exercises selectivity in perception.

Which stimuli get selected depends on two major factors in addition to the nature of the stimulus itself: (1) consumers' previous *experience* as it affects their expectations (what they are prepared, or "set," to see) and (2) their *motives* at the time (their needs, desires, interests, and so on.) Each of these factors can serve to increase or decrease the probability that a stimulus will be perceived.

Nature of the Stimulus

Marketing stimuli include an enormous number of variables that affect the consumer's perception, such as the nature of the product, its physical attributes, the package design, the brand name, the advertisements and commercials (including copy claims, choice and sex of model, positioning of model, size of ad, typography), the position of a print ad or a commercial, and the editorial environment.

In general, *contrast* is one of the most attention-compelling attributes of a stimulus. Advertisers often use extreme attention-getting devices to achieve maximum contrast and thus penetrate the consumer's perceptual "screen." For example, a number of magazines and newspapers carry ads that readers can unfold to reveal oversized, posterlike advertisements for products ranging from cosmetics to automobiles, because of the "stopping power" of giant ads among more traditional sizes. However, advertising does not have to be unique to achieve a high degree of differentiation; it simply has to contrast with the environment in which it is run. The use of lots of white space in a print advertisement, the absence of sound in a commercial's opening scene, a 60-second commercial within a string of 20-second spots—all offer sufficient contrast from their environments to achieve differentiation and merit the consumer's attention. Figure 6-5 illustrates the attention-getting nature of white space in an advertisement. In an effort to achieve contrast, advertisers are also using splashes of color in black-and-white print ads to highlight the advertised product. Eye-catching ads, some using surrealistic imagery for either humorous effect or mood enhancement, attract attention because of their contrast to consumer expectations (see Figure 6-6).

With respect to packaging, astute marketers usually try to differentiate their packages to ensure rapid consumer perception. Since the average package on the supermarket shelf has about 1/10th of a second to make an impression on the consumer, it is important that every aspect of the package—the name, shape, color, label, and copy—provide sufficient sensory stimulation to be noted and remembered.

Sometimes advertisers capitalize on the *lack* of contrast. For example, a technique that has been used effectively in TV commercials is to position the commercial so close to the storyline of a program that viewers are unaware they are watching an ad

FIGURE 6-5
White Space Attracts
Attention

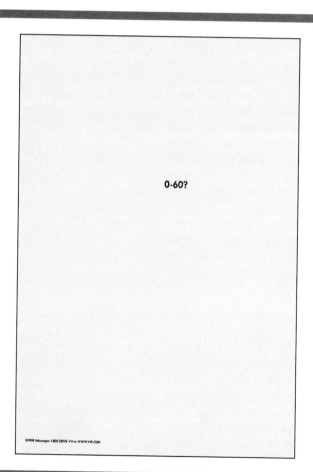

FIGURE 6-6
Surreal Images Attract
Attention

until they are well into it. In the case of children's programming, the Federal Trade Commission has strictly limited the use of this technique. TV stars or cartoon characters are prohibited from promoting products during the children's shows in which they appear.

Advertisers are producing 30-minute commercials (called *infomercials*) that appear to the average viewer as documentaries and thus command more attentive viewing than obvious commercials would receive. Advertisers are also running print ads (called *advertorials*) that closely resemble editorial material, making it increasingly difficult for readers to tell them apart.

Expectations

People usually see what they expect to see, and what they expect to see is usually based on familiarity, previous experience, or preconditioned set (expectations). In a marketing context, people tend to perceive products and product attributes according to their own expectations. A man who has been told by his friends that a new Scotch malt whiskey has a bitter taste will probably perceive the taste to be bitter; a teenager who attends a horror movie that has been billed as terrifying will probably find it so. On the other hand, stimuli that conflict sharply with expectations often receive more attention than those that conform to expectations (see Figure 6-7).

For years, certain advertisers have used blatant sexuality in advertisements for products to which sex was not relevant, in the belief that such advertisements would attract a high degree of attention. However, ads with irrelevant sexuality often defeat the

Bye-Bye, Crocodile.

The LUBRIDERM® Body Bar and
LUBRIDERM Lotion. Think of them as Shampoo
and Conditioner for your skin.

FIGURE 6-7
The Unexpected Attracts
Attention

marketer's objectives, because readers tend to remember the sexual aspects of the ad (e.g., the innuendo or the model), not the product or brand advertised. Nevertheless, some advertisers continue to use erotic appeals in promoting a wide variety of products, from office furniture to jeans. (The use of sex in advertising is discussed in chapter 9.)

Motives

People tend to perceive the things they need or want; the stronger the need, the greater the tendency to ignore unrelated stimuli in the environment. A woman interested in a portable computer is more likely to notice and read carefully ads for computer laptops than her neighbor, who uses a desktop computer. In general, there is a heightened awareness of stimuli that are relevant to one's needs and interests, and a decreased awareness of stimuli that are irrelevant to those needs. An individual's perceptual process simply attunes itself more closely to those elements in the environment that are important to that person. Someone who is hungry is more likely to spot a restaurant sign; a sexually repressed person may perceive sexual symbolism where none exists.

Marketing managers recognize the efficiency of targeting their products to the perceived needs of consumers. For example, a marketer can determine through marketing research what consumers consider to be the ideal attributes of the product category, or what consumers perceive their needs to be in relation to the product category. The marketer can then segment the market on the basis of those needs and vary the product advertising so that consumers in each segment will perceive the product as meeting their own special needs, wants, and interests.

Important Concepts Concerning Selective Perception

As the preceding discussion illustrates, the consumer's "selection" of stimuli from the environment is based on the interaction of expectations and motives with the stimulus itself. These factors give rise to four important concepts concerning perception.

Selective Exposure Consumers actively seek out messages that they find pleasant or with which they are sympathetic, and they actively avoid painful or threatening ones. They also selectively expose themselves to advertisements that reassure them of the wisdom of their purchase decisions.

Selective Attention Consumers exercise a great deal of selectivity in terms of the attention they give to commercial stimuli. They have a heightened awareness of stimuli that meet their needs or interests and minimal awareness of stimuli irrelevant to their needs. Thus, consumers are likely to note ads for products that would satisfy their needs and disregard those in which they have no interest. People also vary in terms of the kinds of information in which they are interested and the form of message and type of medium they prefer. Some people are more interested in price, some in appearance, and some in social acceptability. Some people like complex, sophisticated messages; others like simple graphics.

Perceptual Defense Consumers subconsciously screen out stimuli that they find psychologically threatening, even though exposure has already taken place. Thus, threatening or otherwise damaging stimuli are less likely to be consciously perceived than are neutral stimuli at the same level of exposure.[12] Furthermore, individuals sometimes unconsciously distort information that is not consistent with their needs, values, and beliefs.

Perceptual Blocking Consumers protect themselves from being bombarded with stimuli by simply "tuning out"—blocking such stimuli from conscious awareness. They do so out of self-protection, because of the visually overwhelming nature of the world in which we live. This perceptual blocking is comparable to the "zapping" of TV commercials with remote controls.

PERCEPTUAL ORGANIZATION

People do not experience the numerous stimuli they select from the environment as separate and discrete sensations; rather, they tend to organize them into groups and perceive them as unified wholes. Thus, the perceived characteristics of even the simplest stimulus are viewed as a function of the whole to which the stimulus appears to belong. This method of perceptual organization simplifies life considerably for the individual.

The specific principles underlying perceptual organization are often referred to by the name given the school of psychology that first developed it: *Gestalt* psychology. (Gestalt, in German, means pattern or configuration.) Three of the most basic principles of perceptual organization are *figure and ground*, *grouping*, and *closure*.

Figure and Ground

As was noted earlier, stimuli that contrast with their environment are more likely to be noticed. A sound must be louder or softer, a color brighter or paler. The simplest visual illustration consists of a figure on a ground (that is, *background*). The figure is perceived more clearly because, in contrast to its ground, it appears to be well defined, solid, and in the forefront. The ground is usually perceived as indefinite, hazy, and continuous. The common line that separates the figure and the ground is generally attributed to the figure, rather than to the ground, which helps give the figure greater definition. Consider the stimulus of music. People can either "bathe" in music, or listen to music. In the first case, music is simply background to other activities; in the sec-

FIGURE 6-8
Closeup Silhouette Has
Stopping Power

Whiskers grow .01 inch per day. Razors coated with DuPont Teflon® keep them comfortably at bay.

www.dupont.com

DU PONT

Better things for better living

Teflon® is a DuPont registered trademark for its brand of coatings. Only DuPont makes Teflon® © 1997 DuPont

ond, it is figure. Figure is more clearly perceived because it appears to be dominant; in contrast, ground appears to be subordinate and, therefore, less important.

People have a tendency to organize their perceptions into figure-and-ground relationships. How a reversible figure-ground pattern is perceived can be influenced by prior pleasant or painful associations with one or the other element in isolation. The consumer's physical state also affects how he or she perceives reversible figure-ground illustrations.

Advertisers have to plan their advertisements carefully to make sure that the stimulus they want noted is seen as figure and not as ground. The musical background must not overwhelm the jingle; the background of an advertisement must not detract from the product. Print advertisers often silhouette their products against a white background to make sure that the features they want noted are clearly perceived (see Figure 6-8). Others use reverse lettering (white letters on a black background) to achieve contrast; however, in such cases they are flirting with the problem of figure-ground reversal.

Marketers sometimes run advertisements that confuse the consumer because there is no clear indication of which is figure and which is ground. Of course, in some cases, the blurring of figure and ground is deliberate. The well-known Absolut Vodka campaign, started over 25 years ago, often runs print ads in which the figure (the shape of the Absolut bottle) is poorly delineated against its ground, challenging readers to search for the bottle; the resulting audience "participation" results in more intense ad scrutiny.

Grouping

Individuals tend to group stimuli so that they form a unified picture or impression. The perception of stimuli as *groups* or *chunks* of information, rather than as discrete bits of information, facilitates their memory and recall. Grouping can be used advantageously by marketers to imply certain desired meanings in connection with their products. For example, an advertisement for tea may show a young man and woman sipping tea in a beautifully appointed room before a blazing hearth. The overall mood implied by the grouping of stimuli leads the consumer to associate the drinking of tea with romance, fine living, and winter warmth.

Most of us can remember and repeat our Social Security numbers because we automatically group them into three "chunks," rather than try to remember nine separate numbers. Years ago, when AT&T introduced the idea of all-digit telephone numbers, consumers objected strenuously on the grounds that they would not be able to recall or repeat a long string of numbers. However, because we automatically group telephone numbers into two chunks (or three, with the area code), the anticipated problems never occurred.

Closure

Individuals have a need for closure. They express this need by organizing their perceptions so that they form a complete picture. If the pattern of stimuli to which they are exposed is incomplete, they tend to perceive it, nevertheless, as complete; that is, they consciously or subconsciously fill in the missing pieces. Thus, a circle with a section of its periphery missing is invariably perceived as a circle, not an arc.

A classic study found that incomplete tasks are better remembered than complete tasks. One explanation for this phenomenon is that the person who begins a task develops a need to complete it. If he or she is prevented from doing so, a state of tension is created that manifests itself in improved memory for the incomplete task. This has been called the **Zeigernik effect**. Hearing the beginning of a message leads to the need to hear the rest of it—like waiting for the second shoe to drop.[13]

There are numerous examples of concept closure, where viewers react to background cues by "filling in" more information than the commercial provides. For example, a TV commercial for Cudahy Bar S bacon showed a close-up of bacon frying in an iron skillet while a voice-over in a deep cowboy twang said what a fine bacon it was. Beneath the laid-back delivery was the sound of a harmonica playing a soft, mournful cowboy tune. A telephone survey 24 hours later found that people remembered far more than the simple commercial had shown them. One respondent recalled bacon frying on a campfire with cowboys sitting around; another recalled horses standing in the background and the light of the campfire reflecting on the faces of the cowboys eating bacon. The viewers filled in the story "painted" by the background cues, in effect creating their own more effective, more memorable commercial than the one aired.

The need for closure has some interesting implications for marketers. The presentation of an incomplete advertising message "begs" for completion by consumers, and the very act of completion serves to involve them more deeply in the message. That is why many advertisers deliberately seek audience articipation in their ads. In a related vein, advertisers have discovered that they can achieve excellent results by using the soundtrack of a frequently shown television commercial on radio. Consumers who are familiar with the TV commercial perceive the audio track alone as incomplete; in their need for completion, they mentally play back the visual content from memory. (Chapter 9 discusses the effectiveness of audience participation as a communications technique.)

In summary, it is clear that perceptions are not equivalent to the raw sensory input of discrete stimuli, nor to the sum total of discrete stimuli. Rather, people tend to add to or subtract from stimuli to which they are exposed on the basis of their expectations and motives, using generalized principles of organization based on Gestalt theory.

PERCEPTUAL INTERPRETATION

The preceding discussion has emphasized that perception is a personal phenomenon. People exercise selectivity as to which stimuli they perceive, and they organize these stimuli on the basis of certain psychological principles. The interpretation of stimuli is also uniquely individual, because it is based on what individuals expect to see in light of their previous experience, on the number of plausible explanations they can envision, and on their motives and interests at the time of perception.

Stimuli are often highly ambiguous. Some stimuli are weak because of such factors as poor visibility, brief exposure, high noise level, or constant fluctuation. Even stimuli that are strong tend to fluctuate dramatically because of such factors as different angles of viewing, varying distances, and changing levels of illumination. Consumers usually attribute the sensory input they receive to sources they consider most likely to have caused the specific pattern of stimuli. Past experiences and social interactions help to form certain expectations that provide categories (or alternative explanations) that individuals use in interpreting stimuli. The narrower the individual's experience, the more limited the access to alternative categories.

When stimuli are highly ambiguous, an individual will usually interpret them in such a way that they serve to fulfill personal needs, wishes, interests, and so on. It is this principle that provides the rationale for the projective tests discussed in chapter 2. Such tests provide ambiguous stimuli (such as incomplete sentences, unclear pictures, untitled cartoons, or ink blots) to respondents who are asked to interpret them.

How a person describes a vague illustration, or what meaning the individual ascribes to an ink blot, is a reflection not of the stimulus itself, but of the subject's own needs, wants, and desires. Through the interpretation of ambiguous stimuli, respondents reveal a great deal about themselves.

How close a person's interpretations are to reality, then, depends on the clarity of the stimulus, the past experiences of the perceiver, and his or her motives and interests at the time of perception.

Distorting Influences

Individuals are subject to a number of influences that tend to distort their perceptions; some of these are discussed below.

Physical Appearances People tend to attribute the qualities they associate with certain people to others who may resemble them, whether or not they consciously recognize the similarity. For this reason, the selection of models for print advertisements and for television commercials can be a key element in their ultimate persuasiveness. Studies on physical appearance have found that attractive models are more persuasive and have a more positive influence on consumer attitudes and behavior than average-looking models; attractive men are perceived as more successful businessmen than average-looking men. Some studies suggest that models influence consumer perceptions of physical attractiveness, and through comparisons, their own self perceptions.[14]

Stereotypes Individuals tend to carry "pictures" in their minds of the meanings of various kinds of stimuli. These stereotypes serve as expectations of what specific situations, people, or events will be like, and they are important determinants of how such stimuli are subsequently perceived. For example, Figure 6-9 presents a stereotypical authority figure with which parochial school alumni can identify.

Irrelevant Cues When required to form a difficult perceptual judgment, consumers often respond to irrelevant stimuli. For example, many high-priced automobiles are purchased because of their color, style, or luxury options, rather than on the basis of mechanical or technical superiority.

First Impressions First impressions tend to be lasting; yet, in forming such impressions, the perceiver does not yet know which stimuli are relevant, important, or predictive of later behavior. A shampoo commercial effectively used the line, "You'll never have a second chance to make a first impression." Since first impressions are often lasting, introducing a new product before it has been perfected may prove fatal to its ultimate success; subsequent information about its advantages, even if true, will often be negated by the memory of its early performance.

Jumping to Conclusions Many people tend to jump to conclusions before examining all the relevant evidence. For example, the consumer may hear just the beginning of a commercial message and draw conclusions regarding the product or service being advertised. For this reason, some copywriters are careful to give their most persuasive arguments first.

Halo Effect Historically, the halo effect has been used to describe situations in which the evaluation of a single object or person on a multitude of dimensions is based on the evaluation of just one or a few dimensions (for example, a man is trustworthy, fine, and noble because he looks you in the eye when he speaks). Consumer

FIGURE 6-9
Ad Using a Stereotypical
Authority Figure

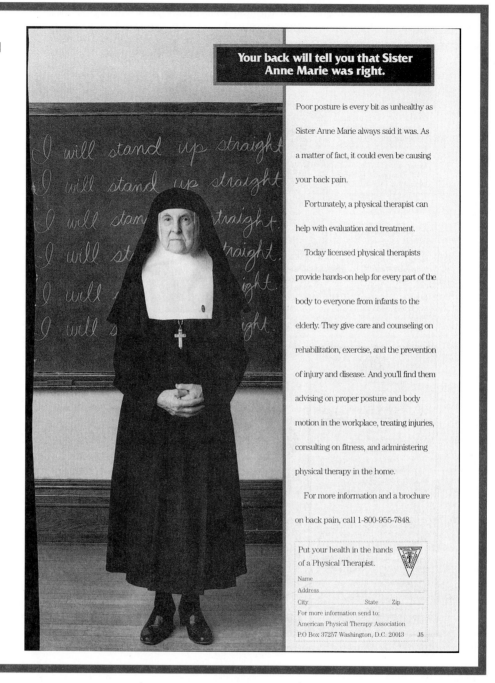

behaviorists broaden the notion of the halo effect to include the evaluation of multiple objects (e.g., a product line) on the basis of the evaluation of just one dimension (a brand name or a spokesperson). Using this broader definition, marketers take advantage of the halo effect when they extend a brand name associated with one line of products to another. The lucrative field of *licensing* is based on the halo effect. Manufacturers and retailers hope to acquire instant recognition and status for their products by associating them with a well-known name. (Chapter 7 discusses licensing in greater detail.)

The reader may well ask how "realistic" perceptions can be, given the many subjective influences on perceptual interpretation. It should be somewhat reassuring to remember that previous experiences usually serve to resolve stimulus ambiguity in a realistic way and to help in its interpretation. Only in situations of unusual or changing stimulus conditions do expectations lead to wrong interpretations.

CONSUMER IMAGERY

Consumers have a number of enduring perceptions, or images, that are particularly relevant to the study of consumer behavior. Chapter 5 discussed consumer self-images; the following section examines consumers' perceived images of products, brands, services, prices, product quality, retail stores, and manufacturers.

Products and brands have symbolic value for individuals, who evaluate them on the basis of their consistency (congruence) with their personal pictures of themselves. Some products seem to match an individual's self-image; others do not. Consumers attempt to preserve or enhance their self-images by buying products and patronizing retail stores that they believe are congruent with their self-images, and by avoiding those that are not.

PRODUCT POSITIONING AND REPOSITIONING

The image that a product has in the mind of the consumer—that is, its **positioning**—is probably more important to its ultimate success than are its actual characteristics. Marketers try to differentiate their products by stressing attributes that they claim will fulfill the consumer's needs better than competing brands. They strive to create a product image consistent with the relevant self-image of the targeted consumer segment.

Positioning strategy is the essence of the marketing mix; it complements the company's segmentation strategy and selection of target markets. Positioning conveys the concept, or meaning, of the product or service in terms of how it fulfills a consumer need. The same product (or service) can be positioned differently to different market segments, or can be repositioned to the same audience, without being physically changed.

The result of successful positioning strategy is a distinctive brand image on which consumers rely in making product choices. Furthermore, research suggests that advertisers' positioning strategies affect consumer beliefs about their brands' attributes and the prices consumers are willing to pay.[15] In today's highly competitive environment, a distinctive product image is most important. As products become more complex and the marketplace more crowded, consumers rely more on the product's image than on its actual attributes in making purchase decisions.

A positive brand image is associated with consumer loyalty, consumer beliefs about positive brand value, and a willingness to search for the brand. A positive brand image also serves to promote consumer interest in future brand promotions, and inoculates against competitors' marketing activities.

Regardless of how well positioned a product appears to be, the marketer may be forced to **reposition** it in response to market events, such as a competitor cutting into the brand's market share. For example, rather than trying to meet the lower prices of high-quality private label competition, some premium brand marketers have repositioned their brands to justify their higher prices, playing up brand attributes that had previously been ignored. At the same time, many upscale department stores have created their own brands to compete with designer brands.

When Evian Natural Spring Water decided to reposition its brand as integral to the act of living well, it ran a series of ads noting the source of Evian's water in the French Alps. The ads concluded with such lines as "Within me lives the power of nature. Pure, natural spring water from the French Alps that's perfect for replenishing a superhero."

Another reason to reposition a product or service is to satisfy changing consumer preferences. For example, when health-oriented consumers began to avoid high-fat foods, many fast-food chains acted swiftly to reposition their images by offering salad bars and other health-oriented foods. Kentucky Fried Chicken changed its well-known corporate name to KFC in order to omit the dread word "fried" from its advertising. Weight Watchers repositioned its line of frozen foods from "dietetic" to "healthy," maintaining its diet-thin imagery while responding to a perceived shift in consumer values. The Avon Company decided to reposition its image from that of a company with legions of women selling their products from door-to-door with self deprecation and irony. Its new campaign showed pictures of accomplished women celebrities with the tag line, "Just another Avon lady."

Perceptual Mapping

The technique of **perceptual mapping** helps marketers to determine just how their products or services appear to consumers in relation to competitive brands on one or more relevant characteristics. It enables them to see gaps in the positioning of all brands in the product or service class and to identify areas in which consumer needs are not being adequately met. For example, if a magazine publisher wants to introduce a new magazine to Generation Xers, he may use perceptual mapping to uncover a niche of consumers with a special set of interests that are not being adequately or equally addressed by other magazines targeted to the same demographic segment. This insight allows him to position the new magazine as specifically focused on these interests. Or, a publisher may discover through perceptual mapping that consumers perceive its magazine (let's call it *Splash*) to be very similar in editorial content and format to its closest competitors, *Bash* and *Crash* (see Figure 6-10). By changing the focus of its editorial features to appeal to a new market niche, the publisher can reposition the magazine (e.g., from *Splash* to *Fashion Splash*).

POSITIONING OF SERVICES

Compared with manufacturing firms, service marketers face several unique problems in positioning and promoting their offerings. Because services are intangible, image becomes a key factor in differentiating a service from its competition. Thus, the marketing objective is to enable the consumer to link a specific image with a specific brand name. Many service marketers have developed strategies to provide customers with visual images and tangible reminders of their service offerings. These include painted delivery vehicles, restaurant matchbooks, packaged hotel soaps and shampoos, and a variety of other specialty items. A number of image consultants have tried to persuade United Parcel Service to change the color of its delivery trucks from dark brown to a more cheerful color, but management has resisted because of the ready identification the brown trucks have achieved with fast and reliable service.

Sometimes companies market several versions of their service to different market segments by using a differentiated positioning strategy. However, they must be careful to avoid perceptual confusion among their customers. The American Express Company offers its regular (green) card to consumers as a short-term credit instrument, and the Gold and more prestigious Platinum cards, each with increased services, to the affluent cardholder. Private banks that target upscale consumers focus on

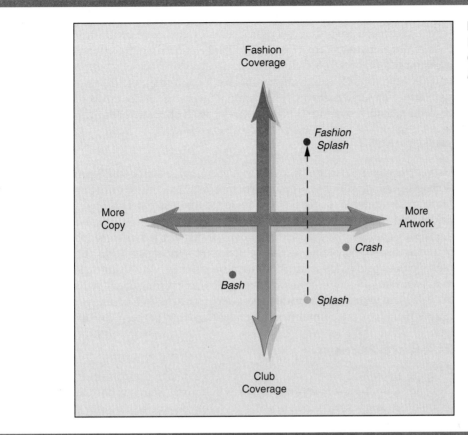

FIGURE 6-10

Perceptual Map of Competitors Facilitates Magazine Repositioning

estate planning, investments, and trust funds to maintain an exclusive image; commercial banks stress cash machines and overdraft privileges to consumers with more modest financial means.

The Service Environment

The design of the service environment is an important aspect of service positioning strategy and sharply influences consumer impressions and consumer and employee behavior. The physical environment is particularly important in creating a favorable impression for such services as banks, retail stores, and professional offices, because there are so few objective criteria by which consumers can judge the quality of the services they receive.[16] The service environment conveys the image of the service provider with whom the service is so closely linked. Thus, at the Chase Private Banking offices, expensive mahogany desks, leather chairs, and silk draperies project stability, solidity, wealth, and power.

The Polo Ralph Lauren store in its renovated 1895 mansion on New York's Upper East Side is the embodiment of the image Lauren wants to create for his clothes: traditionalism and Old World values. All the trappings of what one imagines to be the high-class and well-heeled ways of the very, very rich are here, from the baronial, hand-carved staircase lined with "family" portraits to the plush sitting rooms with working fireplaces. The Polo store image artfully extends the image of the clothing it sells, and projects an Old World quality of living and shopping that its upscale target market finds appealing.

One study of service environments identified five environmental variables most important to bank customers: (1) privacy (both visually and verbally, with enclosed offices, transaction privacy, etc.); (2) efficiency/convenience (transaction areas that are easy to find, directional signs, etc.); (3) ambient background conditions (temperature, lighting, noise, music); (4) social conditions (the physical appearance of other people in the bank environment, such as bank customers and bank personnel); and (5) aesthetics (e.g., color, style, use of materials, artworks).[17] Clearly, a favorable service environment creates the perception among consumers that the service itself better satisfies their needs.

PERCEIVED PRICE

How a consumer perceives a price—as high, as low, as fair—has a strong influence on both purchase intentions and purchase satisfaction. Consider the perception of price fairness, for example. There is some evidence that customers do pay attention to the prices paid by other customers (such as senior citizens, frequent flyers, affinity club members), and that the differential pricing strategies used by some marketers are perceived as unfair by customers not eligible for the special prices. No one is happy knowing he or she paid twice as much for an airline ticket or a theater ticket as the person in the next seat. Perceptions of price unfairness affect consumers' perceptions of product value, and ultimately, their willingness to patronize a store or a service. Strategies that reduce perceived price unfairness ultimately enhance perceived product value.[18]

Reference Prices

Products advertised as "on sale" tend to create enhanced customer perceptions of savings and value. Different formats used in sales advertisements have differing impacts, based on consumer reference prices. A **reference price** is any price that a consumer uses as a basis for comparison in judging another price. Reference prices can be *external* or *internal*. An advertiser generally uses a higher *external reference price* ("sold elsewhere at . . .") in an ad in which a lower sales price is being offered, to persuade the consumer that the product advertised is a really good buy. *Internal reference prices* are those prices (or price ranges) retrieved by the consumer from memory. Internal reference points are thought to play a major role in consumers' evaluations and perceptions of value of an advertised (external) price deal, as well as in the believability of any advertised reference price. Advertised prices (both reference and sales prices) affect consumers' reference prices (that is, higher advertised prices lead to higher internal reference prices.)[19]

According to *acquisition-transaction utility theory*, two types of utility are associated with consumer purchases. *Acquisition utility* represents the consumer's perceived economic gain or loss associated with a purchase, and is a function of product utility and purchase price. *Transaction utility* concerns the perceived pleasure or displeasure associated with the financial aspect of the purchase, and is determined by the difference between the internal reference price and the purchase price.[20] For example, if a consumer wants to purchase a television set for which her internal reference price is approximately $500, and she buys a set that is sale-priced at $500, she receives no transaction utility. However, if either her internal reference price is increased, or the sales price of the set is decreased, she will receive positive transaction utility, which increases the total utility she experiences with the purchase. Research findings indicate that transaction utility is significant only when the consumer is certain about consistency of quality.[21]

Several studies have investigated the effects on consumer price perceptions of three types of advertised reference prices: plausible low, plausible high, and implausible high. *Plausible low* prices are well within the range of acceptable market prices;

plausible high are near the outer limits of the range but not beyond the realm of believability, and *implausible high* are well above the consumer's perceived range of acceptable market prices. As long as an advertised reference price is within a given consumer's acceptable price range, it is considered plausible and is *assimilated*. (See *assimilation-contrast theory* in chapter 8.) If the advertised reference point is outside the range of acceptable prices (that is, implausible), it will be *contrasted* and thus will not be perceived as a valid reference point.[22] Findings show that an implausible high reference price can affect both consumer evaluations and the advertiser's image of credibility. By setting the reference price at the highest price recently offered for identical or comparable merchandise, the advertiser can enhance consumer perceptions of value while minimizing negative effects.

Tensile and Objective Price Claims

The semantic cues (i.e., specific wording) of the phrase used to communicate the price-related information may affect consumers' price perceptions. *Tensile price claims* (for example, "save 10 to 40%," "save up to 60%," "save 20% or more") are used to promote a range of price discounts for a product line, an entire department, or sometimes an entire store. In contrast with tensile cues, *objective price claims* provide a single discount level (such as "save 25%"). Because of the broader range of sale merchandise that is covered by both tensile and objective price claims, they potentially have a greater effect on consumer shopping and on store traffic than a reference price advertisement that promotes a single product.[23]

Consumer evaluations and shopping intentions are least favorable for advertisements stating the minimum discount level ("save 10% or more"). Ads that state a maximum discount level ("save up to 40%") either equal or exceed the effectiveness of ads stating a discount range ("save 10 to 40%"). When different levels of savings are advertised across a product line, the maximum discount level has been found to be the most effective at influencing consumers' perceptions of savings.

Consumer reactions to tensile price claims are affected by the width of the discount range. Several studies examined the effects of the three forms of tensile price claims—advertising a minimum, a maximum, or a range of savings—on consumers' price perceptions and their search and shopping intentions. The studies found that, for broader discount ranges, tensile claims stating the maximum level of savings have more positive effects than those stating the minimum level or the entire savings range. For more narrow discount ranges, tensile claims stating the maximum level of savings appear to be no more effective than claims stating the minimum level or the entire savings range.[24]

An experiment examining the effects of a "bundle price" (the marketing of two or more products or services in a single package for a special price) on consumer price perceptions found that additional savings offered directly on the bundle have a greater relative impact on buyers' perceptions of transaction value than savings offered on the bundle's individual items.[25]

Consumers are less sensitive to price when using credit cards than when they use cash. Similarly, a recent study reported that consumers tend to be less sensitive to price when they shop on-line than when they shop in stores.[26]

PERCEIVED QUALITY

Consumers often judge the quality of a product or service on the basis of a variety of informational cues that they associate with the product. Some of these cues are intrinsic to the product or service, others are extrinsic. Either singly or in composite, such cues provide the basis for perceptions of product and service quality.

Perceived Quality of Products

Cues that are **intrinsic** concern physical characteristics of the product itself, such as size, color, flavor, or aroma. In some cases, consumers use physical characteristics (e.g., the flavor of ice cream or cake) to judge product quality. Consumers like to believe that they base their evaluations of product quality on intrinsic cues, because that enables them to justify their product decisions (either positive or negative) as being "rational" or "objective" product choices. More often than not, however, the physical characteristics they use to judge quality have no intrinsic relationship to the product's quality. For example, though many consumers claim they buy a brand because of its superior taste, they are often unable to identify that brand in blind taste tests. *Consumer Reports* found that consumers often cannot differentiate among various cola beverages and base their preferences on such **extrinsic** cues as pricing, packaging, advertising, and even peer pressure.[27] In the absence of actual experience with a product, consumers often "evaluate" quality on the basis of cues that are external to the product itself, such as price, brand image, manufacturer's image, retail store image, or even the country of origin.

Many consumers use country-of-origin stereotypes to evaluate products (e.g., "German engineering is excellent" or "Japanese cars are reliable").[28] Many consumers believe that a "Made in the U.S.A." label means a product is "superior" or "fairly good." Yet for food products, a foreign image is often more enticing. For example, the elegant image of vichyssoise, a soup created in New York in 1917, is based on the perception that it is a French delicacy. Häagen-Dazs, an American-made ice cream, has been incredibly successful with its made-up (and meaningless) Scandinavian-sounding name. The success of Smirnoff Vodka, made in Connecticut, can be related to its so-called Russian derivation. Sorbet has become a very popular and chic dessert, now that it is no longer called sherbet. There are many other examples that support the notion that American consumers are much more impressed with foreign foods than they are with domestic foods.

Perceived Quality of Services

It is more difficult for consumers to evaluate the quality of services than the quality of products. This is true because of certain distinctive characteristics of services: They are *intangible*, they are *variable*, they are *perishable*, and they are *simultaneously produced and consumed*. To overcome the fact that consumers are unable to compare services side-by-side as they do with competing products, consumers rely on surrogate cues (i.e., extrinsic cues) to evaluate service quality. In evaluating a doctor's services, for example, they note the quality of the office and examining room furnishings, the number (and source) of framed degrees on the wall, the pleasantness of the receptionist and the professionalism of the nurse; all contribute to the consumer's overall evaluation of service quality.

Because the actual quality of services can vary from day to day, from service employee to service employee, and from customer to customer (e.g., in food, in waiter service, in haircuts, even in classes taught by the same professor), marketers try to standardize their services in order to provide consistency of quality. The downside of service standardization is the loss of customized services, which many consumers value.

Unlike products, which are first produced, then sold, and then consumed, most services are first sold, then produced and consumed simultaneously. While a defective product is likely to be detected by factory quality control inspectors before it ever reaches the consumer, a "defective" service is consumed as it is being produced; thus there is little opportunity to correct it. For example, a defective haircut is difficult to correct, just as the negative impression caused by an argument between two service employees in the presence of a customer is difficult to correct.

During peak demand hours, the interactive quality of services often declines, because both the customer and the service provider are hurried and under stress. Without special effort by the service provider to ensure consistency of services during peak hours, service image is likely to decline. Some marketers try to change demand patterns in order to "distribute" the service more equally over time. Long-distance telephone services, for instance, traditionally have offered a discount on telephone calls placed during off-peak hours (for example, after 11:00 p.m. or on weekends); some restaurants offer a significantly less expensive "early-bird" dinner for consumers who come in before 7 p.m. Research suggests that service providers can reduce the perceived waiting time and consequent negative service evaluation by filling the consumer's time. Diners may be invited to study the menu while waiting for a table; patients can view informative videos in the doctor's waiting room.[29]

Some researchers believe that a consumer's evaluation of service quality is a function of the magnitude and direction of the gap between the customer's expectations of service and the customer's assessment (perception) of the service actually delivered.[30] For example, a brand-new graduate student may have certain expectations about the intellectual abilities of her classmates, the richness of classroom discussions, and the school's libraries. Her assessment of the quality of the university is based on her expectations, which in turn are largely based on her own background and experiences. If the university services fall below her expectations, she will view the university as a service provider of poor quality. If her expectations are exceeded, she will view the university as a high-quality educational institution. Some researchers believe that service quality perceptions are a function of the gap between perceived performance and a combination of expectations and desires.[31]

The SERVQUAL scale was designed to measure the gap between customers' expectations of services and their perceptions of the actual service delivered, based upon the following five dimensions: tangibles, reliability, responsiveness, assurance, and empathy.[32] Table 6-1 presents a description of these factors. Since its development, the SERVQUAL scale has been used in numerous studies, though not all of its empirical findings correspond precisely to the five dimensions that the scale is designed to measure. Furthermore, some researchers believe that there are problems in conceptualizing service quality as a "difference" score.[33]

Another scale that measures service quality, called SERVPERF, is based on the consumer's perception of service performance. The SERVPERF scale results in a summated overall service quality score that can be plotted relative to time and specific consumer subgroups (demographic segments).[34] The dimensions along which

TABLE 6-1 SERVQUAL Dimensions for Measuring Service Quality

DIMENSION	DESCRIPTION
• Tangibles	Appearance of physical facilities, equipment, personnel, and communication materials
• Reliability	Ability to perform the promised service dependably and accurately
• Responsiveness	Willingness to help customers and provide prompt service
• Assurance	Knowledge and courtesy of employees and their ability to convey trust and confidence
• Empathy	Caring, individualized attention the firm provides its customers.

Source: Adapted with permission of The Free Press, a division of Simon & Schuster, from Valarie A. Zeithaml, A. Parasuraman, and Leonard L. Berry, *Delivering Quality Service: Balancing Customer Perceptions and Expectations* (New York: The Free Press, 1990). Copyright © 1990 by The Free Press.

consumers evaluate service quality are divided into two groups: the *outcome* dimension (which focuses on the reliable delivery of the core service) and the *process* dimension (which focuses on how the core service is delivered).[35] The process dimension offers the service provider a significant opportunity to exceed customer expectations. For example, while Federal Express provides the same core service as other couriers (the outcome dimension), it provides a superior process dimension through its advanced tracking system, which can provide customers with instant information about the status of their packages at any time between pickup and delivery. Thus, FedEx uses the process dimension to exceed customers' expectations, and has acquired the image of a company that has an important, customer-focused competitive advantage among the many companies providing the same core service.

Researchers have tried to integrate the concepts of *product quality* and *service quality* into an overall *transaction satisfaction index*, on the basis that all product (that is, tangible) purchases contain some element of service beyond the core tangible offering. For example, satisfaction with a retail purchase would include evaluation of the helpfulness and efficiency of the salesperson and the pleasantness of the surroundings. Figure 6-11 presents a conceptual model that proposes that the consumer's overall satisfaction with the transaction is based on an evaluation of service quality, product quality, and price.[36] A study of the relationship between service quality, consumer satisfaction, and purchase intentions found that perceptions of high service quality and high service satisfaction result in a very high level of purchase intentions.[37]

Some consumer theorists believe that service quality and consumer behavioral intentions are related, and that service quality is a determinant of whether the consumer ultimately remains with the company or defects to a competitor.[38] When service quality evaluations are high, the customer's behavioral intentions are favorable to the company, and they are likely to remain customers. When service evaluations are low, the customer's relationship is more likely to weaken, resulting in defection to a competitor. The resulting financial implications should motivate the service provider to give quality service. Figure 6-12 is a conceptual model that depicts the behavioral and financial consequences of service quality as it affects the retention or defection of customers.

FIGURE 6-11

A Conceptual Model of the Components of Transaction Satisfaction

Source: A. Parasuraman, Valarie A. Zeithaml, and Leonard L. Berry, "Reassessment of Expectations as a Comparison Standard in Measuring Service Quality," *Journal of Marketing* 58 (January 1994), 121. Reprinted by permission of the American Marketing Association.

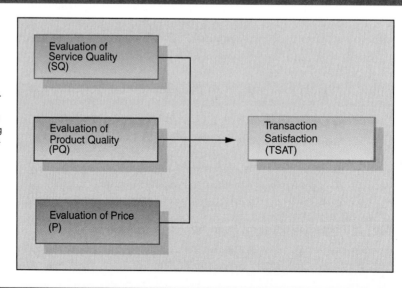

PERCEIVED RISK

Consumers must constantly make decisions regarding what products or services to buy and where to buy them. Because the outcomes (or consequences) of such decisions are often uncertain, the consumer perceives some degree of "risk" in making a purchase decision. **Perceived risk** is defined as the uncertainty that consumers face when they cannot foresee the consequences of their purchase decisions. This definition highlights two relevant dimensions of perceived risk: *uncertainty* and *consequences*.

The degree of risk that consumers perceive and their own tolerance for risk taking are factors that influence their purchase strategies. It should be stressed that consumers are influenced by risks that they *perceive*, whether or not such risks actually exist. Risk that is not perceived—no matter how real or how dangerous—will not influence consumer behavior. Furthermore, the amount of money involved in the purchase is not directly related to the amount of risk perceived. Selecting a new color printer may present as great a risk to a consumer as selecting a new car.

Types of Perceived Risk

The major types of risks that consumers perceive when making product decisions include functional risk, physical risk, financial risk, social risk, psychological risk, and time risk.

> *Functional Risk* is the risk that the product will not perform as expected. ("Will the new electric car operate a full day without needing to be recharged?")
>
> *Physical Risk* is the risk to self and others that the product may pose. ("Is a cellular phone really safe, or does it emit harmful radiation?")
>
> *Financial Risk* is the risk that the product will not be worth its cost. ("Will a new $3,000 computer become obsolescent before the year is over?")
>
> *Social Risk* is the risk that a poor product choice may result in social embarrassment. ("Will my buddies laugh at my new electronic organizer?")
>
> *Psychological Risk* is the risk that a poor product choice will bruise the consumer's ego. ("Will I be embarrassed to invite friends to this tiny apartment?")
>
> *Time Risk* is the risk that the time spent in product search may be wasted if the product does not perform as expected. ("Will I have to go through the shopping effort all over again?")

Perception of Risk Varies

Consumer perception of risk varies, depending on the person, the product, the situation, and the culture. The *amount* of risk perceived depends on the specific consumer. Some consumers tend to perceive high degrees of risk in various consumption situations; others tend to perceive little risk. For example, studies of risk perception among adolescents have found that adolescents who engage in high-risk consumption activities (such as drug use) differ significantly from those who do not engage in high-risk activities.[48] *High-risk perceivers* are often described as *narrow categorizers* because they limit their choices (e.g., product choices) to a few safe alternatives. They would rather exclude some perfectly good alternatives than chance a poor selection. *Low-risk perceivers* have been described as *broad categorizers* because they tend to make their choices from a much wider range of alternatives. They would rather risk a poor selection than limit the number of alternatives from which they can choose. One study concluded that risk preference may be a stable personality trait, with experience a mediating factor in risk perception.[49] For example, individuals who have made money in the stock market are more likely to continue investing (e.g., to perceive less risk) than those who have lost money.

An individual's perception of risk varies with *product categories*. For example, consumers are likely to perceive a higher degree of risk (e.g., functional risk, financial risk, time risk) in the purchase of a high-definition television set than in the purchase of an automobile. In addition to product-category perceived risk, researchers have identified product-specific perceived risk.[50] One study found that consumers perceive service decisions to be riskier than product decisions, particularly in terms of social risk, physical risk, and psychological risk.[51]

The degree of risk perceived by a consumer is also affected by the *shopping situation* (e.g., a traditional retail store, on-line, from catalogs or direct-mail solicitations, or from door-to-door salespeople.) The sharp increase in mail-order catalog sales in recent years suggests that on the basis of positive experiences and word of mouth, consumers now tend to perceive less risk in mail-order shopping than they once did, despite their inability to physically inspect the merchandise before ordering. High risk perceivers are unlikely to purchase items on-line despite the geometric expansion of on-line retail stores.

Culture also affects risk perception. Many Americans feel insecure in shopping center parking lots because of news reports of crimes and carjackings, and the very act of shopping results in a high degree of perceived risk.[52] Not all people around the world exhibit the same level of risk perception. For this reason, marketers who do business in several countries should not generalize the results of consumer risk perception studies conducted in one country to other countries without additional research.

How Consumers Handle Risk

Consumers characteristically develop their own strategies for reducing perceived risk. These risk-reduction strategies enable them to act with increased confidence when making product decisions, even though the consequences of such decisions remain somewhat uncertain. Some of the more common risk-reduction strategies are discussed in the following sections.

Consumers Seek Information Consumers seek information about the product and product category through word-of-mouth communication (from friends and family and from other people whose opinions they value), from salespeople, and from the general media. They spend more time thinking about their choice and search for more information about the product alternatives when they associate a high degree of risk with the purchase. This strategy is straightforward and logical, because the more information the consumer has about the product and the product category, the more predictable the probable consequences, and thus the lower the perceived risk.

Consumers Are Brand Loyal Consumers avoid risk by remaining loyal to a brand with which they have been satisfied instead of purchasing new or untried brands. High-risk perceivers, for example, are more likely to be loyal to their old brands and less likely to purchase newly introduced products.

Consumers Select by Brand Image When consumers have had no experience with a product, they tend to "trust" a favored or well-known brand name. Consumers often think well-known brands are better and are worth buying for the implied assurance of quality, dependability, performance, and service. Marketers' promotional efforts supplement the perceived quality of their products by helping to build and sustain a favorable brand image.

Consumers Rely on Store Image If consumers have no other information about a product, they often trust the judgment of the merchandise buyers of a reputable store and depend on them to have made careful decisions in selecting products for resale. Store image also imparts the implication of product testing and the assurance of service, return privileges, and adjustment in case of dissatisfaction.

Consumers Buy the Most Expensive Model When in doubt, consumers may feel that the most expensive model is probably the best in terms of quality; that is, they equate price with quality. (The price/quality relationship was discussed earlier in this chapter.)

Consumers Seek Reassurance Consumers who are uncertain about the wisdom of a product choice seek reassurance through money-back guarantees, government and private laboratory test results, warranties, and prepurchase trial.[53] For example, it is unlikely that anyone would buy a new model car without a "test drive." Products that do not easily lend themselves to free or limited trial present a challenge to marketers.

The concept of perceived risk has major implications for the introduction of new products. Because high-risk perceivers are less likely to purchase new or innovative products than low-risk perceivers, it is important for marketers to provide such consumers with persuasive risk-reduction strategies, such as a well-known brand name (sometimes achieved through licensing), distribution through reputable retail outlets, informative advertising, publicity stories in the media, impartial test results, free samples, and money-back guarantees.

SUMMARY

Perception is the process by which individuals select, organize, and interpret stimuli into a meaningful and coherent picture of the world. Perception has strategy implications for marketers, because consumers make decisions based on what they perceive, rather than on the basis of objective reality.

The lowest level at which an individual can perceive a specific stimulus is that person's absolute threshold. The minimal difference that can be perceived between two stimuli is called the differential threshold, or just noticeable difference (j.n.d.). Most stimuli are perceived by consumers above the level of their conscious awareness; however, weak stimuli can be perceived below the level of conscious awareness (that is, subliminally). Research refutes the notion that subliminal stimuli affect consumer buying decisions.

Consumers' selection of stimuli from the environment is based on the interaction of their expectations and motives with the stimulus itself. The principle of selective perception includes the following concepts: selective exposure, selective attention, perceptual defense, and perceptual blocking. People usually perceive things they need or want and block the perception of unnecessary, unfavorable, or painful stimuli.

Consumers organize their perceptions into unified wholes according to the principles of Gestalt psychology: figure and ground, grouping, and closure. The interpretation of stimuli is highly subjective and is based on what the consumer expects to see in light of previous experience, on the number of plausible

explanations he or she can envision, on motives and interests at the time of perception, and on the clarity of the stimulus itself. Influences that tend to distort objective interpretation include physical appearances, stereotypes, halo effects, irrelevant cues, first impressions, and the tendency to jump to conclusions.

Just as individuals have perceived images of themselves, they also have perceived images of products and brands. The perceived image of a product or service (that is, its symbolic meaning) is probably more important to its ultimate success than are its actual physical characteristics. Products and services that are perceived favorably have a much better chance of being purchased than products or services with unfavorable or neutral images.

Compared with manufacturing firms, service marketers face several unique problems in positioning and promoting their offerings, such as the service environment and service characteristics (e.g., services are intangible, variable, perishable, and are simultaneously produced and consumed). Regardless of how well positioned a product or service appears to be, the marketer may be forced to reposition it in response to market events, such as new competitive strategies or changing consumer preferences.

Consumers often judge the quality of a product or service on the basis of a variety of informational cues; some are intrinsic to the product (such as color, size, flavor, aroma), while others are extrinsic (e.g., price, store image, brand image, service environment). In the absence of direct experience or other information, consumers often rely on price as an indicator of quality. How a consumer perceives a price—as high, low, or fair—has a strong influence on purchase intentions and satisfaction. Consumers rely on both internal and external reference prices when assessing the fairness of a price. The images of retail stores influence the perceived quality of products they carry, as well as the decisions of consumers as to where to shop.

Consumer imagery extends beyond perceived price and store image to the producers themselves. Manufacturers who enjoy a favorable image generally find that their new products are accepted more readily than those of manufacturers with less favorable or even neutral images.

Consumers often perceive risk in making product selections because of uncertainty as to the consequences of their product decisions. The most frequent types of risk that consumers perceive are functional risk, physical risk, financial risk, social risk, psychological risk, and time risk. Consumer strategies for reducing perceived risk include increased information search, brand loyalty, buying a well-known brand, buying from a reputable retailer, buying the most expensive brand, and seeking reassurance in the form of money-back guarantees, warranties, and prepurchase trial. The concept of perceived risk has important implications for marketers, who can facilitate the acceptance of new products by incorporating risk reduction strategies in their new product promotional campaigns.

DISCUSSION QUESTIONS

1. How does sensory adaptation affect advertising effectiveness? How can marketers overcome sensory adaptation?

2. Describe how manufacturers of chocolate bars can apply their knowledge of the differential threshold to packages and prices during periods of: (a) rising ingredient costs, (b) increasing competition, and (c) consumer nutrition concerns.

3. Does subliminal advertising work? Support your view.

4. How do advertisers use contrast to make sure that their ads are noticed? Would the lack of contrast between the ad and the medium in which it appears help or hinder the effectiveness of the ad? What are the ethical considerations in employing such strategies?

5. a. Discuss the differences between the absolute threshold and the differential threshold.

   b. What is consumer reality?

6. What are the implications of figure-ground relationships for print ads and for on-line ads? How can the figure-ground construct help or interfere with the communication of advertising messages?

7. How is perceptual mapping used in consumer research? Why are marketers sometimes "forced" to reposition their products or services? Illustrate your answers with examples.

8. Why is it more difficult for consumers to evaluate the quality of services than the quality of products?

9. Discuss the roles of extrinsic cues and intrinsic cues in the perceived quality of:

   a. wines   b. restaurants,
   c. shampoo   d. medical services
   e. graduate education.

EXERCISES

1. Find five examples of print advertisements that use emotional stimulus factors to garner attention. For each example, evaluate the effectiveness of the stimulus factors used.

2. What roles do actual product attributes and perceptions of attributes play in positioning a product? Find three different computer ads that stress different product attributes and discuss whether each marketer has effectively positioned its product to communicate a specific image.

3. Construct a two-dimensional perceptual map of your college using the two attributes that were most influ-

ential in your selection. Then, mark the position of your school on the diagram relative to that of another school you considered. Discuss the implications of this perceptual map for the student recruitment function of the university that you did not choose.

4. Select a restaurant where you have recently eaten. Analyze the atmosphere and physical environment of this service establishment. What image does the environment convey? Should the owner change anything to make the environment more appealing to customers? Explain.

KEY TERMS

- **Absolute threshold**
- **Differential threshold (j.n.d.)**
- **Intrinsic versus extrinsic cues**
- **Perceived risk**
- **Perceptual distortion**
- **Perceptual selection, organization, and interpretation**

- **Perceptual mapping**
- **Positioning versus repositioning**
- **Price/quality relationship**
- **Reference prices**
- **Selective perception**
- **Sensory adaptation**

- **Sensory receptors**
- **Subliminal perception**
- **Weber's law**
- **Zeigernik effect**

NOTES

1. C. Douglas Olsen, "Observations: The Sound of Silence: Functions and Use of Silence in Television Advertising," *Journal of Advertising Research* (September–October 1994): 89–95.
2. Eric R. Spangenberg, Ayn E. Crowley, and Pamela W. Henderson, "Improving the Store Environment: Do Olfactory Cues Affect Evaluations and Behaviors?" *Journal of Marketing* 60 (April 1996): 67–80.
3. Bernard Berelson and Gary A. Steiner, *Human Behavior: An Inventory of Scientific Findings* (New York: Harcourt, Brace & World, 1964), 87–130.
4. W. Bevan, "Subliminal Stimulation: A Pervasive Problem for Psychology," *Psychological Bulletin* 61, 2 (1964): 81–99.
5. Sharon E. Beatty and Del I. Hawkins, "Subliminal Stimulation: Some New Data and Interpretation," *Journal of Advertising* 18 (1989): 4–8.
6. Wilson Bryan Key, *Subliminal Seduction* (New York: New American Library, 1973).
7. Myron Gable, Henry T. Wilkens, Lynn Harris, and Richard Feinberg, "An Evaluation of Subliminally Embedded Sexual Stimuli in Graphics," *Journal of Advertising* 16, 1 (1987): 26–31.
8. Kirk H. Smith and Martha Rogers, "Effectiveness of Subliminal Messages in Television Commercials: Two Experiments," *Journal of Applied Psychology* 19, 6 (1994): 866–74.
9. Kathryn T. Theus, "Subliminal Advertising and the Psychology of Processing Unconscious Stimuli: A Review of Research," *Psychology and Marketing* 11, 3 (May–June 1994): 271–90. See also Dennis L. Rosen and Surenra N. Singh, "An Investigation of Subliminal Embed Effect on Multiple Measures of Advertising Effectiveness," *Psychology and Marketing* 9, 2 (March–April 1992): 157–73.
10. Carl L. Witte, Madhavan Parthasarathy, and James W. Gentry, "Subliminal Perception Versus Subliminal Persuasion: A Re-Examination of the Basic Issues," *American Marketing Association* (Summer 1995): 133–38.

See also Jack Haberstroh, *Ice Cube Sex: The Truth about Subliminal Advertising* (Notre Dame, IN: Cross Cultural Publications), 1994.
11. Martha Rogers and Christine A. Seiler, "The Answer Is No: A National Survey of Advertising Practitioners and Their Clients about Whether They Use Subliminal Advertising," *Journal of Advertising Research* (March–April 1994): 36–45; Martha Rogers and Kirk H. Smith, "Public Perceptions of Subliminal Advertising: Why Practitioners Shouldn't Ignore This Issue," *Journal of Advertising Research* (March–April 1993): 10–18. See also Nicolas E. Synodinos, "Subliminal Stimulation: What Does the Public Think about It?" in *Current Issues and Research in Advertising*, vol. 11 (1 and 2), ed. James H. Leigh and Claude R. Martin Jr. (1988): 157–87.
12. Theus, "Subliminal Advertising," 273–74.
13. James T. Heimbach and Jacob Jacoby, "The Zeigernik Effect in Advertising," in *Proceedings of the Third Annual Conference* (Association for Consumer Research), ed. M. Venkatesan (1972): 746–58.
14. Marsha L. Richins, "Social Comparison and the Idealized Images of Advertising," *Journal of Consumer Research* 18 (June 1991): 71–83. See also Mary C. Martin and James W. Gentry, "Stuck in the Model Trap: The Effects of Beautiful Models in Ads on Female Pre-Adolescents and Adolescents," *Journal of Advertising* 26, 2 (Summer 1997): 19–33.
15. Ajay Kalra and Ronald C. Goodstein, "The Impact of Advertising Positioning Strategies on Consumer Price Sensitivity," *Journal of Marketing Research* 35 (May 1998): 210–24.
16. Mary Jo Bitner, "Servicescapes: The Impact of Physical Surroundings on Customers and Employees," *Journal of Marketing* 56 (April 1992): 57–71.
17. Julie Baker, Leonard L. Berry, and A. Parasuraman, "The Marketing Impact of Branch Facility Design," *Journal of Retail Banking* 10, 2 (Summer 1988): 33–42.

18. Marielza Martins and Kent B. Monroe, "Perceived Price Fairness: A New Look at an Old Construct," *Advances in Consumer Research* 21 (1994): 75–78.

19. Dhruv Grewal et al., "The Effects of Price-Comparison Advertising on Buyers' Perceptions of Acquisition Value, Transaction Value, and Behavioral Intentions," *Journal of Marketing* 62 (April 1998): 46–59.

20. Katherine Fraccastoro, Scot Burton, and Abhijit Biswas, "Effective Use of Advertisements Promoting Sales Prices," *Journal of Consumer Marketing* 10, 1 (1993): 61–79.

21. Joel E. Urbany et al., "Transaction Utility Effects: When Quality Is Uncertain," *Journal of the Academy of Marketing Science* 25, 1 (Winter 1997): 45–55.

22. Fraccastoro, "Effective Use of Advertisements," 61–79.

23. Ibid.

24. Abhijit Biswas and Scot Burton, "Consumer Perceptions of Tensile Price Claims in Advertisements: An Assessment of Claim Types Across Different Discount Levels," *Journal of the Academy of Marketing Science* 21, 3 (1993): 217–29.

25. Manjit S. Yadav and Kent B. Monroe, "How Buyers Perceive Savings in a Bundle Price: An Examination of a Bundle's Transaction Value," *Journal of Marketing Research* 30 (August 1993): 350–58.

26. Robert D. Hershey Jr., "Information Age? Maybe Not, When It Comes to Prices," *New York Times*, 23 August 1998, D10.

27. Michael J. McCarthy, "Forget the Ads: Cola Is Cola, Magazine Finds," *The Wall Street Journal*, 24 February 1991, B1.

28. Durairaj Maheswaron, "Country of Origin as a Stereotype: Effects of Consumer Expertise and Attribute Strength on Product Evaluations," *Journal of Consumer Research* 21 (September 1994): 354–65.

29. Shirley Taylor, "Waiting for Service: The Relationship Between Delay and Evaluations of Service," *Journal of Marketing* 58 (April 1994): 56–69. See also Michael K. Hui and David K. Tse, "What to Tell Consumers in Waits of Different Lengths: An Integrative Model of Service Evaluation," *Journal of Marketing* 60 (April 1996): 81–90.

30. Valarie A. Zeithaml, A. Parasuraman, and Leonard L. Berry, *Delivering Quality Service: Balancing Customer Perceptions and Expectations* (New York: The Free Press, 1990).

31. Richard A. Spreng et al., "A Reexamination of the Determinants of Consumer Satisfaction," *Journal of Marketing* 60 (July 1996): 15–32.

32. A. Parasuraman, Leonard L. Berry, and Valarie A. Zeithaml, "Refinement and Reassessment of the SERVQUAL Scale," *Journal of Retailing* 67, 4 (Winter 1991): 420–50. See also James M. Carman, "Consumer Perceptions of Service Quality: An Assessment of the SERVQUAL Dimensions," *Journal of Retailing* 66, 1 (Spring 1990): 33–55.

33. J. Joseph Cronin Jr. and Steven A. Taylor, "SERVPERF versus SERVQUAL: Reconciling Performance-Based and Perceptions-Minus-Expectations Measurement of Service Quality," *Journal of Marketing* 58 (January 1994): 125–31; also William Boulding, Ajay Kalra, Richard Staelin, and Valarie A. Zeithaml, "A Dynamic Process Model of Service Quality: From Expectations to Behavioral Intentions," *Journal of Marketing Research* 30 (February 1993): 7–27; and Kenneth Teas, "Expectations as a Comparison Standard in Measuring Service Quality: An Assessment of a Reassessment," *Journal of Marketing* 58 (January 1994): 132–39.

34. Cronin and Taylor, "SERVPERF versus SERVQUAL," 130.

35. Ibid.

36. A. Parasuraman, Valarie A. Zeithaml, and Leonard L. Berry, "Reassessment of Expectations as a Comparison Standard in Measuring Service Quality: Implications for Further Research," *Journal of Marketing* 58 (January 1994): 111–24.

37. Steven A. Taylor, "Assessing Regression-Based Importance Weights for Quality Perceptions and Satisfaction Judgments in the Presence of Higher Order and/or Interaction Effects," *Journal of Retailing* 73, 1 (1997): 135–39.

38. Valarie A. Zeithaml, Leonard L. Berry, and A. Parasuraman, "The Behavioral Consequences of Service Quality," *Journal of Marketing* 60 (April 1996): 31–46.

39. William Dodds, Kent Monroe, and Dhruv Grewal, "Effects of Price, Brand, and Store Information on Buyers' Product Evaluations," *Journal of Marketing Research* 28 (August 1991): 307–19; Kent Monroe, *Pricing: Making Profitable Decisions*, 2d ed. (New York: McGraw-Hill, 1990). See also Tung-Zong Chang and Albert R. Wildt, "Price, Product Information, and Purchase Intention: An Empirical Study," *Journal of the Academy of Marketing Science* 22, 1 (1994): 16–27.

40. Indrajit Sinha and Wayne S. DeSasrbo, "An Integrated Approach toward the Spatial Model of Perceived Customer Value," *Journal of Marketing Research* 35 (May 1998): 236–49.

41. Donald R. Liechtenstein, Nancy M. Ridgway, and Richard G. Nitemeyer, "Price Perception and Consumer Shopping Behavior: A Field Study," *Journal of Marketing Research* 30 (May 1993): 242.

42. Dodds, Monroe, and Grewal, "Effects of Price," 307–19. See also Noel Mark Lavenka, "Measurement of Consumers' Perceptions of Product Quality, Brand Name and Packaging: Candy Bar Comparisons by Magnitude Estimation," *Marketing Research* 3, 2 (June 1991): 38–45.

43. Joseph W. Alba, Susan M. Broniarczyk, Terence A. Shimp, and Joel E. Urbany, "The Influence of Prior Beliefs, Frequency Cues, and Magnitude Cues on Consumers' Perceptions of Comparative Price Data," *Journal of Consumer Research* 21 (September 1994): 219–35.

44. Ibid.

45. Susan M. Broniarczyk et al., "Consumers' Perceptions of the Assortment Carried in a Grocery Category: The Impact of Item Reduction," *Journal of Marketing Research* 35 (May 1998): 166–76.

46. Julie Baker, Dhruv Grewal, and A. Parasuraman, "The Influence of Store Environment on Quality Inferences and Store Image," *Journal of the Academy of Marketing Science* 22, 4 (1994): 328–39.

47. Frank H. Alpert and Michael A. Kamins, "An Empirical Investigation of Consumer Memory, Attitude and Perceptions Toward Pioneer and Follower Brands," *Journal of Marketing* 59 (October 1995): 34–45.

48. Herbert H. Severson, Paul Slovic, and Sarah Hampson, "Adolescents' Perception of Risk: Understanding and Preventing High Risk Behavior," *Advances in Consumer Research* 20 (1993): 177–82.

49. Elke U. Weber and Richard A. Milliman, "Perceived Risk Attitudes: Relating Risk Perception to Risky Choice," *Management Science* 43, 2 (February 1997): 123–44.

50. Grahame R. Dowling and Richard Staelin, "A Model of Perceived Risk and Intended Risk-Handling Activity," *Journal of Consumer Research* 21 (June 1994): 119–34.

51. Keith B. Murray and John L. Schlacter, "The Impact of Services versus Goods on Consumers' Assessment of Perceived Risk and Variability," *Journal of the Academy of Marketing Sciences* 18 (Winter 1990): 51–65.

52. Arjun Chaudhuri, *Journal of Business Research* 39 (1997): 81–92.

53. Jagdish Agraswal et al., "The Relationship Between Warranty and Product Reliability," *Journal of Consumer Affairs* 30, 2 (Winter 1996): 421–43.

CHAPTER 7
Consumer Learning

■ ■

How individuals learn is a matter of great interest and importance to academicians, to psychologists, to consumer researchers, and to marketers. The reason that marketers are concerned with how individuals learn is that they are vitally interested in teaching them, in their roles as consumers, about products—product attributes and potential consumer benefits; where to buy them, how to use them, how to maintain them, and even how to dispose of them. They are also vitally interested in how effectively they have taught consumers to prefer their brands and to differentiate their products from competitive offerings. Marketing strategies are based on communicating with the consumer—directly, through advertisements, and indirectly, through product appearance, packaging, price, and distribution channels. Marketers want their communications to be noted, believed, remembered, and recalled. For these reasons, they are interested in every aspect of the learning process.

However, despite the fact that learning is all-pervasive in our lives, there is no single, universal theory of how people learn. Instead, there are two major schools of thought concerning the learning process: one consists of behavioral theories, the other of cognitive theories. Cognitive theorists view learning as a function of purely mental processes, whereas behavioral theorists focus almost exclusively on observable behaviors (responses) that occur as the result of exposure to stimuli.

In this chapter, we examine the two general categories of learning theory: behavioral learning theory and cognitive learning theory. Although these theories differ markedly in a number of essentials, each theory offers insights to marketers on how to shape their messages to consumers to bring about desired purchase behavior. We also discuss how consumers store, retain, and retrieve information, and how learning is measured. The chapter concludes with a discussion of how marketers use learning theories in their marketing strategies.

CONSUMER LEARNING

Since not all learning theorists agree on how learning takes place, it is difficult to come up with a generally acceptable definition of learning. From a marketing perspective, however, consumer learning can be thought of as the process by which individuals acquire the purchase and consumption knowledge and experience that they apply to future related behavior. Several points in this definition are worth noting.

First, consumer learning is a *process*; that is, it continually evolves and changes as a result of newly acquired *knowledge* (which may be gained from reading, from discussions, from observation, from thinking) or from actual *experience*. Both newly acquired knowledge and personal experience serve as feedback to the individual and provide the basis for future behavior in similar situations. The definition makes clear that learning results from acquired knowledge or experience. This qualification distinguishes learning from instinctive behavior, such as sucking in infants.

The role of *experience* in learning does not mean that all learning is deliberately sought. Though much learning is *intentional* (that is, it is acquired as the result of a careful search for information), a great deal of learning is also *incidental*, acquired by accident or without much effort. For example, some ads may induce learning (e.g., of brand names), even though the consumer's attention is elsewhere (on a magazine article rather than on the advertisement on the facing page). Other ads are sought out and carefully read by consumers contemplating an important purchase decision.

The term *learning* encompasses the total range of learning, from simple, almost reflexive responses to the learning of abstract concepts and complex problem solving. Most learning theorists recognize the existence of different types of learning and explain the differences through the use of distinctive models of learning.

Despite their different viewpoints, learning theorists in general agree that in order for learning to occur, certain basic elements must be present. The elements included in most learning theories are *motivation, cues, response*, and *reinforcement*. These concepts are discussed first because they tend to recur in the theories discussed later in this chapter.

MOTIVATION

The concept of **motivation** is important to learning theory. Remember, motivation is based on needs and goals. Motivation acts as a spur to learning. For example, men and women who want to become good tennis players are motivated to learn all they can about tennis and to practice whenever they can. They may seek information concerning the prices, quality, and characteristics of tennis racquets if they "learn" that a good racquet is instrumental to playing a good game. Conversely, individuals who are not interested in tennis are likely to ignore all information related to the game. The goal object (proficiency in tennis) simply has no relevance for them. The degree of relevance, or *involvement*, determines the consumer's level of motivation to search for knowledge or information about a product or service. Uncovering consumer motives is one of the prime tasks of marketers, who then try to teach motivated consumer segments why and how their products will fulfill the consumer's needs. (Involvement theory, as it has come to be known, will be discussed later in the chapter.)

CUES

If motives serve to stimulate learning, **cues** are the stimuli that give direction to these motives. An advertisement for a tennis camp may serve as a cue for tennis buffs, who may suddenly "recognize" that attending tennis camp is a concentrated way to improve their game while taking a vacation. The ad is the cue, or stimulus, that suggests a specific way to satisfy a salient motive. In the marketplace, price, styling, packaging, advertising, and store displays all serve as cues to help consumers fulfill their needs in product-specific ways.

Cues serve to direct consumer drives when they are consistent with consumer expectations. Marketers must be careful to provide cues that do not upset those expectations. For example, consumers expect designer clothes to be expensive and to be sold in upscale retail stores. Thus, a high-fashion designer should sell his or her clothes only through exclusive stores and advertise only in upscale fashion magazines. Each aspect of the marketing mix must reinforce the others if cues are to serve as the stimuli that guide consumer actions in the direction desired by the marketer.

RESPONSE

How individuals react to a drive or cue—how they behave—constitutes their **response**. Learning can occur even when responses are not overt. The automobile manufacturer who provides consistent cues to a consumer may not always succeed in stimulating a purchase. However, if the manufacturer succeeds in forming a favorable image of a particular automobile model in the consumer's mind, when the consumer is ready to buy, it is likely that he or she will consider that make or model.

A response is not tied to a need in a one-to-one fashion. Indeed, as was discussed in chapter 4, a need or motive may evoke a whole variety of responses. For example, there are many ways to respond to the need for physical exercise besides playing tennis. Cues provide some direction, but there are many cues competing for the consumer's attention. Which response the consumer makes depends heavily on previous learning; that, in turn, depends on how related responses were reinforced previously.

REINFORCEMENT

Reinforcement increases the likelihood that a specific response will occur in the future as the result of particular cues or stimuli. If a college student finds that an advertised brand of pain remedy has enabled him to run in a marathon despite a knee injury, he is more likely to buy the advertised brand should he suffer another injury. Clearly, through positive reinforcement, learning has taken place, since the pain remedy lived up to expectations. On the other hand, if the pain remedy had not alleviated his pain when he first used it, the student would have no reason to associate the brand with pain relief in the future. Because of the absence of reinforcement, it is unlikely that he would buy that brand again, despite extensive advertising or store display cues for the product.

With these basic principles established, we can now discuss some well-known theories or models of how learning occurs.

■■■■ BEHAVIORAL LEARNING THEORIES

Behavioral learning theories are sometimes referred to as **stimulus-response** theories because they are based on the premise that observable responses to specific external stimuli signal that learning has taken place. When a person acts (responds) in a predictable way to a known stimulus, he or she is said to have "learned." Behavioral theories are not so much concerned with the process of learning as they are with the inputs and outcomes of learning; that is, in the stimuli that consumers select from the environment and the observable behaviors that result. Two behavioral theories with great relevance to marketing are **classical conditioning** and **instrumental** (or **operant**) **conditioning**.

CLASSICAL CONDITIONING

Early classical conditioning theorists regarded all organisms (both animal and human) as relatively passive entities that could be taught certain behaviors through repetition (or "conditioning"). In everyday speech, the word *conditioning* has come to mean a

FIGURE 7-3
A. Product Line Extensions;
B. Product Form Extensions;
C. Product Category
Extension

Researchers report that the number of different products affiliated with a brand may actually strengthen the brand name, as long as the company maintains a quality image across all brand extensions. Failure to do so is likely, in the long run, to negatively affect consumer confidence and evaluations of all the brand offerings.

Family Branding. Family branding—the practice of marketing a whole line of company products under the same brand name—is another strategy that capitalizes on the consumer's ability to generalize favorable brand associations from one product to the next. The Campbell's Soup Company, for example, continues to add new food products to its product line under the Campbell's brand name, achieving ready acceptance for the new products from satisfied consumers of other Campbell's food products. The Ralph Lauren designer label on men's and women's clothing helps to achieve ready acceptance for these products in the upscale sportswear market.

Procter & Gamble (P&G) was built on the strength of its many individual brands in the same product category (such as laundry detergents and cleansers). Now it focuses on the category-wide benefits of its products, using the combined weight of its brands to come up with a more powerful message directed against competitive products. P&G has effectively moved from *brand management* to *category management*. At the same time, it is consolidating its product lines, selling off marginal and second-tier brands, and standardizing product formulas. By simplifying their product offerings, P&G management has cut costs and increased market share in many categories.[10]

Retail private branding often achieves the same effect as family branding. For example, Wal-Mart used to advertise that its stores carried only "brands you trust." Now, the name Wal-Mart itself has become a "brand" that consumers have confidence in, and the name confers brand value on Wal-Mart's store brands.

Licensing. Licensing—allowing a well-known brand name to be affixed to products of another manufacturer—is a marketing strategy that operates on the principle of stimulus generalization. The names of designers, manufacturers, celebrities, corporations, and even cartoon characters are attached for a fee (i.e., "rented") to a variety of products, enabling the licensees to achieve instant recognition and implied quality for the licensed products. Some successful licensors include Liz Claiborne, Tommy Hilfiger,

Calvin Klein, and Christian Dior, whose names appear on an exceptionally wide variety of products, from sheets to shoes and luggage to perfume. Figure 7-4 shows an ad for eyeglasses bearing the name of the well-known shoe manufacturer Kenneth Cole.

Corporations also license their names and trademarks, usually for some form of brand extension, where the name of the corporation is licensed to the maker of a related product and thereby enters a new product category (e.g., Godiva Chocolates licensed its name for Godiva Liqueur). Corporations also license their names for purely promotional licensing, in which popular company logos (such as "Always Coca-Cola") are stamped on clothing, toys, coffee mugs, and the like. Recently, magazines have been licensing their names to manufacturers of products similar to the magazines' own publishing focus: *Better Homes and Gardens* gardening tools, *Popular Mechanics* work boots, and *Martha Stewart Living* flowerpots. According to the Licensing Industry Manufacturers Association, licensed branded goods accounted for $80 billion in retail sales in the United States in 1997.[11]

Municipal and state governments have begun licensing their names to achieve new sources of revenue. For example, the city of Atlanta licensed its name to Visa USA for the 1996 Summer Olympics. The Vatican Library licenses its name for a variety of products from luggage to bed linens, the Mormon Church has expanded its licensing activities to apparel and home decorating items, and Britain's Queen Elizabeth II has agreed to extend the licensed name "House of Windsor" to furniture and Scottish throw rugs.

FIGURE 7-4
Shoe Manufacturer
Licenses Its Name

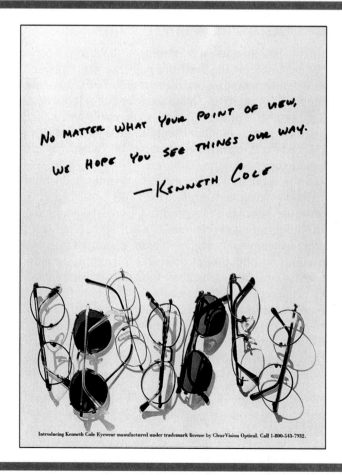

The increase in licensing has made *counterfeiting* a booming business, as counterfeiters add well-known licensor names to a variety of products without benefit of contract or quality control. Aside from the loss of sales revenue because of counterfeiting, the authentic brand also suffers the consequences associated with zero quality control over counterfeit products that bear their names. For example, a counterfeit beer sold in China under the label Pabst Blue Ribbon was contaminated and resulted in at least one death and dozens of illnesses, thus endangering the quality image of Pabst worldwide.[12] Counterfeiting has spread to many product categories, and a great deal of counterfeit merchandise is virtually identical to the original.

Generalizing Usage Situations. Not only are marketers trying to generalize positive associations for their brand name through product line extensions and product category extensions, but some marketers are also trying to generalize the usage situations of their well-known brands. For example, Kellogg's is trying to persuade consumers that its dry cereals are good snack foods for any time of the day. Similarly, Florida citrus growers tried to persuade consumers that orange juice was "not just for breakfast anymore," and Coca-Cola tried to persuade consumers that Coke provided a good caffeine boost at breakfast.

Stimulus Discrimination Stimulus discrimination is the opposite of stimulus generalization and results in the selection of a specific stimulus from among similar stimuli. The consumer's ability to discriminate among similar stimuli is the basis of *positioning* strategy (discussed in chapter 6), which seeks to establish a unique image for a brand in the consumer's mind.

Positioning. In our overcommunicated society, the key to stimulus discrimination is effective positioning, a major competitive advantage. The image—or position—that a product or service holds in the mind of the consumer is critical to its success. When a marketer targets consumers with a strong communications program that stresses the unique ways in which its product will satisfy the consumer's needs, it wants the consumer to differentiate its product from among competitive products on the shelf. Unlike the imitator who hopes consumers will *generalize* their perceptions and attribute special characteristics of the market leader's products to its own products, market leaders want the consumer to *discriminate* among similar stimuli. Major marketers are constantly vigilant concerning store brand look-alikes, and they quickly file suit against retailers that they believe are cannibalizing their sales. They want their products to be recognized as uniquely fulfilling consumers' needs. The favorable attitudes resulting from effective positioning and stimulus discrimination are usually retained long enough to influence future purchase behavior.[13]

Product Differentiation. Most product differentiation strategies are designed to distinguish a product or brand from that of competitors on the basis of an attribute that is relevant, meaningful, and valuable to consumers. However, many marketers also successfully differentiate their brands on an attribute that may actually be irrelevant to creating the implied benefit, such as a noncontributing ingredient or a color.[14]

It often is quite difficult to unseat a brand leader once stimulus discrimination has occurred. One explanation is that the leader is usually first in the market and has had a longer period to "teach" consumers (through advertising and selling) to associate the brand name with the product. In general, the longer the period of learning—of associating a brand name with a specific product—the more likely the consumer is to discriminate and the less likely to generalize the stimulus. Figure 7-5 is an example of stimulus discrimination.

FIGURE 7-5
Stimulus Discrimination

The principles of classical conditioning provide the theoretical underpinnings for many marketing applications. Repetition, stimulus generalization, and stimulus discrimination are all major applied concepts that help to explain consumer behavior in the marketplace. However, they do not explain all behavioral consumer learning. Although a great deal of consumer behavior (for example, the purchase of branded convenience goods) is shaped to some extent by repeated advertising messages stressing a unique competitive advantage, other purchase behavior results from evaluation of product alternatives. Our assessments of products are often based on the degree of satisfaction—the rewards—we experience as a result of making specific purchases—in other words, from *instrumental conditioning*.

INSTRUMENTAL CONDITIONING

Like classical conditioning, instrumental conditioning requires a link between a stimulus and a response. However, in instrumental conditioning, the stimulus that results in the most satisfactory response is the one that is learned.

Instrumental learning theorists believe that learning occurs through a trial-and-error process, with habits formed as a result of rewards received for certain responses or behaviors. This model of learning applies to many situations in which consumers learn about products, services, and retail stores. For example, consumers learn which stores carry the type of clothing they prefer at prices they can afford to pay by shopping in a number of stores. Once they find a store that carries clothing that meets their needs, they are likely to patronize that store to the exclusion of others. Every time they purchase a shirt or a sweater there that they really like, their store loyalty is rewarded (reinforced), and their patronage of that store is more likely to be repeated. While classical conditioning is useful in explaining how consumers learn very simple kinds of behaviors, instrumental conditioning is more helpful in explaining complex, goal-directed activities.

The name most closely associated with **instrumental (operant) conditioning** is that of the American psychologist B. F. Skinner. According to Skinner, most individual learning occurs in a controlled environment in which individuals are "rewarded" for choosing an appropriate behavior. In consumer behavior terms, instrumental conditioning suggests that consumers learn by means of a trial-and-error process in which some purchase behaviors result in more favorable outcomes (i.e., rewards) than other purchase behaviors. A favorable experience is *instrumental* in teaching the individual to repeat a specific behavior.

Like Pavlov, Skinner developed his model of learning by working with animals. Small animals, such as rats and pigeons, were placed in his "Skinner box"; if they made appropriate movements (for instance, if they depressed levers or pecked keys), they received food (a positive reinforcement). Skinner and his many adherents have done amazing things with this simple learning model, including teaching pigeons to play Ping-Pong, and even to dance. In a marketing context, the consumer who tries several brands and styles of jeans before finding a style that fits her figure (positive reinforcement) has engaged in instrumental learning. Presumably, the brand that fits best is the one she will continue to buy. This model of instrumental conditioning is presented in Figure 7-6.

Reinforcement of Behavior

Skinner distinguished two types of reinforcement (or reward) that influence the likelihood that a response will be repeated. The first type, *positive reinforcement*, consists of events that strengthen the likelihood of a specific response. Using a shampoo that leaves your hair feeling silky and clean is likely to result in a repeat purchase of the shampoo. *Negative reinforcement* is an unpleasant or negative outcome that also serves to *encourage* a specific behavior. An advertisement that shows a model with wrinkled skin is designed to encourage consumers to buy and use the advertised skin cream.

Fear appeals in ad messages are examples of negative reinforcement. Many life insurance commercials rely on negative reinforcement to encourage the purchase of life insurance: The ads warn husbands of the dire consequences to their wives and children in the event of their sudden death. Marketers of headache remedies use negative reinforcement when they illustrate the unpleasant symptoms of an unrelieved headache, as do marketers of mouthwash when they show the loneliness suffered by someone with bad breath. In each of these cases, the consumer is encouraged to avoid the negative consequences by buying the advertised product.

FIGURE 7-6

A Model of Instrumental Conditioning

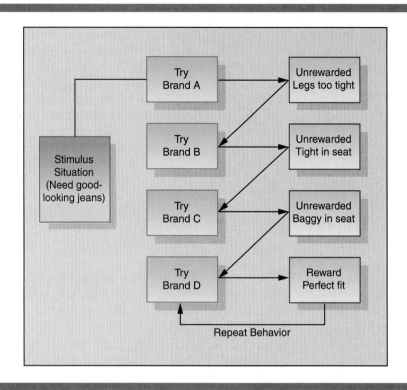

Either positive or negative reinforcement can be used to elicit a desired response. However, negative reinforcement should not be confused with punishment, which is designed to *discourage* behavior. For example, parking tickets are not negative reinforcement; they are a form of "punishment" designed to discourage drivers from parking illegally.

Forgetting and Extinction When a learned response is no longer reinforced, it diminishes to the point of *extinction*; that is, to the point at which the link between the stimulus and the expected reward is eliminated. If a consumer is no longer satisfied with the service a retail store provides, the link between the stimulus (the store) and the response (expected satisfaction) is no longer reinforced, and there is little likelihood that the consumer will return. When behavior is no longer reinforced, it is "unlearned." There is a difference, however, between extinction and *forgetting*. A person who has not visited a once-favorite restaurant for a very long time may simply forget how much he used to enjoy eating there, and not think to return. Thus, his behavior is unlearned because of lack of use, rather than lack of reinforcement. Forgetting is often related to the passage of time; this is known as the process of *decay*. Marketers can overcome forgetting through repetition, and can combat extinction through the deliberate enhancement of consumer satisfaction.

Strategic Applications of Instrumental Conditioning

Marketers effectively utilize the concepts of consumer instrumental learning when they provide positive reinforcement by assuring consumer satisfaction with the product, the service, and the total buying experience.

Customer Satisfaction (Reinforcement) The objective of all marketing efforts should be to maximize customer satisfaction. Marketers must be certain to provide the best possible product for the money, and to avoid raising consumer expectations for product performance beyond what the product can deliver. Aside from the experience of using the product itself, consumers can receive reinforcement from other elements in the purchase situation, such as the environment in which the transaction or service takes place, the attention and service provided by employees, and the amenities provided. For example, an upscale beauty salon may provide a beautiful environment, have attentive stylists and manicurists, serve coffee and other soft drinks to waiting clients, and provide free local telephone service at each hairdressing station. Even if the styling outcome is not so great, the client may feel so pampered with the atmosphere and service that she looks forward to returning. On the other hand, even with all of the other positive reinforcements in place, if the salon's employees are so busy talking with each other while the service is being rendered that the client feels ignored, she is not likely to return.

Some hotels provide reinforcement to guests in the form of small amenities, such as chocolates on the pillow or bottled water on the dresser; others send platters of fruit or even bottles of wine to returning guests to show their appreciation for continued patronage. Most frequent shopper programs are based on enhancing positive reinforcement and encouraging continued patronage. The more a consumer uses the service, the greater the rewards. Kellogg's provides a frequent user program by including coupons on the top of its cereal boxes that can be accumulated and exchanged for various premiums, such as a coffee mug or denim shirt emblazoned with the company's logo.

Relationship marketing—developing a close personalized relationship with customers—is another form of nonproduct reinforcement. Knowing that she will be advised of a forthcoming sale, or that selected merchandise will be set aside for her next visit, cements the loyalty that a consumer may have for a retail store. The ability to telephone his "personal" banker to transfer funds between accounts or to make other banking transactions without coming into the bank reinforces the satisfaction a consumer may have with his bank.

Reinforcement Schedules Marketers have found that product quality must be consistently high and provide customer satisfaction with each use for desired consumer behavior to continue. However, they have also discovered that some nonproduct rewards do not have to be offered each time the transaction takes place; even an occasional reward provides reinforcement and encourages consumer patronage. For example, airlines may occasionally upgrade a passenger at the gate, or a clothing discounter may from time to time announce a one-hour sale over the store loudspeaker. The promise of possibly receiving a reward provides positive reinforcement and encourages consumer patronage.

Marketers have identified three types of reinforcement schedules: total (or continuous) reinforcement, systematic (fixed ratio) reinforcement, and random (variable ratio) reinforcement. Needless to say, the basic product or service rendered is expected to provide total reinforcement each time it is used. Another example of a total (or continuous) reinforcement schedule is the free after-dinner drink always served to patrons at certain restaurants.

A *fixed ratio* reinforcement schedule provides reinforcement every "nth" time the product or service is purchased (say, every third time). For example, Staples sends a credit voucher to account holders every 3 months based on a percentage of the previous quarter's purchases. A *variable ratio* reinforcement schedule rewards consumers on a random basis or on an average frequency basis (such as every third or tenth transaction.) Gambling casinos operate on the basis of variable ratios. People pour money into slot machines (which are programmed to pay off on a variable ratio), hoping for the big win. Variable ratios tend to engender high rates of desired behavior and are somewhat resistant to extinction—perhaps because, for many consumers, hope springs eternal. Other examples of variable ratio schedules include lotteries, sweepstakes, door prizes, and contests that require certain consumer behaviors for eligibility.

Shaping. The reinforcement of behaviors that must be performed by consumers *before* the desired behavior can be performed is called *shaping*. Shaping increases the probabilities that certain desired consumer behavior will occur. For example, retailers recognize that they must first attract customers to their stores before they can expect them to do the bulk of their shopping there. Many retailers provide some form of preliminary reinforcement ("shaping") to encourage consumers to just visit their store. For example, some retailers offer "loss leaders"—popular products at severely discounted prices—to the first hundred or so customers to arrive, since those customers are likely to stay to do much of their shopping there. By reinforcing the behavior that's needed to enable the targeted consumer behavior to take place, marketers increase the probability that the desired behavior will occur. Car dealers recognize that in order to sell new model cars, they must first encourage people to visit their showrooms and to test-drive their cars. Hopefully, the test-drive will result in a sale. Using shaping principles, many car dealers encourage showroom visits by providing small gifts (such as key chains and lotteries), larger gifts (a $10 check) to test-drive the car, and a rebate check upon placement of an order. They use a multistep shaping process to achieve desired consumer learning.

Massed versus Distributed Learning As illustrated previously, *timing* has an important influence on consumer learning. Should a learning schedule be spread out over a period of time (*distributed learning*), or should it be "bunched up" all at once (*massed learning*)? The question is an important one for advertisers planning a media schedule, because massed advertising produces more initial learning, whereas a distributed schedule usually results in learning that persists longer. When advertisers want an immediate impact (e.g., to introduce a new product or to counter a competitor's blitz campaign), they generally use a massed schedule to hasten consumer learning. However, when the goal is long-term repeat buying on a regular basis, a distributed schedule is preferable. A distributed schedule, with ads repeated on a regular basis, usually results in more long-term learning and is relatively immune to extinction.

MODELING OR OBSERVATIONAL LEARNING

Learning theorists have noted that a considerable amount of learning takes place in the absence of direct reinforcement, either positive or negative, through a process psychologists call **modeling** or **observational learning** (also called *vicarious learning*). They observe how others behave in response to certain situations (stimuli) and the ensuing results (reinforcement) that occur, and they imitate (model) the positively-reinforced behavior when faced with similar situations.

Modeling, then, is the process through which individuals learn behavior by observing the behavior of others and the consequences of such behavior. Their role models are usually people they admire because of such traits as appearance, accomplishment, skill, even social class.

Children learn much of their social behavior and consumer behavior by observing their older siblings or their parents. They imitate the behavior of those they see rewarded, expecting to be rewarded similarly if they adopt the same behavior.

Advertisers recognize the importance of observational learning in their selection of models—whether celebrities or unknowns. If a teenager sees an ad that depicts social success as the outcome of using a certain brand of shampoo, she will want to buy it. If her brother sees a commercial that shows a muscular young athlete eating Wheaties—"the breakfast of champions"—he will want some too. Indeed, vicarious (or observational) learning is the basis of much of today's advertising. Consumer models with whom the target audience can identify are shown achieving positive outcomes to common problem situations through the use of the advertised product (see Figure 7-7.)

FIGURE 7-7
Vicarious Learning

Sometimes ads depict negative consequences for certain types of behavior. This is particularly true of public policy ads, which may show the negative consequences of smoking, of driving too fast, of taking drugs. By observing the actions of others and the resulting consequences, consumers learn vicariously to recognize appropriate behavior.

■■■■ COGNITIVE LEARNING THEORY

Not all learning takes place as the result of repeated trials. A considerable amount of learning takes place as the result of consumer thinking and problem solving. Sudden learning is also a reality. When confronted with a problem, we sometimes see the solution instantly. More often, however, we are likely to search for information on which to base a decision, and we carefully evaluate what we learn in order to make the best decision possible for our purposes.

Learning based on mental activity is called **cognitive learning**. Cognitive learning theory holds that the kind of learning most characteristic of human beings is problem solving, which enables individuals to gain some control over their environment. Unlike *behavioral learning theory*, *cognitive theory* holds that learning involves complex mental processing of information. Instead of stressing the importance of repetition or the association of a reward with a specific response, cognitive theorists emphasize the role of motivation and mental processes in producing a desired response.[15] Figure 7-8 presents an ad designed to appeal to cognitive processing.

INFORMATION PROCESSING

Just as a computer processes information received as input, so too does the human mind process the information it receives as input. **Information processing** is related to both the consumer's cognitive ability and the complexity of the information to be processed. Consumers process product information by attributes, brands, comparisons between brands, or a combination of these factors. While the attributes included in the brand's message and the number of available alternatives influence the intensity or degree of information processing, consumers with higher cognitive ability apparently acquire more product information and are more capable of integrating information on several product attributes than consumers with lesser ability.

Individuals also differ in terms of imagery—that is, in their ability to form mental images—and these differences influence their ability to recall information. Individual differences in imagery processing can be measured with tests of imagery vividness (the ability to evoke clear images), processing style (preference for and frequency of visual versus verbal processing), and tests of daydream (fantasy) content and frequency.[16]

The more experience a consumer has with a product category, the greater his or her ability to make use of product information. Greater familiarity with the product category also increases cognitive ability and learning during a new purchase decision, particularly with regard to technical information. Some consumers learn by analogy; that is, they transfer knowledge about products they are familiar with to new or unfamiliar products in order to enhance their understanding.[17] One study found that when people exert more cognitive effort in processing information about an alternative, they experience a process-induced negative affect toward that alternative, and are more likely to choose a product that requires less effort to evaluate. However, the negative affect did not influence product choice when there was a clearly superior alternative.[18]

FIGURE 7-8
Cognitive Appeal

How Consumers Store, Retain and Retrieve Information

Of central importance to the processing of information is the human memory. A basic research concern of most cognitive scientists is discovering how information gets stored in memory, how it is retained, and how it is retrieved.

Structure of Memory Because information processing occurs in stages, it is generally believed that there are separate and sequential "storehouses" in memory where information is kept temporarily before further processing: a *sensory store*, a *short-term store*, and a *long-term store*.

Sensory Store. All data come to us through our senses; however, the senses do not transmit whole images as a camera does. Instead, each sense receives a fragmented piece of information (such as the smell, color, shape, and feel of a flower) and transmits it to the brain in parallel, where the perceptions of a single instant are synchronized and perceived as a single image, in a single moment of time.[19] The image of a sensory input lasts for just a second or two in the mind's sensory store. If it is not processed, it is lost immediately. As noted in chapter 6, we are constantly bombarded with stimuli from the environment, and subconsciously block out a great deal of information that we do not "need" or cannot use. For marketers, this means that although it is relatively easy to get information into the consumer's sensory store, it is difficult to make a lasting impression. Furthermore, studies suggest that the brain automatically and unconsciously "tags" all perceptions with a value, either positive or negative; this evaluation, added to the initial perception in the first microsecond of cognition, tends to remain unless further information is processed.[20] This would explain why first impressions tend to last and why it's hazardous to introduce a product prematurely into the marketplace.

Short-Term Store. The short-term store (known as *working memory*) is the stage of real memory in which information is processed and held for just a brief period. Anyone who has ever looked up a number in a telephone book, only to forget it just before dialing, knows how briefly information lasts in short-term storage. If information in the short-term store undergoes the process known as *rehearsal* (that is, the silent, mental repetition of information), it is then transferred to the long-term store. The transfer process takes from 2 to 10 seconds. If information is not rehearsed and transferred, it is lost in about 30 seconds or less. The amount of information that can be held in short-term storage is limited to about four or five items.

Long-Term Store. In contrast to the short-term store, where information lasts only a few seconds, the long-term store retains information for relatively extended periods of time. Although it is possible to forget something within a few minutes after the information has reached long-term storage, it is more common for data in long-term storage to last for days, weeks, or even years. Almost all of us, for example, can remember the name of our first-grade teacher. Figure 7-9 depicts the transfer of information received by the sensory store, through the short-term store, to long-term storage.

Rehearsal and Encoding. The amount of information available for delivery from short-term storage to long-term storage depends on the amount of **rehearsal** it is given. Failure to rehearse an input, either by repeating it or by relating it to other data, can result in fading and eventual loss of the information. Information can also be lost because of competition for attention. For example, if the short-term store receives a great number of inputs simultaneously from the sensory store, its capacity may be reduced to only two or three pieces of information.

The purpose of rehearsal is to hold information in short-term storage long enough for encoding to take place. **Encoding** is the process by which we select a word or visual image to represent a perceived object. Marketers, for example, help consumers encode brands by using brand symbols. Kellogg's uses Tony the Tiger on its Frosted Flakes; the Green Giant Company has its Jolly Green Giant. Dell Computer turns the *e* in its logo on its side for quick name recognition; Microsoft uses a stylized window, presumably on the world.

FIGURE 7-9
Information Processing and Memory Stores

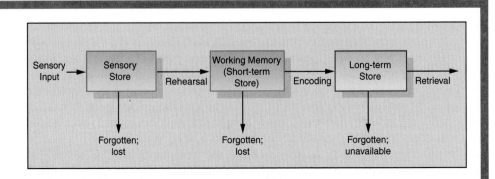

"Learning" a picture takes less time than learning verbal information, but both types of information are important in forming an overall mental image. A print ad with both an illustration and body copy is more likely to be encoded and stored than an illustration without verbal information. A study that examined the effects of visual and verbal advertising found that when advertising copy and illustrations focus on different product attributes, the illustrations disproportionately influence consumer inferences.[21] Another study found that high-imagery copy had greater recall than low-imagery copy, whether or not it was accompanied by an illustration; for low-imagery copy, however, illustrations were an important factor in audience recall.[22]

Researchers have found that the encoding of a commercial is related to the context of the TV program during (or adjacent to) which it is shown. Some parts of a program may require viewers to commit a larger portion of their cognitive resources to processing (for example, when a dramatic event takes place versus a casual conversation). When viewers commit more cognitive resources to the program itself, they encode and store less of the information conveyed by a commercial. This suggests that commercials requiring relatively little cognitive processing may be more effective within or adjacent to a dramatic program setting than commercials requiring more elaborate processing.[23] Other research indicates that viewers who are very involved with a television show respond more positively to commercials adjacent to that show, and have more positive purchase intentions.[24]

Men and women exhibit different encoding patterns. For example, although women are more likely than men to recall TV commercials depicting a social relationship theme, there is no difference in recall among men and women for commercials that focus on the product itself.[25]

When consumers are presented with too much information (called *information overload*), they may encounter difficulty in encoding and storing it all. Findings suggest that it is difficult for consumers to remember product information from ads for new brands in heavily advertised categories.[26] Consumers can become cognitively overloaded when they are given a lot of information in a limited time. The result of this overload is confusion, resulting in poor purchase decisions.

Retention Information does not just sit in long-term storage waiting to be retrieved. Instead, information is constantly organized and reorganized as new links between chunks of information are forged. In fact, many information-processing theorists view the long-term store as a network consisting of nodes (i.e., concepts), with links among them. Figure 7-10 is a representation of long-term storage of information about personal computers, showing nodes (e.g., the concepts: *models*, *monitors*, *manufacturers*, *software*, *operating systems*, *printers*) connected by links (e.g., for software: *word processing*, *databases*, *graphics*, *games*, *spreadsheets*). As individuals gain more knowledge about computers, they expand their network of relationships, and sometimes their search for additional information. This process is known as *activation*, which involves relating new data to old to make the material more meaningful. Consumer memory for the name of a product may also be activated by relating it to the spokesperson used in its advertising. For many people, Michael Jordan means Nike sneakers. The total package of associations brought to mind when a cue is activated is called a *schema*. Research has found that older adults appear to be more reliant on schema-based information-processing strategies than younger adults.[27]

Product information stored in memory tends to be brand based, and consumers interpret new information in a manner consistent with the way in which it is already organized.[28] Consumers are confronted with thousands of new products each year, and their information search is often dependent upon how similar or dissimilar (discrepant) these products are to product categories already stored in memory. One

FIGURE 7-10

Conceptualization of Long-Term Storage of Personal Computer Information

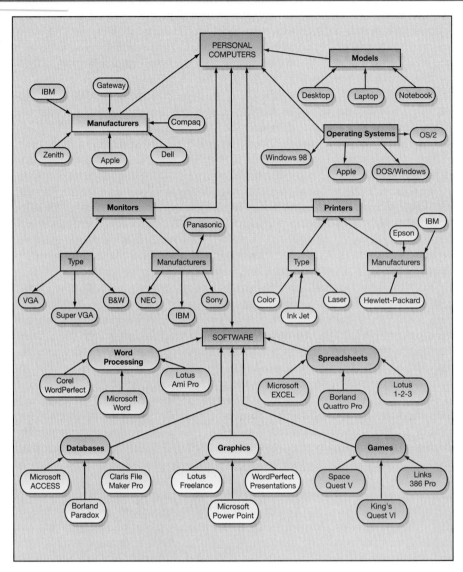

study found that at a moderate level of discrepancy, consumers are more likely to examine a relevant set of attributes in greater depth than to search for new information on a broader range of attributes.[29] Another study found that consumers have better recall of new product information for familiar brands.[30] This underscores the fact that established brands have important advantages in advertising: Consumers are more likely to recall the information they receive on new products bearing a familiar brand name, and their memory is less affected by exposure to competitive ads.

Consumers recode what they have already encoded to include larger amounts of information (*chunking*). For example, those individuals new to a computer keyboard must type letter by letter. Those with more experience type in groups of whole words or phrases. It is important for marketers to discover the kinds and numbers of groupings (chunks) of information that consumers can handle. Recall may be hampered when the chunks offered in an advertisement do not match those in the consumer's frame of reference. The degree of prior knowledge is an important consideration. Knowledgeable consumers can take in more complex chunks of information than those who are less knowledgeable in the product category. Thus, the amount and type of technological information contained in a computer ad can be much more detailed in a magazine, such as *PC Magazine* or *Wired*, than in a general-interest magazine such as *Time*.

Information is stored in long-term memory in two ways: *episodically* (by the order in which it is acquired) and *semantically* (according to significant concepts). We may remember having gone to a movie last Saturday because of our ability to store data episodically, and we may remember the plot, the stars, and the director because of our ability to store data semantically. A recent study found that when consumers have little knowledge about brands, sequential exposure to information about different brands produces different degrees of learning, depending on the order in which the information is received. The product attributes of later entries in a product category—although regarded as novel and attention-getting for the initial brand—seem to be redundant and uninteresting for the later entrants.[31] That helps to explain why the first brand in a new product category tends to retain the largest market share.

Many learning theorists believe that memories stored semantically are organized into frameworks by which we integrate new data with previous experience. For information about a new brand or model of printer to enter our memory, for example, we would have to relate it to our previous experience with printers in terms of such qualities as speed, print quality, resolution, and memory.

Retrieval Retrieval is the process by which we recover information from long-term storage. Most people have had the experience of being unable to remember something with which they are very familiar.[32] Information-processing theorists look on such forgetting as a failure of the **retrieval** system. A great deal of research is focused on how individuals retrieve information from memory. Studies show that consumers tend to remember the product's *benefits*, rather than its *attributes*, suggesting that advertising messages are most effective when they link the product's attributes with the benefits that consumers seek from the product.

Motivated consumers are likely to spend time interpreting and elaborating on information they find relevant to their needs; and are likely to activate such relevant knowledge from long-term memory.[33] When consumers lack the ability to engage in extensive information processing, however, relatively low-level information may become influential, particularly when motivation is high.[34]

One stream of research has investigated the ability of incongruent advertising elements to provoke consumer memory. The findings suggest that incongruent (or unexpected) elements pierce consumers' perceptual screens and improve the memorability of an ad when these elements are relevant to the advertising message.[35] For example, an ad for a brand of stain-resistant, easy-to-clean carpet shows an elegantly dressed couple in a beautiful dining room setting where the man inadvertently knocks the food, the flowers, and the china crashing to the floor. The elegance of the actors and the upscale setting make the accident totally incongruent and unexpected, whereas the message remains highly relevant: The mess can be cleaned up easily without leaving a stain on the carpet.

Incongruent elements that are not relevant to an ad also pierce the consumer's perceptual screen but provide no memorability for the product. An ad showing a nude woman sitting on a piece of office furniture would very likely attract readers' attention, but would provide no memorability for the product or the advertiser because of the irrelevance of the nudity to the advertising message.

Interference. The greater the number of competitive ads in a product category, the lower the recall of brand claims in a specific ad. These *interference* effects are caused by confusion with competing ads and result in a failure to retrieve.[36] Ads can also act as retrieval cues for a competitive brand. An example of such consumer confusion occurred when consumers attributed the long-running and attention-getting television campaign featuring the Eveready Energizer Bunny to the leader in the field, Duracell.

Advertisements for competing brands or for other products made by the same manufacturer can lower the consumer's ability to remember advertised brand information. Such effects occur in response to even a small amount of advertising for similar products. The level of interference experienced can depend on the consumer's previous experiences, prior knowledge of brand attribute information, and the amount of brand information available at the time of choice. There are actually two kinds of interference. *New learning* can interfere with the retrieval of previously stored material, and *old learning* can interfere with the recall of recently learned material. With both kinds of interference, the problem is the similarity of old and new information. Advertising that creates a distinctive brand image can assist in the retention and retrieval of message contents.

Limited and Extensive Information Processing

For a long time, consumer researchers believed that all consumers passed through a complex series of mental and behavioral stages in arriving at a purchase decision. These stages ranged from awareness (exposure to information), to evaluation (preference, attitude formation), to behavior (purchase), to final evaluation (adoption or rejection). This same series of stages often is presented as the *consumer adoption process*.

A number of models have been developed over the years to express the same notion of sequential processing of information by consumers (see Table 7-1). Initially, marketing scholars believed that extensive and complex processing of information by consumers was applicable to all purchase decisions. However, on the basis of their own subjective experiences as consumers, some theorists began to realize that there were some purchase situations that simply did not call for extensive information processing and evaluation; that sometimes consumers simply went from awareness of a need to a routine purchase, without a great deal of information search and mental evaluation. Such purchases were considered of minimal personal relevance, as opposed to highly relevant, search-oriented purchases. Purchases of minimal personal importance were called *low-involvement purchases*, and complex, search-oriented purchases were considered *high-involvement purchases*. The following section describes the development of **involvement theory** and discusses its applications to marketing strategy.

TABLE 7-1 Models of Cognitive Learning

	PROMOTIONAL MODEL	TRICOMPONENT MODEL	DECISION-MAKING MODEL	INNOVATION ADOPTION MODEL	INNOVATION DECISION PROCESS
SEQUENTIAL STAGES OF PROCESSING	Attention	Cognitive	Awareness Knowledge	Awareness	Knowledge
	Interest Desire	Affective	Evaluation	Interest Evaluation	Persuasion
	Action	Conative	Purchase Postpurchase Evaluation	Trial Adoption	Decision Confirmation

INVOLVEMENT THEORY

Involvement theory developed from a stream of research called **hemispheral lateralization**, or **split-brain theory**. The basic premise of split-brain theory is that the right and left hemispheres of the brain "specialize" in the kinds of information they process. The left hemisphere is primarily responsible for cognitive activities such as reading, speaking, and attributional information processing. Individuals who are exposed to verbal information cognitively analyze the information through left-brain processing and form mental images. Unlike the left hemisphere, the right hemisphere of the brain is concerned with nonverbal, timeless, pictorial, and holistic information.[37] Put another way, the left side of the brain is rational, active, and realistic; the right side is emotional, metaphoric, impulsive, and intuitive. Figure 7-11 shows an ad based on split-brain theory.

Involvement Theory and Media Strategy

Building on the notion of hemispheral lateralization, a pioneer consumer researcher theorized that individuals passively process and store right-brain (nonverbal, pictorial) information—that is, without active involvement.[38] Because TV is primarily a pictorial medium, TV viewing was considered a right-brain activity (passive and holistic processing of images viewed on the screen), and TV itself was therefore considered a low-involvement medium. Passive learning was thought to occur through repeated exposures to a TV commercial (i.e., low-involvement information processing,) and to produce a change in consumer behavior (e.g., a product purchase) prior to a change in the consumer's attitude toward the product.

FIGURE 7-11
Ad Based on Split-Brain Theory

To extend this line of reasoning, cognitive (verbal) information is processed by the left side of the brain; thus, print media (e.g., newspapers and magazines) and interactive media are considered high-involvement media. According to this theory, print advertising is processed in the complex sequence of cognitive stages depicted in classic models of information processing (i.e., high-involvement information processing).

The right-brain, passive-processing-of-information theory is consistent with classical conditioning. Through repetition, the product is paired with a visual image (for example, a distinctive package) to produce the desired response: purchase of the advertised brand. According to this theory, in situations of passive learning (generated by low-involvement media), repetition is all that is needed to produce purchase behavior. In marketing terms, the theory suggests that television commercials are most effective when they are of short duration and repeated frequently, thus ensuring brand familiarity without provoking detailed evaluation of the message content. A study of Web banner advertising found important attitudinal effects among viewers even when they didn't click through to the hyperlinked ad.[39]

The right-brain processing theory stresses the importance of the visual component of advertising, including the creative use of symbols. Under this theory, highly visual TV commercials, packaging, and in-store displays generate familiarity with the brand and induce purchase behavior. Peripheral cues related to the product category lead to more attitude persistence than unrelated peripheral cues.[40] Pictorial cues are more effective at generating recall and familiarity with the product, whereas verbal cues (which trigger left-brain processing) generate cognitive activity that encourages consumers to evaluate the advantages and disadvantages of the product.

There are limitations to the application of split-brain theory to media strategy. Research suggests that the right and left hemispheres of the brain do not operate independently of each other, but work together to process information. Some individuals are *integrated processors* (they readily engage both hemispheres during information processing). Integrated processors show greater overall recall of both the verbal and the visual portions of print ads than individuals who exhibit more "specialized" processing (that is, right or left hemispheral processing).[41] Figure 7-12 presents an ad that builds on the notion of integrated processing; it shows an illustration and provocative headline on one page and a block of body copy explaining the headline on the facing page. One stream of research suggests that, despite hemispheral specialization, both sides of the brain are capable of high and low involvement—the left side of the brain in high and low *cognitive* processing, the right side in high and low *affective* processing.[42]

Involvement Theory and Consumer Relevance

From the conceptualization of high- and low-involvement media, involvement theory next focused on the consumer's involvement with products and purchases. It was briefly hypothesized that there are high- and low-involvement consumers; then, that there are high- and low-involvement purchases. These two approaches led to the notion that a consumer's level of involvement depends on the degree of personal *relevance* that the product holds for that consumer. Under this definition, high-involvement purchases are those that are very important to the consumer (e.g., in terms of perceived risk) and thus provoke extensive problem solving (information processing). An automobile and a dandruff shampoo both may represent high-involvement purchases under this scenario; the automobile because of high perceived financial risk, the shampoo because of high perceived social risk. Low-involvement purchases are purchases that are not very important to the consumer, hold little relevance, and have little perceived risk, and thus provoke very limited information processing. Highly

It's been suggested since the dawn of the computer age. A future in which everything worth knowing is accessible on screen.

But as it turns out, people don't just want information at their fingertips. They want it on their fingertips. They want to be able to touch, fold and dog-ear; to fax, copy and refer to; scribble in the margins or post proudly on the refrigerator door. And, above all, they want to print out - quickly, flawlessly and in vibrant color, please.

So today, as people require more (and more types of) paper than ever, our research centers are responding with new papers for home and business. Printing papers such as our Hammermill® brand Jet Print Ultra® are one example. They enable anyone with an ink jet printer to print with the sort of brightness and smoothness you'd expect from fine magazines.

The introduction of a lightweight paper called Accolade® is another example. It results in superior printing quality for catalogs, magazines, brochures and the like, at less cost for paper and postage. From printing paper to fine art paper to digital photography paper, we're committed to providing the "Paperless Society" with all the paper it needs.

The digital age hasn't created a paperless society. Just a revolution in paper.

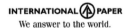

INTERNATIONAL PAPER
We answer to the world.

www.internationalpaper.com

FIGURE 7-12
Encouraging Right- and Left-Brain Processing

involved consumers find fewer brands acceptable (they are called *narrow categorizers*); uninvolved consumers are likely to be receptive to a greater number of messages regarding the purchase and will consider more brands (they are *broad categorizers*).

Central and Peripheral Routes to Persuasion

The **central and peripheral routes to persuasion** theory illustrates the concepts of extensive and limited problem solving for high- and low-involvement purchase situations. The major premise of this theory is that consumers are more likely to carefully evaluate the merits and weaknesses of a product when the purchase is of high relevance to them. Conversely, the likelihood is great that consumers will engage in very limited information search and evaluation when the purchase holds little relevance or importance for them.[43] Thus, for high-involvement purchases, the *central route to persuasion*—which requires considered thought and cognitive processing—is likely to be the most effective marketing strategy. For low-involvement purchases, the *peripheral route to persuasion* is likely to be more effective. In this instance, because the consumer is less motivated to exert cognitive effort, learning is more likely to occur through repetition, the passive processing of visual cues, and holistic perception.

Various researchers have addressed the relationship between the central and peripheral routes to persuasion theory and consumer information processing. A number of studies have found that high involvement with an issue produces more extensive processing of information. In these situations, the quality of the argument presented in the persuasive message is very influential to the decision outcome.[44] That would explain why highly involved consumers tend to use more attributes to evaluate brands, whereas less involved consumers apply very simple decision rules.

The Elaboration Likelihood Model The **Elaboration Likelihood Model (ELM)** suggests that a person's level of involvement during message processing is a critical factor in determining which route to persuasion is likely to be effective. For example, as the message becomes more personally relevant (that is, as involvement increases), people are more willing to expend the cognitive effort required to process the message arguments. Thus, when involvement is high, consumers follow the central route and base their attitudes or choices on the message arguments. When involvement is low, they follow the peripheral route and rely more heavily on other message elements (such as spokespersons or background music) to form attitudes or make product choices. Figure 7-13 shows an ad using the central route to persuasion; Figure 7-14 shows an ad that takes the peripheral route. One study found that comparative ads (see chapter 9) are more likely to be processed centrally (purposeful processing of message arguments), whereas noncomparative ads are commonly processed peripherally (with little message elaboration and a response derived from other executional elements in the ad).[45]

The marketing implications of the *elaboration likelihood model* are clear: For high-involvement purchases, marketers should use arguments stressing the strong, solid, high-quality attributes of their products—thus using the central (or highly cognitive) route. For low-involvement purchases, marketers should use the peripheral route to persuasion, focusing on the method of presentation rather than on the content of the message (e.g., through the use of celebrity spokespersons or highly visual and symbolic advertisements).

Measures of Involvement

Given that involvement theory evolved from the notion of high- and low-involvement media, to high- and low-involvement consumers, to high- and low-involvement products and purchases, to appropriate methods of persuasion in situations of high and low involvement, it is not surprising to find there is great variation in the conceptualization and measurement of *involvement* itself. Researchers have defined and conceptualized involvement in a variety of ways, including ego involvement, commitment, communication involvement, purchase importance, extent of information search, persons, products, situations, and purchase decisions.[46] Some studies have tried to differentiate between brand involvement and product involvement.[47] Others differentiate between situational, enduring, and response involvement.[48]

The lack of a clear definition about the essential components of involvement poses some measurement problems. Researchers who regard involvement as a *cognitive* state are concerned with the measurement of ego involvement, risk perception, and purchase importance. Researchers who focus on the *behavioral* aspects of involvement measure such factors as the search for and evaluation of product information. Others argue that involvement should be measured by the degree of importance the product has to the buyer.

Because of the many different dimensions and conceptualizations of involvement, many researchers agree that it makes more sense to develop an *involvement profile*, rather than to measure a single involvement level. The suggested profile would include interest in the product category, the rewarding nature (perceived pleasure) of the product, its perceived ability to reflect the purchaser's personality, and the perceived risk associated with the purchase.[49] This view is consistent with the notion that involvement should be measured on a continuum, rather than as a dichotomy consisting of two mutually exclusive cat-

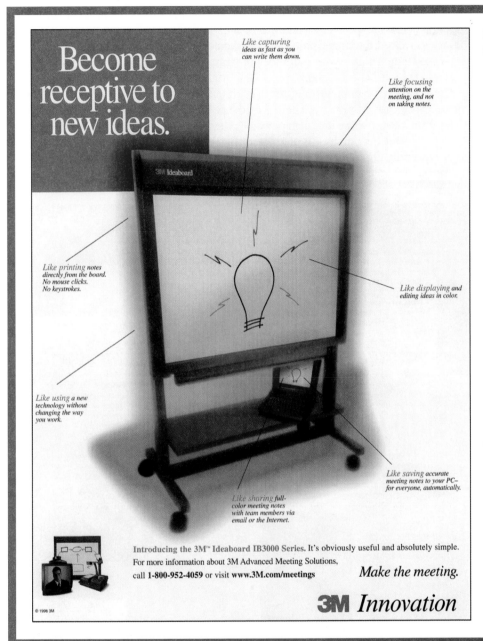

FIGURE 7-13
Central Route to Persuasion

egories of "high" and "low" involvement.[50] Table 7-2 presents a semantic differential scale designed to measure involvement.[51] Table 7-3 shows a personal involvement inventory developed to measure consumers' "enduring involvement" with a product.[52]

A new conceptualization of involvement proposes that involvement be defined as the *mobilization of behavioral resources* (physical, mental, and energy resources) for the achievement of a personally relevant goal to the extent that three conditions are met: The goal is subjectively relevant, the perceived ability to reach the goal is favorable, and the perceived opportunity to achieve that goal is also viewed as favorable.[53] A college student may want to take a round-the-world trip after graduation (a subjectively relevant goal) and perceives her ability and opportunity to earn sufficient money to do so as favorable. Thus, she would engage in extensive problem solving to find a way to achieve her goal. Another student may have the same desire to travel around the world, but perceives his chances of having enough money to do so as an impossible dream; thus, he is unlikely to spend much time in problem solving. The extensive problem solver would be highly involved; the limited problem solver would have little involvement.

Involvement theory has a number of strategic applications for the marketer. For example, the left-brain (cognitive processing)/right-brain (passive processing) paradigm seems to have strong implications for the content, length, and presentation of both print and television advertisements. There is evidence that people process information extensively when the purchase is of high personal relevance, and engage in limited information processing when the purchase is of low personal relevance. Uninvolved consumers appear to be susceptible to different kinds of persuasion than highly involved consumers.

FIGURE 7-14
Peripheral Route
to Persuasion

TABLE 7-2 Measuring Involvement on a Semantic Differential Scale

TO ME, [INSERT PRODUCT OR PRODUCT CATEGORY] **IS:**

	1	2	3	4	5	6	7	
1. Important	—	—	—	—	—	—	—	Unimportant
2. Interesting	—	—	—	—	—	—	—	Boring
3. Relevant	—	—	—	—	—	—	—	Irrelevant
4. Exciting	—	—	—	—	—	—	—	Unexciting
5. Meaningful	—	—	—	—	—	—	—	Meaningless
6. Appealing	—	—	—	—	—	—	—	Unappealing
7. Fascinating	—	—	—	—	—	—	—	Ordinary
8. Priceless	—	—	—	—	—	—	—	Worthless
9. Involving	—	—	—	—	—	—	—	Uninvolving
10. Necessary	—	—	—	—	—	—	—	Unnecessary

Adapted from Judith Lynne Zaichowsky, "The Personal Involvement Inventory: Reduction, Revision, and Application to Advertising," *Journal of Advertising* 23, 4 (December 1994): 59–70. Reprinted by permission.

TABLE 7-3 Product Involvement Inventory Measuring Consumers' Enduring Involvement with Products

1. I would be interested in reading about this product.
2. I would read a *Consumer Reports* article about this product.
3. I have compared product characteristics among brands.
4. I usually pay attention to ads for this product.
5. I usually talk about this product with other people.
6. I usually seek advice from other people prior to purchasing this product.
7. I usually take many factors into account before purchasing this product.
8. I usually spend a lot of time choosing what kind to buy.

Source: Edward F. McQuarrie and J. Michael Munson, "A Revised Product Involvement Inventory: Improved Usability and Validity," *Diversity in Consumer Behavior: Advances in Consumer Research*, vol. 19 (Provo, UT: Association for Consumer Research, 1992): pp. 108–15. Reprinted by permission.

■■■■■ MEASURES OF CONSUMER LEARNING

Increased market share and *brand-loyal consumers* are, for many marketers, the dual goals of consumer learning. These goals are interdependent: Brand-loyal customers provide the basis for a stable and growing market share, and brands with larger market shares have proportionately larger groups of loyal buyers.[54] Marketers focus all of their promotional monies on trying to teach consumers that their brands are best and that their products will best solve the consumer's problems and satisfy consumer needs. Thus, it is important for the marketer to measure how effectively consumers have "learned" its message. The following sections will examine various measures of consumer learning: recognition and recall measures, cognitive measures, and the attitudinal and behavioral measures of brand loyalty.

RECOGNITION AND RECALL MEASURES

Recognition and recall tests are conducted to determine whether consumers remember seeing an ad, the extent to which they have read it or seen it and can recall its content, their resulting attitudes toward the product and the brand, and their purchase intentions. **Recognition tests** are based on *aided recall*, whereas **recall tests** use *unaided recall*. In recognition tests, the consumer is shown an ad and asked whether he or she remembers seeing it and can remember any of its salient points. In recall tests, the consumer is asked whether he or she has read a specific magazine or watched a specific television show, and if so, can recall any ads or commercials seen, the product advertised, the brand, and any salient points about the product. One study found that a brand name explicitly conveying a product benefit (such as Manhattan Mini-storage) leads to higher recall of an advertised benefit claim than a nonsuggestive brand name (Acme Storage).[55] A number of syndicated research services conduct recognition and recall tests. For example, the Starch Readership Service evaluates the effectiveness of magazine advertisements. After qualifying as having read a given issue of a magazine, respondents are presented with the magazine and asked to point out which ads they noted, which they associated with the advertiser, and which they read most. They are also asked which parts of the ads they noted and read most. The resulting readership recognition score is meaningful when compared to similar-sized ads, to competitive ads, and to the marketer's own prior ads. Figure 7-15 shows an example of a "Starched" ad.

COGNITIVE RESPONSES TO ADVERTISING

Another measure of consumer learning is the degree to which consumers accurately comprehend the intended advertising message. *Comprehension* is a function of the message characteristics, the consumer's opportunity and ability to process the information, and the consumer's motivation (or level of involvement).[56] When the target market is clearly defined, marketers have a much better opportunity to develop advertising messages and highlight needs to which the targeted consumers can closely relate.

To ensure a high level of comprehension, many marketers conduct *copy testing* either before the advertising is actually run in media (called *pretesting*) or after it appears (*posttesting*). Pretests are used to determine which, if any, elements of an advertising message should be revised before major media expenses are incurred. Posttests are used to evaluate the effectiveness of an ad that has already run and to identify which elements, if any, should be changed to improve the impact and memorability of future ads.

ATTITUDINAL AND BEHAVIORAL MEASURES OF BRAND LOYALTY

Attitudinal measures are concerned with consumers' overall feelings (i.e., evaluation) about the product and the brand, and their purchase intentions. Behavioral measures are based on observable responses to promotional stimuli—purchase behavior, rather than attitude toward the product or brand. A basic issue among researchers is whether to define **brand loyalty** in terms of consumer *behavior* or consumer *attitudes*.

Behavioral scientists who favor the theory of instrumental conditioning believe that brand loyalty results from an initial product trial that is reinforced through satisfaction, leading to repeat purchase. Cognitive researchers, on the other hand, emphasize the role of mental processes in building brand loyalty. They believe that consumers engage in extensive problem-solving behavior involving brand and attribute comparisons, leading to a strong brand preference and repeat purchase behavior.

To cognitive learning theorists, behavioral definitions (such as frequency of purchase or proportion of total purchases) lack precision, because they do not distinguish

Skylark. It's one thing I can always count on.

STARCH™ AD-AS-A-WHOLE		
Noted %	Associated %	Read Most %
W 47	45	11

...raction control system

→ 4-wheel anti-lock brakes

→ Dual air bags

→ Battery Rundown Protection system

→ 150-hp Twin Cam engine

→ Passlock™ theft-deterrent system

→ Premium Roadside Assistance

→ To learn more, call 1-800-4A-BUICK.
Or visit http://www.buick.com

Premium In
Everything But Price.
$15,995.*

BUICK

USA
Official Sponsor of the
1996 U.S. Olympic Team

GM ©1995 GM Corp. All rights reserved. Skylark is a registered trademark of GM Corp.
Buckle up, America! * MSRP including dealer prep. Tax, license and optional equipment additional.

FIGURE 7-15

Starch Readership Scores
Measure Learning Through
Ad Recognition Tests

between the "real" brand-loyal buyer who is intentionally faithful, and the spurious brand-loyal buyer who repeats a brand purchase because it is the only one available at the store. Such theorists say that brand loyalty must be measured by *attitudes toward a brand*, rather than by *purchase consistency*.

One study measured brand loyalty in three different ways: brand market share, the number of same-brand purchases in a 6-month period, and the average number of brands bought per buyer. Findings suggest that consumers buy from a mix of brands within their acceptable range (that is, their *evoked set*). The greater the number of acceptable brands in a specific product category, the less likely the consumer is to be brand loyal to one specific brand. Conversely, products having few competitors, as well as those purchased with great frequency, are likely to have greater brand loyalty.[57] Thus, a more favorable *attitude* toward a brand, service, or store, compared to potential alternatives, together with *repeat patronage*, are seen as the requisite components of customer loyalty.

An integrated conceptual framework views consumer loyalty as the relationship between an individual's relative attitude toward an entity (brand, service, store, or vendor) and patronage behavior.[58] The consumer's relative attitude consists of two dimensions: the strength of the attitude and the degree of attitudinal differentiation among competing brands. As Figure 7-16 indicates, a consumer with a high relative attitude and high degree of repeat purchase behavior would be defined as *brand loyal*; a consumer with a low relative attitude and high repeat patronage would be considered *spuriously loyal*. An example of such spurious loyalty would be a consumer who perceives little differentiation among brands in a low-involvement category but who undertakes repeat brand purchases on the basis of situational cues, such as package familiarity, shelf positioning, or special prices.

Some theorists suggest that brand loyalty is correlated with the consumer's degree of involvement: High involvement leads to extensive information search and, ultimately, to brand loyalty, whereas low involvement leads to exposure and brand awareness, and then possibly to brand habit. As a customer's satisfaction with a product increases along with repeat purchases, the search for information about alternative brands decreases. Evidence suggests that loyal consumers—those who have a strong commitment to a brand, a service, or a retail store—show strong resistance to counterpersuasion attempts. A syndicated research company reported that 74 percent of its respondents resist promotional efforts by rival brands once they find a brand with which they are satisfied.[59]

Marketers are interested not only in *how* brand loyalty develops, but also in *when* it develops. Research evidence suggests that a great deal of brand loyalty develops quite early, in the context of family life. Classic toys—Lego blocks, Barbie dolls, Lionel trains, GI Joes—have enjoyed renewed popularity as baby boomers flocked to buy their children the toys they best remembered. Indeed, nostalgia has become an important advertising appeal for the baby boomer market. Marketers are also interested in finding out what stimulus factors in their promotion affected purchase behavior. They correlate the results of syndicated consumer panel data (compiled from the diaries of consumer panelists who have agreed to provide purchase data for all their purchases over a set period of time) with their advertising, sales promotion, and price data to develop an understanding of consumer purchase "triggers."

FIGURE 7-16

Brand Loyalty as a Function of *Relative Attitude* and *Patronage Behavior*

Source: Alan S. Dick and Kunal Basu, "Customer Loyalty: Toward an Integrated Conceptual Framework," *Journal of the Academy of Marketing Science* 22, 2 (1994): 101. Copyright © 1994 by *Journal of the Academy of Marketing Science*. Reprinted by permission of Sage Publications.

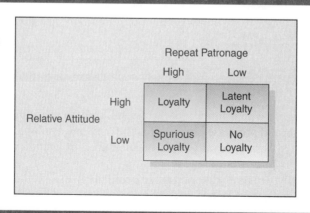

Some marketing scholars have noted a recent decline in brand loyalty; some of the reasons include consumer boredom or dissatisfaction with the products they use, consumer variety-seeking, the constant availability of new product offerings, and an increased concern with price.[60] In an era of lower-priced "value" brands, the market share of private label brands in a variety of product categories has increased; at the same time, patronage of traditional department stores has declined in favor of discount stores. Some marketers have started to promote consistency of operation and convenience in an effort to combat shifting loyalties. Others have adopted such sales promotion devices as frequent-user credits to encourage brand loyalty. Because of the importance of brand imagery to brand loyalty, many marketers develop a simple, descriptive promotional line (for instance, "The Friendly Skies") and, through heavy repetition, engrave it in consumers' memories.[61]

Developing a highly consistent market share of brand-loyal consumers is the ultimate goal of all marketers. Discovering how consumers learn about brands and become attached to certain brands assists marketers in achieving this goal.

BRAND EQUITY

The term **brand equity** refers to the value inherent in a well-known brand name. From a consumer's perspective, brand equity is the added value bestowed on the product by the brand name.[62] Brand equity facilitates the acceptance of new products and the allocation of preferred shelf space and enhances perceived value, perceived quality, and premium pricing options. For many companies, their most valuable assets are their brand names.[63] Because of the escalation of new product costs and the high rate of new product failures, many companies prefer to leverage their brand equity through brand extensions, rather than risk launching a new brand.

Because a brand that has been promoted heavily in the past retains a cumulative level of name recognition, companies buy, sell, and rent (i.e., license) their brand names, knowing that it is easier to buy than to create a brand name with enduring strength. Brand equity enables companies to charge a price premium—an additional amount over and above the price of an identical store brand.

A relatively new strategy among some marketers is *co-branding* (also called double branding). The basis of co-branding, in which two brand names are featured on a single product, is to use another product's brand equity to enhance the primary brand's equity. For example, Cranberry Newtons is a product of Nabisco and Ocean Spray, bearing both brand names. Some experts believe that using a second brand's equity may imply that the host brand can no longer stand on its own. Others question whether a co-branded product causes consumer confusion as to who actually makes the product and whether the host brand can survive if the second brand endorsement is taken away.

Well-known brand names are referred to as *megabrands*. Among the best known brands are Coca-Cola, Campbell's Soup, Hallmark Cards, and United Parcel Service. Their names have become "cultural icons" and enjoy powerful advantages over the competition. To enhance the brand equity of their largest brands, some marketers have adopted a strategy of brand consolidation.

Brand equity is important to marketers because it leads to brand loyalty, which in turn leads to increased market share and greater profits. To marketers, the major function of learning theory is to teach consumers that their product is best, to encourage repeat purchase, and, ultimately, to develop loyalty to the brand name.

SUMMARY

Consumer learning is the process by which individuals acquire the purchase and consumption knowledge and experience they apply to future related behavior. Although some learning is intentional, much learning is incidental. Basic elements that contribute to an understanding of learning are motivation, cues, response, and reinforcement.

There are two schools of thought as to how individuals learn—behavioral theories and cognitive theories. Both contribute to an understanding of consumer behavior. Behavioral theorists view learning as observable responses to stimuli, whereas cognitive theorists believe that learning is a function of mental processes.

Three major behavioral learning theories are classical conditioning, instrumental conditioning, and observational (vicarious) learning. The principles of classical conditioning that provide theoretical underpinnings for many marketing applications include repetition, stimulus generalization, and stimulus discrimination. Neo-Pavlovian theories view traditional classical conditioning as cognitive associative learning rather than as reflexive action.

Instrumental learning theorists believe that learning occurs through a trial-and-error process in which positive outcomes (i.e., rewards) result in repeat behavior. Both positive and negative reinforcement can be used to encourage the desired behavior. The timing of repetitions influences how long the learned material is retained. Reinforcement schedules can be total (consistent) or partial (fixed ratio or random.) Massed repetitions produce more initial learning than distributed repetitions; however, learning usually persists longer with distributed (that is, spread-out) reinforcement schedules.

Cognitive learning theory holds that the kind of learning most characteristic of humans is problem solving. Cognitive theorists are concerned with how information is processed by the human mind: how it is stored, retained, and retrieved. A simple model of the structure and operation of memory suggests the existence of three separate storage units: the sensory store, short-term store (or working memory), and long-term store. The processes of memory include rehearsal, encoding, storage, and retrieval.

Involvement theory proposes that people engage in limited information processing in situations of low importance or relevance to them and in extensive information processing in situations of high relevance. Hemispheral lateralization theory gave rise to the theory that television is a low-involvement medium that results in passive learning, and that print and interactive media encourage more cognitive information processing.

Measures of consumer learning include recall and recognition tests, cognitive responses to advertising, and attitudinal and behavioral measures of brand loyalty. A basic issue among researchers is whether to define brand loyalty in terms of the consumer's behavior or the consumer's attitude toward the brand. Brand equity refers to the inherent value a brand name has in the marketplace.

For marketers, the purposes of understanding how consumers learn are to teach them that their brand is best and to develop brand loyalty.

DISCUSSION QUESTIONS

1. How can the principles of (a) classical conditioning theory and (b) instrumental conditioning theory be applied to the development of marketing strategies?

2. Kraft Foods uses family branding, but Procter & Gamble (which makes Crest, Duncan Hines, Charmin, and Tide) does not. Yet, both companies are successful. Describe in learning terms the conditions under which family branding is a good policy and those under which it is not. What do you think are the reasons for the difference in family-branding policies between Kraft and P&G?

3. Estée Lauder, the cosmetics company, has introduced an exensive line of skin creams to enhance its product line. How can the company use stimulus generalization to market these products? Is instrumental conditioning applicable to this marketing situation? If so, how?

4. Which theory of learning (classical conditioning, instrumental conditioning, observational learning, or cognitive learning) best explains the following consumption behaviors: (a) buying a six-pack of Evian water, (b) preferring to fly on a particular airline, (c) buying a personal computer for the first time, and (d) buying a new car? Explain your choices.

5. a. Define the following memory structures: sensory store, working memory, and long-term store. Discuss how each of these concepts can be used in the development of an advertising strategy.

    b. How does information overload affect the consumer's ability to comprehend an ad and store it in his or her memory?

6. Discuss the differences between low- and high-involvement media. How would you apply the knowledge of hemispheral lateralization to the design of TV commercials and print advertisements?

EXERCISES

1. Imagine you are the instructor in this course and that you are trying to increase student participation in class discussions. How would you use reinforcement to achieve your objective?

2. Visit a supermarket. Can you identify any packages where you think the marketer's knowledge of stimulus generalization or stimulus discrimination was incorporated into the package design? Note these examples and present them in class.

3. Discuss a recent product purchase you regard as high involvement and another one you view as low involvement with three classmates. Do they agree with your selections? Describe how their points of view may be related to (a) brand loyalty, (b) frequency of use, (c) price paid, and (d) perceived risk associated with the purchase.

KEY TERMS

- **Behavioral learning theory**
- **Brand loyalty versus brand equity**
- **Central and peripheral routes to persuasion**
- **Classical versus instrumental conditioning**
- **Cognitive associative learning**
- **Cognitive learning theory**
- **Elaboration Likelihood Model (ELM)**

- **Hemispheral lateralization**
- **Information processing**
- **Involvement theory**
- **Limited versus extensive information processing**
- **Modeling, observational, and vicarious learning**
- **Operant conditioning**
- **Rehearsal**

- **Reinforcement**
- **Retention**
- **Retrieval**
- **Sensory, short-term, and long-term stores**
- **Split-brain theory**
- **Stimulus discrimination**
- **Stimulus generalization**
- **Stimulus-response theories**

NOTES

1. Robert A. Rescorla, "Pavlovian Conditioning, It's Not What You Think It Is," *American Psychologist* 43, 3 (March 1988): 151–60.

2. N. J. Mackintosh, *Conditioning and Associative Learning* (New York: Oxford University Press, 1983), 10.

3. Terence A. Shimp, "Neo-Pavlovian Conditioning and Its Implications for Consumer Theory and Research," in *Handbook of Consumer Behavior*, ed. Thomas S. Robertson and Harold H. Kassarjian (Upper Saddle River, NJ: Prentice Hall, 1991): 162–87.

4. Chris Janiszewski and Luk Warlop, "The Influence of Classical Conditioning Procedures on Subsequent Attention to the Conditioned Brand," *Journal of Consumer Research* 20 (September 1993): 171–89.

5. Dana Canedy, "Where Nothing Lasts Forever," *New York Times*, 24 April 1998, D1.

6. David W. Schumann, Richard E. Petty, and D. Scott Clemons, "Predicting the Effectiveness of Different Strategies of Advertising Variation: A Test of the Repetition-Variation Hypothesis," *Journal of Consumer Research* 17 (September 1990): 192–202; See also H. Rao Unnava and Robert E. Burnkrant, "Effects of Repeating Varied Ad Executions on Brand Name Memory," *Journal of Marketing Research* 28 (November 1991): 406–16.

7. Curtis P. Haugtvedt, David W. Schumann, Wendy L. Schneier, and Wendy L. Warren, "Advertising Repetition and Variation Strategies: Implications for Understanding Attitude Strength," *Journal of Consumer Research* 21 (June 1994): 176–89.

8. Youssef M. Ibrahim, "As Trademarks Multiply, Infringement Does, Too," *New York Times*, 12 November 1998, D2.

9. Peter A. Dacin and Daniel C. Smith, "The Effect of Brand Portfolio Characteristics on Consumer Evaluations of Brand Extensions," *Journal of Marketing Research* 31 (May 1994): 229–42; Susan M. Broniarczyk and Joseph W. Alba, "The Importance of the Brand in Brand Extension," *Journal of Marketing Research* 31 (May 1994): 214–28.

10. Zachary Schiller et al., "Make it Simple: P&G's New Marketing Mantra," *Business Week*, 9 September 1996, 96–104. See also Fara Warner, "P&G is Promoting Products as a Category," *Wall Street Journal*, 25 April 1995, B10.

11. William L. Hamilton, "For Whom the Sell Tolls? It Tolls for Thee," *New York Times*, 8 October 1998, F1, 8.

12. Craig S. Smith, "A Beer Tampering Scare in China Shows a Peril of Global Marketing," *Wall Street Journal*, 3 November 1995, B1.

13. Randi Priluck Grossman and Brian D. Till, "The Persistance of Classically Conditioned Brand Attitudes," *Journal of Advertising* 27, 1 (Spring 1998): 23–31.

14. Gregory S. Carpenter, Rashi Glazer, and Kent Nakamoto, "Meaningful Brands from Meaningless Differentiation: The Dependence on Irrelevant Attributes," *Journal of Marketing Research* 31 (August 1994): 339–50.

15. S. Ratneshwar, "New Directions in Exploring the Interface of Consumer Cognition and Motivation," *Advances in Consumer Research* 22 (1995): 271–72; Jerome B. Kernan, "The Interface of Consumer Cognition and Motivation," *Advances in Consumer Research* 22 (1995): 273–74. See also Cynthia Huffman and Michael J. Houston, "Goal-Oriented Experiences and the Development of Knowledge," *Journal of Consumer Research* 20 (September 1993): 190–207.

16. Michael D. Johnson and Claes Fornell, "The Nature and Methodological Implications of the Cognitive Representation of Products," *Journal of Consumer Research* 14 (September 1987): 214–27.

17. Jennifer Gregan-Paxton and Deborah Roedder John, "Consumer Learning by Analogy: A Model of Internal Knowledge Transfer," *Journal of Consumer Research* 24 (December 1997): 266–84.

18. Ellen C. Garbarino and Julie A. Edell, "Cognitive Effort, Affect, and Choice," *Journal of Consumer Research* 24 (September 1997): 147–58.

19. Sandra Blakeslee, "How the Brain Might Work: A New Theory of Consciousness," *New York Times*, 21 March 1995, C1.

20. Daniel Goleman, "Brain May Tag All Perceptions with a Value," *New York Times*, 8 August 1995, C1.

21. Ruth Ann Smith, "The Effects of Visual and Verbal Advertising Information on Consumers' Inferences," *Journal of Advertising* 20, 4 (December 1991): 13–23.

22. H. Rao Unnava and Robert E. Burnkrant, "An Imagery-Processing View of the Role of Pictures in Print Advertisements," *Journal of Marketing Research* 28 (May 1991): 226–31.

23. Kenneth R. Lord and Robert E. Burnkrant, "Television Program Elaboration Effects on Commercial Processing," in *Advances in Consumer Research*, vol. 15, ed. Michael Houston (Provo, UT: Association for Consumer Research, 1988): 213–18.

24. Kevin J. Clancy, "CPMs Must Bow to 'Involvement' Measurement," *Advertising Age*, 20 January 1992, 26.

25. Joan Meyers-Levy and Durairaj Maheswasran, "Exploring Differences in Males' and Females' Processing Strategies," *Journal of Consumer Research* 18 (June 1991): 63–70.

26. Robert J. Kent and Chris T. Allen, "Competitive Interference Effects in Consumer Memory for Advertising: The Role of Brand Familiarity," *Journal of Marketing* 58 (July 1994): 97–105.

27. Carolyn Yoon, "Age Differences in Consumers' Processing Strategies: An Investigation of Moderating Influences," *Journal of Consumer Research* 24 (December 1997): 229–42.

28. Itamar Simonson, Joel Huber, and John Payne, "The Relationship Between Prior Brand Knowledge and Information Acquisition Order," *Journal of Consumer Research* 14 (March 1988): 566–78.

29. Julie L. Ozanne, Merrie Brucks, and Dhruv Grewal, "A Study of Information Search Behavior During the Categorization of New Products," *Journal of Consumer Research* 18 (March 1992): 452–63.

30. Kent and Allen, "Competitive Interference Effects," 97–105.

31. Frank R. Kardes and Gurumurthy Kalya-Naram, "Order-of-Entry Effects on Consumer Memory and Judgment: An Information Integration Perspective," *Journal of Marketing Research* 29 (August 1992): 343–57.

32. Daniel L. Schacter, *The Brain, The Mind, and the Past*, (New York: Basic Books), 1998; also Stephen S. Hall, "Our Memories, Our Selves," *The New York Times Magazine*, 15 February 1998, 26–39.

33. Kevin Lane Keller, "Memory and Evaluation Effects in Competitive Advertising Environments," *Journal of Consumer Research* 17 (March 1991): 463–76.

34. Carolyn L. Costley and Merrie Brucks, "Selective Recall and Information Use in Consumer Preferences," *Journal of Consumer Research* 18 (March 1992): 464–73.

35. Susan E. Heckler and Terry L. Childers, "The Role of Expectancy and Relevancy in Memory for Verbal and Visual Information: What Is Incongruency?" *Journal of Consumer Research* 18 (March 1992): 475–92.

36. Joseph W. Alba, Howard Marmorstein, and Amitava Chattopadhyay, "Transitions in Preference Over Time: The Effects of Memory on Message Persuasiveness," *Journal of Marketing Research* 29 (November 1992): 406–16.

37. Flemming Hansen, "Hemispheral Lateralization: Implications for Understanding Consumer Behavior," *Journal of Consumer Research* 8 (June 1981): 23–36; Peter H. Lindzay and Donald Norman, *Human Information Processing* (New York: Academic Press, 1977); and Merlin C. Wittrock, *The Human Brain* (Upper Saddle River, NJ: Prentice Hall, 1977).

38. Herbert E. Krugman, "The Impact of Television Advertising: Learning Without Involvement," *Public Opinion Quarterly* 29 (Fall 1965): 349–56; "Brain Wave Measures of Media Involvement," *Journal of Advertising Research* 11 (February 1971): 3–10; and "Memory Without Recall, Exposure Without Perception," *Journal of Advertising Research*, Classics 1 (September 1982): 80–85.

39. Rex Briggs and Nigel Hollis, "Advertising on the Web: Is There Response Before Click-Through?" *Journal of Advertising Research* 37, 2 (March–April 1997): 33–45.

40. Jaideep Sengupta, Ronald C. Goodstein, and David S. Boninger, "All Cues Are Not Created Equal: Obtaining Attitude Persistence under Low-Involvement Conditions," *Journal of Consumer Research* 23 (March 1997): 351–61.

41. Susan E. Heckler and Terry L. Childers, "Hemispheric Lateralization: The Relationship of Processing Orientation with Judgment and Recall Measures for Print Advertisements," in *Advances in Consumer Research*, vol. 14, ed. M. Wallendorf and P. F. Anderson (Provo, UT: Association for Consumer Research, 1987): 46–50.

42. Banwari Mittal, "A Framework for Relating Consumer Involvement to Lateral Brain Functioning," in *Advances in Consumer Research*, vol. 14, ed. M. Wallendorf and P. F. Anderson (Provo, UT: Association for Consumer Research, 1987): 41–45.

43. John T. Cacioppo, Richard E. Petty, Chuan Feng Kao, and Regina Rodriguez, "Central and Peripheral Routes to Persuasion: An Individual Difference Perspective," *Journal of Personality and Social Psychology* 51, 5 (1986): 1032–43.

44. See, for example, Richard E. Petty and John T. Cacioppo, "Issues Involvement Can Increase or Decrease Persuasion by Enhancing Message-Relevant Cognitive Responses," *Journal of Personality and Social Psychology* 37 (1979): 1915–26; Cacioppo and Petty, "The Need for Cognition," *Journal of Personality and Social Psychology* 42 (1982): 116–31; and Cacioppo, Petty, and Katherine J. Morris, "Effects of Need for Cognition on Message Evaluation, Recall and Persuasion," *Journal of Personality and Social Psychology* 45 (1983): 805–18.

45. Sanjay Putrevu and Kenneth R. Lord, "Comparative and Noncomparative Advertising: Attitudinal Effects Under Cognitive and Affective Involvement Conditions," *Journal of Advertising* 23, 2 (June 1994): 77–91.

46. Theo B. C. Poiesz and J. P. M. de Bont, "Do We Need Involvement to Understand Consumer Behavior?" *Advances in Consumer Research* 22 (1995): 448–52. See also the following articles in *Advances in Consumer Research*, 11 ed. Thomas C. Kinnear, (Provo, UT: Association for Consumer Research, 1984): James A. Muncy and Shelby D. Hunt, "Consumer Involvement: Definitional Issues and Research Directions," 193–96; John H. Antil, "Conceptualization and Operationalization of Involvement," 203–9; and Michael L. Rothschild, "Perspectives on Involvement: Current Problems and Future Directions," 216–17; Judith L. Zaichkowsky, "Conceptualizing Involvement," *Journal of Advertising* 15, 2 (1986): 4–34.

47. Banwari Mittal and Myung Soo Lee, "Separating Brand Choice Involvement from Product Involvement via Consumer Involvement Profiles," in *Advances in Consumer Research*, vol. 15, ed. Michael Houston, (Provo, UT: Association for Consumer Research, 1988): 43–49.

48. See Marsha L. Richins, Peter H. Bloch, and Edward F. McQuarrie, "How Enduring and Situational Involvement Combine to Create Involvement Responses," *Journal of Consumer Psychology* 1, 2 (1992): 143–53.

49. Gilles Laurent and Jean-Noel Kapferer, "Measuring Consumer Involvement Profiles," *Journal of Marketing Research* 22 (February 1985): 41–53; Jean Noel Kapferer and Gilles Laurent, "Consumer Involvement Profiles: A New Practical Approach to Consumer Involvement," *Journal of Advertising Research*, 25, 6 (December 1985–January 1986): 48–56.

50. Kenneth Schneider and William Rodgers, "An 'Importance' Subscale for the Consumer Involvement Profile," *Advances in Consumer Research*, vol. 23, ed. Kim Corfman and John Lynch (Provo, Utah: Association for Consumer Research, 1996): 249–54.

51. Judith Lynne Zaichkowsky, "The Personal Involvement Inventory: Reduction, Revision, and Application to Advertising," *Journal of Advertising* 23, 4 (December 1994): 59–69; also Robert N. Stone, "The Marketing Characteristics of Involvement," in *Advances in Consumer Research*, 11 ed. Thomas C. Kinnear, (Provo, UT: Association for Consumer Research, 1984): 210–15.

52. Edward F. McQuarrie and J. Michael Munson, "A Revised Product Involvement Inventory: Improved Usability and Validity," *Diversity in Consumer Behavior: Advances in Consumer Research*, 19 (Provo, Utah: Association for Consumer Research, 1992): 108–15; also Edward F. McQuarrie and J. Michael Munson, "The Zaichkowsky Personal Involvement Inventory: Modification and Extension," in *Advances in Consumer Research*, vol. 14, ed. M. Wallendorf and P. F. Anderson (Provo, UT: Association for Consumer Research, 1987): 36–40.

53. Poiesz and deBont. "Do We Need Involvement to Understand Consumer Behavior?"

54. Alan Dick and Kunai Basu, "Customer Loyalty: Toward an Integrated Conceptual Framework," *Journal of the Academy of Marketing Science* 22 (Spring 1994): 99–113.

55. Kevin Lane Keller, Susan E. Heckler, and Michael J. Houston, "The Effects of Brand Name Suggestiveness on Advertising Recall," *Journal of Marketing* 62 (January 1998): 48–57.

56. David Glen Mick, "Levels of Subjective Comprehension in Advertising Processing and Their Relations to Ad Perceptions, Attitudes, and Memory," *Journal of Consumer Research* 18 (March 1992): 411–24.

57. Thomas Exter, "Looking for Brand Loyalty," *American Demographics* (April 1986): 33.

58. Alan S. Dick and Kunal Basu, "Customer Loyalty: Toward an Integrated Conceptual Framework," *Journal of the Academy of Marketing Science* 22, 2 (1994): 99–113.

59. Diane Crispell and Kathleen Brandenburg, "What's in a Brand," *American Demographics* (May 1993): 28.

60. Hans C. M. Van Trup, Wayne D. Hoyer, and J. Jeffrey Inman, "Why Switch? Product Category-Level Explanations for True Variety-Seeking Behavior," *Journal of Marketing Research* 33 (August 1996): 281–92.

61. Scott A. Hawkins and Stephen J. Hoch, "Low-Involvement Learning: Memory Without Evaluation," *Journal of Consumer Research* 19 (September 1992): 212–25.

62. Chan Su Park and V. Srinivasan, "A Survey-Based Method for Measuring and Understanding Brand Equity and Its Extendibility," *Journal of Marketing Research* 31 (May 1994): 271–288.

63. Gillian Oakenfull and Betsy Gelb, "Research-Based Advertising to Preserve Brand Equity but Avoid Genericide," *Journal of Advertising Research* (September–October 1996): 65–72.

CHAPTER 8
Consumer Attitude Formation and Change

As consumers, each of us has a vast number of attitudes toward products, services, advertisements, direct mail, the Internet, and retail stores. Whenever we are asked whether we like or dislike a product (e.g., Windows 2000), a service (such as Poland Springs Water—Home and Office Delivery Service), a particular retailer (e.g., the Sharper Image), a specific direct marketer (CDW®—Computer Discount Warehouse), or an advertising theme (Colgate Total toothpaste "The Brushing That Works Between Brushings™"), we are being asked to express our **attitudes**.

Within the context of consumer behavior, an appreciation of prevailing attitudes has considerable strategic merit. For instance, there has been very rapid growth in the sales of natural ingredient bath, body, and cosmetic products throughout the world. This trend seems linked to the currently popular attitude that things "natural" are good and things "synthetic" are bad. Yet, in reality, the positive attitude favoring things natural is not based on any systematic evidence that natural cosmetic products are any safer or better for consumers.

To get at the heart of what is driving consumers' behavior, *attitude research* has been used to study a wide range of strategic marketing questions. For example, attitude research is frequently undertaken to determine whether consumers will accept a proposed new-product idea, to gauge why a firm's target audience has not reacted more favorably to its new promotional theme, or to learn how target customers are likely to react to a proposed change in the firm's packaging design. To illustrate, Fruit of the Loom frequently conducts research among male and female target consumers to determine their attitudes about size, fit, comfort, and fashion elements of its active wear clothing (T-shirts, sweatshirts, sweatpants, and sweatshorts), as well as testing reactions to potential active wear designs. The goal of this research is often to *identify current attitudes* as a basis to better satisfying customer needs. In a similar fashion, Fruit of the Loom's consumer advertising seeks to *modify attitudes* in ways that stimulate sales of its products.[1]

In this chapter we will discuss the reasons why attitude research has had such a pervasive impact on consumer behavior. We also will discuss the properties that have made attitudes so attractive to consumer researchers, as well as some of the common frustrations encountered in attitude research. Particular attention will be paid to the central topics of attitude formation, attitude change, and related strategic marketing issues.

WHAT ARE ATTITUDES?

Consumer researchers assess attitudes by asking questions or making inferences from behavior. For example, if a researcher determines from questioning a consumer that she consistently buys Cover Girl Lipcolor products and even recommends them to friends, the researcher is likely to infer that the consumer possesses a positive attitude toward Cover Girl Lipcolor products. This example illustrates that attitudes are not directly observable, but must be inferred from what people say or what they do.

Moreover, the illustration suggests that a whole universe of consumer behaviors—consistency of purchases, recommendations to others, top rankings, beliefs, evaluations, and intentions—are related to attitudes. What, then, are attitudes? In a consumer behavior context, an attitude is a learned predisposition to behave in a consistently favorable or unfavorable way with respect to a given object. Each part of this definition describes an important property of an attitude and is critical to understanding the role of attitudes in consumer behavior.

THE ATTITUDE "OBJECT"

The word *object* in our consumer-oriented definition of attitude should be interpreted broadly to include specific consumption- or marketing-related concepts, such as product, product category, brand, service, possessions, product use, causes or issues, people, advertisement, Internet site, price, medium, or retailer.

In conducting attitude research, we tend to be *object-specific*. For example, if we were interested in learning consumers' attitudes toward three major brands of cellular telephones, our "object" might include Motorola, Ericsson, and Nokia; if we were examining consumer attitudes toward major brands of laptop computers, our "object" might include IBM, Toshiba, Compaq, Sony, Dell, and Hitachi.

ATTITUDES ARE A LEARNED PREDISPOSITION

There is general agreement that attitudes are *learned*. This means that attitudes relevant to purchase behavior are formed as a result of direct experience with the product, word-of-mouth information acquired from others, or exposure to mass-media advertising, the Internet, and various forms of direct marketing (such as a retailer's catalog). It is important to remember that whereas attitudes may result from behavior, they are not synonymous with behavior. Instead, they reflect either a favorable or an unfavorable evaluation of the attitude object. As *learned predispositions*, attitudes have a motivational quality; that is, they might propel a consumer *toward* a particular behavior or repel the consumer *away* from a particular behavior.

ATTITUDES HAVE CONSISTENCY

Another characteristic of attitudes is that they are relatively consistent with the behavior they reflect. However, despite their *consistency*, attitudes are not necessarily permanent; they do change. (Attitude change is explored later in this chapter.)

It is important to illustrate what we mean by consistency. Normally, we expect consumers' behavior to correspond with their attitudes. For example, if a Dutch consumer reported preferring German over Japanese automobiles, we would expect that the individual would be more likely to buy a German car when next in the market for a new car. In other words, when consumers are free to act as they wish, we anticipate that their actions will be consistent with their attitudes. However, circumstances often preclude consistency between attitudes and behavior. For example, in the case of our Dutch consumer, the matter of affordability may intervene, and the consumer would find a particular Japanese car to be a more realistic choice than a German car. Therefore, we must consider possible *situational* influences on consumer attitudes and behavior.

ATTITUDES OCCUR WITHIN A SITUATION

It is not immediately evident from our definition that attitudes occur within and are affected by the *situation*. By situation, we mean events or circumstances that, at a particular point in time, influence the relationship between an attitude and behavior. A specific situation can cause consumers to behave in ways that are seemingly inconsistent with their attitudes. For instance, let us assume that Noah purchases a different brand of shaving cream each time the brand he is using runs low. Although his brand-switching behavior may seem to reflect a negative attitude or dissatisfaction with the brands he tries, it actually may be influenced by a specific situation. For example, if his wish is to economize, he will buy whatever is the least expensive brand.

The opposite can also be true. If Paul rents a car from Value each time he goes out of town on business, we may erroneously infer that he has a particularly favorable attitude toward Value. On the contrary, Paul may find Value car rental to be "just okay" (because more often than not they are inconveniently located away from the airport). However, since he owns his own business and travels at his own expense, he may feel that Value is "good enough," given that he may be paying a little less than he would be paying if he rented from one of the major business-oriented car rental companies located at the airport.

Indeed, individuals can have a variety of attitudes toward a particular behavior, each corresponding to a particular situation. Stan may feel it is all right to eat lunch at McDonald's but does not consider it appropriate for dinner. In this case, McDonald's has its "time and place," which functions as a boundary delineating the situations when Stan considers McDonald's acceptable. However, if Stan is coming home late from school one night, feels exhausted and hungry, and spots a McDonald's, he may decide to just have "dinner" there. Why? Because it is late, he is tired and hungry, and McDonald's is convenient. Has he changed his attitude? Probably not.

It is important to understand how consumer attitudes vary from situation to situation. For instance, it is useful to know whether consumer preferences for different burger chains (for instance, Burger King, McDonald's, or Wendy's) vary in terms of eating situations (that is, lunch or snack, evening meal when rushed for time, or evening meal with family when not rushed for time). Consumer preferences for the various burger restaurants might depend on the anticipated eating situation. Wendy's, for example, might be favored by some consumers as a good place to have dinner with their families. This suggests that its management might position Wendy's restaurants as a nice place to take the family for a leisurely (and inexpensive) dinner.

Clearly, when measuring attitudes, it is important to consider the situation in which the behavior takes place, or we can misinterpret the relationship between attitudes and behavior. Table 8-1 presents some additional examples of how specific situations might influence consumer attitudes toward specific brands of products or services.

TABLE 8-1 Examples of How Situations Might Influence Attitudes

PRODUCT/SERVICE	SITUATION	ATTITUDE
Coppertone Oil Free Sunscreen	Active sports in the sun	"It sounds like a good idea to use an oil free sunscreen when involved in summer sports activities."
Cannon Color Printers	Old PC printer ceases to work	"Now that they have gone down in price so much, it's time for me to buy a color printer."
Hilton Resorts and Casinos	Exhausted, time for a weekend get-a-way	"I worked hard; I earned a couple of days away to relax."
Altoids Mints	Bad taste in one's mouth	"I really need a strong mint after I drink a large cup of coffee."
Sports Illustrated for Kids	It's my nephew's birthday	"He loves sports; I should get a one-year subscription."
Omega Seamaster Professional	Old wristwatch is lost	"Now I have an opportunity to get the watch James Bond wears."
Claritin-D 24 Hour	Summer allergy	"I need something that really works. I've heard good things about Claritin."
Kraft Fat-Free Salad Dressings	Going on a diet	"I really should try using more fat-free products."

▪▪▪▪ STRUCTURAL MODELS OF ATTITUDES

Motivated by a desire to understand the relationship between attitudes and behavior, psychologists have sought to construct models that capture the underlying dimensions of an attitude.[2] To this end, the focus has been on specifying the composition of an attitude to better explain or predict behavior. The following section examines several important attitude models: the *tricomponent attitude model*, the *multiattribute attitude models*, the *trying-to-consume model*, and the *attitude-toward-the-ad model*. Each of these models provides a somewhat different perspective on the number of component parts of an attitude and how those parts are arranged or interrelated.

TRICOMPONENT ATTITUDE MODEL

According to the **tricomponent attitude model**, attitudes consist of three major components: a *cognitive* component, an *affective* component, and a *conative* component (see Figure 8-1).

The Cognitive Component

The first component of the tricomponent attitude model consists of a person's *cognitions*, that is, the knowledge and perceptions that are acquired by a combination of direct experience with the *attitude object* and related information from various sources. This knowledge and resulting perceptions commonly take the form of *beliefs*, that is, the consumer believes that the attitude object possesses various attributes and that specific behavior will lead to specific outcomes.

Although it captures only a part of Dana's belief system about two brands of pocket digital organizers (for example, the PalmPilot and Casio Casiopeia), Figure 8-2 illustrates the composition of a consumer's belief system about two alternatives. Dana's belief system for both brands consists of the same basic four attributes: ease of use, handwriting feature, PC backup, and "other" features. However, Dana has somewhat different beliefs about the two brands for these attributes. For instance, she knows from colleagues at work that the PalmPilot is famous for being easy to use and

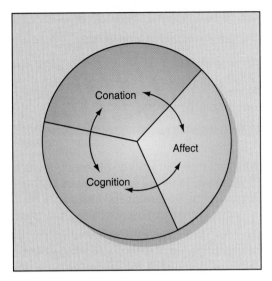

FIGURE 8-1
A Simple Representation of the Tricomponent Attitude Model

easy to back up; she feels from what she has read in an on-line review of the two machines that Casio is also good, but not as good on these two features. However, the Casio has a built-in drawing and doodling feature, as well as a built-in voice recording capability. These are two features that the PalmPilot did not have. Before she really makes her selection, she is thinking of asking a few friends and going on-line to the two companies' Web sites to check things out (www.palmpilot.com and www.casio.com).

The Affective Component

A consumer's *emotions* or *feelings* about a particular product or brand constitute the *affective component* of an attitude. These emotions and feelings are frequently treated by consumer researchers as primarily *evaluative* in nature; that is, they capture an individual's direct or global assessment of the attitude-object (or the extent to which the

FIGURE 8-2
A Consumer's Belief System for Two Brands of Pocket Digital Organizers

PRODUCT	POCKET DIGITAL ORGANIZERS							
BRAND	3Com PalmPilot				Casio Cassiopeia			
ATTRIBUTES	Ease of use	Handwriting feature	PC backup	Other features	Ease of use	Handwriting feature	PC backup	Other features
BELIEFS	Known to be a snap to use	A little effort to learn a few rules	Simple one button	Doesn't have built-in drawing feature	A longer learning curve	Easy, but a little learning	Some learning	Has drawing and voice-record features
EVALUATIONS	(++++)	(+++)	(++)	(–)	(+)	(++)	(++)	(+++)

TABLE 8-2 Selected Evaluative Scale Used to Gauge Consumers' Attitudes toward Old Spice After Shave

Compared to other after shave products, Old Spice is:

Good	[1]	[2]	[3]	[4]	[5]	[6]	[7]	Bad
Positive	[1]	[2]	[3]	[4]	[5]	[6]	[7]	Negative
Pleasant	[1]	[2]	[3]	[4]	[5]	[6]	[7]	Unpleasant
Appealing	[1]	[2]	[3]	[4]	[5]	[6]	[7]	Unappealing

individual rates the attitude-object as "favorable" or "unfavorable," "good" or "bad"). To illustrate, Table 8-2 shows a series of evaluative (affective) scale items that might be used to assess consumers' attitudes toward Old Spice After Shave.

Affect-laden experiences also manifest themselves as *emotionally charged states* (such as happiness, sadness, shame, disgust, anger, distress, guilt, or surprise). Research indicates that such emotional states may enhance or amplify positive or negative experiences and that later recollections of such experiences may impact what comes to mind and how the individual acts.[3] For instance, a person visiting an outlet mall is likely to be influenced by his or her emotional state at the time. If the outlet mall shopper is feeling particularly joyous at the moment, a positive response to the outlet mall may be amplified. The emotionally enhanced response to the outlet mall may lead the shopper to recall with great pleasure the time spent at the outlet mall. It also may influence the individual shopper to persuade friends and acquaintances to visit the same outlet mall and to make the personal decision to revisit the mall.

In addition to using direct or global evaluative measures of an attitude-object (for example, from "good to bad," or "pleasant to unpleasant," as depicted in Table 8-2), consumer researchers can also use a battery of affective response scales that measure feelings and emotions to construct a picture of consumers' overall feelings about a product, service, or ad. Table 8-3 gives an example of a five-point scale that measures affective responses.

TABLE 8-3 Measuring Consumers' Feelings and Emotions with Regard to Using Old Spice After Shave

For the past 10 days you have had a chance to try Old Spice After Shave. We would appreciate it if you would identify how your face felt after using the product during this 10-day trial period.

For each of the words below, we would appreciate it if you would mark an "X" in the box corresponding to how your face felt after using Old Spice during the past 10 days.

	VERY				NOT AT ALL
My face felt relaxed	[ ]	[ ]	[ ]	[ ]	[ ]
My face felt handsome	[ ]	[ ]	[ ]	[ ]	[ ]
My face felt tight	[ ]	[ ]	[ ]	[ ]	[ ]
My face felt smooth	[ ]	[ ]	[ ]	[ ]	[ ]
My face felt supple	[ ]	[ ]	[ ]	[ ]	[ ]
My face felt clean	[ ]	[ ]	[ ]	[ ]	[ ]
My face felt refreshed	[ ]	[ ]	[ ]	[ ]	[ ]
My face felt revived	[ ]	[ ]	[ ]	[ ]	[ ]
My face felt pampered	[ ]	[ ]	[ ]	[ ]	[ ]
My face felt renewed	[ ]	[ ]	[ ]	[ ]	[ ]

The Conative Component

Conation, the final component of the tricomponent attitude model, is concerned with the *likelihood* or *tendency* that an individual will undertake a specific action or behave in a particular way with regard to the attitude object. According to some interpretations, the conative component may include the actual behavior itself.

In marketing and consumer research, the conative component is frequently treated as an expression of the consumer's *intention to buy*. Buyer intention scales are used to assess the likelihood of a consumer purchasing a product or behaving in a certain way. Table 8-4 provides several examples of common **intention-to-buy scales**. Interestingly, consumers who are asked to respond to an intention-to-buy question appear to be more likely to actually make a brand purchase for positively evaluated brands (such as "I will buy it"), as contrasted to consumers who are not asked to respond to an intention question.[4] This suggests that a positive brand commitment in the form of a positive answer to an attitude intention question impacts in a positive way on the actual brand purchase.

MULTIATTRIBUTE ATTITUDE MODELS

Multiattribute attitude models portray consumers' attitudes with regard to an attitude "object" (such as a product, a service, a direct-mail catalog, or a cause or issue)[5] as a function of consumers' perception and assessment of the key attributes or beliefs held with regard to the particular attitude "object." Although there are many variations of this type of attitude model, we have selected the following three models to briefly consider here: the *attitude-toward-object model*, the *attitude-toward-behavior model*, and the *theory-of-reasoned-action model*.

The Attitude-Toward-Object Model

The attitude-toward-object model is especially suitable for measuring attitudes toward a *product* (or *service*) category or specific *brands*.[5] According to this model, the consumer's attitude toward a product or specific brands of a product is a function of the presence (or absence) and evaluation of certain product-specific beliefs or attributes. In other words, consumers generally have favorable attitudes toward those brands that they believe have an adequate level of attributes that they

TABLE 8-4 Two Examples of Intention-to-Buy Scales

Which of the following statements best describes the chance that you will buy Old Spice the next time you purchase an after shave product?

____ I definitely will buy it.
____ I probably will buy it.
____ I am uncertain whether I will buy it.
____ I probably will not buy it.
____ I definitely will not buy it.

How likely are you to buy Old Spice After Shave during the next three months?

____ Very likely
____ Likely
____ Unlikely
____ Very unlikely

evaluate as positive, and they have unfavorable attitudes toward those brands they feel do not have an adequate level of desired attributes or have too many negative or undesired attributes. As an illustration, we return to the pocket digital organizer (see Figure 8-2). Currently, there are about a half dozen or so brands of pocket digital organizers available on the market. The available brands each have a different "mix" of features (a "feature set"). The defining features might include: simplicity of general use, backup with one's PC, accuracy of the handwriting recognition program, e-mailing capacity, brightness of the backlit screen, drawing/doodling, and recording voice message. Some brands are likely to excel on the core features; some are really good on a few features; others are only adequate, but have more features; and some other brands are really no more than second-rate. However, what consumers will purchase is a function of how much they know, what they feel are the important features for them, and their awareness as to whether particular brands possess (or lack) these valued attributes.

The Attitude-Toward-Behavior Model

The **attitude-toward-behavior model** is the individual's *attitude toward behaving* or *acting* with respect to an object, rather than the attitude toward the object itself.[6] The appeal of the attitude-toward-behavior model is that it seems to correspond somewhat more closely to actual behavior than does the attitude-toward-object model. For instance, knowing Howard's attitude about the act of purchasing a top-of-the-line BMW (that is, his attitude toward the *behavior*) reveals more about the potential act of purchasing than does simply knowing his attitude toward expensive German cars, or specifically BMWs (or the attitude toward the *object*). This seems logical, for a consumer might have a positive attitude toward an expensive BMW, but a negative attitude as to his prospects for purchasing such an expensive vehicle.

Theory-of-Reasoned-Action Model

The **theory of reasoned action** represents a comprehensive integration of attitude components into a structure that is designed to lead to both better explanations and better predictions of behavior. Like the basic tricomponent attitude model, the theory-of-reasoned-action model incorporates a *cognitive* component, an *affective* component, and a *conative* component; however, these are arranged in a pattern different from that of the tricomponent model (see Figure 8-3).

In accordance with this expanded model, to understand *intention* we also need to measure the *subjective norms* that influence an individual's intention to act. A subjective norm can be measured directly by assessing a consumer's feelings as to what relevant others (family, friends, roommates, co-workers) would think of the action being contemplated; that is, would they look favorably or unfavorably on the anticipated action? For example, if a graduate student was considering purchasing a new VW Beetle and stopped to ask himself what his parents or girlfriend would think of such behavior (that is, approve or disapprove), such a reflection would constitute his subjective norm.

Consumer researchers can get behind the *subjective norm* to the underlying factors that are likely to produce it. They accomplish this by assessing the *normative beliefs* that the individual attributes to relevant others, as well as the individual's *motivation to comply* with each of the relevant others. For instance, consider the graduate student contemplating the purchase of a new VW Beetle. To understand his subjective norm about the desired purchase, we would have to identify his relevant others (parents and girlfriend); his beliefs about how each would respond to his pur-

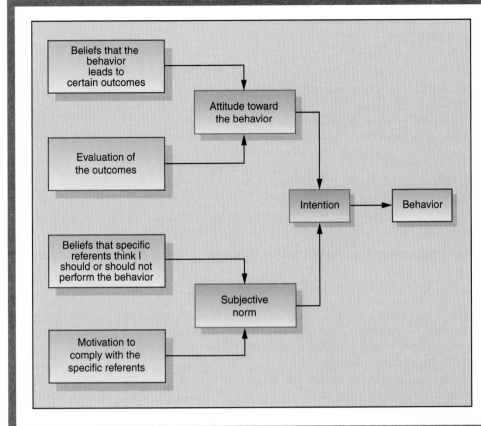

FIGURE 8-3
A Simplified Version of the Theory of Reasoned Action

Source: Adapted from Icek Ajzen and Martin Fishbein, *Understanding Attitudes and Predicting Social Behavior* (Upper Saddle River, NJ: Prentice Hall, 1980), 84. © 1980. Adapted by permission of Prentice-Hall, Inc.

chase of the Beetle (such as "Dad would consider the car an unnecessary luxury, but my girlfriend would love it"); and finally, his motivation to comply with his parents or his girlfriend.[7]

THEORY OF TRYING TO CONSUME

There has been an effort underway to extend attitude models so that they might better accommodate consumers' goals as expressed by their "trying" to consume.[8] The **theory of trying to consume** is designed to account for the many cases where the action or outcome is not certain, but instead reflects the consumer's attempts to consume (or purchase). In such cases, there are often *personal impediments* (a consumer is trying to find just the right eyeglass frames for under $200 or trying to lose weight but loves desserts) and/or *environmental impediments* (only the first 500 in line will be able to purchase tickets for the rock concert) that might prevent the desired action or outcome from occurring. Again, the key point is that in these cases of trying, the outcome (purchase, possession, use, or action) is not, and cannot be assumed to be, certain. Table 8-5 lists a few examples of possible personal and environmental impediments that might negatively impact the outcome for a consumer trying to consume. Researchers have recently extended this inquiry by examining those situations where consumers do *not* try to consume—that is *failing to try to consume*. In this case, consumers appear to: (1) fail to see or are too ignorant of their options; and (2) make a conscious effort not to consume; that is, they might seek to self-sacrifice or defer gratification to some future time.[9]

TABLE 8-5 Selected Examples of Potential Impediments That Might Impact on Trying

POTENTIAL PERSONAL IMPEDIMENTS

"I wonder whether my fingernails will be longer by the time of my wedding."
"I want to try to lose fifteen pounds by next summer."
"I'm going to try to get tickets for a Broadway show for your birthday."
"I'm going to attempt to give up smoking by my birthday."
"I am going to increase how often I go to the gym from two to four times a week."
"Tonight, I'm not going to have dessert at the restaurant."

POTENTIAL ENVIRONMENTAL IMPEDIMENTS

"The first ten people to call in will receive a free T-shirt."
"Sorry, the shoes didn't come in this shipment from Italy."
"There are only three bottles of champagne in our stockroom. You better come in sometime today."
"I am sorry. We cannot serve you. We are closing the restaurant because of a problem with the oven."

ATTITUDE-TOWARD-THE-AD MODELS

In an effort to understand the impact of advertising or some other promotional vehicle (such as a catalog) on consumer attitudes toward particular products or brands, considerable attention has been paid to developing what has been referred to as **attitude-toward-the-ad models**.

Figure 8-4 presents a schematic of some of the basic relationships described by an attitude-toward-the-ad model. As the model depicts, the consumer forms various feelings (affects) and judgments (cognitions) as the result of exposure to an ad. These feelings and judgments in turn affect the consumer's attitude toward the ad and beliefs about the brand acquired from exposure to the ad. Finally, the consumer's attitude toward the ad and beliefs about the brand influence his or her attitude toward the brand.[10]

FIGURE 8-4

A Conception of the Relationship among Elements in an Attitude-Toward-the-Ad Model

Source: Inspired by and based on Julie A. Edell and Marian Chapman Burke, "The Power of Feelings in Understanding Advertising Effects," *Journal of Consumer Research* 14 (Dec 1987), 431. Reprinted by permission of University of Chicago Press as publisher.

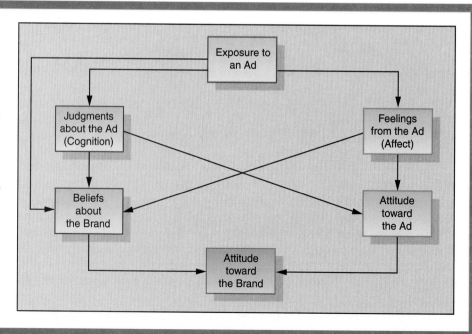

It appears that for a novel product, such as a "contact lens for pets," the consumer's attitude toward the ad has a *stronger* impact on brand attitude and purchase intention than for a familiar product, such as pet food.[11] This same research found that beliefs about a brand (brand cognition) that result from ad exposure play a much stronger role in determining attitudes toward the brand for a familiar product. This research points up the importance of considering the nature of the attitude object in assessing the potential impact of advertising exposure.

ATTITUDE FORMATION

How do people, especially young people, form their initial *general* attitudes toward "things"? Consider their attitudes toward clothing they wear, for example, such as underwear, casual wear, and business attire. On a more specific level, how do they form attitudes toward Fruit of the Loom or Calvin Klein underwear, or Levi's or Gap casual wear, or Anne Klein or Emporium Armani business clothing? Also, what about where such clothing is purchased? Would they buy their underwear, casual wear, and business clothing at K-Mart, Sears, JC Penney, or Macy's? How do family members and friends, admired celebrities, mass-media advertisements, even cultural memberships, influence the formation of their attitudes concerning consuming or not consuming each of these types of apparel items? Why do some attitudes seem to persist indefinitely, while others change fairly often? The answers to such questions are of vital importance to marketers, for without knowing how attitudes are formed, they are unable to understand or to influence consumer attitudes or behavior.

Our examination of attitude formation is divided into three areas: how attitudes are learned, the sources of influence on attitude formation, and the impact of personality on attitude formation.

HOW ATTITUDES ARE LEARNED

When we speak of the formation of an attitude, we refer to the shift from having no attitude toward a given object (for instance, a notebook computer) to having *some* attitude toward it (such as a notebook computer is useful when traveling). The shift from no attitude to an attitude (or the *attitude formation*) is a result of learning (see chapter 7 for a detailed exploration of learning theories).

Consumers often purchase new products that are associated with a favorably viewed brand name. Their favorable attitude toward the brand name is frequently the result of repeated satisfaction with other products produced by the same company. In terms of *classical conditioning*, an established brand name is an *unconditioned* stimulus that through past positive reinforcement has resulted in a favorable brand attitude. A new product, yet to be linked to the established brand, would be the *conditioned* stimulus. To illustrate, by giving a new skin-smoothing lotion the benefit of its well-known and respected family name, Jergens® is counting on an extension of the favorable attitude already associated with the brand name to the new product. They are counting on *stimulus generalization* from the brand name to the new product. Research suggests that the "fit" between a parent brand (for instance, Jergens) and a brand extension (for instance, Jergens' skin-smoothing lotion) is a function of two factors: (1) the similarity between the pre-existing product categories already associated with the parent brand and the new extension, and (2) the "fit" or match between the images of the parent brand and the new extension.[12]

Sometimes, attitudes follow the purchase and consumption of a product. For example, a consumer may purchase a brand-name product without having a prior attitude toward it, because it is the only product of its kind available (such as the last tube of toothpaste in a hotel drugstore). Consumers also make trial purchases of new brands from product categories in which they have little personal involvement (see chapter 7). If they find the purchased brand to be satisfactory, then they are likely to develop a favorable attitude toward it.

In situations in which consumers seek to solve a problem or satisfy a need, they are likely to form attitudes (either positive or negative) about products on the basis of information exposure and their own cognition (knowledge and beliefs). In general, the more information consumers have about a product or service, the more likely they are to form attitudes about it, either positive or negative. However, regardless of the available information, consumers are not always ready or willing to process product-related information. Furthermore, consumers often use only a limited amount of the information available to them. Research suggests that only two or three important beliefs about a product dominate in the formation of attitudes and that less important beliefs provide little additional input.[13] This finding suggests that marketers should fight off the impulse to include *all* the features of their products and services in their ads; rather, they should focus on the few key points that are at the heart of what distinguishes their product from the competition.

SOURCES OF INFLUENCE ON ATTITUDE FORMATION

The formation of consumer attitudes is strongly influenced by personal experience, the influence of family and friends, direct marketing, and mass media.

The primary means by which attitudes toward goods and services are formed is through the consumer's direct experience in trying and evaluating them.[14] Recognizing the importance of direct experience, marketers frequently attempt to stimulate trial of new products by offering cents-off coupons or even free samples. Figure 8-5 illustrates this strategy; the ad for Diet Snapple includes a coupon for 55¢ off when the consumer buys two 16-ounce bottles to encourage trial. In such cases, the marketer's objective is to get consumers to try the product and then to evaluate it. If a product proves to their liking, then it is probable that consumers will form a positive attitude and be likely to purchase the product. In addition, from the information on the coupon (such as name and address) the marketer is able to create a database of interested consumers.

As we come in contact with others, especially family, close friends, and admired individuals (such as a respected teacher), we form attitudes that influence our lives. The family is an extremely important source of influence on the formation of attitudes, for it is the family that provides us with many of our basic values and a wide range of less-central beliefs. For instance, young children who are "rewarded" for good behavior with sweet foods and candy often retain a taste for (and positive attitude toward) sweets as adults.

Marketers are increasingly using highly focused direct-marketing programs to target small consumer niches with products and services that fit their interests and lifestyles. (Niche marketing is sometimes called *micromarketing*.) Marketers very carefully target customers on the basis of their demographic, psychographic, or geo-demographic profiles with highly personalized product offerings (such as golf clubs for left-handed people) and messages that show they understand their special needs and desires. Direct marketing efforts have an excellent chance of favorably influencing target consumers' attitudes, because the products and services offered and the

FIGURE 8-5
Snapple Uses a Cents-Off
Coupon to Encourage Trial

promotional messages conveyed are very carefully designed to address the individual segment's needs and concerns. Thus, they are able to achieve a higher "hit rate" than mass marketing.

In countries where people have easy access to newspapers and a variety of general and special-interest magazines and television channels, consumers are constantly exposed to new ideas, products, opinions, and advertisements. These mass-media communications provide an important source of information that influences the formation of consumer attitudes.

PERSONALITY FACTORS

Personality also plays a critical role in attitude formation. For example, individuals with a *high need for cognition* (that is, those who crave information and enjoy thinking) are likely to form positive attitudes in response to ads or direct mail that are rich in product-related information. On the other hand, consumers who are relatively *low in need for cognition* are more likely to form positive attitudes in response to ads that feature an attractive model or well-known celebrity. In a similar fashion, attitudes toward new products and new consumption situations are strongly influenced by specific personality characteristics of consumers.

■■■■ ATTITUDE CHANGE

It is important to recognize that much that has been said about *attitude formation* is also basically true of attitude change. That is, attitude changes are learned; they are influenced by personal experience and other sources of information, and personality affects both the receptivity and the speed with which attitudes are likely to be altered.

■■■■ STRATEGIES OF ATTITUDE CHANGE

Altering consumer attitudes is a key strategy consideration for most marketers. For marketers who are fortunate enough to be market leaders and to enjoy a significant amount of customer goodwill and loyalty, the overriding goal is to fortify the existing positive attitudes of customers so that they will not succumb to competitors' special offers and other inducements designed to win them over. For instance, in many product categories (greeting cards, in which Hallmark has been the leader, or wet shaving systems, in which Gillette has dominated), most competitors take aim at the market leaders when developing their marketing strategies. Their objective is to change the attitudes of the market leaders' customers and win them over. Among the *attitude-change strategies* that are available to them are: (1) changing the consumer's basic motivational function, (2) associating the product with an admired group or event, (3) resolving two conflicting attitudes, (4) altering components of the multiattribute model, and (5) changing consumer beliefs about competitors' brands.

CHANGING THE BASIC MOTIVATIONAL FUNCTION

An effective strategy for changing consumer attitudes toward a product or brand is to make particular needs prominent. One method for changing motivation is known as the **functional approach**.[15] According to this approach, attitudes can be classified in terms of four functions: the **utilitarian function**, the **ego-defensive function**, the **value-expressive function**, and the **knowledge function**.

The Utilitarian Function

We hold certain brand attitudes partly because of a brand's utility. When a product has been useful or helped us in the past, our attitude toward it tends to be favorable. One way of changing attitudes in favor of a product is by showing people that it can serve a utilitarian purpose that they may not have considered. For example, as its market positioning,

Comet cleaner with bleach stresses its utilitarian benefit in terms of superior cleaning ability. Similarly, Scripto Aim'n Flame lighter also stresses its superiority (to the match) as a means of safely lighting fireplaces, barbecues, or pilot lights (a utilitarian benefit).

The Ego-Defensive Function

Most people want to protect their self-images from inner feelings of doubt—they want to replace their uncertainty with a sense of security and personal confidence. Ads for cosmetics and personal care products, by acknowledging this need, increase both their relevance to the consumer and the likelihood of a favorable attitude change by offering reassurance to the consumer's self-concept. For example, Figure 8-6 for Ortho's Retin-A counter argues a number of common parental stalemates about teenage acne (e.g., "There's nothing you can do about it") with the statement "No matter what anybody says, it's your face and you can take action." Ortho's response shows understanding and it's reassuring to potential consumers.

The Value-Expressive Function

Attitudes are an expression or reflection of the consumer's general values, lifestyle, and outlook. If a consumer segment generally holds a positive attitude toward owning the latest personal communications devices (owning the smallest cellular telephone currently on the market), then their attitudes toward new electronic devices are likely to reflect that orientation. Similarly, if a segment of consumers has a positive attitude toward being "in fashion," then their attitudes toward high-fashion clothing are likely to reflect this viewpoint. Thus, by knowing target consumers' attitudes, marketers can better anticipate their values, lifestyle, or outlook and can reflect these characteristics in their ads and direct-marketing efforts. Advertisements for Tommy Hilfiger's Tommy fragrance are targeted to young individuals who pursue a clean-cut, sociable, and outdoors lifestyle.

The Knowledge Function

Individuals generally have a strong need to know and understand the people and things with whom they come in contact. The consumer's "need to know," a cognitive need, is important to marketers concerned with product positioning. Indeed, many product and brand positionings are attempts to satisfy the *need to know* and to improve the consumer's attitudes toward the brand by emphasizing its advantages over competitive brands. For instance, a message for an advanced design toothbrush might point out *how* it is superior to other toothbrushes in controlling gum disease by removing more plaque and why this is so important to good overall health. The message might even use a bar graph to contrast its plaque removal abilities to other leading toothbrushes. Figure 8-7 is an ad for Activin™, the natural extract of red grape seeds that helps fight free radicals by providing antioxidant power that helps promote good health. The presentation of scientific evidence and graphic comparative information about Activin™ all are an appeal to consumers's *need to know*.

Combining Several Functions

Because different consumers may like or dislike the same product or service for different reasons, a functional framework for examining attitudes can be very useful. For instance, three consumers may all have positive attitudes toward Suave hair care products. However, one may be responding solely to the fact that the products work well (the utilitarian function); the second may have the inner confidence to agree with the point "When you know beautiful hair doesn't have to cost a fortune" (an ego-defensive function). The third consumer's favorable attitudes might reflect the realization that Suave has for many years stressed "value" (equal or better products for less)—the knowledge function.

FIGURE 8-6
Appeal to the Ego-
Defensive Function

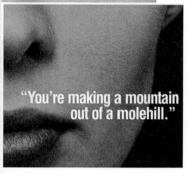

No matter what anybody says,
it's your face and you can take action.

You can make it clearer. You can make it more healthy-looking. You can even make it blemish-free. Whether you have five pimples or fifteen.

Retin-A is a proven prescription treatment you can only get from your healthcare provider. Unlike other products that simply cover up or dry out pimples, Retin-A works at the source where blemishes begin.

It contains tretinoin, a vitamin A derivative much like the naturally occurring one in your body. Retin-A is thought to help lift excess oil and pore-clogging skin cells to the surface. It also helps prevent this cell build-up from recurring, so you can maintain the improvement in your skin.

Retin-A doesn't work overnight. However, with continued use you may start to notice an overall improvement. So be patient.

During the first few weeks, some irritation, including redness and peeling, will be experienced by most patients. Generally, these effects are manageable and diminish over time. However, some people with sensitive skin may experience excessive irritation. Since Retin-A may make your skin more sensitive to the sun's rays, be sure to protect your skin from natural or artificial sunlight. For more information, ask your healthcare provider about Retin-A or call: **1-800-99RETIN-A**.

Retin-A for the skin you want to have.
See additional important information on the following page.

ASSOCIATING THE PRODUCT WITH A SPECIAL GROUP, EVENT, OR CAUSE

Attitudes are related, at least in part, to certain groups, social events, or causes. It is possible to alter attitudes toward products, services, and brands by pointing out their relationships to particular social groups, events, or causes. For instance, A.T. Cross provides a fixed amount of financial support to Literacy Volunteers of America when consumers purchase their fine writing instruments. This link with a literacy enhancing program is a logical step

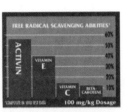

The French eat rich foods. They smoke more, exercise less, and live longer.

(Is there no justice?)

In France, the pursuit of pleasure does not include trips to the gym or avoiding fatty foods. (Life is good.) So why do the French have the lowest rate of heart disease of any Westernized society? This is the French Paradox.

Some scientists believe they have traced the mystery of the French Paradox to the red wine they drink, which contains powerful antioxidants called biologically active flavonoids. Antioxidants help protect the body against free radicals, which can destroy cell membrane molecules and damage DNA. Many scientists believe that free radicals may be a root cause of certain types of cancer, heart disease and the aging process.

Inspired by the research behind the French Paradox, ActiVin™ is a natural extract of red grape seeds, where flavonoids are concentrated. ActiVin helps fight free radicals by delivering the antioxidant power of flavonoids without the alcohol of red wine.

In fact, university studies show that the antioxidant activity of ActiVin is significantly greater than that of vitamins E, C or beta-carotene, which means that ActiVin may be more effective in fighting free radicals and maintaining a healthier, active life.

ActiVin promotes good health in other ways as well.

It is made by a unique process called *Acti-Pure*™, which eliminates the need for toxic chemicals used in extracting flavonoids. So it's safe to consume and environmentally friendly to produce.

ActiVin is a nutritional ingredient found in quality health and dietary products. Make sure you see the ActiVin™ logo on the label, or call 1-800-783-4636 for more information. It's not just about better health; it's about living better.

FREE RADICAL SCAVENGING ABILITIES

ACTIVIN — 60%
VITAMIN E — 50%
VITAMIN C — BETA-CAROTENE — 10%
COMPOSITE IN VIVO TEST DATA   100 mg/kg Dosage

ACTIVIN™
THE POWER TO STAY HEALTHY™

©1997 InterHealth Nutritionals Incorporated, Concord, CA 94520 (510) 827-4400 fax/(510) 827-4086 www.InterHealthUSA.com

FIGURE 8-7
Appeal to the Knowledge Function

on the part of a writing instrument company like A.T. Cross. It also has the potential of augmenting consumers' positive attitudes toward A.T. Cross, among consumers who perceive the Literacy Volunteers of America as a worthwhile not-for-profit service organization.

RESOLVING TWO CONFLICTING ATTITUDES

Attitude-change strategies can sometimes resolve actual or potential conflict between two attitudes. Specifically, if consumers can be made to see that their negative attitude toward a product, a specific brand, or its attributes, is really not in conflict with another attitude, they may be induced to change their evaluation of the brand (or move from negative to positive).

For example, Charles loves the idea of making video documentaries of his frequent vacations to exotic faraway places (attitude #1), but he may feel that purchasing a camcorder is an unwise investment because these cameras are inadequate when it comes to low-light environments that he repeatedly finds himself in (attitude #2). However, if Charles learns that Sony makes camcorders with a "NightShot™" feature that makes it possible to record in even complete darkness, he might change his mind, thus resolving his conflicting attitudes (see Figure 8-8).

ALTERING COMPONENTS OF THE MULTIATTRIBUTE MODEL

Earlier in this chapter we discussed a number of multiattribute attitude models. These models have implications for attitude-change strategies; specifically, they provide us with additional insights as to how to bring about attitude change: (1) changing the relative evaluation of attributes, (2) changing brand beliefs, (3) adding an attribute, and (4) changing the overall brand rating.

FIGURE 8-8

Resolving Two Conflicting Attitudes

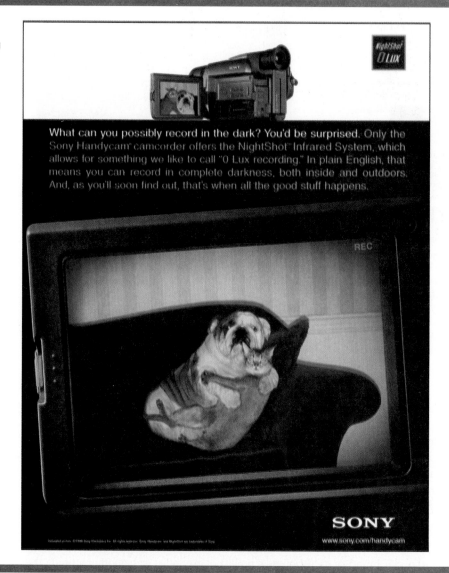

Changing the Relative Evaluation of Attributes

The overall market for many product categories is often set out so that different consumer segments are offered different brands, with different features or benefits. For instance, within a product category such as headache remedies, there are brands like Extra-Strength Anacin that stress potency and brands like Tylenol that stress gentleness (or contain no aspirin). These two brands of headache remedy historically have appealed to different segments of the overall headache remedy market. Similarly, when it comes to chewing gum, the market can be divided into regular gum and sugar-free gum or into regular gum and bubble gum.

In general, when a product category is naturally divided according to distinct product features or benefits that appeal to a particular segment of consumers, marketers usually have an opportunity to persuade consumers to "cross over," that is, to persuade consumers who prefer one version of the product (such as a 35-mm single-lens reflex camera) to shift their favorable attitudes toward another version of the product (for instance, a highly automatic point-and-shoot camera), and possibly vice versa.

Changing Brand Beliefs

A second cognitive-oriented strategy for changing attitudes concentrates on changing beliefs or perceptions about the brand itself. This is by far the most common form of advertising appeal. Advertisers are constantly reminding us that their product has "more" or is "better" or "best" in terms of some important product attribute. As a variation on this theme of "more," ads for Palmolive dishwashing liquid are designed to *extend* consumers' brand attitudes with regard to the product's gentleness by suggesting that it be used for hand washing of fine clothing items. Dr Pepper's ads challenge consumers to taste any difference between regular Dr Pepper (with sugar) and Diet Dr Pepper (sugar free). One version visually portrays the idea of the same taste by using identical twins each with a can of one of the two types of soft drinks in their hand. Moreover, it offers a $1.00-off coupon to give consumers an incentive to try Diet Dr Pepper. The purpose is to change consumers' attitudes about Diet Dr Pepper (that is, that it tastes as good as regular Dr Pepper).

Adding an Attribute

Another cognitive strategy consists of *adding an attribute*. This can be accomplished either by adding an attribute that previously has been ignored or one that represents an improvement or technological innovation.

The first route, adding a previously ignored attribute, is illustrated by the point that yogurt has more potassium than a banana (a fruit associated with a high quantity of potassium). For consumers interested in increasing their intake of potassium, the comparison of yogurt and bananas has the power of enhancing their attitudes toward yogurt.

The second route of adding an attribute that reflects an actual product change or technological innovation is easier to accomplish than stressing a previously ignored attribute. An example is Pantene Pro-V hair spray, which makes the point that because of the new ingredient Elastesse® its product is able to hold hair in place without a stiff or sticky feel. Thus, by adding an ingredient, Pantene may favorably alter consumers' attitudes. In a similar fashion, Dove's decision to introduce an unscented version of its popular moisturizing bar may help women with a strong preference for unscented cosmetic products to now shift their attitude toward Dove and consider purchasing the unscented Dove soap (*deleting an ingredient*).

Changing the Overall Brand Rating

Still another cognitive-oriented strategy consists of attempting to alter consumers' *overall assessment of the brand* directly, without attempting to improve or change their evaluation of any single brand attribute. Such a strategy frequently relies on some form of global statement that "this is the largest-selling brand" or "the one all others try to imitate," or a similar claim that sets the brand apart from all its competitors. This strategy has regularly been part of Honda's advertising approach of affirming that its cars are used by other auto manufacturers as the "standard" to live up to.

CHANGING BELIEFS ABOUT COMPETITORS' BRANDS

Another approach to attitude change strategy involves changing consumer beliefs about the *attributes of competitive* brands or product categories. For instance, an ad for Advil makes a dramatic assertion of product superiority over aspirin and Tylenol: The ad claims that Advil lasts longer and is gentler than aspirin and that two Advil work better than Extra Strength Tylenol. Similarly, Vicks 44 claimed that it works longer at fighting coughs than Robitussin-DM (see Figure 8-9). Clearly, the purpose of this ad is to create the attitude that Vicks 44 is a longer-lasting product than a principal competitor. In general, this strategy must be used with caution. Comparative advertising can boomerang by giving visibility to competing brands and claims. (Chapter 9 discusses comparative advertising in greater depth.)

THE ELABORATION LIKELIHOOD MODEL (ELM)

Compared to the various specific strategies of attitude change that we have reviewed, the **elaboration likelihood model (ELM)** proposes the more global view that consumer attitudes are changed by two distinctly different "routes to persuasion"—a central route or a peripheral route (see also chapter 7).[16] The *central route* is particularly relevant to attitude change when a consumer's motivation or ability to assess the attitude object is high; that is, attitude change occurs because the consumer actively seeks out information relevant to the attitude object itself. When consumers are willing to exert the effort to comprehend, learn, or evaluate the available information about the attitude object, learning and attitude change occur via the central route.

In contrast, when a consumer's motivation or assessment skills are low (low-involvement), learning and attitude change tend to occur via the peripheral route without the consumer focusing on information relevant to the attitude object itself. In such cases, attitude change is often an outcome of secondary inducements (such as cents-off coupons, free samples, beautiful background scenery, great package, or the encouragement of a celebrity endorsement). Current research indicates that even in low-involvement conditions (like exposure to most advertising), where both central and secondary inducements are initially equal in their ability to evoke similar attitudes, it is the central inducement that has the greatest "staying power"—that is over time it is more persistent.[17]

∷ ## BEHAVIOR CAN PRECEDE
OR FOLLOW ATTITUDE FORMATION

Our discussion of attitude formation and attitude change has stressed the traditional "rational" view that consumers develop their attitudes before taking action (or "Know what you are doing before you do it"). There are alternatives to this "attitude precedes

FIGURE 8-9
Changing Attitudes by
Changing Beliefs About a
Competitor's Brand

behavior" perspective, alternatives that, on careful analysis, are likely to be just as logical and rational. For example, *cognitive dissonance theory* and *attribution theory* each provide a different explanation as to why behavior might precede attitude formation.

COGNITIVE DISSONANCE THEORY

According to **cognitive dissonance theory**, discomfort or dissonance occurs when a consumer holds conflicting thoughts about a belief or an attitude object. For instance, when consumers have made a commitment—made a down payment or placed an order for a product, particularly an expensive one such as an automobile or a personal computer—they often begin to feel cognitive dissonance when they think of the unique, positive qualities of the brands not selected ("left behind"). When cognitive dissonance occurs after a purchase, it is called **postpurchase dissonance**. Because purchase decisions often require some amount of compromise, postpurchase dissonance is quite normal. Nevertheless, it is likely to leave consumers with an uneasy feeling about their prior beliefs or actions—a feeling that they tend to resolve by changing their attitudes to conform with their behavior.

Thus, in the case of postpurchase dissonance, attitude change is frequently an *outcome* of an action or behavior. The conflicting thoughts or dissonant information that follow a purchase are prime factors that induce consumers to change their attitudes so that they will be consonant with their actual purchase behavior.

What makes postpurchase dissonance relevant to marketing strategists is the premise that *dissonance* propels consumers to reduce the unpleasant feelings created by the rival thoughts. A variety of tactics are open to consumers to reduce postpurchase dissonance. The consumer can rationalize the decision as being wise, seek out advertisements that support the choice (while avoiding dissonance-creating competitive ads), try to "sell" friends on the positive features of the brand, or look to known satisfied owners for reassurance.

In addition to such consumer-initiated tactics to reduce postpurchase uncertainty, a marketer can relieve consumer dissonance by including messages in its advertising specifically aimed at reinforcing consumers' decisions by "complimenting their wisdom," offering stronger guarantees or warranties, increasing the number and effectiveness of its services, or providing detailed brochures on how to use its products correctly. Beyond these dissonance-reducing tactics, marketers increasingly are developing *affinity* or *relationship programs* (see chapter 16) designed to reward good customers and to build customer loyalty and satisfaction. As noted earlier, the airlines, hotel chains, and major car rental companies have all developed such programs for their best customers.

ATTRIBUTION THEORY

As a group of loosely interrelated social psychological principles, **attribution theory** attempts to explain how people assign causality (that is, blame or credit) to events on the basis of either their own behavior or the behavior of others.[18] In other words, a person might say, "I contributed to Care, Inc., because it really helps people in need," or "She tried to persuade me to buy that unknown autofocus camera because she'd make a bigger commission." In attribution theory, the underlying question is why: "Why did I do this?" "Why did she try to get me to switch brands?" This process of making inferences about one's own or another's behavior is a major component of attitude formation and change.

Attribution theory describes attitude formation and change as an outgrowth of people's speculations as to their own behavior (self-perception) and experiences.

Self-Perception Theory

Of the various perspectives on attribution theory that have been proposed, **self-perception theory**—individuals' inferences or judgments as to the causes of their own behavior—is a good beginning point for a discussion of attribution.

In terms of consumer behavior, self-perception theory suggests that attitudes develop as consumers look at and make judgments about their own behavior. Simply stated, if a woman observes that she routinely purchases the *Wall Street Journal* on her way to work, she is apt to conclude that she likes the *Wall Street Journal* (or has a pos-

EXERCISES

1. Find two print ads, one illustrating the use of the affective component and the other illustrating the cognitive component. Discuss each ad in the context of the tri-component model. In your view, why has each marketer taken the approach in each of these ads?

2. What sources influenced your attitude about this course before classes started? Has your initial attitude changed since the course started? If so, how?

3. Describe a situation in which you acquired an attitude toward a new product through exposure to an advertisement for that product. Describe a situation where you formed an attitude toward a product or brand on the basis of personal influence.

4. Find advertisements that illustrate each of the four motivational functions of attitudes. Distinguish between ads that are designed to reinforce an existing attitude and those aimed at changing an attitude.

5. Think back to the time when you were selecting a college. Did you experience dissonance immediately after you made a decision? Why or why not? If you did experience dissonance, how did you resolve it?

KEY TERMS

- **Attitude-toward-object model**
- **Attitude-toward-the-ad model**
- **Attitude-toward-behavior model**
- **Attitudes**
- **Attribution theory**
- **Attributions toward things**
- **Attributions toward others**
- **Cognitive dissonance theory**
- **Defensive attribution**
- **Ego-defensive function**
- **Elaboration Likelihood Model**
- **Foot-in-the-door technique**
- **Functional approach**
- **Intention-to-buy scales**
- **Internal and external attributions**
- **Knowledge function**
- **Multiattribute attitude models**
- **Postpurchase dissonance**
- **Self-perception theory**
- **Theory-of-reasoned-action model**
- **Theory of trying to consume**
- **Tricomponent attitude model**
- **Utilitarian function**
- **Value-expressive function**

NOTES

1. Stuart Elliott, "Fruit of the Loom Redesigns Its Sales Pitches with a Modern Edge—No Surprise—'Fruitness,'" *New York Times*, 2 June 1998, D6.
2. Richard J. Lutz, "The Role of Attitude Theory in Marketing," in *Perspectives in Consumer Behavior*, 4th ed., ed. Harold H. Kassarjian and Thomas S. Robertson (Upper Saddle River, NJ: Prentice Hall, 1991), 317–39.
3. Joel B. Cohen and Charles S. Areni, "Affect and Consumer Behavior," in *Perspectives in Consumer Behavior*, 4th ed., ed. Harold H. Kassarjian and Thomas S. Robertson (Upper Saddle River, NJ: Prentice Hall, 1991), 188–240; and Madeline Johnson and George M. Zinkhan, "Emotional Responses to a Professional Service Encounter," *Journal of Service Marketing* 5 (Spring 1991): 5–16. Also see: John Kim, Jeen-Su Lim, and Mukesh Bhargava, "The Role of Affect in Attitude Formation: A Classical Condition Approach," *Journal of the Academy of Marketing Science* 26 (1998): 143–52.
4. Jaideep Sengupta, "Perspectives on Attitude Strength" (a special session summary), in *Advances in Consumer Research*, vol. 25, ed. Joseph W. Alba and J. Wesley Hutchinson (Provo, UT: Association for Consumer Research, 1998), 63–64.
5. Martin Fishbein, "An Investigation of the Relationships between Beliefs about an Object and the Attitude toward the Object," *Human Relations* 16 (1963): 233–40; and Martin Fishbein, "A Behavioral Theory Approach to the Relations between Beliefs about an Object and the Attitude toward the Object," in *Readings in Attitude Theory and Measurement*, ed. Martin Fishbein (New York: Wiley, 1967), 389–400.

6. Icek Ajzen and Martin Fishbein, *Understanding Attitudes and Predicting Social Behavior* (Upper Saddle River, NJ: Prentice Hall, 1980); and Martin Fishbein and Icek Ajzen, *Belief, Attitude, Intentions, and Behavior* (Reading, MA: Addison-Wesley, 1975), 62–63. Also, see: Robert E. Burnkrant, H. Rao Unnava, and Thomas J. Page Jr., "Effects of Experience on Attitude Structure," in *Advances in Consumer Research*, vol. 18, ed. Rebecca H. Holman and Michael R. Solomon (Provo, UT: Association for Consumer Research, 1991), 28–29.

7. Terence A. Shimp and Alican Kavas, "The Theory of Reasoned Action Applied to Coupon Usage," *Journal of Consumer Research* 11 (December 1984): 795–809; Blair H. Sheppard, Jon Hartwick, and Paul R. Warshaw, "The Theory of Reasoned Action: A Meta-Analysis of Past Research with Recommendations for Modifications and Future Research," *Journal of Consumer Research* 15 (September 1986): 325–43; Sharon E. Beatly and Lynn R. Kahle, "Alternative Hierarchies of the Attitude-Behavior Relationship: The Impact of Brand Commitment and Habit," *Journal of the Academy of Marketing Science* 16 (Summer 1988): 1–10; and Richard P. Bagozzi, Hans Baumgartner, and Youjae Yi, "Coupon Usage and the Theory of Reasoned Action," in *Advances in Consumer Research*, vol. 18, ed. Rebecca H. Holman and Michael R. Solomon (Provo, UT: Association for Consumer Research, 1991), 24–27.

8. Richard P. Bagozzi and Paul R. Warshaw, "Trying to Consume," *Journal of Consumer Research* 17 (September 1990): 127–40; Richard P. Bagozzi, Fred D. Davis, and Paul R. Warshaw, "Development and Test of a Theory of Technological Learning and Usage," *Human Relations* 45, 7 (July 1992): 659–86; and Anil Mathur, "From Intentions to Behavior: The Role of Trying and Control," in *1995 AMA Educators' Proceedings*, ed. Barbara B. Stern and George M. Zinkan (Chicago: American Marketing Association, 1995), 374–75.

9. Stephen J. Gould, Franklin S. Houston, and Jonel Mundt, "Failing to Try to Consume: A Reversal of the Usual Consumer Research Perspective," in *Advances in Consumer Research*, ed. Merrie Brucks and Deborah J. MacInnis (Provo, UT: Association for Consumer Research, 1997), 211–16.

10. Rajeev Batra and Michael L. Ray, "Affective Responses Mediating Acceptance of Advertising," *Journal of Consumer Research* 13 (September 1986): 236–39; Julie A. Edell and Marian Chapman Burke, "The Power of Feelings in Understanding Advertising Effects," *Journal of Consumer Research* 14 (December 1987): 421–33; and Marian Chapman Burke and Julie A. Edell, "The Impact of Feelings on Ad-Based Affect and Cognition," *Journal of Marketing Research* 26 (February 1989): 69–83.

11. Dena Saliagas Cox and William B. Locander, "Product Novelty: Does It Moderate the Relationship between Ad Attitudes and Brand Attitudes?" *Journal of Advertising* 16 (1987): 39–44. Also see: Cynthia B. Hanson and Gabriel J. Biehal, "Accessibility Effects on the Relationship between Attitude toward the Ad and Brand Choice," in *Advances in Consumer Research*, vol. 22, ed. Frank R. Kardes and Mita Sujan (Provo, UT: Association for Consumer Research, 1995), 152–58.

12. Subodh Bhat and Srinivas K. Reddy, "Investigating the Dimensions of the Fit between a Brand and Its Extensions," *1997 AMA Winter Educators' Conference Proceedings*, vol. 8 (Chicago: American Marketing Association, 1997), 186–94.

13. Morris B. Holbrook, David A. Velez, and Gerard J. Tabouret, "Attitude Structure and Search: An Integrative Model of Importance-Directed Information Processing," in *Advances in Consumer Research*, vol. 8, ed. Kent B. Monroe (Ann Arbor, MI: Association for Consumer Research, 1981), 35–41.

14. Richard P. Bagozzi, Hans Baumgartner, and Yougae Yi, "Coupon Usage and the Theory of Reasoned Action," in *Advances in Consumer Research*, vol. 18, ed. Rebecca H. Holman and Michael R. Solomon (Provo, UT: Association for Consumer Research, 1991), 24–27.

15. Daniel Katz, "The Functional Approach to the Study of Attitudes," *Public Opinion Quarterly* 24 (Summer 1960): 163–91; Sharon Shavitt, "Products, Personality and Situations in Attitude Functions: Implications for Consumer Behavior," in *Advances in Consumer Research*, vol. 16, ed. Thomas K. Srull (Provo, UT: Association for Consumer Research, 1989), 300–305; and Richard Ennis and Mark P. Zanna, "Attitudes, Advertising, and Automobiles: A Functional Approach," in *Advances in Consumer Research*, vol. 20, ed. Leigh McAlister and Michael L. Rothschild (Provo, UT: Association for Consumer Research 1992), 662–66.

16. Richard E. Petty et al., "Theories of Attitude Change," in *Handbook of Consumer Theory and Research*, ed. Harold Kassarjian and Thomas Robertson (Upper Saddle River, NJ: Prentice Hall, 1991); and Richard E. Petty, John T. Cacioppo, and David Schumann, "Central and Peripheral Routes to Advertising Effectiveness: The Moderating Role of Involvement," *Journal of Consumer Research* 10 (September 1983): 135–46. Also see Curtis P. Haugtvedt and Alan J. Strathman, "Situational Product Relevance and Attitude Persistence," in *Advances in Consumer Research*, vol. 17, ed. Marvin E. Goldberg, Gerald Gorn, and Richard W. Pollay (Provo, UT: Association for Consumer Research, 1990), 766–69; and Scott B. Mackenzie and Richard A. Spreng, "How Does Motivation Moderate the Impact of Central and Peripheral Processing on Brand Attitudes and Intentions?" *Journal of Consumer Research* 18 (March 1992): 519–29.

17. Jaideep Sengupta, Ronald C. Goldstein and David S. Boninger, "All Cues Are Not Created Equal: Obtaining Attitude Persistence Under Low-Involvement Conditions," *Journal of Consumer Research* 23 (March 1997): 351–61.

18. Edward E. Jones et al., Attribution: Perceiving the Causes of Behavior (Morristown, NJ: General Learning Press, 1972).

19. Chris T. Allen and William R. Dillon, "Self-Perception Development and Consumer Choice Criteria: Is There a Linkage?" in *Advances in Consumer Research*, vol. 10, ed. Richard P. Bagozzi and Alice M. Tybout (Ann Arbor, MI: Association for Consumer Research, 1983), 45–50.

20. See, for example, Leslie Lazar Kanuk, *Mail Questionnaire Response Behavior as a Function of Motivational Treatment* (New York: CUNY, 1974).

21. John R. O'Malley Jr., "Consumer Attributions of Product Failtures to Channel Members," in *Advances in Consumer Research*, vol. 23, ed. Kim P. Corfman and John F. Lynch Jr. (Provo, UT: Association for Consumer Research, 1996), 342–45. Also see: Charmine Hartel, Janet R. McColl-Kennedy and Lyn McDonald, "Incorpoating Attributional Theory and the Theory of Reasoned Action within an Affective Events Theory Framework to Produce a Contingency Predictive Model of Consumer Reactions to Organizational Mishaps," in *Advances in Consumer Research*, vol. 25, ed. Joseph W. Alba and J. Wesley Hutchinson (Provo, UT: Association for Consumer Research, 1998), 428–32.

22. Valerie S. Folkes, "Consumer Reactions to Product Failure: Attributional Approach," *Journal of Consumer Research* 10 (March 1984): 398–409; and "Recent Attribution Research in Consumer Behavior: A Review and New Dimensions," *Journal of Consumer Research* 14 (March 1988): 548–65.

23. Harold H. Kelley, "Attribution Theory in Social Psychology," in *Nebraska Symposium on Motivation*, vol. 15, ed. David Levine (Lincoln, NE: University of Nebraska Press, 1967), 197.

CHAPTER 9
Communication and Consumer Behavior

▪ ▪

Communication is the unique tool that marketers use to persuade consumers to act in a desired way (e.g., to vote, to make a purchase, to make a donation, to patronize a retail store). Communication takes many forms: It can be verbal (either written or spoken), visual (an illustration, a picture, a product demonstration, a frown), or a combination of the two. It can also be symbolic—represented, say, by a high price, premium packaging, or a memorable logo—and convey special meaning that the marketer wants to impart. Communication can evoke emotions that put consumers in a more receptive frame of mind, and it can encourage purchases that help consumers solve problems or avoid negative outcomes. In short, communication is the bridge between marketers and consumers and between consumers and their sociocultural environments.

COMPONENTS OF COMMUNICATION

Although there are many ways to define communication, most marketers would agree that communication is the transmission of a *message* from a *sender* to a *receiver* via a *medium* (or channel) of transmission. In addition to these four basic components—sender, receiver, medium, and message—most communicators would also agree to a fifth essential component of communication—*feedback*—which alerts the sender as to whether the intended message was, in fact, received. Figure 9-1 depicts this basic communication model.

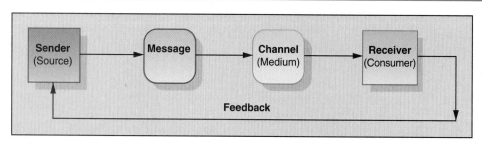

FIGURE 9-1
Basic Communication Model

THE SENDER

The sender, as the initiator of the communication, can be a formal or an informal source. A **formal communications source** is likely to represent either a for-profit (commercial) or a not-for-profit organization; an **informal source** can be a parent or a friend who gives product information or advice. Consumers often rely on informal communications sources in making purchase decisions because, unlike formal sources, the sender is perceived as having nothing to gain from the receiver's subsequent actions. For that reason, informal **word-of-mouth communications** tend to be highly persuasive.

THE RECEIVER

The receiver of formal marketing communications is likely to be a targeted prospect or a customer (e.g., a member of the marketer's target audience). *Intermediary* and *unintended* audiences are also likely to receive marketers' communications. Examples of intermediary audiences are wholesalers, distributors, and retailers, who receive *trade advertising* from marketers designed to persuade them to order and stock merchandise, and relevant professionals (such as architects or physicians), who are sent *professional advertising* in the hopes that they will specify or prescribe the marketer's products. Unintended audiences include everyone who is exposed to the message who is not specifically targeted by the sender. Unintended receivers of marketing communications often include publics that are important to the marketer, such as shareholders, creditors, suppliers, employees, bankers, and the local community.[1] It is important to remember that the audience—no matter how large or how diverse—is composed of individual receivers, each of whom interprets the message according to his or her own personal perceptions and experiences.

THE MEDIUM

The medium, or communications channel, can be **impersonal** (e.g., a mass medium) or **interpersonal** (a formal conversation between a salesperson and a customer or an *informal* conversation between two or more people that takes place face-to-face, by telephone, by mail, or on-line).

Mass media are generally classified as print (newspapers, magazines, billboards), broadcast (radio, television), or electronic (primarily the Internet). Most marketers today include their Web addresses in their print and television ads—encouraging consumers to "visit" their Web site to find out more about the product or service being advertised or to order on-line. New modes of interactive communication that permit the audiences of mass media to provide direct feedback are beginning to blur the distinction between interpersonal and impersonal communication. For example, in some communities consumers can do their grocery shopping electronically as the TV camera scans the grocery shelves. Home shopping networks are expanding dramatically, as consumers demonstrate their enthusiasm for TV shopping. Books, greeting cards, securities, and every other imaginable commodity are being bought on-line. Direct marketers—often called *database marketers*—seek individual responses from advertisements placed in all the mass media: broadcast, print, and electronic, as well as from direct mail.

THE MESSAGE

The message can be verbal (spoken or written), nonverbal (a photograph, an illustration, or a symbol), or a combination of the two. A verbal message, whether it is spoken or written, can usually contain more specific product (or service) information than a nonverbal message. A verbal message combined with a nonverbal message often provides more information to the receiver than either would alone.

Nonverbal information takes place in both interpersonal channels and in impersonal channels, and often takes the form of symbolic communication. The study of semiotics, discussed in chapter 2, is the study of the meanings implied by signs and symbols. Marketers often try to develop logos or symbols that are associated exclusively with their products and achieve high recognition.[2] The Coca-Cola Company, for example, has trademarked both the word *Coke* in a specific typographic style and the shape of the traditional Coke bottle, and both are instantly recognizable to consumers as symbols of the company's best-selling soft drink. In 1994, the Supreme Court ruled that even a color that distinguishes a product (and serves no other function) can be registered as a trademark.[3]

FEEDBACK

Feedback is an essential component of both interpersonal and impersonal communications. Prompt feedback permits the sender to reinforce, to change, or to modify the message to ensure that it is understood in the intended way. For example, a good salesperson usually is alert to nonverbal feedback provided by consumer prospects. Such feedback may take the form of facial expressions (a smile, a frown, a look of total boredom, an expression of disbelief) or body movements (finger tapping, head nodding, head shaking, or clenched hands). Because senders often can "read" meaning into such bodily reactions, these nonverbal actions sometimes are referred to as "body language." Generally, it is easier to obtain feedback (both verbal and nonverbal) from interpersonal communications than impersonal communications. However, because of the high cost of space and time in impersonal media, it is very important for sponsors of impersonal communications to devise some method to obtain feedback as promptly as possible, so that they may revise a message if its meaning is not being received as intended.

THE COMMUNICATIONS PROCESS

In general, a company's marketing communications are designed to make the consumer aware of the product, induce purchase or commitment, create a positive attitude toward the product, give the product a symbolic meaning, or show how it can solve the consumer's problem better than a competitive product (or service).

THE MESSAGE INITIATOR (THE SOURCE)

The sponsor, or initiator, of the message first must decide to whom the message should be sent and what meaning it should convey, and then must **encode** the message in such a way that its meaning is interpreted by the targeted audience in precisely the intended way. The sources of *impersonal communications* usually are organizations (either for-profit or not-for-profit) that develop and transmit appropriate messages through special departments (e.g., public relations) or spokespersons. The targets, or receivers, of such messages usually are a specific audience or several audiences that the organization is trying to inform, influence, or persuade. For example, an Internet server may want to attract both on-line users and advertisers, a museum may wish to target both donors and visitors. A travel company may want to persuade consumers to book its adventure tours, a mail-order retailer may want to persuade consumers to call a toll-free telephone number for a copy of its catalog.

Marketers have a large arsenal from which to draw in encoding their messages: They can use words, pictures, symbols, spokespersons, and special channels. They can buy space or time in carefully selected media to advertise or broadcast their message, or they can try to have their message appear in space or time usually reserved for editorial messages. (The latter, called *publicity*, usually is the result of public relations efforts and tends to be more believable because its commercial origins or intent are not readily apparent.)

Credibility

The **credibility of the source** affects the **decoding** of the message. The sponsor of the communication—and his or her perceived honesty and objectivity—has an enormous influence on how the communication is accepted by the receiver(s). When the source is well respected and highly thought of by the intended audience, the message is much more likely to be believed. Conversely, a message from a source considered unreliable or untrustworthy is likely to be received with skepticism, and may be rejected.

Credibility is built on a number of factors, of which the most important are the perceived intentions of the source. Receivers ask themselves, "Just what does he (or she) stand to gain if I do what is suggested?" If the receiver perceives any type of personal gain for the message sponsor as a result of the proposed action or advice, the message itself becomes suspect: "He wants me to buy that product just to earn a commission."

Credibility of Informal Sources One of the major reasons that informal sources such as friends, neighbors, and relatives have such a strong influence on a receiver's behavior is simply that they are perceived as having nothing to gain from a product transaction that they recommend. That is why *word-of-mouth communication* is so effective. Interestingly enough, informal communications sources, called *opinion leaders*, often do profit psychologically, if not tangibly, by providing product information to others (see chapter 15). A person may obtain a great deal of ego satisfaction by providing solicited as well as unsolicited information and advice to friends. This ego gratification may actually improve the quality of the information provided, because the opinion leader often deliberately seeks out the latest detailed information in order to enhance his or her position as "expert" in a particular product category. The fact that the opinion leader does not receive material gain from the recommended action increases the likelihood that the advice will be seriously considered.

Even with informal sources, however, intentions are not always what they appear to be. Individuals who experience *postpurchase dissonance* often try to alleviate their uncertainty by convincing others to make a similar purchase (see chapter 8). Each time they persuade a friend or an acquaintance to make the same brand selection as they did, they are somewhat reassured that their own product choice was a wise one. The receiver, on the other hand, regards product advice from "the person who owns one" as totally objective, because the source is able to speak from actual experience. Thus, the increased credibility accorded the informal source may not really be warranted, despite the aura of perceived objectivity.

Credibility of Formal Sources Not-for-profit sources generally have more credibility than for-profit (commercial) sources. Formal sources that are perceived to be "neutral"—such as *Consumer Reports* or newspaper articles—have greater credibility than commercial sources because of the perception that they are more objective in their product assessments. That is why publicity is so valuable to a manufacturer: Citations of a product in an editorial context, rather than in a paid advertisement, give the reader much more confidence in the message.

Because consumers recognize that the intentions of commercial sources (manufacturers, service companies, financial institutions, retailers) are clearly profit-oriented, they judge commercial source credibility on such factors as past performance, the kind and quality of service they are known to render, the quality and image of other products they manufacture, the image and attractiveness of the spokesperson used, the type of retail outlets through which they sell, and their position in the community (e.g., evidence of their commitment to such issues as social responsibility or equal employment).

Firms with well-established reputations generally have an easier time selling their products than do firms with lesser reputations. The ability of a quality image to invoke credibility is one of the reasons for the growth of family brands. Manufacturers with favorable brand images prefer to give their new products the existing brand name in order to obtain ready acceptance from consumers. Furthermore, a quality image permits a company to experiment more freely in many more areas of marketing than would otherwise be considered prudent, such as self-standing retail outlets, new price levels, and innovative promotional techniques. Recognizing that a manufacturer with a good reputation generally has high credibility among consumers, many companies spend a sizable part of their advertising budget on *institutional advertising*, which is designed to promote a favorable company image rather than to promote specific products.

Many companies sponsor special entertainment and sports events to enhance their image and credibility with their target audiences. The nature and quality of these sponsorships constitute a subtle message to the consumer: "We're a great (kind, good-natured, socially-responsible) company; we deserve your business." For example, such firms as the American Express Company, Chase Manhattan Bank, and Estée Lauder sponsor concerts in the park, athletic events, and walks to support cancer research. Other kinds of corporate-sponsored special events include marching bands, fireworks displays, computerized skywriting, laser shows, and traveling art exhibits.[4]

Credibility of Spokespersons and Endorsers Consumers sometimes regard the spokesperson who gives the product message as the source (or initiator) of the message. Thus, the "pitchman"—whether he or she appears in person or in a commercial or advertisement—has a major influence on message credibility. This accounts for the increasing use of celebrities to promote products. However, marketers who use celebrities to give testimonials or endorse products must be sure that the specific wording of the endorsement lies within the recognized competence of the spokesperson. A football star can believably endorse an analgesic product with comments about how it relieves sore muscle pain; however, a recitation of its chemical properties is beyond his expected knowledge and expertise, and thus reduces (rather than enhances) message credibility.

Researchers have studied the relationship between consumers' comprehension of the message and persuasion, and have found that when comprehension is low, receivers rely on the spokesperson's credibility in forming attitudes toward the product, but when comprehension (and thus systematic information processing) is high, the expertise of the source has far less impact on a receiver's attitudes.[5]

In *interpersonal* communications, consumers are more likely to be persuaded by salespersons who engender confidence and who give the impression of honesty and integrity. Consumer confidence in a salesperson is created in diverse ways, whether warranted or not. A salesperson who "looks you in the eye" often is perceived as more honest than one who evades direct eye contact. For many products, a sales representative who dresses well and drives an expensive, late-model car may have more credibility than one without such outward signs of success (and inferred representation of a best-selling product). For some products, however, a salesperson may achieve more credibility by dressing in the role of an expert. For example, a man selling home improvements may achieve more credibility by looking like someone who just climbed off a roof or out of a basement than by looking like a banker. One study found that, for attractiveness-related products (such as cosmetics), the use of a physically attractive celebrity significantly enhanced spokesperson credibility and attitude toward the ad; for attractiveness-unrelated products (e.g., a camera) an attractive endorser had little or no effect. This suggests a "match-up" hypothesis for celebrity advertising.[6]

The reputation of the *retailer* who sells the product has a major influence on message credibility. Products sold by well-known quality stores seem to carry the added endorsement (and implicit guarantee) of the store itself: "If Macy's carries it, it must be good." The aura of credibility generated by reputable retail advertising reinforces the manufacturer's message as well. That is why so many national ads (i.e., manufacturer-initiated ads) carry the line, "Sold at better stores everywhere."

The reputation of the *medium* that carries the advertisement also enhances the credibility of the advertiser. For example, the image of a prestige magazine like *Fortune* confers added status on the products advertised within. The reputation of the medium for honesty and objectivity also affects the believability of the advertising. Consumers often think that a medium they respect would not accept advertising for products it did not "know" were good. Because specialization in an area implies knowledge and expertise, consumers tend to regard advertising they see in special-interest magazines with more credibility than those they note in general-interest magazines.

Message Credibility   The consumer's previous experience with the product or the retailer has a major impact on the credibility of the message. Fulfilled product expectations tend to increase the credibility accorded future messages by the same advertiser; unfulfilled product claims or disappointing products tend to reduce the credibility of future messages. The significant increase in mail-order sales in the last decade has been attributed to the fact that reputable catalog houses have lived up to their advertised claims of providing full and prompt refunds on all merchandise returns.

Effects of Time on Source Credibility: The Sleeper Effect

The persuasive effects of high-credibility sources do not endure over time. Although a high-credibility source is initially more influential than a low-credibility source, research suggests that both positive and negative credibility effects tend to disappear after 6 weeks or so. This phenomenon has been termed the **sleeper effect**.[7] Consumers simply forget the source of the message faster than they forget the message itself. However, reintroduction of a similar message by the source serves to jog the audience's memory, and the original effect remanifests itself—that is, the high-credibility source remains more persuasive than the low-credibility source.[8] The implication for marketers who use high-credibility spokespersons is that they must repeat the same series of ads or commercials regularly in order to maintain the high level of persuasiveness their spokespersons have achieved. Studies attribute the sleeper effect to *disassociation* (that is, the consumer disassociates the message from its source) over time, leaving just the message content. The theory of *differential decay* suggests that the memory of a negative cue (e.g., a low-credibility source) simply decays faster than the message itself, leaving behind the primary message content.[9]

THE TARGET AUDIENCE (THE RECEIVERS)

Receivers decode the messages they receive on the basis of their personal experience and personal characteristics. If Mrs. Brown signed a contract to have her apartment painted because she received a well-designed, convincing direct-mail brochure and a follow-up call from a sincere-sounding, respectable-looking contractor, and then was dissatisfied with the quality of work done, she might end up distrusting all direct-mail communications, all home contractors and, perhaps, all smooth-talking salesmen. She is likely to decode any subsequent communications received through the mail with great skepticism. At the same time, her neighbor, Mrs. Greene, ordered a jacket and gloves from the L.L. Bean catalog and was so pleased with the quality, the service, and the fit that she studies all subsequent direct-mail catalogs with great care and decides to do all her shopping by direct mail. The level of trust each neighbor displays toward direct-mail communications is based on her own prior experience.

Comprehension

The amount of meaning accurately derived from the message is a function of the message characteristics, the receiver's opportunity and ability to process the message, and the receiver's motivation.[10] In fact, all of an individual's personal characteristics (described in earlier chapters) influence the accuracy with which an individual decodes a message. A person's *demographics* (such as age, gender, marital status), *sociocultural* memberships (social class, race, religion), and *lifestyle* are all key determinants in how a message is interpreted. A bachelor may interpret a friendly comment from his unmarried neighbor as a "come-on"; a student may interpret a professor's comments as an indication of grading rigor. Personality, attitudes, and prior learning all affect how a message is decoded. Perception, based as it is on expectations, motivation, and past experience, certainly influences message interpretation. Not everyone reads and understands the marketing communications they receive in the same way that the sender intended. For example, a study on the comprehension of direct-mail advertising written at an eighth-grade reading level found that fully one-third of the direct-mail recipients were unable to comprehend the intended message.[11]

A person's level of involvement (see chapter 7) plays a key role in how much attention is paid to the message and how carefully it is decoded. People who have little interest (e.g., a low level of involvement) in golf, for example, may not pay much attention to an ad for a specially designed putter; people who are very interested (highly involved) in golf may read every word of a highly technical advertisement describing the new golf club. Thus, a target audience's level of involvement is an important consideration in the design and content of persuasive communications.

Mood

Mood, or affect, plays a significant role in how a message is decoded. A consumer's mood (e.g., cheerfulness or unhappiness) affects the way in which an advertisement is perceived, recalled, and acted upon.[12] Research indicates that the consumer's mood often is influenced by the *context* in which the advertising message appears (such as the adjacent TV program or newspaper story) and the *content* of the ad itself; these in turn affect the consumer's evaluation and recall of the message.[13] Research also suggests that the consumer's state of arousal (or excitement) limits cognitive (that is, central) processing of the ad and increases reliance on peripheral cues.[14] Positive feelings induced by a commercial that depicts positive outcomes may enhance the likelihood that consumers will buy the advertised product (e.g., a large-screen TV), while negative (or depressing) commercials may induce negative moods. Of course, this outcome may be congruent with the marketer's objectives; consumers may be persuaded that a negative outcome will occur if they do not buy the advertised product (e.g., accident insurance.) In addition to inducing positive or negative *cognitive* moods, marketers can also induce *noncognitive* (or affective) moods through the use of advertising stimuli such as background cues. Ralph Lauren creates a mood of timeless elegance and tradition in multipage advertisements that serve to enhance consumer attitudes toward the company's merchandise. Figure 9-2 creates a happy

FIGURE 9-2
Ad Creates Happy Mood

mood with its visual, colorful treatment. Other extrinsic factors that influence consumer moods and affect the decoding of marketing communications include the retail store image, the climate, and even the weather.

Barriers to Communication

Various "barriers" to communication may affect the accuracy with which consumers interpret messages. These include selective perception and psychological noise.

Selective Perception   Consumers selectively perceive advertising messages. They tend to ignore advertisements that have no special interest or relevance to them. TV remote controls offer viewers the ability to "wander" among program offerings with ease (often referred to as *grazing*), to zap commercials by muting the audio, and to *channel surf*—switch channels to check out other program offerings during the commercial break. Some marketers try to overcome channel surfing during commercials by *roadblocking* (i.e., playing the same commercial simultaneously on competing channels).[15]

The VCR created problems for television advertisers by enabling viewers to fast-forward, or *zip* through commercials on prerecorded programs. Researchers have found that a majority of consumers zip indiscriminately through videotapes to avoid all commercials, without first evaluating the commercials they zap.[16] Some marketers make the mistake of playing theme music at the beginning and end of a commercial break, thus signaling viewers that they can attend to other needs without missing program content.

Psychological Noise Just as telephone static can impair reception of a message, so too can *psychological noise* (e.g., competing advertising messages or distracting thoughts). A viewer faced with the clutter of nine successive commercial messages during a program break may actually receive and retain almost nothing of what he has seen. Similarly, an executive planning a department meeting while driving to work may be too engrossed in her thoughts to "hear" a radio commercial. On a more familiar level, a student daydreaming about a Saturday night date may simply not "hear" a direct question by the professor. The student is just as much a victim of noise—albeit psychological noise—as another student who literally cannot hear a question because of construction noises in the building next door. The best way for a sender to overcome noise is simply to repeat the message several times, much as a sailor does when sending an SOS over and over again to make sure it is received. (The effects of repetition on learning were discussed in chapter 7.) The principle of redundancy also is seen in advertisements that use both illustrations and copy to emphasize the same points. Repeated exposure to an advertising message (redundancy of the advertising appeal) helps surmount psychological noise and thus facilitates message reception.

In addition to redundancy, copywriters often use *contrast* (discussed in chapter 6) to break through the noise and clutter. Two general ways to achieve contrast are called *subverting* and *forcing*. *Subverting* involves the presentation of something unexpected (or disconcerting) in an ad; *forcing* attempts to jolt the viewer into paying some initial notice to the advertisement (e.g., through a teaser appeal).[17]

FEEDBACK—THE RECEIVER'S RESPONSE

Since marketing communications are usually designed to persuade a target audience to act in a desired way (for example, to purchase a branded product, to vote for a presidential candidate, to pay income taxes early), the ultimate test of marketing communications is the receiver's response. For this reason, it is essential for the sender to obtain feedback as promptly and as accurately as possible. Only through feedback can the sender determine whether and how well the message has been received.

As noted earlier, an important advantage of *interpersonal* communications is the ability to obtain immediate feedback through verbal as well as nonverbal cues. Experienced communicators are very attentive to feedback and constantly modify their messages based on what they see or hear from the audience. Immediate feedback is the factor that makes personal selling so effective. It enables the salesperson to tailor the sales pitch to the expressed needs and observed reactions of each prospect. Similarly, it enables a political candidate to stress specific aspects of his or her platform selectively in response to questions posed by prospective voters in face-to-face meetings. Immediate feedback in the form of inattention serves to alert the college professor to the need to jolt awake a dozing class; thus, the professor may make a deliberately provocative statement such as: "This material will probably appear on your final exam."

argument.) Using a two-sided argument, the candidate may say something favorable about the reasonableness of an opponent's position before attacking it, thus gaining credibility by appearing objective, open-minded, and fair in examining the issues.

Comparative Advertising Comparative advertising is a widely used marketing strategy in which a marketer claims product superiority for its brand over one or more explicitly named or implicitly identified competitors, either on an overall basis or on selected product attributes (see Figure 9-8). Comparative advertising is useful for

FIGURE 9-8
Comparative Advertising

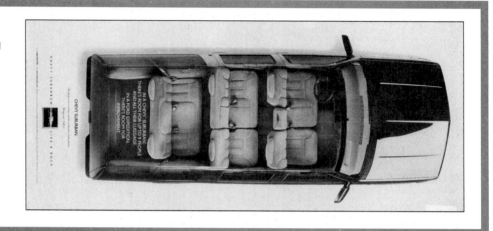

product positioning, for target market selection, and for brand positioning strategies that stress the differential advantage of the "underdog" product over leading brands. Figure 9-9 positions *Wired* magazine as the favored magazine of young CEOs, in comparison to *Fortune* magazine, which was shown as appealing to "old" CEOs. Comparative data supplied by an independent research organization tends to reinforce the credibility of the claim. Some critics of the technique maintain that comparative ads

FIGURE 9-9
Comparative Advertising

often assist recall of the competitor's brand at the expense of the advertised brand. There has been a great deal of interest and research into the effects of comparative advertising. In general, though, studies have found that comparative ads are capable of exerting more positive effects on brand attitudes, purchase intentions, and purchase than noncomparative advertisements.[34]

A study of comparative advertising using an information-processing perspective found that comparative ads elicited higher levels of cognitive processing, had better recall, and were perceived as more relevant than noncomparative ads.[35] Figure 9-10 presents an ad where Saab compares its automobile to the Saab military aircraft, thus positioning the car as a precision-manufactured road military aircraft. Comparative

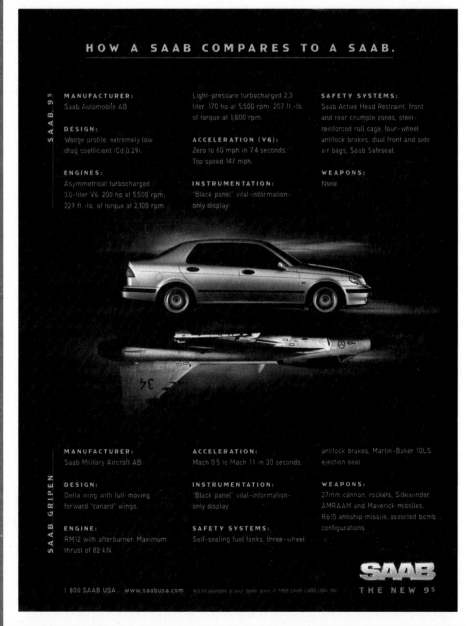

FIGURE 9-10
Comparative Ad Used for Positioning

ads were also found to be more effective than noncomparative ads when the advertised brand had a low market share or was unknown.[36]

Political campaigns provide some very blatant examples of comparative advertising. In recent election campaigns, for every level of public office, most candidates name their opponents and condemn their actions, their platforms, their voting history, and their behavior. Or, they may assert that various misfortunes will befall the country (or state or city) if the opponent is elected.

Order Effects Is it best to present your commercial first or last? Should you give the bad news first or last? Communications researchers have found that the order in which a message is presented affects audience receptivity. For this reason, politicians and other professional communicators often jockey for position when they address an audience sequentially; they are aware that the first and last speeches are more likely to be retained in the audience's memory than those in between. On TV, the position of a commercial in a commercial pod can be critical. The commercials shown first are recalled best, those in the middle the least. There is also evidence to suggest that television commercials that interrupt an exciting or suspenseful part of a program tend to have lower recall than those presented during a less gripping moment.[37] Another study found that order of presentation is more likely to affect the recall of audio messages (e.g., radio commercials) than visual messages (e.g., print ads).[38]

When just two competing messages are presented, one after the other, the evidence as to which position is more effective is somewhat conflicting. Some researchers have found that the material presented first produces a greater effect (the *primacy effect*), whereas others have found that the material presented last is more effective (the *recency effect*). One study found that in situations that foster high levels of cognitive processing, the initial message tends to be more influential (the primacy effect), while in situations of low message elaboration, the second message had a greater impact (the recency effect).[39] Magazine publishers recognize the impact of order effects by charging more for ads on the front, back, and inside covers of magazines than for the inside magazine pages, because of their greater visibility and recall.

Order is also important in listing product benefits within an ad. If audience interest is low, the most important point should be made first to attract attention. However, if interest is high, it is not necessary to pique curiosity, and so product benefits can be arranged in ascending order, with the most important point mentioned last. When both favorable information and unfavorable information are to be presented (as in an annual stockholders' report), placing the favorable material first often produces greater tolerance for the unfavorable news. It also produces greater acceptance and better understanding of the total message.

Repetition Repetition is an important factor in learning (see chapter 7). Thus, it is not surprising that repetition, or frequency of the ad, affects persuasion, ad recall, brand name recall, and brand preferences. It also increases the likelihood that the brand will be included in the consumer's *consideration set*. One study found that multiple message exposures gave consumers more opportunity to internalize product attributes, to develop more or stronger cue associations, more positive attitudes, and increased willingness to resist competitive counterpersuasion efforts.[40] Another study found that in low-involvement situations, individuals are more likely to regard message claims that are repeated frequently as more truthful than those that are not; the truth effect increased when subjects engaged in rote *rehearsal* that increased message familiarity without increasing evaluative processing of the information.[41] A study that examined the effects of repetition of the same ad versus repetition of varied ad executions (holding the number of repetitions for each variable constant) found that varied ad executions enhanced memory for the brand name over repeated same-ad executions. The study also supported the *encoding variability hypothesis*, which attributes the superior memorability of varied executions to the multiple paths laid down in memory between the brand name and other concepts, providing alternative retrieval routes that increase access to the brand name.[42]

Advertising Appeals

Sometimes objective, *factual appeals* are more effective in persuading a target audience, sometimes *emotional appeals* are more effective. It depends on the kind of audience to be reached and their degree of involvement in the product category. In general, however, logical, reason-why appeals are more effective in persuading educated audiences, and emotional appeals are more effective in persuading less-educated consumers. The following section examines the effectiveness of several frequently used emotional appeals.

Fear Fear is an effective appeal often used in marketing communications. Some researchers have found a negative relationship between the intensity of fear appeals and their ability to persuade, so that strong fear appeals tend to be less effective than mild fear appeals. (See also the discussion of *assimilation-contrast* theory in chapter 8.) A number of explanations have been offered for this phenomenon. Strong fear appeals concerning a highly relevant topic (such as cigarette smoking) cause the individual to experience cognitive dissonance, which is resolved either by rejecting the practice or by rejecting the unwelcome information. Because giving up a comfortable habit is difficult, consumers more readily reject the threat. This they do by a variety of techniques, including denial of its validity ("There still is no real proof that smoking causes cancer"), the belief that they are immune to personal disaster ("It can't happen to me"), and a diffusing process that robs the claim of its true significance ("I play it safe by smoking only filter cigarettes"). A study of the impact of low-fear appeals versus high-fear appeals on oven cleaner warning labels found that subjects were able to recall more information from the low-fear appeal label than from the high-fear appeal label.[43] Another study of warning and information labels affixed to full-fat, reduced-fat, and nonfat products concluded that, for products with credible and familiar risks, information labels were more effective than warning labels because they do not arouse *psychological reactance*.[44]

Some researchers have found a positive relationship between fear and persuasiveness. They believe that when individuals focus on controlling the danger (a cognitive response) rather than controlling their fear (an emotional response), there is a greater likelihood that they will accept the message.[45] One theory proposes that individuals cognitively appraise the available information regarding the severity of the threat, then they appraise the likelihood that the threat will occur; they evaluate whether coping behavior can eliminate the threat's danger, and if so, whether they have the ability to perform the coping behavior. This theory is called the *Ordered Protection Motivation (OPM)* model.[46] A recent study of adolescent responses to fear communications found that adolescents are more persuaded to avoid drug use by messages that depict negative social consequences of drug use rather than physical threats to their bodies.[47] The study also found that the personality variable *sensation-seeking* affected the processing of antidrug communications. A high sensation seeker is not only more likely to use drugs, but reacts negatively to antidrug messages, feeling he or she is immortal.

There is some indication that the mention of possible harmful effects of using a product category while proclaiming the benefits of the advertised product results in negative attitudes toward the product itself.[48] For example, when a luxury automobile company featured a new 24-hour emergency hot-line in a series of advertisements, some consumers were "turned off" by even the suggestion that a brand new, expensive car would experience roadside mechanical problems—particularly late at night on a dark and lonely road.

Humor Many marketers use humorous appeals in the belief that humor will increase the acceptance and persuasiveness of their advertising communications. Indeed, some estimates claim that almost 25 percent of TV commercials and over 30 percent of radio commercials use some form of humor.[49] Some marketers avoid the use of humor because they fear their product will become an object of ridicule, that consumers will laugh *at* them rather than *with* them. Table 9-3 summarizes some research findings on the impact of humor on advertising.[50]

There is some evidence that audience characteristics may confound the effects of humor. For example, younger, better-educated, upscale, and professional people tend to be receptive audiences for humorous messages (see Figure 9-11). The program or editorial matter that surrounds a humorous message also influences its effectiveness. Humorous commercials seem to work best when presented in an action-adventure environment, rather than in a situation-comedy environment. A study that examined the behavioral impact of humorous promotions within a field setting found that relevant humor increased patronage, but that humor not relevant to the object of the promotion either had no impact or a negative impact.[51]

Abrasive Advertising How effective can unpleasant or annoying ads be? Studies of the *sleeper effect*, discussed earlier, suggest that the memory of an unpleasant commercial that antagonizes listeners or viewers may dissipate over time, leaving only the brand name in the minds of consumers.

All of us have at one time or another been repelled by so-called *agony commercials*, which depict in diagrammatic detail the internal and intestinal effects of heartburn, indigestion, clogged sinus cavities, hammer-induced headaches, and the like. Nevertheless, pharmaceutical companies often run such commercials with great success because they appeal to a certain segment of the population that suffers from ailments that are not visible, and which therefore elicit little sympathy from family and friends. Their complaints are legitimized by commercials with which they immediately identify. With the sponsor's cred-

---

TABLE 9-3 Impact of Humor on Advertising

- Humor attracts attention.
- Humor does not harm comprehension. *(In some cases it may even aid comprehension.)*
- Humor is not more effective at increasing persuasion.
- Humor does not enhance source credibility.
- Humor enhances liking.
- Humor that is relevant to the product is superior to humor that is unrelated to the product.
- Audience demographic factors (e.g., gender, ethnicity, age) affect the response to humorous advertising appeals.
- The nature of the product affects the appropriateness of a humorous treatment.
- Humor is more effective with existing products than with new products.
- Humor is more appropriate for low-involvement products and feeling-oriented products than for high-involvement products.

Source: Marc G. Weinberger and Charles S. Gulas, "The Impact of Humor in Advertising: A Review," *Journal of Advertising* 21, 4 (December 1992): 35–59. Reprinted by permission.

FIGURE 9-11
Humorous Ad Targeted to
Baby Boomers

ibility established ("They really understand the misery I'm going through"), the message itself tends to be highly persuasive in getting consumers to buy the advertised product.

Sex in Advertising In our highly permissive society, sensual advertising seems to permeate the print media and the airwaves. Advertisers are increasingly trying to provoke public attention with suggestive illustrations and crude language, and showing more nudity than ever before, in an effort to appear "hip" and contemporary. There is more daring sexual imagery, extending far beyond the traditional product categories of fashion and fragrance, into such categories as shampoo, beer, cars, and resorts.[52] There is little doubt that sexual themes have attention-getting value, but studies show that they rarely encourage curiosity about the product. A study that examined the effects of sexual advertising appeals on cognitive processing and communication effectiveness found that sexual appeals interfere with message comprehension, particularly when there is substantial information to be processed.[53] It also found that more product-related thinking occurs in response to nonsexual appeals, and that visual sexual elements in the ad are more likely to be processed than the verbal content, drawing cognitive processing away from product or message evaluation.[54] These and other findings support the theory that sexual advertising appeals often detract from the processing of message content.

There are strong indications that the type of interest that sex evokes often stops exactly where it started—with sex. If a sexually suggestive or explicit illustration is not relevant to the product advertised, it has little effect on consumers' buying intentions. Some researchers have concluded that nudity may negatively impact the product message.[55] This highlights the potential risk of sexually-oriented advertising: The advertiser may be giving up persuasiveness to achieve "stopping power."

One thread seems to run through all the research findings regarding sex in advertising: The advertiser must be sure that the product, the ad, the target audience, and the use of sexual themes and elements all work together. When sex is relevant to the product, it can be an extremely potent copy theme. Jockey International, Inc. introduced a campaign targeted to young, savvy shoppers, both male and female. The ads show groups of attractive "real" people (not professional models) who share a common profession or interest (e.g., actors, or doctors, or ranchers) with their pants dropped around their ankles, smiling, and showing off their colorful Jockey briefs (see Figure 9-12). The tag line on each ad is "Let 'em know you're Jockey." Despite their obvious sensuality, the ads are highly relevant to the product.

Audience Participation

Earlier, we spoke about the importance of feedback in the communications process. The provision of feedback changes the communications process from one-way to two-

FIGURE 9-12
Sexual Appeal

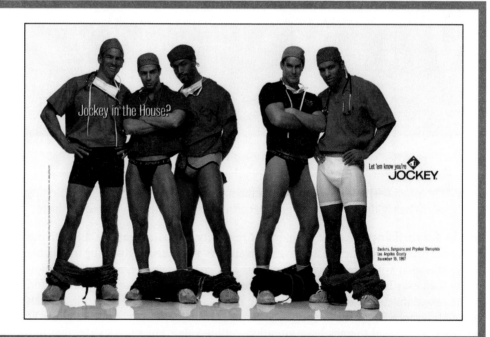

way communication. This is important to senders, because it enables them to determine whether and how well communication has taken place. But feedback also is important to receivers, because it enables them to participate, to be involved, to experience in some way the message itself. Participation by the receiver reinforces the message. An experienced communicator asks questions and opinions of an audience to draw them into the discussion. Many professors use the participative approach in classrooms rather than the more sterile lecture format, because they recognize that student participation tends to facilitate internalization of the information discussed.

Although participation is easily accomplished in interpersonal situations and drives the interactivity of cyber communications, it takes a great deal of ingenuity to achieve in impersonal communications. Thus, it is a challenge for imaginative marketers to get consumers involved in their advertising. Examples of ads inviting audience participation include word games (where the reader fills in the missing letters) and identification games (where the receiver tries to guess the identity of the celebrity spokesperson). American Express used this technique in a series of credit card ads showing a celebrity with the headline "Do You Know Me?" Radio and television commercials achieve this same effect as listeners try to identify the celebrity behind a familiar voice-over.

The increase in interactivity in the marketplace is the foundation for a new communications-based model of relationship marketing. Figure 9-13 shows how interactivity links the company and its communications sources to its customers and other stakeholders (e.g., its intermediary and unintended publics), resulting in increased brand value.[56]

FIGURE 9-13

Communication-Based Model Links Company to Its Public

Source: Tom Duncan and Sandra E. Moriarty, "A Communication-Based Marketing Model for Managing Relationships," *Journal of Marketing* 62 (April 1998): 9. Reprinted by permission.

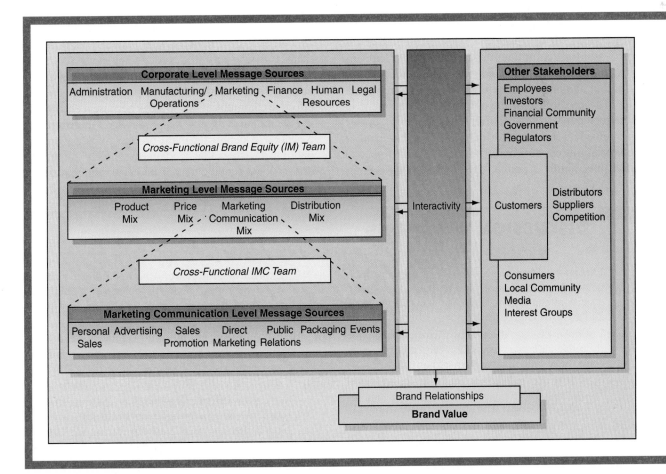

SUMMARY

This chapter has described how the consumer receives and is influenced by marketing communications. There are five basic components of communication: the sender, the receiver, the medium, the message, and some form of feedback (the receiver's response). In the communications process, the sender encodes the message using words, pictures, symbols, or spokespersons, and sends it through a selected channel (or medium). The receiver decodes (interprets) the message based on personal characteristics and experience and responds (or does not respond) based on such factors as comprehension, psychological noise, selective exposure, and selective perception.

There are two types of communications: interpersonal and impersonal (or mass) communications. Interpersonal communications occur on a personal level between two or more people and may be verbal or nonverbal, formal or informal. In mass communications, there is no direct contact between source and receiver. Interpersonal communications take place in person, by telephone, by mail, or by e-mail; mass communications through such impersonal media as television, radio, newspapers, and magazines. Feedback is an essential component of all communications because it provides the sender with some notion as to whether and how well the message has been received.

The credibility of the source, a vital element in message persuasiveness, often is based on his or her perceived intentions. Informal sources and neutral or editorial sources are considered to be highly objective and thus, highly credible. The credibility of a commercial source is more problematic, and usually is based on a composite evaluation of its reputation, expertise, and knowledge, and that of the medium, the retail channel, and company spokespersons.

Media selection depends on the product, the audience, and the advertising objectives of the campaign. In addition to consumers, a marketer's audiences include selling intermediaries and other publics that are relevant to the organization's success, as well as unintended audiences.

The manner in which a message is presented influences its impact. For example, one-sided messages are more effective in some situations and with some audiences; two-sided messages are more effective with others. High-involvement products (those with great relevance to a consumer segment) are best advertised through the central route to persuasion, which encourages active cognitive effort. Low-involvement products are best promoted through peripheral cues, such as background scenery, music, or celebrity spokespersons.

Emotional appeals frequently used in advertising include fear, humor, and sexual appeals. When sexual themes are relevant to the product, they can be very effective; when used solely as attention-getters, they rarely achieve brand recall. Audience participation is a very effective communications strategy because it encourages internalization of the advertising message. Future research is needed to identify the many product, audience, and situational variables that mediate the effects of message order and presentation in persuading consumers to buy.

DISCUSSION QUESTIONS

1. Explain the differences between feedback from interpersonal communications and feedback from impersonal communications. How can the marketer obtain and use each kind of feedback?

2. List and discuss the effects of psychological barriers on the communications process. How can a marketer overcome the communications barrier known as "noise"?

3. a. What factors influence the perceived credibility of an informal communications source? List and discuss factors that determine the credibility of formal communications sources of product information.
   b. What are the implications of the sleeper effect for the selection of spokespersons and the scheduling of advertising messages?

4. Explain the difference(s) between direct mail and direct marketing. Discuss the objectives of direct marketing and the reasons for its continued growth.

5. a. Should marketers use more body copy than artwork in print ads? Explain your answer.
   b. For what kinds of audiences would you consider using comparative advertising? Why?

6. You are the marketing manager for a headache remedy. Your advertising agency has just presented you with two different promotional strategies, one using a humorous approach and one taking an "agony" approach. Which approach would you adopt? Why?

EXERCISES

1. Bring two advertisements to class: one illustrating a one-sided message and the other a two-sided message. Explain why each marketer may have chosen that specific message strategy and evaluate each ad's effectiveness.

2. Find three print ads, one using a fear appeal, the second a sex appeal, and the third an audience participation appeal, and present them in class. For each ad, discuss whether you think the appeal used is effective and why.

3. Watch one hour of TV on a single channel during prime time and record the broadcast. List all the commercials you can recall seeing. For each commercial, identify (a) the message framing approach used, and (b) whether the message was one-sided or two-sided. Compare your list with the actual taped broadcast. Explain any discrepancies between your recollections and the actual broadcast on the basis of concepts discussed in this chapter.

4. For three of the commercials you watched in the above exercise, identify whether the marketer used the central or peripheral route to persuasion. Explain your answer and speculate on why each marketer chose the approach it used to advertise the product or service.

KEY TERMS

- **Audience versus consumer profiles**
- **Central and peripheral routes to persuasion**
- **Communications objectives**
- **Direct mail versus direct marketing**
- **Encoding and decoding**
- **Feedback**
- **Formal versus informal communications sources**
- **Interpersonal versus impersonal communications**
- **Media strategies**
- **Message framing strategies**
- **One-sided versus two-sided messages**
- **Precision targeting**
- **Sleeper effect**
- **Source credibility**
- **Word-of-mouth communications**

NOTES

1. See, for example, Mary C. Gilly and Mary Wolfinbarger, "Advertising's Internal Audience," *Journal of Marketing* 62 (January 1998): 69–88; and Stewart Shapiro et al., "The Effects of Incidental Ad Exposure on the Formation of Considersation Sets," *Journal of Consumer Research* 24 (June 1997): 94–104.

2. For an empirical analysis of some 200 logos designed to achieve corporate image and communication goals, see Pamela W. Henderson and Joseph A. Cote, "Guidelines for Selecting or Modifying Logos," *Journal of Marketing* (April 1998): 14–30.

3. See Paul N. Bloom and Torger Reve, "Transmitting Signals to Consumers for Competitive Advantage," *Business Horizons* (July–August 1990): 58–66; and Linda Greenhouse, "High Court Ruling Upholds Trademarking of a Color," *New York Times*, 29 March 1994, D1.

4. Jeff Jensen, "Is Olympic Sponsor Pie Sliced Too Thin?" *Business Marketing* 80 (December 1995): 1.

5. S. Ratneshwar and Shelly Chaiken, "Comprehension's Role in Persuasion: The Case of Its Moderating Effect on the Persuasive Impact of Source Cues," *Journal of Consumer Research* 18 (June 1991): 52–62.

6. Michael A. Kamins, "An Investigation into the 'Match-Up' Hypothesis in Celebrity Advertising: When Beauty May Be Only Skin Deep," *Journal of Advertising* 19, 1 (1990): 4–13. See also Marsha L. Richins, "Social Comparison and the Idealized Images of Advertising," *Journal of Consumer Research* 18 (June 1991): 71–83.

7. Carl I. Hovland, Arthur A. Lumsdaine, and Fred D. Sheffield, *Experiments on Mass Communication* (New York: Wiley, 1949), 182–200.

8. Darlene B. Hannah and Brian Sternthal, "Detecting and Explaining the Sleeper Effect," *Journal of Consumer Research* 11 (September 1984): 632–42.

9. See Joseph W. Alba, Howard Marmorstein, and Amitava Chattopadhyay, "Transitions in Preference over Time: The Effects of Memory on Message Persuasiveness," *Journal of Marketing Research* 29 (November 1992): 414.

10. David Glen Mick, "Levels of Subjective Comprehension in Advertising Processing and Their Relations to Ad Perceptions, Attitudes, and Memory," *Journal of Consumer Research* 18 (March 1992): 411–24.

11. Jean Harrison-Walker, "The Import of Illiteracy to Mar-

keting Communication," *Journal of Consumer Marketing* 12, 1 (1995): 50–64.

12. William R. Swinyard, "The Effects of Mood, Involvement, and Quality of Store Experience on Shopping Intentions," *Journal of Consumer Research* 20 (September 1993): 271–80.

13. See Mahima Mathur and Amitava Chattopadhyay, "The Impact of Moods Generated by Television Programs on Responses to Advertising," *Psychology and Marketing* 8, 1 (Spring 1991): 59–77.

14. Michel Tuan Pham, "Cue Representation and Selection Effects of Arousal on Persuasion," *Journal of Consumer Research* 22 (March 1996): 373–87.

15. Carol Felker Kaufman and Paul M. Lane, "In Pursuit of the Nomadic Viewer," *Journal of Consumer Marketing* 11, 4 (1994): 4–17.

16. John J. Cronin and Nancy E. Menelly, "Discrimination vs. Avoidance: Zipping of Television Commercials," *Journal of Advertising* 21, 2 (June 1992): 1–7.

17. Arthur J. Kover, "Copywriters' Implicit Theories of Communication: An Exploration," *Journal of Consumer Research* 21 (March 1995): 596–611.

18. Joseph C. Philport and Jerry Arbittier, "Advertising Brand Communications Styles in Established Media and the Internet," *Journal of Advertising Research* 37, 2 (March–April 1997): 68–76.

19. Stuart Elliott, "Advertising," *New York Times*, 14 January 1994, D15.

20. Alan J. Bush, Victoria Bush, and Sharon Harris, "Advertiser Perceptions of the Internet as a Marketing Communications Tool," *Journal of Advertising Research* 38, 2 (March–April 1998): 17–26. See also Sabra Chartrand, "Patents," *New York Times*, 5 October 1998, C8; and Teresa Riordan, "Patents," *New York Times*, 7 December 1998, C9.

21. Ibid.

22. Gary Hennerberg, "The Righteous, Social, and Pragmatic Buyer," *Direct Marketing* (May 1993): 31–34.

23. H. Rao Unnava and Robert E. Burnkrant, "An Imagery-Processing View of the Role of Pictures in Print Advertisements," *Journal of Marketing Research* 28 (May 1991): 226–31.

24. Tina M. Lowrey, "The Relation Between Syntactic Complexity and Advertising Persuasiveness," *Advances in Consumer Research* 19 (1992): 270–74.

25. Edward F. McQuarrie and David Glen Mick, "Figures of Rhetoric in Advertising Language," *Journal of Consumer Research* 22 (March 1996): 424–38.

26. Edward F. McQuarrie and David Glen Mick, "On Resonance: A Critical Pluralistic Inquiry into Advertising Rhetoric," *Journal of Consumer Research* 19 (September 1992): 180–97.

27. Ibid.

28. J. Craig Andrews and Terence A. Shimp, "Effects of Involvement, Argument Strength, and Source Characteristics on Central and Peripheral Processing of Adver-

tising," *Psychology & Marketing* 7, 3 (Fall 1990): 195–214.

29. Alan G. Sawyer and Daniel J. Howard, "Effects of Omitting Conclusions in Advertisements to Involved and Uninvolved Audiences," *Journal of Marketing Research* 28 (November 1991): 467–74.

30. Durairaj Maheswaran and Joan Meyers-Levy, "The Influence of Message Framing and Issue Involvement," *Journal of Marketing Research* 27 (August 1990): 361–67.

31. Yoav Ganzach and Nili Karsahi, "Message Framing and Buying Behavior: A Field Experiment," *Journal of Business Research* 32 (1995): 11–17.

32. Baba Shiv et al., "Factors Affecting the Impact of Negatively and Positively Framed Ad Messages," *Journal of Consumer Research* 24 (December 1997): 285–94.

33. Ayn E. Crowley and Wayne D. Hoyer, "An Integrative Framework for Understanding Two-Sided Persuasion," *Journal of Consumer Research* 20 (March 1994): 561–74.

34. Randall L. Rose, Paul W. Miniard, Michael J. Barone, Kenneth C. Manning, and Brian D. Till, "When Persuasion Goes Undetected: The Case of Comparative Advertising," *Journal of Marketing Research* 30 (August 1993): 315–30; see also Cornelia Pechmann and S. Ratneshwar, "The Use of Comparative Advertising for Brand Positioning: Association versus Differentiation," *Journal of Consumer Research* 18 (September 1991): 145–60, and Cornelia Pechmann and David W. Stewart, "The Effects of Comparative Advertising on Attention, Memory, and Purchase Intentions," *Journal of Consumer Research* 17 (September 1990): 180–91.

35. Darrel D. Muehling, Jeffrey J. Stoltman, and Sanford Grossbart, "The Impact of Comparative Advertising on Levels of Message Involvement," *Journal of Advertising* 19, 4 (1990): 41–50; see also Jerry B. Gotlieb and Dan Sarel, "Comparative Advertising Effectiveness: The Role of Involvement and Source Credibility," *Journal of Advertising* 20, 1 (1991): 38–45.

36. Paul W. Miniard, Michael J. Barone, Randall L. Rose, and Kenneth C. Manning, "A Re-Examination of the Relative Persuasiveness of Comparative and Noncomparative Advertising," *Advances in Consumer Behavior* 21 (1994): 299–302.

37. Valerie Starr and Charles A. Lowe, "The Influence of Program Context and Order of Ad Presentation on Immediate and Delayed Responses to Television Advertisements," *Advances in Consumer Research* 22 (1995): 184–90.

38. H. Rao Unnava, Robert E. Burnkrant, and Sunil Erevelles, "Effects of Presentation Order and Communication Modality on Recall and Attitude," *Journal of Consumer Research* 21 (December 1994): 481–90.

39. Curtis P. Haugtvedt and Duane T. Wegener, "Message Order Effect in Persuasion: An Attitude Strength Perspective," *Journal of Consumer Research* 21 (June 1994): 205–18.

40. Curtis P. Haugtvedt et al., "Advertising Repetition and Variation Strategies: Implications for Understanding

Attitude Strength," *Journal of Consumer Research* 21 (June 1994): 176–89.

41. Scott A. Hawkins and Stephen J. Hoch, "Low-Involvement Learning: Memory Without Evaluation," *Journal of Consumer Research* 19 (September 1992): 212–25.

42. H. Rao Unnava and Robert E. Burnkrant, "Effects of Repeating Varied Ad Executions on Brand Name Memory," *Journal of Marketing Research* 28 (November 1991): 406–16.

43. Mark A. DeTurck, Robert A. Rachline, and Melissa J. Young, "Effects of a Role Model and Fear in Warning Label on Perceptions of Safety and Safety Behavior," *Advances in Consumer Research* 21 (1994): 208–12.

44. Brad J. Bushman, "Effects of Warning and Information Labels on Consumption of Full-Fat, Reduced-Fat, and No-Fat Products," *Journal of Applied Psychology* 83, 1 (1998): 97–101.

45. Ken Chapman, "Fear Appeal Research: Perspective and Application," *Proceedings of the American Marketing Association* (Summer 1992): 1–9; also John F. Tanner Jr., James B. Hunt, and David R. Eppright, "The Protection Motivation Model: A Normative Model of Fear Appeals," *Journal of Marketing* 55 (July 1991): 36–45.

46. James B. Hunt, John F. Tanner Jr., and David R. Eppright, "Forty Years of Fear Appeal Research: Support for the Ordered Protection Motivation Model," *American Marketing Association* 6 (Winter 1995): 147–53.

47. Denise D. Schoenbachler and Tommy E. Whittler, "Adolescent Processing of Social and Physical Threat Communications," *Journal of Advertising* 35, 4 (Winter 1996): 37–54.

48. Meryl P. Gardner and Rosalyn S. Levin, "Truth and Consequences: The Effects of Disclosing Possibly Harmful Results of Product Use," in *An Assessment of Marketing Thought and Practice*, ed. Bruce J. Walker et al. (*1992 Educators' Conference Proceedings*), 39–42.

49. Hyongoh Cho, "Humor Mechanisms, Perceived Humor and Their Relationships to Various Executional Types in Advertising," *Advances in Consumer Research* 22 (1995): 191–97.

50. Marc G. Weinberger and Charles S. Gulas, "The Impact of Humor in Advertising: A Review," *Journal of Advertising* 21, 4 (December 1992): 35–59.

51. Ibid.

52. Stuart Elliott, "A Vivid-Livid Divide: Madison Avenue's New Explicitness is Open to Debate," *New York Times*, 29 June 1998, C1, 4. See also Michael S. LaTour and Tony L. Henthorne, "Ethical Judgments of Sexual Appeals in Print Advertising," *Journal of Advertising* 23, 3 (September 1994): 81–90.

53. Jessica Severn, George E. Belch, and Michael A. Belch, "The Effects of Sexual and Non-Sexual Advertising Appeals and Information Level on Cognitive Processing and Communication Effectiveness," *Journal of Advertising* 19, 1 (1990): 14–22.

54. Ibid.

55. Michael S. LaTour, Robert E. Pitts, and David C. Snook-Luther, "Female Nudity, Arousal, and Ad Response: An Experimental Investigation," *Journal of Advertising* 19, 4 (1990): 51–62.

56. Tom Duncan and Sandra E. Moriarty, "A Communication-Based Marketing Model for Managing Relationships," *Journal of Marketing* 62 (April 1998): 1–13.

PART

CONSUMERS IN THEIR SOCIAL AND CULTURAL SETTINGS

3

The five chapters in Part 3 are designed to provide the reader with a detailed picture of the social and cultural dimensions of consumer behavior. Chapters 10 through 14 explain how social and cultural concepts affect the attitudes and behavior of individuals in the United States and the world beyond, and show how these concepts are employed by marketing practitioners to achieve their marketing objectives.

CHAPTER 10
Reference Groups and Family Influences

■■■■■■■■■■■■■■■■■■■■■■■■■■■■■■

With the exception of those very few people who are classified as hermits, most individuals interact with other people on a daily basis, especially with members of their own families.

In the first part of this chapter, we will consider how group involvements and memberships influence our actions as consumers—that is, to impact consumers' decision making, shopping activities, and actual consumption. The second part of this chapter deals with how the family influences its members' consumer behavior. For instance, a child learning the uses and value of money is often a "family matter"; so are decisions about a new car, a vacation trip, or whether to go to a local or an out-of-town college. The family commonly provides the opportunity for product exposure and trial and imparts consumption values to its members. As a major consumption group, the family is also a prime target for many products and services.

This chapter begins with a discussion of the basic concepts of group dynamics and how reference groups both directly and indirectly influence consumer behavior. We then examine some basic family concepts. Next we discuss family consumer decision making and consumption behavior; last we explore the marketing implications of the family life cycle. (The four chapters that follow discuss other social and societal *groupings* that influence consumer buying processes: social class, culture, subculture, and cross-cultural exposure.)

WHAT IS A GROUP?

A **group** may be defined as two or more people who interact to accomplish either individual or mutual goals. The broad scope of this definition includes an intimate "group" of two next-door neighbors who three times a week take exercise classes together and a larger, more formal group, such as a neighborhood homeowners association, whose members are mutually concerned with the schools, roads, taxes, and types of businesses in their neighborhood. Included in this definition, too, are a kind of "one-sided grouping" in which an individual consumer observes the appearance or actions of others, who unknowingly serve as consumption-related role models.

Sometimes, groups are classified by membership status. A group to which a person either belongs or would qualify for membership in is called a *membership group*. For example, the group of men with whom a young executive plays golf weekly would be considered, for him, a membership group. There are also groups in which an individual is not likely to receive membership, despite acting like a member by adopting the group's values, attitudes, and behavior. This is considered a **symbolic group**. For instance, professional bowlers may constitute a symbolic group for an amateur bowler who identifies with certain players by imitating their behavior whenever possible (for example, by purchasing a specific brand of bowling ball or bowling shoes). The amateur bowler does not, however (and probably never will), qualify for membership as a professional bowler, because he has neither the skills nor the opportunity to compete professionally.

░░░░ UNDERSTANDING THE POWER OF REFERENCE GROUPS

Within the context of consumer behavior, the concept of reference groups is an extremely important and powerful idea. A **reference group** is any person or group that serves as a point of comparison (or reference) for an individual in forming either general or specific values, attitudes, or a specific guide for behavior. This basic concept provides a valuable perspective for understanding the impact of other people on an individual's consumption beliefs, attitudes, and behavior. It also provides some insight into the methods marketers sometime use to effect desired changes in consumer behavior.

From a marketing perspective, *reference groups* are groups that serve as *frames of reference* for individuals in their purchase or consumption decisions. The usefulness of this concept is enhanced by the fact that it places no restrictions on group size or membership, nor does it require that consumers identify with a tangible group (that is, the group can be symbolic: owners of successful small businesses, leading corporate chief executive officers, rock stars, or golf celebrities).

Reference groups that influence general or broadly defined values or behavior are called **normative reference groups**. An example of a child's normative reference group is the immediate family, which is likely to play an important role in molding the child's general consumer values and behavior (such as which foods to select for good nutrition, appropriate ways to dress for specific occasions, how and where to shop, or what constitutes "good" value).

Reference groups that serve as benchmarks for specific or narrowly defined attitudes or behavior are called **comparative reference groups**. A comparative reference group might be a neighboring family whose lifestyle appears to be admirable and worthy of imitation (the way they maintain their home, their choice of home furnishings and cars, their taste in clothing, or the number and types of vacations they take).

Both normative and comparative reference groups are important. Normative reference groups influence the development of a basic code of behavior; comparative reference groups influence the expression of specific consumer attitudes and behavior. It is likely that the specific influences of comparative reference groups to some measure depend on the basic values and behavior patterns established early in a person's development by normative reference groups.

A BROADENED PERSPECTIVE ON REFERENCE GROUPS

The meaning of "reference group" has changed over the years. As originally used, reference groups were narrowly defined to include only those groups with which a person interacted on a direct basis (like family and close friends). However, the concept gradually has broadened to include both direct and indirect individual or group influences. **Indirect reference groups** consist of those individuals or groups with whom a person does not have direct face-to-face contact, such as movie stars, sports heroes, political leaders, TV personalities, or even a well-dressed and interesting looking person on a street corner.

Referents a person might use in evaluating his or her own general or specific attitudes or behavior vary from one individual, to several family members, to a broader kinship or from a voluntary association to a social class, a profession, an ethnic group, a community, an age category, or even a nation or culture. As Figure 10-1 indicates, the major societal groupings that influence an individual's consumer behavior are, in order: family, friends, social class, various subcultures, one's own culture, and even other cultures. For instance, within the scope of "selected subcultures," we would include various age categories (teenagers or baby boomers) that might serve as a reference group for their own or others' behavior.

FACTORS THAT AFFECT REFERENCE GROUP INFLUENCE

The degree of influence that a reference group exerts on an individual's behavior usually depends on the nature of the individual and the product and on specific social factors. This section discusses how and why some of these factors influence consumer behavior.

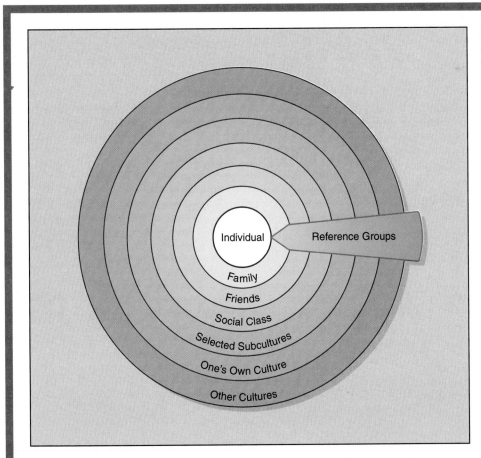

FIGURE 10-1
Major Consumer Reference Groups

Information and Experience

An individual who has firsthand experience with a product or service, or can easily obtain full information about it, is less likely to be influenced by the advice or example of others. On the other hand, a person who has little or no experience with a product or service and does not expect to have access to objective information about it (for example, a person who believes that advertising may be misleading or deceptive) is more likely to seek out the advice or example of others. For instance, when a young corporate sales rep wants to impress his client, he may take her to a restaurant that he knows from experience to be good or to one that has been highly recommended by the local newspaper's Dining Out Guide. If he has neither personal experience nor information he regards as valid, he may seek the advice of a friend or a parent or imitate the behavior of others by taking her to a restaurant he knows is frequented by young business executives whom he admires.

Credibility, Attractiveness, and Power of the Reference Group

A reference group that is perceived as credible, attractive, or powerful can induce consumer attitude and behavior change. For example, when consumers are concerned with obtaining accurate information about the performance or quality of a product or service, they are likely to be persuaded by those whom they consider trustworthy and knowledgeable. That is, they are more likely to be persuaded by sources with *high credibility*.

When consumers are primarily concerned with the acceptance or approval of others they like, with whom they identify, or who offer them status or other benefits, they are likely to adopt their product, brand, or other behavioral characteristics. When consumers are primarily concerned with the power that a person or group can exert over them, they might choose products or services that conform to the norms of that person or group in order to avoid ridicule or punishment. However, unlike other reference groups that consumers follow because they are credible or because they are attractive, *power groups* are not as likely to cause attitude change. Individuals may conform to the behavior of a powerful person or group, but are not as likely to experience a change in their own attitudes.

Different reference groups may influence the beliefs, attitudes, and behavior of an individual at different points in time or under different circumstances. For example, the dress habits of a young male executive may vary, depending on his place and role. He may conform to the dress code of his office by wearing dress shirts and conservative business suits by day and drastically alter his mode of dress after work by wearing more trendy, flamboyant styles.

Conspicuousness of the Product

The potential influence of a reference group on a purchase decision varies according to how visually or verbally conspicuous the product is to others. A visually **conspicuous product** is one that will stand out and be noticed (such as a luxury item or novelty product); a verbally conspicuous product may be highly interesting, or it may be easily described to others. Products that are especially conspicuous and status-revealing (a new automobile, fashion clothing, sleek laptop computer, or home furniture) are most likely to be purchased with an eye to the reactions of relevant others, as shown in Figure 10-2. Privately consumed products that are less conspicuous (canned fruits or laundry soaps) are less likely to be purchased with a reference group in mind.

FIGURE 10-2

Conspicuousness Aids the Acceptance of Some Products

REFERENCE GROUPS AND CONSUMER CONFORMITY

Marketers may have divergent goals with regard to **consumer conformity**. Some marketers, especially market leaders, are interested in the ability of reference groups to change consumer attitudes and behavior by encouraging *conformity*. To be capable of such influence, a reference group must accomplish the following:

1. Inform or make the individual aware of a specific product or brand
2. Provide the individual with the opportunity to compare his or her own thinking with the attitudes and behavior of the group
3. Influence the individual to adopt attitudes and behavior that are consistent with the norms of the group
4. Legitimize the decision to use the same products as the group

In contrast, marketers, especially those responsible for a new brand or a brand that is not the market leader, may wish to elect a strategy that asks consumers to strike out and be different and *not just follow the crowd* when making a purchase decision.

In reality the nonconformity appeal can be thought of as a request to shift one's reference (attitudes or behavior) from one grouping (brand A users) to another reference (non-A users or brand B users).

■■■■■ SELECTED CONSUMER-RELATED REFERENCE GROUPS

As already mentioned, consumers are potentially influenced by a diverse range of people that they come in contact with or observe. We will consider the following five specific reference groups because they give us a kind of cross-section of the types of groups that influence consumers' attitudes and behavior: (1) friendship groups, (2) shopping groups, (3) work groups, (4) virtual groups or communities; and (5) consumer-action groups. The family, possibly the most compelling reference group for consumer behavior, will be fully covered in the second part of this chapter.

FRIENDSHIP GROUPS

Friendship groups are typically classified as **informal groups**, because they are usually unstructured and lack specific authority levels. In terms of relative influence, after an individual's family, his or her friends are most likely to influence the individual's purchase decisions.

Seeking and maintaining friendships is a basic drive of most people. Friends fulfill a wide range of needs: they provide companionship, security, and opportunities to discuss problems that an individual may be reluctant to discuss with family members. Friendships are also a sign of maturity and independence, for they represent a breaking away from the family and the forming of social ties with the outside world.

The opinions and preferences of friends are an important influence in determining the products or brands a consumer ultimately selects. Marketers of products such as brand-name clothing, fine jewelry, snack foods, and alcoholic beverages recognize the power of peer group influence and frequently depict friendship situations in their ads.

SHOPPING GROUPS

Two or more people who shop together, whether for food, for clothing, or simply to pass the time, can be called a **shopping group**. Such groups are often offshoots of family or friendship groups, and therefore they function as what has been referred to as *purchase pals*.[1] The motivations for shopping with a purchase pal range from a primarily social motive (to share time together and enjoy lunch after shopping), to helping reduce the risk when making an important decision (have someone along whose expertise will reduce the chance of making an incorrect purchase). In instances where none of the members of the shopping group knows much about the product under consideration (such as an expensive home entertainment center), a shopping group may form for defensive reasons; members may feel more confident with a collective decision.

A special type of shopping group is the in-home shopping party, which typically consists of a group who gathers together in the home of a friend to attend a "party" devoted to demonstrating and evaluating a specific line of products. The in-home party approach provides marketers with an opportunity to demonstrate the features of their products simultaneously to a group of potential customers. Early purchasers tend to create a *bandwagon effect*: Undecided guests often overcome a reluctance to buy when they see their friends make positive purchase decisions. Furthermore, some of the guests may feel obliged to buy because they are in the home of the sponsoring host or hostess.

WORK GROUPS

The sheer amount of time that people spend at their jobs, frequently more than 35 hours per week, provides ample opportunity for *work groups* to serve as a major influence on the consumption behavior of members.

Both the formal work group and the informal friendship-work group can influence consumer behavior. The **formal** work **group**, consists of individuals who work together as part of a team, and, thus, have a sustained opportunity to influence each other's consumption-related attitudes and actions. Informal friendship-work groups consist of people who have become friends as a result of working for the same firm, whether or not they work together as a team. Members of informal work groups may influence the consumption behavior of other members during coffee or lunch breaks or at after-work meetings.

Recognizing that work groups influence consumers' brand choices and that most women now work outside of their homes, firms that in the past sold their products exclusively through direct calls on women in their homes now are redirecting their sales efforts to offices and plants during lunch hour visits. For instance, Avon and Tupperware, two leading direct-to-home marketers, encourage their sales representatives to reach working women at their places of employment.

VIRTUAL GROUPS OR COMMUNITIES

Thanks to computers and the Internet, we are witnessing the beginnings of a new type of group—*virtual groups* or *communities*. Both adults and children are turning on their computers, logging onto the Web, and visiting special interest Web sites, often with chat rooms. If you're a skier, you can chat, on-line, with other skiers; if you're an amateur photographer, you can chat on-line with others who share your interest. Local newspapers everywhere run stories from time to time about singles who met on-line, typically accompanied by a picture of their wedding. An Internet provider like America Online even lets its members create *Buddy Lists*™, so when they sign onto AOL they immediately know which of their friends are currently on-line and can send and receive instant messages.

Whereas 50 years ago the definition of a community stressed the notion of geographic proximity and face-to-face relationships, today's communities are much more broadly defined as "sets of social relations among people."[2] In this spirit, there is also today rather wide-scale access to what is known as "Internet Communities" (e.g., www.well.com, www.geocities.com, www.ivillage.com, www.bigplanet.com, www.planetall.com, and www.icq.com). These communities provide their members with access to extensive amount of information and fellowship and social interaction covering an extremely wide range of topics and issues (for instance, vegetarianism, cooking, collecting, trading, finance, filmmaking, romance, politics, technology, art, hobbies, spiritualism, age grouping, on-line game playing, voice-video chats, free e-mail, tech assistance, travel and vacations, educational opportunities, living with illnesses, and a host of lifestyle options).

When visiting such communities, it does not matter if you are tall or short, thin or fat, handsome or plain-looking. On the Internet, people are free to express their thoughts, to be emotional and intimate with those they do not know and have never met, and even to escape from those they normally interact with by spending time on the Internet. The anonymity of the Net gives its users the freedom to express whatever views they wish, and to also benefit from savoring the views of others. Because of this anonymity, Internet users can say things to others that they would not say in face-to-face interactions.[3] Communicating over the Internet permits people to explore the boundaries of their personalities (see the related discussion in chapter 5), and to shift from one persona to another. For example, investigators have found that there are a surprisingly large number of men who adopt female personae on-line ("gender swapping").[4]

CONSUMER-ACTION GROUPS

A particular kind of consumer group—a **consumer-action group**—has emerged in response to the consumerist movement. Today, there are a very large number of such groups who are dedicated to providing consumers with assistance in their effort to make the right purchase decisions, consume products and services in a healthy and responsible manner, and to generally add to the overall quality of their lives. The following are just a few examples of the diverse range of consumer concerns being addressed by private and public consumer action groups: neighborhood crime watch, youth development, forests and wildlife concerns, children and advertising, race and ethnicity, community volunteerism, legal assistance, public health, disaster relief, energy conservation, education, smoking, the environment, access to telecommunications, science in the public interest, credit counseling, and privacy issues.

Consumer-action groups can be divided into two broad categories: (1) those that organize to correct a specific consumer abuse and then disband and (2) those that organize to address broader, more pervasive problem areas and operate over an extended or indefinite period of time. A group of irate neighbors who band together to protest the opening of a topless bar in their neighborhood or a group of parents who attend a meeting of the local school board to question some of the decisions made by the high school principal are examples of temporary, cause-specific consumer-action groups. An example of an enduring consumer-action group is Mothers Against Drunk Driving (MADD), a group founded in 1980, and operating today throughout the United States within local community groups. MADD representatives serve on numerous public advisory boards and help establish local task forces to combat drunk driving. Additionally, the organization supports actions to restrict alcoholic beverage advertising and is opposed in general to any advertising and products that may have a negative impact on youth.

The overriding objective of many consumer-action groups is to bring sufficient pressure to bear on selected members of the business community to make them correct perceived consumer abuses.

CELEBRITIES AND OTHER REFERENCE GROUP APPEALS

Celebrities and other similar reference group appeals are used very effectively by advertisers to communicate with their markets. Celebrities can be a powerful force in creating interest or actions with regard to purchasing or using selected goods and services. This identification may be based on admiration (of an athlete), on aspiration (of a celebrity or a way of life), on empathy (with a person or a situation), or on recognition (of a person—real or stereotypical—or of a situation). In some cases, the prospective consumer may think, "If she uses it, it must be good. If I use it, I'll be like her." In other cases, the prospective consumer says to himself, "He has the same problems that I have. What worked for him will work for me."

Five major types of reference group appeals in common marketing usage are *celebrity appeals*, *expert appeals*, *common-man appeals*, *executive and employee appeals*, and *trade or spokes-character appeals*. These appeals, as well as less frequently employed appeals, are often operationalized in the form of testimonials or endorsements. In the case of the common man, they may be presented as *slice-of-life* commercials.

CELEBRITIES

Celebrities, particularly movie stars, TV personalities, popular entertainers, and sports icons, provide a very common type of reference group appeal. To their loyal followers and to much of the general public, celebrities represent an idealization of life that most people imagine that they would love to live. Advertisers spend enormous sums of money to have celebrities promote their products, with the expectation that the reading or viewing audience will react positively to the celebrity's association with their products. Do you remember when Michael Jordan first retired from basketball for about 2 years? His return to the NBA resulted in the firms whose products he endorses to increase their stock market value by $1 billion.[5]

A firm that decides to employ a celebrity to promote its product or service has the choice of using the celebrity to give a **testimonial**, to give an **endorsement**, as an **actor** in a commercial, or as a company **spokesperson**. Table 10-1 distinguishes between these different types of celebrity appeals, and Table 10-2 lists some currently popular celebrity endorsers and the client products or services they have represented.

Of all the benefits that a celebrity might contribute to a firm's advertising program—fame, talent, credibility, or charisma—celebrity credibility with the consumer audience is the most important. By **celebrity credibility** we mean the audience's perception of both the celebrity's expertise (how much the celebrity knows about the product area) and *trustworthiness* (how honest the celebrity is about what he or she says about the product).[6] To illustrate, when a celebrity endorses only one product, consumers are likely to perceive the product in a highly favorable light and indicate a greater intention to purchase it. In contrast, when a celebrity endorses a variety of products, his or her perceived credibility is reduced because of the apparent economic motivation underlying the celebrity's efforts.[7]

Not all companies feel that using celebrity endorsers is the best way to advertise. For example, Gap, Inc., used celebrities throughout the 1980s in its "Individuals of Style campaign"; however, its current ads focus more heavily on the clothes. Some companies avoid

TABLE 10-1 Types of Celebrity Appeals

TYPE	DEFINITION	EXAMPLE
Testimonial	Based on personal usage, a celebrity attests to the quality of the product or service	Pat Riley for 1-Day Accuvue® disposable contact lenses
Endorsement	Celebrity lends his name and appears on behalf of a product or service with which he or she may or may not be an expert	Senior pro golfer Larry Laoretti for TE-AMO cigars
Actor	Celebrity presents a product or service as part of a character endorsement	Jason Alexander (George on "Seinfeld") for Rold Gold pretzels
Spokesperson	Celebrity represents the brand or company over an extended period of time	Lee Trevino for Motorola telecommunications products

TABLE 10-2 Popular Celebrities and Their Products/Services

CELEBRITY	PRODUCT/SERVICE
June Allyson	Depends
Pierce Brosnan	Omega Watches
Bill Cosby	Jell-O
Cindy Crawford	Revlon, Omega Watches
Kareem Abdul-Jabbar	Pepperidge Farm Goldfish crackers
Michael Jordan	McDonald's, Nike
Lorenzo Lamas	Elizabeth Taylor's White Diamonds
Heather Locklear	L'Oreal
Rosie O'Donnell and Penny Marshall	Kmart
Paul Reiser	AT&T
Jerry Seinfeld	American Express
Jaclyn Smith	Kmart
Jonathan Winters	Choice Hotels

celebrities because they fear that if the celebrity gets involved in some undesirable act or event (e.g., an ugly matrimonial problem, a scandal, or a criminal case), the negative news or press coverage will negatively impact on the sale of the endorsed brand.

THE EXPERT

A second type of reference group appeal used by marketers is the expert, a person who, because of his or her occupation, special training, or experience, is in a unique position to help the prospective consumer evaluate the product or service that the advertisement promotes. For example, an advertisement for a quality frying pan may feature the endorsement of a chef; an ad for fishing tackle may contain the endorsement of a professional fishing guide; or an ad for volleyball shoes might feature the endorsement of a champion volleyball team (see Figure 10-3).

THE "COMMON MAN"

A reference group appeal that uses the testimonials of satisfied customers is known as the *common-man* approach. The advantage of the common-man appeal is that it demonstrates to prospective customers that someone just like them uses and is satisfied with the product or service being advertised. The common-man appeal is especially effective in public-health announcements (such as antismoking or high-blood pressure messages), for most people seem to identify with people like themselves when it comes to such messages.[8]

The Saturn Corporation consistently has used a variation of the common-man approach, when it tells of the interesting experiences of satisfied Saturn customers—often showing the consumers in a dramatization of the customer's unique experience. In one example, Darlene and Tom Robison were "run off the highway, rolled their car," and yet were able to walk away from the accident.

Many television commercials show a typical person or family solving a problem by using the advertised product or service. These commercials are known as *slice-of-life commercials* because they focus on "real-life" situations with which the viewer can identify. For example, one commercial focuses on how a laundry detergent can deodorize clothes; another talks about how a certain breakfast cereal provides enough energy to get an indi-

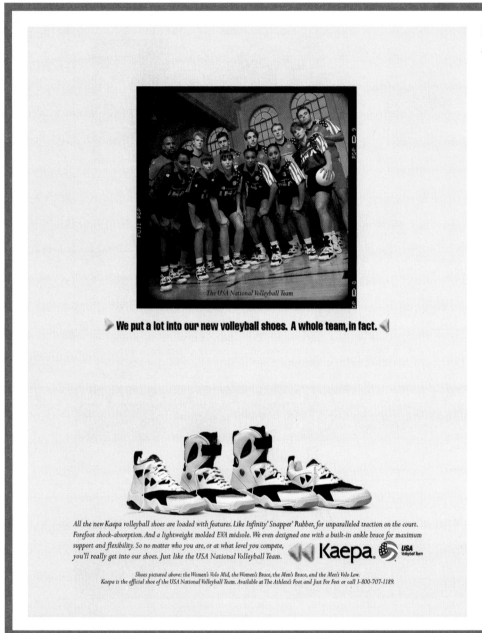

FIGURE 10-3
An Expert Appeal

vidual through a hectic morning. When viewers identify with the situation, they are likely to adopt the solution that worked in the TV commercial. Figure 10-4 presents an ad for Jenny Craig™ Personal Weight Management that effectively uses the endorsement of a satisfied customer who personally lost 22 pounds in three and half months.

THE EXECUTIVE AND EMPLOYEE SPOKESPERSON

During the past two decades, an increasing number of firms have used their top executives as spokespersons in consumer ads. The popularity of this type of advertising probably is due to the success and publicity received by a number of innovative executive spokespersons. For instance, Lee Iacocca was highly effective in persuading consumers

FIGURE 10-4
Customers Providing
Testimonials

Denise before she lost 21 lbs. with Jenny Craig.*

Diana before she lost 35 lbs. with Jenny Craig.*

"Together, we lost 56 pounds with Jenny Craig!*"

"As twins, we're always together. But when you're losing weight, you want to be treated as an individual. At Jenny Craig, your very own Consultant helps customize a weight loss plan just for you. Jenny Craig can work for you, too. Don't wait. Call Jenny Craig today!"

Join Jenny Craig now and lose all the weight you want for just
$1 a pound**

St. Catharines
353 Lake Street, #12B

Jenny Craig ®

*Results not typical. ****Plus the cost of food.

New clients only. Offer expires 10/31/98. At participating Centres. No cash value. ©1998 Jenny Craig Inc. Denise Peterein lost 21 lbs. in 3 1/2 months. Diana Chipps lost 35 lbs. in 8 1/2 months.

To be directly connected to your nearest Centre,
CALL 1-800-68-JENNY
or visit us at www.jennycraig.com

that Chrysler automobiles were worthy of their purchase consideration. Similarly, Frank Perdue spoke about the superiority of his Perdue chickens; Victor Kiam, the president of Remington Products, spoke about the benefits of his made-in-America shavers; Bill Marriott, the president of the Marriott Corporation, promoted the chain's hotels; and founder Dave Thomas is prominent in most Wendy's TV commercials.

Like the celebrity spokesperson, executive spokespersons seem to be admired by the general population because of their achievements and the status implicitly conferred on business leaders in the United States. The appearance of a company's chief executive in its advertising seems to imply that someone at the top is watching over the consumers' best interests, and it encourages consumers to have more confidence in the firm's products or services.

TRADE OR SPOKES-CHARACTERS

Trade or spokes-characters (for example, Mr. Peanut, Tony the Tiger, or Cap 'n Crunch), as well as familiar cartoon characters (Ninja Turtles, Mr. Magoo, Bart Simpson), serve as quasicelebrity endorsers. These trade spokes-characters present an idealized image and dispense information that can be very important for the product or service that they "work for."[9]

With few exceptions, trade characters serve as an exclusive spokesperson for a particular product or service. They sometimes provide a kind of personality for the product or service and make the product appear more friendly (Ronald McDonald) or less complex (when IBM PCs used the little tramp). Betty Crocker now even has her own Web site to offer recipes, personalized weekly menus, and household hints. This Web site is the modern-day extension of the fact that Betty Crocker started answering letters from consumers in the 1920s and got her own toll-free telephone number in 1980. According to the company, the purpose of the Web site "is not to push Betty Crocker, not to sell product, but to provide content that offers ideas and solves problems, so people consider the site a valuable resource."[10]

OTHER REFERENCE GROUP APPEALS

A variety of other promotional strategies can function creatively as frames of reference for consumers. Respected retailers and the editorial content of selected special-interest magazines can also function as frames of reference that influence consumer attitudes and behavior. For instance, a customer might feel that if a leading fashion specialty store such as Bergdorf Goodman depicts men's single-breasted suits with peaked lapels as "in," then the style must be acceptable and in good taste. Similarly, a regular reader of *GQ* might see unstructured and relaxed sport coats as appropriate to wear to work if the magazine were to feature them in office surroundings. In these two instances, the retailer and the magazine are functioning as frames of reference that influence consumer behavior.

Finally, *seals of approval* and even objective product ratings can serve as positive endorsements that encourage consumers to act favorably toward certain products. For instance, many parents of young children look for the American Dental Association's seal of approval before selecting a brand of toothpaste. A high rating by an objective rating magazine, such as *Consumer Reports*, can also serve as an endorsement for a brand.

The remainder of this chapter concentrates on the family—arguably the most important group influencing human behavior in general and consumer behavior in particular.

THE FAMILY IS A CONCEPT IN FLUX

Although the term **family** is a basic concept, it is not easy to define because family composition and structure, as well as the roles played by family members, are almost always in transition. Traditionally, however, *family* is defined as *two or more persons related by blood, marriage, or adoption who reside together*. In a more dynamic sense, the individuals who constitute a family might be described as members of the most basic social group who live together and interact to satisfy their personal and mutual needs. Today in the United States, 70 percent of the just over 100 million households are families.[11] According to many sources, the *family* remains the central or dominant

FIGURE 10-5
The Appeal of a Family
Shared Meal

institution in providing for the welfare of it members. Figure 10-5 presents an ad for Stouffer's Family Style Favorites (feeding about 12 people) that depicts in a grand style a family gathering to enjoy the celebration of a shared meal.

Although **families** sometimes are referred to as **households**, not all households are families. For example, a household might include individuals who are not related by blood, marriage, or adoption, such as unmarried couples, family friends, roommates, or boarders. However, within the context of consumer behavior, households and families usually are treated as synonymous, and we will continue this convention.

In most Western societies, three types of families dominate: the married couple, the nuclear family, and the extended family. The simplest type of family, in number of members, is the *married couple*—a husband and a wife. As a household unit, the married couple generally is representative of either new marrieds who have not yet started a family and older couples who have already raised their children.

A husband and wife and one or more children constitute a **nuclear family**. This type of family is still commonplace, but has been on the decline. The nuclear family, together with at least one grandparent living within the household, is called an **extended family**. Within the past 30 years the incidence of the extended family has also declined because of the geographic mobility that split-up families. Moreover, because of divorce, separation, and out-of-wedlock births, there has been a rapid increase in the number of **single-parent family** households consisting of one parent and at least one child.

Not surprisingly, the type of family which is most "typical" can vary considerably from culture to culture. For instance, in an individualistic society such as that in Canada, the nuclear family is most common. In a kinship culture (with extended families) such as that in Thailand, a family would commonly include a head of household, married adult children, and grandchildren.[12]

■ SOCIALIZATION OF FAMILY MEMBERS

The **socialization of family members**, ranging from young children to adults, is a central family function. In the case of young children, this process includes imparting to children the basic values and modes of behavior consistent with the culture. These generally include moral and religious principles, interpersonal skills, dress and grooming standards, appropriate manners and speech, and the selection of suitable educational and occupational or career goals. To illustrate how this socialization responsibility is expanding, parents are increasingly anxious to see their young children possess adequate computer skills, almost before they are able to talk or walk—as early as 12 months after their birth. Because parents seem to be so intensively interested in their young children learning about using a computer, hardware and software developers are rapidly creating products targeted at parents seeking to buy such items for their very young children (see Figure 10-6).

Marketers frequently target parents looking for assistance in the task of socializing their children. To this end, marketers are sensitive to the fact that the socialization of young children provides an opportunity to establish a foundation on which later experiences continue to build throughout life. These experiences are reinforced and modified as the child grows into adolescence, the teenage years, and eventually into adulthood.

CONSUMER SOCIALIZATION OF CHILDREN

The aspect of childhood socialization that is particularly relevant to the study of consumer behavior is **consumer socialization**, which is defined as *the process by which children acquire the skills, knowledge, and attitudes necessary to function as consumers*. A variety of studies have focused on how children develop consumption skills. Many preadolescent children acquire their *consumer behavior norms* through observation of their parents and older siblings, who function as role models and sources of cues for basic consumption learning. In contrast, adolescents and teenagers are likely to look to their friends for models of acceptable consumption behavior.[13]

Shared shopping experiences (that is, coshopping when mother and child shop together) also give children the opportunity to acquire in-store shopping skills. Possibly because of their more harried lifestyles, working mothers are more likely to undertake coshopping with their children than are nonworking mothers. Coshopping is a way of spending time with one's children while at the same time accomplishing a necessary task.

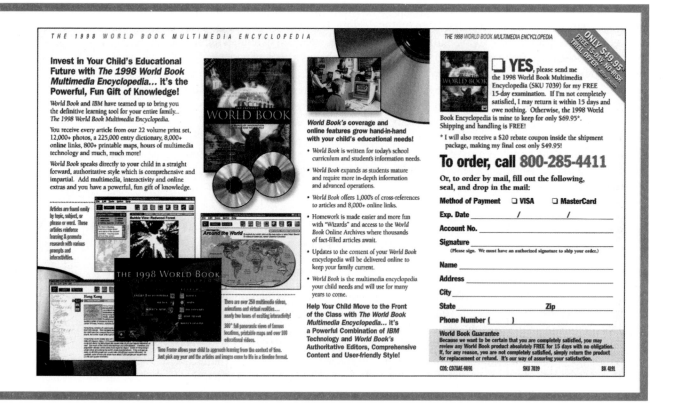

FIGURE 10-6

Computer Related Products Are Sought After by Parents of Young Children

Consumer socialization also serves as a tool by which parents influence other aspects of the socialization process. For instance, parents frequently use the promise or reward of material goods as a device to modify or control a child's behavior. A mother may reward her child with a gift when the child does something to please her, or she may withhold or remove it when the child disobeys. Research conducted by one of the authors supports this behavior-controlling function. Specifically, adolescents reported that their parents frequently used the promise of chocolate candy as a means of controlling their behavior (such as getting them to complete homework or to clean their rooms).

ADULT CONSUMER SOCIALIZATION

The socialization process is not confined to childhood; rather, it is an ongoing process. It is now accepted that socialization begins in early childhood and extends throughout a person's entire life. For example, when a newly married couple establishes a separate household, their adjustment to living and consuming together is part of this continuing process. Similarly, the adjustment of a retired couple who decide to move to Florida or Arizona is also part of the ongoing socialization process. Even a family that is welcoming a pet into their home, as a new family member, must face the challenge of socializing the pet so that it fits into the family environment.

INTERGENERATIONAL SOCIALIZATION

It appears that it is quite common for selected product loyalty or brand preferences to be *transferred* from one generation to another—*intergeneration brand transfer*—maybe for even three or four generations within the same family. For instance, specific brand preferences for products like peanut butter, mayonnaise, ketchup, coffee, and canned soup are all product categories that are frequently "passed on" from one generation to another generation. The following are several verbatims from research with college-aged consumers as to how they feel about product usage extending over several generations:[14]

> *My mother stills buys almost every brand that her mother did. She is scared to try anything else, for it will not meet the standards, and (she) would feel bad not buying something that has been with her so long. (Respondent is an Italian-American male in his early twenties.)*

> *I find it hard to break away from the things I've been using since I was little; like Vaseline products, Ivory soap, Lipton tea, and corn flakes. I live on campus so I have to do my own shopping, and when I do I see a lot of my mother in myself. I buy things I'm accustomed to using . . . products my mother buys for the house. (Respondent is West Indian–American female.)*

Figure 10-7 presents a simple model of the socialization process that focuses on the socialization of young children but that can be extended to family members of all ages. Note that the arrows run both ways between the young person and other family members and between the young person and his or her friends. This two-directional arrow signifies that socialization is really a two-way street, in which the young person is both socialized and influences those who are doing the socializing. Supporting this view is the reality that children of all ages often influence the opinions and behavior of their parents.

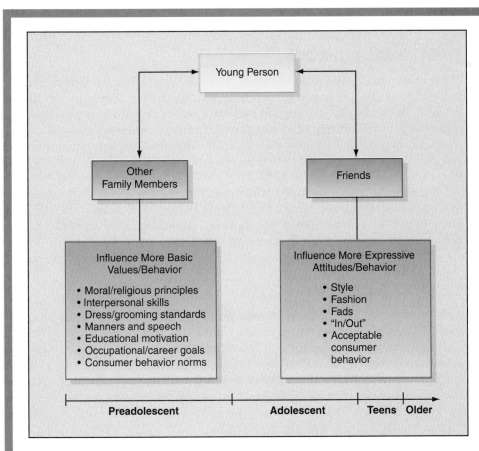

FIGURE 10-7
A Simple Model of the Socialization Process

▪▪▪▪ OTHER FUNCTIONS OF THE FAMILY

Three other basic functions provided by the family are particularly relevant to a discussion of consumer behavior. These include economic well-being, emotional support, and suitable family lifestyles.

ECONOMIC WELL-BEING

Although families in affluent nations of North America, Europe, and Asia are no longer formed primarily for economic security, providing financial means to its dependents is unquestionably a basic family function (see Figure 10-8). How the family divides its responsibilities for providing economic well-being has changed considerably during the past 25 years. No longer are the traditional roles of husband as economic provider and wife as homemaker and child rearer still valid. For instance, it is very common for married women with children in the United States and other industrial countries to be employed outside the home and for their husbands to share household responsibilities. In part, this may be why more than 70 percent of women in the United States who are over the age of 18 claim that it is more difficult to be a mother now than it was 20 or 30 years ago.[15]

The economic role of children also has changed. Today, despite the fact that many teenage children work, they rarely assist the family financially. Instead, many teenagers are expected to pay for their own amusements; others contribute to the costs of their formal education and prepare themselves to be financially independent.

EMOTIONAL SUPPORT

The provision of emotional nourishment (including love, affection, and intimacy) to its members is an important core function of the contemporary family. In fulfilling this function, the family provides support and encouragement and assists its members in coping with decision making and with personal or social problems.[16] To make it easier for working parents to show their love, affection, and support to their children, greeting card companies have been increasingly creating cards for parents to give to their children (or vice versa).

If the family cannot provide adequate assistance when it is needed, it may turn to a counselor, psychologist, or other helping professional as an alternative. For instance, in most communities, educational and psychological centers are available that are designed to assist parents who want to help their children improve their learning and communication skills or to generally better adjust to their environments.

SUITABLE FAMILY LIFESTYLES

Another important family function in terms of consumer behavior is the establishment of a suitable *lifestyle* for the family. Upbringing, experience, and the personal and jointly held goals of the spouses determine the importance placed on education or career, on reading, on television viewing, on the learning of computer skills, on the frequency and quality of dining out, and on the selection of other entertainment and recreational activities. Researchers have identified a shift in the nature of family "togetherness." Whereas a family being together once meant doing things together, today it means being in the same household and each person doing his or her own thing.[17]

Family lifestyle commitments, including the allocation of time, is greatly influencing consumption patterns. For example, a series of diverse pressures on moms has reduced the time that they have available for household chores and has created a market for convenience products and fast-food restaurants. Also, with both parents working, an increased emphasis is being placed on the notion of "quality time," rather than on the "quantity of time" spent with children and other family members. Realizing the scarcity of quality family time, Hilton hotels feature a variety of vacation and weekend packages targeted to couples and their children (see Figure 10-9).

FIGURE 10-9
An Ad Telling Readers That
a Great Vacation Is Family
Time Together

FAMILY DECISION MAKING AND CONSUMPTION-RELATED ROLES

Although many marketers recognize the family as the basic decision-making unit, they most frequently examine the attitudes and behavior of the one family member whom they believe to be the major decision maker. In some cases, they also examine the attitudes and behavior of the person most likely to be the primary user of the product or service. For instance, in the case of men's underwear, which is frequently purchased by women for their husbands and unmarried sons, it is commonplace to seek the views of both the men who wear the underwear and the women who buy it. By considering both the likely user and the likely purchaser, the marketer obtains a richer picture of the consumption process.

KEY FAMILY CONSUMPTION ROLES

For a family to function as a cohesive unit, tasks such as doing the laundry, preparing meals, setting the dinner table, taking out the garbage, and walking the dog must be carried out by one or more family members. In a dynamic society, family-related duties are constantly changing (such as the greater assumption of household tasks by

TABLE 10-3 The Eight Roles in the Family Decision-Making Process

ROLE	DESCRIPTION
Influencers	Family member(s) who provide information to other members about a product or service
Gatekeepers	Family member(s) who control the flow of information about a product or service into the family
Deciders	Family member(s) with the power to determine unilaterally or jointly whether to shop for, purchase, use, consume, or dispose of a specific product or service
Buyers	Family member(s) who make the actual purchase of a particular product or service
Preparers	Family member(s) who transform the product into a form suitable for consumption by other family members
Users	Family member(s) who use or consume a particular product or service
Maintainers	Family member(s) who service or repair the product so that it will provide continued satisfaction
Disposers	Family member(s) who initiate or carry out the disposal or discontinuation of a particular product or service

men). However, we can identify eight distinct roles in the *family decision-making process*, as presented in Table 10-3. A look at these roles provides further insight into how family members interact in their various consumption-related roles.

The number and identity of the family members who fill these roles vary from family to family and from product to product. In some cases, a single family member will independently assume a number of roles; in other cases, a single role will be performed jointly by two or more family members. In still other cases, one or more of these basic roles may not be required. For example, a family member may be walking down the snack food aisle at a local supermarket when he picks out an interesting new chocolate candy. His selection does not directly involve the influence of other family members. He is the *decider*, the *buyer* and, in a sense, the *gatekeeper*; however, he may or may not be the sole consumer (or user). Products may be consumed by a single family member (beer, lipstick), consumed or used directly by two or more family members (frozen vegetables, shampoo), or consumed indirectly by the entire family (central air conditioning, a home security alarm system, or an art glass collection).

DYNAMICS OF HUSBAND-WIFE DECISION MAKING

Marketers are interested in the relative amount of influence that a husband and a wife have when it comes to family consumption choices. Most husband-wife influence studies classify family consumption decisions as **husband-dominated**, **wife-dominated**, **joint** (either equal or syncratic), and **autonomic** (either solitary or unilateral).[18]

The relative influence of a husband and wife on a particular consumer decision depends in part on the product and service category. For instance, during the 1950s, the purchase of a new automobile was strongly husband-dominated, while food and financial-banking decisions more often were wife-dominated. Forty years later, the purchase of the family's principal automobile is still often husband-dominated in many households. However, in other contexts or situations (such as a second car or a car for a single or working woman), female car buyers are a rapidly expanding segment of the automobile market, a segment to which many car manufacturers are currently paying separate marketing attention. Also, in case of financial decision making, there has been a general trend away from wife-dominated decisions to joint decisions (see Figure 10-10).[19]

FIGURE 10-10

Husband-Wife Influence in Financial Tasks and Decisions

Source: JoAnne Stilley Hopper, "Family Financial Decision Making: Implications for Marketing Strategy," *Journal of Services Marketing* 9(1), 1995, 28. First published by MCB University Press Ltd. Reprinted by permission.

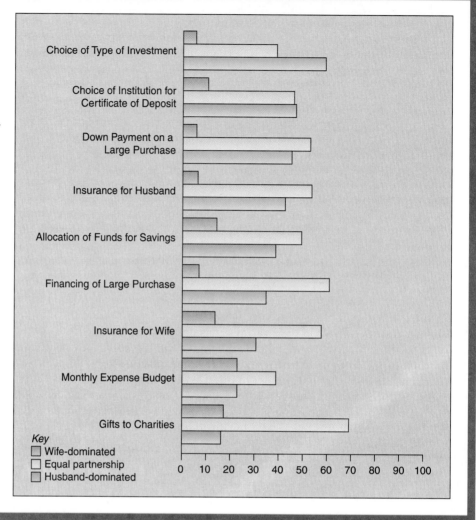

Husband-wife decision making also appears to be related to *cultural influence*. Research comparing husband-wife decision making patterns in the People's Republic of China and in the United States reveals that among Chinese there were substantially fewer "joint" decisions and more "husband-dominated" decisions for many household purchases.[20] However, when limiting the comparison to urban and rural Chinese households (or a "within-China" comparison), the research showed that in a larger city like Beijing, married couples were more likely than rural couples to share equally in purchase decisions. Still further, because of China's "one child" policy and the ensuing custom of treating a single child as a "little emperor," many of the parents' purchase decisions are influenced by the input of their child.[21]

In another recent cross-cultural study, husband-wife decision making was studied among three groups: Asian-Indians living in India, Asian-Indians living in the United States, and American nationals. Results show a decrease in husband-dominated decisions and an increase in wife-dominated decisions, going from Asian-Indians in India, to Asian-Indians in the United States, to American nationals. This pattern seems to indicate the impact of assimilation on decision making.[22]

A BETTER WAY TO LIVE.

Olympic-Size and
Resort-Style Pools.
Indoor and
Outdoor Pools.

What could be better than
diving into clear blue waters
under a sunny Arizona sky?
How about doing laps in an
Olympic-size pool? Or enjoying
a light lunch poolside?

We have indoor pools. Outdoor
pools. Pools for people who like
to dangle their feet. And pools
to lounge by. With five pools, it's
easy to see why Sun City West
gives you more.

Besides more pools, we have
more pool tables (30), seven golf
courses, and more than 200
clubs and classes.

You'll find up to $15,000 in
incentives on over 200 homes, too.
So go ahead and add landscaping,
window treatments, or even a spa.
It's not just a better way to buy a
home, it's a better way to live. For
a closer look, tour Sun City West
today. Models open daily from
9 a.m. to 5 p.m.

Del Webb's
Sun City West®

TAKE I-17 TO BELL ROAD WEST
CALL 602-546-5149 or 800-341-6121
FOR INFORMATION.

FIGURE 10-12
Targeting the Postparent-
hood Stage

lifestyle arrangements.[27] Figure 10-13 presents an FLC model that depicts along the main horizontal row the stages of the traditional FLC and above and below the main horizontal row are selected alternative FLC stages that account for some important nontraditional family households that marketers are increasingly targeting. The underlying sociodemographic forces that drive this expanded FLC model include divorce and later marriages, with and without the presence of children. Although somewhat greater reality is provided by this modified FLC model, it only recognizes families that started in marriage, ignoring such single-parent households as unwed mothers and families formed because a single person or single persons adopt a child.

FIGURE 10-13

An Extended Family Life Cycle Schema Accounts for Alternative Consumer Lifestyle Realities

Source: Patrick E. Murphy and William A. Staples, "A Modernized Family Life Cycle," *Journal of Consumer Research* 6 (June 1979), 17. Reprinted by permission of The University of Chicago Press as publisher.

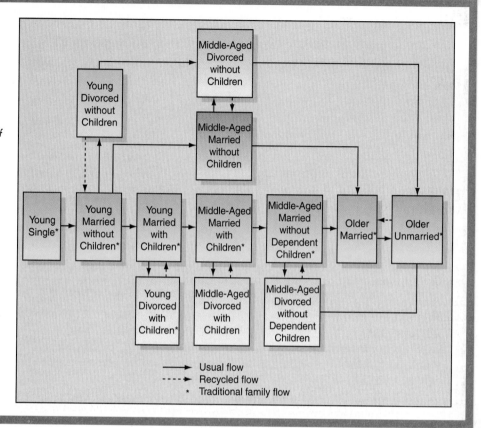

Nontraditional FLC Stages

Table 10-4 presents an extensive categorization of nontraditional FLC stages that are derived from the dynamic sociodemographic forces operating during the past 25 years or so. These nontraditional stages include not only family households but also nonfamily households: those consisting of a single individual and those consisting of two or more unrelated individuals. At one time, nonfamily households were so uncommon that it was not really important whether they were considered or not. However, as Table 10-5 reveals, nearly 30 percent of all households are currently nonfamily households (that is, men or women living alone or with another person as an unmarried couple). The table points out how FLC stages have shifted so that today nonfamily households actually outnumber married couples with children, the once stereotypical family.

Consumption in Nontraditional Families

When households undergo status changes (divorce, temporary retirement, a new person moving into the household, or the death of a spouse), they often undergo spontaneous changes in consumption-related preferences and, thus, become attractive targets for many marketers. For example, divorce often requires that one (or both) former spouses find a new residence, get new telephones (with new telephone numbers), buy new furniture, and perhaps find a job. These requirements mean that a divorced person might need to contact real estate agents, call the local and long-distance telephone companies, visit furniture stores, and possibly contact a personnel agency or career consultant. There are also the special needs of the children who are experiencing the divorce (see Figure 10-14).

types of categories used for each of these income variables. Recent evidence suggests that income works best in accounting for leisure consumption when measured in terms of (engaging in either "doing or not doing") a particular leisure activity (such as snow skiing, bowling, or playing basketball or golf).[7]

Although income is a popular estimate of social-class standing, not all consumer researchers agree that it is an appropriate index of social class. Some argue that a blue-collar automobile mechanic and a white-collar assistant bank manager may both earn $48,000 a year, yet because of (or as a reflection of) social-class differences, each will spend that income in a different way. How they decide to spend their incomes reflects different values. Within this context, it is the difference in values that is an important discriminant of social class between people, not the amount of income they earn.

Supporting this viewpoint is the marketplace behavior of "underprivileged" upper-class and "overprivileged" middle-class American families with the same basic annual incomes. Specifically, overprivileged middle-class consumers can be differentiated from underprivileged upper-class consumers by their more likely ownership of such products as campers, motorboats, pickup trucks, tractor lawnmowers, and backyard swimming pools. In contrast, underprivileged upper-class consumers with the same income spend relatively greater amounts on private club memberships, special educational experiences for their children, and cultural objects and events.[8]

Further substantiating the importance of consumers' personal values, rather than amount of income, is the observation that affluence may be more a function of attitude or behavior than of income level.[9] These "attitudinally affluent" consumers represent a broad segment who do not have the income needed to be considered affluent in today's society, yet they desire to have the best. They buy less but buy better quality, assigning priorities and gradually working their way toward having everything they want.

Other Variables Quality of neighborhood and dollar value of residence are rarely used as sole measures of social class. However, they are used informally to support or verify social-class membership assigned on the basis of occupational status or income.

Finally, *possessions* have been used by sociologists as an index of social class.[10] The best-known and most elaborate rating scheme for evaluating possessions is **Chapin's Social Status Scale**, which focuses on the presence of certain items of furniture and accessories in the living room (types of floor or floor covering, drapes, fireplace, library table, telephone, or bookcases) and the condition of the room (cleanliness, organization, or general atmosphere).[11] Conclusions are drawn about a family's social class on the basis of such observations. To illustrate how home decorations reflect social-class standing, studies reveal that lower-class families are likely to place their television sets in the living room, while middle- and upper-class families usually place their television sets in the bedroom or family room.[12] The marketing implications of such insights suggest that advertisements for television sets targeted at lower-class consumers should show the set in a living room, whereas advertisements directed to middle- or upper-class consumers should show the set in a bedroom, a family room, or a media room. Figure 11-2 presents an ad for HotSpring Portable Spas that is aimed at upper-class consumers seeking to create a personal home spa.

Composite-Variable Indexes

Composite indexes systematically combine a number of socioeconomic factors to form one overall measure of social-class standing. Such indexes are of interest to consumer researchers because they may better reflect the complexity of social class than single-variable indexes. For instance, research exploring consumers' perceptions of mail and phone order shopping reveals that the *higher* the socioeconomic status (in terms

FIGURE 11-2
Targeting the Upper-Class
Consumer

of a composite of income, occupational status, and education), the more positive are the consumers' ratings of mail and phone order buying, relative to in-store shopping.[13] The research also found that downscale consumers (a composite of lower scores on the three variables) were less positive toward magazine and catalog shopping and more positive toward in-store shopping than more upscale socioeconomic groupings.[14] Armed with such information, retailers like Kmart, Wal-Mart, and Target that especially target their stores' merchandise to working-class (more downscale) consumers would have a real challenge using direct marketing catalogs and telephone selling approaches. In contrast, retailers concentrating on upscale consumers, such as Neiman Marcus, have been especially effective in developing catalog programs targeted to specific segments of affluent or upscale consumers.

Two of the more important composite indexes are the **Index of Status Characteristics** and the **Socioeconomic Status Score**:

1. **Index of Status Characteristics.** A classic composite measure of social class is Warner's Index of Status Characteristics (ISC).[15] The ISC is a weighted measure of the following socioeconomic variables: occupation, source of income (not amount of income), house type, and dwelling area (quality of neighborhood).

2. **Socioeconomic Status Scores.** The United States Bureau of the Census developed the Socioeconomic Status Score (SES), which combines three basic socioeconomic variables: occupation, family income, and educational attainment.[16]

LIFESTYLE PROFILES OF THE SOCIAL CLASSES

Consumer research has found evidence that within each of the social classes, there is a constellation of specific lifestyle factors (shared beliefs, attitudes, activities, and behaviors) that tend to distinguish the members of each class from the members of all other social classes.

To capture the lifestyle composition of the various social-class groupings, Table 11-7 presents a consolidated portrait, pieced together from numerous sources, of the members of the following six social classes: upper-upper class, lower-upper class, upper-middle class, lower-middle class, upper-lower class, and lower-lower class. Each of these profiles is only a generalized picture of the class. People in any class may possess values, attitudes, and behavioral patterns that are a hybrid of two or more classes.

SOCIAL-CLASS MOBILITY

Social-class membership in the United States is not so hard and fixed as it is in some other countries and cultures. Although individuals can move either up or down in social-class standing from the class position held by their parents, Americans have primarily thought in terms of **upward mobility** because of the availability of free education and opportunities for self-development and self-advancement. Indeed, the classic Horatio Alger tale of a penniless young orphan who managed to achieve great success in business and in life is depicted over and over again in American novels, movies, and television shows. Today, many young men and women with ambition to get ahead dream of going to college and eventually starting their own successful businesses.

Because upward mobility has commonly been attainable in American society, the higher social classes often become reference groups for ambitious men and women of lower social status. Familiar examples of upward mobility are: the new management trainee who strives to dress like the boss; the middle manager who aspires to belong to the status country club; or the graduate of a municipal college who wants to send his daughter to Princeton. The ad for the Ritz-Carlton San Juan Hotel & Casino in Figure 11-3 is targeted to successful upwardly mobile individuals striving to express their personal attainment. The supporting description of the history of the resort and its range of services are additional clues to the status appeal.

Recognizing that individuals often aspire to the lifestyle and possessions enjoyed by members of a higher social class, marketers frequently incorporate the symbols of higher-class membership, both as products and props in advertisements targeted to lower social-class audiences. For example, ads often present or display marketers' products within an upper-class setting: the products are displayed on a table in front of a fireplace with a beautiful mantle (a board game), being shown on the desk of an elegantly appointed executive office (a new desktop computer), shown being consumed by fashionably (European) dressed models (a domestic wine), shown appearing on an

TABLE 11-7 Social-Class Profiles

THE UPPER-UPPER CLASS—COUNTRY CLUB ESTABLISHMENT

- Small number of well-established families
- Belong to best country clubs and sponsor major charity events
- Serve as trustees for local colleges and hospitals
- Prominent physicians and lawyers
- May be heads of major financial institutions, owners of major long-established firms
- Accustomed to wealth, so do not spend money conspicuously

THE LOWER-UPPER CLASS—NEW WEALTH

- Not quite accepted by the upper crust of society
- Represent "new money"
- Successful business executive
- Conspicuous users of their new wealth

THE UPPER-MIDDLE CLASS—ACHIEVING PROFESSIONALS

- Have neither family status nor unusual wealth
- Career-oriented
- Young successful professionals, corporate managers, and business owners
- Most are college graduates, many with advanced degrees
- Active in professional, community, and social activities
- Have a keen interest in obtaining the "better things in life"
- Their homes serve as symbols of their achievements
- Consumption is often conspicuous
- Very child-oriented

THE LOWER-MIDDLE CLASS—FAITHFUL FOLLOWERS

- Primary nonmanagerial white-collar workers and highly paid blue-collar workers
- Want to achieve "respectability" and be accepted as good citizens
- Want their children to be well-behaved
- Tend to be churchgoers and are often involved in church-sponsored activities
- Prefer a neat and clean appearance and tend to avoid faddish or highly-styled clothing
- Constitute a major market for do-it-yourself products

THE UPPER-LOWER CLASS—SECURITY-MINDED MAJORITY

- The largest social-class segment
- Solidly blue collar
- Strive for security (sometimes gained from union membership)
- View work as a means to "buy" enjoyment
- Want children to behave properly
- High wage earners in this group may spend impulsively
- Interested in items that enhance their leisure time (e.g., TV sets, hunting equipment)
- Husbands typically have a strong "macho" self-image
- Males are sports fans, heavy smokers, beer drinkers

THE LOWER-LOWER CLASS—ROCK BOTTOM

- Poorly educated, unskilled laborers
- Often out of work
- Children are often poorly treated
- Tend to live a day-to-day existence

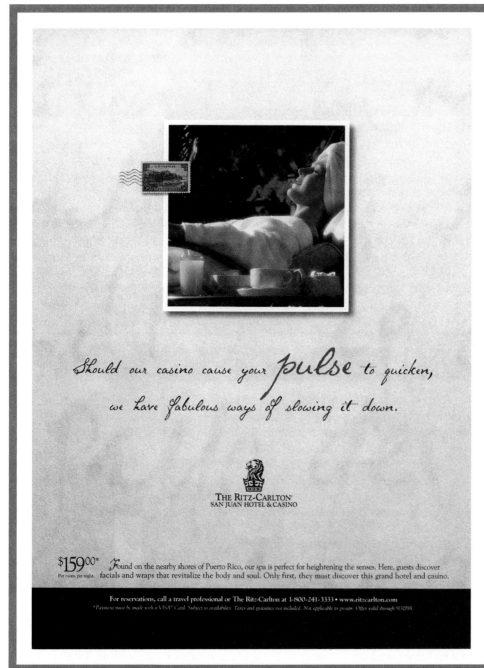

FIGURE 11-3
Appealing to Upward
Mobility

exquisitely set dining room table (a bottle of jam), and shown parked outside of a famous exclusive restaurant (a new model automobile). Sometimes a more direct appeal to consumers' sense of having products that are normally restricted to members of other social classes is an affective message. For instance, if a direct marketer of consumer electronics were to promote a top-of-the-line laptop (such as a high-end model of an IBM ThinkPad), usually purchased by senior business executives, as "now it's your turn to have what Fortune 500 executives have enjoyed" (its been marked down about 50 percent of original price), this would be a marketing message that encourages "ordinary consumers" to own a "dream machine."

Another characteristic of social-class mobility is that products and services traditionally within the realm of one social class may filter down to lower social classes. For instance, plastic surgery was once affordable only for movie stars and other wealthy consumers. Today, however, consumers of all economic strata undergo cosmetic procedures.

SIGNS OF DOWNWARD MOBILITY

Although the United States is frequently associated with *upward mobility*, because it was the rule for much of its history, there now are signs of some **downward mobility**. Social commentators have suggested that some young adults (such as members of the X-Generation described in chapter 13) are not only likely to find it difficult to "do better" than their parents (better jobs, own homes, more disposable income, more savings) but may not even do as well as their parents.

There is evidence of a slide in social-class mobility. Defining middle class as households having an after-tax income between $24,000 and $72,000, researchers found that the chance of becoming either affluent or poor has increased, whereas the chance of staying middle class has been declining.[17] Moreover, the same research indicates that the odds that young men's income will reach middle-class levels by the time they reach their thirtieth birthday has also been declining. This regressive pattern holds true, regardless of race, parents' income, and young persons' educational level.

GEODEMOGRAPHIC CLUSTERING

In recent years, traditional social-class measures have been enhanced by the linkage of geographic and socioeconomic consumer data to create more powerful **geodemographic clusters**. The underlying rationale for geodemographic clustering is that "birds of a feather flock together."

One of the most popular clustering services is **PRIZM**, which identifies a variety of socioeconomic and demographic factors (education, income, occupation, family life cycle, ethnicity, housing, and urbanization) drawn from U.S. Census data. This material is combined with survey and panel data on actual consumer behavior (for example, product purchase and usage, mail-order buying, and media-exposure habits) to locate concentrations of consumers with similar characteristics.

PRIZM assigns every one of the United States microneighborhoods (zip code + 4 areas) to one of 62 PRIZM clusters, which can be further collapsed into 15 groups (S1 through R3). Table 11-8 shows an example of a PRIZM cluster from each of the seven socioeconomic categories. Marketers can superimpose these geodemographic clusters onto a host of product and service usage data, media-exposure data, and lifestyle data (such as VALS, discussed in chapter 5) to create a sharp, refined picture of their target markets. To illustrate the usefulness of such information, Table 11-9 presents an overview profile of the Young Literati PRIZM cluster.

THE AFFLUENT CONSUMER

Affluent households constitute an especially attractive target segment because its members have incomes that provide them with a disproportionately larger share of all discretionary income—the "extras" that allow the purchase of luxury cruises, foreign sports cars, time-sharing ski-resort condos, fine jewelry, and ready access to home PCs, laptops and surfing on the Internet.

TABLE 11-8 Sample PRIZM Cluster Segments Drawn from All 62 Clusters to Reflect a Range of Socioeconomic Groups

GROUP CODES	CLUSTER NUMBER	CLUSTER NICKNAME/ DESCRIPTION	PERCENT OF UNITED STATES HOUSEHOLDS	SOCIOECONOMIC CATEGORY/INCOME RANGE OF HEAD-OF-HOUSEHOLD	KEY EDUCATION LEVEL	KEY OCCUPATIONAL LEVEL
S1 Elite Suburbs (Suburban)	01	Blue Blood Estates/ Privileged super-rich families	1.18	Elite (1)*	College grad	Professional
	02	Winner's Circle/ Executive suburban families	2.15	Wealthy (2)	College grad	Professional
U1 Urban Uptown (Urban)	06	Urban Gold Coast/ Professional urban singles and couples	0.59	Affluent (3)	College grad	Professional
C1 2nd City Society (City)	12	Upward Bound/Young upscale white-collar families	1.83	Upper middle (13)	College grad/ Some college	Professional
S2 The Affluentials (Suburban)	21	Suburban Sprawl/ Young midscale suburban townhouse couples	1.50	Middle (24)	Some college	White collar
T2 Exurban Blues (Town)	40	Military Quarters/GIs and surrounding off-base families	.42	Lower middle (40)	Some college	Service White collar
R3 Rustic Living (Rural)	62	Hardscrabble/Families in poor isolated areas	2.0	Poor (58)	Grade school/ High school	Farm Blue collar

*Socioeconomic rank, e.g., "(1)" = ranked first out of 62 clusters, and "(58)" = ranked 58 out of 62 clusters.

Source: ©1999, Claritas, Inc. PRIZM and Claritas are registered trademarks of Claritas, Inc. The 62 PRIZM cluster nicknames ("Blue Blood Estates," "Big Sky Families," "Country Squires," etc.) are trademarks of Claritas. Reprinted by permission.

TABLE 11-9 A Profile of PRIZM Cluster: "Young Literati" (Cluster 08)

SOCIOECONOMIC FACTORS:

Percent of U.S. households	0.94%
Predominant age range	25–34, 35–44
Socioeconomic group	Upper-middle
Demographic caption	Upscale urban singles and couples
Housing type	Renter
Education	College graduates
Occupation	Professional

LIFESTYLE:

Plan for large purchases
Take vitamins
Use a discount-broker
Watch Bravo
Read *GQ*

Source: Courtesy of Claritas Inc. (PRIZM and the 62 Cluster nicknames are registered trademarks of Claritas Inc.). Reprinted by permission.

For almost 25 years, Mendelsohn Media Research has conducted an annual study of the **affluent market** (currently defined in terms of three affluent segments: those with household incomes of $70,000 to $99,999 per year—the "least affluent," those with incomes of $100,000 to $199,999 per year—the "medium affluent," and those with incomes of $200,000 or more per year—the "most affluent"). While it consists of only 21 percent of all households, this upscale market segment consumed more wine (2.5 drinks per week per adult), took more domestic airline flights (8.4 flights annually per adult), owned more vehicles (2.5 per household), and held more securities ($190,000 per household) than nonaffluent households. The average household income for these consumers is $119,300, and 63 percent of those who are employed work in either a professional or managerial capacity.[18] Figure 11-4 presents additional information as to average household expenditures for selected purchases for the three affluent segments. The results reveal that although the first two segments of affluent consumers certainly spend ample amounts purchasing a wide variety of products, in most cases the "most affluent" purchasers spend significantly more. For instance, when it comes to desktop and laptop computers, the "least affluent" spent $2,230 and the medium affluent spent $2,760, while the "most affluent" spent $4,660. Figure 11-5 presents some further insights about affluent consumers in terms of a comparison of the sports participation of the three segments of affluent consumers. The results reveal that the "most affluent" are more likely than members of the two other affluent consumer segments to participate in a sample of sports.[19] An examination of these two tables explains why marketers are eager to target affluent consumers.

Still further, a growing subcategory of the affluent are *millionaires*. Currently, more than 3 million American households have a net worth of more than $1 million.[20] Contrary to common stereotypes, these millionaires are quite similar to nonmillionaires. They are typically first generation wealthy; often working for themselves in "ordinary" nonglamour businesses. They work hard and frequently live in nonpretentious homes, often next door to nonmillionaires.

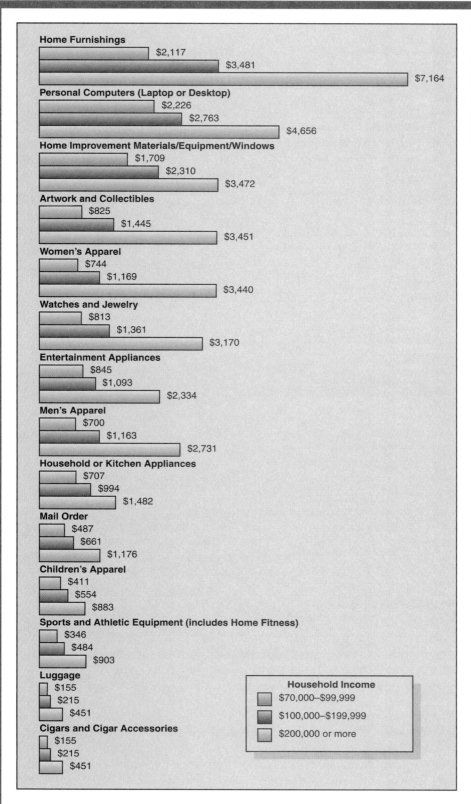

FIGURE 11-4

Three Segments of Affluent Consumers' Average Household Expenditures (among purchasing households)

Source: 1998 Mendelsohn Affluent Survey (New York: Mendelsohn Media Research, Inc., 1998), 11.

Home Furnishings
$2,117
$3,481
$7,164

Personal Computers (Laptop or Desktop)
$2,226
$2,763
$4,656

Home Improvement Materials/Equipment/Windows
$1,709
$2,310
$3,472

Artwork and Collectibles
$825
$1,445
$3,451

Women's Apparel
$744
$1,169
$3,440

Watches and Jewelry
$813
$1,361
$3,170

Entertainment Appliances
$845
$1,093
$2,334

Men's Apparel
$700
$1,163
$2,731

Household or Kitchen Appliances
$707
$994
$1,482

Mail Order
$487
$661
$1,176

Children's Apparel
$411
$554
$883

Sports and Athletic Equipment (includes Home Fitness)
$346
$484
$903

Luggage
$155
$215
$451

Cigars and Cigar Accessories
$155
$215
$451

Household Income
$70,000–$99,999
$100,000–$199,999
$200,000 or more

FIGURE 11-5

Affluent Consumers' Participation in Selected Sports (number of days in past year, indexed to each of the three income segments)

Source: 1998 Mendelsohn Affluent Survey (New York: Mendelsohn Media Research, Inc., 1998).

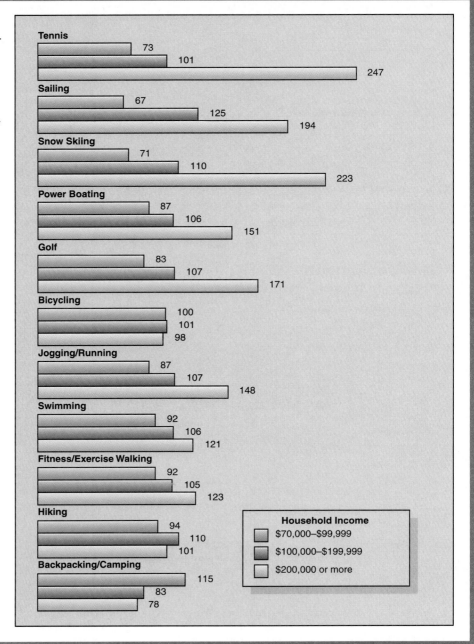

THE MEDIA EXPOSURE OF THE AFFLUENT CONSUMER

As might be expected, the media habits of the affluent differ from those of the general population.[21] For example, those households earning more than $70,000 a year view less TV per day than less-affluent households. A profile of the media habits of $70,000-plus affluent adult householders shows they read 6.6 different publications; they listen to 12.8 hours of weekday radio and watch 23 hours of TV per week; and 88 percent of them subscribe to cable TV. Magazines that cater to the tastes and interests of the affluent include *Architectural Digest*, *Condé Nast Traveler*, *Gourmet*, *Southern Accents*, and *Town & Country*. Table 11-10 presents a selection of magazines

TABLE 11-10 Affluent Readers' ($70,000+ Median Household Income) for Selected Publications

NEWSPAPER/MAGAZINE	MEDIAN HOUSEHOLD INCOME ($)
Allure	115,400
Architectural Digest	125,400
Art & Antiques	103,200
Better Homes and Gardens	96,600
Boating	101,400
Bon Appétit	119,200
Business Week	121,500
Cigar Aficionado	115,100
Condé Nast Traveler	123,500
Elle	119,900
Esquire	108,200
Fortune	121,900
Golf Magazine	102,200
Good Housekeeping	94,800
Gourmet	120,600
GQ/Gentlemen's Quarterly	103,500
House & Garden	100,300
Martha Stewart Living	100,000
National Geographic	97,000
Newsweek	109,000
Self	103,800
Southern Accents	120,800
Town & Country	124,200
Travel & Leisure	111,100
U.S. News & World Report	99,900
Vanity Fair	124,700
Vogue	119,800
W	138,000

Source: From 1998 Mendelsohn Affluent Survey (New York: Mendelsohn Media Research, Inc.). Reprinted by permission.

and reveals the median household incomes of their readers who have incomes of $70,000 or more (see Table 11-3 for a more general selection of print media and corresponding median incomes).

SEGMENTING THE AFFLUENT MARKET

The affluent market is not one single market. Contrary to popular stereotypes, the wealth in America is not found only behind "the tall, cloistered walls of suburban country clubs."[22] Wealth is spread among niches, including Asian immigrants, single women, and young Cuban Americans, to name a few.

Because not all affluent consumers share the same lifestyles (that is, activities, interests, and opinions), various marketers have tried to isolate meaningful segments of the affluent market. To assist the many marketers interested in reaching subsegments of the affluent market, Mediamark Research, Inc. (MRI) has developed the following affluent market-segmentation schema (or the *Upper Deck*—defined as the top 10 percent of households in terms of income).[23]

1. *Well-feathered nests:* Households that have at least one high-income earner and children present (37% of the Upper Deck).
2. *No strings attached:* Households that have at least one high-income earner and no children (32% of the Upper Deck).
3. *Nanny's in charge:* Households that have two or more earners, none earning high incomes, and children present (11% of the Upper Deck).
4. *Two careers:* Households that have two or more earners, neither earning high incomes, and no children present (14% of the Upper Deck).
5. *The good life:* Households that have a high degree of affluence with no person employed or with the head of household not employed (6% of the Upper Deck).

Armed with such affluent lifestyle segments, MRI provides subscribing firms with profiles of users of a variety of goods and services frequently targeted to the affluent consumer (for instance, domestic and foreign travel, leisure clothing, lawn-care services, rental cars, and various types of recreational activities). For instance, in terms of recreation, the well-feathered nester can be found on the tennis court, the good lifer may be playing golf, while the two-career couple may be off sailing.[24]

With few local marketers vying for their business, the rural affluent represent an untapped (and somewhat difficult to pinpoint) subsegment of the affluent market. The rural affluent fall into four categories:[25]

1. *Suburban transplants:* Those who move to the country but still commute to a high-paying urban job.
2. *Equity-rich suburban expatriates:* Urbanites who sell their homes for a huge profit, buy a far less expensive home in a small town, and live off the difference.
3. *City folks with country homes:* Wealthy snowbirds and vacationers who spend winters or summers in scenic rural areas, especially mountainous and coastal areas.
4. *Wealthy landowners:* Wealthy farmers and other natives who make a comfortable living off the land.

THE NONAFFLUENT CONSUMER

Although many advertisers would prefer to show their products as part of an affluent lifestyle, blue-collar and other nonprofessional people represent a vast group of consumers that marketers cannot ignore. In fact, households earning $34,000 or less control more than 30 percent of the total income in the United States. Lower-income, or **downscale**, **consumers** (frequently defined as having household incomes of $30,000 or less) may actually be more brand loyal than wealthier consumers, because they can ill afford to make mistakes by switching to unfamiliar brands. They also are more likely to be either younger or older than upscale consumers, as well as being single or divorced.

Understanding the importance of speaking to (not at) the downscale consumers, companies such as RC Cola, MasterCard and McDonald's target "average Joes" (and Janes) with ads reflecting the modest lifestyles of some of their customers.[26]

THE ARRIVAL OF "TECHNO-CLASS"

The degree of literacy, familiarity, and competency with technology, especially computers and the Internet, appears to be a new basis for a kind of "class standing," or status or prestige. Those who are unfamiliar with or lack computer skills are being referred to as "technological underclassed."[27] Educators, business leaders, and government officials have warned that the inability to adequately use technology is negatively impacting lifestyles and quality of life of those who are not computer literate.

Fueling this reality, the business press regularly runs cover stories featuring technological superstar Bill Gates or other ultra-successful Silicon Valley achievers. These stories describe their accomplishments and enviable lifestyles that include $30-million residences and other luxuries that serve to motivate others to duplicate their accomplishments. Even factory workers in highly successful start-up technology firms have become millionaires on their employee profit sharing and stock option programs.

These extraordinary stories of entrepreneurial and technological accomplishments, when coupled with a general sense of not wanting to be left out of the "sweep of computer technology," have propelled parents to seek out computer training for their children, even their infant children ("They are never too young to learn about computers"). Parents sense that an understanding of computer usage is a necessary tool of "competitive achievement" and "success." Moreover, even 55-year-old professionals, who were initially reluctant to "learn computers," are now seeking "personal computer training"—they no longer want to be left out, nor do they want to be further embarrassed by having to admit that they "don't know computers."

Consumers throughout the world have come to believe that it is critical to acquire a functional understanding of computers in order to ensure that they do not become obsolete or hinder themselves socially or professionally. In this sense, there is a "technological class structure" that centers around the amount of computer skills that one possesses. It appears that those without necessary computer skills will increasingly find themselves to be "underclassed" and "disadvantaged."

SELECTED CONSUMER BEHAVIOR APPLICATIONS OF SOCIAL CLASS

Social class profiles provide a broad picture of the values, attitudes, and behavior that distinguish the members of various social classes. This section focuses on specific consumer research that relates social class to the development of marketing strategy.

CLOTHING, FASHION, AND SHOPPING

A Greek philosopher once said, "Know, first, who you are; and then adorn yourself accordingly."[28] This bit of wisdom is relevant to clothing marketers today, because most people dress to fit their self-images, which includes their perceptions of their own social-class membership.

Members of specific social classes differ in terms of what they consider fashionable or in good taste. For instance, lower middle-class consumers have a strong preference for T-shirts, caps, and other clothing that offer an *external point of identification*, such as the name of an admired person or group (Michael Jordan), a respected company or brand name (Heineken), or a valued trademark (Nike). These consumers are prime targets for licensed goods. In contrast, upper-class consumers are likely to buy clothing that is free from such supporting associations. Upper-class consumers also seek clothing with a more subtle look, such as the kind of sportswear found in an L.L. Bean catalog, rather than designer jeans.

In Shanghai, the public wearing of pajamas is a sign of status and possibly a signal of an economically developing society (for its citizens historically could not afford the luxury of wearing pajamas).[29] In a similar manner, in Asia, people can be observed wearing outer clothing with the well-known designer labels still on the garment's sleeves. Again, this is a sign of status or being able to afford such expensive luxury clothing. More research is needed to examine the relationship between various appearance-related purchase behaviors and social-class membership.

Social class is also an important variable in determining where a consumer shops. People tend to avoid stores that have the image of appealing to a social class very different from their own. In the past, some mass merchandisers who tried to appeal to a higher class of consumers found themselves alienating their traditional customers. This implies that retailers should pay attention to the social class of their customer base and the social class of their store appeal to ensure that they send the appropriate message through advertising. For instance, Gap has been rapidly rolling out the Old Navy clothing stores in an effort to attract working-class families who usually purchased their casual and active wear clothing from general merchandise retailers like Kmart, Wal-Mart, or Target.

THE PURSUIT OF LEISURE

Social-class membership is also closely related to the choice of recreational and leisure-time activities. For instance, upper-class consumers are likely to attend the theater and concerts, to play bridge, and to attend college football games. Lower-class consumers tend to be avid television watchers and fishing enthusiasts, and they enjoy drive-in movies and baseball games. Furthermore, the lower-class consumer spends more time on commercial types of activities (bowling, playing pool or billiards, or visiting taverns) and craft activities (model building, painting, and woodworking projects), rather than cerebral activities (reading, visiting museums). In any case, regardless if we are describing middle-class or working-class consumers, there appears to be a trend toward more spending on "experiences" that bring the family together (family vacations or activities) and less spending on "things."[30]

SAVING, SPENDING, AND CREDIT

Saving, spending, and credit-card usage all seem to be related to social-class standing. Upper-class consumers are more future oriented and confident of their financial acumen; they are more willing to invest in insurance, stocks, and real estate. In comparison, lower-class consumers are generally more concerned with immediate gratification; when they do save, they are primarily interested in safety and security. Therefore, it is not surprising that when it comes to bank credit-card usage, members of the lower social classes tend to use their bank credit cards for installment purchases, while members of the upper social classes pay their credit card bills in full each month. In other words, lower-class purchasers tend to use their credit cards to "buy now and pay later" for things they might not otherwise be able to afford, while upper-class purchasers use their credit cards as a convenient substitute for cash.

SOCIAL CLASS AND COMMUNICATION

Social-class groupings differ in terms of their media habits and in how they transmit and receive communications. Knowledge of these differences is invaluable to marketers who segment their markets on the basis of social class.

When it comes to describing their world, lower-class consumers tend to portray it in rather personal and concrete terms, while middle-class consumers are able to describe their experiences from a number of different perspectives. A simple example illustrates that members of different social classes tend to see the world differently. The following responses to a question asking where the respondent usually purchases gasoline were received:

Upper-middle-class answer: At Mobil or Shell.
Lower-middle-class answer: At the station on Main and Fifth Street.
Lower-class answer: At Ed's.

Such variations in response indicate that middle-class consumers have a *broader* or more general view of the world, while lower-class consumers tend to have a *narrow* or personal view—seeing the world through their own immediate experiences.

Regional differences in terminology, choice of words and phrases, and patterns of usage also tend to increase as we move down the social-class ladder. Therefore, in creating messages targeted to the lower classes, marketers try to word advertisements to reflect particular regional preferences that exist (for example, "soda" is "pop" in the Midwest).

Selective exposure to various types of mass media differs by social class. In the selection of specific television programs and program types, higher-social-class members tend to prefer current events and drama, while lower-class individuals tend to prefer soap operas, quiz shows, and situation comedies. Higher-class consumers tend to have greater exposure to magazines and newspapers than do their lower-class counterparts. Lower-class consumers are likely to have greater exposure to publications that dramatize romance and the lifestyles of movie and television celebrities. For example, magazines such as *True Story* appeal heavily to blue-collar or working-class women ("Middle America"), who enjoy reading about the problems, fame, and fortunes of others.

SUMMARY

Social stratification, the division of members of a society into a hierarchy of distinct social classes, exists in all societies and cultures. Social class usually is defined by the amount of status that members of a specific class possess in relation to members of other classes. Social-class membership often serves as a frame of reference (a reference group) for the development of consumer attitudes and behavior.

The measurement of social class is concerned with classifying individuals into social-class groupings. These groupings are of particular value to marketers, who use social classification as an effective means of identifying and segmenting target markets. There are three basic methods for measuring social class: subjective measurement, reputational measurement, and objective measurement. Subjective measures rely on an individual's self-perception; reputational measures rely on an individual's perceptions of others; and objective measures use specific socioeconomic measures, either alone (as a single-variable index) or in combination with others (as a composite-variable index). Composite-variable indexes, such as the Index of Status Characteristics and the Socioeconomic Status Score, combine a number of socioeconomic factors to form one overall measure of social-class standing.

Class structures range from two-class to nine-class systems. A frequently used classification system consists of six classes: upper-upper, lower-upper, upper-middle, lower-middle, upper-lower, and lower-lower. Profiles of these classes indicate that the socioeconomic differences between classes are reflected in differences in attitudes, in leisure activities, and in consumption habits. This is why segmentation by social class is of special interest to marketers.

In recent years, some marketers have turned to geodemographic clustering as an alternative to a strict social-class typology. Geodemographic clustering is a technique that combines geographic and socioeconomic factors to locate concentrations of consumers with particular characteristics. Particular attention currently is being directed to affluent consumers, who represent the fastest-growing segment in our population; however, some marketers are finding it extremely profitable to cater to the needs of non-affluent consumers.

Research has revealed social-class differences in clothing habits, home decoration, and leisure activities, as well as saving, spending, and credit habits. Thus, astute marketers tailor specific product and promotional strategies to each social-class target segment.

DISCUSSION QUESTIONS

1. Marketing researchers generally use the objective method to measure social class, rather than the subjective or reputational methods. Why is the objective method preferred by researchers?

2. Under what circumstances would you expect income to be a better predictor of consumer behavior than a composite measure of social class (for example, based on income, education, and occupation)? When would you expect the composite social-class measure to be superior?

3. Describe the correlation between social status (or prestige) and income. Which is a more useful segmentation variable? Discuss.

4. Which status-related variable, occupation, education, or income is the most appropriate segmentation base for: (a) expensive vacations, (b) opera subscriptions, (c) *People* magazine subscriptions, (d) fat-free foods, (e) personal computers, (f) pocket-size cellular telephones, and (g) health clubs?

5. Consider the Rolex watch, which has a retail price range starting at about $2,000 for a stainless-steel model to thousands of dollars for a solid-gold model. How might the Rolex company use geodemographic clustering in its marketing efforts?

6. How would you use the research evidence on affluent households presented in this chapter to segment the market for: (a) home exercise equipment, (b) vacations, and (c) banking services?

7. How can a marketer use knowledge of consumer behavior to develop financial services for affluent consumers? For "downscale" consumers?

8. You are the owner of two furniture stores, one catering to upper-middle-class consumers and the other to lower-class consumers. How do social-class differences influence each store's: (a) product lines and styles, (b) advertising media selection, (c) the copy and communications style used in the ads, and (d) payment policies?

EXERCISES

1. Copy the list of occupations in Table 11-4 and ask students majoring in areas other than marketing (both business and nonbusiness) to rank the relative prestige of these occupations. Are any differences in the rankings related to the students' majors? Explain.

2. Find three print ads in one of the publications listed in Table 11-3. Using the social-class characteristics listed in Table 11-7, identify the social class targeted by each ad and evaluate the effectiveness of the advertising appeals used.

3. Select two households featured in two different TV series or sitcoms. Classify each household into one of the social classes discussed in the text and analyze its lifestyle and consumption behavior.

KEY TERMS

- **Affluent consumers**
- **Chapin's Social Status Scale**
- **Class consciousness**
- **Composite-variable indexes**
- **Downscale consumers**
- **Downward mobility**
- **Geodemographic clustering**
- **Index of Status Characteristics**
- **Objective measures**
- **PRIZM**
- **Reputational measures**
- **Single-variable index**
- **Social class**
- **Social prestige**
- **Social status**
- **Socioeconomic Status Score**
- **Subjective measures of social class**
- **Upward mobility**

NOTES

1. Douglas B. Holt, "Does Cultural Capital Structure American Consumption?" *Journal of Consumer Research* 25 (June 1998): 19.
2. Elia Kacapyr, "Are You Middle Class?" *American Demographics* (October 1996): 31.
3. Home Arts On-Line Media Kit, "Audience Demographics," (derived from National Market Measures Study), The Hearst Corporation (Fall–Winter 1997) (www.homearts.com/adsite/ aol.htm).
4. Rebecca Piirto Heath, "The New Working Class," *American Demographics* (January 1998): 52.
5. Rebecca Piirto Heath, "Life on Easy Street," *American Demographics* (April 1997): 33–38.
6. Diane Crispell, "The Real Middle Americans," *American Demographics* (October 1994): 28–35.
7. Eugene Sivadas, George Mathew, and David J. Curry, "A Preliminary Examination of the Continued Significance of Social Class to Marketing: A Geodemographic Replication," *Journal of Consumer Marketing* 14, 6 (1997): 469.
8. Richard P. Coleman, "The Continuing Significance of Social Class to Marketing," *Journal of Consumer Research* 10 (December 1983): 274.
9. Dennis Rodkin, "Wealthy Attitude Wins over Healthy Wallet: Consumers Prove Affluence Is a State of Mind," *Advertising Age*, 9 July 1990, S4, S6.
10. Janeen Arnold Costa and Russell W. Belk, "Nouveaux Riches as Quintessential Americans: Case Studies of Consumption in an Extended Family," *Advances in Nonprofit Marketing*, vol. 3 (Greenwich, CT: JAI Press, 1990), 83–140.
11. F. Stuart Chapin, *Contemporary American Institutions* (New York: Harper, 1935), 373–97.
12. Joan Kron, *Home-Psych* (New York: Potter, 1983), 90–102.
13. Robert B. Settle, Pamela L. Alreck, and Denny E. McCorkle, "Consumer Perceptions of Mail/Phone Order Shopping Media," *Journal of Direct Marketing* 8 (Summer 1994): 30–45.
14. Ibid.
15. W. Lloyd Warner, Marchia Meeker, and Kenneth Eells, *Social Class in America: Manual of Procedure for the Measurement of Social Status* (New York: Harper & Brothers, 1960).
16. *Methodology and Scores of Socioeconomic Status*, Working Paper No. 15 (Washington, DC: U.S. Bureau of the Census, 1963).
17. Randy Kennedy, "For Middle Class, New York Shrinks as Home Prices Soar," *New York Times*, 1 April 1998, A1, B6; "Two Tier Marketing," *Business Week*, 17 March 1997, 82–90; and Keith Bradsher, "America's Opportunity Gap," *New York Times*, 4 June 1995, 4.
18. *The Mendelsohn Affluent Survey 1998* (New York: Mendelsohn Media Research, Inc., 1998).
19. Ibid.
20. Anita Sharpe, "The Rich Aren't So Different After All," *Wall Street Journal*, 12 November 1996, B1, B10; and Rebecca Piirto Heath, "Life on Easy Street," *Wall Street Journal*, 12 November 1996, 33.
21. *The Mendelsohn Affluent Survey 1998.*
22. "Marketing to Affluents: Hidden Pockets of Wealth," *Advertising Age*, 9 July 1990, S1.
23. *The Upper Deck* (Mediamark Research, Inc., 1998).
24. For some further insights about the affluence of dual-income households, see: Diane Crispell, "The Very Rich Are Sort of Different," *American Demographics* (March 1994): 11–13.
25. Sharon O'Malley, "Country Gold," *American Demographics* (July 1992): 26–34.
26. Karen Benezra, "Hardworking RC Cola," *BrandWeek*, 25 May 1998, 18–19.
27. Steve Rosenbush, "Techno Leaders Warn of 'Great Divide'" *USAToday*, 17 June 1998, B1.
28. Epictetus, Discourses (second century) in *The Enchiridon*, 2d ed., trans. Thomas Higginson (Indianapolis: Bobbs-Merrill, 1955).
29. Seth Faison, "A City of Sleepwalkers? No, They Just Like PJ's," *New York Times*, 6 August 1997, A4.
30. Christina Duff, "Indulging in Inconspicuous Consumption," *Wall Street Journal*, 14 April 1997, B1, B2; and Christina Duff, "Two Family Budgets: Different Means, Similar Ends," *Wall Street Journal*, 14 April 1997, B1, B2;

CHAPTER 12

The Influence of Culture on Consumer Behavior

■ ■

The study of culture is a challenging undertaking, because its primary focus is on the broadest component of social behavior—*an entire society*. In contrast to the psychologist, who is principally concerned with the study of individual behavior, or the sociologist, who is concerned with the study of groups, the anthropologist is primarily interested in identifying the very fabric of society itself.

This chapter explores the basic concepts of culture, with particular emphasis on the role that culture plays in influencing consumer behavior. We will first consider the specific dimensions of culture that make it a powerful force in regulating human behavior. After reviewing several measurement approaches that researchers use to understand the impact of culture on consumption behavior, we will show how a variety of core American cultural values influence consumer behavior.

This chapter is concerned with the general aspects of culture; the following two chapters focus on subculture and on cross-culture and show how marketers can use such knowledge to shape and modify their marketing strategies.

■■■■ WHAT IS CULTURE?

Given the broad and pervasive nature of **culture**, its study generally requires a detailed examination of the character of the total society, including such factors as language, knowledge, laws, religions, food customs, music, art, technology, work patterns, products, and other artifacts that give a society its distinctive flavor. In a sense, culture is a society's personality. For this reason, it is not easy to define its boundaries.

Because our objective is to understand the influence of culture on consumer behavior, we define culture as the *sum total of learned beliefs, values, and customs that serve to direct the consumer behavior of members of a particular society.*

The *belief* and *value* components of our definition refer to the accumulated feelings and priorities that individuals have about "things" and possessions. More precisely, *beliefs* consist of the very large number of mental or verbal statements (that is, "I believe . . .") that reflect a person's particular knowledge and assessment of something (another person, a store, a product, a brand). *Values* also are beliefs. Values differ from other beliefs, however, because they meet the following criteria: (1) they are relatively few in number; (2) they serve as a guide for culturally appropriate behavior; (3) they are enduring or difficult to change; (4) they are not tied to specific objects or situations; and (5) they are widely accepted by the members of a society.

Therefore, in a broad sense, both values and beliefs are mental images that affect a wide range of specific attitudes that, in turn, influence the way a person is likely to respond in a specific situation.[1] For example, the criteria a person uses to evaluate alternative brands in a product category (such as Kodak versus Fuji 35-mm film), or his or her eventual preference for one of these brands over the other, are influenced by both a person's general values (perceptions as to what constitutes quality and the meaning of country of origin) and specific beliefs (particular perceptions about the quality of American-made versus Japanese-made film).

In contrast to beliefs and values, *customs* are *overt modes of behavior that constitute culturally approved or acceptable ways of behaving in specific situations.* Customs consist of everyday or routine behavior. For example, a consumer's routine behavior, such as adding sugar and milk to coffee, putting ketchup on hamburgers, and putting mustard on frankfurters, are customs. Thus, while beliefs and values are guides for behavior, customs are *usual and acceptable ways of behaving.*

By our definition, it is easy to see how an understanding of various cultures of a society helps marketers predict consumer acceptance of their products.

THE INVISIBLE HAND OF CULTURE

The impact of culture is so natural and automatic that its influence on behavior is usually taken for granted. For instance, when consumer researchers ask people why they do certain things, they frequently answer, "Because it's the right thing to do." This seemingly superficial response partially reflects the ingrained influence of culture on our behavior. Often, it is only when we are exposed to people with different cultural values or customs (as when visiting a different region or a different country) that we become aware of how culture has molded our own behavior. Thus, a true appreciation of the influence that culture has on our daily life requires some knowledge of at least one other society with different cultural characteristics. For example, to understand that brushing our teeth twice a day with flavored toothpaste is a cultural phenomenon requires some awareness that members of another society either do not brush their teeth at all or do so in a distinctly different manner than our own society.

CULTURE SATISFIES NEEDS

Culture exists to satisfy the needs of the people within a society. It offers order, direction, and guidance in all phases of human problem solving by providing "tried-and-true" methods of satisfying physiological, personal, and social needs. For example, culture provides standards and "rules" about when to eat ("not between meals"), where to eat ("in a busy restaurant, because the food is likely to be good"), what is appropriate to eat for breakfast (juice and cereal), lunch (a sandwich), dinner ("something hot and good and healthy"), and snacks ("something with quick energy"); and what to serve to guests at a dinner party ("a formal sit-down meal"), at a picnic (barbecued "franks and hamburgers"), or at a wedding (champagne). Culture is also associated with what a society's members consider to be a "necessity" and what they view as a "luxury." For instance, 55 percent of American adults consider a microwave to be a necessity, and 36 percent consider a remote control for a TV or VCR to be a necessity.[2] In contrast, only 17 percent currently consider voice mail at work to be a necessity.

Similarly, culture also provides insights as to suitable dress for specific occasions (such as what to wear around the house, what to wear to school, to work, to church, at a fast-food restaurant, or to a movie theater). Dress codes are shifting dramatically; people are dressing more casually all the time and in most situations. Today, only a few big-city restaurants and clubs have business dress requirements. With the relaxed dress code in the corporate work environment, fewer men are wearing dress shirts, ties, and business suits, and fewer women are wearing dresses, suits, and panty hose.[3] In their place casual slacks, sports shirts and blouses, jeans, and the emerging category of "dress casual" have been increasing in sales.

Soft-drink companies would prefer that consumers received their morning "jolt" of caffeine from one of their products, rather than from coffee. Because most Americans do not consider soda a suitable breakfast beverage, the real challenge for soft-drink companies is to overcome culture, not competition. In fact, coffee accounts for more than 45 percent of the morning beverage market. However, it has been challenged on all fronts by juices, milk, teas (hot and iced), a host of different types of soft drinks, and now caffeinated waters.

Cultural beliefs, values, and customs continue to be followed as long as they yield satisfaction. When a specific standard no longer satisfies the members of a society, however, it is modified or replaced, so that the resulting standard is more in line with current needs and desires. For instance, it was once considered a sign of a fine hotel that they provided down or goose feather pillows in rooms. Today, with so many guests allergic to such materials, synthetic polyfill pillows are becoming the rule. Thus, culture gradually but continually evolves to meet the needs of society.

■■■■■ CULTURE IS LEARNED

Unlike innate biological characteristics (e.g., sex, skin, hair color, or intelligence), culture is learned. At an early age, we begin to acquire from our social environment a set of beliefs, values, and customs that make up our culture. For children, the learning of these acceptable cultural values and customs is reinforced by the process of playing with their toys. As children play, they act out and rehearse important cultural lessons and situations. This cultural learning prepares them for later real-life circumstances.

How Culture Is Learned

Anthropologists have identified three distinct forms of cultural learning: *formal learning*, in which adults and older siblings teach a young family member "how to behave"; *informal learning*, in which a child learns primarily by imitating the behavior of selected others, such as family, friends, or TV heroes; and *technical learning*, in which teachers instruct the child in an educational environment about what should be done, how it should be done, and why it should be done (see Figure 12-1). Although a firm's advertising can influence all three types of cultural learning, it is likely that many product advertisements enhance informal cultural learning by providing the audience with a model of behavior to imitate. This is especially true for visible or conspicuous products and products that are evaluated in public settings (such as clothing, or beepers, or portable cellular telephones), where peer influence is likely to play an important role.[4]

FIGURE 12-1
Ad Expressing Dimensions
of Formal Cultural Learning

The repetition of advertising messages creates and reinforces cultural beliefs and values. For example, many advertisers continually stress the same selected benefits of their products or services. Ads for portable cellular telephone service often stress the convenience of scheduling and rescheduling appointments, as well as the security of having a phone at all times in case of some emergency. It is difficult to say whether cellular phone subscribers *inherently* desire these benefits from their cellular telephone service or whether, after several years of cumulative exposure to advertising appeals, they have been taught by marketers to desire them. In a sense, although specific product advertising may reinforce the benefits that consumers want from the product (as determined by consumer behavior research), such advertising also "teaches" future generations of consumers to expect the same benefits from the product category.

Figure 12-2 shows that cultural meaning moves from the culturally constituted world to consumer goods and from there to the individual consumer by means of various consumption-related vehicles. Imagine the ever-popular T-shirt and how it can furnish cultural meaning and identity for wearers. T-shirts can function as *trophies* (as

FIGURE 12-2

The Movement of Cultural Meaning

Source: Grant McCracken, "Culture and Consumption: A Theoretical Account of the Structure and Movement of the Cultural Meaning of Consumer Goods," *Journal of Consumer Research* 13 (June 1986), 72. Reprinted by permission of The University of Chicago Press as publishers.

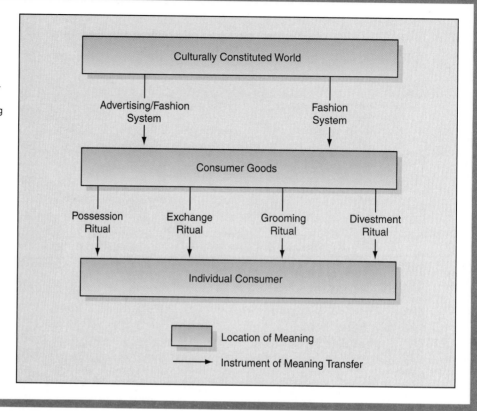

proof of participation in sports or travel) or as self-proclaimed labels of *belonging to a cultural category* ("49er," "native Floridian"). T-shirts can also be used as a means of *self-expression*, which may provide wearers with the additional benefit of serving as a "topic" initiating social dialogue with others.

ENCULTURATION AND ACCULTURATION

When discussing the acquisition of culture, anthropologists often distinguish between the learning of one's own, or native, culture and the learning of some "new" (other) culture. The learning of one's own culture is known as **enculturation**. The learning of a new or foreign culture is known as **acculturation**. In chapter 14, we will see that acculturation is an important concept for marketers who plan to sell their products in foreign or multinational markets. In such cases, marketers must study the specific culture(s) of their potential target markets to determine whether their products will be acceptable to its members and, if so, how they can best communicate the characteristics of their products to persuade the target market to buy.

LANGUAGE AND SYMBOLS

To acquire a common culture, the members of a society must be able to communicate with each other through a common language. Without a common language, shared meaning could not exist, and true communication would not take place (see chapter 9).

To communicate effectively with their audiences, marketers must use appropriate **symbols** to convey desired product images or characteristics (see Figure 12-3). These symbols can be verbal or nonverbal. Verbal symbols may include a television

FIGURE 12-3
Ad Using Visual Imagery
as a Symbol

announcement or an advertisement in a magazine. Nonverbal communication includes the use of such symbols as figures, colors, shapes, and even textures to lend additional meaning to print or broadcast advertisements, to trademarks, and to packaging or product designs.

Basically, the symbolic nature of human language sets it apart from all other animal communication. A symbol is anything that stands for something else. Any word is a symbol. The word *razor* calls forth a specific image related to an individual's own knowledge and experience. The word *hurricane* calls forth the notion of wind and rain and also has the power to stir us emotionally, arousing feelings of danger and the need for protection and safety. Similarly, the word *jaguar* has symbolic meaning: to some it suggests a fine luxury automobile, to others it implies wealth and status; to still others it suggests a sleek, wild animal to be seen at the zoo.

Because the human mind can process symbols, it is possible, for example, for a person to "experience" cognitively a visualization for a product, like the advertisement for Edge skin moisturizing gel, which contrasts two scenes—one of a parched desert without the gel and one of a rich green landscape with the gel. Such a comparison presents the idea that a skin-moisturizing gel will transform a person's dry skin to a comfortable moist state. The capacity to learn symbolically is primarily a human phenomenon; most other animals learn by direct experience. Clearly, the ability of humans to understand symbolically how a product, service, or idea can satisfy their needs makes it easier for marketers to "sell" the features and benefits of their offerings. Through a shared language and culture, individuals already know what the image means; thus, an association can be made without actively thinking about it.

A symbol may have several, even contradictory, meanings, so the advertiser must ascertain exactly what the symbol is communicating to its intended audience. For example, the advertiser who uses a trademark depicting an old craftsman to symbolize careful workmanship may instead be communicating an image of outmoded methods and lack of style. The marketer who uses slang in an advertisement to attract a teenage audience must do so with great care; slang that is misused or outdated will symbolically date the marketer's firm and product.

Price and channels of distribution also are significant symbols of the marketer and the marketer's product. For example, price often implies quality to potential buyers. For certain products (such as clothing), the type of store in which the product is sold also is an important symbol of quality. In fact, all the elements of the marketing mix—the product, its promotion, price, and the stores at which it is available—are symbols that communicate ranges of quality to potential buyers.

RITUAL

In addition to language and symbols, culture includes various ritualized experiences and behaviors that until recently have been neglected by consumer researchers. A **ritual** is a type of symbolic activity consisting of a series of steps (*multiple behaviors*) occurring in a fixed sequence and repeated over time.[5]

In practice, rituals extend over the human life cycle from birth to death, including a host of intermediate events (like confirmation, graduations, and marriage). These rituals can be very public, elaborate, religious, or civil ceremonies, or they can be as mundane as an individual's grooming behavior or flossing.[6] Ritualized behavior is typically rather formal and often is scripted behavior (as a religious service requiring a prayer book or the code of proper conduct in a court of law). It is also likely to occur repeatedly over time (such as singing the national anthem before a baseball game).

Most important from the standpoint of marketers is the fact that rituals tend to be replete with ritual *artifacts* (products) that are associated with or somehow enhance the performance of the ritual. For instance, tree ornaments, stockings, and various food items are linked to the ritual of Christmas celebration; other rituals (such as a graduation, a wedding or wedding anniversary, a Thursday night card game, or a Saturday afternoon visit to the hair salon) have their own specific artifacts associated with them. For special occasions, such as wedding anniversaries, some types of artifacts are perceived as more appropriate and are appreciated more than others, such as jewelry versus household goods (Table 12-1).

In addition to a ritual, which is the way that something is traditionally done, there is also **ritualistic behavior**, which can be defined as any behavior that is made into a ritual. For example, a baseball player may swing his bat a certain number of times and kick the dirt near home plate before a pitch to ensure a good swing. Table 12-2 describes a young woman's ritualistic behavior with respect to nightly beauty care.

TABLE 12-1 Selected Rituals and Associated Artifacts

SELECTED RITUALS	TYPICAL ARTIFACTS
Wedding	White gown (something old, something new, something borrowed, something blue)
Birth of child	U.S. savings bond, silver baby spoon
Birthday	Card, present, cake with candles
50th wedding anniversary	Catered party, card and gift, display of photos of the couple's life together
Graduation	Pen, U.S. savings bond, card, wristwatch
Valentine's Day	Candy, card, flowers
New Year's Eve	Champagne, party, fancy dress
Thanksgiving	Prepare a turkey meal for family and friends
Going to the gym	Towel, exercise clothes, water, portable tape player
Sunday football	Beer, potato chips, pretzels
Super Bowl party	Same as Sunday football (just more)
Starting a new job	Get a haircut, buy some new clothing
Get a job promotion	Taken out to lunch by coworkers, receive token gift
Retirement	Company party, watch, plaque
Death	Send a card, give to charity in the name of the deceased

CULTURE IS SHARED

To be considered a cultural characteristic, a particular belief, value, or practice must be shared by a significant portion of the society. Thus, culture frequently is viewed as *group customs* that link together the members of a society. Of course, common language is the critical cultural component that makes it possible for people to share values, experiences, and customs.

Various social institutions within a society transmit the elements of culture and make the sharing of culture a reality. Chief among such institutions is the *family*, which serves as the primary agent for enculturation—the passing along of basic cultural beliefs, values, and customs to society's newest members. A vital part of the enculturation role of the family is the consumer socialization of the young (see chapter 10). This includes teaching such basic consumer-related values and skills as the meaning of money; the relationship between price and quality; the establishment of product tastes, preferences, and habits; and appropriate methods of response to various promotional messages.

TABLE 12-2 Nightly Facial Beauty Ritual of a Young Internet Sales Representative

1. I pull my hair back with a headband.
2. I wash my face with tepid water using Dove facial cleanser to remove all makeup.
3. Next, I use a Q-tip with some moisturizer around my eyes to make sure all eye makeup is removed.
4. I apply Dermacil facial cream to my face to heavily moisturize and Clinique Dramatically Different Lotion on my neck and throat.
5. If I have a blemish, I apply Clearasil Treatment to the area to dry it out.
6. Twice weekly (or as necessary) I use Aapri Facial Scrub to remove dry and dead skin.
7. Once a week I apply Clinique Clarifying Lotion 2 with a cotton ball to my face and throat to remove deep down dirt and oils.
8. Once a month I get a professional salon facial to deep clean my pores.

In addition to the family, two other institutions traditionally share much of the responsibility for the transfer of selected aspects of culture: *educational institutions* and *houses of worship*. Educational institutions specifically are charged with imparting basic learning skills, history, patriotism, citizenship, and the technical training needed to prepare people for significant roles within society. Religious institutions provide and perpetuate religious consciousness, spiritual guidance, and moral training. Although the young receive much of their consumer training within the family setting, the educational and religious systems reinforce this training by teaching economic and ethical concepts.

A fourth, frequently overlooked, social institution that plays a major role in the transfer of culture throughout society is the mass media. Given the extensive exposure of the American population to both print and broadcast media, as well as the easily ingested, entertaining format in which the contents of such media usually are presented, it is not surprising that the mass media are powerful vehicles for imparting a wide range of cultural values.

We are exposed daily to advertising, an important component of the media. Advertising not only underwrites, or makes economically feasible, the editorial or programming contents of the media, but it also transmits much about our culture. Without advertising, it would be almost impossible to disseminate information about products, ideas, and causes.

Consumers receive important cultural information from advertising. For example, it has been hypothesized that one of the roles of advertising in sophisticated magazines such as *Vanity Fair* is to instruct readers how to dress, how to decorate their homes, and what foods and wines to serve guests; in other words, what types of behavior are most appropriate to their particular social class.

Thus, while the scope of advertising is often considered to be limited to influencing the demand for specific products or services, in a cultural context advertising has the expanded mission of reinforcing established cultural values and aiding in the dissemination of new tastes, habits, and customs. In planning their advertising, marketers should recognize that advertising is an important agent for social change in our society.

■■■■ CULTURE IS DYNAMIC

To fulfill its need-gratifying role, culture continually must evolve if it is to function in the best interests of a society. For this reason, the marketer must carefully monitor the sociocultural environment in order to market an existing product more effectively or to develop promising new products.

This is not an easy task, because many factors are likely to produce cultural changes within a given society (new technology, population shifts, resource shortages, wars, changing values, and customs borrowed from other cultures). For example, a major ongoing cultural change in American society is the expanded role options open to women. Today, most women work outside the home, frequently in careers that once were considered exclusively male oriented. These career women are increasingly not waiting for marriage and a man to buy them luxury items—like fur coats, expensive wristwatches, and diamond rings. More and more such women are saying, "I earn a good living, why wait? I will buy it for myself."[7]

The changing nature of culture means that marketers have to consistently reconsider *why* consumers are now doing what they do, *who* are the purchasers and the users of their products (males only, females only, or both), *when* they do their shopping, *how* and *where* they can be reached by the media, and *what* new product and service needs are emerging. Marketers who monitor cultural changes also often find new opportunities to

increase corporate profitability. For example, marketers of such products and services as life insurance, financial and investment advice, casual clothing, toy electric trains, and cigars are among those who have attempted to exploit the dramatically shifting sense of what is feminine and how to communicate with female consumers (Figure 12-4).

THE MEASUREMENT OF CULTURE

A wide range of measurement techniques are used in the study of culture. Some of these techniques were described in chapter 2. For example, the projective tests used by psychologists to study motivation and personality and the attitude measurement techniques used by social psychologists and sociologists are relatively popular tools in the study of culture.

In addition, *content analysis*, *consumer fieldwork*, and *value measurement instruments* are three research approaches that are frequently used to examine culture and to spot cultural trends. There are also several commercial services that track emerging values and social trends for businesses and governmental agencies.

CONTENT ANALYSIS

Conclusions about a society, or specific aspects of a society, sometimes can be drawn from examining the content of its messages. **Content analysis**, as the name implies, focuses on the content of verbal, written, and pictorial communications (such as the copy and art composition of an ad).

Content analysis can be used as a relatively objective means of determining what social and cultural changes have occurred in a specific society. A content analysis of *Ms.* magazine advertising, for example, found that the portrayal of women as subordinate to men or as merely decorative had decreased over time.[8]

Content analysis is useful to both marketers and public-policy makers interested in comparing the advertising claims of competitors within a specific industry, as well as for evaluating the nature of advertising claims targeted to specific audiences (for instance, women, the elderly, or children).

CONSUMER FIELDWORK

When examining a specific society, anthropologists frequently immerse themselves in the environment under study through **consumer fieldwork**. As trained researchers, they are likely to select a small sample of people from a particular society and carefully observe their behavior. Based on their observations, researchers draw conclusions about the values, beliefs, and customs of the society under investigation. For example, if researchers were interested in how people select compact discs (CDs), they might position trained observers in record stores and note how specific types of CDs are selected (rap versus country, jazz versus classical, rock versus sound tracks). The researchers also may be interested in the degree of search that accompanies the choice; that is, how often consumers tend to take a CD off the display, read the description, and place it back again before selecting the CD that they finally purchase.

The distinct characteristics of **field observation** are that (1) it takes place within a natural environment; (2) it is performed sometimes without the subject's awareness; and (3) it focuses on observation of behavior. Because the emphasis is on a natural environment and observable behavior, field observation concerned with consumer behavior often focuses on in-store shopping behavior and, less frequently, on in-home preparation and consumption.

In some cases, instead of just observing behavior, researchers become **participant-observers** (that is, they become active members of the environment that they are studying). For example, if researchers were interested in examining how consumers select computer software, they might take a sales position in a computer superstore to observe directly and even to interact with customers in the transaction process.

Both field observation and participant-observer research require highly skilled researchers who can separate their own emotions from what they actually observe in their professional roles. Both techniques provide valuable insight that might not easily be obtained through survey research that simply asks consumers questions about their behavior.

In addition to fieldwork methods, depth interviews and focus-group sessions (see chapter 2) are also often used by marketers to get a "first look" at an emerging social or cultural change. In the relatively informal atmosphere of focus group discussions, consumers are apt to reveal attitudes or behavior that may signal a shift in values that, in turn, may affect the long-run market acceptance of a product or service. For instance, focus group studies can be used to identify marketing programs that reinforce established customer loyalty and goodwill (or relationship marketing). A common thread running throughout these studies showed that established customers, especially for services (such as investment and banking services), want to have their loyalty acknowledged in the form of *personalized* services. These observations have led various service and product companies to refine or establish loyalty programs that are more personalized in the way that they treat their established customers (for instance, by recognizing the individuality of such core customers). This is just one of numerous examples showing how focus groups and depth interviews are used to spot social trends.

VALUE MEASUREMENT SURVEY INSTRUMENTS

Anthropologists have traditionally observed the behavior of members of a specific society and inferred from such behavior the dominant or underlying values of the society. In recent years, however, there has been a gradual shift to measuring values directly by means of survey (questionnaire) research. Researchers use data collection instruments called *value instruments* to ask people how they feel about such basic personal and social concepts as freedom, comfort, national security, and peace.

A variety of popular value instruments have been used in consumer behavior studies, including: the **Rokeach Value Survey**, the *List of Values* (LOV), and the *Values and Lifestyles—VALS* (discussed in chapter 3). The widely used Rokeach Value Survey is a self-administered value inventory that is divided into two parts, each part measuring different but complementary types of personal values (see Table 12-3). The first part consists of 18 *terminal value* items, which are designed to measure the relative importance of end-states of existence (or personal goals). The second part consists of 18 *instrumental value* items, which measure basic approaches an individual might take to reach end-state values. Thus, the first half of the measurement instrument deals with ends, and the second half considers means.

Using the Rokeach Value Survey, adult Brazilians were categorized into six distinctive value segments.[9] For example, Segment A (representing 13 percent of the sample) was most concerned with "world peace," followed by "inner harmony" and "true friendship." Members of this segment were found to be especially involved in domestic-oriented activities (such as gardening, reading, and going out with the family to visit relatives). Because of their less materialistic and nonhedonistic orientation, this segment also may be the least prone to experiment with new products. In contrast, Segment B (representing 9 percent of the sample) was most concerned with self-centered values such as self-respect, a comfortable life, pleasure, an exciting life, a sense of accomplishment, and social recognition. They were least concerned with values related to the family, such as friendship, love, and equality. These self-centered, achievement-oriented, pleasure seekers were expected to prefer provocative clothes in the latest fashion, to enjoy an active lifestyle, and to be more likely to try new products.

The LOV is a related measurement instrument that is also designed to be used in surveying consumers' personal values. The LOV scale asks consumers to identify their two most important values from a nine-value list (such as "warm relationships with others," "a sense of belonging," or "a sense of accomplishment") that is based on the terminal values of the Rokeach Value Survey.[10]

TABLE 12-3 The Rokeach Value Survey Instrument

TERMINAL VALUES	INSTRUMENTAL VALUES
A COMFORTABLE LIFE (a prosperous life)	AMBITIOUS (hardworking, aspiring)
AN EXCITING LIFE (a stimulating, active life)	BROAD-MINDED (open-minded)
A WORLD AT PEACE (free of war and conflict)	CAPABLE (competent, effective)
EQUALITY (brotherhood, equal opportunity for all)	CHEERFUL (lighthearted, joyful)
FREEDOM (independence and free choice)	CLEAN (neat, tidy)
HAPPINESS (contentedness)	COURAGEOUS (standing up for your beliefs)
NATIONAL SECURITY (protection from attack)	FORGIVING (willing to pardon others)
PLEASURE (an enjoyable life)	HELPFUL (working for the welfare of others)
SALVATION (saved, eternal life)	HONEST (sincere, truthful)
SOCIAL RECOGNITION (respect and admiration)	IMAGINATIVE (daring, creative)
TRUE FRIENDSHIP (close companionship)	INDEPENDENT (self-reliant, self-sufficient)
WISDOM (a mature understanding of life)	INTELLECTUAL (intelligent, reflective)
A WORLD OF BEAUTY (beauty of nature and the arts)	LOGICAL (consistent, rational)
FAMILY SECURITY (taking care of loved ones)	LOVING (affectionate, tender)
MATURE LOVE (sexual and spiritual intimacy)	OBEDIENT (dutiful, respectful)
SELF-RESPECT (self-esteem)	POLITE (courteous, well-mannered)
A SENSE OF ACCOMPLISHMENT (lasting contribution)	RESPONSIBLE (dependable, reliable)
INNER HARMONY (freedom from inner conflict)	SELF-CONTROLLED (restrained, self-disciplined)

Source: Modified and reproduced by special permission of the publisher, Consulting Psychologists Press, Inc., Palo Alto, CA 94303 from *Rokeach Value Survey* by Milton Research. Copyright 1983 by Milton Rokeach. All rights reserved. Further reproduction is prohibited without the publisher's written consent.

▪▪▪▪ AMERICAN CORE VALUES

What is the American culture? In this section, we identify a number of **core values** that both affect and reflect the character of American society. This is a difficult undertaking for several reasons. First, the United States is a diverse country, consisting of a variety of **subcultures** (religious, ethnic, regional, racial, and economic groups), each of which interprets and responds to society's basic beliefs and values in its own specific way. Second, America is a dynamic society that has undergone almost constant change in response to the development of new technology. This element of rapid change makes it especially difficult to monitor changes in cultural values. Finally, the existence of contradictory values in American society is somewhat confusing. For instance, Americans traditionally embrace freedom of choice and individualism, yet simultaneously they show great tendencies to conform (in dress, in furnishings, and in fads) to the rest of society. In the context of consumer behavior, Americans like to have a wide choice of products and prefer those that uniquely express their personal lifestyles. Yet, there is often a considerable amount of implicit pressure to conform to the values of family members, friends, and other socially important groups. It is difficult to reconcile these seemingly inconsistent values; their existence, however, demonstrates that America is a complex society with numerous paradoxes.

When selecting the specific core values to be examined, we were guided by three criteria:

1. *The value must be pervasive.* A significant portion of the American people must accept the value and use it as a guide for their attitudes and actions.
2. *The value must be enduring.* The specific value must have influenced the actions of the American people over an extended period of time (as distinguished from a short-run trend).
3. *The value must be consumer-related.* The specific value must provide insights that help us to understand the consumption actions of the American people.

Meeting these criteria are a number of basic values that expert observers of the American scene consider the "building blocks" of that rather elusive concept called the "*American character*."

ACHIEVEMENT AND SUCCESS

In a broad cultural context, achievement is a major American value, with historical roots that can be traced to the traditional religious belief in the Protestant work ethic, which considers hard work to be wholesome, spiritually rewarding, and an appropriate end in itself. Indeed, substantial research evidence shows that the achievement orientation is closely associated with the technical development and general economic growth of American society.[11]

Individuals who consider a "sense of accomplishment" an important personal value tend to be achievers who strive hard for success. Although historically associated with men, especially male business executives, today *achievement* is very important for women, who are increasingly enrolled in undergraduate and graduate business programs and are more commonly seeking top level business careers.

Success is a closely related American cultural theme. However, achievement and success do differ. Specifically, achievement is its own direct reward (it is implicitly satisfying to the individual achiever), whereas success implies an extrinsic reward (such as luxury possessions, financial compensation, or status improvement).

Both achievement and success influence consumption. They often serve as social and moral justification for the acquisition of goods and services. For example, "You owe it to yourself," "You worked for it," and "You deserve it" are popular achievement themes used by advertisers to coax consumers into purchasing their products (see Figure 12-5). Regardless of gender, achievement-oriented people often enjoy conspicuous consumption, because it allows them to display symbols of their personal achievement. When it comes to personal development and preparation for future careers, the themes of achievement and success are also especially appropriate.

ACTIVITY

Americans attach an extraordinary amount of importance to being *active* or *involved*. Keeping busy is widely accepted as a healthy and even necessary part of the American lifestyle. The hectic nature of American life is attested to by foreign visitors, who frequently comment that they cannot understand why Americans are always "on the run" and seemingly unable to relax.

The premium placed on *activity* has had both a positive and a negative effect on the popularity of various products. For example, a principal reason for the enormous growth of fast-food chains, such as McDonald's and Kentucky Fried Chicken, is that so many people want quick, prepared meals when they are away from the house. Americans rarely eat a full breakfast, because they usually are too rushed in the morning to prepare and consume a traditional morning meal. In fact, bagels, which can be prepared quickly and easily, are stealing sales away from sit-down cereal breakfasts because they can be eaten on the run.[12]

FIGURE 12-5
Incorporating Achievement
and Success Appeals

EFFICIENCY AND PRACTICALITY

With a basic philosophy of down-to-earth pragmatism, Americans pride themselves on being efficient and practical. When it comes to *efficiency*, they admire anything that saves time and effort. In terms of *practicality*, they generally are receptive to any new product that makes tasks easier and can help solve problems. For example, today it is possible for manufacturers of many product categories to offer the public a wide range of interchangeable components. Thus, a consumer can design his or her own "customized" wall unit from such standard components as compatible metals and woods, legs, door facings, and style panels at a cost not much higher than a completely standardized unit. The capacity of manufacturers to create mass-produced components offer consumers the practical option of a customized product at a reasonable price.

Another illustration of Americans' attentiveness to efficiency and practicality is the extreme importance attached to *time* (see Figure 12-6). Americans seem to be convinced that "time waits for no one," which is reflected in their habitual attention to being prompt. Another sign of America's preoccupation with time is the belief that time is in increasingly short supply.[13] Americans place a great deal of importance on getting there first, on the value of time itself, on the notion that time is money, on the importance of not wasting time, and on identifying "more" time.

FIGURE 12-6
Scarcity of Time as Need to be Efficient and Practical

The frequency with which Americans look at their watches, and the importance attached to having an accurate timepiece, tend to support the American value of *punctuality*. Similarly, the broad consumer acceptance of the microwave oven and microwaveable foods are also examples of Americans' love affair with products that save time and effort by providing efficiency and practicality.

PROGRESS

Progress is another watchword of American society. Americans respond favorably to the promise of "progress." Our receptivity to progress appears to be closely linked to the other core values already examined (*achievement* and *success*, *efficiency* and *practicality*) and to the central belief that people can always improve themselves, that tomorrow should be better than today. In a consumption-oriented society, such as that of the United States, progress often means the acceptance of change, new products, or services designed to fulfill previously undersatisfied or unsatisfied needs (Figure 12-7). In the name of progress, Americans appear to be receptive to product claims that stress "new," "improved," "longer-lasting," "speedier," "quicker," "smoother and closer," and "increased strength."

FIGURE 12-7
Progress Is an Attractive
Appeal

MATERIAL COMFORT

For most Americans (even young children), *material comfort* signifies the attainment of "the good life," a life that may include a new car, a dishwasher, a microwave oven, an air conditioner, a hot tub, and an almost infinite variety of other convenience-oriented and pleasure-providing goods and services.[14] It appears that consumers' idea of material comfort is largely a *relative* view; that is, consumers tend to define their own satisfaction with the amount of material goods they have in terms of a comparison of what they have to what others have. If a comparison suggests that they have more than others do, then they are more likely to be satisfied.[15] On the other hand, as many popular songs point out, the ownership of material goods does not always lead to happiness. For instance, many people, especially affluent people, might be willing to trade money for more free time to spend with family and friends.

INDIVIDUALISM

Americans place a strong value on "being themselves." Self-reliance, self-interest, self-confidence, self-esteem, and self-fulfillment are all exceedingly popular expressions of *individualism*. Striving for individualism seems to be linked to the rejection of dependency; that is, it is better to rely on oneself than on others.

In terms of consumer behavior, an appeal to individualism frequently takes the form of reinforcing the consumer's sense of identity with products or services that both reflect and emphasize that identity. For example, advertisements for high-style clothing and cosmetics usually promise that their products will enhance the consumer's exclusive or distinctive character and set him or her apart from others.

FREEDOM

Freedom is another very strong American value, with historical roots in such democratic ideals as "freedom of speech," "freedom of the press," and "freedom of worship." As an outgrowth of these democratic beliefs in freedom, Americans have a strong preference for *freedom of choice*, the opportunity to choose from a wide range of alternatives. This preference is reflected in the large number of competitive brands and product variations that can be found on the shelves of the modern supermarket or department store. For many products, consumers can select from a wide variety of sizes, colors, flavors, features, styles, and even special ingredients (such as all-natural-ingredient toothpaste without sugar). It also explains why many companies offer consumers many choices.

EXTERNAL CONFORMITY

Although Americans deeply embrace *freedom of choice* and *individualism*, they nevertheless accept the reality of *conformity*. External conformity is a necessary process by which the individual adapts to society.

In the realm of consumer behavior, conformity (or uniformity) takes the form of standardized goods and services. Standardized products have been made possible by mass production. The availability of a wide choice of standardized products places the consumer in the unique position of being *individualistic* (by selecting specific products that close friends do not have) or of *conforming* (by purchasing a similar product). In this context, individualism and conformity exist side by side as choices for the American consumer.

An interesting example of the "Ping-Pong" relationship between seeking individualism and accepting conformity is the trend for more casual dressing in the workplace (already discussed in this chapter). For instance, male and female executives are conforming less to workplace dress codes (that is, there are more dress options open to business executives). For instance, some male executives are wearing casual slacks and sport shirts to work; others are wearing blazers and slacks, rather than business suits. Greater personal confidence and an emphasis on comfort appear to be the reasons that many executives are wearing less-traditional business attire. Nevertheless, in some companies the appearance of male executives in blue blazers and gray slacks does seem like a "business uniform" (which is a kind of conformity). Figure 12-8 presents the findings of consumer research that reveals the types of clothing that men and women wear to the office. The evidence suggests that the majority of American workers are wearing some type of casual clothing to work.[16] For men, it is commonly "everyday casual" (jeans, shorts, T-shirts, etc.); for women it is "casual" (casual pants with or without a jacket, sweaters, separates, and pantsuits). Moreover, more than 50 percent of workers surveyed feel that it increases their productivity to wear casual clothing to work.

FIGURE 12-8

What Are Men and
Women Wearing to the
Office?

Source: Kari Van Hoof, "Casual
Clothing Are Workspace Trend,"
BrandWeek, July 18, 1994, 17.
© 1996 ASM Communications,
Inc. Used with permission from
BrandWeek.

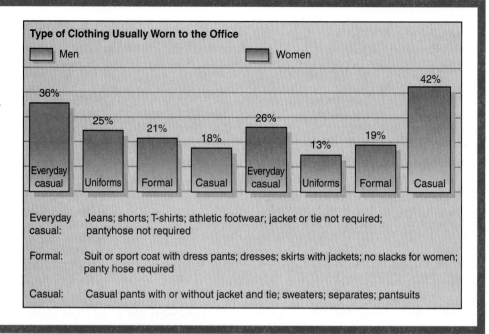

Type of Clothing Usually Worn to the Office

Everyday
casual: Jeans; shorts; T-shirts; athletic footwear; jacket or tie not required;
           pantyhose not required

Formal: Suit or sport coat with dress pants; dresses; skirts with jackets; no slacks for women;
           panty hose required

Casual: Casual pants with or without jacket and tie; sweaters; separates; pantsuits

HUMANITARIANISM

Americans are generous when it comes to those in need. They support with a passion many humane and charitable causes, and they sympathize with the "underdog" who must overcome adversity to get ahead. They also tend to be charitable and willing to come to the aid of people less fortunate. Additionally, social issues have an impact on both what consumers buy and where they invest. For example, some investors prefer mutual funds that screen companies for such social concerns as military contracts, pollution problems, and equal-opportunity employment. Investments in socially conscious mutual funds are now quite commonplace. Many companies try to appeal to consumers by emphasizing their concern for environmental or social issues.

YOUTHFULNESS

Americans tend to place an almost sacred value on *youthfulness.* This emphasis is a reflection of America's rapid technological development. In an atmosphere where "new" is constantly stressed, "old" is often equated with being "outdated." This is in contrast to traditional European, African, and Asian societies, in which the elderly are revered for having the wisdom of experience that comes with age.

Youthfulness should not be confused with youth, which describes an age grouping. Americans are preoccupied with *looking* and *acting* young, regardless of their chronological age. For Americans, youthfulness is a state of mind and a state of being, sometimes expressed as being "young at heart," "young in spirit," or "young in appearance." Figure 12-9 presents an ad for Quaker Oats that features a profile of a mature woman who very much typifies an individual with a youthful state of mind.

A great deal of advertising is directed to creating a sense of urgency about retaining one's youth and fearing aging.[17] Hand-cream ads talk about "young hands"; skin-treatment ads state "I dreaded turning 30 . . . "; fragrance and makeup ads stress looking "sexy and young" or "denying your age"; detergent ads ask the reader, "Can

FIGURE 12-9
Ad Stressing Youthfulness
Is a "State of Mind"

you match their hands with their ages?" These advertising themes, which promise the consumer the benefits of youthfulness, reflect the high premium Americans place on appearing and acting young.

FITNESS AND HEALTH

Americans' preoccupation with *fitness* and *health* has emerged as a core value. This value has manifested itself in a number of ways, including tennis, racquetball, and jogging, and the continued increases in sales of vitamins. Add to these trends an enhanced consciousness on the part of Americans that "You are what you eat (or drink)."

Fitness and health are becoming lifestyle choices for many consumers. This trend has stimulated Reebok to open a series of exercise-retail complexes that seek to build a cultural connection with consumers that goes beyond the normal marketing approach. Traditional food manufacturers have begun modifying their ingredients to cater to the health-conscious consumer. Frozen dinners have become more nutritious in recent years, and manufacturers of traditional "junk food" are trying to make them more healthful. "Light" or "fat-free" versions of snack chips or pretzels, along with "low-sodium," "no-cholesterol," "no-preservative" snack products, are an attempt to provide consumers with tasty and healthy options.

While there is no denying the *fitness and healthy living* trend in American society, there is evidence that consumers find it difficult "to be good." For instance, people miss their desserts. Research suggests that more than 75 percent of American consumers think about dessert between one and eight times a day. The main activities that seem to put people in the "mood" for desserts are: exercise, working, entertainment, eating, and studying.[18] Also, many Americans are unwilling to compromise on flavor for health benefits, with the result being a kind of reverse trend toward full-flavored, rich foods. This countertrend reveals the diversity of preferences that exist side by side within the marketplace.[19] It points up that low-fat and low-cholesterol food products are not for everyone and that there is an important market segment whose members seek to indulge their taste buds and their waistlines.

CORE VALUES ARE NOT AN AMERICAN PHENOMENON

The cultural values just examined are not all uniquely or originally American. Some were borrowed, particularly from European society, as people emigrated to the United States. Some values that originated in America are now part of the fabric of other societies. For example, there is evidence that the good life may be a universal notion and that global brands are used as an external sign of attaining the good life.[20]

In addition, not all Americans necessarily accept each of these values. However, as a whole, these values do account for much of the American character. Table 12-4 summarizes a number of American core values and indicates their relevance to consumer behavior.

TABLE 12-4 Summary of American Core Values

VALUE	GENERAL FEATURES	RELEVANCE TO CONSUMER BEHAVIOR
ACHIEVEMENT AND SUCCESS ACTIVITY	Hard work is good; success flows from hard work	Acts as a justification for acquisition of goods ("You deserve it")
	Keeping busy is healthy and natural	Stimulates interest in products that are time-savers and enhance leisure time
EFFICIENCY AND PRACTICALITY	Admiration of things that solve problems (e.g., save time and effort)	Stimulates purchase of products that function well and save time
	People can improve themselves; tomorrow should be better than today	Stimulates desire for new products that fulfill unsatisfied needs; ready acceptance of products that claim to be "new and improved"
MATERIAL COMFORT	"The good life"	Fosters acceptance of convenience and luxury products that make life more comfortable and enjoyable
INDIVIDUALISM	Being oneself (e.g, self-reliance, self-interest, self-esteem)	Stimulates acceptance of customized or unique products that enable a person to "express his or her own personality"
FREEDOM	Freedom of choice	Fosters interest in wide product lines and differentiated products
EXTERNAL CONFORMITY	Uniformity of observable behavior; desire for acceptance	Stimulates interest in products that are used or owned by others in the same social group
HUMANITARIANISM	Caring for others, particularly the underdog	Stimulates patronage of firms that compete with market leaders
YOUTHFULNESS	A state of mind that stresses being "young at heart" and having a youthful appearance	Stimulates acceptance of products that provide the illusion of maintaining or fostering youthfulness
FITNESS AND HEALTH	Caring about one's body, including the desire to be physically fit and healthy	Stimulates acceptance of food products, activities, and equipment perceived to maintain or increase physical fitness

SUMMARY

The study of culture is the study of all aspects of a society. It is the language, knowledge, laws, and customs that give that society its distinctive character and personality. In the context of consumer behavior, culture is defined as the sum total of learned beliefs, values, and customs that serve to regulate the consumer behavior of members of a particular society. Beliefs and values are guides for consumer behavior; customs are usual and accepted ways of behaving.

The impact of culture on society is so natural and so ingrained that its influence on behavior is rarely noted. Yet, culture offers order, direction, and guidance to members of society in all phases of human problem solving. Culture is dynamic and gradually and continually evolves to meet the needs of society.

Culture is learned as part of social experience. Children acquire from their environments a set of beliefs, values, and customs that constitute culture (that is, they are encultured). These are acquired through formal learning, informal learning, and technical learning. Advertising enhances formal learning by reinforcing desired modes of behavior and expectations; it enhances informal learning by providing models for behavior.

Culture is communicated to members of society through a common language and through commonly shared symbols. Because the human mind has the ability to absorb and to process symbolic communi-

cation, marketers can successfully promote both tangible and intangible products and product concepts to consumers through mass media.

All the elements in the marketing mix serve to communicate symbolically with the audience. Products project an image of their own; so does promotion. Price and retail outlets symbolically convey images concerning the quality of the product.

The elements of culture are transmitted by three pervasive social institutions: the family, the church, and the school. A fourth social institution that plays a major role in the transmission of culture is the mass media, both through editorial content and through advertising.

A wide range of measurement techniques is used to study culture. The range includes projective techniques, attitude measurement methods, field observation, participant observation, content analysis, and value measurement survey techniques.

A number of core values of the American people are relevant to the study of consumer behavior. These include achievement and success, activity, efficiency and practicality, progress, material comfort, individualism, freedom, conformity, humanitarianism, youthfulness, and fitness and health.

Because each of these values varies in importance to the members of our society, each provides an effective basis for segmenting consumer markets.

DISCUSSION QUESTIONS

1. Distinguish between beliefs, values, and customs. Illustrate how the clothing a person wears at different times or for different occasions is influenced by customs.

2. A manufacturer of fat-free granola bars is considering targeting school-age children by positioning its product as a healthy, nutritious snack food. How can an understanding of the three forms of cultural learning be used in developing an effective strategy to target the intended market?

3. The Citrus Growers of America is planning a promotional campaign to encourage the drinking of orange and grapefruit juice in situations in which many consumers normally consume soft drinks. Using the Rokeach Value Survey Instrument (Table 12-3), identify relevant cultural, consumption-specific, and product-specific values for citrus juices as an alternative to soft drinks. What are the implications of these values for an advertising campaign designed to increase the consumption of citrus juices?

4. For each of the products and activities listed below:
   a. Identify the core values most relevant to their purchase and use.
   b. Determine whether these values encourage or discourage use or ownership.
   c. Determine whether these core values are shifting and, if so, in what direction.
   The products and activities are:

   1. Donating money to charities
   2. Donating blood
   3. Compact disc players
   4. Telephone answering machines
   5. Toothpaste
   6. Diet soft drinks
   7. Foreign travel
   8. Suntan lotion
   9. Cellular phones
   10. Interactive TV home-shopping services
   11. Fat-free foods
   12. Products in recyclable packaging

EXERCISES

1. Identify a singer or singing group whose music you like and discuss the symbolic function of the clothes that person (or group) wears.

2. Think of various routines in your everyday life (like grooming or food preparation). Identify one ritual and describe it. In your view, is this ritual shared by others? If so, to what extent? What are the implications of your ritualistic behavior to the marketer(s) of the product(s) you use during your routine?

3. a. Summarize an episode of a weekly television series that you watched recently. Describe how the program transmitted cultural beliefs, values, and customs.

   b. Select and describe three commercials that were broadcast during the program mentioned in 3a. Do these commercials create or reflect cultural values? Explain your answer.

4. a. Find two different advertisements for deodorants in two magazines that are targeted to different audiences. Content-analyze the written and pictorial aspects of each ad, using any core values discussed in this chapter. How are these values portrayed to the target audiences?

   b. Identify symbols used in these ads and discuss their effectiveness in conveying the desired product image or characteristics.

KEY TERMS

- **Acculturation**
- **American core values**
- **Consumer fieldwork**
- **Content analysis**
- **Culture**

- **Enculturation**
- **Field observation**
- **Participant-observers**
- **Ritualistic behavior**

- **Rituals**
- **Rokeach Value Survey**
- **Subculture**
- **Symbols**

NOTES

1. Thomas C. O'Guinn and L. J. Shrum, "The Role of Television in the Construction of Consumer Reality," *Journal of Consumer Research* 23 (March 1997): 278–95.

2. "Demo Memo," *American Demographics* (February 1998): 41.

3. "Remember When Bras Were for Burning," *Business Week*, 16 January 1995, 37; and Cyndee Miller, "Casual Affair," *Marketing News*, 13 March 1995, 1; and "Casual Clothes are Workplace Trend," *BrandWeek*, 18 July 1994, 17.

4. Gwen Rae Bachmann, Deborah Roedder John, and Akshay Rao, "Children's Susceptibility to Peer Group Purchase Influence: An Exploratory Investigation," in *Advances in Consumer Research*, vol. 20, ed. Leigh McAlister and Michael L. Rothschild (Provo, UT: Association for Consumer Research 1993): 463–68.

5. Dennis W. Rook, "The Ritual Dimension of Consumer Behavior," *Journal of Consumer Research* 12 (December 1985): 251–64.

6. Dennis W. Rook, "Ritual Behavior and Consumer Symbolism," in *Advances in Consumer Research*, vol. 11, ed. Thomas C. Kinnear, (Ann Arbor, MI: Association for Consumer Research, 1984): 279–84.

7. Tara Parker-Pope, "All That Glitters Isn't Purchased by Men," *Wall Street Journal*, 7 January 1997, B1; and Dana Canedy, "As the Purchasing Power of Women Rises, Marketers Start to Pay Attention to Them," *New York Times*, 2 July 1998, D6.

8. Jill Hicks Ferguson, Peggy J. Kreshel, and Spencer F. Tinkham, "In the Pages of *Ms.*: Sex Role Portrayals of Women in Advertising," *Journal of Advertising* 19 (1990): 20–51. Also, see Shay Sayre, "Content Analysis as a Tool for Consumer Research," *Journal of Consumer Marketing* 9 (Winter 1992): 15–25.

9. Wagner A. Kamakura and Jose Afonso Mazzon, "Value Segmentation: A Model for the Measurement of Values and Value Systems," *Journal of Consumer Research* 18 (September 1991): 208–18.

10. Lynn R. Kahle, ed., *Social Values and Social Change: Adaption of Life in America* (New York: Praeger, 1983); Sharon E. Beatty et al., "Alternative Measurement Approaches to Consumer Values: The List of Values and the Rokeach Value Survey," *Psychology & Marketing* 2 (1985): 181–200; and Lynn R. Kahle and Roger P. McIntyre, Reid P. Claxton, and David B. Jones, "Empirical Relationships Between Cognitive Style and LOV: Implications for Values and Value Systems," in *Advances in Consumer Research*, vol. 22, ed. Frank R. Kardes and Mita Sujan, (Provo, UT: Association for Consumer Research 1995): 141–46.

11. David C. McClelland, *The Achieving Society* (New York: Free Press, 1961), 150–51.

12. James P. Miller, "Cereal Makers Fight Bagels with Price Cuts," *Wall Street Journal*, 20 June 1996, B1.

13. Corina Cristea, "Now Everybody's a Busy Body," *BrandWeek*, 6 July 1998, 18–19.

14. William J. Havlena and Susan L. Holak, "Children's Images and Symbols of Wealth: An Exploration Using Consumer Collages," *1997 AMA Winter Educators' Conference*, ed. Debbie Thorne LeClair and Michael Hartline (Chicago: American Marketing Association, 1997), 1–2.

15. Ramesh Venkat and Harold J. Ogden, "Material Satisfaction: The Effects of Social Comparison and Attribution," in *1995 AMA Educators' Proceedings*, ed. Barbara B. Stern and George M. Zinkan (Chicago: American Marketing Association, 1995), 314–49.

16. "Casual Clothes Are Workplace Trend," *BrandWeek*, 18 July 1994, 17. Also, see: Ellen Neuborne, "Fashion on Menu at T.G.I. Friday's," *USA Today*, 27 February 1996, B1.

17. Richard A. Lee, "The Youth Bias in Advertising," *American Demographics* (January 1997): 47–50.

18. "The Big Scoop on Just Desserts," *Advertising Age*, 2 October 1995, 3.

19. Sean Mehegan, "As Indulgence Roars Back with a Vengeance, Low-Fat Candies Beat a Strategic Retreat," *BrandWeek*, 2 March 1998, 12.

20. George M. Zinkhan and Penelope J. Prenshaw, "Good Life Images and Brand Name Associations: Evidence from Asia, America, and Europe," in *Advances in Consumer Research*, vol. 21, ed. Chris T. Allen and Deborah Roedder John (Provo, UT: Association for Consumer Research, 1994), 496–500.

CHAPTER 13

Subcultures and Consumer Behavior

■ ■

Culture has a potent influence on all consumer behavior. Individuals are brought up to follow the beliefs, values, and customs of their society and to avoid behavior that is judged "unacceptable" or considered taboo. In addition to segmenting in terms of cultural factors, marketers also segment overall societies into smaller subgroups (subcultures) that consist of people who are similar in terms of their ethnic origin, their customs, and the ways they behave. These subcultures provide important marketing opportunities for astute marketing strategists.

Our discussion of subcultures, therefore, has a narrower focus than the discussion of culture. Instead of examining the dominant beliefs, values, and customs that exist within an entire society, this chapter explores the marketing opportunities created by the existence of certain beliefs, values, and customs shared by members of specific subcultural groups within a society.

These subcultural divisions are based on a variety of sociocultural and demographic variables, such as nationality, religion, geographic locality, race, age, sex, and even working status.

■■■■ WHAT IS SUBCULTURE?

The members of a specific **subculture** possess beliefs, values, and customs that set them apart from other members of the same society. In addition, they adhere to most of the dominant cultural beliefs, values, and behavioral patterns of the larger society. We define subculture, then, as *a distinct cultural group that exists as an identifiable segment within a larger, more complex society*.

Thus, the cultural profile of a society or nation is a composite of two distinct elements: (1) the unique beliefs, values, and customs subscribed to by members of specific subcultures; and (2) the central or core cultural themes that are shared by most of the population, regardless of specific subcultural memberships. Figure 13-1 presents a simple model of the relationship between two subcultural groups (Hispanic Americans and Asian Americans) and the larger culture. As the figure depicts, each subculture has its own unique traits, yet both groups share the dominant traits of the overall American culture.

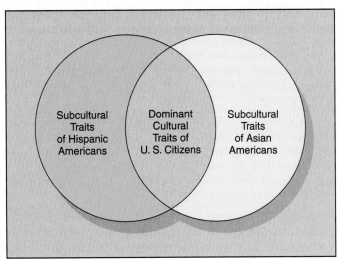

FIGURE 13-1

Relationship between Culture and Subculture

Let us look at it in another way: Each American is, in large part, a product of the "American way of life." Each American, however, is at the same time a member of various subcultures. For example, a 13-year-old girl may simultaneously be African American, Baptist, a teenager, and a Texan. We would expect that membership in each different subculture would provide its own set of specific beliefs, values, attitudes, and customs. Table 13-1 lists typical subcultural categories and corresponding examples of specific subcultural groups. This list is by no means exhaustive: college students, environmentalists, Boy Scouts, and retirees—in fact, any group that shares common beliefs and customs—may be classified as a subculture.

Subcultural analysis enables the marketing manager to focus on sizable and "natural" market segments. When carrying out such analyses, the marketer must determine whether the beliefs, values, and customs shared by members of a specific subgroup make them desirable candidates for special marketing attention. Subcultures, therefore, are relevant units of analysis for market research.

The following sections examine a number of important subcultural categories: nationality, religion, geographic location, race, age, and sex. (Occupational and social-class subgroups were discussed in detail in chapter 11.)

TABLE 13-1 Examples of Major Subcultural Categories

CATEGORIES	EXAMPLES
Nationality (i.e., birthplace of ancestors)	French, Puerto Rican, Korean
Religion	Catholic, Hindu, Jew
Geographic region	Southeastern, Midwestern, Eastern
Race	African American, Caucasian, Asian American
Age	Teens, Xers, middle age, elderly
Gender	Female, male
Occupation	Engineer, cook, plumber
Social class	Lower, middle, upper

■■■■ NATIONALITY SUBCULTURES

The United States has been in the midst of one of its largest immigration waves in decades. Although the 1990 census found almost 20 million foreign-born persons living in the United States, about 25 percent of them had arrived within a single 5-year period.

Adding to the importance of **nationality** as a subcultural reference, although most U.S. citizens, especially those born in the United States, see themselves as Americans, they frequently retain a sense of identification and pride in the language and customs of their ancestors. When it comes to consumer behavior, this ancestral pride is manifested most strongly in the consumption of ethnic foods, in travel to the "homeland," and in the purchase of numerous cultural artifacts (ethnic clothing, art, music, foreign-language newspapers). Interest in these goods and services has expanded rapidly as younger Americans attempt to better understand and more closely associate with their ethnic roots. To illustrate the importance of ethnic origin as a subcultural market segment, the following section examines the **Hispanic American subculture**.

HISPANIC SUBCULTURES

Hispanic Americans represent almost 11 percent of the United States population (29 million people, with buying power of $348 billion).[1] In contrast to other American population segments, Hispanic Americans are younger (the median age of Hispanics is about 10 years younger than the median age of non-Hispanic whites), they are members of larger families, and they are more likely to live in an "extended family" household—consisting of several generations of family members. Not only are Hispanic households more likely than black or non-Hispanic white families to contain children, Hispanics spent more time caring for their children.[2]

With the number of Hispanic Americans expected to grow to over 32 million by the year 2001, this subculture is anticipated to comprise the largest minority in the United Stated by the year 2005 (supplanting African Americans as the largest American minority group).[3] Indeed, Hispanics have already become the dominant minority in New York, Los Angeles, San Diego, Phoenix, San Francisco, and Denver; they represent the majority in San Antonio, Texas; and it has been estimated that the Hispanic market is growing six and a half times faster than the general market.[4] The 10 metro areas with the largest Hispanic populations are also the cities with the greatest gains in their Hispanic populations; they attracted more than half of all new Hispanic residents and together are the home to 58 percent of the Hispanic population of the United States.[5]

This subcultural group can be considered as a single market, based on a common language and culture, or as separate subcultural markets that correspond to different Hispanic countries of origin. There are 12 Hispanic subgroups now identified in the United States. The three largest Hispanic subcultural groups consist of Mexican Americans (about 64 percent of total Hispanic Americans), Puerto Ricans (approximately 10 percent of the total), and Cubans (about 4 percent of the total). These subcultures are heavily concentrated geographically, with more than 70 percent of their members residing in California, Texas, New York, and Florida; Los Angeles alone is home to one-fifth of the Hispanic population of the United States. Also, whereas more than 60 percent of all Mexican Americans (the largest Hispanic group) were born in the United States, 72 percent of Cuban Americans were born in Cuba.[6]

Understanding Hispanic Consumer Behavior

Available evidence indicates that Hispanic and Anglo consumers differ in terms of a variety of important buyer behavior variables. For instance, Hispanic consumers have a strong preference for well-established brands and traditionally prefer to shop at smaller stores. In the New York metropolitan area, for example, Hispanic consumers spend 55 percent of their food budgets in over 8,000 *bodegas* (relatively small food specialty stores), despite the fact that supermarket prices generally are lower. Table 13-2 presents, in list form, these and other distinctive characteristics of the overall Hispanic market.

While mindful of their tradition, Hispanic Americans, like other major subcultural groups, are a dynamic and evolving portion of the overall society. For this reason, a growing number of Hispanic consumers are shifting their food shopping to nonethnic large American-style supermarkets. They appear to be engaged in a process of acculturation; that is, they are gradually adopting the consumption patterns of the majority of United States consumers. Similarly, when it comes to clothes shopping, Hispanic youths are more fashion-conscious and are more likely to seek out and be loyal to well-known brands and to generally like the act of shopping more than their non-Hispanic counterparts.[7]

Defining and Segmenting the Hispanic Market

Marketers who are targeting the diversity within the Hispanic subcultures are concerned with finding the best ways to define and segment this overall subculture. In terms of definition, Table 13-3 presents six variables marketers have used to determine who is Hispanic.

TABLE 13-2 Traditional Characteristics of the Hispanic American Market

Prefer well-known or familiar brands
Buy brands perceived to be more prestigious
Are fashion-conscious
Historically prefer to shop at smaller personal stores
Buy brands advertised by their ethnic-group stores
Tend not to be impulse buyers (i.e., are deliberate)
Increasingly clipping and using cents-off coupons
Likely to buy what their parents bought
Prefer fresh to frozen or prepared items
Tend to be negative about marketing practices and government intervention in business

---

TABLE 13-3 Ways in Which "Hispanic" Has Been Defined

NAME OF INDICATOR	NATURE/SCOPE AND COMMENTARY
Spanish surname	Not a definitive; since a non-Hispanic person might have a Spanish surname, or a Hispanic person might have a non-Spanish surname.
Country of origin	The birthplace of persons born in the United States of Hispanic parents (e.g., of Puerto Rican parentage) would not reveal their Hispanic background.
Country of family ancestry	Includes those individuals who may not be Hispanic despite coming from a particular Spanish-Latin country (e.g., people of German parentage who may be brought up in a Latin country).
Spanish spoken at home	A significant minority of Hispanic households may speak English at home, yet consider themselves to be culturally Hispanic.
Self-identification	It is reasonable that if an adequnate number of self-report choices are offered, a person might identify himself or herself as "Hispanic."
Degree of identification	This measure captures the "degree" of personal identification as "Hispanic" and augments the self-identification measure.

Of these measures, the combination of *self-identification* and *degree of identification* are particularly appealing, because they permit consumers to define or label themselves. Research shows that those who strongly identify with being Hispanic (or *Strong Hispanic Identifiers*) are more frequent users of Spanish-language media, are more brand loyal, are more likely to buy prestige brands, are more likely to seek the advice of another and to more often be influenced by friends or family, and are more likely to buy brands advertised to Hispanics than *Weak Hispanic Identifiers*.[8] This pattern suggests that the degree of Hispanic identification is a useful segmentation variable when targeting the Hispanic market.

In addition, the Hispanic market can be segmented by using a combination of *country of origin* and *geographic concentration in the United States* (for example, 74 percent of Hispanic Americans of Mexican origin are concentrated in California and Texas; almost 40 percent of those of Puerto Rican origin live in New York).[9] Some marketers feel that it is worthwhile to target each Hispanic American market separately. Other marketers, including Procter & Gamble, Anheuser-Busch, Coca-Cola, American Honda, Sears, Coors, Colgate-Palmolive, McDonald's, Toyota, Philip Morris, and the "Big Three" United States car companies (GM, Ford, and Chrysler) have targeted the Hispanic market as a single market, using Spanish-language mass media. Taco Bell has recently more than doubled its Hispanic advertising budget in an attempt to woo the Hispanic consumer, who is already a frequent visitor to fast-food restaurants, and Colgate-Palmolive has introduced two of its Mexican brands of cleaning products to the U.S. Hispanic market.[10]

The Spanish language is often regarded as the bridge that links the various Hispanic subcultures. Even with this common language, however, there is considerable variation among Hispanics regarding their language preferences (such as Spanish only, Spanish preferred, English only, or English preferred). This language framework provides still another basis for segmenting the Hispanic American market. Available research indicates that Hispanic Americans spend the most time with mass media in the first language that they learn to speak. So those whose first language is Spanish tend to prefer TV, radio, magazines, and newspapers in Spanish (see Figure 13-2), whereas those Hispanic Americans who first learn English prefer their media exposure to be in English.[11] However, there is also some evidence that "Hispanic assimilation is a myth," especially with regard to Spanish-language television. Even second- and third-generation Hispanics in the United States, people who are completely bilingual and who speak English without a trace of an accent, are big viewers of Spanish-language television. This fact seems to hold true regardless of the Hispanic household's income. As the program director of Telemundo (one of the two Spanish-language TV networks operating in the U.S.) has observed, "After nearly 40 years, Spanish remains a more powerful force than assimilation."[12]

Each of the major Hispanic subcultural groups appears to have some distinct beliefs, values, and customs; thus, a marketing strategy that may be successful with Puerto Ricans in New York might fail with Cubans in Miami. For this reason some marketers segment the Hispanic market by appealing to the distinct cultural values of a specific nationality. Others segment the Hispanic market in terms of the degree of *acculturation* to the dominant American cultural values, customs, artifacts, and rituals.

▪▪▪▪▪ RELIGIOUS SUBCULTURES

The United States reportedly has more than 200 different organized **religious** groups. Of this number, Protestant denominations, Roman Catholicism, and Judaism are the principal organized religious faiths. The members of all these religious groups at

FIGURE 13-2
Targeting the Hispanic
American Consumer

times are likely to make purchase decisions that are influenced by their religious identity. Commonly, consumer behavior is directly affected by religion in terms of products that are *symbolically* and *ritualistically* associated with the celebration of various religious holidays. For example, Christmas has become the major gift-purchasing season of the year.

Religious requirements or practices sometimes take on an expanded meaning beyond their original purpose. For instance, dietary laws for an observant Jewish family represent an obligation. For example, there is a Kosher lipstick manufactured by Cinema Beauté.[13] The *U* and *K* marks on food packaging are symbols that the food meets Jewish dietary laws. For nonobservant Jews and an increasing number of non-Jews, however, these marks often signify that the food is pure and wholesome—a kind of "Jewish *Good Housekeeping* Seal of Approval." In response to the broader meaning given to kosher-certified products, a number of national brands, such as Coors beer and Pepperidge Farm cookies, have secured kosher certification for their products.[14] The kosher certification secured by Dannon yogurt resulted in a 25 percent increase in the brand's Jewish household penetration, as well as $2 million in annual revenue.[15] Targeting specific religious groups with specially designed marketing programs can be really profitable. Table 13-4 presents some of the differences between the Jewish consumers and the population of the United States as a whole in terms of travel-related behavior.

TABLE 13-4 A Comparison of Jewish and General Population with Respect to Travel-Related Behavior

BEHAVIOR	JEWISH MEDIA READER	TOTAL U.S. AVERAGE
Taken a trip outside the U.S. within the past 3 years	60.3%	18.4%
Taken 10 or more trips outside the U.S. within the last 3 years	6.9%	1.2%
Taken a cruise within the past 3 years	31.4%	6.4%
Belong to a frequent flier program	67.5%	9.1%
Personally rented a car within the past 12 months	48.1%	11.4%

Source: Lisa Skriloff, "Targeting Travelers," *BrandWeek*, March 17, 1997, 20. Reprinted by permission.

▪▪▪▪▪ GEOGRAPHIC AND REGIONAL SUBCULTURES

The United States is a large country, one that enjoys a wide range of climatic and geographic conditions. Given the country's size and physical diversity, it is only natural that many Americans have a sense of **regional** identification and use this identification as a way of describing others (such as "He is a true New Englander"). These labels often assist us in developing a mental picture and supporting *stereotype* of the person in question.

Anyone who has traveled across the United States has probably noted many regional differences in consumption behavior, especially when it comes to food and drink. For example, a *mug* of black coffee typifies the West, while a *cup* of coffee with milk and sugar is preferred in the East. There also are geographic differences in the consumption of a staple food such as bread. Specifically, in the South and Midwest, soft white bread is preferred, while on the East and West coasts, firmer breads (rye, whole wheat, and French and Italian breads) are favored. And regional differences also include brand preferences. Why do you suppose Skippy is the best selling brand of peanut butter on both the East and West coasts, while Peter Pan sells best in the South and Jif sells best in the Middle West?[16]

Consumer research studies document regional differences in consumption patterns. For instance, Table 13-5 illustrates that differences in product purchase, own-

TABLE 13-5 Product Purchase/Usage by Leading Metropolitan Market

PRODUCT PURCHASE/USAGE	HIGHEST PURCHASE/USAGE	LOWEST PURCHASE/USAGE
Own Rollerblades/in-line skates	Detroit	Dallas
New domestic car	Detroit	San Francisco
New imported car	Washington, DC	Detroit
Have life insurance	Cleveland	San Francisco
Drink Scotch whiskey	Dallas	Cleveland
Purchased men's jeans (past 12 months)	Cleveland	New York
Have a bowling ball	Detroit	Boston
Use eyeliner	Dallas	Philadelphia
Use artificial sweeteners	Dallas-Fort Worth	San Francisco
Used cough syrup (past 6 months)	Chicago	Washington, DC
Popcorn (past 6 months)	Detroit	New York
Lottery tickets (past 12 months)	Cleveland	Washington, DC

Source: Mediamark Research, Inc. *Doublebase 1998 Report.* All rights reserved. Reprinted by permission.

ership, or usage levels occur between major metropolitan areas. This distinction helps redefine local markets in terms of specific urban lifestyle. Moreover, such regional variations provide additional support for marketers who argue that it is important to take geographic consumption patterns into account when planning marketing and promotional efforts.

In general, large metropolitan areas, with a substantial number of affluent middle-age households, dominate many, but not all, consumer-spending categories. Two examples are the San Jose, California, metro area, that lead in apparel purchasing, and Nassau-Suffolk counties in New York that lead in purchasing of insurance and pension programs.[17] Also, demonstrating local and regional differences, consumer research reveals that Irwindale, California, is the "king of the Big Mac." This California community is home of the greatest per capita sales of Big Macs—double or triple the sales of the four next largest markets.[18] Does anyone know why?

▪▪▪▪ RACIAL SUBCULTURES

The major **racial subcultures** in the United States are Caucasian, African American, Asian American, and American Indian. Although differences in lifestyles and consumer-spending patterns exist among these groups, the vast majority of racially oriented consumer research has focused on consumer differences between African Americans and Caucasians. Only recently has particular research attention been given to Asian American consumers.

THE AFRICAN AMERICAN CONSUMER

Consisting of about 34 million people, **African American consumers** currently constitute the largest racial minority in the United States (almost 13 percent of the population). With a purchasing power estimated to be $469 billion, African American consumers are sought after by marketers who target about $1 billion in advertising and promotions to communicate specifically with them.[19] However, this important subcultural grouping is frequently portrayed as a single, undifferentiated "African American market," consisting of consumers who have a uniform set of consumer needs. In reality they are a diverse group, consisting of numerous subgroups, each with distinctive backgrounds, needs, interests, and opinions. Therefore, just as the white majority has been divided into a variety of market segments, each with its own distinctive needs and tastes, so, too, can the African American market be segmented.

It is also of interest to point out that the 1990s have witnessed a migration of African Americans back to the South from the cities of the Midwest and the Northeast. The African American populations in the suburbs of such fast-growing cities as Atlanta, Dallas-Fort Worth, and Washington-Baltimore, as well as in parts of Florida, have been rapidly increasing during this decade.[20]

Consumer Behavior Characteristics of African American Consumers

Although there are many similarities between African Americans and the rest of America in terms of consumer behavior, there are also some meaningful differences in terms of product preferences and brand purchase patterns. African American consumers tend to prefer popular or leading brands, are brand loyal, and are unlikely to purchase private-label and generic products. A recent study found that almost two-thirds of African Americans are willing to pay more to get "the best," even if the brand or product is not widely recognized (only 51 percent of whites were reported to feel this way).[21] Also, to satisfy a valid need in the marketplace, cosmetic and hair-care companies have developed a stream of products aimed at African American women, such as Almay's Darker Tones, African Pride's® Body Bar, Dark & Lovely's® hair color, Revlon's Herba Rich with oils and African herbs, and Maybelline's Shades of You.

Some meaningful differences exist among Anglo white, African American, and Hispanic American consumers in the purchase, ownership, and use of a diverse group of products (see Table 13-6). For marketers, these findings confirm the wisdom of targeting racial market segments.

Reaching the African American Audience

A question of central importance to marketers is how to best reach *African American consumers*. Traditionally, marketers have subscribed to one of two distinct marketing strategies. Some have followed the policy of running all their advertising in general mass media in the belief that African Americans have the same media habits as whites; others have followed the policy of running additional advertising in selected media directed exclusively to African Americans.

Both strategies may be appropriate in specific situations and for specific product categories. For products of very broad appeal (as aspirin or toothpaste), it is possible that the mass media (primarily television) may effectively reach all relevant consumers, including African American and white. For other products (such as personal grooming products or food products), marketers may find that mass media do not communicate effectively with the African American market. Because the media habits of African American consumers differ from those of the general population, media specifically targeted to African Americans are likely to be more effective. The notion that African Americans have cultural values subtly different from the U.S. population as a whole is supported by a Yankelovich survey in which a majority of African Americans believe that most advertising is designed for white people.[22]

TABLE 13-6 Comparison of Purchase Patterns of White, African American, and Hispanic American Households

PRODUCT/ACTIVITY	ANGLO WHITE	AFRICAN AMERICAN	HISPANIC AMERICAN
Purchased men's jeans (past 12 months)	105	69	104
Dress shoes	99	104	85
Women's designer jeans	96	118	117
Regular women's jeans	103	80	100
Have a bowling ball	109	40	58
Have a rifle	112	22	72
Noncola soft drink 2+ glasses in past 7 days	104	69	92
Diet-cola soft drink 2+ glasses in past 7 days	108	59	82
Cough syrup 2+ times in past 30 days	92	155	120
Baby powder 5+ times in past 7 days	97	129	146
Hair coloring past 6 months	98	116	126
Women's eyeliner	100	95	117

Index: All adults = 100

Source: Mediamark Research, Inc., *Doublebase 1998 Report.* All rights reserved. Reprinted by permission.

FIGURE 13-3
Ad Targeting African
American Consumers

Many marketers supplement their general advertising with advertisements in magazines, newspapers, and other media directed specifically to African Americans (see Figure 13-3). For example, L'eggs especially targets African American women by running ads in such publications as *Ebony*, *Essence*, and *Heart & Soul*. This is the first time since the mid-1980s that L'eggs has conducted such a targeted campaign, which makes sense because African American women wear panty hose at twice the rate of other women.[23] In recent years, major advertisers targeting the African American market have increasingly used the specialized services of African American advertising agencies. These specialized agencies generally provide marketers wanting to target African Americans with the distinctive advantage of access to a staff of African American marketing professionals who thoroughly know the values and customs of this market and its specific subsegments.

ASIAN AMERICAN CONSUMERS

The **Asian American** population (primarily Chinese, Filipinos, Japanese, Asian-Indians, Koreans, and Vietnamese) is currently about 10 million in size and is the fastest-growing American minority. It is expected that immigration should push the Asian American population to 10.9 million or more in 2001, which represents a gain of almost 50 percent since 1990.[24]

The current Asian American market, which represents close to 4 percent of the United States population, is composed of almost 23 percent Chinese, 19 percent Filipino, 12 percent Japanese, 11 percent Asian-Indians, and 11 percent Korean, with the remainder being drawn from a variety of Asian countries. Because Asian Americans are largely family-oriented, highly industrious, and strongly driven to achieve a middle-class lifestyle, they are an attractive market for increasing numbers of marketers. Indeed, while the median income for non-Hispanic white households in the mid-1990s was $37,200, the Asian American median household income was $40,600.[25]

Where Are the Asian Americans?

Asian Americans are largely urban people, who are presently concentrated in and around a small number of large American cities. About 58 percent of Asian Americans live in greater Los Angeles, San Francisco, and Hawaii, while another 18 percent reside in greater New York, Philadelphia, and Washington, DC. At present, more than 10 percent of California's population is Asian, and it is expected that by the year 2001, approximately 13.2 percent of California's population will be Asian American.[26] Marketers can be misled by these numbers if they treat the Asian American market as one single market. For instance, the stereotype that most Chinese live in "Chinatown" is incorrect. Most Chinese, as well as most other Asian Americans, do not live in downtown urban areas; they live in the suburbs.[27]

Understanding the Asian American Consumer

Local newspapers and weekly news magazines frequently portray the accomplishments of Asian Americans, who have shown themselves to be hardworking, very family-oriented, and strivers for excellence in educational pursuits (for themselves and their children). Indeed, throughout the United States, Asian American children have consistently won a substantial share of academic awards and scholarships.

Supporting this profile, United States Census Bureau data reveal that more Asian Americans, on a per capita basis, own their own businesses than non-Asian American minorities. Those who do not own their own businesses are largely in professional, technical, or managerial occupations. They also tend to be better educated and more computer literate than the general population. Additionally, many Asian Americans are young and live a good part of their lives in multi-income households.

Asian Americans as Consumers

The buying power of Asian Americans amounts to about $110 billion annually.[28] They value quality (frequently associated with well-known brands) and are willing to pay for it (Figure 13-4). This population segment tends to be loyal customers, frequently more male oriented when it comes to consumption decisions, and attracted to retailers who make it known that they welcome Asian American patronage.

It is important to remember that Asian Americans are really drawn from diverse cultural backgrounds. Therefore, although Asian Americans have many similarities, marketers should approach this overall group with caution, as they are not completely homogeneous. For example, Vietnamese Americans are more likely to follow the traditional model, wherein the man makes the decision for large purchases; whereas Chinese American husbands and wives are more likely to share in the decision-making process.[29] Retailers and other service businesses can benefit from niche marketing to specific subsegments of the overall Asian American market. As an example of such niche marketing, a life insurance manager in Forest Hills, New York, turned the agency into one of the leading producing offices of MONY Financial Services by focusing on Asian-Indians.[30] However, with 29 major ethnic groups between the Indian subcontinent and the Pacific Ocean, Asian Americans cannot be efficiently targeted as a single homogeneous group.

FIGURE 13-4
Ad Targeting Asian
American Consumers

The use of Asian American models in advertising is effective in reaching this market segment. A research study found that responses to an advertisement for stereo speakers featuring an Asian model were significantly more positive than responses to the same ad using a Caucasian model.[31] There is also a Web site targeted specifically to Asian Americans and offering culture, products, and services. *Channel A* receives more than 1.5 million "hits" a month and wants to serve the 1.7 million adult Asian Americans who use the Internet (see Figure 13-5). The most popular areas on the site are entertainment and food.[32]

AGE SUBCULTURES

It's not difficult to understand why each major age subgrouping of the population might be thought of as a separate subculture. After all, don't you listen to different music than your parents and grandparents, dress differently, read different magazines, and enjoy different TV shows? Clearly, important shifts occur in an individual's demand for specific types of products and services as he or she goes from being a dependent child to a retired senior citizen. In this chapter, we will limit our examination of **age subcultures** to three

FIGURE 13-5
Appealing to Asian
American Consumers'
Interest in the Internet

adult age groups: **Generation X**, **baby boomers**, and **seniors**. These three adult age segments have been singled out because their distinctive lifestyles qualify them for consideration as subcultural groups.

THE GENERATION X MARKET

This age grouping, often referred to as *Xers*, *busters*, or *slackers* (as opposed to boomers) is continually being defined as the approximately 46 million 18- to 29-year-olds who spend about $125 billion yearly. They do not like labels and do not want to be singled out and marketed to.

Also, unlike their parents, who are frequently baby boomers, they are in no rush to marry, start a family, or work excessive hours to earn high salaries. For *Generation X consumers*, job satisfaction is typically much more important than salary. Xers reject the values of older coworkers who may neglect their families while striving to secure higher salaries and career advancement. For Generation X, it is more important to enjoy life and to have a lifestyle that provides freedom and flexibility. Many Xers are much more interested in tennis shoes, furniture for their apartments, and camping equipment than in BMWs or oceanfront condos. Owning one's own home is often considered a negative that reduces an individual's flexibility. Although upward mobility has traditionally been the American dream, Xers often find good jobs either difficult or impossible to find.

Appealing to Generation X

Members of Generation X often pride themselves on their sophistication. Although they are not necessarily materialistic, they do purchase good brand names (such as Sony) but not necessarily designer labels. They want to be recognized by marketers as a group in their own right and not as mini-baby boomers. Therefore, advertisements targeted to this audience must focus on their style in music, fashions, and language (see Figure 13-6). One

FIGURE 13-6
Ad Appealing to Generation X Consumers

key for marketers appears to be sincerity. Xers are not against advertising but only opposed to insincerity. Consequently, including Cindy Crawford and an animated duck in advertisements for the Cadillac Catera did not appeal to the Gen X car buyer.[33]

Baby boomer media does not work with Generation X members. For example, 18- to 24-year-olds have the lowest percentage of daily newspaper readership of all age groups. Xers are the MTV generation, and whereas the three major United States TV networks attract an average of only 18 percent of the 18-to-29 group, the Fox network claims that 38 percent of its viewers are in this age group. The success Fox has had with Xers may be due to such programs as *Married with Children*, *The Simpsons*, *In Living Color*, and *Beverly Hills 90210*. Furthermore, a number of cable TV networks such as MTV, Comedy Central, and E! have been very successful in reaching this audience. It appears that a low-key approach works best in reaching this market segment. Table 13-7 presents a comparison of Gen X versus baby boomers that has been circulated on the Internet by Xers.

THE BABY BOOMER MARKET

Marketers have found baby boomers a particularly desirable target audience because (1) they are the single largest distinctive age category alive today; (2) they frequently make important consumer purchase decisions; and (3) they contain a small subsegment of trendsetting consumers (sometimes known as *yuppies*, or young upwardly mobile professionals) who have influence on the consumer tastes of other age segments of society.[34]

Who Are the Baby Boomers?

The term *baby boomers* refers to the age segment of the population that was born between 1946 and 1964. Thus, baby boomers are in the broad age category that extends from about mid-30s to mid-50s. Baby boomers represent more than 40 percent of the adult population. The magnitude of this statistic alone would make them a much sought-after market segment. However, they also are valued because they comprise about 50 percent of all those in professional and managerial occupations and more than one-half of those with at least a college degree.

TABLE 13-7 A Comparison of Generation X and Baby Boomers: As Seen by Xers

CATEGORY	GENERATION X	BABY BOOMERS
Favorite TV Mom	Mrs. Brady	June Cleaver
Scariest Movie	*Silence of the Lambs*	*The Blob*
Lost Poet Musician	Kurt Cobain	Jim Morrison
Childhood Athlete	Michael Jordan	O. J. Simpson
Life Changing Movie	*Heathers*	*Easy Rider*
Haunting Assassination	John Lennon	John F. Kennedy
Most Annoying Fad	Body Piercing	Hula Hoops
Way Back When . . .	Vanilla Ice	Barry Manilow
Fashion Faux Pas	Parachute Pants	Bell Bottoms
Rallying Cry	AIDS, Crime	Vietnam
Kennedy?	MTV-VJ	Former President

Source: Based on information from the Collegiate Marketing Company, as appears in: David Ashley Morrison, "Beyond the Gen X Label," *BrandWeek*, March 17, 1997, 24. Reprinted by permission.

In addition, although each year more *baby boomers* turn 50 years of age, they do not necessarily like the idea. Increases in health club memberships and a boom in the sales of vitamin and health supplements are evidence that these consumers are trying hard to look and feel "young."

Consumer Characteristics of Baby Boomers

Baby boomers tend to be motivated consumers. They enjoy buying for themselves, for their homes or apartments, and for others—they are consumption-oriented. As baby boomers age, the nature of the products and services they most need or desire changes. For example, because of the aging of this market segment, Levi Strauss is featuring "relaxed fit" jeans, sales of "lineless" bifocal glasses to new customers are up substantially, and sales of walking shoes have grown rapidly. Men's and women's pants with elastic waistbands are also enjoying strong sales. Recently, bank marketers and other financial institutions are also paying more attention to assisting boomers who are starting to think about retirement.

Yuppies are by far the most sought-after subgroup of baby boomers. Although constituting only 5 percent of the population, they generally are well off financially, well educated, and in enviable professional or managerial careers. They often are associated with status brand names, such as BMWs or Volvo station wagons, Rolex watches, cable TV, and Cuisinart food processors. Today, as many yuppies are maturing, they are shifting their attention away from expensive status-type possessions to travel, physical fitness, planning for second careers, or some other form of new directions for their lives (see Figure 13-7).

OLDER CONSUMER

America is aging. Some baby boomers are in their 50s (or "mature adults"), there are plenty of preboomers (those 55 to 65 years), and the number of **elderly consumers** is growing twice as fast as the overall U.S. population. Thus, we will explore the 50-plus market and elderly market, two age subcultures. It should also be remembered, as Table 13-8 indicates, that the single longest life stage for most consumers begins when they turn 50 years of age, and that people over age 50 comprise fully one-third of the adult U.S. market. Additionally, 75 percent of the people born today will live to age 65, and half are expected to live to be 80 years of age.[35]

While some people think of older consumers as consisting of people without substantial financial resources, in generally poor health, and with plenty of free time on their hands, the fact is that one in four seniors between the ages of 65 and 72 is still employed full-time, many more have part-time jobs, 14 million seniors are involved in the daily care of a grandchild, and almost 60 percent of this group volunteer. The annual discretionary income of this group amounts to $150 billion, and they spent billions of dollars more on necessities, such as housing and food.[36]

Defining "Older" in Older Consumer

About 33 million Americans are within the 65-plus age category, representing 12 percent of the country's population. This number is expected to double by the year 2030, with the elderly segment eventually accounting for about 20 percent of the American population. This expected growth in the elderly population can be explained by the declining birthrate, the aging of the huge baby boomer segment, and improved medical diagnoses and treatment. One expert has called this phenomenon the "Age Wave."[37]

In the United States, "old age" is officially assumed to begin with a person's 65th birthday (or when the individual qualifies for full Social Security and Medicare). However, people who are 70 years old still tend to view themselves as "middle-aged." After

FIGURE 13-7
Appealing to Yuppies'
Sense of Seeking Enriching
Experiences

TABLE 13-8 Length of Lifestyle for the U.S. Consumer

AGE COHORT	LENGTH OF LIFESTYLE
Childhood (0–17)	17
Early adulthood (18–34)	16
Middle adulthood (35–49)	14
Later adulthood (50+)	29+

Source: John Nielson and Kathy Curry, "Creative Strategies for Connecting with Mature Individuals," *Journal of Consumer Marketing* 14, 4 (1997): 320.

all, former President George Bush parachuted into the Arizona desert at the age of 72, and the Duke University Center for Demographic Studies has noted that between 1982 and 1994 there has been a 15 percent drop in chronic disability rates (which measures things like ability to feed oneself).[38]

Research consistently suggests that people's perceptions of their ages are more important in determining behavior than their chronological ages (or the number of years lived).[39] In fact, people may at the same time have a number of different perceived or **cognitive ages**. Specifically, elderly consumers perceive themselves to be younger than their chronological ages on four perceived age dimensions: *feel age* (how old they feel); *look age* (how old they look); *do age* (how involved they are in activities favored by members of a specific age group); and *interest age* (how similar their interests are to those of members of a specific age group).[40] The results support other research that indicates that elderly consumers are more likely to consider themselves younger (to have a younger cognitive age) than their chronological age.

For marketers, these findings underscore the importance of looking beyond chronological age to perceived or cognitive age when appealing to mature consumers and to the possibility that cognitive age might be used to segment the mature market (see Figure 13-8).

Segmenting the Elderly Market

The elderly are by no means a homogeneous subcultural group. There are those who, as a matter of choice, do not have color TVs or Touch-Tone telephone service, whereas others have the latest desktop computers and spend their time surfing the Internet. In fact, the 38 hours a month that 55-plus computer owners spend on their "machines," is 60 percent higher than the national average for all computer owners, regardless of age.[41]

One consumer gerontologist has suggested that the elderly are more diverse in interests, opinions, and actions than other segments of the adult population.[42] Although this view runs counter to the popular myth that the elderly are uniform in terms of attitudes and lifestyles, both gerontologists and market researchers have repeatedly demonstrated that age is not necessarily a major factor in determining how older consumers respond to marketing activities.

With an increased appreciation that the elderly constitute a diverse age segment, more attention is now being given to identifying ways to segment the elderly into meaningful groupings.[43] One relatively simple segmentation scheme partitions the elderly into three chronological age categories: the *young-old* (65 to 74 years of age), the *old* (those 75 to 84); and the *old-old* (those 85 years of age and older). This market segmentation approach provides useful consumer-relevant insights.

The elderly can also be segmented in terms of motivations and *quality-of-life orientation*. Table 13-9 presents a side-by-side comparison of *new-age elderly* consumers and the more traditional older consumers. The increased presence of the new-age elderly suggests that marketers need to respond to the value orientations of older consumers whose lifestyles remain relatively ageless. Clearly, the new-age elderly are individuals who feel, think, and do according to a cognitive age that is younger than their chronological age.

Shopping Experiences of the Older Consumer

Householders in the 65- to 74-year-old age range tend to spend more per capita on most major categories of goods and services than members of the 25- to 34-year-old age group.[44] To illustrate, householders aged 55 to 64 spend 56 percent more on women's clothing than the average U.S. household. For this reason it is not surprising to find that marketers have been especially attuned to the needs of elderly consumers and see them as valued customers.

FIGURE 13-8
Appealing to Older
Consumers' Sense of
Cognitive Age

SEX AS A SUBCULTURE

Because sex roles have an important cultural component, it is quite fitting to examine **gender** as a subcultural category.

TABLE 13-9 Comparison of New-Age and Traditional Elderly

NEW-AGE ELDERLY	TRADITIONAL/STEREOTYPICAL ELDERLY
• Perceive themselves to be different in outlook from other people their age	• Perceive all older people to be about the same in outlook
• Age is seen as a state of mind	• See age as more of a physical state
• See themselves as younger than their chronological age	• See themselves at or near their chronological age
• Feel younger, think younger, and "do" younger	• Tend to feel, think, and do things that they feel match their chronological age
• Have a genuinely youthful outlook	• Feel that one should act one's age
• Feel there is a considerable adventure to living	
• Feel more in control of their own lives	• Normal sense of being in control of their own lives
• Have greater self-confidence when it comes to making consumer decisions	• Normal range of self-confidence when it comes to making consumer decisions
• Less concerned that they will make a mistake when buying something	• Some concern that they will make a mistake when buying something
• Especially knowledgeable and alert consumers	• Low-to-average consumer capabilities
• Selectively innovative	• Not innovative
• Seek new experiences and personal challenges	• Seek stability and a secure routine
• Less interested in accumulating possessions	• Normal range of interest in accumulating possessions
• Higher measured life satisfaction	• Lower measured life satisfaction
• Less likely to want to live their lives over differently	• Have some regrets as to how they lived their lives
• Perceive themselves to be healthier	• Perceive themselves to be of normal health for their age
• Feel financially more secure	• Somewhat concerned about financial security

Source: Reprinted by permission from "The Value Orientation of New-Age Elderly: The Coming of an Ageless Market" by Leon G. Schiffman and Elaine Sherman in *Journal of Business Research* 22 (April 1991), 187–94. Copyright 1991 by Elsevier Science Publishing Co., Inc.

SEX ROLES AND CONSUMER BEHAVIOR

All societies tend to assign certain traits and roles to males and others to females. In American society, for instance, aggressiveness and competitiveness often were considered traditional *masculine traits*; neatness, tactfulness, gentleness, and talkativeness were considered traditional *feminine traits*. In terms of role differences, women have historically been cast as homemakers with responsibility for child care and men as the providers or breadwinners. Because such traits and roles are no longer relevant for many individuals, marketers are increasingly appealing to consumers' broader vision of gender-related role options (see Figure 13-9).

Consumer Products and Sex Roles

Within every society, it is quite common to find products that are either exclusively or strongly associated with the members of one sex. In the United States, for example, shaving equipment, cigars, pants, ties, and work clothing were historically male products; bracelets, hair spray, hair dryers, and sweet-smelling colognes generally were considered feminine products. For most of these products, the **sex role** link has either diminished or disappeared; for others, the prohibition still lingers. An interesting product category with regard to the blurring of a gender appeal is men's fragrances. Although men are increasingly wearing fragrances, it is estimated that 30 percent of men's fragrances are worn by women.[45] Also, although women have historically been the major market for vitamins, men are increasingly being targeted for vitamins exclusively formulated for men.

Who says
you can't
own the
future?

There are no limits to
what a woman can
accomplish. Especially
when you have a plan
and the right financial
advice.

An American Express
financial advisor can
help you with education
planning, retirement
planning, and making
sure your money will
last. We offer you the
expertise and insight
you need to make smart
decisions. So you can
take charge of your
financial future.

Plan to do more.
Call I-800-GET-ADVICE.
and own your world.
www.americanexpress.com/advisors

do more

AMERICAN
EXPRESS
**Financial
Advisors**

THE WORKING WOMAN

Marketers and consumer researchers have been increasingly interested in the **working woman**, especially the married working woman. They recognize that married women who work outside of the home are a large and growing market segment, one whose needs differ from those of women who do not work outside the home (frequently self-labeled "stay-at-home Moms"). It is the size of the working woman market that makes it so attractive. Approximately 72 percent of American women work full-time, and only 3.5 percent of American families consist of the traditional arrangement of a breadwinning husband and a homemaking wife.[46] Young women with young children have been the fastest-growing segment in the female workforce.

Segmenting the Working Woman Market

To provide a richer framework for segmentation, marketers have developed categories that differentiate the motivations of working and nonworking women. For instance, a number of studies have divided the female population into four segments: *stay-at-home* housewives; *plan-to-work* housewives; *just-a-job* working women; and *career-oriented* working women.[47] The distinction between "just-a-job" and "career-oriented" working women is particularly meaningful. "Just-a-job" working women seem to be motivated to work primarily by a sense that the family requires the additional income, whereas "career-oriented" working women, who tend to be in a managerial or professional position, are driven more by a need to achieve and succeed in their chosen careers. Today, though, with more and more female college graduates in the workforce, the percentage of career-oriented working women is on the rise. As evidence of this fact, 25 percent of all working women bring home a paycheck that is larger than their husband's (10 years ago it was only 17 percent), and 40 percent of all business travelers today are women (up from only 1 percent in 1970).[48] Table 13-10 presents information illustrating the influence of women on spending for selected types of products and services, as well as how their influence has been changing.

Shopping Patterns of Working Women

Working women spend less time shopping than nonworking women. They accomplish this "time economy" by shopping less often and by being brand- and store-loyal. Not surprisingly, working women also are likely to shop during evening hours and on the weekend, as well as to buy through direct-mail catalogs.

A relatively new way for working women to shop is via the Internet. More than 40 percent of all on-line users are female; 64 percent of these women are employed full-time, and they average about 6 hours a week on-line. Considering that women account for 70 percent of retail sales, it is especially important to point out a recent survey that found new products are the primary motivation why women click on banners (74 percent) and visit new Web sites (79 percent). These female Internet users are both early adopters and opinion leaders (two concepts that will be fully discussed in chapter 15).[49]

TABLE 13-10 How Women Control the Purse Strings

Women control or influence...

80% of all purchase decisions
80% of new vehicle purchases
46% of menswear purchases
82% of supermarket purchases
53% of investment decisions
70% of appliance choices

Women also...

handle 75% of family finances
constitute 40% of business travel
are 43% of the persons with assets over $500,000

Source: Adopted from Alice Z. Cuneo, "Advertisers Target Women, but Market Remains Elusive," *Advertising Age*, 10 November 1997, 24. (Based in part on information from N. W. Ayer & Partner et al.).

▪▪▪▪ SUBCULTURAL INTERACTION

All consumers are simultaneously members of more than one subcultural segment (for example, a consumer may be a young, Hispanic, Catholic homemaker living in the Midwest). For this reason, marketers should strive to understand how multiple **subcultural** memberships **interact** to influence target consumers' relevant consumption behavior. Promotional strategy should not be limited to target a single subcultural membership.

SUMMARY

Subcultural analysis enables marketers to segment their markets to meet the specific needs, motivations, perceptions, and attitudes shared by members of a specific subcultural group. A subculture is a distinct cultural group that exists as an identifiable segment within a larger, more complex society. Its members possess beliefs, values, and customs that set them apart from other members of the same society; at the same time, they hold to the dominant beliefs of the overall society. Major subcultural categories in this country include nationality, religion, geo-graphic location, race, age, and sex. Each of these can be broken down into smaller segments that can be reached through special copy appeals and selective media choices. In some cases (such as the elderly consumer), product characteristics can be tailored to the specialized needs of the market segment. Because all consumers simultaneously are members of several subcultural groups, the marketer must determine for the product category how specific subcultural memberships interact to influence the consumer's purchase decisions.

DISCUSSION QUESTIONS

1. Why is subcultural analysis especially significant in a country such as the United States?

2. Discuss the importance of subcultural segmentation to marketers of food products. Identify a food product for which the marketing mix should be regionalized. Explain why and how the marketing mix should be varied across geographic areas of the United States.

3. How can marketers of the following products use the material presented in this chapter to develop promotional campaigns designed to increase market share among African American, Hispanic, and Asian American consumers? The products are: (a) compact disk players, (b) ready-to-eat cereals, and (c) designer jeans.

4. Asian Americans are a small proportion of the total United States population. Why are they an important market segment? How can a marketer of personal computers effectively target Asian Americans?

5. Sony is introducing a new 27-inch TV with a picture-in-picture feature. How should the company position and advertise the product to: (a) Generation X consumers and (b) affluent baby boomers?

6. In view of the anticipated growth of the over-50 market, a leading cosmetics company is reevaluating the marketing strategy for its best-selling moisturizing face cream for women. Should the company market the product to younger (under-50) as well as older women? Would it be wiser to develop a new brand and formula for consumers over 50 rather than target both age groups with one product? Explain your answer.

7. Marketers realize that people of the same age often exhibit very different lifestyles. Using the evidence presented in this chapter, discuss how developers of retirement housing can use older Americans' lifestyles to more effectively segment their markets.

8. a. How should marketers promote products and services to working women? What appeals should they use? Explain.

   b. As the owner of a Saturn automobile dealership, what kind of marketing strategies would you use to target working women?

EXERCISES

1. Using one of the subculture categories listed in Table 13-1, identify a group that can be regarded as a subculture within your university or college.
   a. Describe the norms, values, and behaviors of the subculture's members.
   b. Interview five members of that subculture regarding attitudes toward the use of credit cards.
   c. What are the implications of your findings for marketing credit cards to the group you selected?

2. Interview one baby boomer and one Generation X consumer regarding the purchase of a car. Prepare a report on the differences in attitudes between the two individuals. Do your findings support the text's discussion of the differences between "boomers" and "busters"? Explain.

3. Many of *your* perceptions regarding price versus value are likely to be different from those of your parents or grandparents. Researchers attribute such differences to "cohort effects," which are based on the premise that consumption patterns are determined early in life. Therefore, individuals who experienced different economic, political, and cultural environments during their youth are likely to be different types of consumers as adults. Describe instances in which your parents or grandparents disagreed with or criticized purchases you had made. Describe the cohort effects that explain each party's position during these disagreements.

4. Find two good and two bad examples of advertising directed toward elderly consumers. To what degree are these ads stereotypical? Do they depict the concept of perceived age? How could these ads be improved by applying some of this chapter's guidelines for advertising to elderly consumers?

KEY TERMS

- **African American consumers**
- **Age subcultures**
- **Asian American consumers**
- **Baby boomers**
- **Cognitive ages**
- **Elderly consumers**

- **Gender subcultures**
- **Generation X consumers**
- **Hispanic subcultures**
- **Nationality subcultures**
- **Racial subcultures**
- **Regional subcultures**

- **Religious subcultures**
- **Sex roles**
- **Subcultural interaction**
- **Subculture**
- **Working woman subcultures**

NOTES

1. Nancy Coltun Webster, "Multicultural," *Advertising Age*, 17 November 1997, S4.
2. John Robinson, Bart Landry, and Ronica Rooks, "Time and the Melting Pot," *American Demographics* (June 1998): 18–24.
3. Brad Edmondson, "Hispanic Americans in 2001," *American Demographics* (January 1997): 17; and "Using Research to Tap into the Hispanic Market," *Advertising Age*, 31 March 1997, A14.
4. Victoria Seitz, "Acculturation and Direct Purchasing Behavior among Ethnic Groups in the US: Implications for Business Practitioners," *Journal of Consumer Marketing* 15 (1998): 23–31.
5. William H. Frey, "The Diversity Myth," *American Demographics* (June 1998): 39.

6. Edmondson, "Hispanic Americans," 17.
7. Soyeon Shim and Kenneth C. Gehrt, "Native American and Hispanic Adolescent Consumers: Examination of Shopping Orientation, Socialization Factors and Social Structure Variables," in *1995 AMA Educators' Proceedings*, ed. Barbara B. Stern and George M. Zinkan (Chicago: American Marketing Association, 1995), 297–98.
8. Rohit Deshpande, Wayne D. Hoyer, and Naveen Donthu, "The Intensity of Ethnic Affiliation: A Study of the Sociology of Hispanic Consumption," *Journal of Consumer Research* 13 (September 1986): 214–20; and Cynthia Webster, "The Role of Hispanic Ethnic Identification on Reference Group Influence," in *Advances in Consumer Research*, vol. 21, ed. Chris T. Allen and Deb-

orah Roedder John (Provo, UT: Association for Consumer Research, 1994), 458–63.

9. Otto Johnson, ed., *1995 Information Please Almanac* (Boston: Houghton Mifflin, 1995).

10. Louise Kramer, "Taco Bell's Hispanic Strategy," *Advertising Age*, 20 October 1997, 12; and Jack Neff, "Colgate's Latin Strength Recruited to Prod U.S. Foes," *Advertising Age*, 29 September 1997, 4.

11. Marcia Mogelonsky, "First Language Comes First," *American Demographics* (October 1995): 21.

12. "Assimilation No Threat to Hispanic Media," *Advertising Age*, 31 March 1997, A2, A4.

13. Marcia Mogelonsky, "Kiss Me, You Kosher Fool," *American Demographics* (May 1994): 17.

14. Laura Bird, "Major Brands Look for the Kosher Label," *Adweek's Marketing Week*, 1 April 1991, 18–19; and Judith Waldrop, "Everything's Kosher," *American Demographics* (March 1991): 4.

15. Elie Rosenfeld, "Kosher Consumers," *BrandWeek*, 19 May 1997, 29–32.

16. Florence Fabricant, "The Geography of Taste," *The New York Times Magazine*, 10 March 1996, 40–41.

17. Marcia Mogelonsky, "America's Hottest Market," *American Demographics* (January 1996): 20–31, 55.

18. Anne R. Curey and Sam Ward, "Big Mac Capital of the USA," *USA Today*, 9 September 1998, 1B.

19. Webster, "The Role of Hispanic Ethnic Identification," S4.

20. Frey, "The Diversity Myth," 43.

21. Christy Fisher, "Black, Hip, and Primed (to Shop)," *American Demographics* (September 1996): 52–58.

22. Kari Van Hoof, "Surveys Point to Group Differences," *BrandWeek*, 7 March 1994, 32–33.

23. Becky Ebenkamp, "L'eggs Goes Multicultural in Spring," *BrandWeek*, 16 February 1998, 4.

24. Brad Edmondson, "Asian Americans in 2001," *American Demographics* (February 1997): 16–17.

25. Ibid.

26. William P. O'Hare, William H. Frey, and Dan Fost, "Asians in the Suburbs," *American Demographics* (May 1994): 32–38; and Edmondson, "Asian Americans," 17.

27. O'Hare, Frey, and Fost, "Asians in the Suburbs," 35.

28. Webster, "The Role of Hispanic Ethnic Identification," S4.

29. John Steere, "How Asian-Americans Make Purchase Decisions," *Marketing News*, 13 March 1995, 9.

30. Harvey Braum, "Marketing to Minority Consumers," *Discount Merchandiser* (February 1991): 44–46, 74; Chui Li, "The Asian-American Market for Personal Products," *Drug and Cosmetic Industry* (November 1992): 32–36; and Ashok Pradhan, "Ethnic Markets: Sales Niche of the Future," *National Underwriter*, 6 November 1989, 18.

31. Judy Cohen, "White Consumer Response to Asian Models in Advertising," *Journal of Consumer Marketing* (Spring 1992): 17–27.

32. Leon E. Wynter, "Asian Web Site Reaches Wide Range of Buyers," *Wall Street Journal*, 4 June 1997, B1.

33. Karen Richie, "Marketing to Generation X," *American Demographics* (April 1995): 34–39; and Gerry Myers, "Mutual Respect," *American Demographics* (April 1997): 20–23.

34. "Boomer Facts," *American Demographics* (January 1996): 14. Also see: Diane Crispell, "U.S. Population Forecasts Decline for 2000, but Rise Slightly for 2050," *Wall Street Journal*, 25 March 1996, B3.

35. Cary Silvers, "Smashing Old Stereotypes of 50-Plus America," *Journal of Consumer Marketing* 14, 4 (1997): 303–9; George P. Moschis, Euehun Lee, and Anil Mathur, "Targeting the Mature Market: Opportunities and Challenges," *Journal of Consumer Marketing* 14, 7 (1997): 282–93.

36. Rich Adler, "Stereotypes Won't Work with Seniors Anymore," *Advertising Age*, 11 November 1996, 32; and Myers, "Mutual Respect," 20.

37. For a discussion of various demographic trends affecting the elderly, see Ken Dychtwald and Joe Flower, *Age Wave* (Los Angeles: Jeremy P. Tarcher, 1989); and Ken Dychtwald, "Baby Boomers Catch the Age Wave," *Marketing Review* (January 1996): 16–19. Also, see George P. Moschis, "Consumer Behavior in Later Life Multidisciplinary Contributions and Implications for Research," *Journal of the Academy of Marketing Science* (1994): 195–204; and Moschis, Lee, and Mathur, "Targeting the Mature Market," 283.

38. Allen R. Myerson, "Acting Their Attitude, Not Their Age," *New York Times*, 30 March 1977, E3.

39. Kelly Tepper, "The Role of Labeling Processes in Elderly Consumers' Responses to Age Segmentation Cues," *Journal of Consumer Research* (March 1994): 503–19; and Candace Corlett, "Building a Successful 50+ Marketing Program," *Marketing Review* (January 1996): 10–11, 19.

40. Benny Barak and Leon G. Schiffman, "Cognitive Age: A Nonchronological Age Variable," in *Advances in Consumer Research*, vol. 8, ed. Kent B. Monroe (Ann Arbor, MI: Association for Consumer Research, 1981), 602–6; Elaine Sherman, Leon G. Schiffman, and William R. Dillon, "Age/Gender Segments and Quality of Life Differences," in *1988 Winter Educators' Conference*, ed. Stanley Shapiro and A. H. Walle (Chicago: American Marketing Association, 1988), 319–20; Stuart Van Auken and Thomas E. Barry, "An Assessment of the Trait Validity of Cognitive Age," *Journal of Consumer Psychology* (1995): 107–32; Robert E. Wilkes, "A Structural Modeling Approach to the Measurement and Meaning of Cognitive Age," *Journal of Consumer Research* (September 1992): 292–301; and Chad Rubel, "Mature Market Often Misunderstood," *Marketing News*, 28 August 1995, 28–29.

41. Catherine McGrath, "Mature and Wired," *American Demographics* (June 1998): 30.

42. Elaine Sherman, quoted in David B. Wolfe, "The Ageless Market," *American Demographics* (July 1987): 26–28, 55–56.

43. Carol M. Morgan and Doran J. Levy, "Understanding Mature Consumers," *Marketing Review* (January 1996):

12–13, 25; and Elaine Sherman and Leon G. Schiffman, "Quality-of-Life (QOL) Assessment of Older Consumers: A Retrospective Review," *Journal of Business and Psychology* (Fall 1991): 107–119.

44. Cheryl Russell, "The Ungraying of America," *American Demographics* (July 1997): 12–15.

45. Maxine Wilkie, "Scent of a Market," *American Demographics* (August 1995): 40–49.

46. "America's Vanishing Housewife," *Adweek's Marketing Week*, 24 June 1991, 28–29.

47. Thomas Barry, Mary Gilly, and Lindley Doran, "Advertising to Women with Different Career Orientations," *Journal of Advertising Research* 25 (April–May 1985): 26–35.

48. Alice Z. Cuneo, "Advertisers Target Women, but Market Remains Elusive," *Advertising Age*, 10 November 1997, 1, 24–26.

49. Bernadette Tracy, "Survey Says Women Want Web Sites That Build Relationships," *Advertising Age*, 22 September 1997, 32.

CHAPTER 14

Cross-Cultural Consumer Behavior: An International Perspective

■ ■

In our examination of psychological, social, and cultural factors, we have consistently pointed out how various segments of the American consuming public differ. If so much diversity exists among segments of a single society, then even more diversity is likely to exist among the members of two or more societies. To succeed, international marketers must understand the nature and extent of differences between the consumers of different societies—"cross-cultural" differences—so that they can develop effective targeted marketing strategies to use in each foreign market of interest.

In this chapter, we broaden our scope of analysis and consider the marketing implications of cultural differences and similarities that exist between the people of two or more nations. We also compare the views that pit a global marketing perspective—one that stresses the *similarities* of consumers worldwide—against a localized marketing strategy that stresses the *diversity* of consumers in different nations and their specific cultural orientations. Our own view is that marketers must be aware of and sensitive to cross-cultural similarities and differences that can provide expanded sales and profit opportunities. Multinational marketers must be ready to tailor their marketing mixes to the specific customs of each nation that they want to target.

■ ■ ■ ■ ■ THE IMPERATIVE TO BE MULTINATIONAL

Today, almost all major corporations are actively marketing their products beyond their original homeland borders. In fact, the issue is generally not *whether* to market a brand in other countries but rather *how* to do it (as the same product, the same ("global") advertising campaign, or "tailored" products and localized ads for each country). Because of this emphasis on operating multinationally, the vocabulary of marketing now includes terms such as *glocal*, which refers to companies that are both "global" and "local"; that is, they include in their marketing efforts a blend of standardized and local elements in order to secure the benefits of each strategy.[1]

This challenge has been given special meaning by the efforts of the **European Union** (EU) to form a single market. Although the movement of goods and services among community members has been eased, it is unclear whether this diverse market will be transformed into a single market of homogeneous "Euroconsumers" with the same or very similar wants and needs. Many people hope that the introduction of the "euro" as a common currency among a number of EU members, and its scheduled replacement of many of Europe's existing currencies in 2002, will help shape Europe into a huge, powerful, single market.[2] The opening up of Eastern Europe to capitalism also presents a major opportunity and challenge to marketers. Firms like Coca-Cola, General Motors, Nabisco, Gillette, and R.J. Reynolds are now investing extensive sums on product development and marketing to satisfy the needs of awakening Eastern European consumer markets.[3]

The **North American Free Trade Agreement** (NAFTA), which currently consists of the United States, Canada, and Mexico, provides free-market access to 400 million consumers representing an $8 trillion market. The emerging Association of Southeast Asian Nations (ASEAN), consisting of Indonesia, Singapore, Thailand, the Philippines, Malaysia, Brunei, and Vietnam, is another important economic alliance that offers marketers new global markets. The members of this group have formed the ASEAN Free Trade Area (AFTA) to promote regional trade.[4]

Many firms are developing strategies to take advantage of these and other emerging economic opportunities. A substantial number of firms are now jockeying for market share in foreign markets. Reebok, for example, in its desire to become a global brand, has recently appointed a global advertising director and plans to spend $100 million plus on a global advertising campaign. And Gap has launched a global ad campaign in an effort to battle Dockers for a larger share of the fast-growing khaki market.[5]

With the buildup of this multinational fever and the general attractiveness of multinational markets, products or services originating in one country are increasingly being sought out by consumers in other parts of the world. For instance, in Japan, there are over 2,000 McDonald's restaurants, and the best-selling brand of dishwashing detergent is Proctor & Gamble's Joy. In addition to Avon's 7.2 million door-to-door salespeople in the United States, the firm has 2 million salespeople in Japan, 2 million in Taiwan, 1 million in Mexico, and half a million in China.[6]

Firms are selling their products worldwide for a variety of reasons. First, many firms have learned that overseas markets represent the single most important opportunity for their future growth when their home markets reach maturity. This realization is propelling them to expand their horizons and seek consumers scattered all over the world. Moreover, consumers all over the world are increasingly eager to try "foreign" products that are popular in different and far-off places.

ACQUIRING EXPOSURE TO OTHER CULTURES

As more and more consumers come in contact with the material goods and lifestyles of people living in other parts of the world, they have the opportunity to adopt these different products and practices. How consumers in one culture secure exposure to the goods of other people living in other cultures is an important part of consumer behavior. It impacts the well-being of consumers worldwide and of marketers trying to gain acceptance for their products in countries that are often quite different from their home country.

A portion of consumers' exposure to different cultures tends to come about through consumers' own initiatives—their travel, their living and working in foreign countries, or even their immigration to a different country. Additionally, consumers obtain a "taste" of different cultures from contact with foreign movies, theater, art and artifacts and, most certainly, from exposure to unfamiliar and different products. This second major category of cultural exposure is often undertaken by marketers seeking to expand their markets by "bringing" new products, services, practices, and ideas to potential consumers residing in a different country and possessing a different cultural view. Within this context, international marketing provides a form of "culture transfer." As a twist on this theme of "cultural transfer," Hertz advertises in the United States that it is ready to serve its U.S. customers who are anticipating traveling in Europe. Hertz promises the American traveler the same high-quality service that they are used to in the United States, which should substantially reduce the uncertainty of renting a car in Europe (Figure 14-1).

FIGURE 14-1

Hertz Appeals to the U.S. Traveler Planning to Visit Europe in This 1998 Advertisement

In Europe, the one face you'll always recognize.

Hertz. The name you can trust no matter where you go.

Whether you're traveling to Brussels or Berlin, enjoy the peace of mind knowing that Hertz is there, just like at home.

And knowing English is spoken at each of our 2,000-plus locations in Europe, there's no need to phone home for directions or help, because we already speak your language. Call your travel agent or Hertz at **1-800-654-3001** for reservations or details. Or stop by our website at **www.hertz.com**. Hertz in Europe, another reason nobody does it exactly like Hertz.

Hertz europe

Hertz rents Fords and other fine cars.
® REG. U.S. PAT. OFF. © HERTZ SYSTEM INC., 1998/012-98

COUNTRY-OF-ORIGIN EFFECTS

When consumers are making purchase decisions, they may take into consideration the countries of origin of their choices. Researchers have shown that consumers use their knowledge of where products are made in the evaluation of their purchase options.[7] Such a "country-of-origin" effect seems to come about because consumers are often aware that a particular firm or brand name is associated with a particular country (as Rolls Royce and Bentley are associated with England and Nikon is associated with Japan). In general, many consumers associate France with wine, perfume, and clothing (see Figure 14-2); Italy with fine designer clothing, furniture, shoes, and sports cars;

FIGURE 14-2
The Importance of Country of Origin

CHAMPS-ELYSEES

GUERLAIN
PARIS

Japan with cameras and consumer electronics; and Germany with cars, tools, and machinery.[8] Moreover, consumers tend to have an *attitude* or even a preference when it comes to a particular product being made in a particular country. This attitude might be positive, negative, or neutral, depending on perceptions or experience. For instance, a consumer in one country might positively value a particular product made in another country (for example, affluent American consumers may feel that Italian shoes or Louis Vuitton luggage from France are worthwhile investments). In contrast, another consumer might be negatively influenced when he learns that a VCR he is looking at in a store is made in a country he does not associate with fine electronics (such as a VCR from any country other than Japan). Such "country-of-origin" effects influence how consumers rate quality and which brands they will ultimately select.[9]

In addition to perceptions of a product's attributes based upon its country of manufacture, research evidence exists that some consumers may refrain from purchasing products from particular countries due to animosity. A recent study of this issue found that *high-animosity consumers* in the People's Republic of China owned fewer Japanese products than *low-animosity consumers* (during World War II, Japan occupied parts of China). Although some Chinese consumers might consider Sony to be a high-end, high-quality brand (or perceptions of the product itself might be very positive), they might nevertheless refuse to bring a product manufactured in Japan into the home. Similarly, some Jewish consumers might avoid purchasing German-made products due to the Holocaust, and some New Zealand and Australian consumers might boycott French products due to France's nuclear tests in the South Pacific.[10]

CROSS-CULTURAL CONSUMER ANALYSIS

To determine whether and how to enter a foreign market, marketers need to conduct some form of **cross-cultural consumer analysis**. Within the scope of this discussion, cross-cultural consumer analysis is defined as the effort to determine to what extent the consumers of two or more nations are similar or different. Such analyses can provide marketers with an understanding of the psychological, social, and cultural characteristics of the foreign consumers they wish to target, so that they can design effective marketing strategies for the specific national markets involved.

In a broader context, cross-cultural consumer analysis might also include a comparison of subcultural groups (see chapter 13) within a single country (such as English and French Canadians, Cuban Americans and Mexican Americans in the United States, or Protestants and Catholics in Northern Ireland). For our purposes, however, we will limit our discussion of cross-cultural consumer analysis to comparisons of consumers of *different* countries.

SIMILARITIES AND DIFFERENCES AMONG PEOPLE

A major objective of cross-cultural consumer analysis is to determine how consumers in two or more societies are similar and how they are different. For instance, Table 14-1 presents the insights of two Japanese advertising executives on the difference between Japanese and American cultural traits. Such an understanding of the similarities and differences that exist between nations is critical to the multinational marketer, who must devise appropriate strategies to reach consumers in specific foreign markets. The greater the similarity between nations, the more feasible it is to use relatively similar strategies in each nation. On the other hand, if the cultural beliefs,

TABLE 14-1 Observations on the Differences between Japanese and American Cultural Traits

JAPANESE CULTURE, TRAITS	AMERICAN CULTURE, TRAITS
• Japanese language	• English language
• Homogeneous	• Diverse
• Harmony to be valued and preserved	• Fight for one's beliefs/positions
• Group, not individual, important	• Individualistic
• Ambiguous	• Clearcut
• General	• Specific
• Unspoken agreement	• Get the facts straight
• Hold back emotions in public	• Display emotions in public
• Process-oriented	• Result-oriented
• Fun-oriented	• Humor-oriented
• Make a long story short	• Make a short story long
• Nonverbal communication important	• Verbal communication important
• Interested in who is speaking	• Interested in what is spoken

Source: Hideo Ishikawa and Koich Naganuma, "Exploring Differences in Japanese, U.S. Culture," *Advertising Age*, September 18, 1995, 1–8. Reprinted with permission from the September 18, 1995 issue of *Advertising Age*. Copyright 1995 by Crain Communications.

values, and customs of specific target countries are found to differ widely, then a highly *individualized* marketing strategy is indicated for each country. To illustrate, the management of the Discovery Channel (the cable TV channel) found, in their effort to bring the correct programming to viewers in specific countries, that they should emphasize history and architecture in Mexico; military technology in China and Brazil; a do-it-yourself series in Russia; and science and technology in Australia.[11]

A firm's success in marketing a product or service in a number of foreign countries is likely to be influenced by how similar the beliefs, values, and customs are that govern the use of the product in the various countries. For example, the worldwide TV commercials of major international airlines (American Airlines, Continental Airlines, Air France, Lufthansa, SAS, Sabena, Swissair, United Airlines, and US Airways/British Airways) tend to depict the luxury and pampering offered their business-class and first-class international travelers. The reason for its general cross-cultural appeal is that it speaks to the same type of individual worldwide—the upscale international business traveler—who share much in common.

Time Effects

When American businesspeople start dealing with their counterparts in other countries, one of the first things they must realize is that the pace of life differs from one nation to another. For example, whereas the average children's birthday party in the United States lasts approximately 2 hours, Brazilians are willing to wait a little more than 2 hours for a late arriver to show up at a birthday party. Consequently, Brazilians are still waiting for guests to arrive as parents of American children are coming to take their kids home. Interestingly, in contrast to the United States, fewer Brazilians wear watches.[12]

How time is spent on the job is also an issue that varies from country to country. In the United States, about 80 percent of work time is spent on the task and perhaps 20 percent is used for social activities. But in countries like India and Nepal, the balance is closer to 50 percent on each; and in Japan, social time, such as having tea with peers in the middle of the day, is considered to be a part of work.[13] Research on pace of life in 31 countries (basing overall pace on how long pedestrians take to walk 60

TABLE 14-2 The Pace of Life in 31 Countries

SPEED IS RELATIVE
(rank of 31 countries for overall pace of life and for three measures: minutes downtown pedestrians take to walk 60 feet; minutes it takes a postal clerk to complete a stamp-purchase transaction; and accuracy in minutes of public clocks)

	OVERALL PACE	WALKING 60 FEET	POSTAL SERVICE	PUBLIC CLOCK
Switzerland	1	3	2	1
Ireland	2	1	3	11
Germany	3	5	1	8
Japan	4	7	4	6
Italy	5	10	12	2
England	6	4	9	13
Sweden	7	13	5	7
Austria	8	23	8	3
Netherlands	9	2	14	25
Hong Kong	10	14	6	14
France	11	8	18	10
Poland	12	12	15	8
Costa Rica	13	16	10	15
Taiwan	14	18	7	21
Singapore	15	25	11	4
United States	16	6	23	20
Canada	17	11	21	22
South Korea	18	20	20	16
Hungary	19	19	19	18
Czech Republic	20	21	17	23
Greece	21	14	13	29
Kenya	22	9	30	24
China	23	24	25	12
Bulgaria	24	27	22	17
Romania	25	30	29	5
Jordan	26	28	27	19
Syria	27	29	28	27
El Salvador	28	22	16	31
Brazil	29	31	24	28
Indonesia	30	26	26	30
Mexico	31	17	31	26

Source: Robert Levine, "The Pace of Life in 31 Countries," *American Demographics*, November 1997, 20–29. Reprinted by permission.

feet, the minutes it takes a postal clerk to complete a stamp-purchase transaction, and the accuracy of public clocks) reveals substantial cross-cultural differences—while Switzerland had the fastest pace of life, Mexico had the slowest. Table 14-2 presents a summary of these findings.

THE GROWING GLOBAL MIDDLE CLASS

The growing middle class in developing countries is a phenomenon that is very attractive to global marketers who are often eager to identify new customers for their products. The news media has given considerable coverage to the idea that the rapidly expanding middle class in countries of Asia, South America, and Eastern Europe is based on the reality that although per capita income may be low, there is nevertheless considerable buying power in a country like China, where $1,500 of income is largely discretionary income. This means that a Chinese family with $1,500 is middle class and is a target customer for TVs, VCRs, and computers. Indeed, this same general pattern of the growing middle class has also been observed in many parts of South America, Asia, and Eastern Europe.[14]

While a growing middle class may provide a market for products like Big Macs and fries, it should always be remembered that the same product may have different meanings in different countries. For example, while a U.S. consumer wants his or her "fast food" to be fast, a Korean consumer is more likely to view a meal as a social or family-related experience. Consequently, convenient store hours may be valued more by a Korean consumer than shorter service time.[15]

ACCULTURATION IS A NEEDED MARKETING VIEWPOINT

Too many marketers, contemplating international expansion, make the strategic error of believing that "if its product is liked by local or domestic consumers, then everyone will like it." This biased viewpoint increases the likelihood of marketing failures abroad. It reflects a lack of appreciation of the unique psychological, social, cultural, and environmental characteristics of distinctly different cultures. To overcome such a narrow and culturally myopic view, marketers must also go through a kind of *acculturation process*. They must learn everything that is relevant about the usage or potential usage of their products and product categories in the foreign countries in which they plan to operate. Take the Chinese culture, for example. For Western marketers to succeed in China it is important for them to take into consideration *guo qing* (pronounced "gwor ching"), which means "to consider the special situation or character of China."[16] An example of *guo qing* for Western marketers is the Chinese policy of limiting families to one child. An appreciation of this policy means that foreign businesses will understand that Chinese families are open to particularly high-quality baby products for their single child (or "the little emperor").[17]

In a sense, cross-cultural **acculturation** is a dual process for marketers. First, marketers must thoroughly orient themselves to the values, beliefs, and customs of the new society to appropriately position and market their products (being sensitive to and consistent with traditional or prevailing attitudes and values). Second, to gain acceptance for a culturally new product in a foreign society, they must develop a strategy that encourages members of that society to modify or even break with their own traditions (to change their attitudes and possibly alter their behavior). To illustrate the point, a social marketing effort designed to encourage consumers in developing nations to secure polio vaccinations for their children would require a two-step acculturation process. First, the marketer must obtain an in-depth picture of a society's present attitudes and customs with regard to preventive medicine and related concepts. Then, the marketer must devise promotional strategies that will convince the members of a target market to have their children vaccinated, even if doing so requires a change in current attitudes.

Two other examples are useful. According to Gillette, the shaving industry giant, only about 30 percent of European women "wet shave," as compared to 75 percent of U.S. women. And in some European nations, like Spain and Italy, women wanting to remove hair go to waxing salons, rather than shaving themselves with a razor. So, not only do many European women feel that it is unnecessary to remove hair, but many of those who do believe in hair removal do not view shaving as the preferred way to do this.[18] Such insights are a necessary prerequisite to identifying a strategy that encourages European women to consider shaving as means of removing unwanted hair. And then there is Tambrands, the maker of Tampax tampons. One of this company's greatest challenges is addressing certain religious and cultural mores that suggest that the use of this product results in a violation of the body. In order for Tambrands to market effectively in countries like Brazil, it must effectively address this issue.[19]

Distinctive Characteristics of Cross-Cultural Analysis

It is often difficult for a company planning to do business in foreign countries to undertake **cross-cultural consumer research**. For instance, it is difficult in the Islamic countries of the Middle East to conduct Western-style market research. In Saudi Arabia it is illegal to stop people on the streets, and focus groups are impractical, because most gatherings of four or more people (with the exception of family and religious gatherings) are outlawed.[20] American firms desiring to do business in Russia have found a limited amount of information regarding consumer and market statistics. Similarly, marketing research information on China is generally inadequate, and surveys that ask personal questions arouse suspicion. So marketers have tried others ways to elicit the data they need. For example, Grey Advertising has given cameras to Chinese children so they can take pictures of what they like and don't like, rather than having to explain it to a stranger; A.C. Nielsen conducts focus groups in pubs and children's playrooms, rather than in conference rooms; and Leo Burnett has sent researchers to China to simply "hang out" with consumers.[21]

Applying Research Techniques

Although the same basic research techniques used to study domestic consumers are useful in studying consumers in foreign lands (see chapter 2), in cross-cultural analysis an additional burden exists, because language and word usage often differ from nation to nation. Another issue in international marketing research concerns scales of measurement. In the United States, a 5- or 7-point scale may be adequate, but in other countries, a 10- or even 20-point scale may be needed. Still further, research facilities, such as telephone interviewing services, may or may not be available in particular countries or areas of the world (Table 14-3).

TABLE 14-3 The Feasibility of Consumer Telephone Research in Asia

COUNTRY	FEASIBILITY
Australia	yes
China, Mainland	no, but within five years in big cities
Hong Kong	yes, best method by far
India	yes, for big cities and in English
Indonesia	yes, in Java, Bali, and Sumatra
Japan	yes
South Korea	yes
Malaysia	yes, Peninsula
New Zealand	yes
Philippines	yes
Singapore	yes
Taiwan	yes
Thailand	yes
Vietnam	no

Source: Bjorn Huysman, "Telephone Research in Asia—The Wave of the Future?" *Quirks Marketing Research Review* 12 (November 1998): 35. Reprinted by permission.

TABLE 14-8 Six Global Consumer Market Segments

SEGMENT NAME	GLOBAL SIZE	DESCRIPTION
Strivers	23%	Value wealth, status, ambition, and power, and products like cellular telephones and computers. They consider material things extremely important.
Devouts	22%	Have more traditional values, like faith, duty, obedience, and respect for elders. Least involved with the media and least likely to want Western brands. Concentrated in the Mideast, Africa, and Asia.
Altruists	18%	Very outer focused—interested in social issues and causes. Generally well educated, older (median age 44), and more female than the norm. Found in Russia and Latin America.
Intimates	15%	These are "people people," and focus on relationships close to home, such as spouses, significant others, family, and friends. Often found in England, Hungary, the Netherlands, and the U.S. Very heavy users of media—gives them something to talk about to others.
Fun Seekers	12%	The youngest group. They value excitement, adventure, pleasure, and looking good, and spend time at bars, clubs, and restaurants. The group loves electronic media and is more global in its lifestyle, especially in music.
Creatives	10%	Dedicated to technology, knowledge, and learning, and are the highest consumers of media, especially books, magazines, and newspapers. Members of this group are global trendsetters in owning and using a PC and in surfing the Web.

Source: Stuart Elliott, "Research Finds Consumers Worldwide Belong to Six Basic Groups That Cross National Lines," *New York Times*, 25 June 1998, D8. Copyright ©1998 The New York Times. Reprinted by permission.

TABLE 14-9 Eight Socioeconomic-Psychographic Segments of the Latin-American Market

BEYOND NATIONAL BOUNDARIES Gallup's eight socioeconomic segments of Latin-American consumers:

EMERGING PROFESSIONAL ELITE

14% of total; occupies top professional executive positions:
- 51% graduated from university or technical college.
- 55% are married.
- 98% have color TV; 96%, VCR; 97%, car; 98%, credit card; 90%, vacuum cleaner.

TRADITIONAL ELITE

11%; almost half in top professional, executive positions:
- 53% finished secondary education.
- 54% married.
- All have color TV; 91%, VCR; 89%, car; 60%, credit card; 60%, vacuum cleaner.

PROGRESSIVE UPPER-MIDDLE CLASS

13%; 36% in top or middle management:
- 75% studied beyond primary education, 30% studied beyond secondary school.
- 48% married.
- 99% have a color TV; 77%, VCR; 74%, car; 31%, credit card; 30%, vacuum cleaner.

SELF-MADE MIDDLE CLASS

11%; skills gained through entrepreneurship:
- Most ended education with primary school, "virtually none" went beyond secondary school.
- Half married.
- 98% have color TV; 72%, VCR; 81%, car; 46%, credit card; 51%, vacuum cleaner.

SKILLED MIDDLE CLASS

9%; 45% have top operational jobs, 14% own small businesses:
- 60% completed secondary education; 18% completed university or technical college.
- Half married.
- 96% have color TV; 60%, VCR; 28%, car, 29%, credit card; 32%, vacuum cleaner.

SELF-SKILLED LOWER-MIDDLE CLASS

13%; 58% employed in operational jobs:
- 42% went beyond primary school, 11% went beyond secondary education.
- Half married.
- 97% have color TV; 50%, VCR; 4%, car; 8%, credit card; none, vacuum cleaner.

INDUSTRIAL WORKING CLASS

14%; a third are in skilled worker positions and another third in average operational jobs:
- 16% went beyond secondary school, 26% completed secondary, 35% completed primary.
- 57% married.
- 92% have color TV; 13%, VCR; 5%, credit card; 15%, vacuum cleaner.

STRUGGLING WORKING CLASS

15%; most in operational, skilled and unskilled jobs:
- 29% completed primary school, 24% completed secondary school.
- 53% married.
- 63% have color TV; no more than 10% have VCR, car, credit card, or vacuum cleaner.

Source: Jeffrey D. Zbar, "Gallup Offers New Take on Latin America," *Advertising Age*, November 13, 1995, 21. Reprinted with permission from the November 13, 1995 issue of Advertising Age. Copyright 1995 by Crain Communications.

ket. The following examples of some international marketing blunders illustrate that failure to adapt marketing strategy to the target market's distinctive cultural traits can lead to costly mistakes.

PRODUCT PROBLEMS

International marketers frequently neglect to modify their products to meet local customs and tastes. American marketers who sell food products in Japan frequently learn the hard way (through poor sales performance) that they must alter traditional product characteristics. For example, Snapple failed to sustain sales momentum in Japan because consumers preferred clearer, less sweet iced tea. It appears that Snapple was either unwilling or too slow to alter its ingredients to conform to local Japanese tastes.[37] Kellogg's, the giant cereal company, has attempted to avoid the numerous "cultural traps" that are associated with cross-cultural marketing of foodstuff in its international expansion. It has learned to draw careful distinctions between the Irish, who consume 17 pounds of cereal per person per year (the highest rate in the world), and the French, Italians, and Greeks, whose meager breakfasts tend not to include cereal.[38] Indeed, a recent article discussing Kellogg's attempt to market cereals in Europe was titled "Europe Is Deaf to Snap! Crackle! Pop!" The story did note that some European Moms were purchasing cereal for their children, and that cultural changes on the Continent might make bigger breakfasts essential.[39]

Still another example showed that when Oreos were introduced in Japan, Nabisco reduced the amount of sugar in the cookie batter (the box promoted them as having a "bitter twist") to meet Japanese tastes. However, some Japanese consumers still considered them too sweet and told the company that they "just wanted to eat the base" without the cream. Nabisco belatedly introduced new Petit Oreo Non-Cream cookies that consisted of single wafers without the cream.[40] To avoid such problems, marketers must ascertain in advance whether the physical characteristics of their products will be acceptable to the new market. When IKEA opened its first store in the Philadelphia area, it sold European-sized curtains that did not fit American windows. The founder of IKEA once remarked, jokingly, that "Americans just won't lower their ceilings to fit our curtains."[41]

Color is also a critical variable in international marketing, because the same color often has different meanings in different cultures. For example, consider the color blue. In Holland, it stands for warmth; in Iran, it represents death; in Sweden, it connotes coldness; in India, it means purity. Furthermore, yellow, which represents warmth in the United States, connotes infidelity in France.[42] Pepsodent erred when it tried to sell its toothpaste in Southeast Asia by promising white teeth. In that part of the world, chewing betel nuts is considered an elite habit and, consequently, brownish-red teeth are viewed as a status symbol. Thus, Pepsodent's slogan, "You'll wonder where the yellow went," did not help to sell the product.[43] It is critical that the colors of products and packages convey the proper meaning in the countries in which they are marketed. For example, just before an American necktie manufacturer shipped its first order to Japan, their customer asked about the color of the gift boxes. When told they were white, the Japanese customer requested red. In Japan, the color white is associated with death.[44]

PROMOTIONAL PROBLEMS

When communicating with consumers in different parts of the world, the promotional message must be consistent with the language and customs of the particular target society. International marketers have faced various problems in communicating with widely different customer groups. For example, the 7-Up Company's highly successful "uncola" theme, developed for the U.S. market, was considered inappropriate for many foreign markets because it did not translate well into other languages. Similarly, learning from earlier mistakes, multinational firms like P&G and Ford now work harder to be responsive to particular tastes and values of local markets. For instance, they recently withdrew their sponsorship of television programming in some countries when the sex and violence of the shows were judged to be too strong.[45]

Product names and promotional phrases can also cause considerable problems for international marketers. The word *clock* in Chinese sounds like the word *death*. The Chevrolet Nova did not sell well in Latin America because in Spanish the words *no va* mean "It doesn't run." GM also blundered with its "body by Fisher" tag line, which in Flemish translates into "corpse by Fisher." The U.S. government made a miscalculation when it moved to drop the word *North* from North American Free Trade Agreement (or to move from NAFTA to AFTA) so as to make it more inclusive. The trouble began when Brazil pointed out that in Portuguese "AFTA" sounded like the words that mean "an open mouth sore."[46]

Consider some other examples of recent cross-cultural blunders:

- A soft-drink company attempted to translate its popular Western slogan into Chinese. The resulting translation informed consumers that if they drank the soft drink, their ancestors would come out of their graves.[47]
- The Rolls Royce Silver Mist is called the Silver Shadow in Germany, because mist in German means manure.[48]
- Reebok named a women's running shoe the *Incubus*, which in one of the countries in which the shoe was being sold translated into "a monster that rapes women in their sleep."[49]
- Japan's number-one cosmetic maker, Shiseido, is a name that "is unpronounceable for Americans and hard to remember."[50]
- A U.S. baby care company advertising in Hungary showed a young woman holding her baby. But to the people of Hungary, the mother was unwed, because her wedding ring was on her left hand. Hungarians wear their wedding bands on their right hand.[51]

PRICING AND DISTRIBUTION PROBLEMS

International marketers must adjust their pricing and distribution policies to meet local economic conditions and customs. For instance, in many developing nations, small-sized product packages often are a necessity, because consumers cannot afford the cash outlay required for the larger sizes popular in the United States and other affluent countries. Even in developed nations, important differences do exist. For example, supermarkets are very popular in Switzerland, but in France, which is just across the border, consumers prefer smaller and more intimate stores for grocery shopping.

It should also be remembered that what Americans view as "low-cost" may not be viewed similarly in other countries. For example, the U.S. fast-food franchises that operate in Mexico, such as Burger King, Wendy's, and McDonalds, are all considered upscale to the Mexican consumer. When Taco Bell tried to enter the Mexican market, it found that its taco prices were much higher than the standard Mexican taco (10 pesos versus 3 pesos). Moreover, what Taco Bell considered to be a taco was more in line with what Mexican consumers would call a burrito.[52]

Japan's traditional distribution system differs from the United States in that a close, complex relationship exists among the larger Japanese manufacturers and their distributors and retailers. For example, it took 24 years from the time Japan allowed the introduction of United States apples, until they actually reached the marketplace where Japanese consumers could buy them.[53] Thus, marketers must vary their distribution channels by nation.

SUMMARY

With so much diversity present among the members of just one nation (as in the United States), it is easy to appreciate that numerous larger differences may exist between citizens of different nations having different cultures, values, beliefs, and languages. If international marketers are to satisfy the needs of consumers in potentially very distinct markets effectively, they must understand the relevant similarities and differences that exist between the peoples of the countries they decide to target.

When consumers make purchase decisions, they seem to take into consideration the countries of origin of the brands that they are assessing. Consumers frequently have specific attitudes or even preferences for products made in particular countries. These "country-of-origin" effects influence how consumers rate quality and, sometimes, which brands they will ultimately select.

As increasing numbers of consumers from all over the world come in contact with the material goods and lifestyle of people living in other countries and as the number of middle-class consumers grows in developing countries, marketers are eager to locate these new customers and to offer them their products. The rapidly expanding middle class in countries of Asia, South America, and Eastern Europe possess relatively substantial buying power because their incomes are largely discretionary (for necessities like housing and medical care are often provided by the state at little or no cost).

For some international marketers, acculturation is a dual process: First, marketers must learn everything that is relevant to the product and product category in the society in which they plan to market, then they must persuade the members of that society to break with their traditional ways of doing things to adopt the new product. The more similar a foreign target market is to a marketer's home market, the easier is the process of acculturation. Conversely, the more different a foreign target market, the more difficult the process of acculturation.

Some of the problems involved in cross-cultural analysis include differences in language, consumption patterns, needs, product usage, economic and social conditions, marketing conditions, and market research opportunities. There is an urgent need for more systematic and conceptual cross-cultural analyses of the psychological, social, and cultural characteristics concerning the consumption habits of foreign consumers. Such analyses would identify increased marketing opportunities that would benefit both international marketers and their targeted consumers.

DISCUSSION QUESTIONS

1. Will the elimination of trade barriers among the countries of the European Union change consumer behavior in these countries? How can U.S. companies take advantage of the economic opportunities emerging in Europe?

2. With all the problems facing companies that go global, why are so many companies choosing to expand internationally? What are the advantages of expanding beyond the domestic market?

3. Are the cultures of the world becoming more similar or more different? Discuss.

4. What is cross-cultural consumer analysis? How can a multinational company use cross-cultural research to design each factor in its marketing mix? Illustrate your answer with examples.

5. What are the advantages and disadvantages of global promotional strategies?

6. Should Head & Shoulders shampoo be sold worldwide with the same formulation? In the same package? With the same advertising theme? Explain your answers.

7. a. If you wanted to name a new product that would be acceptable to consumers throughout the world, what cultural factors would you consider?
   b. What factors might inhibit an attempt by Apple to position a new laptop computer as a "world brand"?

8. An American company is introducing a line of canned soups in Poland. (a) How should the company use cross-cultural research? (b) Should the company use the same marketing mix it uses in the United States to target Polish consumers? (c) Which, if any, marketing mix components should be designed specifically for marketing canned soups in Poland? Explain your answers.

9. Mercedes-Benz, a German car manufacturer, is using cross-cultural psychographic segmentation to develop marketing campaigns for a new two-seater sports car directed at consumers in different countries. How should the company market the car in the United States? How should it market the car in Japan?

10. What advice would you give to an American retailer who wants to sell women's clothing in Japan?

11. Select two of the marketing mistakes discussed in the text. Discuss how these mistakes could have been avoided if the companies involved had adequately researched some of the issues listed in Table 14-4.

EXERCISES

1. Have you ever traveled outside the United States? If so, please identify some of the differences in values, behavior, and consumption patterns you noted between people in a country you visited and Americans.

2. Interview a student from another culture about his or her use of: (a) credit cards, (b) fast-food restaurants, (c) shampoo, and (d) sneakers. Compare your consumption behavior to that of the person you interviewed and discuss any similarities and differences you found.

3. Much has been written about the problems at Euro Disney, the Walt Disney Company's theme park and resort complex, which opened in France in April of 1992. These difficulties were largely attributed to Disney's lack of understanding of European (particularly French) culture and the company's failure to modify its American theme-park concept to fit the preferences and customs of European visitors. Discuss how the Walt Disney Company could have used input from cross-cultural analysis in better designing and operating Euro Disney, using a computerized literature search about Euro Disney from your school's library.

4. Select one of the following countries: Mexico, Brazil, Germany, Italy, Israel, Kuwait, Japan, or Australia. Assume that a significant number of people in the country you chose would like to visit the United States and have the financial means to do so. Now, imagine you are a consultant for your state's tourism agency and that you have been charged with developing a promotional strategy to attract tourists from the country you chose. Conduct a computerized literature search of the databases in your school's library and select and read several articles about the lifestyles, customs, and consumption behavior of people in the country you chose. Prepare an analysis of the articles and, on the basis of what you read, develop a promotional strategy designed to persuade tourists from that country to visit your state.

KEY TERMS

- **Acculturation**
- **Cross-cultural consumer analysis**
- **Cross-cultural consumer research**
- **Cross-cultural psychographic segmentation**
- **European Union**
- **Global versus localized marketing**
- **Multinational strategies**
- **North American Free Trade Agreement**
- **Product standardization**
- **World brands**

NOTES

1. Thomas L. Friedman, "Big Mac II," *New York Times*, 11 December 1996, A27.
2. Douglas Lavin, "Europe Starts Spending to Sell the Euro," *Wall Street Journal*, 25 November 1997, B6.
3. Betsy McKay and Steven Gutterman, "For Ads, Russian Revolution Lives," *Advertising Age*, 7 March 1994, 40.
4. Michael H. Mescon, Courtland L. Bovée, and John V. Thill, *Business Today*, 9 ed. (Upper Saddle River, NJ: Prentice Hall, 1998), 47.
5. Juliana Koranteng, "Reebok Finds Its Second Wind as It Pursues Global Presence," *Advertising Age International* (January 1998): 18; and Alice Z. Cuneo, "Gap's 1st Global Ads Confront Dockers on a Khaki Battlefield," *Advertising Age*, 20 April 1998, 3.
6. Friedman, "Big Mac II," A27; Tara Parker-Pope, "Avon's New Calling: Selling Barbie in China," *Wall Street Journal*, 1 May 1997, B1.
7. Sharyne Merritt and Vernon Staubb, "A Cross-Cultural Exploration of Country-of-Origin Preference," in *1995 AMA Winter Educators' Proceedings*, ed. David W. Stewart and Naufel J. Vilcassim (Chicago: American Marketing Association, 1995), 380; Jill Gabrielle Klein, Richard Ettenson, and Marlene D. Morris, "The Animosity Model of Foreign Product Purchase: An Empirical Test in the People's

Republic of China," *Journal of Marketing* 62 (January 1998): 89–100.

8. Shlomo I. Lampert and Eugene D. Jaffe, "Dynamic Approach to Country-of-Origin Effect," *European Journal of Marketing*, forthcoming.

9. Israel D. Nebenzahl, Eugene D. Jaffe, and Shlomo I. Lampert, "Towards a Theory of Country Image Effect on Product Evaluation," *Management International Review* 37 (1997): 27–49.

10. Klein, Ettenson, and Morris, "The Animosity Model," 89–100.

11. Wayne Walley, "Programming Globally—with Care," *Advertising Age*, 18 September 1995, 1–14.

12. Robert Levine, "The Pace of Life in 31 Countries," *American Demographics* (November 1997): 20–29.

13. Robert Levine, "Re-Learning to Tell Time," *American Demographics* (January 1998): 20–25.

14. Chip Walker, "The Global Middle Class," *American Demographics* (September 1995): 40–46; Paula Kephart, "How Big Is the Mexican Market?" *American Demographics* (October 1995): 17–18; and Rahul Jacob, "The Big Rise," *Fortune*, 30 May 1994, 74–90.

15. Mookyu Lee and Francis M. Ulgado, "Consumer Evaluations of Fast-Food Services: A Cross-National Comparison," *The Journal of Services Marketing* 11, 1 (1997): 39–52.

16. Rick Yan, "To Reach China's Consumers, Adapt to Guo Qing," *Harvard Business Review* (September–October 1994): 66–67.

17. Kathy Chen, "Chinese Babies Are Coveted Consumers," *Wall Street Journal*, 15 May 1998, B1; and Fara Warner, "Western Markets Send Researchers to China to Plumb Consumers' Minds," *Wall Street Journal*, 28 March 1997, B5.

18. Ernest Beck, "Shaving Firms Turn to European Women," *Wall Street Journal*, 12 May 1997, B1.

19. Yumiko Ono, "Tampax Ads Address Cultural Obstacles," *Wall Street Journal*, 17 March 1997, B8.

20. Tara Parker-Pope, "Nonalcoholic Beer Hits the Spot in Mideast," *Wall Street Journal*, 6 December 1995, B1.

21. Warner, "Western Markets Send Researchers," B5.

22. Robert L. Wehling, "Even at P&G, Only 3 Brands Make Truly Global Grade So Far," *Advertising Age International* (January 1998): 8.

23. Friedman, "Big Mac II," A27.

24. Martin S. Roth, "The Effects of Culture and Socioeconomics on the Performance of Global Brand Image Strategies," *Journal of Marketing Research* 32 (1995): 163–75.

25. Yumiko Ono, "PepsiCo's Pitch in Japan Has New Twist," *Wall Street Journal*, 23 May 1997, B10.

26. Suzanne Cassidy, "Defining the Cosmo Girl: Check Out the Passport," *New York Times*, 12 October 1992, D8.

27. Sharon Shavitt, Michelle R. Nelson, and Rose Mei Len Yuan, "Exploring Cross-Cultural Differences in Cognitive Responding to Ads," in *Advances in Consumer Research*, vol. 24, ed. Merrie Brucks and Deborah J. MacInnis (Provo, UT: Association for Consumer Research, 1997), 245–50.

28. Michael A. Callow, Dawn B. Lerman, and Mayo de Juan Vigaray, "Motivational Appeals in Advertising: A Comparative Content Analysis of United States and Spanish Advertising," in *Proceedings of the Sixth Symposium on Cross-Cultural Consumer and Business Studies*, ed. Scott M. Smith (Honolulu, HI: 1997), 392–96.

29. Dean Foster, "Playing with China Dollars," *BrandWeek*, 10 November 1997, 20–23.

30. Robert Frank, "Potato Chips to Go Global—or So Pepsi Bets," *Wall Street Journal*, 30 November 1995, B1.

31. Teresa Domzal and Lynette Unger, "Emerging Positioning Strategies in Global Marketing," *Journal of Consumer Marketing* 4 (Fall 1987): 27–29.

32. David Kirkpatrick, "Europe's Technology Gap Is Getting Scary," *Fortune*, 17 March 1997, 26–27.

33. Jack Russel, "Working Women Give Japan Culture Shock," *Advertising Age*, 16 January 1995, 1–24.

34. Sidney J. Levy, "Myth and Meaning in Marketing," in *1974 Combined Proceedings*, ed. Ronald C. Curhan (Chicago: American Marketing Association, 1975), 555–56.

35. Stuart Elliott, "Research Finds Consumers Worldwide Belong to Six Basic Groups That Cross National Lines," *New York Times*, 25 June 1998, D8.

36. Jeffrey D. Zbar, "Gallup Offers New Take on Latin America," *Advertising Age*, 13 November 1995, 21.

37. Norihiko Shirouzu, "Snapple in Japan: Splash Dried Up," *Wall Street Journal*, 15 April 1996, B1, B6.

38. John Tagliabue, "Spoon-to-Spoon Combat Overseas," *New York Times*, 7 January 1995, 17.

39. Ernest Beck and Rekha Balu, "Europe Is Deaf to Snap! Crackle! Pop!" *Wall Street Journal*, 22 June 1998, B1, B2.

40. Yumiko Ono, "Some Kids Won't Eat the Middle of an Oreo," *Wall Street Journal*, 20 November 1991, B1.

41. Julia Flynn and Lori Bongiorno, "IKEA's New Game Plan," *Business Week*, 6 October 1997, 99–102.

42. Linda J. Coleman, Ernest F. Cooke, and Chandra M. Kochunny, "What Is Meant by Global Marketing?" in *Developments in Marketing Science*, ed. J. M. Hawes and G. B. Gilsan (Akron, OH: Academy of Marketing Science, 1987), 10, 178.

43. Ibid., 179.

44. Toddi Gutner, "Never Give a Mandarin a Clock, and Other Rules," *Business Week*, 9 December 1996, 192.

45. Deborah Klosky, "Spanish Viewership Cries 'Foul' on Lurid TV," *Advertising Age*, 17 April 1995, 1–20.

46. David E. Sanger, "An Epidemic Adverted: Foot-in-Mouth Disease," *New York Times*, 11 December 1994, 22.

47. Dean Foster, "Playing with China Dollars," *BrandWeek*, 10 November 1997, 20–23.

48. Cacilie Rohwedder, "Name-Finders Save New Products from Fiascoes in Global Market," *Wall Street Journal*, 11 April 1996, B8.

49. Kay Stout, "Thinking Global?" *BrandWeek*, 3 March 1997, 22–25.

50. Norihiko Shirouzu, "How One Woman Is Shaking Up Shiseido," *Wall Street Journal*, 19 May 1997, B1, B7.

51. Tara Parker-Pope, "Ad Agencies Are Stumbling in East Europe," *Wall Street Journal*, 10 May 1996, B1, B5.

52. Gustavo Mendex-Kuhn, "MEXICO: What Bell?" *BrandWeek*, 5 May 1997, 26.

53. Lisa A. Petrison, Masaru Ariga, and Paul Wang, "Strategies for Penetrating the Japanese Market," *Journal of Direct Marketing* 8 (Winter 1994): 44–58; and Sheryl WuDunn, "Japan Tastes Once-Forbidden Fruit," *New York Times*, 11 January 1995, A3.

PART 4

THE CONSUMER'S DECISION-MAKING PROCESS

Chapter 15 begins with a discussion of a personal influence, opinion leadership, and the diffusion of innovations. The final chapter examines in detail a simple model of consumer decision making that ties together the psychological, social, and cultural concepts examined throughout the book. The book concludes with a discussion of various related aspects of consumption behavior (such as gift giving) and explores the outcomes of relationship marketing from the consumer's perspective.

PART 4 EXPLORES THE VARIOUS ASPECTS OF CONSUMER DECISION MAKING.

CHAPTER 15
Consumer Influence and the Diffusion of Innovations

■ ■

This chapter deals with two interrelated issues of considerable importance to consumers and marketers alike—the informal influence that others have on consumers' behavior and the dynamic processes that impact consumers' acceptance of new products and services.

In the first part of this chapter we will examine the nature and dynamics of the influence that friends, neighbors, and acquaintances have on our consumer-related decisions. This influence is often called *word-of-mouth communications* or the *opinion leadership process* (the two terms will be used interchangeably here). We will also consider the personality and motivations of those who influence (opinion leaders) and those who are influenced (opinion receivers). In the second part of this chapter, we will explore factors that encourage and discourage acceptance (or rejection) of new products and services. For consumers, new products and services may represent increased opportunities to satisfy personal, social, and environmental needs and add to their quality of life. For the marketer, new products and services provide an important mechanism for keeping the firm competitive and profitable.

■■■■ WHAT IS OPINION LEADERSHIP?

The power and importance of personal influence is captured in the following comment by an ad agency executive: "Perhaps the most important thing for marketers to understand about word of mouth is its huge potential economic impact."[1]

Opinion leadership (or word-of-mouth communications) is the process by which one person (the opinion leader) informally influences the actions or attitudes of others, who may be opinion seekers or merely opinion recipients. The key characteristic of the influence is that it is interpersonal and informal and takes place between two or more people, none of whom represents a commercial selling source that would gain directly from the sale of something. Word of mouth implies personal, or face-to-face, communication, although it may also take place in a telephone conversation or within the context of a chat group on the Internet. This communication process is likely, at times, to also be reinforced by nonverbal observations of the appearance and behavior of others.

One of the parties in a word-of-mouth encounter usually offers advice or information about a product or service, such as which of several brands is best or how a particular product may be used. This person, the **opinion leader**, may become an **opinion receiver** when another product or service is brought up as part of the discussion.

Individuals who actively seek information and advice about products sometimes are called **opinion seekers**. For purposes of simplicity, the terms *opinion receiver* and *opinion recipient* will be used interchangeably in the following discussion to identify both those who actively seek product information from others and those who receive unsolicited information. Simple examples of opinion leadership at work include the following:

1. During lunch, a coworker mentions the desire to purchase a car, and the colleague recommends a particular brand.
2. A person shows a friend photographs of his recent skiing vacation, and the friend suggests that a different type of film might produce better pictures of outdoor scenery.
3. A woman who recently moved into a new house wants more light in her family room and calls her neighbor for the name of "a good electrician."

Most studies of opinion leadership are concerned with the measurement of the behavioral impact that opinion leaders have on the consumption habits of others. Available research, for example, suggests that "influentials" or opinion leaders are almost four times more likely than others to be asked about political and government issues, as well as how to handle teens; three times more likely to be asked about computers or investments; and twice as likely to be asked about health issues and restaurants.[2] There is also research to suggest that when an information seeker feels that he or she knows little about a particular product or service, a strong-tie source will be sought (such as a friend or family member), but when the consumer has some prior knowledge of the subject area, then a weak-tie source is acceptable (acquaintances or strangers).[3]

▪▪▪▪ DYNAMICS OF THE OPINION LEADERSHIP PROCESS

The opinion leadership process is a very dynamic and powerful consumer force. As informal communication sources, opinion leaders are remarkably effective at influencing consumers in their product-related decisions. Some of the reasons for the effectiveness of opinion leaders are discussed below.

CREDIBILITY

Opinion leaders are highly credible sources of information because they usually are perceived as objective concerning the product or service information or advice they dispense. Their intentions are perceived as being in the best interests of the opinion recipients because they receive no compensation for the advice and apparently have no "ax to grind." Because opinion leaders often base their product comments on firsthand experience, their advice reduces for opinion receivers the perceived risk or anxiety inherent in buying new products.

POSITIVE AND NEGATIVE PRODUCT INFORMATION

Information provided by marketers is invariably favorable to the product. Thus, the very fact that opinion leaders provide both favorable and unfavorable information adds to their credibility. An example of an unfavorable or negative product comment is, "The problem with those little subnotebook computers is that they have external disk drives that you have to stop and hook up." Compared with positive or even neutral comments, negative comments are relatively uncommon. For this reason, consumers are especially likely to note such information and to avoid products or brands that receive negative evaluations.

INFORMATION AND ADVICE

Opinion leaders are the source of both information and advice. They may simply talk about their *experience* with a product, relate what they know about a product, or, more aggressively, *advise* others to buy or to avoid a specific product. The kinds of product or service information that opinion leaders are likely to transmit during a conversation include the following:

1. *Which of several brands is best*:
   "In my opinion, Nike sneakers are the best sneakers you can buy."
2. *How to best use a specific product*:
   "I find that my car runs best when I add a can of fuel injector cleaner to the gas tank every three months."
3. *Where to shop*:
   "When Nordstrom's has a sale, the values are terrific."
4. *Who provides the best service*:
   "Over the last 10 years, I've called Sal's Appliance Repair every time I've had a problem, and I think their service can't be beat."

OPINION LEADERSHIP IS CATEGORY-SPECIFIC

Opinion leadership tends to be *category-specific*; that is, opinion leaders often "specialize" in certain product categories about which they offer information and advice. When other product categories are discussed, however, they are just as likely to reverse their roles and become opinion receivers. A person who is considered particularly knowledgeable about tennis equipment may be an opinion leader in terms of this subject, yet when it comes to purchasing a car, the same person may seek advice from someone else—perhaps even from someone who has sought his advice on tennis rackets.

OPINION LEADERSHIP IS A TWO-WAY STREET

As the preceding example suggests, consumers who are opinion leaders in one product-related situation may become opinion receivers in another situation, even for the same product. Consider the following example. Burt, a new homeowner contemplating the purchase of a snowblower, may seek information and advice from other people to reduce his indecision about which brand to select. Once the snowblower has been bought, however, he may experience postpurchase dissonance (see chapter 8) and have a compelling need to talk favorably about the purchase to other people to confirm the correctness of his own choice. In the first instance, he is an opinion receiver (seeker); in the second, he assumes the role of opinion leader.

An opinion leader may also be influenced by an opinion receiver as the result of a product-related conversation. For example, a person may tell a friend about a favorite hotel getaway in Cozumel, Mexico, and, in response to comments from the opinion receiver, come to realize that the hotel is too small, too isolated, and offers vacationers fewer amenities than other hotels.

▪▪▪▪ THE MOTIVATION BEHIND OPINION LEADERSHIP

To understand the phenomenon of opinion leadership, it is useful to examine the motivation of those who provide and those who receive product-related information.

THE NEEDS OF OPINION LEADERS

What motivates a person to talk about a product or service? Motivation theory suggests that people may provide information or advice to others to satisfy some basic need of their own (see chapter 4). However, opinion leaders may be unaware of their own underlying motives. As suggested earlier, opinion leaders may simply be trying to reduce their own postpurchase dissonance. For instance, if Chester buys a new satellite TV dish system and then is uncertain that he made the right choice, he may try to reassure himself by "talking up" the product's advantages to others. In this way, he relieves his own psychological discomfort. Furthermore, when he can influence a friend or neighbor to also buy that brand, he confirms his own good judgment in selecting the product first. Thus, the opinion leader's true motivation may really be self-confirmation or self-involvement. Furthermore, the information or advice that an opinion leader dispenses may provide all types of tangential personal benefits: it may confer attention, imply some type of status, grant superiority, demonstrate awareness and expertise, and give the feeling of possessing inside information and the satisfaction of "converting" less-adventurous souls.

In addition to *self*-involvement, the opinion leader may also be motivated by *product* involvement, *social* involvement, and *message* involvement. Opinion leaders who are motivated by product involvement may find themselves so pleased or so disappointed with a product that they simply must tell others about it. Those who are motivated by social involvement need to share product-related experiences. In this type of situation, opinion leaders use their product-related conversations as expressions of friendship, neighborliness, and love.

The pervasiveness of advertising in our society encourages message involvement. Individuals who are bombarded with advertising messages and slogans tend to discuss them and the products they are designed to sell. Such word-of-mouth conversation is typified by the popular use in everyday conversation of slogans such as Microsoft's "Where do you want to go today?" Nike's "Just do it!" or Chevrolet truck's "Like a rock."

THE NEEDS OF OPINION RECEIVERS

Opinion receivers satisfy a variety of needs by engaging in product-related conversations. First, they obtain new-product or new-usage information. Second, they reduce their perceived risk by receiving firsthand knowledge from a user about a specific product or brand. Third, they reduce the search time entailed in the identification of a needed product or service. Moreover, opinion receivers can be certain of receiving the approval of the opinion leader if they follow that person's product endorsement or advice and purchase the product. For all of these reasons, people often look to friends, neighbors, and other acquaintances for product information. Indeed, when a recent study examined the importance of four specific information sources on a hypothetical $100 purchase of consumer services, *advice from others* proved to be more important than the combined impact of sales representatives, advertising and promotion, and other sources.[4]

Research reveals that women and men differ with respect to the types of products and services they are likely to seek advice about. For example, whereas an approximately equal percentage of men and women will seek advice about a new doctor, where to eat out, and what movies to see, significantly more women will seek advice about where to get their hair cut (24 percent versus 10 percent for men) and what car to buy (22 percent versus 15 percent).[5] In general, women are more likely to trust the advice of other individuals, especially other women. Table 15-1 compares the motivations of opinion receivers with those of opinion leaders.

PURCHASE PALS

Researchers have also examined the influence of "purchase pals" as information sources who actually accompany consumers on shopping trips. Although purchase pals were used only 9 percent of the time for grocery items, they were used 25 percent of the time for purchases of electronic equipment (computers, VCRs, TV sets).[6] Interestingly, male purchase pals are more likely to be used as sources of product category expertise, product information, and retail store and price information. Female purchase pals are more often used for moral support and to increase confidence in the buyer's decisions. Similarly, research evidence suggests that when a weak tie exists between the purchase pal and the shopper (for instance, neighbor, classmate, or work colleague), the purchase pal's main contribution tends to be functional—the source's specific product experiences and general marketplace knowledge are being relied on. In contrast, when strong ties exist (such as mother, son, husband, or wife), what is relied on is the purchase pal's familiarity and understanding of the buyer's individual characteristics and needs (or tastes and preferences).[7]

SURROGATE BUYERS VERSUS OPINION LEADERS

While the traditional model of new product adoption shows opinion leaders influencing the purchase of many new products and services, there are instances in which surrogate buyers replace opinion leaders in this role. For example, working women are increasingly

---

TABLE 15-1 A Comparison of the Motivations of Opinion Leaders and Opinion Receivers

OPINION LEADERS	OPINION RECEIVERS
SELF-IMPROVEMENT MOTIVATIONS	
• Reduce postpurchase uncertainty or dissonance	• Reduce the risk of making a purchase commitment
• Gain attention or status	• Reduce search time (e.g., avoid the necessity of shopping around)
• Assert superiority and expertise	
• Feel like an adventurer	
• Experience the power of "converting" others	
PRODUCT-INVOLVEMENT MOTIVATIONS	
• Express satisfaction or dissatisfaction with a product or service	• Learn how to use or consume a product
	• Learn what products are new in the marketplace
SOCIAL-INVOLVEMENT MOTIVATIONS	
• Express neighborliness and friendship by discussing products or services that may be useful to others	• Buy products that have the approval of others, thereby ensuring acceptance
MESSAGE-INVOLVEMENT MOTIVATIONS	
• Express one's reaction to a stimulating advertisement by telling others about it	

TABLE 15-2 Key Differences between Opinion Leaders and Surrogate Buyers

OPINION LEADER	SURROGATE BUYER
1. Informal relationship with end-users	1. Formal relationship; occupation-related status
2. Information exchange occurs in the context of a casual interaction	2. Information exchange in the form of formal instructions/advice
3. Homophilous (to a certain extent) to end-users	3. Heterophilus to end-users (that in fact, is the source of power)
4. Does not get paid for advice	4. Usually hired, therefore gets paid
5. Usually socially more active than end-users	5. Not necessarily socially more active than end-users
6. Accountability limited regarding the outcome of advice	6. High level of accountability
7. As accountability limited, rigor in search and screening of alternatives low	7. Search and screening of alternatives more rigorous
8. Likely to have (although not always) used the product personally	8. May not have used the product for personal consumption
9. More than one can be consulted before making a final decision	9. Second opinion taken on rare occasions
10. Same person can be an opinion leader for a variety of related product categories	10. Usually specializes for a specific product/service category

Source: Praveen Aggarwal and Taihoon Cha, "Surrogate Buyers and the New Product Adoption Process: A Conceptualization and Managerial Framework," *Journal of Consumer Marketing*, 14, 5 (1997): 394.

turning to wardrobe consultants for help in purchasing business attire, most new drugs start out requiring a doctor's prescription, and many service providers make decisions for their clients (for instance, your service station decides which brand of disk brake pads to install on your car). Consequently, in an increasing number of decision situations, it is a surrogate buyer, and not an opinion leader, who primarily influences the purchase.[8] Table 15-2 presents the key differences between opinion leaders and surrogate buyers.

MEASUREMENT OF OPINION LEADERSHIP

Consumer researchers are interested in identifying and measuring the impact of the opinion leadership process on consumption behavior. In measuring opinion leadership, the researcher has a choice of four basic measurement techniques: (1) the *self-designating method*, (2) the *sociometric method*, (3) the *key informant method*, and (4) the *objective method*.

In the self-designating method, respondents are asked to evaluate the extent to which they have provided others with information about a product category or specific brand or have otherwise influenced the purchase decisions of others. Figure 15-1 shows two types of self-designating question formats that can be used to determine a consumer's opinion leadership activity. The first consists of a single question, whereas the second consists of a series of questions. The use of multiple questions enables the researcher to determine a respondent's opinion leadership more reliably, because the statements are interrelated.[9] The self-designating technique is used more often than other methods for measuring opinion leadership because consumer researchers find it easy to include in market research questionnaires. Because this method relies on the respondent's self-evaluation, however, it may be open to bias, should respondents perceive "opinion leadership" (even though the term is not used) to be a desirable characteristic and thus overestimate their own roles as opinion leaders.

present a profile of **consumer innovators**, those who are the first to purchase a new product. The ability of marketers to identify and reach this important group of consumers plays a major role in the success or failure of new-product introductions.

▪▪▪▪▪ THE DIFFUSION PROCESS

The diffusion process is concerned with how innovations spread, that is, how they are assimilated within a market. More precisely, diffusion is the process by which the acceptance of an innovation (a new product, new service, new idea, or new practice) is spread by communication (mass media, salespeople, or informal conversations) to members of a social system (a target market) over a period of time. This definition includes the four basic elements of the diffusion process: (1) the innovation, (2) the channels of communication, (3) the social system, and (4) time.

THE INNOVATION

No universally accepted definition of the terms *product* **innovation** or *new product* exists. Instead, various approaches have been taken to define a new product or a new service; these can be classified as *firm-*, *product-*, *market-*, and *consumer-oriented definitions of innovations*.

Firm-Oriented Definitions

A *firm-oriented* approach treats the newness of a product from the perspective of the company producing or marketing it. When the product is "new" to the company, it is considered *new*. This definition ignores whether or not the product is actually new to the marketplace (that is, to competitors or consumers). Consistent with this view, copies or modifications of a competitor's product would qualify as new. Although this definition has considerable merit when the objective is to examine the impact that a "new" product has on the firm, it is not very useful when the goal is to understand consumer acceptance of a new product.

Product-Oriented Definitions

In contrast to firm-oriented definitions, a *product-oriented* approach focuses on the features inherent in the product itself and on the effects these features are likely to have on consumers' established usage patterns. One product-oriented framework considers the extent to which a new product is likely to disrupt established behavior patterns. It defines the following three types of product innovations:[23]

1. A **continuous innovation** has the least disruptive influence on established patterns. It involves the introduction of a modified product, rather than a totally new product. Examples include the redesigned Honda Accord, the latest version of Microsoft Office, or reduced-fat Ritz crackers. See Figure 15-5 for a BOSE ad that reflects how the radio is even today a continuous innovation.
2. A **dynamically continuous innovation** is somewhat more disruptive than a continuous innovation but still does not alter established behavior patterns. It may involve the creation of a new product or the modification of an existing product. Examples include 8-mm camcorders, compact disc players, antilock automobile brakes, erasable-ink pens, and disposable diapers.
3. A **discontinuous innovation** requires consumers to adopt new behavior patterns. Examples include airplanes, radios, TVs, automobiles, fax machines, home computers, videocassette recorders, medical self-test kits, and the Internet.

FIGURE 15-5

The Radio as an Example
of a Continuous Innovation

Figure 15-6 shows how the telephone, a discontinuous innovation of major magnitude, has produced a variety of both dynamically continuous and continuous innovations and has even stimulated the development of other discontinuous innovations. Iridium—the world's first handheld global satellite phone and paging network—is a vivid illustration that dynamically continuous innovations are still being created for telecommunications related products and services.

Market-Oriented Definitions

A *market-oriented* approach judges the newness of a product in terms of how much exposure consumers have to the new product. Two market-oriented definitions of product innovation have been used extensively in consumer studies:

extensive problem solving. At this level, the consumer needs a great deal of information to establish a set of criteria on which to judge specific brands and a correspondingly large amount of information concerning each of the brands to be considered.

LIMITED PROBLEM SOLVING

At this level of problem solving, consumers already have established the basic criteria for evaluating the product category and the various brands in the category. However, they have not fully established preferences concerning a select group of brands. Their search for additional information is more like "fine-tuning"; they must gather additional brand information to discriminate among the various brands.

ROUTINIZED RESPONSE BEHAVIOR

At this level, consumers have some experience with the product category and a well-established set of criteria with which to evaluate the brands they are considering. In some situations, they may search for a small amount of additional information; in others, they simply review what they already know.

Just how extensive a consumer's problem-solving task is depends on how well established his or her criteria for selection are, how much information he or she has about each brand being considered, and how narrow the set of brands is from which the choice will be made. Clearly, extensive problem solving implies that the consumer must seek more information to make a choice, whereas routinized response behavior implies little need for additional information.

All decisions in our lives cannot be complex and require extensive search and consideration—we just cannot exert the level of effort required. Some decisions have to be "easy ones."

■■■■ MODELS OF CONSUMERS: FOUR VIEWS OF CONSUMER DECISION MAKING

Before presenting an overview model of how consumers make decisions, we will consider several schools of thought that depict consumer decision making in distinctly different ways. The term *models of consumers* refers to a general "view" or perspective as to how (and why) individuals behave as they do. Specifically, we will examine models of consumers in terms of the following four views: (1) an *economic view*, (2) a *passive view*, (3) a *cognitive view*, and (4) an *emotional view*.

AN ECONOMIC VIEW

In the field of theoretical economics, which portrays a world of perfect competition, the consumer has often been characterized as making rational decisions. This model, called the *economic man* theory, has been criticized by consumer researchers for a number of reasons. To behave rationally in the economic sense, a consumer would have to: (1) be aware of all available product alternatives, (2) be capable of correctly ranking each alternative in terms of its benefits and disadvantages, and (3) be able to identify the one best alternative. Realistically, however, consumers rarely have all of the information or sufficiently accurate information or even an adequate degree of involvement or motivation to make the so-called "perfect" decision.

It has been argued that the classical economic model of an all-rational consumer is unrealistic for the following reasons: (a) people are limited by their existing skills, habits, and reflexes; (b) people are limited by their existing values and goals; and (c) people are limited by the extent of their knowledge.[3] Consumers operate in an imperfect world in which they do not maximize their decisions in terms of economic considerations, such as price–quantity relationships, marginal utility, or indifference curves. Indeed, the consumer generally is unwilling to engage in extensive decision-making activities and will settle, instead, for a "satisfactory" decision, one that is "good enough."[4] For this reason, the economic model is often rejected as too idealistic and simplistic. As an example, recent research has found that consumers' primary motivation for price haggling, which was long thought to be the desire to obtain a better price (that is, better dollar value for the purchase), may instead be related to the need for achievement, affiliation, and dominance.[5]

A PASSIVE VIEW

Quite opposite to the rational economic view of consumers is the *passive* view that depicts the consumer as basically submissive to the self-serving interests and promotional efforts of marketers. In the passive view, consumers are perceived as impulsive and irrational purchasers, ready to yield to the aims and arms of marketers. At least to some degree, the passive model of the consumer was subscribed to by the hard-driving supersalespeople of old, who were trained to regard the consumer as an object to be manipulated.

The principal limitation of the passive model is that it fails to recognize that the consumer plays an equal, if not dominant, role in many buying situations—sometimes by seeking information about product alternatives and selecting the product that appears to offer the greatest satisfaction and at other times by impulsively selecting a product that satisfies the mood or emotion of the moment. All that we have studied about motivation (see chapter 4), selective perception (chapter 6), learning (chapter 7), attitudes (chapter 8), communication (chapter 9), and opinion leadership (chapter 15) serves to support the proposition that consumers are rarely objects of manipulation. Therefore, this simple and single-minded view should also be rejected as unrealistic.

A COGNITIVE VIEW

The third model portrays the consumer as a *thinking problem solver*. Within this framework, consumers frequently are pictured as either receptive to or actively searching for products and services that fulfill their needs and enrich their lives. The cognitive model focuses on the processes by which consumers seek and evaluate information about selected brands and retail outlets.

Within the context of the cognitive model, consumers are viewed as information processors. Information processing leads to the formation of preferences and, ultimately, to purchase intentions. The cognitive view also recognizes that the consumer is unlikely to even attempt to obtain all available information about every choice. Instead, consumers are likely to cease their information-seeking efforts when they perceive that they have sufficient information about some of the alternatives to make a "satisfactory" decision. As this information-processing viewpoint suggests, consumers often develop shortcut decision rules (called **heuristics**) to facilitate the decision-making process. They also use decision rules to cope with exposure to too much information (i.e., **information overload**).

The cognitive, or problem-solving, view describes a consumer who falls somewhere between the extremes of the economic and passive views, who does not (or cannot) have total knowledge about available product alternatives and therefore cannot make *perfect* decisions, but who nonetheless actively seeks information and attempts to make *satisfactory* decisions.

AN EMOTIONAL VIEW

Although long aware of the *emotional* or *impulsive* model of consumer decision making, marketers frequently prefer to think of consumers in terms of either economic or passive models. In reality, however, each of us is likely to associate deep feelings or emotions, such as joy, fear, love, hope, sexuality, fantasy, and even a little "magic," with certain purchases or possessions. These feelings or emotions are likely to be highly involving. For instance, a person who misplaces a favorite fountain pen might go to great lengths to look for it, despite the fact that he or she has six others at hand.

Possessions also may serve to preserve a sense of the past and act as familiar transitional objects when one is confronted with an uncertain future. For example, members of the armed forces invariably carry photographs of "the girl (or guy) back home," their families, and their lives in earlier times. These memorabilia frequently serve as hopeful reminders that normal activities will someday resume.

If we were to reflect on the nature of our recent purchases, we might be surprised to realize just how impulsive some of them were. Rather than carefully searching, deliberating, and evaluating alternatives before buying, we are just as likely to have made many of these purchases on impulse, on a whim, or because we were "emotionally driven."

When a consumer makes what is basically an emotional purchase decision, less emphasis is placed on the search for prepurchase information. Instead, more emphasis is placed on current mood and feelings ("Go for it!"). This is not to say that emotional decisions are not rational. As chapter 4 pointed out, buying products that afford emotional satisfaction is a perfectly rational consumer decision. Some emotional decisions are expressions that "you deserve it," or "treat yourself" (see Figure 16-1).

For instance, many consumers buy designer label clothing, not because they *look* any better in them, but because status labels make them *feel* better. This is a rational decision. Of course, if a man with a wife and three children purchases a two-seater Mazda Miata for himself, the neighbors might wonder about his level of rationality (although some might think it was deviously high). No such question would arise if the same man selected Ben & Jerry's ice cream instead of Sealtest ice cream, although in both instances, each might be an impulsive, emotional purchase decision.

Consumers' **moods** are also important to decision making. Mood can be defined as a "feeling state" or state of mind.[6] Unlike an emotion, which is a response to a particular environment, a mood is more typically an unfocused, pre-existing state—already present at the time a consumer "experiences" an advertisement, a retail environment, a brand, or a product.[7]

Mood appears to be important to consumer decision making, because it impacts on *when* consumers shop, *where* they shop, and *whether* they shop alone or with others. It also is likely to influence *how* the consumer responds to actual shopping environments (i.e., at point of purchase).[8] Some retailers attempt to create a mood for shoppers, even though shoppers enter the store with a pre-existing mood. Research suggests that a store's image or atmosphere can affect shoppers' moods; in turn, shoppers' moods can influence how long they stay in the store, as well as other behavior that retailers wish to encourage.[9]

In general, individuals in a positive mood recall more information about a product than those in a negative mood. As the results of one study suggest, however, inducing a positive mood at the point-of-purchase decision (as through background music, point-of-purchase displays, etc.) is unlikely to have a meaningful impact on specific brand choice unless a previously stored brand evaluation already exists.[10]

FIGURE 16-1
Emotional Decision May
Stress "Reward Yourself"

A MODEL OF CONSUMER DECISION MAKING

This section presents an overview model of consumer decision making (briefly introduced in chapter 1) that reflects the *cognitive* (or *problem-solving*) consumer and, to some degree, the *emotional consumer*. The model is designed to tie together many of the ideas on consumer decision making and consumption behavior discussed through-

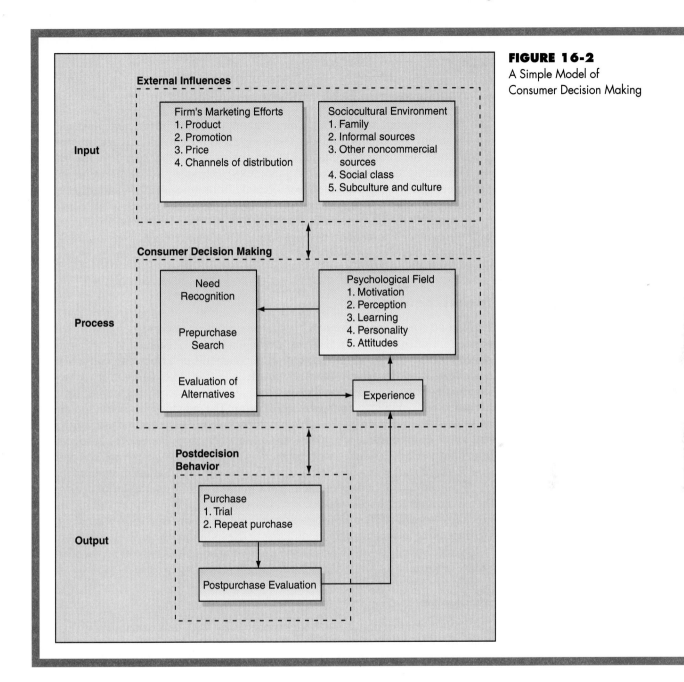

FIGURE 16-2
A Simple Model of
Consumer Decision Making

out the book. It does not presume to provide an exhaustive picture of the complexities of consumer decision making. Rather, it is designed to synthesize and coordinate relevant concepts into a significant whole. The model, presented in Figure 16-2, has three major components: input, process, and output.

INPUT

The *input* component of our consumer decision-making model draws on external influences that serve as sources of information about a particular product and influence a consumer's product-related values, attitudes, and behavior. Chief among these input factors are the *marketing mix activities* of organizations that attempt to communicate the benefits of their products and services to potential consumers and the nonmarketing *sociocultural influences*, which, when internalized, affect the consumer's purchase decisions.

Marketing Inputs

The firm's marketing activities are a direct attempt to reach, inform, and persuade consumers to buy and use its products. These inputs to the consumer's decision-making process take the form of specific marketing mix strategies that consist of the product itself (including its package, size, and guarantees); mass-media advertising, direct marketing, personal selling, and other promotional efforts; pricing policy; and the selection of distribution channels to move the product from the manufacturer to the consumer.

Ultimately, the impact of a firm's marketing efforts in large measure is governed by the consumer's perception of these efforts. Thus, marketers do well to remain diligently alert to consumer perceptions by sponsoring consumer research, rather than to rely on the *intended* impact of their marketing messages.

Sociocultural Inputs

The second type of input, the *sociocultural environment*, also exerts a major influence on the consumer. Sociocultural inputs (examined in part III) consist of a wide range of noncommercial influences. For example, the comments of a friend, an editorial in the newspaper, usage by a family member, an article in *Consumer Reports*, or the views of experienced consumers participating in a special-interest discussion group on the Internet are all noncommercial sources of information. The influences of social class, culture, and subculture, although less tangible, are important input factors that are internalized and affect how consumers evaluate and ultimately adopt (or reject) products. The unwritten codes of conduct communicated by culture subtly indicate which consumption behavior should be considered "right" or "wrong" at a particular point in time.

The cumulative impact of each firm's marketing efforts; the influence of family, friends, and neighbors; and society's existing code of behavior are all inputs that are likely to affect what consumers purchase and how they use what they buy. Because these influences may be directed to the individual or actively sought by the individual, a two-headed arrow is used to link the *input* and *process* segments of the model (Figure 16-2).

PROCESS

The *process* component of the model is concerned with how consumers make decisions. To understand this process, we must consider the influence of the psychological concepts examined in part II. The *psychological field* represents the internal influences (motivation, perception, learning, personality, and attitudes) that affect consumers' decision-making processes (what they need or want, their awareness of various product choices, their information-gathering activities, and their evaluation of alternatives). As pictured in the *process* component of the overview decision model (Figure 16-2), the act of making a consumer decision consists of three stages: (1) **need recognition**, (2) **prepurchase search**, and (3) **evaluation of alternatives**.

Need Recognition

The *recognition of a need* is likely to occur when a consumer is faced with a "problem." For example, consider the case of Steve and Charlene, a young couple with a two-year-old son. Because both Steve and Charlene want to have a "large" family, they realized that their city apartment was just too small. So they have just moved from St. Louis to a four-bedroom home (a resale) in Clayton, Missouri (a suburb of St. Louis). And since Charlene is home all day with their son while Steve is at work, the couple feels that it is very important that they have a security alarm system installed as quickly as possible.

One problem facing both Steve and Charlene is that neither grew up in a home with a security alarm system, and they are therefore unfamiliar with the functioning and range of options that such a system can provide. They know that some of their new neighbors have home security systems, because several houses on their block have either a lawn placard or a door decal that announces such protection.

The issue facing Steve and Charlene is not whether or when to purchase a home security system—they want one and they want it now. Consequently, it is fair to say that they have *recognized the need for a home security system*.

Among consumers, there seem to be two different need or problem recognition styles. Some consumers are *actual state* types, who perceive that they have a problem when a product fails to perform satisfactorily (as a cordless telephone that develops constant static). In contrast, other consumers are *desired state* types, for whom the desire for something new may trigger the decision process.[11] Steve and Charlene, in their consideration of a home security system, appear to be desired state consumers.

Prepurchase Search

Prepurchase search begins when a consumer perceives a need that might be satisfied by the purchase and consumption of a product. The recollection of past experiences (drawn from long-term memory storage) might provide the consumer with adequate information to make the present choice. On the other hand, when the consumer has had no prior experience, he or she may have to engage in an extensive search of the outside environment for useful information on which to base a choice.

The consumer usually searches his or her memory (the *psychological field* depicted in the model) before seeking external sources of information regarding a given consumption-related need. Past experience is considered an *internal* source of information. The greater the relevant past experience, the less external information the consumer is likely to need to reach a decision. Many consumer decisions are based on a combination of past experience (internal sources) and marketing and noncommercial information (external sources). The degree of perceived risk can also influence this stage of the decision process (see chapter 6). In high-risk situations, consumers are likely to engage in complex information search and evaluation; in low-risk situations, they are likely to use very simple search and evaluation tactics.

The act of "shopping" is an important form of external information. According to a recent consumer study there is a big difference between men and women in terms of their response to shopping. Whereas most men do not like to shop, most women claim to like the experience of shopping; and although the majority of women found shopping to be relaxing and enjoyable, the majority of men did not have the same response.[12] In addition to gender differences, research reveals that price considerations can also play a role in determining the extent of the search process. For instance, consumers may engage in *smart shopping*, which indicates a willingness to invest a considerable amount of time and effort to seek and use promotion-related information in order to obtain a price savings. For such consumers, this search constitutes doing your "homework" prior to making a purchase.[13]

An examination of the external search effort associated with the purchase of different product categories (TVs, VCRs, or personal computers) found that, as the amount of total search effort increased, consumer attitudes toward shopping became more positive, and more time was made available for shopping. Not surprisingly, the external search effort was greatest for consumers who had the least amount of product category knowledge.[14] It follows that the less consumers know about a product category and the more important the purchase is to them, the more time they will make available and the more extensive their prepurchase search activity is likely to be.

It is also important to point out that the Internet has had a great impact on prepurchase search. Rather than visiting a store to find out about a product or calling the manufacturer and asking for a brochure, manufacturers' Web sites can provide consumers with much of the information they need about the products and services they are considering. For example, many automobile Web sites provide product specifications, sticker prices and dealer cost information, reviews, and even comparisons with competing vehicles. Saab's Web site even includes an "interactive showroom," to let the "shopper" browse as if he or she were actually visiting a Saab dealership. Some Web sites will even list a particular auto dealer's new and used car inventory.

With respect to surfing the Internet for information, consider one consumer's comments drawn from a recent research study: "I like to use the Web because it's so easy to find information, and it's really easy to use. The information is at my fingertips and I don't have to search books in libraries."[15]

How much information a consumer will gather also depends on various situational factors. Getting back to Steve and Charlene, since they want their home security system installed as soon as possible, they might open their local Yellow Pages, turn to "Burglar Alarm Systems," and telephone a number of the listed companies that install such systems. The purpose of such telephone calls would be to arrange to have security company sales representatives visit their home to talk to them about security systems. They might also talk to their neighbors who have home security systems, and/or Steve might talk to some of his coworkers. Additionally, Steve and Charlene might go to their local public library to find a number of magazine articles about home security systems, or search the Internet for such information. On the basis of selective perception, Steve and Charlene might start seeing and hearing advertising messages and paying attention to direct mail for home security systems.

As Table 16-2 indicates, a number of factors are likely to increase consumers' prepurchase search. For some product and services, the consumer may have ongoing experience on which to draw (such as a computer user purchasing a "faster" computer), or the purchase may essentially be discretionary in nature (rather than a necessity), so there is no rush to make a decision. Steve and Charlene, though, associate the home security system with safety, and therefore have no desire to postpone the purchase.

Let's consider several of the prepurchase search alternatives open to prospective home security system buyers. At the most fundamental level, search alternatives can be classified as either personal or impersonal. *Personal* search alternatives include more than a consumer's past experience with the product or service. They also include asking for information and advice from friends, relatives, coworkers, and sales representatives. For instance, Steve might speak with a coworker and ask her what she knows about security systems. Then Steve and Charlene might also investigate whether *Consumer Reports*, *Popular Science*, or some other publications might have rated the various brands or types of security systems.

Table 16-3 presents some of the sources of information that the couple might use as part of their prepurchase search. Any or all of these sources might be used as part of a consumer's search process.

Evaluation of Alternatives

When evaluating potential alternatives, consumers tend to use two types of information: (1) a "list" of brands from which they plan to make their selection (the

TABLE 16-2 Factors That Are Likely to Increase Prepurchase Search

PRODUCT FACTORS

Long interpurchase time (a long-lasting or infrequently used product)
Frequent changes in product styling
Frequent price changes
Volume purchasing (large number of units)
High price
Many alternative brands
Much variation in features

SITUATIONAL FACTORS

Experience
    First-time purchase
    No past experience because the product is new
    Unsatisfactory past experience within the product category
Social Acceptability
    The purchase is for a gift
    The product is socially visible
Value-Related Considerations
    Purchase is discretionary rather than necessary
    All alternatives have both desirable and undesirable consequences
    Family members disagree on product requirements or evaluation of alternatives
    Product usage deviates from important reference group
    The purchase involves ecological considerations
    Many sources of conflicting information

PRODUCT FACTORS

Demographic Characteristics of Consumer
    Well-educated
    High-income
    White-collar occupation
    Under 35 years of age
Personality
    Low dogmatic
    Low-risk perceiver (broad categorizer)
    Other personal factors, such as high product involvement and enjoyment of shopping and search

TABLE 16-3 Alternative Prepurchase Information Sources for a Home Security System

PERSONAL	IMPERSONAL
Friends	Newspaper articles
Neighbors	Magazine articles
Relatives	*Consumer Reports*
Coworkers	Direct-mail brochures
Security system salespeople	Information from product advertisements
Calling the security alarm company	Internal Web site

evoked set) and (2) the criteria they will use to evaluate each brand. Making a selection from a *sample* of all possible brands is a human characteristic that helps simplify the decision-making process.

Evoked Set Within the context of consumer decision making, the **evoked set** refers to the specific brands a consumer considers in making a purchase within a particular product category. (The evoked set is also called the *consideration set*.) A consumer's evoked set is distinguished from his or her **inept set**, which consists of brands the consumer excludes from purchase consideration because they are felt to be unacceptable (or they are seen as "inferior"), and from the **inert set**, which consists of brands the consumer is indifferent toward because they are perceived as not having any particular advantages. Regardless of the total number of brands in a product category, a consumer's evoked set tends to be quite small on average, often consisting of only three to five brands. However, research indicates that a consumer's consideration set increases in size as experience with a product category grows.[16]

The evoked set consists of the small number of brands the consumer is familiar with, remembers, and finds acceptable. Figure 16-3 depicts the evoked set as a subset of all available brands in a product category. As the figure indicates, it is essential that a product be part of a consumer's evoked set if it is to be considered at all. The five terminal positions in the model that do *not* end in purchase would appear to have perceptual problems. For example: (1) brands may be *unknown* because of the consumer's selective exposure to advertising media and selective perception of advertising stimuli; (2) brands may be *unacceptable* because of poor qualities or attributes or inappropriate positioning in either advertising or product characteristics; (3) brands may be perceived as not having any special benefits and are regarded *indifferently* by the consumer; (4) brands may be *overlooked* because they have not been clearly positioned or sharply targeted at the consumer market segment under study; and (5) brands may not be selected because they are perceived by consumers as *unable to satisfy* perceived needs as fully as the brand that is chosen.

In each of these instances, the implication for marketers is that promotional techniques should be designed to impart a more favorable, perhaps more relevant, product image to the target consumer. This may also require a change in product fea-

FIGURE 16-3

The Evoked Set as a Subset of All Brands in a Product Class

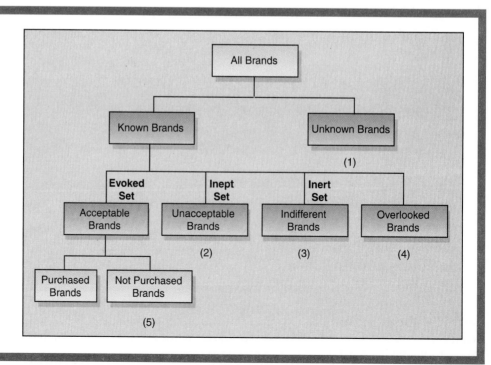

tures or attributes (more or better features). An alternative strategy is to invite consumers in a particular target segment to consider a specific brand and possibly put in their evoked set.

Criteria Used for Evaluating Brands The criteria consumers use to evaluate the brands that constitute their evoked sets usually are expressed in terms of important product attributes. Examples of product attributes that consumers have used as criteria in evaluating nine product categories are listed in Table 16-4.

When a company knows that consumers will be evaluating alternatives, they sometimes advertise in a way that recommends the criteria that consumers should use in assessing product or service options. For example, Figure 16-4 presents an ad for the Dodge Stratus that suggests to potential car buyers, "These are the questions." The ad continues by presenting information and raising a series of questions for readers to consider. Finally, it suggests that the Stratus is the answer. Still further, according to a recent study, if evaluations are made on-line, information acquired later (the recency effect) is given more weight than information that had been acquired earlier (although this decreases with the amount of knowledge that consumers already possess).[17] In another study, the mere possession of a rebate coupon (whether it is used or not) for a product purchase enhances consumers' preference for that object.[18]

We have probably all had the experience of comparing or evaluating different brands or models of a product and finding the one that just feels, looks, and/or performs "right." Interestingly, research shows that when consumers discuss such "right products," there is little or no mention of price; brand names are not often top-of-mind; items often reflect personality characteristics or childhood experiences; and it is often "love at first sight." In one recent study, the products claimed by research participants to "just feel right" included Big Bertha golf clubs, old leather briefcases, Post-it notes, and the Honda Accord.[19]

TABLE 16-4 Possible Product Attributes Used as Purchase Criteria for Nine Product Categories

PERSONAL COMPUTERS	CD PLAYER	WRISTWATCHES
Processing speed	Mega bass	Watchband
Price	Electronic shock protection	Alarm feature
Type of display	Length of play on batteries	Price
Hard-disk size	Random play feature	Water-resistant
Amount of memory	Water resistant	Quartz movement
Laptop or desktop		Size of dial
VCRS	**COLOR TVS**	**FROZEN DINNERS**
Ease of programming	Picture quality	Taste
Number of heads	Length of warranty	Type of main course
Number of tape speeds	Cable-ready	Type of side dishes
Slow-motion feature	Price	Price
Automatic tracking	Size of screen	Preparation requirements
35-mm CAMERAS	**FOUNTAIN PENS**	**COLOR INKJET PRINTER**
Autofocus	Balance	Output speed
Built-in flash	Price	Number of ink colors
Automatic film loading	Gold nib	Resolution (DPI)
Lens type	Smoothness	Length of warranty
Size and weight	Ink reserve	USB capability

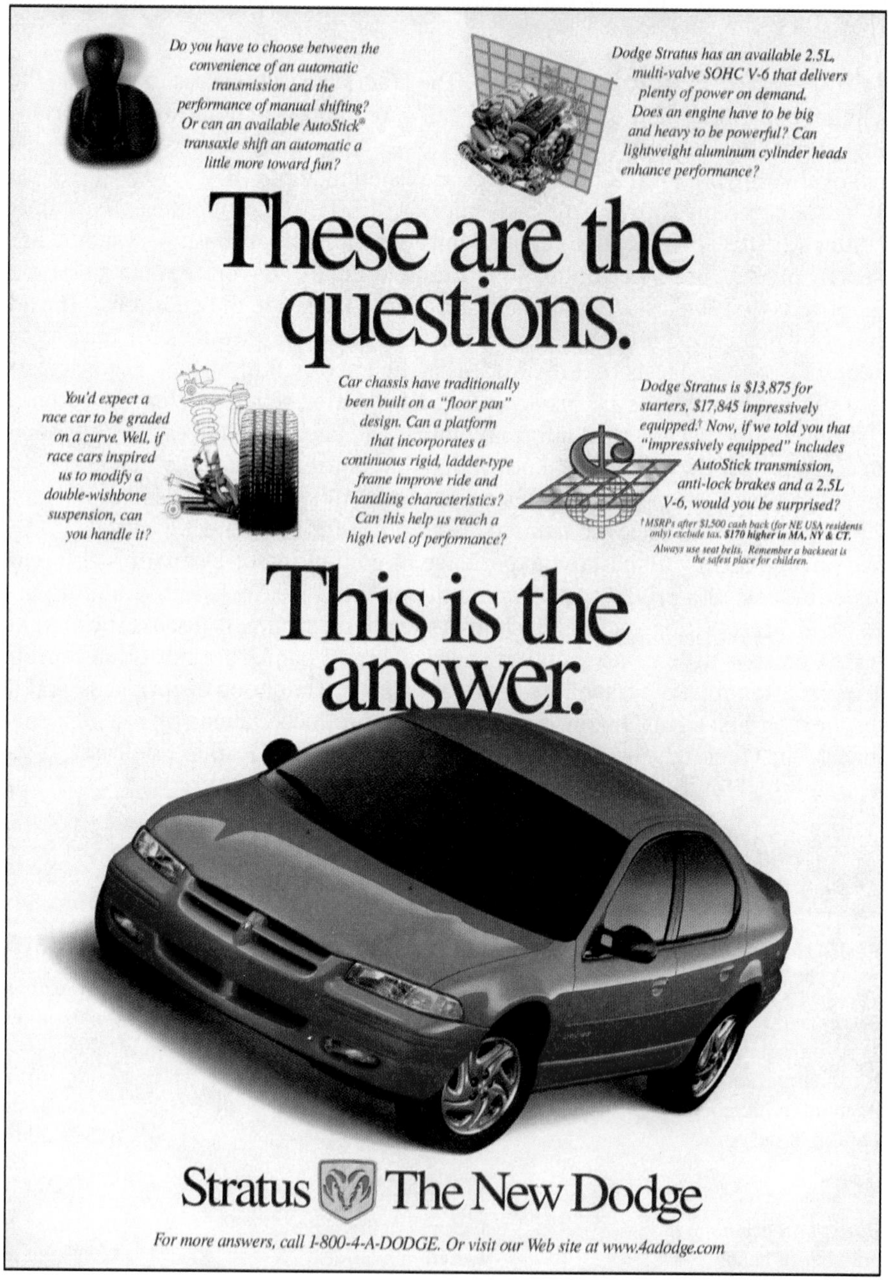

FIGURE 16-4
Ad Suggesting Criteria for Decision Making

Let's return for a moment to Steve and Charlene, who want to have a security system installed in their new suburban home. They have read a few magazine articles they found at their local library, spoken with salespeople from three different security alarm installation companies in their area, and carefully read several security system ads in their local newspaper. As a result of this information search, they have come to the realization that a security system for their home can range from almost free up to about two thousand dollars.

As in other parts of the country, there is a local security alarm dealer, St. Louis Alarm Systems, that is willing to install a security system in Steve and Charlene's home for $99, as long as they are willing to sign a 5-year contract for central station monitoring (at $24.95 a month). At the other end of the spectrum, Clayton Security Services is asking $1,950 to install a complete home security system and is recommending that it be connected to a central monitoring station that the company feels is reliable (at $19.95 per month). And then there is Missouri Burglary, Inc., a firm willing to install a security system in Steve and Charlene's home for $999 (again, central station monitoring, if desired, would be an additional monthly fee). These three firms, St. Louis Alarm Systems, Clayton Security Services, and Missouri Burglary, Inc., constitute Steve and Charlene's evoked set.

Steve and Charlene liked the presentations made in their home by representatives of each of these three companies. Based on what they learned during these presentations and what they read in magazine articles about home security systems, the couple decided that the system they have installed in their home should include the following features: have central station monitoring, all exterior doors and windows must be wired to the system, and three keypads (to activate and deactivate the alarm system and its various features) are needed (one at the front door, one by the door to the home's two-car garage, and one in the master bedroom). To evaluate the information provided by the three security firms, Steve and Charlene might mentally or on paper construct a table that compares the availability of specific features of the three home security systems in their evoked set (see Table 16-5).

As part of their search process, Steve and Charlene have also acquired information about other relevant issues (or attributes) that could influence their final choice (again, see Table 16-5). For example, they have learned that the $99 system includes only motion detectors inside the home (rather than separate security protection for each of the home's windows), and only includes security coverage for their home's front and back door. Only the most expensive system, from Clayton Security Services, includes smoke detection (with a smoke detector on each level of the home, wired into the security system and monitored by the central station).

Consumer Decision Rules Consumer decision rules, often referred to as *heuristics, decision strategies*, and *information-processing strategies*, are procedures used

TABLE 16-5 Comparison of Selected Characteristics of Home Security Systems

FEATURE	ST. LOUIS ALARM SYSTEMS	CLAYTON SECURITY SERVICES	MISSOURI BURGLARY
System Price	$99	$1,950	$999
Monthly monitoring fee	$19.95	$19.95	$19.95
Number of entry doors protected (the home has three—a front door, a garage door, and a patio door)	1	3	2
Number of keypads included	1	3	2
Price for each additional keypad	($90)	(no more needed)	($75)
Number of included smoke detectors wired to system	0 ($100 each, if desired)	3	0
How home is protected	2 motion detectors plus contact on front door	2 motion detectors plus contacts on all windows and outer doors	2 motion detectors plus contacts on all outer doors

by consumers to facilitate brand (or other consumption-related) choices. These rules reduce the burden of making complex decisions by providing guidelines or routines that make the process less taxing.

Consumer decision rules have been broadly classified into two major categories: **compensatory** and **noncompensatory decision rules**. In following a compensatory decision rule, a consumer evaluates brand options in terms of each relevant attribute and computes a weighted or summated score for each brand. The computed score reflects the brand's relative merit as a potential purchase choice. The assumption is that the consumer will select the brand that scores highest among the alternatives evaluated. Referring to Table 16-6, it is clear that using a compensatory decision rule, Clayton Security Services scores highest.

A unique feature of a compensatory decision rule is that it allows a positive evaluation of a brand on one attribute to balance out a negative evaluation on some other attribute. For example, a positive assessment of the energy savings made possible by a particular brand or type of lightbulb may offset an unacceptable assessment in terms of the bulb's diminished light output.

In contrast, noncompensatory decision rules do not allow consumers to balance positive evaluations of a brand on one attribute against a negative evaluation on some other attribute. For instance, in the case of an energy-saving lightbulb, the product's negative (unacceptable) rating on its light output would not be offset by a positive evaluation of its energy savings. Instead, this particular lightbulb would be disqualified from further consideration. If Steve and Charlene's choice of a home security system was based on their desire to have smoke detection as part of their system (refer again to Table 16-6), a noncompensatory decision rule would have eliminated Missouri Burglary.

Three noncompensatory rules are considered briefly here: the *conjunctive* rule, the *disjunctive* rule, and the *lexicographic* rule.

In following a **conjunctive decision rule**, the consumer establishes a separate, minimally acceptable level as a cutoff point for each attribute. If any particular brand falls below the cutoff point on any one attribute, the brand is eliminated from further consideration. Because the conjunctive rule can result in several acceptable alternatives, it becomes necessary in such cases for the consumer to apply an additional decision rule to arrive at a final selection; for example, to accept the first satisfactory brand. The conjunctive rule is particularly useful in quickly reducing the number of alternatives to be considered. The consumer can then apply another, more refined, decision rule to arrive at a final choice.

TABLE 16-6 Hypothetical Ratings for Security Systems

FEATURE	ST. LOUIS ALARM SYSTEMS	CLAYTON SECURITY SERVICES	MISSOURI BURGLARY
System price	10	1	5
Monthly monitoring fee	4	6	5
Number of entry doors protected (the home has three—a front door, a garage door, and a patio door)	1	10	5
Number of keypads included	3	10	6
Price for each additional keypad	3	10	6
Number of included smoke detectors wired to system	3	10	1
How home is protected	2	10	6
	27	56	34

The **disjunctive rule** is the "mirror image" of the conjunctive rule. In applying this decision rule, the consumer establishes a separate, minimally acceptable cutoff level for each attribute (which may be higher than the one normally established for a conjunctive rule). In this case, if a brand alternative meets or exceeds the cutoff established for any one attribute, it is accepted. Here again, a number of brands might exceed the cutoff point, producing a situation in which another decision rule is required. When this occurs, the consumer may accept the first satisfactory brand as the final choice or apply some other, perhaps more suitable, decision rule.

In following a **lexicographic decision rule**, the consumer first ranks the attributes in terms of perceived relevance or importance. The consumer then compares the various brand alternatives in terms of the single attribute that is considered most important. If one brand scores sufficiently high on this top-ranked attribute (regardless of the score on any of the other attributes), it is selected and the process ends. When there are two or more surviving brand alternatives, the process is repeated with the second highest-ranked attribute (and so on), until reaching the point that one of the brands is selected because it exceeds the others on a particular attribute.

With the lexicographic rule, the highest-ranked attribute (the one applied first) may reveal something about the individual's basic consumer (or shopping) orientation. For instance, a "buy the best" rule might indicate that the consumer is *quality oriented*; a "buy the most prestigious brand" rule might indicate that the consumer is *status oriented*; a "buy the least expensive" rule might reveal that the consumer is *economy minded*.

A variety of decision rules appear quite commonplace. According to a consumer survey, 9 out of 10 shoppers who go to the store for frequently purchased items possess a specific shopping strategy for saving money. The consumer segment and the specific shopping rules that these segments employ are:[20]

1. Practical loyalists—those who look for ways to save on the brands and products they would buy anyway.
2. Bottom-line price shoppers—those who buy the lowest-priced item, with little or no regard for brand.
3. Opportunistic switchers—those who use coupons or sales to decide among brands and products that fall within their evoked set.
4. Deal hunters—those who look for the best "bargain" and are not brand-loyal.

We have considered only the most basic of an almost infinite number of consumer decision rules. Most of the decision rules described here can be combined to form new variations, such as conjunctive-compensatory, conjunctive-disjunctive, or disjunctive-conjunctive. It is likely that for many purchase decisions, consumers maintain in long-term memory overall evaluations of the brands in their evoked sets. This would make assessment by individual attributes unnecessary. Instead, the consumer would simply select the brand with the highest perceived overall rating. This type of synthesized decision rule is known as the **affect referral decision rule** and may represent the simplest of all rules.

Table 16-7 summarizes the essence of many of the decision rules considered in this chapter, in terms of the kind of mental statements that Steve and Charlene might make in selecting a home security system.

Lifestyles as a Consumer Decision Strategy An individual's or family's decisions to be committed to a particular lifestyle (for instance, devoted followers of a particular religion) impacts on a wide range of specific everyday consumer behavior. For instance, The Trends Research Institute has identified "voluntary simplicity" as one of the top 10 lifestyle trends of the 1990s.[21] They estimate that by the year 2000, 15 percent of all "boomers" will be seeking a simpler lifestyle with reduced emphasis on ownership and

TABLE 16-7 Hypothetical Use of Popular Decision Rules in Making a Decision to Purchase a Home Security System

DECISION RULE	MENTAL STATEMENT
Compensatory rule	"We selected the security system that came out best when we balanced the good ratings against the bad ratings."
Conjunctive rule	"We picked the security system that had no bad features."
Disjunctive rule	"We selected the security system that excelled in at least one attribute."
Lexicographic rule	"We looked at the feature that was most important to us and chose the security system that ranked highest on that attribute."
Affect referral rule	"Everything they do is outstanding, so we decided to have them install our security system."

possessions. Voluntary simplifiers are making do with less clothing and fewer credit cards (with no outstanding balances) and moving to smaller, yet still adequate, homes or apartments in less populated communities. Most importantly, it is not that these consumers can no longer afford their affluence or "lifestyle of abundance"; rather, they are seeking new, "reduced," less-extravagant lifestyles. As part of this new lifestyle commitment, some individuals are seeking less stressful and lower salary careers or jobs. In a telephone survey, for example, 33 percent of those contacted claimed that they would be willing to take a 20 percent pay cut in return for working fewer hours.[22]

Incomplete Information and Noncomparable Alternatives In many choice situations, consumers face incomplete information on which to base decisions and must use alternative strategies to cope with the missing elements. Missing information may result from advertisements or packaging that mentions only certain attributes, the consumer's own imperfect memory of attributes for nonpresent alternatives, or because some attributes are experiential and can only be evaluated after product use.[23] There are at least four alternative strategies that consumers can adopt for coping with missing information:[24]

1. Consumers may delay the decision until missing information is obtained. This strategy is likely to be used for high-risk decisions.
2. Consumers may ignore missing information and decide to continue with the current decision rule (e.g., compensatory or noncompensatory), using the available attribute information.
3. Consumers may change the customarily used decision strategy to one that better accommodates missing information.
4. Consumers may infer ("construct") the missing information.

In discussing consumer decision rules, we have assumed that a choice is made from among the brands evaluated. Of course, a consumer also may conclude that none of the alternatives offers sufficient benefits to warrant purchase. If this were to occur with a necessity, such as a refrigerator, the consumer would probably either lower his or her expectations and settle for the best of the available alternatives or seek information about additional brands, hoping to find one that more closely meets predetermined criteria. On the other hand, if the purchase is more discretionary (a second or third pair of sneakers), the consumer probably would postpone the purchase. In this case, information gained from the search up to that point would be transferred to long-term storage (in the psychological field) and retrieved and reintroduced as input if and when the consumer regains interest in making such a purchase.

It should be noted that, in applying decision rules, consumers may at times attempt to compare dissimilar (noncomparable) alternatives. For example, a consumer may be undecided about whether to take a Caribbean vacation or remodel a bathroom, because the budget can afford either, but not both, expenditures. Another example: A consumer may try to decide between buying a new blue blazer or a new pair of boots. When there is great dissimilarity in the alternative ways of allocating available funds, consumers abstract the products to a level in which comparisons are possible. In the examples cited above, a consumer might weigh the alternatives (vacation versus remodeled bathroom or blazer versus boots) in terms of which alternative would offer the most pleasure or which, if either, is more of a "necessity."

A Series of Decisions Although we have discussed the purchase decision as if it were a single decision, in reality, a purchase can involve a number of decisions. For example, when purchasing an automobile, consumers are involved in multiple decisions such as choosing the make or country of origin of the car (foreign versus domestic), the dealer, the financing, and particular options. In the case of a replacement automobile, these decisions must be preceded by a decision as to whether or not to trade in one's current car. A study found that the attitudes and search behavior of consumers who replace their cars after only a few years (early replacement buyers) differ greatly from those who replace their cars after many years (late replacement buyers). In particular, early car replacement buyers were more concerned with the car's styling and image or status and were less concerned with cost. In contrast, late car replacement buyers undertook a greater amount of information and dealer search and were greatly influenced by friends.[25]

Decision Rules and Marketing Strategy An understanding of which decision rules consumers apply in selecting a particular product or service is useful to marketers concerned with formulating a promotional program. A marketer familiar with the prevailing decision rule can prepare a promotional message in a format that would facilitate consumer information processing. The promotional message might even suggest how potential consumers should make a decision. For instance, a direct-mail piece for a 22-inch wheeled "carry-on" bag (luggage) might tell potential consumers "what to look for in a new piece of luggage." This mail piece might specifically ask consumers to consider the attributes of size of wheels, composition of wheels (plastic versus rubber), sturdiness of the pull-up handle, fabric, and number of outside pockets in their purchase decision process.

Consumption Vision Researchers have recently proposed "consumption vision" as a nonorthodox, but potentially accurate, portrayal of decision making for those situations in which the consumer has little experience and the problems are not well-structured, as well as those in which there is a considerable amount of emotion. Under such circumstances, the consumer may turn to a consumption vision, a mental picture or visual image of specific usage outcomes and/or consumption consequences."[26] Such visions (such as a high school senior envisioning attending college at a small liberal arts school versus attending a major university or a consumer visualizing driving a new car to the office) allow consumers to imagine or vicariously participate in the consumption of the product or service prior to making an actual decision. After "trying out" a number of different alternatives in one's mind, so to speak, the consumer then makes his or her decision.[27] In a recent study, consumers were more likely to construct consumption visions when they saw an advertisement presenting the product's attributes in concrete and detailed language or visually with a picture.[28]

OUTPUT

The *output* portion of the consumer decision-making model concerns two closely associated kinds of postdecision activity: **purchase behavior** and **postpurchase evaluation**. The objective of both activities is to increase the consumer's satisfaction with his or her purchase.

Purchase Behavior

Consumers make three types of purchases: *trial purchases*, *repeat purchases*, and *long-term commitment purchases*. When a consumer purchases a product (or brand) for the first time and buys a smaller quantity than usual, this purchase would be considered a trial. Thus, a trial is the exploratory phase of purchase behavior in which consumers attempt to evaluate a product through direct use. For instance, when consumers purchase a new brand of laundry detergent about which they may be uncertain, they are likely to purchase smaller trial quantities than if it were a familiar brand. Consumers can also be encouraged to try a new product through such promotional tactics as free samples, coupons, and/or sale prices.

When a new brand in an established product category (toothpaste, chewing gum, or cola) is found by trial to be more satisfactory or better than other brands, consumers are likely to repeat the purchase. Repeat purchase behavior is closely related to the concept of *brand loyalty*, which most firms try to encourage, because it contributes to greater stability in the marketplace (see chapter 7). Unlike trial, in which the consumer uses the product on a small scale and without any commitment, a repeat purchase usually signifies that the product meets with the consumer's approval and that he or she is willing to use it again and in larger quantities.

Trial, of course, is not always feasible. For example, with most durable goods (refrigerators, washing machines, or electric ranges), a consumer usually moves directly from evaluation to a long-term commitment (through purchase), without the opportunity for an actual trial.

It is also important that some observers believe that eventually there will be almost universal Internet access, at least in the United States. As a result, some authorities are forecasting that early in the twenty-first century, consumers will be purchasing food and other basic household needs via in-home television computer systems. Choices will be made by the shopper after viewing brands and prices on the screen. So the purchasing process itself will change dramatically in the coming decades.[29]

Consider Steve and Charlene and their decision concerning the selection of a home security system. There is really no way that the couple can try each of the three systems that they have been considering. Instead, they ask each of the three security companies that they have spoken with to supply them with names of individuals in their local area who have recently had that type of system installed. They then telephone these homeowners to find out how satisfied they are with their security systems and whether they would recommend the installation company. After this process has been completed, Steve and Charlene are both in agreement that they are interested in maximizing their protection—both when they are at home and when the home is vacant—and want protection from both burglary and fire. Therefore, they decided that in the long run it would pay for them to purchase the more expensive of the three systems they have been considering, the one from Clayton Security Services. Moreover, they recall being impressed by the comments of the family who had purchased their system from Clayton Security that this particular local firm was an authorized First Alert Professional Security Systems dealer. They were told this meant that Clayton Security installed a very well regarded national name brand quality security system. Thus, Steve and Charlene both felt that with this system, they would feel "safe," and have "peace of mind."

Postpurchase Evaluation

As consumers use a product, particularly during a trial purchase, they evaluate its performance in light of their own expectations. There are three possible outcomes of these evaluations: (1) actual performance matches expectations, leading to a neutral feeling; (2) performance exceeds expectations, causing what is known as *positive disconfirmation of expectations* (which leads to satisfaction); and (3) performance is below expectations, causing *negative disconfirmation of expectations* and dissatisfaction.[30] For each of these three outcomes, consumers' expectations and satisfaction are closely linked; that is, consumers tend to judge their experience against their expectations when performing a *postpurchase evaluation*. The two go hand in hand.

An important component of postpurchase evaluation is the reduction of any uncertainty or doubt that the consumer might have had about the selection. As part of their postpurchase analyses, consumers try to reassure themselves that their choice was a wise one; that is, they attempt to reduce *postpurchase cognitive dissonance*. As chapter 8 indicated, they do this by adopting one of the following strategies: They may rationalize the decision as being wise; they may seek advertisements that support their choice and avoid those of competitive brands; they may attempt to persuade friends or neighbors to buy the same brand (and thus confirm their own choice); or they may turn to other satisfied owners for reassurance.

The degree of postpurchase analysis that consumers undertake depends on the importance of the product decision and the experience acquired in using the product. When the product lives up to expectations, they probably will buy it again. When the product's performance is disappointing or does not meet expectations, however, they will search for more suitable alternatives. Thus, the consumer's postpurchase evaluation "feeds back" as *experience* to the consumer's psychological field and serves to influence future related decisions. Although it would be logical to assume that customer satisfaction is related to customer retention (that is, if a consumer is satisfied with his RCA TV he will buy other RCA products), a recent study found no direct relationship between satisfaction and retention. The findings show that customer retention may be more a matter of the brand's reputation—especially for products consumers find difficult to evaluate.[31]

What was Steve and Charlene's postpurchase evaluation of their new home security system? Because the system protects all their doors (front door, garage door, and patio door), and they have security system contacts on all their windows as well as motion detectors to detect an intruder when the house is empty, they both feel much safer than they thought they could ever feel. Additionally, because they can turn off the motion detectors when they are at home, they can keep the system armed 24 hours a day, should they choose to do so. They are also enjoying the convenience of having a keypad both at the front door and the garage door, so that whenever they enter their home they can quickly reset the alarm system. They realize that if they had only one keypad, by the front door, they would have to rush to that door every time they entered their home through the garage (often with their hands filled with supermarket bags). They also appreciate the convenience of being able to arm, disarm, and check the status of their security system from their bedroom keypad.

In summary, Steve and Charlene are thus far very satisfied with their new home security system and feel that the extra money they spent for this particular system pays them back daily in terms of both extra peace of mind and added convenience.

▪▪▪▪▪ CONSUMER GIFTING BEHAVIOR

In terms of both dollars spent each year and how they make givers and receivers feel, gifts are a particularly interesting part of consumer behavior. Products and services chosen as gifts represent more than ordinary "everyday" purchases. Because of their symbolic meaning, they are associated with such important events as Mother's Day, births and birthdays, engagements, weddings, graduations, and many other accomplishments and milestones.

Gifting behavior has been defined as "the process of *gift exchange* that takes place between a giver and a recipient."[32] The definition is broad in nature and embraces gifts given voluntarily ("Just to let you know I'm thinking of you"), as well gifts that are an obligation ("I had to get him a gift").[33] It includes gifts given to (and received from) others and gifts to oneself, or **self-gifts**.

Still further, gifting is an act of symbolic communication, with explicit and implicit meanings ranging from congratulations, love, and regret, to obligation and dominance. The nature of the relationship between gift giver and gift receiver is an important consideration in choosing a gift. Table 16-8 presents a model of the relationships between various combinations of gift givers and gift receivers in the consumer gifting process. The model reveals the following five gifting subdivisions: (1) intergroup gifting, (2) intercategory gifting, (3) intragroup gifting, (4) interpersonal gifting, and (5) intrapersonal gifting.

Intergroup gifting behavior occurs whenever one group exchanges gifts with another group (such as one family and another). You will recall from chapter 10 that the process and outcome of family decision making is different from individual decision making. Similarly, gifts given to families will be different than those given to individual family members. For example, a "common" wedding gift for a bride *and* a groom may include products for setting up a household, rather than a gift that would personally be used by either the bride or the groom. When it comes to *intercategory gifting*, either an individual is giving a gift to a group (a single friend is giving a couple an anniversary gift) or a group is giving an individual a gift (friends chip in and give another friend a joint birthday gift). The gift selection strategies "buy for joint recipients" or "buy with someone" (creating intercategory gifting) are especially useful when it comes to a difficult recipient situation (when "nothing seems to satisfy her").[34] These strategies can also be applied to reduce some of the time pressure associated with shopping for the great number of gifts exchanged during the American Christmas season gift-giving ritual. For example, a consumer may choose to purchase 5 intercategory gifts for five aunt and uncle pairs (intercategory gifting), instead of buying 10 personal gifts for five aunts and five uncles (interpersonal gifting). In this way, less time, money, and effort may be expended.

An *intragroup gift* can be characterized by the sentiment "we gave this to ourselves"; that is, a group gives a gift to itself or its members. For example, a dual-income couple may find that their demanding work schedules limit leisure time spent together as husband and wife. Therefore, an anniversary gift ("to us") of a cruise to Bermuda would be an example of an intragroup gift. It would also remedy the couple's problem

TABLE 16-8 Five Giver-Receiver Gifting Subdivisions

GIVERS	INDIVIDUAL	RECEIVERS "OTHER" GROUP	SELF*
INDIVIDUAL	Interpersonal gifting	Intercategory gifting	Intrapersonal gifting
GROUP	Intercategory gifting	Intergroup gifting	Intragroup gifting

*This "SELF" is either singular self ("me") or plural self ("us").

Source: Based on Deborah Y. Cohn and Leon G. Schiffman, "Gifting: A Taxonomy of Private Realm Giver and Recipient Relationships," Working Paper, City University of New York, Baruch College, 1996, 2–7.

of not spending enough time together. In contrast, *interpersonal gifting* occurs between just two individuals, a gift giver and gift receiver. By their very nature, interpersonal gifts are "intimate" because they provide an opportunity for a gift giver to reveal what he or she thinks of the gift receiver. Successful gifts are those that communicate that the giver knows and understands the receiver and their relationship. For example, a shirt or blouse given to a friend in just the right color and size can be viewed as "she really knows me." In contrast, a computer modem given as a Valentine's Day gift, when the recipient is expecting a more "intimate" gift, can mean a deterioration of a relationship.[35] Still further, researchers that have explored the gender of gift givers and their feelings about same-sex gifting (female-to-female or male-to-male) and opposite-sex gifting (male-to-female or female-to-male) have found that both male and female gift givers feel more comfortable in giving gifts to the same sex; however, they also reported that they felt more intense feeling with respect to gifts given to members of the opposite sex.[36] Knowledge of such gender differences are useful for marketers to know, because they imply that additional support might be appreciated at the point of purchase (while in a store) when a consumer is considering a gift for an opposite-sex recipient.

A recent study examined mothers giving gifts to their children (*interpersonal gifting*) across three different cultures: (1) Anglo-Celtic (mothers born in Australia), (2) Sino-Vietnamese (mothers born in Vietnam), and (3) Israeli (mothers born in Israel).[37] Whereas in all three of these cultures the mother plays a central role in family gift giving, Table 16-9 presents the major differences between these groups.

Intrapersonal gifting, or a self-gift (also called "monadic giving"), occurs when the giver and the receiver are the same individual.[38] To some extent a self-gift is a "state of mind." If a consumer sees a purchase as the "buying of something I need," then it is simply a "purchase." On the other hand, if the same consumer sees the same purchase as a "self-gift," then it is something special, with special meaning. Consumers may "treat" themselves to self-gifts that are products (clothing, compact discs, or jewelry), services (hair styling, restaurant meals, spa membership), or experiences (socializing with friends).[39] For example, while purchasing holiday gifts for others, some consumers find themselves in stores that they might not otherwise visit, or find themselves looking at merchandise (such as a scarf) that they want but would not ordinarily buy.[40] Such intrapersonal gifts have their own special range of meaning and context. Table 16-10 illustrates specific circumstances and motivations that might lead a consumer to engage in self-gift behavior. Research focusing on college students' self-gifting behavior found that when they had the money to spend and when they either felt good or wished to cheer themselves up, they were particularly likely to purchase self-gifts.[41]

Finally, Table 16-11 summarizes the five gifting behavior subdivisions explored above.

▪▪▪▪▪ BEYOND THE DECISION: CONSUMING AND POSSESSING

Historically, the emphasis in consumer behavior studies has been on product, service, and brand choice decisions. As shown throughout this book, however, there are many more facets to consumer behavior. The experience of using products and services, as well as the sense of pleasure derived from *possessing, collecting,* or *consuming* "things" and "experiences" (a VCR, rare stamps or coins, or a faraway vacation) contribute to consumer satisfaction and overall quality of life. These consumption outcomes or experiences, in turn, affect consumers' future decision processes.

TABLE 16-9 Major Differences between Gift-Giving Behavior of Anglo-Celtic, Sino-Vietnamese, and Israeli Mothers

GIFT-GIVING ELEMENTS:	ANGLO-CELTIC MOTHERS	SINO-VIETNAMESE MOTHERS	ISRAELI MOTHERS
1. MOTIVATION			
Justification	Short-term goals	Long-term goals	Long-term/short-term goals
Significance	Prestige gifts Birthday gifts	Practical gifts Lucky money	Importance to recipient
Timing	Special occasions, e.g. birthdays, Christmas	Chinese New Year and academic reward	Birthdays and general needs
2. SELECTION			
Involvement	High priority Social and psychological risks	Low priority Financial risks	Low priority
Family Influences	Children	Mother	Mother dominant with younger children and influenced by older children
Promotional Influences	Status symbols	Sale items	Sale items
Gift Attributes	Quality Money unsuitable	Price Money suitable	Price Money suitable
3. PRESENTATION			
Presentation Messages	Immediate self-gratification	Delayed self-gratification	Immediate self-gratification
Allocation Messages	Multiple gifts Mothers favored	Single gifts Eldest child favored	Single gifts
Understanding of Messages	Always	Not always	Never
4. REACTION			
Achievement	Often	Most of the time	Never
Feedback	More expressive	Less expressive	Least expressive
Usage	Often private	Often shared	Never shared

Source: Constance Hill and Celia T. Romm, "The Role of Mothers as Gift Givers: A Comparison Across Three Cultures," in *Advances in Consumer Research*, 23, ed. Kim P. Corfman and John G. Lynch, Jr. (Provo, UT: Association for Consumer Research, 1996), 26. Reprinted by permission.

Thus, given the importance of possessions and experiences, a broader perspective of consumer behavior might view consumer choices as the beginning of a **consumption process**, not merely the end of a consumer decision-making effort. In this context, the choice or purchase decision is an *input* into a process of consumption. The input stage includes the establishment of a *consumption set* (an assortment or portfolio of products and their attributes) and a *consuming style* (the "rules" by which the individual or household fulfills consumption requirements). The *process* stage of a simple model of consumption might include (from the consumer's perspective) the *using, possessing* (or having), *collecting*, and *disposing* of things and experiences. The *output* stage of this process would include changes in a wide range of feelings, moods, attitudes, and behavior, as well as reinforcement (positive or negative) of a particular lifestyle (for instance, a devotion to physical fitness), enhancement of a sense of self, and the level of consumer satisfaction and quality of life.[42] Figure 16-5 presents a simple *model of consumption* that reflects the ideas discussed here and throughout the book.

TABLE 16-10 Reported Circumstances and Motivations for Self-Gift Behavior

CIRCUMSTANCES	MOTIVATIONS
Personal accomplishment	To reward oneself
Feeling down	To be nice to oneself
Holiday	To cheer oneself up
Feeling stressed	To fulfill a need
Have some extra money	To celebrate
Need	To relieve stress
Had not bought for self in a while	To maintain a good feeling
Attainment of a desired goal	To provide an incentive toward a goal
Others	Others

Source: David Glen Mick and Mitchelle DeMoss, "To Me from Me: A Descriptive Phenomenology of Self-Gifts," in *Advances in Consumer Research* 23. Marvin E. Goldberg, Gerald Gorn, and Richard W. Pollay, ed., (Provo, UT: Association for Consumer Research, 1990), 677–82. Reprinted by permission.

TABLE 16-11 Gifting Relationship Categories: Definitions and Examples

GIFTING RELATIONSHIP	DEFINITION	EXAMPLE
Intergroup	A group giving a gift to another group	A Christmas gift from one family to another family
Intercategory	An individual giving a gift to a group or a group giving a gift to an individual	A group of friends chips in to buy a new mother a baby gift
Intragroup	A group giving a gift to itself or its members	A family buys a VCR for itself as a Christmas gift
Interpersonal	An individual giving a gift to another individual	Valentine's Day chocolates presented from a boyfriend to a girlfriend
Intrapersonal	Self-gift	A woman buys herself jewelry to cheer herself up

Source: Adapted from Deborah Y. Cohn and Leon G. Schiffman, "Gifting: A Taxonomy of Private Realm Giver and Recipient Relationships," Working Paper, City University of New York, Baruch College, 1996, 2.

PRODUCTS HAVE SPECIAL MEANING AND MEMORIES

Consuming is a diverse and complex concept.[43] It includes the simple utility derived from the continued use of a superior toothpaste, the stress reduction of an island holiday, the stored memories of a video reflecting one's childhood, the "sacred" meaning or "magic" of a grandparent's wristwatch, the symbol of membership gained from wearing a school tie, the pleasure and sense of accomplishment that comes from building a model airplane, and the fun and even financial rewards that come from collecting almost anything (even jokers from decks of cards). In fact, one man's hobby of collecting old earthenware drain tiles has become the "Mike Weaver Drain Tile Museum."[44]

Consider how some consumers have a fascination with Swatch watches. For example, there is the story of how one woman hid in a department store for the lunch shift, so that the person filling in at the Swatch counter would sell her a second Swatch watch, or the man who paid someone $100 to stand in line overnight in front of a New York City food store where 999 special edition Swatch watches were to go on sale the next morning. Such collecting can be "both rational and irrational, deliberate and uncontrollable, cooperative and competitive, passive and aggressive, and tension producing and tension reducing."[45]

FIGURE 16-5
A Simple Model of
Consumption

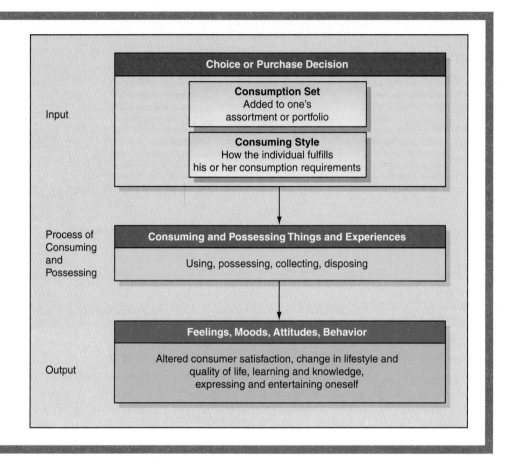

Some possessions (such as photographs, souvenirs, trophies, and everyday objects) serve to assist consumers in their effort to create "personal meaning" and to maintain a sense of the past, which is essential to having a sense of self.[46] For instance, "objects of the past" are often acquired and retained intentionally (some become antiques or even heirlooms) to "memorialize" pleasant or momentous times and people in one's past.

Why are some consumers so interested in the past? It has been suggested that nostalgia permits people to maintain their identity after some major change in their life. This nostalgia can be based on family and friends; on objects such as toys, books, jewelry, and cars; or on special events, such as graduations, weddings, and holidays.[47] Providing the triple benefits of a sense of nostalgia, the fun of collecting, and the attraction of a potential return on investment, there is a strong interest in collecting Barbie® dolls. It is estimated that there are currently more than 100,000 Barbie® doll collectors, who are dedicated to hunting down rare and valuable Barbie® dolls to add to their collections. To encourage interest in Barbie® collecting, Mattel has an ad campaign that plays up the nostalgia and fun of collecting Barbie® dolls—there is even a Barbie® collectors' 800 hotline (Figure 16-6).

▪▪▪▪ RELATIONSHIP MARKETING

We will complete our discussion of consumer decision making with a brief consideration of **relationship marketing**. Many firms have established relationship marketing programs (sometimes called *loyalty programs*) to foster usage loyalty and a commitment to their

FIGURE 16-6

Mattel Targeting Mature Women Through Nostalgia to Ignite Interest in Barbies

company's products and services. Relationship marketing is exceedingly logical when we realize credit card research has shown that "75 percent of college students keep their first card for 15 years, and 60 percent keep that card for life."[48] This kind of loyalty is enhanced by relationship marketing, which at its heart is all about building *trust* (between the firm and its customers) and keeping *promises* ("making promises," "enabling promises," and "keeping promises" on the part of the firm and, possibly, on the part of the customer).[49]

Indeed, it is the aim of relationship marketing to create strong, lasting relationships with a core group of customers. The emphasis is on developing long-term bonds with customers by making them feel good about how the company interacts (or does business) with them and by giving them some kind of "personal connection" to the business. A review of the composition of 66 consumer relationship marketing programs revealed three elements shared by more than 50 percent of the programs. They are: (1) fostering ongoing communication with customers (73 percent of the programs), (2) furnishing loyalty by building in extras like upgrades and other perks (68 percent of the programs); and (3) stimulating a sense of belonging by providing a "club membership" format (50 percent of the programs).[50]

An analogy can be drawn between two individuals who build an interpersonal relationship and the type of relationship marketers attempt to build between the company (or its products) and the consumer. Like personal relationships between individuals who are willing to do favors for each other, "relationship" marketers offer loyal customers special services, discounts, increased communications, and attention beyond the core product or service, *without* expecting an immediate payback. However, they are hoping that, over time, they will reap the advantages of sustained and increasing transactions with a core group of loyal customers.

Although direct marketing, sales promotion, and general advertising may be used as part of a relationship marketing strategy, relationship marketing stresses long-term commitment to the individual customer. Advances in technology (such as UPC scanning equipment, relational databases) have provided techniques that make tracking customers simpler, thus influencing the trend toward relationship marketing. Indeed, Wal-Mart's database is second in size only to the U.S. government's.[51] Still further, a recent study suggests that relationship marketing programs are more likely to succeed if the product or service is one that buyers consider to be high involvement, due to its association with financial, social, or physical risk.[52]

As illustrated in Table 16-12, relationship marketing can be seen in a wide variety of product and service categories. Many companies call their relationship programs a "club," and some even charge a fee to join. Membership in a club may serve as a means to convey to customers the notions of permanence and exclusivity inherent in a "committed relationship." Additionally, those firms that charge a fee (such as the American Express Platinum card) increase customers' investment in the relationship that may, in turn, lead to greater commitment to the relationship and increased usage loyalty.

Airlines and major hotel chains, in particular, use relationship marketing techniques by awarding points to frequent customers that can be used to obtain additional goods or services from the company. This kind of point system may act as an exit barrier, because starting a new relationship would mean giving up the potential future value of the points and starting from ground zero with a new service provider. Moreover, companies have recently been broadening the scope of such relationship programs. For example, Table 16-13 lists the many products and services offered to participants in the American Airlines AAdvantage Mileage Program.

Ultimately, it is to a firm's advantage to develop long-term relationships with existing customers, because it is easier and less expensive to make an additional sale to an existing customer than to make a new sale to a new consumer.[53] This is why, for example, Lands' End tells consumers that if they are not 100 percent satisfied with their purchase, they can return it at any time, for any reason.[54] However, the effort

TABLE 16-12 Examples of Relationship Marketing Techniques

COMPANY	PROGRAM TYPE AND MEMBERSHIP CRITERIA	BENEFITS
AT&T	"True Rewards" points earned for dollarsspent on long distance calling (no fee to join)	Points may be redeemed for free minutes, frequent flier miles, and other rewards. Toll-free number for member questions, quarterly point statement, and informational mailings.
American Express	Platinum Card Program "By invitation only"offered to the top 1 percent of AmEx cardholders (fee to join)	Invitations to special cultural, culinary, and artistic events based on member's personal profile.
Road Runner Sports (catalog that caters to runners, bikers, and other sports)	"Run America Club" (fee to join)	Discounts on merchandise and "shoe analysis program," quarterly newsletter "Running Shorts," free shipping upgrades, and travel and car rental discounts.
World Yacht (restaurant and cruises)	"World Yacht club" "flags" earned each time a member dines aboard World Yacht	"Flags" redeemed for awards such as free brunch, caviar, champagne, and discounts on dinner cruises. Five "flags" earn VIP status for preferred seating and additional discounts.
Neiman Marcus	"InCircle" point system (minimum purchases of $3,000 per year to join)	Quarterly newsletter, travel discounts, credit card registration, perfume, magazine subscriptions, special offer mailings, and dedicated toll-free telephone number.
Pacific Bell	"California Gold" points earned for dollars spent	Newsletter, toll-free customer service number, and third-party discounts.

Source: Adapted by Mary M. Long, Drexel University, from issues of *Colloquy*.

TABLE 16-13 A Broad-based Relationship Program

AIRLINES

Canadian Airlines International
Cathay Pacific Airlines
Hawaiian Airlines
Qantas Airways
Keno Air
Singapore Airlines
TWA
US Airways

HOTELS

Conrad Hotels
Forte Hotels
Forum Hotels
Hilton Hotels & Resorts
Hilton International Hotels
Holiday Inns

HOTELS *continued*

Inter-Continental Hotels
ITT Sheraton Hotels, Inns, Resorts, and All-Suites
Marriott Hotels, Resorts, and Suites
Vista Hotels
Wyndham Hotels & Resorts

CAR RENTAL

Avis Rent A Car
Hertz

OTHER

Citibank AAdvantage Visa or MasterCard application
MCI Long-Distance
American AAdvantage Money Market Fund
The American Traveler Catalog

involved in developing and maintaining a customer relationship must be weighed against the expected long-term benefits. Marketers must determine the "lifetime value" of a customer to ensure that the costs of obtaining, servicing, and communicating with the customer do not exceed the potential profits.[55] Figure 16-7 portrays some of the characteristics of the relationship between the firm and the customer within the "spirit" of relationship marketing.

Why is relationship marketing so important? Research indicates that consumers today are less loyal than in the past, due to six major forces: (1) the abundance of choice, (2) availability of information, (3) entitlement (consumers repeatedly ask "What have you done for me lately?"), (4) commoditization (most products/services appear to be similar—nothing stands out), (5) insecurity (consumer financial problems reduce loyalty), and (6) time scarcity (not enough time to be loyal). These six forces result in consumer defections, complaints, cynicism, reduced affiliation, greater price sensitivity, and litigiousness.[56] Consequently, relationship programs that can retain customers are a vital part of a company's marketing program.

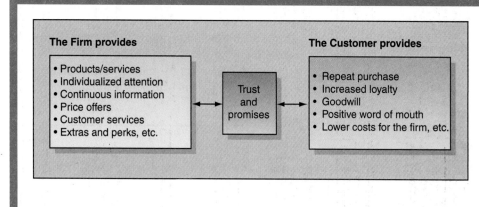

FIGURE 16-7

A Portrayal of the Characteristics of Relationship Marketing

Source: In part, this portrayal was inspired by: Mary Long, Leon Schiffman, and Elaine Sherman, "Understanding the Relationships in Consumer Marketing Relationship Programs: A Content Analysis," in *Proceedings of the World Marketing Congress* VII-II, ed. K. Grant and Walker (Melbourne, Australia: Academy of Marketing Science, 1995), 10/27–10/26.

SUMMARY

The consumer's decision to purchase or not to purchase a product or service is an important moment for most marketers. It can signify whether a marketing strategy has been wise, insightful, and effective, or whether it was poorly planned and missed the mark. Thus, marketers are particularly interested in the consumer's decision-making process. For a consumer to make a decision, more than one alternative must be available. (The decision not to buy is also an alternative.)

Theories of consumer decision making vary, depending on the researcher's assumptions about the nature of humankind. The various models of consumers (economic view, passive view, cognitive view, and emotional view) depict consumers and their decision-making processes in distinctly different ways.

An overview consumer decision-making model ties together the psychological, social, and cultural concepts examined in parts II and III into an easily understood framework. This decision model has three sets of variables: input variables, process variables, and output variables.

Input variables that affect the decision-making process include commercial marketing efforts, as well as noncommercial influences from the consumer's sociocultural environment. The decision process variables are influenced by the consumer's psychological field, including the evoked set (or the brands in a particular product category considered in making a purchase choice). Taken as a whole, the psychological field influences the consumer's recognition of a need, prepurchase search for information, and evaluation of alternatives.

The output phase of the model includes the actual purchase (either trial or repeat purchase) and postpurchase evaluation. Both prepurchase and postpurchase evaluation feed back in the form of experience into the consumer's psychological field and serve to influence future decision processing.

The process of gift exchange is an important part of consumer behavior. Various gift-giving and gift-receiving relationships are captured by the following five specific categories in the gifting classification scheme: (1) intergroup gifting (a group gives a gift to another group); (2) intercategory gifting (an individual gives a gift to a group or a group gives a gift to an individual); (3) intragroup gifting (a group gives a gift to itself or its members), (4) interpersonal gifting (an individual gives a gift to another individual), and (5) intrapersonal gifting (a self-gift).

Consumer behavior is not just making a purchase decision or the act of purchasing; it also includes the full range of experiences associated with using or consuming products and services. It also includes the sense of pleasure and satisfaction derived from possessing or collecting "things." The outputs of consumption are changes in feelings, moods, or attitudes; reinforcement of lifestyles; an enhanced sense of self; satisfaction of a consumer-related need; belonging to groups; and expressing and entertaining oneself.

Among other things, consuming includes the simple utility of using a superior product, the stress reduction of a vacation, the sense of having a "sacred" possession, and the pleasures of a hobby or a collection. Some possessions serve to assist consumers in their effort to create "personal meaning" and to maintain a sense of the past.

Relationship marketing impacts consumers' decisions and their consumption satisfaction. Firms establish relationship marketing programs (sometimes called loyalty programs) to foster usage loyalty and a commitment to their products and services. At its heart, relationship marketing is all about building trust (between the firm and its customers), and keeping promises made to consumers. Therefore, the emphasis in relationship marketing is almost always on developing long-term bonds with customers by making them feel "special" and by providing them with personalized services.

DISCUSSION QUESTIONS

1. Compare and contrast the economic, passive, cognitive, and emotional models of consumer decision making.

2. What kinds of marketing and sociocultural inputs would influence the purchase of: (a) a TV with a built-in VCR, (b) a concentrated liquid laundry detergent, and (c) fat-free ice cream? Explain your answers.

3. Define extensive problem solving, limited problem solving, and routinized response behavior. What are the differences between the three decision-making approaches? What type of decision process would you expect most consumers to follow in their first purchase of a new product or brand in each of the following areas: (a) chewing gum, (b) sugar, (c) men's after shave lotion, (d) carpeting, (e) paper towels, (f) a cellular telephone, and (g) a luxury car? Explain your answers.

4. a. Identify three different products that you believe require a reasonably intensive prepurchase search by a consumer. Then, using Table 16-2 as a guide, identify the specific characteristics of these products that make an intensive prepurchase search likely.

   b. For each of the products that you listed, identify the perceived risks that a consumer is likely to experience before a purchase. Discuss how the marketers of these products can reduce these perceived risks.

5. Let's assume that this coming summer you are planning to spend a month touring Europe and are therefore in need of a good 35-mm camera. (a) Develop a list of product attributes that you will use as the purchase criteria in evaluating various 35-mm cameras. (b) Distinguish the differences that would occur in your decision process if you were to use compensatory versus noncompensatory decision rules.

6. How can a marketer of very light, very powerful laptop computers use its knowledge of customers' expectations in designing a marketing strategy?

7. How do consumers reduce postpurchase dissonance? How can marketers provide positive reinforcement to consumers after the purchase to reduce their dissonance?

8. The Gillette Company, which produces the highly successful Sensor shaving blade, has recently introduced a clear gel antiperspirant and deodorant for men. Identify the perceived risks associated with the purchase of this new product and outline a strategy designed to reduce these perceived risks during the product's introduction.

9. Albert Einstein once wrote that "the whole of science is nothing more than a refinement of everyday thinking." Do you think that this quote applies to the development of the consumer decision-making model presented in Figure 16-2?

EXERCISES

1. Find two print advertisements, one that illustrates the cognitive model of consumer decision making and one that illustrates the emotional model. Explain your choices. In your view, why did the marketers choose the approaches depicted in the advertisements?

2. Describe the need recognition process that took place before you purchased your last can of soft drink. How did it differ from the process that preceded the purchase of a new pair of sneakers? What role, if any, did advertising play in your need recognition?

3. List the colleges that you considered when choosing which college or university to attend and the criteria that you used to evaluate them. Describe how you acquired information on the different colleges along the different attributes that were important to you and how you made your decision. Be sure to specify whether you used compensatory or noncompensatory decision rules.

4. Select one of the following product categories: (a) compact disc players, (b) fast-food restaurants, or (c) shampoo, and: (1) write down the brands that constitute your evoked set, (2) identify brands that are not part of your evoked set, and (3) discuss how the brands included in your evoked set differ from those that are not included in terms of important attributes.

5. Select a newspaper or magazine advertisement that attempts: (a) to provide the consumer with a decision strategy to follow in making a purchase decision or (b) to reduce the perceived risk(s) associated with a purchase. Evaluate the effectiveness of the ad you selected.

KEY TERMS

- **Affect referral decision rule**
- **Compensatory decision rules**
- **Conjunctive decision rule**
- **Consumer decision making**
- **Consumption process**
- **Disjunctive rule**
- **Evaluation of alternatives**
- **Evoked set**
- **Extensive problem solving**
- **Gifting behavior**
- **Heuristics**
- **Inept set**
- **Inert set**
- **Information overload**
- **Lexicographic decision rule**
- **Limited problem solving**
- **Moods**
- **Need recognition**

- **Noncompensatory decision rules**
- **Postpurchase evaluation**
- **Prepurchase search**
- **Purchase behavior**
- **Relationship marketing**
- **Routinized response behavior**
- **Self-gifts**

NOTES

1. Itamar Simonson, "Shoppers' Easily Influenced Choices," *New York Times*, 6 November 1994, 11.
2. John A. Howard and Jagdish N. Sheth, *The Theory of Buyer Behavior* (New York: Wiley, 1969), 46–47; see also: John Howard, *Consumer Behavior in Marketing Strategy* (Upper Saddle River, NJ: Prentice Hall, 1989).
3. Herbert A. Simon, *Administrative Behavior*, 2d ed. (New York: Free Press, 1965), 40.
4. James G. March and Herbert A. Simon, *Organizations* (New York: Wiley, 1958), 140–41.
5. Michael A. Jones, Philip J. Trocchia, and David L. Mothersbaugh, "Noneconomic Motivations for Price Haggling: An Exploratory Study," in *Advances in Consumer Research*, vol. 24, ed. Merrie Brucks and Deborah J. MacInnis (Provo, UT: Association for Consumer Research, 1997), 388–91.
6. Meryl Paula Gardner, "Mood States and Consumer Behavior: A Critical Review," *Journal of Consumer Research* 12 (December 1985): 281–300; and Robert A. Peterson and Matthew Sauber, "A Mood Scale for Survey Research," in *1983 AMA Educators' Proceedings*, ed. Patrick E. Murphy et al. (Chicago: American Marketing Association, 1983), 409–14.
7. Barry J. Babin, William R. Darden, and Mitch Griffin, "Some Comments on the Role of Emotions in Consumer Behavior," in *1992 AMA Educators' Proceedings*, ed. Robert P. Leone and V. Kumor et al. (Chicago: American Marketing Association, 1992), 130–39; and Patricia A. Knowles, Stephen J. Grove, and W. Jeffrey Burroughs, "An Experimental Examination of Mood Effects on Retrieval and Evaluation of Advertisement and Brand Information," *Journal of the Academy of Marketing Science* 21 (Spring 1993): 135–42.
8. Gardner, "Mood States and Consumer Behavior."
9. Ruth Belk Smith and Elaine Sherman, "Effects of Store Image and Mood on Consumer Behavior: A Theoretical and Empirical Analysis," in *Advances in Consumer Research*, vol. 20, ed. Leigh McAlister and Michael L. Rothschild (Provo, UT: Association for Consumer Research, 1993), 631.
10. Knowles, Grove, and Burroughs, "An Experimental Examination."
11. Gordon C. Bruner, II, "The Effect of Problem-Recognition Style on Information Seeking," *Journal of the Academy of Marketing Science* 15 (Winter 1987): 33–41.
12. Matthew Klein, "He Shops, She Shops," *American Demographics* (March 1998): 34–35.
13. Haim Mano and Michael T. Elliott, "Smart Shopping: The Origins and Consequences of Price Savings," in *Advances in Consumer Research*, ed. Brucks and MacInnis, 504–10.
14. Sharon E. Beatty and Scott M. Smith, "External Search Effort: An Investigation Across Several Product Categories," *Journal of Consumer Research* 14 (June 1987): 83–95.
15. Niranjan V. Raman, "A Qualitative Investigation of Web-Browsing Behavior," in *Advances in Consumer Research*, ed. Brucks and MacInnis, 511–16.
16. Michael D. Johnson and Donald R. Lehmann, "Consumer Experience and Consideration Sets for Brands and Product Categories," in *Advances in Consumer Research*, ed. Brucks and MacInnis, 295–300.
17. Gita Venkataramani Johar, Kamel Jedidi, and Jacob Jacoby, "A Varying-Parameter Averaging Model on On-Line Brand Evaluations," *Journal of Consumer Research* 24 (September 1997): 232–47.
18. Sankar Sen and Eric J. Johnson, "Mere-Possession Effects without Possession in Consumer Choice," *Journal of Consumer Research* 24 (June 1997): 105–17.
19. Jeffrey F. Durgee, "Why Some Products 'Just Fell Right,' or, The Phenomenology of Product Rightness," in *Advances in Consumer Research*, vol. 22, ed. Frank R. Kardes and Mita Sujan (Provo, UT: Association for Consumer Research, 1995), 650–52.
20. Laurie Peterson, "The Strategic Shopper," *Adweek's Marketing Week*, 30 March 1992, 18–20.
21. Carey Goldberg, "Choosing the Joys of a Simplified Life," *New York Times*, 21 September 1995, C1, C9.
22. Ibid.
23. Sandra J. Burke, "The Effects of Missing Information on Decision Strategy Selection," in *Advances in Consumer Research*, vol. 17, ed. Marvin E. Goldberg, Gerald Gorn, and Richard W. Pollay (Provo, UT: Association for Consumer Research, 1990), 250–56.
24. Sarah Fisher Gardial and David W. Schumann, "In Search of the Elusive Consumer Inference," in *Advances in Consumer Research*, ed. Goldberg, Gorn, and Pollay, 283–87; see also Burke.
25. Barry L. Bayus, "The Consumer Durable Replacement Buyer," *Journal of Marketing* 55 (January 1991): 42–51.
26. Diane M. Phillips, Jerry C. Olson, and Hans Baumgartner, "Consumption Visions in Consumer Decision Making," in *Advances in Consumer Research*, vol. 22, ed. Frank R. Kardes and Mita Sujan (Provo, UT: Association for Consumer Research, 1995), 280.
27. Ibid., 280–84.
28. Diane M. Phillips, "Anticipating the Future: The Role of Consumption Visions in Consumer Behavior," in *Advances in Consumer Research*, vol. 23, ed. Kim P.

Corfman and John G. Lynch Jr. (Provo, UT: Association for Consumer Research, 1996), 70–75.

29. Robert A. Peterson, Sridhar Balasubramanian, and Bart J. Bronnenberg, "Exploring the Implications of the Internet for Consumer Marketing," *Journal of the Academy of Marketing Sciences* 25 (1997): 329–46.

30. Ernest R. Cadotte, Robert B. Woodruff, and Roger L. Jenkins, "Expectations and Norms in Models of Consumer Satisfaction," *Journal of Marketing Research*, 24 August 1987, 305–14.

31. Kare Sandvik, Kjell Gronhaug, and Frank Lindberg, "Routes to Customer Retention: The Importance of Customer Satisfaction, Performance Quality, Brand Reputation and Customer Knowledge," in *AMA Winter Conference*, ed. Debbie Thorne LeClair and Michael Hartline (Chicago: American Marketing Association, 1997), 211–17.

32. Deborah Y. Cohn and Leon G. Schiffman, "Gifting: A Taxonomy of Private Realm Giver and Recipient Relationships," Working Paper, City University of New York, Baruch College, 1996, 2.

33. Russell W. Belk and Gregory S. Coon, "Gift Giving as Agapic Love: An Alternative to the Exchange Paradigm Based on Dating Experiences," *Journal of Consumer Research* 20 (December 1993): 393–417.

34. Cele Otnes, Tina M. Lowrey, and Young Chan Kim, "Gift Selection for Easy and Difficult Recipients: A Social Roles Interpretation," *Journal of Consumer Research* 20 (September 1993): 229–44.

35. John F. Sherry Jr., "Reflections on Giftware and Giftcare: Whither Consumer Research?" in *Gift Giving: An Interdisciplinary Anthology*, ed. Cele Otnes and Richard F. Beltramini (Bowling Green, KY: Popular Press, 1996), 220.

36. Stephen J. Gould and Claudia E. Weil, "Gift-Giving and Gender Self-Concepts," *Gender Role* 24 (1991): 617–37.

37. Constance Hill and Celia T. Romm, "The Role of Mothers as Gift Givers: A Comparison Across Three Cultures," in *Advances in Consumer Research*, vol. 23, ed. Kim P. Corfman and John G. Lynch Jr., 21–27.

38. For a really interesting article on self-gifts, see: John F. Sherry Jr., Mary Ann McGrath, and Sidney J. Levy, "Monadic Gifting: Anatomy of Gifts Given to the Self," in *Contemporary Marketing and Consumer Behavior*, ed. John F. Sherry Jr. (Thousand Oaks, CA: Sage, 1995), 399–432.

39. David Glen Mick and Mitchelle DeMoss, "To Me from Me: A Descriptive Phenomenology of Self-Gifts," in *Advances in Consumer Research*, ed., Goldberg, Gorn, and Pollay, 677–82; and Shay Sayre and David Horne, "I Shop, Therefore I Am: The Role of Possessions for Self Definition," in *Advances in Consumer Research*, vol. 23, ed. Kim P. Corfman and John G. Lynch Jr., 323–28 (Provo, UT: Association for Consumer Research, 1996).

40. Cynthia Crossen, "'Merry Christmas to Moi,' Shoppers Say," *Wall Street Journal*, 11 December 1997, B1, B10.

41. Kim K. R. McKeage, Marsha L. Richins, and Kathleen Debevec, "Self-Gifts and the Manifestation of Material Values," in *Advances in Consumer Research*, vol. 20, ed. Leigh McAlister and Michael L. Rothschild (Provo, UT: Association for Consumer Research 1993), 359–64.

42. Kathleen M. Rassuli and Gilbert D. Harrell, "A New Perspective on Choice," in *Advances in Consumer Research*, ed. Goldberg, Gorn, and Pollay, 737–44.

43. For an interesting article on "consumption practices," see: Douglas B. Holt, "How Consumers Consume: A Typology of Consumer Practices," *Journal of Consumer Research* 22 (June 1995): 1–16.

44. James M. Perry, "Mike Weaver Proves That Everything Can Be a Collection," *Wall Street Journal*, 16 August 1995, 1.

45. Mary M. Long and Leon G. Schiffman, "Swatch Fever: An Allegory for Understanding the Paradox of Collecting," *Psychology and Marketing* 14 (August 1997): 495–509.

46. Russell W. Belk, "The Role of Possessions in Constructing and Maintaining a Sense of Past," in *Advances in Consumer Research*, ed. Goldberg, Gorn, and Pollay, 669–76.

47. Stacey Menzel Baker and Patricia F. Kennedy, "Death by Nostalgia: A Diagnosis of Context-Specific Cases," in *Advances in Consumer Research*, vol. 21, ed. Chris T. Allen and Deborah Roedder John (Provo, UT: Association for Consumer Research, 1994), 169–74.

48. Robert Bryce, "Here's a Course in Personal Finance 101, the Hard Way," *New York Times*, 30 April 1995, F11.

49. Leonard L. Berry, "Relationship Marketing of Services—Growing Interest, Emerging Perspectives," *Journal of the Academy of Marketing Science* 23 (Fall 1995): 236–45; and Mary Jo Bitner, "Building Service Relationships: It's All About Promises," *Journal of the Academy of Marketing Science* 23 (Fall 1995): 246–51.

50. Mary Long, Leon Schiffman, and Elaine Sherman, "Understanding the Relationships in Consumer Marketing Relationship Programs: A Content Analysis," in *Proceedings of the World Marketing Congress* VII-II, ed. K. Grant and Walker (Melbourne, Australia: Academy of Marketing Science, 1995), 10/27–10/32.

51. Emily Nelson, "Why Wal-Mart Sings, 'Yes, We Have Bananas,'" *Wall Street Journal*, 6 October 1998, B1, B4.

52. Mary Ellen Gordon and Kim McKeage, "Relationship Marketing Effectiveness: Differences between Women in New Zealand and the United States," in *1997 AMA Educators' Proceedings*, ed. William M. Pride and G. Tomas M. Hult (Chicago: American Marketing Association, 1997), 117–22.

53. Jagdish N. Sheth and Atul Parvatiyar, "Relationship Marketing in Consumer Marketing: Antecedents and Consequences," *Journal of the Academy of Marketing Science* 23 (Fall 1995): 255–71.

54. Barbara B. Stern, "Advertising Intimacy: Relationship Marketing and the Services Consumer, *Journal of Advertising* 26 (Winter 1997): 7–19.

55. Robert F. Dwyer, "Customer Lifetime Valuation to Support Marketing Decision Making," *Journal of Direct Marketing* 3 (1989): 8–15; Jonathan R. Copulsky and Michael J. Wolf, "Relationship Marketing: Positioning for the Future," *The Journal of Business Strategy* (July–August 1990): 16–20; and Philip Kotler, "Marketing's New Paradigm: What's Really Happening Out There," *Planning Review* (September–October 1992): 50–52.

56. Steve Schriver, "Customer Loyalty: Going, Going …," *American Demographics* (September 1997): 20–23.

Absolute Threshold. The lowest level at which an individual can experience a sensation.

Acculturation. The learning of a new or "foreign" culture.

Achievement Need. The need for personal accomplishment as an end in itself.

Acquired Needs. Needs that are learned in response to one's culture or environment (such as the need for esteem, prestige, affection, or power). Also known as *psychogenic* or *secondary needs*.

Actual Self-Image. The image that an individual has of himself or herself as a certain kind of person, with certain characteristic traits, habits, possessions, relationships, and behavior.

Adaptation. Process by which an individual becomes accommodated to a certain level of stimulation.

Adopter Categories. A sequence of categories that describes how early (or late) a consumer adopts a new product in relation to other adopters. The five typical adopter categories are innovators, early adopters, early majority, late majority, and laggards.

Adoption Process. The stages through which an individual consumer passes in arriving at a decision to try (or not to try), to continue using (or discontinue using) a new product. The five stages of the traditional adoption process are awareness, interest, evaluation, trial, and adoption.

Advertising Wearout. Overexposure to repetitive advertising that causes individuals to become satiated and their attention and retention to decline.

Affective Component. The part of the tricomponent attitude model that reflects a consumer's emotions or feelings with respect to an idea or object.

Affect Referral Decision Rule. A simplified decision rule by which consumers make a product choice on the basis of their previously established overall ratings of the brands considered, rather than on specific attributes.

Affiliation Need. The need for friendship, for acceptance, and for belonging.

Affluent Consumers. Consumers with household incomes that provide them with a disproportionately large share of all discretionary income.

Age Subcultures. Age subgroupings of the population.

Aggressive Personality. One of three personality types identified by Karen Horney. The aggressive person is one who moves against others (e.g., competes with others).

Aided Recall and Recognition. A research technique in which the consumer is shown a specific advertisement and is asked whether he or she remembers seeing it and can recall its content.

AIOs. Psychographic variables that focus on activities, interests, and opinions. Also referred to as Lifestyle.

American Core Values. Values that both affect and reflect the character of American society.

Approach Object. A positive goal toward which behavior is directed.

Arousal of Motives. Motives are often aroused on the basis of physiological, emotional, cognitive, or environmental factors.

Aspirational Group. A group to which a nonmember would like to belong.

Assimilation-Contrast Theory. A theory of attitude change that suggests that consumers are likely to accept only moderate attitude changes. If the change suggested is too extreme, the contrast with presently held attitudes will cause rejection of the entire message.

Attitude. A learned predisposition to behave in a consistently favorable or unfavorable manner with respect to a given object.

Attitude-Toward-Behavior Model. A model that proposes that a consumer's attitude toward a specific behavior is a function of how strongly he or she believes that the action will lead to a specific outcome (either favorable or unfavorable).

Attitude-Toward-Object Model. A model that proposes that a consumer's attitude toward a product or brand is a function of the presence of certain attributes and the consumer's evaluation of those attributes.

Attitude-Toward-the-Ad Model. A model that proposes that a consumer forms various feelings (affects) and judgments (cognitions) as the result of exposure to an advertisement, which, in turn, affect the consumer's *attitude toward the ad* and *beliefs and attitudes toward the brand*.

Attribution Theory. A theory concerned with how people assign causality to events and form or alter their attitudes as an outcome of assessing their own or other people's behavior.

Attributions towards Others. Consumers feel that another person is responsible for either positive or negative product performance.

Attributions towards Things. Consumers judge a product's performance and attribute it's success or failure to the product itself.

Audience Profile. Psychographic/demographic profile of the audience of a specific medium.

Autonomic (Unilateral) Decision. A purchase decision in which either the husband or the wife makes the final decision.

Avoidance Object. A negative goal from which behavior is directed away.

Baby Boomers. Individuals born between 1946 and 1964 (approximately 45% of the adult population).

Balance Theory. An attitude-change theory that postulates that individuals avoid inconsistency and seek harmony (consistency) by changing the weaker conflicting attitude to agree with the stronger attitude.

Behavioral Learning Theories. Theories based on the premise that learning takes place as the result of observable responses to external stimuli. Also known as *stimulus response theory*.

Beliefs. Mental or verbal statements that reflect a person's particular knowledge and assessment about some idea or thing.

Benefit Segmentation. Segmentation based on the kinds of benefits consumers seek in a product.

Biogenic Needs. The needs for food, water, air, clothing, shelter, and sex.

Brand Equity. The value inherent in a well-known brand name.

Brand Loyalty. Consumers' consistent preference and/or purchase of the same brand in a specific product or service category.

Brand Personification. Specific "personality-type" traits or characteristics ascribed by consumers to different brands.

Celebrity Credibility. The audience's perception of both the celebrity's expertise and trustworthiness.

Central and Peripheral Routes to Persuasion. A promotional theory that proposes that highly involved consumers are best reached through ads that focus on the specific attributes of the product (the central route) while uninvolved consumers can be attracted through peripheral advertising cues such as the model or the setting (the peripheral route).

Chapin's Social Status Scale. A social class rating scheme that focuses on the presence or absence of certain items of furniture and accessories in the home.

Class Consciousness. A feeling of social-group membership that reflects an individual's sense of belonging or identification with others.

Classical Conditioning. (See Conditioned Learning.)

Closure. A principle of Gestalt psychology that stresses the individual's need for completion. This need is reflected in the individual's subconscious reorganization and perception of incomplete stimuli as complete or whole pictures.

Cognitions. Knowledge that is acquired by a combination of direct experience and related information from various sources.

Cognitive Age. An individual's perceived age (usually 10 to 15 years younger than his or her chronological age).

Cognitive Arousal. A motivating situation in which mental or visual cues (e.g., specific thoughts or an ad) lead to awareness of a need.

Cognitive Associative Learning. The learning of associations among events through classical conditioning that allows the organism to anticipate and represent its environment.

Cognitive Component. A part of the tricomponent attitude model that represents the knowledge, perception, and beliefs that a consumer has with respect to an idea or object.

Cognitive Dissonance. The discomfort or dissonance that consumers experience as a result of conflicting information. (See Balance Theory.)

Cognitive Learning Theory. A theory of learning based on mental information processing, often in response to problem solving.

Cognitive Personality. *Need for cognition* and *visualizers versus verbalizers* are two cognitive personality traits that influence consumer behavior.

Communication. The transmission of a message from a sender to a receiver by means of a signal of some sort sent through a channel of some sort.

Comparative Advertising. Advertising that explicitly names or otherwise identifies one or more competitors of the advertised brand for the purpose of claiming superiority, either on an overall basis or in selected product attributes.

Comparative Reference Group. A group whose norms serve as a benchmark for highly specific or narrowly defined types of behavior. (See also Normative Reference Group.)

Compatibility. The degree to which potential consumers feel that a new product is consistent with their present needs, values, and practices.

Compensatory Decision Rule. A type of decision rule in which a consumer evaluates each brand in terms of each relevant attribute and then selects the brand with the highest weighted score.

Complexity. The degree to which a new product is difficult to comprehend and/or use.

Compliant Personality. One of three personality types identified by Karen Horney. The compliant person is one who moves toward others (e.g., one who desires to be loved, wanted, and appreciated by others).

Composite Variable Index. An index that combines a number of socioeconomic variables (such as education, income, occupation) to form one overall measure of social class standing. (See also Single Variable Index.)

Compulsive Consumption. Consumers who are compulsive buyers have an addiction; in some respects, they are out of control and their actions may have damaging consequences to them and to those around them.

Conative Component. A part of the tricomponent attitude model that reflects a consumer's likelihood or tendency to behave in a particular way with regard to an attitude-object. Also referred to as "intention to buy."

Concentrated Marketing. Targeting a product or service to a single market segment with a unique marketing mix (price, product, promotion, method of distribution).

Concept. A mental image of an intangible trait, characteristic, or idea.

Conditioned Learning. According to Pavlovian theory, conditioned learning results when a stimulus paired with another stimulus that elicits a known response serves to produce the same response by itself.

Conditioned Response. Automatic response to a situation built up through repeated exposures.

Conformity. The extent to which an individual adopts attitudes and/or behavior that are consistent with the norms of a group to which he or she belongs or would like to belong.

Conjunctive Rule. A noncompensatory decision rule in which consumers establish a minimally acceptable cutoff point for each attribute evaluated. Brands that fall below the cutoff point on any one attribute are eliminated from further consideration.

Construct. A term that represents or symbolizes an abstract trait or characteristic, such as motivation or aggression.

Consumer Behavior. The behavior that consumers display in searching for, purchasing, using, evaluating, and disposing of products, services, and ideas.

Consumer Conformity. The willingness of consumers to adopt the norms, attitudes and behavior of reference groups.

Consumer Decision Rules. Procedures adopted by consumers to reduce the complexity of making product and brand decisions.

Consumer Ethnocentrism. A consumer's predisposition to accept or reject foreign-made products.

Consumer Fieldwork. Observational research by anthropologists of the behaviors of a small sample of people from a particular society.

Consumer Innovativeness. The degree to which consumers are receptive to new products, new services, or new practices.

Consumer Innovators. Those who are among the first to purchase a new product.

Consumer Learning. The process by which individuals acquire the purchase and consumption knowledge and experience they apply to future related behavior.

Consumer Materialism. A personality-like trait of individuals who regard possessions as particularly essential to their identities and lives. (See also Materialistic Consumers.)

Consumer-Oriented Definition of Innovation. Any product that a potential consumer judges to be new. Newness is based on the consumer's *perception* of the product, rather than on physical features or market realities.

Consumer-Oriented Legislation. Legislation enacted to protect the public from dishonest or unethical business practices.

Consumer Profile. Psychographic/demographic profile of actual or proposed consumers for a specific product or service.

Consumer Research. Methodology used to study consumer behavior.

Consumer Research Process. The consumer research process generally consists of six steps: defining objectives, collecting secondary data, developing a research design, collecting primary data, analyzing the data, and preparing a report on the findings.

Consumers. A term used to describe two different kinds of consuming entities: *personal consumers* (who buy goods and services for their own use or for household use) and *organizational consumers* (who buy products, equipment, and services in order to run their organizations).

Consumer Socialization. The process, started in childhood, by which an individual first learns the skills and attitudes relevant to consumer purchase behavior.

Consumption Process. A process consisting of three stages: the *input stage* establishes the consumption set and consuming style; the *process* of consuming and possessing, which includes using, possessing, collecting, and disposing of things and experiences; and the *output stage*, which includes changes in feelings, moods, attitudes, and behavior toward the product or service.

Content Analysis. A method for systematically analyzing the content of verbal and/or pictorial communication. The method is frequently used to determine prevailing social values of a society in a particular era under study.

Continuous Innovation. A new product entry that is an improved or modified version of an existing product rather than a totally new product. A continuous innovation has the least disruptive influence on established consumption patterns.

Copy Pretest. A test of an advertisement before the ad is run to determine which, if any, elements of the advertising message should be revised before major media expenses are incurred.

Copy Posttest. A posttest is used to evaluate the effectiveness of an advertisement that has already appeared and to see which elements, if any, should be revised to improve the impact of future advertisements.

Countersegmentation Strategy. A strategy in which a company combines two or more segments into a single segment to be targeted with an individually tailored product or promotion campaign.

Cross-Cultural Consumer Analysis. Research to determine the extent to which consumers of two or more nations are similar in relation to specific consumption behavior.

Cross-Cultural Consumer Research. Research methods designed to find the similarities and differences among consumers in a marketer's domestic market and those it wants to target in a foreign country.

Cross-Cultural Psychographic Segmentation. Tailoring marketing strategies to the needs (psychological, social, cultural, and functional) of specific foreign segments.

Cues. Stimuli that give direction to consumer motives (i.e., that suggest a specific way to satisfy a salient motive).

Cultural Anthropology. The study of human beings that traces the development of core beliefs, values, and customs passed down to individuals from their parents and grandparents.

Culture. The sum total of learned beliefs, values, and customs that serve to regulate the consumer behavior of members of a particular society.

Customs. Overt modes of behavior that constitute culturally acceptable ways of behaving in specific situations.

Decision. A choice made from two or more alternatives.

Decision Time. Within the context of the diffusion process, the amount of time required for an individual to adopt (or reject) a specific new product.

Decoding. Receivers interpret the messages they receive on the basis of their personal experience and personal characteristics.

Defense Mechanisms. Methods by which people mentally redefine frustrating situations to protect their self-images and their self-esteem.

Defensive Attribution. A theory that suggests consumers are likely to accept credit for successful outcomes (internal attribution) and to blame other persons or products for failure (external attribution).

Demographic Characteristics. Objective characteristics of a population (such as age, sex, marital status, income, occupation, and education) which are often used as the basis for market segmentation.

Demographic Segmentation. The division of a total market into smaller subgroups on the basis of such objective characteristics as age, sex, marital status, income, occupation, or education.

Deontology. An ethical philosophy that places greater weight on personal and social values than on economic values.

Dependent Variable. A variable whose value changes as the result of a change in another (i.e., independent) variable. For example, consumer purchases are a dependent variable subject to level and quality of advertising (independent variables).

Depth Interview. A lengthy and relatively unstructured interview designed to uncover a consumer's underlying attitudes and/or motivations.

Detached Personality. One of three personality types identified by Karen Horney. The detached person is one who moves away from others (e.g., who desires independence, self-sufficiency, and freedom from obligations).

Differential Threshold. The minimal difference that can be detected between two stimuli. Also known as the *j.n.d. (just noticeable difference).* (See also Weber's Law.)

Differentiated Marketing. Targeting a product or service to two or more segments, using a specifically tailored product, promotional appeal, price, and/or method of distribution for each.

Diffusion of Innovations. The framework for exploring the spread of consumer acceptance of new products throughout the social system.

Diffusion Process. The process by which the acceptance of an innovation is spread by communication to members of a social system over a period of time.

Direct Mail. Advertising that is sent directly to the mailing address of a target consumer.

Direct Marketing. A marketing technique that uses various media (mail, print, broadcast, telephone interview) to solicit a direct response from a consumer. Also known as database marketing.

Disclaimant Group. A group in which a person holds membership, but with whose values, attitudes, and behavior he or she does not wish to be associated.

Discontinuous Innovation. A dramatically new product entry that requires the establishment of new consumption practices.

Disjunctive Rule. A noncompensatory decision rule in which consumers establish a minimally acceptable cutoff point for each relevant product attribute; any brand meeting or surpassing the cutoff point for any one attribute is considered an acceptable choice.

Distributed Learning. Learning spaced over a period of time to increase consumer retention. (See also Massed Learning.)

Dogmatism. A personality trait that reflects the degree of rigidity a person displays toward the unfamiliar and toward information that is contrary to his or her own established beliefs.

Downscale Consumers. Frequently defined as consumers with annual household incomes of $30,000 or less.

Downward Mobility. Consumers who have a lower social class level than their parents in terms of the jobs they hold, their residences, level of disposable income, and savings.

Drive. An internal force that impels a person to engage in an action designed to satisfy a specific need.

Dynamically Continuous Innovation. A new product entry that is sufficiently innovative to have some disruptive effects on established consumption practices.

Ego. In Freudian theory, the part of the personality that serves as the individual's conscious control. It functions as an internal monitor that balances the impulsive demands of the *id* and the sociocultural constraints of the *superego.*

Ego-Defensive Function. A component of the functional approach to attitude-change that suggests that consumers want to protect their self-concepts from inner feelings of doubt.

Elaboration Likelihood Model (ELM). A theory that suggests that a person's level of involvement during message processing is a critical factor in determining which route to persuasion is likely to be effective. (See also Central and Peripheral Routes to Persuasion.)

Embeds. Disguised stimuli (often sexual in nature) that are "planted" in print advertisements to subconsciously influence consumers to buy the advertised products.

Emotional Arousal. Motives aroused through emotional factors (e.g., anger).

Emotional Motives. The selection of goals according to personal or subjective criteria (e.g., the desire for individuality, pride, fear, affection, status).

Encoding. The process by which individuals select and assign a word or visual image to represent a perceived object or idea.

Enculturation. The learning of the culture of one's own society.

Endorsements. Celebrities who may or may not be users of a particular product or service may lend their names to advertisements for such products or services for a fee.

Environmental Arousal. Motives activated at a particular time by specific cues in the environment.

Evaluation of Alternatives. A stage in the consumer *decision-making process* in which the consumer appraises the benefits to be derived from each of the product alternatives being considered.

Evoked Set. The specific brands a consumer considers in making a purchase choice in a particular product category.

Expected Self-Image. How individuals expect to see themselves at some specified future time.

Experientialism. An approach to the study of consumer behavior that focuses on the consumption experience. (See also Interpretivism and Postmodernism.)

Expert Appeals. The promotional use of a person who, because of his or her occupation, special training, or experience, is able to speak knowledgeably to the consumer about the product or service being advertised.

Extended Family. A household consisting of a husband, wife, offspring, and at least one other blood relative.

Extended Self. Modification or changing of one's self by which a consumer uses self-altering products or services to conform to or take on the appearance of a particular type of person (e.g., a biker, a physician, a lawyer, a college professor).

Extensive Information Processing. A search by the consumer to establish the necessary product criteria to select knowledgeably the most suitable product to fulfill a need.

External Attribution. A theory that suggests that consumers are likely to credit their success to outside sources.

Extinction. The point at which a learned response ceases to occur because of lack of reinforcement. (See also Wearout.)

Extrinsic Cues. Cues external to the product (such as price, store image, or brand image) that serve to influence the consumer's perception of a product's quality.

Family. Two or more persons related by blood, marriage, or adoption who reside together.

Family Branding. The practice of marketing several company products under the same brand name.

Family Gatekeeper. A family member who controls the flow of information to the family about products or services, thereby regulating the related consumption decisions of other family members.

Family Influencer. A family member who provides product-related information and advice to other members of the family, thereby influencing related consumption decisions.

Family Life Cycle. Classification of families into significant stages. The five traditional *FLC* stages are Bachelorhood, Honeymooners, Parenthood, Postparenthood, and Dissolution.

Family Life Cycle (FLC) Analysis. A strategic tool that enables marketers to segment families in terms of a series of stages spanning the life course of a family unit.

Federal Trade Commission (FTC). Federal agency empowered to regulate the substance of commercial communications (i.e., advertising).

Feedback. Communication—either verbal or nonverbal (body language)—that is communicated back to the sender of a message by the receiver.

Field Observation. A cultural measurement technique that focuses on observing behavior within a natural environment (sometimes without the subjects' awareness).

Figure and Ground. A Gestalt principle of perceptual organization that focuses on contrast. Figure is usually perceived clearly because, in contrast to (back) ground, it appears to be well defined, solid, and in the forefront, while the ground is usually perceived as indefinite, hazy, and continuous. Music can be figure or (back) ground.

Financial Risk. The perceived risk that the product will not be worth its cost.

Firm-Oriented Definition of Innovation. Treats the newness of a product from the perspective of how new it is for the company producing or marketing it.

Fixated Consumers. Consumers who have a passionate interest in a specific product category.

Focus Group. A qualitative research method in which about eight to ten persons participate in an unstructured group interview focused on a product or service concept.

Foot-in-the-Door Technique. A theory of attitude change that suggests individuals form attitudes that are consistent with their own prior behavior.

Formal Communications Sources. A source that speaks on behalf of an organization—either a for-profit (commercial) or a not-for-profit organization.

Formal Group. A group that has a clearly defined structure, specific roles and authority levels, and specific goals (e.g., a political party).

Formal Interpersonal Communication. Direct communication between a person representing a profit or non-profit organization and one or more others (e.g., a discussion between a salesman and a prospect).

Freudian Theory. A theory of personality and motivation developed by the psychoanalyst Sigmund Freud. (See Psychoanalytic Theory.)

Functional Approach. An attitude-change theory that classifies attitudes in terms of four functions: *utilitarian*, *ego-defensive*, *value-expressive*, and *knowledge* functions.

Functional Risk. The perceived risk that the product will not perform as expected.

Functions of the Family. Traditional functions of the family include the provision of: economic well-being, emotional support, suitable family lifestyles, and childhood socialization.

Generation X. The 18- to 29-year-old post baby-boomer segment (also referred to as *Xers* or *busters*).

Generic Goals. The general classes or categories of goals that individuals select to fulfill their needs. (See also Product-Specific Goals.)

Geodemographic Clusters. A composite segmentation strategy that uses both geographic variables (zip codes, neighborhoods, or blocks) and demographic variables (e.g., income, occupation, value of residence) to identify target markets.

Geographic Segmentation. The division of a total potential market into smaller subgroups on the basis of geographic variables (e.g., region, state, or city).

Gestalt. A German term meaning "pattern" or "configuration" that has come to represent various principles of perceptual organization. (See also Perceptual Organization.)

Gifting Behavior. The process of gift exchange that takes place between a giver and a recipient.

Global Marketing. A product that is marketed with the same marketing and promotional campaign in all markets throughout the world.

Goals. The sought-after results of motivated behavior. A person fulfills a need through achievement of a goal.

Group. Two or more individuals who interact to accomplish either individual or mutual goals.

Grouping. A Gestalt theory of perceptual organization that proposes that individuals tend to group stimuli automatically so that they form a unified picture or impression. The perception of stimuli as groups or chunks of information, rather than as discrete bits of information, facilitates their memory and recall.

Group Norms. The implicit rules of conduct or standards of behavior which members of a group are expected to observe.

Habit. A consistent pattern of behavior performed without considered thought. Consistent repetition is the hallmark of habit.

Halo Effect. A situation in which the perception of a person on a multitude of dimensions is based on the evaluation of just one (or a few) dimensions (e.g., a man is trustworthy, fine, and noble because he looks you in the eye when he speaks).

Hemispheral Lateralization. Learning theory in which the basic premise is that the right and left hemispheres of the brain "specialize" in the kinds of information that they process. Also called Split Brain theory.

Heuristics. (See Consumer Decision Rules.)

Hierarchy of Needs. (See Maslow's Need Hierarchy.)

High Involvement. A situation where consumers judge a purchase decision to be important enough for them to engage in extensive information search prior to making the decision.

Hybrid Segmentation. The use of several segmentation variables to more accurately define or "fine tune" consumer segments.

Hypothesis. A tentative statement of relationship between two or more variables.

Id. In Freudian theory, the part of the personality that consists of primitive and impulsive drives that the individual strives to satisfy.

Ideal Social Self-Image. How consumers would like others to see them.

Ideal Self-Image. How individuals would *like* to perceive themselves (as opposed to Actual Self-Image—the way they *do* perceive themselves).

Impersonal Communication. Communication directed to a large and diffuse audience, with no direct communication between source and receiver. Also known as *mass communication*.

Independent Variable. A variable that can be manipulated to effect a change in the value of a second (i.e., dependent) variable. For example, price is an independent variable that often affects sales (the dependent variable).

Index of Status Characteristics (ISC). A composite measure of social class that combines occupation, source of income (not amount), house type, and dwelling area into a single weighted index of social class standing. Also known as *Warner's ISC*.

Indirect Reference Groups. Individuals or groups with whom a person identifies but does not have direct face-to-face contact, such as movie stars, sports heroes, political leaders, or TV personalities.

Inept Set. Brands that a consumer excludes from purchase consideration.

Inert Set. Brands that a consumer is indifferent towards because they are perceived as having no particular advantage.

Informal Group. A group of people who see each other frequently on an informal basis, such as weekly poker players or social acquaintances.

Informal Interpersonal Communications. Direct communication between two or more persons who are friends, neighbors, relatives, or co-workers.

Information Overload. A situation in which the consumer is presented with too much product- or brand-related information.

Information Processing. A cognitive theory of human learning patterned after computer information processing that focuses on how information is stored in human memory and how it is retrieved.

Innate Needs. Physiological needs for food, water, air, clothing, shelter, and sex. Also known as *biogenic* or *primary needs*.

Inner-Directed Consumers. Consumers who tend to rely on their own "inner" values or standards when evaluating new products and who are likely to be consumer innovators.

Innovation. A totally new product, new service, new idea, or new practice.

Innovation Decision Process. An update of the traditional *adoption process* model consisting of the following four stages: knowledge, persuasion, decision, and confirmation.

Innovativeness Scale. A measure of a consumer's willingness to try new products.

Innovator. An individual who is among the earliest purchasers of a new product.

Institutional Advertising. Advertising designed to promote a favorable company image rather than specific products.

Instrumental Conditioning. A behavioral theory of learning based on a trial-and-error process, with habits formed as the result of positive experiences (reinforcement) resulting from specific behaviors. (See also Conditioned Learning.)

Intention-to-Buy Scales. A method of assessing the likelihood of a consumer purchasing a product or behaving in a certain way.

Intermediary Audiences. Wholesalers, distributors, and retailers who are sent *trade advertising* designed to persuade them to order and stock merchandise, and relevant professionals (such as architects or physicians) who are sent *professional advertising* in the hopes that they will specify or prescribe the marketers' products.

Internal Attributions. Consumers attribute their success in using a product or source to their own skill.

Interpersonal Communication. Communication that occurs directly between two or more people by mail, by telephone, or in person.

Interpretivism. A postmodernist approach to the study of consumer behavior that focuses on the act of consuming rather than on the act of buying.

Intrinsic Cues. Physical characteristics of the product (such as size, color, flavor, or aroma) that serve to influence the consumer's perceptions of product quality.

Involvement Theory. A theory of consumer learning which postulates that consumers engage in a range of information processing activity, from extensive to limited problem solving, depending on the relevance of the purchase.

Joint Decisions. Family purchase decisions in which the husband and wife are equally influential. Also known as *syncratic decisions*.

Just Noticeable Difference (j.n.d.). The minimal difference that can be detected between two stimuli. (See also Differential Threshold and Weber's Law.)

Key Informant Method. A method of measuring various aspects of consumer behavior (e.g., opinion leadership or social class) by which a knowledgeable person is asked to classify individuals with whom he or she is familiar into specific categories.

Knowledge Function. A component of the functional approach to attitude-change theory that suggests that consumers have a strong need to know and understand the people and things with which they come into contact.

Learning. The process by which individuals acquire the knowledge and experience they apply to future purchase and consumption behavior.

Lexicographic Rule. A noncompensatory decision rule in which consumers first rank product attributes in terms of their importance, then compare brands in terms of the attribute considered most important. If one brand scores higher than the other brands, it is selected; if not, the process is continued with the second ranked attribute, and so on.

Licensing. The use by manufacturers and retailers of well-known celebrity or designer names (for a fee) to acquire instant recognition and status for their products.

Lifestyle. (See Psychographic Characteristics.)

Likert Scale. A summated attitude scale.

Limited Information Processing or Problem Solving. A limited search by a consumer for a product that will satisfy his or her basic criteria from among a selected group of brands.

Localized Marketing. Products and promotional programs are tailored for each market.

Long-Term Store. In information-processing theory, the stage of real memory where information is organized, reorganized and retained for relatively extended periods of time.

Low Involvement. A situation where consumers judge a purchase decision to be so unimportant or routine that they engage in little information search prior to making a decision.

Market Mavens. Individuals whose influence stems from a general knowledge and market expertise that lead to an early awareness of new products and services.

Marketing. Activities designed to enhance the flow of goods, services, and ideas from producers to consumers in order to satisfy consumer needs and wants.

Marketing Concept. A consumer-oriented philosophy that suggests that satisfaction of consumer needs provides the focus for product development and marketing strategy to enable the firm to meet its own organizational goals.

Marketing Ethics. Designing, packaging, pricing, advertising, and distributing products in such a way that negative consequences to consumers, employees, and society in general are avoided.

Marketing Mix. The unique configuration of the four basic marketing variables (product, promotion, price, and channels of distribution) that a marketing organization controls.

Marketing of Social Causes. Advertising campaigns designed to promote socially desirable behavior.

Market-Oriented Definitions of Innovativeness. Judges the newness of a product in terms of how much exposure consumers have had to the new product.

Market Segmentation. The process of dividing a potential market into distinct subsets of consumers and selecting one or more segments as a target market to be reached with a distinct marketing mix.

Maslow's Need Hierarchy. A theory of motivation that postulates that individuals strive to satisfy their needs according to a basic hierarchical structure, starting with physiological needs, then moving to safety needs, social needs, egoistic needs, and finally self-actualization needs.

Mass Communication. (See Impersonal Communication.)

Massed Learning. Compressing the learning schedule into a short time span to accelerate consumer learning. (See also Distributed Learning.)

Mass Marketing. Offering the same product and marketing mix to all consumers.

Media Demassification. Publishers redirecting their focus from large, general-interest audiences to smaller, more specialized audiences.

Media Strategy. An essential component of a communications plan, which calls for the placement of advertisements in the specific media read, viewed, or heard by the selected target audiences.

Medium. A channel through which a message is transmitted (e.g., a television commercial, a newspaper advertisement, or a personal letter). The plural is *media*.

Message. The thought, idea, attitude, image, or other information that a sender wishes to convey to an intended audience.

Message Framing. Positively framed messages (those that specify benefits to be *gained* by using a product) are more persuasive than negatively framed messages (that specify benefits *lost* by not using a product).

Metaphor Analysis. A method of research where respondents are given magazines, scissors, paste, and paper and asked to cut out pictures from magazines that represent their feelings about the product category under study.

Micromarketing. Highly regionalized marketing strategies that use advertising and promotional campaigns specifically geared to local market needs and conditions.

Model. A simplified representation of reality designed to show the relationships between the various elements of a system or process under investigation.

Modeling. (See Observational Learning.)

Models of Man. (See Economic Man, Passive Man, Cognitive Man, and Emotional Man Models.)

Mood/Affect. An individual's subjectively perceived "feeling state."

Motivation. The driving force within individuals that impels them to action.

Motivational Research. Qualitative research designed to uncover consumers' subconscious or hidden motivations. The basic premise of motivational research is that consumers are not always aware of, or may not wish to reveal, the basic reasons underlying their actions.

Multiattribute Attitude Models. Attitude models that examine the composition of consumer attitudes in terms of selected product attributes or beliefs.

Multinational Strategies. Decisions that marketers make on how to reach all potential consumers of their products in countries throughout the world.

Multiple Self or Selves. Consumers have different images of themselves in response to different situations and are quite likely to act differently with different people and in different situations.

Multistep Flow of Communication Theory. A revision of the traditional two-step theory that shows multiple communication flows: from the mass media simultaneously to opinion leaders, opinion receivers, and information receivers (who neither influence nor are influenced by others); from opinion leaders to opinion receivers; and from opinion receivers to opinion leaders.

National Subcultures. Nationality subcultures in a larger society in which members often retain a sense of identification and pride in the language and customs of their ancestors.

Need for Cognition. The personality trait that measures a person's craving for or enjoyment of thinking.

Need Recognition. The realization by the consumer that there is a difference between "what is" and "what should be."

Negative Motivation. A driving force away from some object or condition.

Negative Reinforcement. An unpleasant or negative outcome that serves to encourage a specific behavior. (Not to be confused with punishment, which discourages repetition of a specific behavior.)

Neo-Freudian Personality Theory. A school of psychology that stresses the fundamental role of social relationships in the formation and development of personality.

Noncompensatory Decision Rule. A type of consumer decision rule by which positive evaluation of a brand attribute does not compensate for (i.e., is not balanced against) a negative evaluation of the same brand on some other attribute.

Nonprofit Marketing. The use of marketing concepts and techniques by not-for-profit organizations (such as museums or government agencies) to impart information, ideas, or attitudes to various segments of the public.

Nontraditional FLC Stages. A family life-cycle categorization that includes nontraditional household configurations such as divorced or widowed young adults, homosexual couples, couples without children, unmarried couples, etc.

Normative Reference Group. A group that influences the general values or behavior of an individual. (See Comparative Reference Group.)

Not-for-Profit-Marketing. (See Nonprofit Marketing.)

Nuclear Family. A household consisting of a husband and wife and at least one offspring.

Objective Measurement of Social Class. A method of measuring social class whereby individuals are asked specific socioeconomic questions concerning themselves or their families. On the basis of their answers, people are placed within specific social-class groupings.

Observability. The ease with which a product's benefits or attributes can be observed, visualized, or described to potential customers.

Observational Learning. A process by which individuals observe the behavior of others, remember it, and imitate it. Also known as *modeling.*

Observational Research. A form of consumer research that relies on observation of consumers in the process of buying and using products.

One-Sided Versus Two-Sided Messages. A one-sided message tells only the benefits of a product or service; a two-sided message also includes some negatives, thereby enhancing the credibility of the marketer.

Operant Conditioning. (See Instrumental Conditioning.)

Opinion Leader. A person who informally gives product information and advice to others.

Opinion Leadership. The process by which one person (the *opinion leader*) informally influences the consumption actions or attitudes of others, who may be *opinion seekers* or *opinion recipients.*

Opinion Receiver (Recipient). An individual who either actively seeks product information from others or receives unsolicited information.

Opinion Seeker. Individuals who actively seek information and advice about products from others.

Optimizing Decision Strategy. A strategy whereby a consumer evaluates each brand in terms of significant product criteria. (See also Simplifying Decision Strategy.)

Optimum Stimulation Level (OSL). A personality trait that measures the level or amount of novelty or complexity that individuals seek in their personal experiences. High OSL consumers tend to accept risky and novel products more readily than low OSL consumers.

Organizational Consumer. A business, government agency, or other institution (profit or nonprofit) that buys the goods, services, and/or equipment necessary for the organization to function.

Other-Directed Consumers. Consumers who tend to look to others for direction and for approval.

Other-Directedness. A tendency to look to others for direction and approval on what is right or wrong.

Packaging-to-Price Deceptions. Deception practiced by some marketers who maintain the size and price of their product packages but decrease the quantity in the package.

Participant-Observers. Researchers who participate in the environment that they are studying without notifying those who are being observed.

Perceived Quality. Consumers often judge the quality of a product or service on the basis of a variety of informational cues that they associate with the product; some of these cues are intrinsic to the product or service; others are extrinsic, such as price, store image, service environment, brand image, and promotional messages.

Perceived Risk. The degree of uncertainty perceived by the consumer as to the consequences (outcome) of a specific purchase decision.

Perception. The process by which an individual selects, organizes, and interprets stimuli into a meaningful and coherent picture of the world.

Perceptual Blocking. The subconscious "screening out" of stimuli that are threatening or inconsistent with one's needs, values, beliefs, or attitudes.

Perceptual Defense. The process of subconsciously distorting stimuli to render them less threatening or more consistent with one's needs, values, beliefs, or attitudes.

Perceptual Distortion. The influences on an individual that separate that person's perception of a stimulus from reality.

Perceptual Interpretation. The interpretation of stimuli based on an individual's expectations in light of previous experiences, on the number of plausible explanations that he or she can envision, and on motives and interests at the time of perception.

Perceptual Mapping. A research technique that enables marketers to plot graphically consumers' perceptions concerning product attributes of specific brands.

Perceptual Organization. The subconscious ordering and perception of stimuli into groups or configurations according to certain principles of Gestalt psychology.

Personal Consumer. The individual who buys goods and services for his or her own use, for household use, for the use of a family member, or for a friend. (Also referred to as the Ultimate Consumer or End User.)

Personality. The inner psychological characteristics that both determine and reflect how a person responds to his or her environment.

Personality Scale. A series of questions or statements designed to measure a single personality trait.

Personality Test. A pencil-and-paper test designed to measure an individual's personality in terms of one or more traits or inner characteristics.

Physical Risk. The perceived physical risk to self and others that the product may pose.

Physiological Needs. Innate (i.e., biogenic needs), including the needs for food, water, air, clothing, shelter, and sex. Also known as Primary Needs.

Political Marketing. The use of marketing concepts and techniques by candidates for political office and by those interested in promoting political causes.

Positioning. Establishing a specific image for a brand in relation to competing brands. (See also Product Positioning.)

Positive Motivation. A driving force toward some object or condition.

Positive Reinforcement. A favorable outcome to a specific behavior that strengthens the likelihood that the behavior will be repeated.

Positivism. A consumer behavior research approach that regards the consumer behavior discipline as an applied marketing science. Its main focus is on consumer decision making.

Positivist Research. Research primarily concerned with predicting consumer behavior.

Postivists. Researchers who endorse the assumptions on which positivism (modernism) is based.

Postpurchase Dissonance. Cognitive dissonance that occurs after a consumer has made a purchase commitment. Consumers resolve this dissonance through a variety of strategies designed to confirm the wisdom of their choice. (See Cognitive Dissonance.)

Postpurchase Evaluation. An assessment of a product based on actual trial after purchase.

Power Need. The need to exercise control over one's environment, including other persons.

Prepotent Need. An overriding need, from among several needs, that serves to initiate goal-directed behavior.

Prepurchase Search. A stage in the consumer decision-making process in which the consumer perceives a need and actively seeks out information concerning products that will help satisfy that need.

Price-Quality Relationship. The perception of price as an indicator of product quality (e.g., the higher the price, the higher the perceived quality of the product).

Primacy Effect. A theory that proposes that the first (i.e., the earliest) message presented in a sequential series of messages tends to produce the greatest impact on the receiver. (See also Recency Effect.)

Primary Group. A group of people who interact (e.g., meet and talk) on a regular basis, such as members of a family, neighbors, or coworkers.

Primary Needs. (See Innate Needs.)

Primary Research. Original research undertaken by individual researchers or organizations to meet specific objectives. Collected information is called Primary Data.

PRIZM (Potential Rating Index by Zip Market). A composite index of geographic and socioeconomic factors expressed in residential zip-code neighborhoods from which geodemographic consumer segments are formed.

Product Conspicuousness. The degree to which a product stands out and is noticed.

Product Line Extension. A marketing strategy of adding related products to an already established brand based on the Stimulus Generalization Theory).

Product Positioning. A marketing strategy designed to project a specific image for a product.

Product-Specific Goals. The specifically branded or labeled products that consumers select to fulfill their needs. (See also Generic Goals.)

Projective Techniques. Research procedures designed to identify consumers' subconscious feelings and motivations. These tests often require consumers to interpret ambiguous stimuli such as incomplete sentences, cartoons, or inkblots.

Psychoanalytic Theory. A theory of motivation and personality that postulates that unconscious needs and drives, particularly sexual and other biological drives, are the basis of human motivation and personality.

Psychogenic Need. Needs acquired through socialization, such as the need for status.

Psychographic Characteristics. Intrinsic psychological, sociocultural, and behavioral characteristics that reflect how an individual is likely to act in relation to consumption decisions. Also referred to as Lifestyle or Activities, Interests, and Opinions (AIOs).

Psychographic Inventory. A series of written statements designed to capture relevant aspects of a consumer's personality, buying motives, interests, attitudes, beliefs, and values.

Psychographic Segmentation. Identifying segments of consumers based on their responses to statements about their activities, interests, and opinions.

Psychological Characteristics. The inner or intrinsic qualities of the individual consumer.

Psychological Noise. A barrier to message reception (i.e., competing advertising messages or distracting thoughts).

Psychological Segmentation. The division of a total potential market into smaller subgroups on the basis of intrinsic characteristics of the individual, such as personality, buying motives, lifestyle, attitudes, or interests.

Psychology. The study of the intrinsic qualities of individuals, such as their motivations, perception, personality, and learning patterns.

Purchase Behavior. Behavior that involves two types of purchases: *trial purchases* (the exploratory phase in which consumers attempt to evaluate a product through direct use) and *repeat purchases*, which usually signify that the product meets with consumer's approval and that the consumer is willing to use it again.

Racial Subcultures. The major racial subcultures in the United States are Caucasian, African American, Asian American, and American Indian.

Rank-Order Scale. An attitude scale in which subjects are asked to rank items such as products (or retail stores or companies) in order of performance in terms of some criterion, such as overall quality or value for the money.

Rate of Adoption. The percentage of potential adopters within a specific social system who have adopted a new product within a given period of time.

Rate of Usage. The frequency of use and repurchase of a particular product.

Rational Motives. Motives or goals based on economic or objective criteria, such as price, size, weight, or miles-per-gallon.

Reach. The number of different people or households that are exposed to an advertisement (either because they hear or watch the program or read the newspaper or magazine).

Recency Effect. A theory that proposes that the last (i.e., most recent) message presented in a sequential series of messages tends to be remembered longest. (See also Primacy Effect.)

Reference Group. A person or group that serves as a point of comparison (or reference) for an individual in the formation of either general or specific values, attitudes, or behavior.

Regional Subcultures. Groups who identify with the regional or geographical areas in which they live.

Rehearsal. The silent, mental repetition of material. Also, the relating of new data to old data to make the former more meaningful.

Reinforcement. A positive or negative outcome that influences the likelihood that a specific behavior will be repeated in the future in response to a particular cue or stimulus.

Relationship Marketing. Marketing aimed at creating strong, lasting relationships with a core group of customers by making them feel good about the company and by giving them some kind of personal connection to the business.

Relative Advantage. The degree to which potential customers perceive a new product to be superior to existing alternatives.

Reliability. The degree to which a measurement instrument is consistent in what it measures.

Religious Subcultures. Groups classified by religious affiliation that may be targeted by marketers because they at times make purchase decisions that are influenced by their religious identity.

Repeat Purchase. The act of repurchasing a product or brand purchased earlier.

Repositioning. Changing the way a product is perceived by consumers in relation to other brands or product uses.

Reputational Measurement of Social Class. A method of measuring social class by which a knowledgeable community member is asked to classify the other members of the community into status groupings. (See Key Informant Method.)

Retention. The ability to retain information in the memory.

Retrieval. The stage of information processing in which individuals recover information from long-term storage.

Ritual. A type of symbolic activity consisting of a series of steps (multiple behaviors) occurring in a fixed sequence and repeated over time.

Ritualistic Behavior. Any behavior that becomes a ritual.

Rokeach Value Survey. A self-administered inventory consisting of eighteen "terminal" values (i.e., personal goals) and eighteen "instrumental" values (i.e., ways of reaching personal goals).

Role. A pattern of behavior expected of an individual in a specific social position, such as mother, daughter, teacher, lawyer. One person may have a number of different roles, each of which is relevant in the context of a specific social situation.

Routinized Response Behavior. A habitual purchase response based on predetermined criteria.

Secondary Data. Data that has been collected for reasons other than the specific research project at hand.

Secondary Needs. (See Acquired Needs.)

Secondary Research. Research conducted for reasons other than the specific problem under study. Resulting data are called Secondary Data.

Segmentation Bases. Eight major categories provide the most popular bases for market segmentation: geographic factors, demographic factors, psychological characteristics, sociocultural variables, use-related characteristics, use-situational factors, benefits sought, and hybrid segmentation forms (such as demographic/psychographic profiles, geodemographic factors, and values and lifestyles [VALS2]).

Segment. A cluster of consumers homogeneous in terms of one or more relevant characteristics.

Selective Attention. A heightened awareness of stimuli relevant to one's needs or interests. Also called Selective Perception.

Selective Exposure. Conscious or subconscious exposure by the consumer to certain media or messages, and the subconscious or active avoidance of others.

Selective Perception. (See Selective Attention.)

Self Concept. (See Self-Image.)

Self-Designating Method. A method of measuring some aspect of consumer behavior (such as opinion leadership) in which a person is asked to evaluate or classify his or her own attitudes or actions.

Self-Perception Theory. A theory that suggests that consumers develop attitudes by reflecting on their own behavior.

Self-Report Attitude Scales. The measurement of consumer attitudes by self-scoring procedures, such as Likert scales, semantic differential scales, or rank-order scales.

Self Reports. Pen-and-pencil "tests" completed by individuals concerning their own actions, attitudes, or motivation in regard to a subject or product under study.

Semantic Differential Scale. A series of bipolar adjectives (such as good/bad, hot/cold) that are anchored at the ends of an odd-numbered (e.g., 5- or 7-point) continuum. Respondents are asked to evaluate a concept (e.g., a product or company) on the basis of each attribute by checking the point on the continuum that best reflects their feelings or beliefs.

Semiotics. The study of symbols and the meanings they convey. Often used to discover the meanings of various consumption behaviors and rituals.

Sensation. The immediate and direct response of the sensory organs to simple stimuli (e.g., color, brightness, loudness, smoothness).

Sensory Adaptation. "Getting used to" certain sensations; becoming accommodated to a certain level of stimulation.

Sensory Receptors. The human organs (eyes, ears, nose, mouth, skin) that receive sensory inputs.

Sensory Store. The place in which all sensory inputs are housed very briefly before passing into the short-term store.

Shopping Group. Two or more people who shop together.

Short-Term Store. The stage of real memory in which information received from the sensory store for processing is retained briefly before passing into the long-term store or forgotten.

Single-Parent Family. Households consisting of one parent and at least one child.

Single-Variable Index. The use of a single socioeconomic variable (such as income) to estimate an individual's relative social class. (See also Composite Variable Index.)

Sleeper Effect. The tendency for persuasive communication to lose the impact of source credibility over time (i.e., the influence of a message from a high credibility source tends to *decrease* over time; the influence of a message from a low credibility source tends to *increase* over time).

Slice-of-Life Commercials. Television commercials that depict a typical person or family solving a problem by using the advertised product or service. They focus on "real-life" situations with which the viewer can identify.

Social Character. In the context of consumer behavior, a personality trait that ranges on a continuum from inner-directedness (reliance on one's own "inner" values or standards) to other-directedness (reliance on others for direction).

Social Class. The division of members of a society into a hierarchy of distinct status classes, so that members of each class have either higher or lower status than members of other classes.

Social Judgment Theory. An individual's processing of information about an issue is determined by his or her involvement with the issue.

Social Marketing. The use of marketing concepts and techniques to win adoption of socially beneficial ideas.

Social Psychology. The study of how individuals operate in a group.

Social Risk. The perceived risk that a poor product choice may result in social embarrassment.

Social Self-Image. How consumers feel others see them.

Social Status. The amount of status those members of one social class have in comparison with members of other social classes.

Social System. A physical, social, or cultural environment to which people belong and within which they function.

Socialization of Family Members. A process that includes imparting to children and other family members the basic values and modes of behavior consistent with the culture.

Societal Marketing Concept. A revision of the traditional marketing concept that suggests that marketers adhere to principles of social responsibility in the marketing of their goods and services; that is, they must endeavor to satisfy the needs and wants of their target markets in ways that preserve and enhance the well-being of consumers and society as a whole.

Sociocultural Segmentation. The division of a total potential market into smaller subgroups on the basis of sociological or cultural variables, such as social class, stage in the family life cycle, religion, race, nationality, values, beliefs or customs.

Socioeconomic Status Scores (SES). A multivariable social class measure used by the United States Bureau of the Census that combines occupational status, family income, and educational attainment into a single measure of social class standing.

Sociology. The study of groups.

NAME INDEX

SUBJECT INDEX